Amazing Journey: The Life of Pete Townshend

By

Mark Ian Wilkerson

"Real spirituality is best portrayed in stories of pure lives, selfless service, of truth realized and applied to the most humble circumstances of our daily lives... This is the highest practicality."
- Meher Baba

Bad News Press
Louisville, KY
Printed by Lulu - www.lulu.com/amazingjourney

Library of Congress Control Number: 2006901213

ISBN-10: 1-4116-7700-5
ISBN-13: 978-1-4116-7700-5

Printed in the United States of America

© Mark Wilkerson, 2006

Book cover design by Amy Smith

Cover photo by Ross Halfin. Used with permission.
www.rosshalfin.com

Acknowledgments

I would like to thank the following people for their help/support/encouragement/advice:

Bonnie Bartman, Sheree Bykofsky and Brian Rubin, Brian Cady, Chris Charlesworth, Martin and Christine Cook, Ross Halfin, Sarah Hardin, Stella Hernandez, Nicola Joss, Matt Kent, Sheila Krynski, Lorne and George Patterson, Mark Richardson, Ken Small, Amy Smith, and Scott Smith. I would also like to thank everyone who viewed an earlier version of this biography on my website, www.townshendbio.com. Your support and feedback was greatly appreciated.

I would also like to thank my family, who by now probably know far more about Pete Townshend than they ever really wanted to! This book would never have been completed without their support – it is dedicated to them.

Mark Ian Wilkerson
vimfuego@bellsouth.net

"...I think this "honest" thing really comes from something else: it comes from an openness rather than honesty. I don't think I'm particularly honest. But there's nothing about me that I want to keep secret... I wanna be judged for what I am, and that's why I'm as open as I can possibly be.

"...I don't really talk about my problems because I think people are interested in my problems. I talk about them because I think they might be archetypal, because they may be general, because they might be things that people can identify with, and that my thinking processes might actually allow people to get a look at themselves..."
- Pete Townshend, 1982

Prologue

To the groups of practicing Mods who populated London in the early 1960s, life outside the local dance halls, clubs, clothes shops and other various gathering places and watering holes was of minimal importance. They were consumed with their appearance, from their short, carefully styled hair down to their made-to-measure shoes. The fashions were quite specific: Fred Perry shirts, narrow trousers or Levi's shrink-to-fit jeans, custom-made suits with narrow ties, military parkas. Transportation was provided by scooters, the most fashionable of which were Italian-made Lambretta and Vespa models fitted with as many gaudy accessories as possible, including whip antennas, extra lights and mirrors, and leopard skin seat covers.

Meticulous attention was paid to the smallest of details when it came to the Mod lifestyle, all in the name of being cool. "The mod way of life consisted of total devotion to looking and being 'cool'," Richard Barnes wrote in 1982. "Spending practically all your money on clothes and all your after work hours in clubs and dance halls. To be part-time was really to miss the point."

The Mod's favorite music centered around American soul and R&B ('Mod' is short for 'Modernists', fans of the Modern Jazz music of artists such as Ray Charles and Mose Allison which preceded soul and R&B by a few years) which had been filtering slowly into Britain in the early 1960s. The music was far from mainstream and it was decidedly difficult to obtain copies of the 'in' recordings, which made it all the more appealing to the Mod crowd. Favorites included Ben E. King, Martha and the Vandellas, The Shirelles and Muddy Waters, the more danceable material receiving the majority of the attention at the local clubs.

London's West End, specifically Soho, became a hotbed of Mod activity with clubs such as The Flamingo and The Scene setting many trends and featuring the most prominent and important proponents of Mod, known as 'faces'. The atmosphere in these early R&B clubs was electric as these immaculately dressed, pilled-up adolescents checked each other out.[1] Many important bands played in London's R&B clubs at this time, including The Rolling Stones, The Animals, and a young Shepherds Bush-based outfit named The Detours, who had by mid-1964 already attracted strong Mod attention and changed their name to something that would print larger on posters.

On June 30, 1964, The Detours, now known as The Who, began a twelve week residency in a small R&B club frequented by Mods in Harrow, London. The Railway Hotel was a "very scruffy looking" place according to Kit Lambert, and The Who "were playing there in this room with just one red bulb glowing and an extraordinary audience that they had collected." Ambience management at the Railway fell to Richard Barnes, an Ealing Art School student who ran the club's entertainment bookings. Barnes had seen to it that the atmosphere was just right. "We turned off all the lights except two in which we had put pink bulbs," he wrote in his 1982 book *Maximum R&B*. "The radiators were deliberately turned up and all the windows blacked out...a capacity was fixed at 180 but there had been occasions when we had issued tickets for as many as 1,000, though a couple of hundred of those would have to content themselves with checking out the scooters in the courtyard."

The band, Roger Daltrey, 20, vocals, Pete Townshend, 19, guitar, John Entwistle, 19, bass, and newly acquired drummer Keith Moon, 17, played on a rather wobbly stage made from beer crates and table tops to the Mod audience and their sound was deafening. "They were the loudest group I'd ever heard," said Lambert. The band played rock'n'roll, blues and R&B numbers - a fairly standard set for a local live act at the time, but what set them apart was the presence of Tamla-Motown songs in their repertoire (the Detroit-based label featured black soul artists such as The Miracles, The Marvelettes, Martha and the Vandellas, and Stevie Wonder). The Who's set list and their unparalleled onstage intensity drew the attention of the Mod crowd. Townshend's Rickenbacker guitar, slung high, almost across his chest, responded with crushing volume to every gyration he made as he windmilled his arm, slashing his hand not across but *through* the strings, then facing his huge speaker cabinet and coaxing screeching feedback from the instrument. Moon's drumming left nobody unaffected; he bashed away with wild abandon as though his very life depended on it. The intense energy and power of his style often required the lashing down of his kit with rope prior to a gig. Entwistle, whose bass thundered through a cabinet similar in size to that of Townshend's, stood relatively still and

---

[1] Amphetamine use was rampant among Mods – pills such as 'Purple Hearts' and 'French Blues' maintained the requisite energy level.

expressionless as he observed the proceedings, with Daltrey fronting the ensemble, scowling, pacing, snarling into the microphone.

The Who's stay at the Railway was not particularly long, but prior to the end of their residency, the band had drawn enough attention to warrant the construction of a proper wooden stage. Townshend was beginning to violently manipulate his Rickenbacker guitar and Moon's drumming was inherently chaotic, so the makeshift stage had to go. In late summer, 1964, the band, which had changed their name to The High Numbers in July, took to their new stage at the Railway. "This stage gave them a more solid and secure feeling for their increasingly physical stage act," said Barnes, "and also had a bit more room." The stage was also slightly higher, something which the six-foot tall Townshend discovered during the show. "I started to knock the guitar about a lot, hitting it on the amps to get banging noises and things like that," said Townshend. "...It banged against the ceiling and smashed a hole in the plaster and the guitar head actually poked through the ceiling...When I brought it out the top of the neck was left behind." Not really knowing what to do next, and noticing a few snickers from the crowd, which included a sizeable contingent of his Ealing Art School cohorts, Townshend smashed what was left of the Rickenbacker to pieces. "I had no recourse but to completely look as though I meant to do it, so I smashed the guitar and jumped all over the bits. It gave me a fantastic buzz," Townshend said. "About a month earlier I'd managed to scrape together enough for a 12-string Rickenbacker, which I only used on two or three numbers. It was lying at the side of the stage so I just picked it up, plugged it in and gave them a sort of look and carried on playing, as if I'd meant to do it."

"This went down tremendously well with the audience," Lambert recalled in 1969, "...and that's how the whole thing started."

Chapter 1

"...He is the longest serving, most honest man in rock; eternally idealistic, if occasionally foolish; for the most part incorruptible and always entertaining. He did not, as he once hoped, die before he got old and for that one lie, the greatest in rock, we should be profoundly grateful."
- Chris Charlesworth, 1984

"The guitar player was a skinny geezer with a big nose who twirled his arm like a windmill. He wrote some good songs about mods, but he didn't quite look like one."
- 'Jimmy Cooper', *Quadrophenia*, 1973

Although Pete Townshend's unique talents as a musician and songwriter didn't begin to manifest themselves until he was in his late teens, the process started much earlier; in fact, Pete had been exposed to music practically since the day he was born.

Born on May 19, 1945, in Chiswick, London, Peter Dennis Blandford Townshend (Dennis was his mother's maiden name, Blandford his father's middle name) was immersed in music from the very beginning. Parents Cliff and Betty were members of the entertainment corps of the Royal Air Force; Cliff an alto saxophonist, Betty a singer. They met in London when Cliff was a member of the RAF Dance Orchestra and Betty was a singer with the Sidney Torch Orchestra, which taped programs to be sent to troops deployed overseas. The RAF Dance Orchestra (which became known as The Squadronaires) was immensely popular throughout Britain and during the war had played their brand of Benny Goodman/Glenn Miller-esque swing throughout Allied Europe. After the war, when the band members left the RAF they went on the road to Britain's various coastal holiday resorts, maintaining a busy touring schedule up until 1964, when they disbanded amidst a surge of interest in contemporary popular music, led by the Beatles and the Rolling Stones.

Pete's parents lived in Acton, West London. Their Whitehall Gardens home was sparsely occupied much of the time since the couple were often on the road, especially Cliff, whose Squadronaires were known as the best swing outfit in the country.

Cliff and Betty had a turbulent marriage - both had fiery tempers which were fueled by frequent drinking (a trait which Pete would unfortunately inherit), and Betty had occasional affairs with other men. Pete later referred to her as "unfaithful." The couple separated for a protracted period when Pete was a toddler, sending him to live with his maternal grandmother, Emma Dennis, known as 'Granny Denny'. "...I was dumped with my grandmother for two years," Pete told *Rolling Stone*'s Anthony DeCurtis in 1993. "I was very lonely, never heard from my father at all. My mother used to come down on the weekend for an hour to see me, dressed incredibly seductively. She was beautiful, and I just longed to be with her. I just wanted to be with my fabulous, exciting, brilliant, beautiful parents. Instead I was with this bitter, crotchety, clinically insane grandmother."

Life at Granny Denny's house was "hell," Pete recalled in 1993.

> It was a fucking nightmare. My father used to send me five shillings a week, a fabulous amount of money in those days. And I would go to the shop with my grandmother and buy myself a toy, and she would take the toy and put it in a cupboard. Then when my mother came to see me, my grandmother would make me get all the toys out as though I'd been playing with them. And then when my mother had gone, I'd have to put them all away again. She was a complete head case.

Pete again described his grandmother as "clinically insane" when he spoke with David Letterman in 1993. "...it's kind of been the one ribbon that's run continually through my life", he told Letterman, demonstrating the profound influence wrought by the two year ordeal. "This is my cauldron," Pete told *Minstrel's Dilemma* author Larry David Smith in 1997. "...If I go too deeply into this... opening it up... my relationship with my grandmother is something – which to date – I've not been able to make any sense of whatsoever. It's the only bit of my life that I haven't been able to make any sense of and, in a sense, I feel that if I was able to go into regressive hypnosis and either find some terrible trauma or nothing at all, it would be equally damaging to me as an artist."

Pete's disturbing period of trauma and upheaval ended when Cliff and Betty Townshend eventually reconciled and settled into a spacious two-floor brick house just east of Ealing Common, on Woodgrange Avenue, in a middle-class neighborhood a few miles west of working class Shepherd's

Bush.[2] "...They got back together and had another couple of kids, and my life was fairly normal from then on," said Pete, the eldest of three boys, brothers Paul and Simon born in 1957 and 1960, respectively.

Back in 1946, the Squadronaires had begun to take extended summer bookings at holiday resorts in Britain, the first being in Clacton, a seaside town on the south coast, then a more extended booking at the Isle of Man, an island just offshore in the northwest, which would last about 13 summers. Pete accompanied his mother and father on these trips, soaking in the musical environment, watching rehearsals and shows, and playing on the beach. He traveled extensively with his parents until he reached school age, when his musical excursions were limited to the summer break. But even when Pete was back at the family's Ealing home, music was the common denominator of most of the people he came into contact with. "All our friends were musicians," Betty Townshend told Dave Marsh in 1983. "All our company were musicians. He had a musical background - not only from his family. It was his environment."

"...My father was a musician in a dance band, so I was brought up in two places," Pete said in a 1993 radio interview.

> During the week we were in dance halls, so I know what to do when people start fighting... This is as young as two or three years old, I was running around dance halls. My mother used to sing with my dad's band, I was kind of on the loose with guys that drank. I was a real kind of rock and roll baby... The other thing that they used to do at weekends was these Sunday concerts where there would be like variety shows. So there would be like girls, comedians, big stars from the USA... But my father also took me a little bit further, he took me into the orchestral writing of Duke Ellington which was very very avant-garde in its time. He took me to see the Basie Band.

It was on the Isle of Man in 1956 that Pete's mother took him and a friend to see the film *Rock Around the Clock*, a film featuring music by Bill Haley and The Comets and Little Richard, among others. "Well, they wanted to see it the next day and the next day and in the end we were giving them the money or getting passes for them," Betty told Dave Marsh in 1983. "They were seeing this film daily - practically every rainy day, anyway. Peter really absolutely adored music, and when this Bill Haley and rock and roll thing started, he was right into it. He was very little; he was ten. And he loved it." Soon afterwards, Cliff took Pete to see Haley perform live –

---

[2] This same Woodgrange Avenue address was later used as a studio by Simon Townshend, Pete's brother.

Pete's first concert. "...I was eleven and a half years old," Pete recalled in 1993, "and I remember once my friend Graham who came with me saying to him, "Do you like this music Cliff?" He said, "Graham, I like anything that swings.""

Pete provided some insight regarding his opinion of his parents in 1989, telling the *San Diego Union* that his relationship with his father "wasn't that intimate. He was very busy, and I think that in a Freudian sense, I'm doing the same thing; I don't see half enough of my family because I'm so wrapped up in my work. He was very simple, very loving, very uncomplicated, very straightforward and immensely proud that I was successful at anything. He really didn't like that it was rock because it wasn't really decent in his view; he hated the drugs. But he was an absolutely sterling supporter of anything I did." Pete added in a 1989 interview with *Guitar Player*, "I just wanted to be like my dad; you know, I worshipped him. He was a magnificent player and a fantastic man."

"It was my mother who actually gave us the most moral and vocal support in the early days," Pete told the *San Diego Union* in 1989. "She set up auditions, lent us her van and almost used to roadie for us. I wrote about my mother and the relationship we had. I've continued to write about it, and it still hurts. She's still a very fiery, exciting, stimulating character, and she can hurt you very badly if she wants to. And I find myself doing the same back to her."

From this point, Pete's interest in music began to focus on rock'n'roll rather than the swing music of his parents and their generation. Naturally, as musicians themselves, Cliff and Betty were supportive of their son's tastes in music at a time when many disapproved of the direction that popular music was taking. Up to this point in his life the only musical instrument Pete had really showed an interest in had been the harmonica. "My father was essentially a pop musician in his day," Pete once told an interviewer. "I dread to think what would have happened if I had been brought up in a classical family. He promised me a harmonica which I never got and in the end I think I had to shoplift one a couple of years later." With the impact of *Rock Around The Clock* fresh in his mind, he began to show an interest in the guitar.

Guitars weren't new to the Townshend family. "My father had played the guitar when he was young and my uncle Jack had worked for Kalamazoo [a depression-era offshoot of Gibson], before the war, developing guitar pickups," Pete told *Guitarist* in 1990. "So there was a kind of family thing about the guitar, althought it was considered something of an anomaly then." Pete's original intention was to emulate his father and play saxophone, but "...I couldn't blow a note so he suggested the guitar," he said. "Chromatic harmonica was actually my first instrument and I got very good at it – not quite Stevie Wonder, but very good. Then I hit eleven and decided I did want to try the guitar, so my grandmother bought me one."

In 1956, Pete was placed in Acton County Grammar School. As eleven year-old Pete entered adolescence and started to notice the opposite sex, he began to realize that the size of his nose was becoming an obstacle to his acceptance in the various social circles that existed at grammar school. His nose was often a topic of conversation both at school and at home, and this unwanted attention affected Pete profoundly.

"High school was very painful for me," Pete told *Penthouse* in 1974.

> I was very embarrassed and self-conscious about my nose for quite a while. I got obsessed with it. Music was my escape. My mother was no help, she seemed to think that anybody who wasn't beautiful couldn't be any good. She was gorgeous, of course. My father was very good-looking, too. How they spawned me I'll never know. Dad was kind to me about the nose, but in an unintentionally devastating manner. He used to say things like, 'Don't worry. Arthur Miller married Marilyn Monroe, didn't he?' I didn't want to look like fucking Arthur Miller, I wanted to look like James Dean.

Deciding against wallowing in self pity, Pete grew defiant: the fact that people often baited him about his nose began to serve as personal motivation to succeed at something which would make them forget that his nose was ever there. "...I used to think, "I'll bloody well show them," " he told the *Evening Standard*. " "I'll push my huge hooter out at them from every newspaper in England - then they won't laugh at me." "

> And when I first started singing with a group, I used to go up on stage and forget that I was Pete Townshend who wasn't a success with the ladies, and all of a sudden I'd become aware that there were little girls giggling and pointing at my nose. And I'd think, "Sod 'em - they're not gonna laugh at me!" And I'd get angrier still. My whole absurdly demonstrative stage act was worked out to turn myself into a body instead of a face. Most pop singers were pretty, but I wanted people to look at my body, and not have to bother looking at my head if they didn't like the look of it.[3]

---

[3] Pete's physical appearance haunted him for years. When asked in 1986 to name the biggest obstacle he'd overcome in his life, 40 year-old Townshend replied, "Believing myself to be unattractive." But Townshend's nose was also recognized as a selling point for the band. The Who's 1966 *Observer* magazine cover photo, with Townshend sitting at center, was shot

Pete's grandmother bought him his first guitar for Christmas in 1956, which he remembers as "a cheap Spanish thing," which again brought to the surface Pete's distaste for Granny Denny. "My father was going to buy me a guitar for my 11-year-old Christmas - and he would have bought me a fabulous instrument," Pete said in 1993. "But what fucking happened is that *she* bought it! She bought me a guitar like you see on the wall of a Spanish restaurant, a phony guitar. I was excited for a while, standing in front of the mirror, but I realized very quickly that I was never going to be able to play anything on it." Cliff taught his son some basic chords, but Pete struggled mightily with the instrument, "just a really, really cheap guitar...I fought tooth and nail with it for a year and finally gave up because it was such a bad instrument."

Pete's difficulties learning to play his new guitar and his evolving taste in music soon saw his aspirations drift toward the banjo. "...I started to examine what was happening, listening to Elvis Presley like all my friends," he said in 1990, "...But to be honest I never really liked him, and also I think Scotty Moore was an aberration – it's not my idea of great playing," adding, "I know that's sacrilege to many people and I wouldn't want to slight him as an individual or as a player, because he's cited as a seminal influence by so many people, but for me it was more the sound of Nancy Whiskey. Yes, the sound of strumming guitars; such a glorious sound." Whiskey was a member of the Chas McDevitt Skiffle Group, who were riding the wave of the genre's new popularity with their single *Freight Train*, on which she sang lead vocals. Skiffle (a peppy, uptempo variety of folk music) and a new form of swing known as Trad. Jazz both experienced burgeoning followings during this period. Chief among Skiffle musicians was Lonnie Donegan, who is credited with boosting the genre's popularity with his 1956 hit *Rock Island Line*. Pete was especially taken with the new wave of banjo players which emerged during the upswing of Skiffle and Trad. Jazz. "...the players I looked at were the guys with Acker Bilk, Ken Collier and Kenny Ball," he said in 1990. "English banjo players really were a law unto themselves – you don't find that kind of brisk banjo playing on the original Louis Armstrong or Bix Beiderbecke records. But Acker Bilk's banjo player had this very vital, bright sound. He used a G banjo with a long scale and played it with lots of flourishes, and I copied that until I went back to the guitar a couple of years later." Pete acquired a mandolin banjo, his sights firmly set on joining The Confederates, "...quite a good trad band – we even had a tuba player," at Pete's school featuring trumpet player named John Entwistle.

---

with a fish-eye lens – reportedly Chris Stamp's idea – which greatly exaggerated the size of Pete's nose.

The Confederates, who reportedly devoted more time to rehearsing than actually performing shows, only played to the local church youth club, the Congo Club (short for Congregational Club). Pete was 14. "The central part of it all then was the Congo Club in Acton," Pete recalled later.

> ...It was when I came closest to being part of a gang. I got caught up with a guy called Stewart Dodd. He and I both had big noses at school and he was nicknamed Oscar after some cartoon character with a big nose. He went through an incredible metamorphosis. We didn't see him for some time and I saw him rolling down the street drunk one day. I said hallo Oscar and he smacked me in the teeth and threw a bottle at me. He had turned into a petty villain overnight and was caught up with a local bunch of hardnuts, and just hated being called by his school nickname. I started to live in the real world after that. I had shut myself away plunking away on the banjo at home and suddenly realised that the Congo wasn't just a place where we got together and entertained the troops, as it were. There was a lot of violence and sex and stuff going on.

Pete found being a member of The Confederates attractive for reasons other than music. Adult topics such as political activism and sex were vying for his attention. "We were all very left-wing, or they were – I didn't know what politics was about, but I went on the Aldermaston march – or, again, they did," he said in 1990[4]. "And they were always disappearing into sleeping bags with girls..."

Pete was initially excited about playing for the Confederates, but was rather self-conscious about his abilities as a musician. "I had to rush out and get a chord book," Pete recalls. "As I'd been buggering about playing guitar for nearly two years I wasn't getting anywhere. They expected me to play and were fairly impressed, which I couldn't work out. Perhaps they thought that if you could play three chords you could play the rest." Pete recalled that at one time there were three banjo players - one of whom would eventually bump him out of the lineup. "This guy Alf Maynard had a Vega banjo and was very much the central figure of the band, so I got edged out. I was a better player than him but I didn't really fit and didn't push myself too much," he said in 1982.

---

[4] The Aldermaston March was a Campaign For Nuclear Disarmament march from London to Aldermaston – site of a new atomic weapons plant - which first took place on Good Friday, 1958, to protest Britain's first atomic bomb tests on Christmas Island in the Pacific Ocean. The march, which covered over fifty miles in four days, boasted approximately 10,000 participants, according to the BBC.

Pete's brief tenure with The Confederates came to an end during his last year at grammar school, when an argument erupted with Chris Sherwin, the band's drummer: "...we got into a fight and I hit him over the head with a bag and he had a concussion which I didn't realize," Pete recalled in 1982. "As a result I was sort of ignored by our little school playground clique. They gave me the cold shoulder. I was a little disturbed by it and went more into my shell in a way and transferred it to the guitar. I just decided to use what was really a pretty bleak period for that."

Pete's ouster from the Confederates, combined with a resurgence of his interest in rock'n'roll, saw his banjo playing days come to a close in 1958. The recent successes of Cliff Richard and The Shadows, Chuck Berry, Elvis Presley and Rick Nelson had brought the guitar to the forefront once again, Pete's favorites being The Shadows, especially guitarist Hank Marvin. Chuck Berry, while enjoying immense popularity during this period, did not have an impact on Townshend until the early Sixties, when he was in art school. As previously noted, Elvis did not do much for Pete. "I never got much into roots rock apart from Bill Haley," Pete remembered in 1980. "I never liked Elvis very much or his band. I thought his band was pretty shitty. I used to think the Jordanaires were awful. And I didn't like Scotty Moore. I did like Jimmy Burton who played with Rick Nelson; he was a big influence."

Townshend bought a "reasonably good Czechoslovakian guitar" for £3 at his mother's antique shop and gave up playing his mandolin banjo, but the rapid strumming technique he had learned remained. "I also got myself a little amplifier and went electric," he recalled in 1993. The amplifier was soon treated to what would soon become standard practice for any piece of equipment belonging to Townshend, as he used it to aid in expressing his anger toward his grandmother. "One day, I was about 14, John and I were sitting playing something together in the front room, not very loud, and she came in and she said, "Turn that bloody awful row down,"" Pete told H.P Newquist of *Guitar* in 1996.

> And I said, "Get out now, or I'm going to kill you, you fucking old bag." She yelled, "How dare you talk to me like that!" So I picked up my amplifier and threw it at her. She ran to the other side of the door, and the amplifier landed there in a big heap and it fizzed and went off. And I'd just bought it. I'd worked delivering newspapers for literally three years to buy it. And John looked at me and said in that low voice, "That was good. Done it now, haven't you?" [laughs] But I got it repaired.

He and Entwistle soon formed another band with two school friends, Pete playing guitar and John on bass. "We used to play Shadows numbers," said Pete. "I was terribly happy with it and people quite liked us. It gave me a new confidence. I hadn't made it very well with chicks, and at the time when my mates started to get it together with chicks I was getting into the guitar. It became quite an obsession." The group was reportedly first named the Aristocrats, then the Scorpions. Following the rehearsal-heavy tradition of the Confederates, they only played once in front of an audience, at the Congo Club.

In 1961, John went on to join The Detours, a band fronted by local tough guy Roger Daltrey, a sheet metal worker who made up for his diminutive stature with an abrasive demeanor. The stage was soon set for Townshend's arrival. "We brought in this guy on rhythm guitar because he'd come into a little bit of money and bought himself a Vox amp and a guitar," Entwistle recalled in 1982.

> We figured like if we had him in the group we'd be able to use his amplifier. He could sing a bit as well. The poor guy went on holiday with his fiance and drowned, so we took over his amplifier. We figured he didn't need it any more. We still had this other rhythm guitarist called Reg Bowen, but he only knew about five chords so eventually we started looking for a new rhythm guitarist and that's when I managed to persuade Pete to join. He didn't, however, want to join at first but I told him we had a real Vox amplifier, so he thought 'A Vox amplifier...well...' and he joined.

The five-piece Detours (with Pete playing rhythm guitar while Roger played lead) played numerous songs by Cliff Richard and The Shadows, with the band being "very much a singer with a backing band," according to Pete's friend, Richard Barnes, who wrote *The Who: Maximum R&B* in 1982. Apparently, singer Colin Dawson fancied himself as a bit of a schmoozer, perhaps emulating Cliff Richard; Townshend later complained that Dawson wiggled his backside too much while singing.

Pete left grammar school in the autumn of 1961 at age sixteen for nearby Ealing Art School, a move which allowed him an opportunity to pursue his interests[5]. The school was less than a mile from the Townshend home on Woodgrange Avenue. "It was such a great period for me," Pete recalled. "I had a natural artistic bend which was why I ended up at art school, but basically I should have done something to do with writing I suppose, but if I had I probably wouldn't have ended up sort of so open-endedly creative as I later became. The art side did get my brain going

---

[5] "It was probably the terrible noise I used to make on my first electric guitar that made my father suggest that I go to art school and concentrate on the graphic rather than the musical areas of education," Townshend told Andrew Motion in 1987.

creatively and started me thinking." Ealing Art School was a think-tank containing much local artistic talent, both present and future. Future Stones guitarist Ronnie Wood, an avid painter, attended Ealing Art School at this time, as did late Queen frontman Freddie Mercury. Richard Barnes, who met Pete at the school in 1962 and has remained a close friend, recalled the atmosphere in 1982: "Ealing Art School was a very unusual art school. This normally staid and conservative institution had, in the same year that Pete enrolled [1961], acquired a new head tutor, Roy Ascot. He had replaced most of the staff with young fresh sixties designers and artists and was to begin a revolutionary experiment in art tuition based on the science of Cybernetics." Cybernetics, according to *Webster's*, is "the science dealing with the comparative study of human control systems, as the brain and nervous system, and complex electronic systems." Barnes recalled that Pete, along with many "excited but confused students," jumped right in. "Printmaking, basic design, sculpture and color theory," he added, "were all intermingled with feedback, noise-interference and automation principles," in the interest of studying and comparing the inner workings of man and machine.

One particular art school project involved each member of the class being assigned certain (and in Pete's case, rather debilitating) physical characteristics. Pete's assigned scenario was to face life with no legs and an inability to communicate with others. To tackle the first problem, Pete and some fellow students fashioned a cart out of some old orange boxes and the wheels from a baby carriage. "Not only did I have to push myself about on this cart," Pete said in 1982, "but I also had to communicate in a phonetic alphabet that my group had to think up. In a way it was like fucking acting school."

Prominent artists, designers and playwrights gave lectures at the school[6], including Larry Rivers, Robert Brownjohn, autodestructive art pioneer Gustav Metzger and American pop-artist R.B. Kitaj. Metzger proved particularly influential. Barnes wrote that Metzger "...showed slides of paintings done in acid on sheets of metal showing the stages of 'beauty' as the acid slowly destroyed the metal and was later publicly acknowledged by Pete for his inspiration on autodestruction." Pete recalled that Metzger "turned up at some of our shows when we were smashing stuff up. He really got into it."

"In Britain... art colleges were intense, hothouse places, with brilliant, over-qualified teachers, and pupils who left with a comprehensive avant-garde education and had to find a use for it in a deeply conservative society," wrote *The Guardian*'s Jonathan Jones in 2000. "I came to Britain in the 60s," artist and teacher Michael Craig-Martin told Jones, "and was

---

[6] Pete told an interviewer in 1982 that "...artists like Jackson Pollock..." gave lectures while he was at Ealing Art School. In *Before I Get Old*, Dave Marsh pointed out that this was impossible since Pollock died five years before Pete enrolled.

immediately teaching in a provincial art school, and I couldn't believe how good the school was. They were sophisticated about art. What you often saw were extremely bright students who had failed in the conventional education system. At art college, the things that had been a disadvantage became an advantage. But when people came out of those institutions there was nothing for them. One of the reasons for them going into other fields, including pop music, was that there was nowhere for them to have a career in Britain."

"It was 1962, the time of the Cuban missile crisis," Pete told Jones. "Metzger had a profound effect on me. I was doing my first gig with The Who and took it as an excuse to smash my new Rickenbacker that I had just hocked myself to the eyebrows to buy. I really believed it was my responsibility to start a rock band that would last only three months, an auto-destructive group. The Who would have been the first punk band except that we had a hit."

Music was also a big part of life at art school. "There would be lessons where you sort of listened to jazz. Or listened to classical music. Or explored minimalism," Pete said in 1982. "We had jazz musicians, film writers, playwrights as well as artists… to come and lecture. It was a clearinghouse, and music was something that was very much considered to be okay. And not something that you only did after hours. It was part of life. You could sit in a classroom with people painting *and* playing. I used to do it."

An American photography student at Ealing Art School named Tom Wright approached Pete in 1962 about the possibility of learning some new guitar licks from Townshend, whom he'd overheard playing in the common room. Pete visited Tom's apartment on Sunnyside Road, just across from the school and was blown away by the American's record collection. Wright, who hailed from Alabama, had around 150 blues, R&B and jazz albums, many of which were very difficult to find in Britain. Pete became a regular visitor to Sunnyside Road where he would teach Tom to play the guitar in exchange for access to the record collection, often also delving into Wright's marijuana stash. Many evenings were spent listening to these beautiful, rare recordings while imbibing Wright's imported pot. Pete remembered later, "When I first got into pot I was involved in the environment more; there was a newness about art college, having beautiful girls around for the first time in my life, having all that music around me for the first time, and it was such a great period - with the Beatles exploding and all that all over the place. So it was very exciting, but although pot was important to me, it wasn't the biggest thing: the biggest thing was the fact that pot helped to make incredible things even more incredible."

While Pete Townshend was quickly working on becoming a pot head, the drug saw the end of Tom Wright's stint at Ealing Art School. Tom was busted for possession of marijuana in late 1962 and deported from

England. He asked Pete and Richard Barnes to move in to his flat and keep an eye on the contents, an opportunity that Pete and Richard jumped at. Now Pete had unlimited access to the best record collection around, not to mention the pot stash. "...I got my introduction to the blues and a lot of other stuff too like Mose Allison, Ray Charles, Jimmy Smith, Jimmy Reed and [John Lee] Hooker," Pete recalled in 1980. "A lot of great music in one year."

Pete was especially impressed with John Lee Hooker. "Hooker's chord work convinced me that pinning down a precise and solid chordal structure was far more important for me than learning by rote the solos of virtuosos like B. B. King and Buddy Guy," he said in 1997. Pete saw Hooker perform at the Flamingo Club a few years later.

Pete also mentioned Howling Wolf, Chuck Berry, Little Walter, Bo Diddley, Booker T., Lonnie Mack and Jimmy Smith as some of the artists featured in Tom Wright's collection that left an imprint in his memory, "and a few rather less obvious gems which none the less changed my head, the shape of my fingers, the way I walked and generally improved the appearance of the ladies I associated with," he told *Rolling Stone* in 1970. "Pete's life revolved around art school, playing four or five nights a week, getting stoned and absorbing his new treasure trove of American blues and jazz," recalled Barnes in 1982. "He went to sleep to music and woke up to music, usually the slow lazy rhythm of Jimmy Reed."

In late spring and summer 1962, The Detours played at various company dances, bar mitzvahs and weddings, transportation being provided by drummer Harry Wilson's dad. The band secured their first residency in July, playing five consecutive weeks at The Paradise Club in Peckham. A key addition to the band was made during this residency when Doug Sandom replaced Harry as drummer. Doug, seven years older than the other band members, brought stability and experience into the mix. In late 1962 the Detours played various venues, including a regular booking at Ealing's Jewish Club and various company outings and dance halls. The band often played four or five nights a week, Daltrey driving to shows behind the wheel of a van which was too small to hold both band and equipment. Often, the band members traveled either lying on top of their gear in the van due to the lack of space, or simply taking the train to the show.

It was in November 1962 that Betty Townshend got The Detours their big break. She had gathered an impressive list of musical contacts and acquaintances over the years as a singer, and managed to get her son's band an audition with the area's leading booking agency, Commercial Entertainments, which ran eighteen venues in the west London area. The Detours played three songs at the audition, and gauging audience satisfaction as the deciding factor, Commercial Entertainments manager Bob Druce signed the band. Within two weeks, The Detours were playing regularly on Druce's circuit, which featured venues such as the Grand

Ballroom in Broadstairs, Kent, and the Oldfield Hotel in Greenford, where the band's audition had taken place. Pete's mother also managed to land the band a regular Sunday afternoon booking at Douglas House, Bayswater, a favorite club of American servicemen.

By January 1963, Roger Daltrey had become the leader of The Detours, partly due to his stubbornness and partly due to his penchant for fisticuffs if things weren't going his way. With Daltrey, Entwistle and Townshend leaning toward R&B and blues music and Colin Dawson aspiring to be the next Cliff Richard, it was decided that Dawson's services were no longer needed. After ex-Bel Airs bassist Gabby Connolly (who preferred to sing country and western, particularly Johnny Cash numbers) filled in on vocals for a short time, Daltrey eventually became the frontman[7].

The Detours soon became a lean, powerful four-piece band that provided the prototype for The Who. An event that precipitated this metamorphosis was a 1963 gig at St. Mary's Hall in Putney, southwest London, where The Detours opened for Johnny Kidd and The Pirates, a tough, rockabilly-influenced outfit whose stripped-down vocals/guitar/bass/drums formula and wild stage show (the band dressed as pirates on stage) quickly earned them a reputation as the best rock and roll outfit in the country prior to the emergence of the Beatles. The sheer power and muscle of The Pirates' performance left a deep impression on The Detours, convincing Daltrey that a switch from lead guitar to vocals was necessary. After witnessing Pirates' guitarist Mick Green live, Townshend and Entwistle had a new appreciation for the power that could be elicited from their respective instruments.

"...if I'm going to hit a note or bend it, I really want to have to struggle for it, because I'm so physically wound up on the stage," Pete told *Guitar Player*'s Michael Brooks in 1972.

> If I wanted to, I could pull the string up and break it with my hand. It's really weird, when I'm in the dressing room playing, I can hardly stretch the strings, and then when I go on stage I get a buzz and the strings feel slinky, they feel really slinky. The first guy that I met, my idol in England, was a guy named Mickey Green, who used to play with Johnny Kitten (sic) and the Pirates, and he was the first big note-bender, particularly on the G. And you'd freak over Jimmy Burton and you'd freak over Mickey Green and you wondered how they got that sound. Went to see a guy about it and he said it was the thin G, he uses like two 2nds instead of a G, right? So I got my guitar and I really got

---

[7] Connolly's vocal talents were especially useful during the 3-month Douglas House residency, where the American servicemen preferred country and western music.

into it. I got to see Mickey play, and I went back stage to see him and I asked him if I could play his guitar and he said, "Sure, man." I picked it up, and he's got strings like bloody piano strings, they're huge! And the G isn't plain, it's wound, and he used to stretch it practically to the A string and beyond. Big hands, and he would pull it down and tuck it under as well.

Roger's move to lead vocals paved the way for the band which became The Who to truly develop a unique style. Pete, John and Roger now all had clearly defined roles in the band which over the coming months they would grow into, each member finding his niche. Pete Townshend's position as rhythm guitarist had now become simply *guitarist*, a role which allowed him the freedom to express himself as he wished.

Aspiring to become a 'serious' band rather than simply a group of entertainers, and since their personal tastes in music had evolved, the four-piece Detours progressed from playing top forty hits to R&B, blues and Motown. Their set now began to reflect the contents of Tom Wright's record collection, and included songs by Chuck Berry, Jimmy Reed, Eddie Holland, The Beatles, Mose Allison and blues staples such as *Smokestack Lightning*, *I'm a Man* and *Spoonful*.

Financially strapped, The Detours stopped at nothing to keep up with those bands with better equipment. Handyman Daltrey remembered, "When we first started, I used to make all the bloody guitars. We used to make our amplifiers as well...In them days it was all psychological warfare being in a group, so we hit on the idea of having the biggest cabinets you've ever seen in your life - yet inside we'd have this little 12-inch speaker. It looked like a bloody sideboard. It looked like me mum's front room on stage. People would come and see us and say, 'Hey, they must be good, look at the size of their gear.'" Pete and John began to frequent Marshall's music shop in Ealing, in search of new equipment. "Jim Marshall started manufacturing amplifiers and somebody in his store came up with the idea of building a 4 x 12 cabinet for bass," Pete recalled in 1980. John bought one of the speaker cabinets, "and suddenly John Entwistle doubled in volume," Pete said. "And so I bought one and then later on I bought another one and I stacked it on top of the other one. I was using a Rickenbacker at the time and because the pickup was right in line with the speakers I was instantly troubled by feedback. But I really used to like to hear the sound in my ears."

When the Detours played at the Oldfield Hotel in Greenford, Pete used to place his amplifier on a piano at the back of the stage. "I used to play at this place where I put my amp on the piano, so the speaker was right opposite my guitar. One day, I was hitting this note and I was going *ba-ba-bam* [hitting the guitar] and the amplifier was going *ur-ur-ur-ur* on its own.

I said to myself, 'That's fun. I'll fool around with that.' And I started to pretend I was an airplane. Everyone went completely crazy."

Pete's openness to onstage experimentation was directly attributable to the environment he was exposed to in art school. "...I was an arty little sod and I was actually experimenting," he told *Guitarist* in 1990. He continued:

> I was... surrounded by real intellectuals, people that were experimenting all the time. I was greatly impressed by all this and wanted to please these people. A lot of it was posing, trying to drag something out of the band that it was resisting – this is pre Keith Moon. And as I got louder, John got louder by inventing the 4 x 12 cabinet, which he did with somebody up at Marshall. Then I got a 4 x 12 cabinet and put it on a chair, so then he invented the 8 x 12 cabinet, to get louder than me, and then I invented the stack by getting two 4 x 12s and stacking them up. Marshall were outraged, and one day somebody from Marshall's came and they were nagging me about the fact that the top cabinet was shifting and was going to fall off and get damaged, and I just said, "So what?" and knocked it over! There was a tremendous kind of arrogance...
>
> Our experimentations were all to do with our irritation with the audience, who heckled if you played a rhythm and blues song that they didn't know. You'd get blokes in the back with their pints of beer shouting, "What's all this rubbish? Play some Shane Fenton!" And we just got louder as a result. Then the squeaks and farts did start to occur in the feedback...
>
> Other people stumbled on feedback at the same time as me. Jeff Beck was using it when Roger went to see The Tridents rehearsing. He said, "There's a shit-hot guitar player down the road and he's making sounds like you." Then later, when we supported The Kinks, Dave Davies was adamant, "I invented it, it wasn't John Lennon and it wasn't you!" I worshipped The Kinks and never let a bad word about them pass my lips, so I conceded. But I believe it was something people were discovering all over London. These big amps that Marshall were turning out – you couldn't stop the guitars feeding back!
>
> ...You could control it and it could be very musical – certainly that sort of thing where you hit an open A chord and then take your fingers off the strings... The A string is still banging away but you're hearing the finger-off

harmonics in feedback. Then the vibrating A starts to stimulate harmonics in the other strings and it's just an extraordinary sound, like an enormous airplane. It's a wonderful, optimistic sound and that was something that happened because I was posing – I'd put my arms out, let go of the chord then find that the resulting noise was better.

In mid-1963, Pete attended a lunchtime music show in the Art School lecture theater by an enigmatic post office engineer whose strange demeanor and rumored musical genius had the campus abuzz with gossip. The show, by Andy 'Thunderclap' Newman, playing piano and kazoo was "an incredible experience," recalled Richard Barnes in 1982. "He was a very strange and mysterious person who had never played to an audience before and he played and sung mostly his own weird compositions. He set a metronome going on top of the grand piano and just played for over an hour until he was stopped. He never looked at the audience once. The students went wild at the end."

"Pete became slightly obsessed with him and regarded him as a sort of undiscovered genius," Barnes recalled. Pete obtained a home-made recording of some of Newman's work which was entitled *Ice and Essence*, "...an amazingly inventive album with all sorts of convoluted time changes. It had an eerie, delicate, echoey quality about it and Pete played it constantly... [Once, Newman] visited Sunnyside Road and held forth about the valuable contribution Bix Beiderbecke made to jazz before he died. Pete went through a Bix Beiderbecke period for the next three or four weeks." An important interest Pete picked up from his friendship with Newman was in the methods he used to record music and other sound effects. "Before I even knew what tape recording was he was into it," Pete recalled. "Multi-tracking bird songs and locomotive recordings... special effects, echoes." Newman showed Pete how he could multi-track instruments using two mono single-track tape players, skills which were invaluable to Pete when he set about writing and recording songs in the coming years.

The Detours' first brush with recording occurred at about the same time that Pete was learning the finer points of multi-tracking with Andy Newman. The father of a friend of Pete and John knew composer Barry Gray, who had a home recording studio. "[Gray] ...used to do music for a lot of space programs for kids where they used... models [notably *Fireball XL5*, *Thunderbirds* and *Space: 1999*]," Pete told *Sounds* in 1980. "He did a lot of popular film music and he had his own studio and we did a demo there once." With Gray at the controls, The Detours recorded a song called *It Was You*[8] which Pete had written when he was 16, and another Townshend

---

[8] Although The Detours never released *It Was You*, it was deemed worthy enough to be recorded by The Who the following year. It was later recorded and released by two other groups, Britain's The Fourmost and an American group, The Naturals.

composition entitled *Please Don't Send Me Home*, the only songs he'd penned to this point. They also ran through a cover of Chuck Berry's *Come On*.

While Pete was playing the guitar and learning to experiment with recording at this time, he was composing very little new music for The Detours. *It Was You* and *Please Don't Send Me Home* were the only songs he had written, and the band was strictly playing covers on stage. The next tangible step Pete took toward composing occurred after his exposure to the music and lyrics of Bob Dylan just after *The Freewheelin' Bob Dylan* was released in May, 1963[9]. The eighteen year-old Pete had heard the record at a fellow art school student's apartment and promptly bought the album, along with its predecessor *Bob Dylan* which had appeared the previous year. These records, along with 1964's *Another Side of Bob Dylan*, cemented Dylan's position as an American music icon. Roommate Barnes remembered Dylan's effect on Pete: "When *Another Side of Bob Dylan* was released Pete played it endlessly, especially the track *All I Really Want To Do*. Dylan and particularly this track spurred him on with his own song writing. After this he would sit down with a guitar and a notepad and play around with a few lines he'd written. He kept a book of odd bits of writing, possible lyrics, scribbles and doodles and general plans and ideas." Pete soon found that writing gave him confidence and direction. "As soon as I started to write, I really came together in one piece for the first time," Pete said in 1974.

Sunday, December 22, 1963 marked an impressive coup for The Detours and their agent Bob Druce. The band played support to the Rolling Stones at St. Mary's Hall in Putney, the site of the explosive Johnny Kidd show earlier that year. The Stones, who had been together for eighteen months, were already considered stars at this point and had both a management contract and a recording deal with Decca. Pete was awestruck[10]. Glyn Johns, singer for the Presidents, was acquainted with the Stones and took Pete to their dressing room. "…it was like going into a sacred place after the gig," Pete recalled. Pete was especially impressed with guitarist Brian Jones, who complimented Pete and offered to help the

---

[9] In 2000, when Pete was asked to name his number one musical influence, he said, "Bob Dylan. He told me… that a folk singer is simply a man with a very good memory. I very much appreciate his memory. But I also appreciate his courage and invention. Number two has to be Brian Wilson. Number three Ray Davies who showed me there is an English way too."
[10] "I remember when we were still playing *Can't Buy Me Love* and maybe even the odd Shadows number thrown in when I saw the Stones on Ealing Broadway Station and thought, "Christ almighty, what a motley crew – they should be shot, the lot of them"," Pete told *Sounds*' Penny Valentine in 1972. "And every girl I fell in love with was in love with Jagger – no, come to think of it, my lot were always in love with Bill Wyman."

band in any way he could.[11] It was at this show that Pete saw Keith Richards warming up behind the curtain prior to the gig by swinging his arm in a circular motion, something which Pete would adopt into the famous 'windmill' strum which would be responsible for the loss of countless fingernails, among other injuries, during his long career.

The Detours opened for the Stones again on January 3, this time at the Glenlyn Ballroom in Forest Hill, during which Pete suspended the use of the windmill in case Keith Richards took exception. "I thought I was copying Keith Richards," he said, "so I didn't do it all night, and I watched him and he didn't do it all night either. 'Swing me what?' Keith said. He must have got into it as a warming up thing... but he didn't remember, and it developed into my sort of trademark."

Less than a month later, after a few shows at the Oldfield Hotel, a name change was necessitated when a group called Johnny Devlin and The Detours were spotted on the TV show *Thank Your Lucky Stars*. A meeting was called shortly thereafter at Pete's Sunnyside Road apartment, attended by Townshend, Daltrey, Sandom, Entwistle and Barnes. "...we were kicking around names for a band," Pete told *WNEW*'s Scott Muni in 1978, "and we were after something weird, there was The Zombies and The Beatles and Herman's Hermits, and various other crazy names and Richard Barnes, Barney I call him, came up with The Who."

"I finally thought 'The Who' worked best for many reasons," Barnes wrote in 1982. "It made people think twice when they saw it and it worked well on posters because it was so short and therefore would print up so big. Lou [the announcer at the Oldfield Hotel] would have a field day with it, or a lot of problems." The meeting adjourned without a decision being reached, but Roger reportedly made up his mind the following morning that the band would be named The Who.

Drummer Doug Sandom's sister facilitated the next step in Who history. She worked at a foundry in Shepherd's Bush whose owner, Helmut Gorden, showed some interest in her brother's band, perhaps entertaining thoughts of Brian Epstein's recent successes with the Beatles. Impressed with the band (and, no doubt, the throng of fans and the monetary possibilities they constituted) after seeing one of their Sunday night gigs at the White Hart Hotel in Acton, Helmut met with them after the show and offered to manage them, invest some money in them, and get them into the recording studio. This obviously delighted the band. Someone to provide financial backing, and therefore a new legitimacy to their existence, was sorely needed. A contract was soon signed with Gorden, who solicited parental signatures for the three minors (Pete's parents chose not to sign, rendering the contract legally ineffective).

---

[11] Pete wrote *A Normal Day For Brian, A Man Who Died Everyday* soon after Jones' death in July 1969. The song included the line *I used to play guitar as a kid wishing that I could be like him*.

The Who remained on the Commercial Entertainments circuit, retaining Bob Druce as agent while Helmut Gorden assumed the role of manager. The effects of Gorden's support soon became apparent in the form of a new van, new clothes (including "long, light tan colored leather waistcoats that came down to the knees" designed by Pete, according to Barnes[12]), and the addition of a new booking to their list of venues: The Stork Club. This central London club became Gorden's site to showcase Pete and the band, who did a series of shows there in the spring of 1964. Gorden invited booking agents, entrepreneurs and other potentially influential people along to evaluate the band. A booking with the Arthur Howes Agency, considered one of the top booking agents in the country, occurred after one such night at the Stork Club.

Around March 1964, Pete and Richard Barnes moved out of their Sunnyside Road apartment. "They were forced to move," Dave Marsh noted in his Who biography *Before I Get Old*, presumably for some unforgivable transgression. Without any immediately available lodgings, the two began living in their van. "Our van was an old ambulance that we bought from the father of one of the college students," Barnes recalled in 1982.

> He had cleverly fitted it out for long distance touring and it had seats that folded down into two single beds and one double bed. It had lights inside and sockets for shavers and was a very strange vehicle. We had a lot of fun with it. On lots of occasions we would be waved through traffic lights by policemen or waved down at accidents because, despite the fact that it was fairly dirty and had YARDBIRDS written across the back in lipstick, they thought it was still an ambulance in service. For about three weeks we lived in this ambulance, parking it outside Sid's café opposite the college so that we could get up and go straight to the door and have breakfast.

Soon tiring of living in the back of a van, Townshend and Barnes settled into the two-room apartment situated on the second floor of Pete's parents' house in Ealing Common.

While Helmut Gorden's business acumen and financial position gave The Who a much-needed shot in the arm, his knowledge of the music business, especially the local scene, was questionable at best. Dozens of bands played live in the London area in 1964 following the successes of the Beatles, the Kinks and the Stones, and staying afloat meant keeping at least one step ahead of the competition. It was in April that a freelance publicist

---

[12] Entwistle later remarked that the arty coats made them look like "poof dustmen".

and self-proclaimed 'taste master' named Peter Meaden learned of The Who's new manager at a local barber shop, and arranged to see the band. Meaden, a die hard Mod since 1961, operated an advertising company named 'Image' in partnership with Rolling Stones manager Andrew Loog Oldham, as well as being publicist for Georgie Fame, Chuck Berry and the Crystals.

Peter Meaden possessed the music know-how that Helmut Gorden lacked. As a publicist, Meaden had a good grasp of which clubs were on the cutting edge, who the important local music writers were (and he knew some of them), and precisely what styles of music and clothing were in vogue. The members of The Who took to him instantly, especially Pete. Although Helmut Gorden had supported The Who with business savvy and money, the members of the band did not identify with him at all. He was middle-aged and knew very little about music. Meaden, at least twenty years younger than Gorden, was positively full of ideas, and had the demeanor of someone who knew exactly what he wanted and where he wanted to go. Meaden could fill the role of an important ideas man and provide a crucial contact with the press and the local music scene. The Who's schedule was so busy that they were often playing four and five nights a week and were therefore unable to keep up with what was going on elsewhere in the London clubs. Gorden, although reportedly slightly mistrustful of this new figure, enlisted Meaden to help promote the band.

Helmut Gorden managed to arrange an April 1964 audition with Fontana records A&R man Chris Parmeinter, and hired out a club called the Zanzibar in London's West End for the occasion. Parmeinter was impressed with The Who, but did not like Doug Sandom's drumming and made this fact apparent in front of the band. In a surprising display of emotion, Pete, not particularly known as a leader at this point, reportedly told Sandom in full view of Parmeinter and the rest of the band, "Get it together. What's wrong with you? If you can't get it right, then you're out of the group." The outburst humiliated Doug, who recalled the audition as "The worst day of my life."

"I wasn't so ambitious as the rest of them," Sandom told Tony Fletcher in 1999. "I'd done it longer than what they had. Of course, I loved it. It was very nice to be part of a band that people followed, it was great. But I didn't get on well with Peter Townshend[13]. I was a few years older than him, and he thought I should pack it in more or less because of that." Sandom decided to leave the band, after giving them some time to look for another drummer and even loaning them his kit for about a month after his departure at the end of April.

---

[13] "You couldn't help but like him, but Peter could be a pig, a pig of a man," Sandom told Dave Marsh. "He had a nasty thing about him – he could be so *sarcastic*, it was unbelievable. He could do things that you'd think, 'God, Pete, what are you *doing*?'"

After bickering with Helmut Gorden over a suitable drummer and utilizing both a session drummer from Marshall's and future Jimi Hendrix Experience drummer Mitch Mitchell for a few shows, The Who found their man one Thursday night in late April, 1964, at a gig at the Oldfield Hotel. Keith Moon, the 17 year old drummer for local band The Beachcombers, approached the band and informed them that he could play better than the session drummer who was with them that night[14]. Moon was allowed to play the second half of the show, and proceeded to bash and flail his way through the set with incredible energy and stamina, which, incidentally, caused substantial damage to the session drummer's kit. Moon's violent thrashing of the drums impressed Pete, John and Roger sufficiently for them to ask Moon to come along to the next show, which he did, thus becoming a full-fledged member of The Who.

The Mods hit their stride in the summer of 1964. The Mod invasion had been brewing for a few years, with small factions cropping up in the suburbs, but now it was spreading into central London. Mod-oriented clothes shops and clubs began to emerge to cater to the growing demands of this highly selective subculture. Music writer Nick Cohn recalled the image: "The archetypal Mod was male, sixteen years old, rode a scooter, swallowed pep pills by the hundred, thought of women as a completely inferior race, was obsessed by cool and dug it. He was also one hundred percent hung up on himself, on his clothes and hair and image; in every way, he was a miserable, narcissistic little runt."

But Mod was also the preferred means of many of saying 'up yours' to those in power at the time. "It was fashionable, it was clean and it was groovy," Pete told Dave Marsh. "You could be a bank clerk, it was acceptable. You got them on your ground. They thought, 'Well, there's a smart young lad.' We made the establishment uptight, we made our parents uptight and our employers uptight, because although they didn't like the way we dressed, they couldn't accuse us of not being smart. We had short hair and were clean and tidy."

Peter Meaden lived and breathed Mod, and Pete Townshend soaked it up like a sponge. "He was fascinated by this almost invisible sect," Richard Barnes recalled.

> He was the first of the group to start taking pills - mod fuel [notably Drynamil]. The band had soon realized that Pete Meaden's strange behavior, his never-ending fast slick talking and his constant energy, were down to pills.

---

[14] Moon's advances took place that evening despite the fact that he was intimidated by the band. "They were outrageous," he later remarked. "All the groups at that time were smart, but onstage the Detours had stage things made of leather. Pete looked very sullen. They were a bit frightening and I was scared of them. Obviously they had been playing together for a few years and it showed."

Quite often when the band were walking around the West End with him, he would stop and try to vomit violently in the gutter. Unfortunately as 'pill-heads' hardly ever ate (the pills took away their appetites), there was nothing in his stomach for him to bring up, and after a short time he would continue his journey practically blue from the straining.

Peter Meaden wanted The Who to cater to Mod tastes by dressing in the appropriate fashions, getting the right haircuts, and basically flaunting a Mod image. While Roger and John were hesitant, Pete and Keith jumped right in. Soon, after trips to the barber shop and Carnaby Street (home to several stores which sold acceptable Mod clothing), the members of The Who were joining Meaden at "the high altar of mod", the Scene Club in Soho, West London[15]. Here, they could learn the latest dances and fashions, and soak up the Mod atmosphere. Since Pete and the rest of the band favored Motown, R&B and blues music, their tastes were already tailor made for the Mod audience; however, Meaden felt that the band's name had to go. The Who adopted a more Mod-friendly name, becoming known as The High Numbers.

Now that The Who/High Numbers had replaced their drummer, Chris Parmeinter arranged a recording session with the band in June 1964. Parmeinter reportedly wanted the band to record Eddie Holland's *Leaving Here* and an obscure Bo Diddley song, *Here 'Tis*, both part of The Who's live show at the time, along with two original songs penned by Pete Meaden, *I'm The Face* and *Zoot Suit*. Meaden admitted that these two 'originals' were really rewrites of two existing R&B numbers, the A-side (*I'm The Face*) a reworking of Slim Harpo's *Got Love If You Want It* and the B-side (*Zoot Suit*) a new take on *Country Fool* by The Showmen. Both songs are well performed and Mod-friendly, but the lyrics come across as contrived.

Zoot Suit and *I'm The Face* were released as a single on July 3, but the record failed to make the charts, despite reports that Meaden purchased as many as 250 of the 1,000 copies available. Competition was stiff that summer, and included The Animals' *The House of the Rising Sun*, The Rolling Stones' *It's All Over Now*, and The Beatles' *A Hard Day's Night*.

The High Numbers had made it to the brink. They had played hundreds of live shows over the past two years, polished their set, enlisted two key new personnel in Meaden and Moon to help push them to the next

---

[15] "All I knew was I had to get [the band] established in the West End in a way that they would be recognized by the hardcore cult center, which was the mods that used to hang out in the Scene Club, you know," said Meaden. "You can't get any more authentic than that. So I had to give them the golden seal of authenticity. If they could turn on these kids, then they could turn on the world. And so that's what the next move was."

level, but it hadn't yet happened. After recording two respectable (but unreleased) covers and two weak 'originals', they had stalled.

Chapter 2

> *"Ever since I was in art college, I believed that the elegance of pop music is that it is reflective – it holds up a mirror; and that, in its most exotic and finest sense, it is deeply, deeply philosophically and spiritually reflective, rather than just societally."*
> - Pete Townshend, 2000

Despite the failure of their single, The High Numbers continued to look wide-eyed into the future. "Meaden maintained his unflagging energy," *Melody Maker* writer Chris Charlesworth wrote in 1984. "Helmut Gordon was persuaded to put the group on contract and pay them a weekly wage of twenty pounds each." With the new steady income, Pete approached an art school instructor about the possibility of leaving college early[16]. "When he told the tutor of his intentions, the tutor was astonished to learn that Pete could make twenty pounds a week playing guitar," Charlesworth wrote. "He advised Pete to become a professional musician right away."

The High Numbers (although they were still being billed as The Who almost a month after the name change) enjoyed many successful live shows as the figurehead band of the Mod movement. The Railway Hotel gigs in June and July (one of which featured Pete's inaugural Rickenbacker smashing incident), as well as those at Mod strongholds the Goldhawk Social Club and the Trade Union Hall in Watford also occurred during this period. The High Numbers' live act was now the talk of the town. Although whittling the Detours lineup down from a five- to a four-piece group had allowed the various members the freedom to settle into their

---

[16] His steady income also meant that he didn't need any further part-time jobs – while in art school, he'd reportedly supplemented his income with gigs delivering milk and working for a butcher.

respective roles, it was not until the arrival of Keith Moon that The High Numbers had a distinctly unified stage attack. Pete's intensity on stage had found a match in Moon, who constantly wowed audiences with the speed and power of his drumming. Furthermore, Moon was not averse to kicking over his kit at the end of a show to complement Townshend's guitar smashing. Now the band had a presence on stage which was second to none, even when they refrained from destroying their instruments. They were incredibly loud, violent and energetic and played with an abandon that constantly kept audiences on edge. Their shows always possessed an undercurrent of danger, and rumors of offstage infighting between band members only added to their overall mystique.

"I drifted into using bigger and bigger amps," Pete recalled in 2000. "...Bigger, more powerful, more distorted, more potent." Roger Daltrey added, "Smashing up the guitar was just one element of it: the other was the noise. The sound was just terrifying. It was a total cacophony. Before Pete wrecked his guitar he would jam it in the speaker cone. The noise was unbelievable! Even when the guitar was in a million pieces, it would still be letting out this unearthly, squealing, primeval howl."

It was at this point (July, 1964) in the life of Pete Townshend that Kit Lambert (or, as Richard Barnes referred to him, "...a man who confessed to having been the worst officer in the British Army") happened upon The High Numbers. The band was playing to a packed house at the Railway Hotel when in walked Kit, surveying the scene like a building inspector rather than someone who had come to enjoy the show. "Kit turned up at the Railway Hotel in Harrow Wealdstone, where I was promoting The High Numbers," Barnes told *Mojo* in 2000. "I was shit scared of him, because he looked so straight. He was around 30 years old and was wearing a really expensive Savile Row suit. He looked trouble." When Kit said that he was a director looking for a band for his next film, Barnes breathed a sigh of relief and pointed out Peter Meaden. Following a conversation with Meaden and a typically blistering High Numbers performance which he would later describe as having "a satanic quality," Lambert telephoned his business partner, Chris Stamp, about his discovery of the band. Stamp was in Dublin, Ireland, working as an assistant director on *Young Cassidy*, a film based on the early life of Irish writer Sean O'Casey.

Christopher "Kit" Lambert and Chris Stamp were an interesting pair. Lambert, 26, was the son of noted British composer and conductor Constant Lambert. His accent, dress and mannerisms were strictly upper class. He was also a true eccentric. Described as "an outrageous gay...arrogant, definitely, and very annoying" by producer Shel Talmy, Kit had attended upper-class Oxford University, and served for a short time as an officer in the British army, stationed in Hong Kong. In keeping with his keen sense of adventure, Lambert took part in an expedition to Brazil in 1961 to chart the course of the longest unexplored river in the world, the

Iriri. After nearly seven months, the trip came to a horrific end when Lambert personally discovered his close friend and traveling companion Richard Mason had been ambushed, murdered and partially decapitated by an Indian hunting party.

With this harrowing experience fresh in his memory, Lambert spent six months studying cinematography at the University of Paris, then took a position as a director's assistant at Shepperton Film studios[17], which was where he met Chris Stamp. Chris, five years younger than Kit, had a working class background, as his father worked as a tugboatman on the Thames. He had managed to acquire an assistant director's position by pursuing his brother, actor Terence Stamp, into the world of show business. Lambert and Stamp worked together on several films (including *I Could Go On Singing* starring Judy Garland, Richard Attenborough's *The L-Shaped Room*, and a 1964 remake of the 1934 film *Of Human Bondage*) before deciding to make their own film about popular music. The two, who shared an apartment just west of Baker Street in west London, were described by music writer Nik Cohn as dissimilar a pair as Laurel and Hardy.

"...they were...are...as incongruous a team as [The Who] are," Keith Moon recalled in a 1972 *Rolling Stone* interview:

> You got Chris on one hand [goes into unintelligible East London cockney]: "Oh well, fuck it, jus, jus whack 'im in-a 'ead, 'it 'im in ee balls an' all." And Kit says [slipping into a proper Oxonian]: "Well, I don't agree, Chris; the thing is...the whole thing needs to be thought out in damned fine detail." These people were perfect for us, because there's me, bouncing about, full of pills, full of everything I could get me 'ands on...and there's Pete, very serious, never laughed, always cool, a grass 'ead. I was working at about ten times the speed Pete was. And Kit and Chris were like the epitome of what we were.

Chris Stamp flew back to London for the August Bank Holiday and joined Kit Lambert on Saturday, August 1 in time to catch the last fifteen minutes of The High Numbers' show at the Watford Trade Union Hall. The band had started a series of shows at this Mod stronghold the previous month, opening for Chris Farlowe & The Thunderbirds, but since much of the crowd left after The High Numbers' set, Farlowe was eventually dropped altogether, leaving The High Numbers the sole attraction at a hall with a capacity of over 1,000. "I shall always remember that night we first saw them together," Stamp told George Tremlett.

---

[17] Lambert worked on such films as *From Russia With Love* and *The Guns of Navarone* in this capacity.

I had never seen anything like it. The Who have a hypnotic effect on an audience. I realized that the first time I saw them. It was like a black mass. Even then Pete Townshend was doing all that electronic feedback stuff. Keith Moon was going wild on the drums. The effect on the audience was tremendous. It was as if they were in a trance. They just sat there watching or shuffled around the dance floor, awestruck.

Stamp was obviously as impressed with the band as Lambert, since over the following month the pair ousted Peter Meaden and Helmut Gorden, becoming managing partners of The High Numbers[18]. Pete and the band had mixed emotions about the change: the prospect of leaving the increasingly authoritarian Gorden raised few, if any, objections, but parting with Meaden was not something that The High Numbers desired. Meaden had given the band an identity during the short time he was with them, and the band members felt a distinct affinity toward him. However, his intense personality did not lend itself well to teaming up with the imposing pair taking over the band, so it was eventually accepted among the band that Meaden would have to go.

Ironically, just prior to their departure, Pete Meaden and Helmut Gorden's work was beginning to pay off. As publicist for The High Numbers, Meaden had arranged a five-week residency for the band at one of London's hottest Mod clubs, The Scene. This Soho club featured DJ Guy Stevens, whose stateside musical contacts enabled him to acquire many obscure, small-label recordings by black R&B, blues, and soul artists who the Mods adored. Pete and Richard Barnes used to visit Stevens' apartment and sift through his vast record collection, listening for songs to add to The High Numbers' repertoire[19].

Also around the time of the change in management, Meaden landed The High Numbers an audition with Rolling Stones manager Andrew Loog Oldham at The New Carlton Irish Club. "Andrew was very excited by what he saw as we played R&B songs by Chuck Berry and Bo Diddley, and a few Tamla Motown songs like *Dance To Keep From Crying*, and *Motoring*,"

---

[18] Lambert was informed by The Beatles' attorney, David Jacobs, that the band's contract with Gorden was legally invalid; Meaden, who had no legal claim to the band, received a buyout for relinquishing control to Lambert and Stamp. Meaden reportedly later boasted that Townshend sent him a thousand pounds every Christmas in a gesture of thanks for his early guidance of the band. "I was the fellow who saw the potential in modism, which is the greatest form of lifestyle you can imagine," Meaden told the *NME*'s Steve Turner in 1978. "I got The Who together because I loved the life so much. I got them together and I dressed them in mod clothes, gave them all the jingoism and all the paraphernalia of modism. It was right on the button. The timing was just right. And timing is where it's at."
[19] Stevens went on to produce work by The Clash and Mott the Hoople.

Pete wrote on www.eelpie.com in July, 2001. "He predicted we would be successful... It was a magic day to have the manager of my favorite band tell us we were headed for great things." Despite his enthusiasm, Oldham, aware that Lambert and Stamp were maneuvering to manage the band, decided to defer to them.[20]

Meanwhile, Arthur Howes' agency booked The High Numbers on a series of five consecutive Sunday shows in resort towns Brighton and Blackpool, opening for major acts such as Gerry and The Pacemakers, The Kinks (who had just released *You Really Got Me*), and a two-show stint in support of The Beatles. The residency at the Scene and the Arthur Howes bookings (which came about as a result of the Stork Club shows back in the spring), particularly the shows with The Beatles[21], played a major role in getting The High Numbers noticed.

Kit Lambert and Chris Stamp's first order of business as co-managers of The High Numbers was to get the band members signed under a legal contract. Lambert had a music-savvy lawyer draw up an appropriate document, and the band members signed. Since the entire band consisted of minors, their parents also had to sign the document. This time, Pete's parents consented to the deal, after Cliff reportedly lined out a clause which would have given Kit and Chris a percentage of any writing royalties due his son. The new document marked a significant improvement over the band's last contract, reportedly guaranteeing the band members £1,000 each per year. Lambert would consume his savings and a significant inheritance in very short order keeping this promise.

For the time being, at least, Kit and Chris shelved their ideas for a pop music film in the interest of promoting The High Numbers. The main focus at first was on the band's stage show, naturally, as both Lambert and Stamp were used to working more with visual ideas than auditory ones. The pair compensated for their glaring lack of any knowledge of the popular music scene in London with sheer intestinal fortitude. Many of their first dealings with professionals in the music business involved Lambert and Stamp concocting fictional scenarios in order to glean the necessary

---

[20] Fear of the eccentric Lambert may have aided Oldham in making his decision: "One day, to my horror, I saw Moon and Townshend stepping out of Andrew's [Rolls] with Brian Jones, all of them chatting conspiratorially," Lambert said, according to Andrew Motion in 1987's *The Lamberts*. "So when the boys got to my flat I drew my old service revolver, an enormous Colt Special, lined the boys against the wall, and asked what's up... Andrew with his white Persian cat, tame joint roller and laced-up fly buttons was obviously impressing them, so I sort of cut in in no uncertain way. Next time I saw the Rolls arrive I jumped in, kicked the cat out of the way, and told him hands off or else."

[21] Beatles' fans certainly noticed The High Numbers after an August 16 support stint. "After the Blackpool show, the Beatles made a safe escape, but the High Numbers, who still moved their own equipment, were in the act of loading their van when a horde of Beatlemaniacs approached, screaming, tearing their hair and rending their garments at the sight of a pop group," Dave Marsh wrote in 1983. "Any pop group." The band emerged from the fray with the collars of their jackets ripped off, and Daltrey lost a sleeve.

information. Mike Shaw, a friend of Chris Stamp who was named the band's production manager, explained to Richard Barnes in 1982 some of the lengths to which they had to go in order to obtain the necessary knowledge of the music business:

> I had to pretend that I was a manager of a group that was playing in Essex or Somerset or somewhere. We made up a name, the Ramrods, I think it was, and I went to the Arthur Howes agency and asked them what we should do. You know, we had to find out. How did we get a contract – what did we do? What was the normal sort of deal we could get? How did one get gigs? How did you get an agent? Then I reported back to Chris and Kit. We needed some idea of how much to ask for and so on.

During the five-week Arthur Howes tour Kit insisted that The High Numbers control their own stage lighting, which was largely unheard of in those days, especially at the bigger venues. "We were the first group to have a Production Manager," Pete said in 1987. "Mike ran a small light rig for us – just a couple of towers – but it made a hell of a difference. People were used to a single spot, or a naked bulb." At the Beatles shows in Blackpool on August 16 (at which even The Beatles did not do their own lighting), management of the Opera House refused to let the band handle their own lights. Lambert's bullish character won out. "Well, Kit just forced his way and shouted the man down," Mike Shaw recalled in 1982. "He couldn't stop us. We had every right to do our own lighting... We wanted to put on a show rather than just be another band following on from everybody else. It was meant to be a show in itself."

It was this unconventional approach that led Kit, Chris and Mike to shoot a 16mm promotional film of the band, an unusual idea at the time. They shot footage (on rented equipment) at one of the autumn 1964 Railway Hotel shows, complete with a mono soundtrack, as well as filming Mods hanging around and dancing at the Scene club in Soho. In addition to its use as a promotional tool, Lambert and Stamp would often air this film prior to the band taking the stage at the beginning of a show[22]. Other Lambert/Stamp-inspired ideas involved sending the band to Max Factor on Bond Street for supplies and lessons on applying stage makeup, and a trip to Carnaby Street for enough Mod clothing for the band to be able to maintain their image on and off stage. And, since the Bob Druce and Arthur Howes bookings had waned, the new management duo began the search for new

---

[22] The promotional film, which cost a reported £350 to make, was eventually sold to the television show *That's For Me* – for £25.

venues for their band. Work also began on the hunt for a recording contract as Kit and Chris proceeded to arrange for auditions for the group.

The nucleus of the Lambert/Stamp empire, which had recently been named New Action Limited, was housed in Kit and Chris' apartment on Ivor Court, near Baker Street. The pair had lived there since late 1963. In *Maximum R&B*, Richard Barnes recalled the appearance of "The Who's headquarters" at the time:

> Kit had papers all over the place, maps pinned on the wall and over the floor. I had posters drying on every available surface, as well as a couple of washing lines strung across the main room, which had about fifty shiny wet posters pegged to them to dry. Mike Shaw and Kit would be coming and going constantly on various errands. Kit, when in the flat, would always be planning things. He would never relax. He was always worrying about everything.

"Kit had this Shell map of London on the wall, and he had it covered all over with drawing pins and red and blue circles where the Who was going to play in different clubs," 'Irish' Jack Lyons told Dave Marsh. "The place looked more like Churchill's bloody war room."

New Action's Ivor Court environs were quite cramped, according to Anya Forbes-Adam, Kit's longtime assistant. "Chris slept on a bed in the hall," she told Andrew Motion in his excellent biography *The Lamberts*, published in 1987. "I was on the sofa, and Kit was in the main bedroom. I got £8 a week, but Kit always borrowed it back. Theoretically I was doing publicity, but in fact I was cooking, sewing on Daltrey's symbols, and consoling Moon for not being in The Beach boys. We were a shambles, but we were a happy family."

Lambert and Stamp never seemed to rest – Stamp careening all over London looking for new venues for the band, while Kit thought up the next grandiose plan in the chaos of his office. Kit, especially, was an eccentric, "thriving on sheer nerve," according to Barnes, and "...profligate and flamboyant in both his personal and business behavior," as Dave Marsh put it. But Marsh also pointed out that while his management style may have seemed haphazard or ill-conceived, Lambert was not playing around. "Irrational as much of his behavior undoubtedly was, it would be a mistake not to see Lambert as dead serious. He wanted and needed to make a giant pop success – and a small fortune – to prove himself to his father's memory and for his own satisfaction."

In September, 1964, The High Numbers visited EMI Studios on Abbey Road for an audition. "That was an amazing session," Pete recalled in 1973. "We recorded it in the same room that The Beatles did their first album in. We were overawed by it and incredibly nervous. We did a tape which was bloody dynamite." Unfortunately, EMI's John Burgess did not agree, as Kit received a letter dated October 22 effectively declining to offer the band a contract. An audition with Pye Records around this time yielded similar results.

Meanwhile, after attempts at breaking into new venues in Greenwich and Leytonstone failed due to poor attendance, Chris Stamp's search for new venues produced a weekly slot at the Marquee, a jazz and R&B club located on Wardour Street in Soho. This was a major coup – although the band had performed at the Scene and the 100 Club (both in Soho), both were known more for their DJ's rather than live acts – records were the featured attraction, not bands. The Marquee, although it had recently moved from Oxford Street to Wardour Street, was a well-known, established venue for live R&B and jazz acts. A successful Tuesday night slot there would gain The High Numbers some much-needed press attention.

Just after The High Numbers played their last show in Greenwich Town Hall in late October, 1964, Kit Lambert decided to change the band's name back to The Who. "The Who was easy to remember, made good conversation fuel, provided ready-made gags for the disc jockeys," Lambert said in an interview. "It was so corny it had to be good."

It also looked good on posters. When Kit and Chris sent The High Numbers to try their luck performing in the east end, they had enlisted Richard Barnes to develop and print posters to attract an audience. They employed the same method for the new Marquee shows, this time using a logo designed by a graphic artist hired by Kit, which featured the words 'The Who,' one above the other with the 'h' in the two words joined together. An arrow was drawn coming out of the top of the 'o' in 'Who', like the medical symbol meaning 'male'. A photograph of Pete windmilling his arm over a Rickenbacker guitar appeared in the upper left corner, while the words 'Maximum R&B' adorned the bottom of the poster. This has been a defining image of the band, used repeatedly over the forty-plus years since its creation.

Although their first show at the Marquee on November 24, 1964, drew fewer than thirty hard-core fans from the Goldhawk Social Club, The Oldfield and The Railway, The Who reportedly played a fantastic set and the numbers were more encouraging the following week, with a turnout of almost 300. Soon the band was packing the club, going on to break attendance records set by Manfred Mann and the Yardbirds. The Marquee performances showcased The Who at a time when the band was blossoming into an incredible live act. The effect the band had on its' fans was amazing. One fan, quoted in 1997's *The Who Concert File*, remembered:

> The first time I came out of my shell was when I saw The Who at the Marquee. I'd never seen anything like

it. I couldn't imagine that people could do such things. I went straight out and broke a window, I was that impressed. It broke down so many barriers for me, just that one evening of seeing The Who. The set was so fucking violent and the music so heady it hit you in the head as well as the guts, it did things to you. You'd never heard anything like it. 'Maximum R&B' said the poster...and fuck me, was it!

In 1994, *New Musical Express* writer Keith Altham remembered his first encounter with The Who, which occurred at the Marquee:

> I arrived late and heard what sounded like someone sawing through an aluminum dustbin with a chainsaw to the accompaniment of a drummer who was obviously in time with another group on another planet and the most deafening bass guitar in the world. The vocalist was virtually inaudible amidst the cacophony. I turned on my heel to leave but Kit [Lambert] came up behind me with a brandy, promising in his beautifully fruity public school accent that, "this will be a moment you will remember all your life." He pulled me into the sweaty, smelly confines of the Marquee where a large number of Mods in their vented jackets and Fred Perry shirts leapt about in delight.
>
> I was astonished. The long lanky guitarist with the big hooter was doing a passing impression of a malfunctioning windmill, all the while extracting a tortuous scream from his guitar which sounded as though several Siamese cats were being electrocuted inside his speaker cabinet. This, I was reliably informed, was 'feedback.' Then the surly looking blond thug up front screaming 'I'm A Man' threw his microphone at the drummer who retaliated by hurling sticks at his head and thrashing around his kit like a whirling dervish. The bass player's hair was dyed jet black (his tribute to Elvis) and in his black clothes on a very dark stage was almost invisible. He made up for this by turning his volume control up so high he could be heard in the next world.
>
> Finally the apocalypse arrived on cue when the guitarist raised his guitar above his head and smashed it to splinters on the stage while the drummer kicked his drums in the general direction of the vocalist who made a determined effort to hit him over the head with one of his cymbals.

When the dust finally settled and the cheers subsided Kit turned to me. "Wasn't that wonderful, dear boy?" he asked.

The shows, featuring songs such as *Young Man Blues, You Really Got Me, Smokestack Lightning, Green Onions* (by Booker T. and the MG's: Pete told *Rolling Stone* editor Jann Wenner in 1968 that MG's guitarist Steve Cropper "...really turned me on to aggressive guitar playing.") *Here 'Tis*, and *Pretty Thing*, often also included an extended R&B jam (*Can't Sit Down*) with sparse vocals which featured Pete's overdriven guitar. Townshend, already adorning hundreds of Who posters around London, was becoming the driving force behind The Who.

In late 1964, Pete played Kit the demo tape of *It Was You* that the Detours had recorded the previous year. Kit was sufficiently impressed that he went out and bought Pete two mono tape recorders for his use in composing. Back in the Confederates/Aristocrats/Scorpions days, a friend of Pete's had sparked an interest in tape recording. "The guy had a tape recorder and we used to have such fun with it, doing spoof radio shows and stuff like that, and I set my heart on getting one," Pete told *Guitarist* in 1990. "My mum and dad had a junk shop, in which I worked, and inevitably a tape recorder came in – it was a Grundig or something. I couldn't dub on it but I rapidly realized that all I needed was another tape machine and I'd be able to."

Pete, still sharing the apartment on the top floor of his parents' house with Richard Barnes, set about converting one of the seven spacious rooms into his first home recording studio. In 1982, Barnes remembered the logistics involved:

> A friend of ours from Art School...undertook the task of laying down a 1-inch thick cement floor all over the existing floorboards of this room. It had a layer of chicken wire in to strengthen it. We bought some very expensive sheets of sound-proofing material. These were 8' x 4' sheets of about 3" thick compressed straw or something. Each sheet weighed about a ton. We had to get six volunteers from Art School to help lift each one.

Pete's equipment at the time consisted of the two mono tape machines, a single microphone and a makeshift metronome he'd fashioned out of a variable speed turntable.

One of the first songs that Pete recorded using his new setup (in winter, 1964) was entitled *Call Me Lightning*. "One of the oldest demos I have," Pete wrote in 1982[23]. "Recorded with another song called *You Don't Have To Jerk* at the flat my Art school pal Barney shared with me. The flat was on the floor above my parents' home. It provided a very safe independence, a phony rebellion until I moved to Belgravia in 1965. The song is a very clear example of how difficult it was for me to reconcile what I took to be Roger's need for macho, chauvinist lyrics and Keith Moon's appetite for surf music and fantasy sports car love affairs." The demo of this song (which was released on 1987's *Another Scoop*) is interesting because it demonstrates both Pete's abilities as a musician at the time and the remarkable quality of his demo tapes. Even this example, one of Pete's earliest recordings, has a crisp, clean sound and features multi-tracked acoustic and electric guitar and harmony vocals. Pete remains impressed with the quality of these earliest examples of his demo recordings. "...although those demos are a little brittle-sounding," he told *Guitarist* in 1990, they were the first things I ever did and they sound really good." The Who would release *Call Me Lightning* as a single in 1968.

With the exposure and prominence of their now popular residency at the Marquee, The Who began to garner recognition in the form of reviews in the national music press. In one of The Who's first press appearances, on January 9, 1965, the British national music paper *Melody Maker* wrote:

> ...[the band] should be billed not only as 'Maximum R&B' but as 'far-out R&B'...*Heatwave* – the Martha and the Vandellas hit number – is given typically fiery 'Who' treatment. Another of their outstanding numbers was an instrumental, *Can't Sit Down*. This performance demonstrated the weird and effective techniques of guitarist Paul Townshend [sic], who expertly uses speaker feedback to accompany many of his solos. 'The Who', spurred by a most exhilarating drummer and a tireless vocalist, must surely be one of the trendsetting groups of 1965.

Despite efforts to land a recording contract during the previous autumn, the band still was unable to persuade record executives that they were good enough to produce a hit record. They had no original songs other than the two which they had recorded as The High Numbers, which rendered them merely a cover band with a great stage show. All this would change in 1965, as Pete, with the encouragement of Kit Lambert, was beginning to compose his own material. The year would see the release of *My Generation*, widely regarded as the single that permanently imprinted

---

[23] In 1996, Pete mentioned a song entitled *Silver Stingray* "and a couple of other mock-Jan and Dean things" as other very early examples of his writings in his first demo studio.

the band's image on British pop culture, an anthem for a generation in need of a catalyst.

My Generation was preceded by two singles which stand as milestones in the writing development of Pete Townshend, as well as in the establishment of The Who as a bona fide chart band in the U.K. The first of these, *I Can't Explain*, recorded and released in January 1965, was the band's first hit. It reached number 8 in the British charts and established The Who's national presence, something which had been bolstered almost daily for the past few years with the band's busy gig itinerary.

With his budding composer armed with a small batch of demo tapes fresh from his new home recording studio, Kit Lambert managed to sign The Who with an American record producer named Shel Talmy who had recently produced The Kinks' smash hit *You Really Got Me*.[24] The contract did not specify a particular record company, giving Talmy the authority to choose a label. The assumption was made that the popular Talmy's name as producer would give the band enough leverage to garner acceptance from a record label. With Talmy being the established professional in the situation, he controlled the content of the contract, so it was no surprise that he would stand to make more money than all four members of The Who and their management team combined. However, the deal got the band in the studio, something which they had been trying to do for months.

I Can't Explain was recorded at Pye Studios, London, in early January 1965. The band's first recording session with Talmy was by no means a pleasant experience. "Shel Talmy," Pete recalled in 1971, "...was a great believer in making groups who were nothing into stars. He was also a great believer in pretending the group didn't exist when they were in a recording studio. Despite the fact that... our first few records are among our best, they were the least fun to make... However, dear Shel got us our first single hits. So he was as close to being God for a week as any other unworthy soul has been."

Upon hearing *I Can't Explain*, Talmy added a few choruses to extend the length of the song and rearranged a few lines. Talmy was not impressed with the band's backing vocals and enlisted all-male backing group The Ivy League to do the job. Likewise, Townshend's abilities as a lead guitarist were brought into question and local session whiz Jimmy Page, who went on to forge his own legendary career with Led Zeppelin, was brought in to lend a hand.

Pete was not impressed with this turn of events and insisted that he play lead on the song. He reportedly eventually won the battle since Page

---

[24] In a 2000 interview with *Mojo*, Ray Davies stated that Shel Talmy's role in recording *You Really Got Me* was minimal. Talmy's recording of the song was "swamped in echo. It was horrible," Davies said. The Kinks rerecorded the song (at their own expense), "and we bashed it out with no echo." Talmy "had to be there", Davies said, but his input was minimal. "...he was happy to be named producer."

did not possess a 12-string Rickenbacker, considered key to the song's sound, and Pete would not let Page use his. While reports vary as to whether Page ended up playing rhythm on the song, it's generally accepted that he played on the B-side, *Bald Headed Woman* (a song Talmy wrote), which was recorded in about two hours[25].

Dave Marsh called *I Can't Explain* "...A slight song with a lyric on the edge of moony adolescent cliché, but as a recorded performance, it remains one of the outstanding documents of rock and roll. The sound is sharper, percussive, electric as a live wire."

"It can't be beat for straightforward Kink copying," Pete said in 1971. "It seems to be about the frustrations of a young person who is so incoherent and uneducated that he can't state his case to the bourgeois intellectual blah blah blah. Or, of course, it might be about drugs." Like The Kinks' *You Really Got Me*, The Who's new single was short, sweet and to the point. The timelessness and sheer staying power *of I Can't Explain* is demonstrated by the fact that the song was used as the opener for the vast majority of The Who's live shows over the next forty years.

Chris Charlesworth assessed *I Can't Explain* as capturing the sentiments of youth: "...an explosive debut, a song about the frustration of being unable to express yourself, not just to the girl of your dreams but, in a broader sense, to the world as a whole." Charlesworth touched here on the essence of the song, and on the essence of Pete's writing: As in plenty of examples of Pete's future writing, a tremendous amount of depth lay beneath what was immediately apparent in the lyrics. This phenomenon escaped even the writer himself. "I wrote *I Can't Explain* about a kid who couldn't explain to a girl that he loved her – that was all it was about," Pete later said. "...A couple of months later it was on the charts, and I started to look at it closely... and I realized that the song was on the chart not because it was a little love song, but because it openly paraded a sort of weakness."

I Can't Explain "...was a *desperate* copy of The Kinks," Pete told *Uncut*'s Simon Goddard in 2004. "...I just thought, 'This'll pay the rent for a while and then I'll go back and be an artist.' I had no idea."

> This deputation of kids came up and said, 'This really means something.' I was kind of going [disinterested] 'Yeah, yeah, yeah' and they went, 'No, you don't understand, this really means something.' And I still went, yeah, whatever, but then they got hold of me [shakes

---

[25] "...I was there for the whole session but I wasn't needed," Page told *Mojo* in 2004. "I actually play on *Bald Headed Woman*: just a few fuzzbox phrases. We played it live in the studio but I was just there to augment things. It was such a thrill to suddenly find myself doing a session that was so totally dynamic. Straight after that, I went to see The Who live at the Marquee and we got to know each other better."

fists] and said, 'No! You don't understand!' And I thought, 'No, I *don't* understand.' I remember walking away and thinking, 'This is really significant, I think I'm going to be an artist in the modern world, I've just found that I have an audience, I've just found that I have a role which is that I can reflect this group of people immediately.' Admittedly it was a bunch of pilled-up mods [grins] but it was better than nothing...

Shel Talmy, wanting to make the single a hit in the U.S. (because, he said, "the big bread was in America, not England"), sold the single to Decca's American subsidiary, who released the record in England on their Brunswick label[26]. *I Can't Explain* was released within two weeks of the recording session, and was well received in England, although not a smash hit, starting out at number 33. Competition that month included The Kinks' *Tired of Waiting For You*, Tom Jones' *It's Not Unusual*, and The Righteous Brothers' *You've Lost that Lovin' Feeling*. The single failed to make an impact in the U.S. (American Decca was known as not being particularly receptive to rock'n'roll recordings), reaching only number 93.

Shortly after the release of *I Can't Explain*, while Chris Stamp was working in Norway on the Kirk Douglas movie *The Heroes of Telemark*, Kit Lambert put Pete up in rooms above his own flat, which doubled as their company's new offices in upper class Eaton Place, Belgravia[27]. Lambert did not want his band's songwriter living in Ealing anymore. "Kit had musical ideas and could guide and encourage Pete," Roger Daltrey recalled in 2000. "He had that relationship with him where he could say, 'That's fucking rubbish, Peter! Absolute fucking rubbish!'" Lambert felt that Pete's pot smoking habits stemmed from art school and that the best way to get him to stop such behavior was to remove him from the situation. "Kit dragged me out of that environment because he thought it was decadent," Pete told Richard Barnes. "He took me away from the decadence that was ours to the decadence that was his."

Another factor led to Pete's change of residence at this time: His parents, who were not particularly enamored with Pete's attempts at remodeling and soundproofing one of the rooms of his upstairs flat in order to transform it into a recording studio. "They tried to soundproof it," Pete's

---

[26] Brunswick, incidentally, was Bill Haley's record label.
[27] The move to Belgravia was at least partly motivated by Lambert's wish to project an impression that New Action was a thriving, profitable outfit. An additional ploy was his reported insistence on using hired Rolls-Royces as his preferred mode of travel. The company was actually at least £60,000 in debt at the time, according to Andrew Motion. "At Eaton Place," Lambert later said, "the bailiffs kept coming and going. I used to have a bust of my father's head which I used to put down the loo and make Anya sit on top of it. She would have to sit there for ages. I used to say to her, 'No. No. Make it look authentic. Take your knickers down.'"

younger brother Paul told Dave Marsh in 1983. "They had egg boxes everywhere on the walls, and they knocked a hole in one wall to put in a window. And they didn't put the window in; they didn't get round to that. Then the cement made the ceiling start to bow in downstairs. There was a blazing row, and my mom and dad kicked 'em out."

Life at Eaton Place saw Pete's introduction to the ways of the upper class. "Kit's grooming started with etiquette and showing Keith and me the right wines and so on," Pete told *Mojo* in 2000. "Up to the last years of his life, Keith was still ordering the vintage of Dom Perignon that Kit said was the best." Kit also introduced Pete to a record collection markedly different from that of Tom Wright. Lambert's collection included "Sinatra, Ellington, a good deal of Italian opera, and a fair amount of baroque music including Purcell's *Gordian Knot Untied*, which he played all the time," Pete told Andrew Motion in 1987. "But not much pop."

"Kit Lambert gave me an album by a 17th-century English composer called Henry Purcell," Pete told *Guitar Player* in 1989.

> It was just full of Baroque suspensions, and I was deeply, deeply influenced by it. I remember I'd just written *I Can't Explain*... I was on my way, but I was just copying. Then I sat down and wrote all the demos for the Who's first album, and it's just covered in those suspensions: *The Kids Are Alright, I'm A Boy*, they're full of them. And it's still one of my favorite pieces of music. In that sense, it was another very, very important thing that I got from Kit, because he wasn't just a manager and he wasn't just a record producer; he was a fantastic, extraordinary friend. I remember I was staying at his flat in Belgravia once, and he put it on for the first time. I heard it and went into the room, and there were tears streaming down his face, because it was his father's favorite piece of music, and it reminded him of his dad.

Life with Lambert, a homosexual, also meant that Pete witnessed firsthand London's gay scene. "We used to eat at all the gay restaurants...and dine out with Quentin Crisp and all that," Pete said in 1982. "I didn't care." Pete has been careful to point out that Lambert's motives in inviting Townshend to live with him were purely professional. "...just for the record," Pete told *Rolling Stone*'s Kurt Loder in 1982, "if Kit Lambert was gettin' into rock music 'cause he was looking for boys, there was certainly no approach made to any individual in the Who – *ever*, under any circumstances. Maybe we weren't his type."[28] Lambert biographer Andrew Motion pointed out that "...the truth is that Kit's friendship with Townshend was charged less by sexual attraction than by the appeal of shaping and directing an as yet unrealized talent. ...He regularly pointed out how remarkably unattractive the band were, and agreed with a friend who, on first seeing them, pronounced them 'the ugliest in London'."

On January 18, 1965, three days after *I Can't Explain* was released in the U.K., The Who made their first TV appearance on *The Beat Room*, appropriately aired from the BBC's Lime Grove Studios in Shepherd's Bush, The Who's home turf. Although it was only aired on BBC2 in the London region and the band was not billed in advance, their first appearance certainly gave them an opportunity to further promote their new single, which they performed here. Another more fruitful television appearance was forthcoming. Vicki Wyckham, producer of *Ready Steady Go*, attended one of the band's January shows at the Marquee and was sufficiently impressed to book the band for her show, considered the hippest music program in England and an important trend-setter. The show boasted a viewership of nearly three million. "...It is a very popular programme, revolving around guest pop artists miming to their records; interviews – sometimes last-minute affairs with stars who drop in; film clips; records to demonstrate new dances; and more records just to be danced to," wrote *Melody Maker*'s Chris Roberts in January, 1964. "It has developed, partly unconsciously... into something mysteriously "in", with an avant-garde clannishness... If you have ever read about mods and rockers, and watch the show, you will know why. It is the TV stronghold of mods, the frighteningly clean, sharply dressed arbiters of tomorrow's tastes." Among bands whose first big TV break came on *RSG* were the Dave Clark Five, Manfred Mann, The Rolling Stones, The Kinks, Herman's Hermits, Marianne Faithfull, Cilla Black, and Dusty Springfield.

The band appeared on *RSG* on January 29, 1965, a Friday night, and were accompanied by the '100 faces', a large contingent of their most rabid mod fans whose attendance was orchestrated by Kit Lambert, who had supplied them with Who scarves. *New Musical Express* writer Roy Carr described Lambert's accomplishments that evening:

> As it transpired, Lambert discovered that the one person responsible for assembling the weekly studio audience was ill, and so Lambert *kindly* volunteered to supply a ready-made crowd of *typical teens*. What the *RSG* producers didn't know was that Lambert had herded together the entire audience from The Goldhawk Social

---

[28] While Townshend's statement is crystal clear, Shel Talmy's view after recording with The Who was that Lambert was "hot after Townshend," according to *Mojo*.

Club in Shepherds Bush and that each one was both bona fide Mod and die-hard Who fan. That night, the other acts on the show really didn't stand a chance. But The Who and, in particular their audience, were sensational. In just under three action-packed minutes, the Mod movement had spread the word right across the British Isles, and the word was The Who.

The Who's first national TV appearance was a huge success, with the 100 faces inserting appropriately thunderous vocal support during a mimed *I Can't Explain*.

Pete Townshend and The Who's next big break occurred towards the end of the following month. The Who were asked to perform on *Top of The Pops* (the British equivalent of *American Bandstand* with an average viewership of around 5.5 million at the time) as the replacement for a band who had canceled at the last minute. They were slotted to appear on 'Tip for the Top,' a segment showcasing potential up-and-comers. "It was exciting," Pete wrote in 1970.

> You only got on the show, apart from the plug spot, if your record was in the charts, so it was instant status, and the doors of the studio were always surrounded by lots of pretty young fans who were always waiting for some other band, it seemed. In those days we had to mime to our record, thus, it was a cinch. No worries about throats or atmosphere, or getting in tune, just about what color pants to wear, or what silly outfit to put on to attract the camera's attention.

"Keith would get about 80 per cent of the camera time," Townshend continued, "simply because the director was convinced it was a drummer-led group. Every time the camera swung to me I would swing my arm like a maniac…" This appearance pushed *I Can't Explain* to its highest U.K. chart position – number 8.

With a hit record, The Who now had more live bookings than they could handle, usually performing on stage twenty or more times a month during this period. Now that they had the attention of the public, the challenge was for the band to remain in demand.

April 27, 1965, marked the end of The Who's twenty-three week residency at the Marquee Club. This booking had brought the band the reputation among fans and the press attention it needed to become a successful, nationally recognized act. While they still played regularly throughout the London area, The Who began to perform further afield as word of their live show spread across the country. The band ventured north through Leicester and Nottingham, on to Newcastle and finally to Scotland for the first time in May, 1965.

In June, *Melody Maker* ran an article with the heading, "Every so often a group is poised on the brink of a breakthrough. Word has it it's The Who." The article provides an interesting account of The Who's stage show during this period. "Their music is defiant, and so is their attitude," the article read.

> Their sound is vicious. This is no note-perfect 'showbiz' group, singing in harmony and playing clean guitar runs. The Who lay down a heavy beat...Moon thunders round the drums. Townshend swings full circles with his right arm. He bangs out morse code by switching the guitar pick-ups on and off. Notes bend and whine. He turns suddenly and rams the end of his guitar into the speaker. A chord shudders on the impact. The speaker rocks. Townshend strikes again on the rebound. He rips the canvas covering, tears into the speaker cone, and the distorted solo splutters from a demolished speaker. The crowds watch this violent display spellbound...it's an exhausting act to watch. But also highly original and full of tremendous pace.

The Who began work on their debut album in March, 1965, at London's IBC studios. The album was to contain mostly covers, with 8 or 9 staples from the band's live set recorded at the first session: *I'm A Man, Heatwave, I Don't Mind, Lubie (Come Back Home), Please Please Please, Leaving Here, Motoring*. Reportedly, only one Townshend composition was recorded, the aptly titled *You're Going To Know Me*. The band held further recording sessions in March and April during which they continued work on the proposed album and their next single.

Anyway, Anyhow, Anywhere, the follow-up to *I Can't Explain*, was an important single for The Who in that it was more Townshend than Talmy. The single reflected The Who's biggest strength – their live firepower – effectively, complete with screeching feedback and Moon's now standard anarchic percussion assault. With *Anyway, Anyhow, Anywhere*, Pete pointed The Who firmly in the direction in which he wanted to travel. This was an important step in an era of producer dictatorships.

Roger told Alan Smith of the *New Musical Express* that *Anyway, Anyhow, Anywhere* was written at 3am, the day before it was recorded, "when he and Pete were locked in a room to make them concentrate on songwriting," according to Smith. Daltrey cowrote this song, which became the theme song for *Ready, Steady, Go* for a time. "I wrote the first verse and Roger helped with the rest," Pete recalled. "I was inspired by listening to

Charlie Parker, feeling that this was really a free spirit, and whatever he'd done with drugs and booze and everything else, that his playing released him and freed his spirit, and I wanted us to be like that, and I wanted to write a song about that, a spiritual song."

"I was laying on my mattress on the floor listening to a Charlie Parker record when I thought up the title," Pete wrote in *Rolling Stone* in 1971. "...I just felt the guy was so free when he was playing. He was a soul without a body, riding, flying, on music...The freedom suggested by the title became restricted by the aggression of our tightly defined image when I came to write the words. In fact, Roger was really a hard nut then, and he changed quite a few words himself to toughen the song up to suit his temperament. It is the most excitingly pigheaded of our songs." The song also was one of the first to feature feedback; in fact, Decca records initially returned the master to Shel Talmy, believing it to be defective due to the various roaring and screeching noises.

"Kit realized that we had to be seen before people would begin to buy our records," Entwistle told Dave Marsh.

> *Anyway, Anyhow, Anywhere* was his way of taking a shortcut. The intention was to encapsulate the Who's entire stage act on just one side of a single – to illustrate the arrogance of the mod movement and then, through the feedback, the smashing of the instruments.
>
> We recorded it at IBC Studios in next to no time. After doing the basic backing track, we set up Townshend's stack and let him do the various whooshing, smashing, morse code and feedback effects as overdubs. It was as simple as that.

In mid 1965, as Mod fever began to cool considerably in the London area (due in part to several violent riots involving Mods which had taken place in Britain over the past year), The Who decided that they did not want to go down with the ship. Thus, *Anyway, Anyhow, Anywhere* was described by the band as the 'first pop-art single.' Pete commented at the time that pop-art "is re-presenting something the public is familiar with in a different form. Like clothes. Union Jacks are supposed to be flown. We have a jacket made of one. Keith Moon, our drummer has a jersey with the RAF insignia on it. I have a white jacket, covered in medals."[29] The band had begun to veer off the mod path. "We think the mod thing is dying,"

---

[29] "Kit came up with the idea for that jacket – he should be posthumously knighted for it," Daltrey said in 2000. "Prior to that the Union Jack had only ever been flown on buildings as the national flag. When we walked into a Savile Row tailor and said, 'Will you make a jacket out of this?', they said, 'No.' They thought they'd go to jail."

Pete said. "We don't plan to go down with it, which is why we've become individualists."

Pete espoused the virtues of pop art to anyone who would listen, telling the *Observer* in March, "From valueless objects – a guitar, a microphone, a hackneyed pop tune, we extract a new value. We take objects with one function and give them another. And the auto-destructive element – the way we destroy our instruments – adds immediacy to it all."

"We stand for pop-art clothes, pop-art music and pop-art behavior," Pete told *Melody Maker*'s Nick Jones in July, 1965.

> This is what everybody seems to forget – we don't change off-stage. We live pop-art.
>
> I bang my guitar on my speaker because of the visual effect. It is very artistic. One gets a tremendous sound, and the effect is great... If guitars exploded and went up in a puff of smoke, I'd be happy. The visual effect would be complete.
>
> ...Well, our next single is really pop-art. I wrote it with that intention. Not only is the number pop-art, the lyrics are 'young and rebellious.' It's anti middle-class, anti boss-class, and anti young marrieds! I've nothing against these people really – just making a positive statement.

The 'pop art' idea was obviously the result of some prodding by Kit Lambert. 20 year-old Pete was often in over his head during interviews when he tried to describe pop art to the press. "Kit Lambert described *Anyway, Anyhow, Anywhere* to reporters as, 'A pop art record, containing pop art music,'" Pete later commented. "'The sounds of war and chaos and frustration expressed musically without the use of sound effects.' A bored and then cynical Nick Cohn – Christ he was even more cynical than me – said calmly, 'That's impressionism, not pop art.' I repeated what Kit had briefed me to say, mumbling something about Peter Blake and Lichtenstein and went red. Completely out of order while your record is screaming in the background: *I can go anyway, way I choose, I can live anyhow, win or lose, I can go anywhere, for something new, Anyway, anyhow, anywhere."* *Anyway,* which appeared five months after the release of *I Can't Explain,* reached number 10 in the U.K. charts.

The Who's first trip overseas, a two-show stint in Paris in early June, drove home the pathetic state of New Action's finances. "When the time came to leave, Kit had not even got the money for the train fare home, and had to be bailed out by [Chris] Parmeinter," wrote Andrew Motion in 1987. "...When they got back they found that the bailiffs had become so insistent that Kit was forced to shift the band's offices from Eaton Place back to Ivor Court. His stay there was a brief one; in November he uprooted himself again, this time to an even posher address: Cavendish Square, just north of Oxford Circus. The move had commercial as well as domestic advantages: Robert Stigwood, the highly successful Australian booking agent, had a flat in the same building. He agreed – for £2,000 – to act for the band."

The uprooting of New Action meant that Pete had to relocate. He soon moved into his own apartment in Chesham Place, Belgravia. According to Dave Marsh, Pete "decorated the place with pages torn from a book on pop art which he'd swiped from the Ealing Art School library." Pete equipped the spare room with his second home recording studio, including (eventually) a Vortexion CBL stereo tape machine, several microphones (as opposed to the single mike which graced his Ealing studio) and several guitars. *Melody Maker* reported that Pete possessed nine guitars during this period, all on hire-purchase, and that he was receiving an unemployment check at the time. In 1975, *NME* writer George Tremlett illustrated Pete's lifestyle during this period:

> Whereas in those days Roger, Keith and occasionally John were to be found late most evenings at the clubs that then mattered, the Ad Lib and the Cromwellian, Pete Townshend began living an almost reclusive life up in his Belgravia flat. At first he had just a mattress on the floor to sleep on, his clothes hung from coat hooks, and furniture consisted mainly of a loaded bookshelf, a pile of albums, a telephone, most of the group's cast-off equipment (mended guitars, microphones, amplifiers, etc). There, once his day's work with the group was done, Townshend would while away the night hours, writing, experimenting with sounds.

Pete was in the middle of producing "...a crop of songs," Townshend said in 1971, "which I was, by then, writing using a tape recorder."

> Kit Lambert had bought me two good quality tape decks and suggested I do this. It appealed to me as I had always attempted it using lesser machines and been encouraged by results... Anyway, ensconced in my Belgravia two-room tape recorder and hi-fi showroom, I proceeded to enjoy myself writing ditties with which I could later amuse myself over-dubbing, multitracking, and adding extra parts. It was the way I practiced. I learnt to play with myself. Masturbation comes to mind and, as a concept, making demos is not far off.

With the confidence in their composer that two original hit songs inevitably brings (and a simultaneous wariness brought on by an unfavorable review penned by John Emery in *Beat Instrumental*, who'd heard samples from the initial recording sessions), The Who announced in July, 1965, that more Townshend originals would be included on their debut album. "The Who have delayed the release of their first LP due to a last minute musical policy change," proclaimed the July 17 edition of *Melody Maker*.

> This drastic move has resulted in the group re-recording nearly all of the LP tracks… Says Who manager Kit Lambert: 'The Who are having serious doubts about the state of R&B. Now the LP material will consist of hard pop. They've finished with *Smokestack Lightnin*!' The main contents of the album will now be originals written by guitarist Pete Townshend, and singer Roger Daltrey. The LP should be released in early September.

The inclusion of a larger chunk of Townshend originals on the album meant a power shift within the pecking order of the band. Townshend began supplanting Daltrey, a transfer of power which nearly destroyed the band. "I took the band over when they asked me to write for them…," Pete told Andrew Motion in 1987, "and used them as a mouthpiece, hitting out at anyone who tried to have a say in what the group (mainly Roger) said and then grumbling when they didn't appreciate my dictatorship."

Following a show at the town hall in Torquay on July 17, The Who took a rare ten-day break during which they rehearsed their new onstage song lineup.

It was a long summer of endless TV shows and live appearances throughout England. Notably, the band appeared at the 5th Richmond Jazz and Blues Festival on August 6. Sharing the bill with The Yardbirds and The Moody Blues, The Who played a five song set which included a new number entitled *My Generation*. The version performed here reportedly lacked the trademark stuttering vocals and thundering climax, which made the final product so memorable. Pete smashed a Rickenbacker into his Vox speakers at the end of *Anyway Anyhow Anywhere*, tossing it to the back of the stage.[30]

---

[30] The Who received a consignment of new amplifiers from Vox in early September. Realizing that the brand new equipment could attract unwanted attention, the band visited Battersea Dogs' Home in search of a guard dog. Unfortunately, while they were inside the Dogs' Home, their van, packed with their new equipment, was stolen.

The Who's first European tour, which consisted of two shows in the Netherlands followed by four gigs in just two days in Denmark, began in late September. After the second show in the Netherlands, Pete found himself with two days of free time prior to the beginning of the band's stint in Denmark on September 25:

> I got drinking with a crowd of blokes, and they invited me back to their flat for the night. But when I woke up next morning there was a policeman standing by the bed – and it was then that I discovered they'd all gone, and it wasn't their place at all. It was somebody else's house and that was why the police had been called. At first it was a bit sticky. But after I had shown them my passport and explained who I was and how I happened to be there, they let me off. But it was all still a bit of a shock.

On Sunday, September 26 in Aahus, Denmark, the various arguments between the individual members of The Who which had been simmering since the band's inception – and which had intensified as Townshend's leadership role grew – reached boiling point. Everyone except Roger had been popping pills during the tour (Roger reportedly couldn't partake since the pills affected his voice) and backstage in Denmark Roger dumped Moon's supply of French Blues down the toilet. When Moon tried to retaliate, "Roger badly beat Keith up, knocking him out," Richard Barnes wrote in 1982. "When Keith was revived, they had to go on and do their second show of the evening, which was understandably tense." The band may have actually met their match for outright raucousness in the crowd present for the first show. "In Aahus, they got completely out of hand," Pete told George Tremlett.

> That's a farming area, and the hall was packed with 4 to 5,000 young farmers, a rather rough audience... the group that went on stage before us had had bottles thrown at them, and we'd lost some of our equipment. When this other group came off, they told us we could use some of their equipment... but then we went out on stage, and the bottles started flying again, then the lads started to storm the stage, and this other group dashed back on to rescue their equipment... we had only been on stage for four minutes before the show was stopped, and of course things got worse after that. The fans stormed out of the hall and started to wreck the town... we heard afterwards that they had done £10,000-worth of damage, and that made the front page of all the Danish papers.

When the band returned from their trip, John, Pete and Keith demanded that Daltrey leave The Who after finishing their work promoting *My Generation*. "Originally the group was run by the iron glove of Roger," Pete told *Record World* in 1975. "...he used to be very tough in getting his own way. If he didn't he'd shout and scream and stamp and in the end he'd punch you in the mouth. We'd all got big egos in the group and none of us liked it. We all got together and politely asked Roger to leave." Daltrey reportedly stewed over this ultimatum during recording sessions for The Who's debut album, produced by Shel Talmy, which took place at IBC studios from October to December, 1965.

As the weather cooled towards the end of 1965, Pete Townshend's future brightened and The Who's collective pulse quickened. With the release of their third single, *My Generation* in November, 1965, The Who cemented their reputation as a hard-nosed band who reflected the feelings of thousands of pissed-off adolescents at the time. *My Generation* was the complete package: All of the commercial appeal of *I Can't Explain*, combined with the aggressive feedback and live aura of *Anyway, Anyhow, Anywhere*.

According to Pete, it was Chris Stamp who saw the potential in *My Generation* when Pete played him the demo tape. "He [Stamp] was convinced it could be the biggest Who record yet," Pete recalled in 1971. "Bearing in mind the state of the demo, it shows an astuteness beyond the call. It sounded like (I still of course have it) Jimmy Reed at ten years old suffering from nervous indigestion. Kit made suggestion after suggestion to improve the song. He later said that it was because he was unsure of it. I went on to make two more demos...the first introduced the stutter. The second several key changes, pinched, again, from the Kinks."

In an era of namby-pamby love songs, *My Generation* was an all-out kick in the pants for anyone who wasn't happy with their lot in life. The bite of lyrics such as *why don't you all F-F-F-Fade away*, with its threat of the harsher 'F' word, seemed to sum up the frustration of countless youths across the nation. The song simply *dripped* attitude.

"If *My Generation* was the only record The Who had ever recorded, they would still deserve an honorable mention in any history of rock," wrote Chris Charlesworth in 1995. "[*My Generation*] is still the best known song in their entire catalogue. Pete Townshend has often regretted penning the memorable lines '*Hope I die before I get old*' but *My Generation* remains the hardest hitting single released by any U.K. pop group in 1965. The Beatles and the Stones, remember, were still writing love songs at the time this was released." *My Generation* reached number 2 in the U.K., selling around 300,000 copies despite the fact that it was at first banned by the BBC, who considered Daltrey's stuttering an insult to those who suffered from the affliction. The song was described by the *NME*'s Derek Johnson as "…A storming, raving shake-beat, with crashing cymbals, raucous guitar, reverberating bass and hand-claps throughout – and that's just the backing."

"*My Generation* was very much about trying to find a place in society," Pete told *Rolling Stone*'s David Fricke in 1987.

> I was very, very lost. The band was young then. It was believed that its career would be incredibly brief. The privilege that I had at the time was to be plucked out of bed-sitter land and put in a flat in the middle of Belgravia with two tape machines. It was private, and I could look out at these people who seemed to me to be from another planet.
>
> I remember one of the things I bought when the Who first became successful was a 1963 Lincoln Continental. I was driving with the top down through London, and a woman in a car going in the other direction looked at me. She was wearing a string of pearls, blond hair, very beautiful, about thirty-five. She kind of looked at me as if admiring me in my car. Then her lip curled, and she said, "Driving Mummy's car, are we?" That one incident, among a series of other key incidents, made me hate those people.
>
> I really started to respond to that. "All right, you motherfuckers, I am going to have you. I am going to be bigger and richer, and I'm going to move into your neighborhood. I'm going to buy that house next to you, Lord So-and-So." And I've done it. And I'm afraid I've done it out of a great sickness. I talk to people I really do respect from that way of life now, and I say to them, "Do you realize why it is I'm so driven to operate within the Establishment? It's vengeance." "Hope I die before I get old" is something I still have to live with, but not for the reason many people think. I have to be very, very vigilant not to become one of those people I despised.

Another incident which fueled Pete's anger toward the establishment at the time involved a run-in with the Queen Mother. "Even though I was young and smashing guitars, I still loved the Queen Mother," Pete told *Q*'s David Cavanagh in January, 2000. "Fucking stopped, though."

> It was in 1964[31]. My manager Kit Lambert felt that I was unduly held down by my art school friends, so he

---

[31] I contend that this event occurred during 1965.

moved me into Chesham Place, the road between Clarence House and Buckingham Palace. I had this Packard hearse parked outside my house. One day I came back and it was gone. It turned out that she'd had it moved, because her husband had been buried in a similar vehicle and it reminded her of him. When I went to collect it, they wanted two hundred and fifty quid. I'd only paid thirty for it in the first place.

Accompanying the release of *My Generation*, some rather belated rumors arose in the music press that The Who had fired Roger as a result of friction within the band. Although Roger's altercation with Keith had taken place two months ago, all had been quiet in the press until now. Following the release of the immensely popular *My Generation*, any news on The Who was suddenly catapulted to the front page. The November 20 edition of *Melody Maker* ran a front-page story entitled 'The Who Split Mystery'. "Wild tales in London's in-clubs flashed the news that 20-year-old singer Roger Daltrey would be leaving the group," the article announced[32]. "It was said that young singer Boz, of the Boz People, would be Daltrey's replacement[33]. It was also thought another drummer would be brought into the group so that Keith Moon could 'explore other fields of percussion.'" Chris Stamp – who originally sided with Townshend, Moon and Entwistle in wanting Daltrey out – was quoted in the piece as saying:

> This is absolute c-c-crap! Quite seriously I've never heard such a lot of rubbish. Does anybody in their right mind think the Who would split at a time like this? Everybody knows there is conflict within the group, and there have been some hefty rows lately, but this doesn't mean that the group will bust up. They just argue about their 'sound' and talk about all the things they want to achieve sound-wise…We hear rumors that Roger is leaving everywhere we go…it's just crap. The Who once and for all, are not 'breaking up.'

Roger, indeed, was on his way out of the band just prior to the release of *My Generation*, but the success of the single threw a wrench in The Who's plans. As the single shot up the charts, it became apparent that

---

[32] "There were actually periods when Roger left the group for several weeks and I was The Who's singer," Pete told *Guitarist* in 1990. "Robert Plant talks about the fact that when he first saw us I was the singer. He came to see us three nights in a row and offered himself for the job… as did Steve Gibbons when he came to see us and Roger wasn't there. Obviously none of them thought I was any good!"

[33] Boz Burrell went on to stints with King Crimson and Bad Company.

the band was quickly on its way to stardom – provided that they could stay together. "[Roger] was quickly reinstated when *Generation* leapt up the charts," Chris Charlesworth later wrote, "and its success undoubtedly saved Roger from a life as a tearaway – and The Who from extinction." Friction was not something new to Townshend and company: When *Fabulous* writer Nancy Lewis interviewed the band in early 1965, she predicted they'd split within six months. "They didn't seem to like each other very much and they were such different people, I just could never see them lasting," she told John Swenson. "Our personalities clash, but we argue and get it all out of our system," Townshend told *Melody Maker* in June, 1965. "There's a lot of friction, and offstage we're not particularly matey. But it doesn't matter. If we were not like this it would destroy our stage performance. We play how we feel."

"We get on badly," Pete told *Disc*, going so far as to say, "...Roger is not a very good singer at all in my opinion. He has got a good act, but I think he expects a backing group more than an integrated group. I don't think he will ever understand that he will never have The Who as a backing group."

After Lambert held a meeting and persuaded Stamp and the other three to let Roger stay, Roger promised that he would attempt to curb his anger. "It was an amazing sort of transformation he went through," Pete told Richard Barnes. "...from being one of the most aggressive, violent people I knew, to being one of the most peaceful. He had to learn to live with a lot of things he didn't like, and what I always admired about him was the fact that he managed to do it, because knowing the kind of power he had as a young man that he gave up in a sense, for the sake of the group, took a lot of guts."

A song The Who would record six years later framed the event for Daltrey. "*Behind Blue Eyes* for me, really speaks volumes," Daltrey said in 1999.

When my fist clenches, crack it open, it just all made sense. That's the only way we used to deal with anything in the part of England where I grew up. Everything was solved with a fight, whoever won the fight, that's the way you went, simple as that. But obviously it didn't quite work that way in a band, and they slung me out for fighting, and the band was everything, it was my band, and it meant... it was my whole life, so I had two choices, give up the fighting or give up the band; there's no choice whatsoever.

The Who's debut album, *My Generation*, released in late December 1965, reached number 5 in the U.K. charts. The album flopped in the U.S.

upon its' release four months later. Of the original sessions which took place in March, only three songs made it on to the final album, *Please Please Please* and *I Don't Mind*, both written by James Brown, and Bo Diddley's *I'm A Man*. Townshend penned the remaining tracks, the most notable being *My Generation* and *The Kids Are Alright*, which remain among Pete's most memorable Who compositions[34]. Of the rest, *Out In The Street* (reportedly a renamed manifestation of *You're Going to Know Me*) is a tight, heavy R&B song which suffers somewhat since the introductory guitar flourish is quite similar to that of *Anyway, Anyhow, Anywhere*. Townshend's guitar prowess is demonstrated on *The Good's Gone*[35], while *La La La Lies* and *It's Not True* exhibit the characteristics of a prototypical Who song. The wacky lyrics of the latter provided a glimpse of Townshend's penchant for weird, humor-tinged compositions which would eventually spawn such titles as *I'm A Boy*, *Happy Jack* and *Little Billy*.

A Legal Matter, a twangy, country-tinged number which featured Pete singing lead vocals for the first time, was "...about a guy on the run from a chick about to pin him down for breach of promise," Pete told *Rolling Stone* in 1971. "What this song was screaming from behind lines like, "It's a legal matter baby, marrying's no fun, it's a legal matter baby, you got me on the run," was "I'm lonely, I'm hungry, and the bed needs making." I wanted a maid I suppose. It's terrible feeling like an eligible bachelor but with no women seeming to agree with you."

The album was rounded out with a thunderous instrumental entitled *The Ox*, John's nickname. "In the studio it was possible – with a bit of frigging around – to get the sound and energy we had on stage, and this is the first Who record where we really caught that," Pete recalled. "Because this is an instrumental, what you get is *The Band*, the sound of this tremendous machine working almost by itself, that incredible chemistry we had in The Who, and that we kept right up until Keith Moon dropped dead." The song, which features a great performance by Moon, who "...simply eclipses every surf drummer in history on a song that is nothing so much as an Anglo 'wipe out,'" Dave Marsh wrote in 1983.

---

[34] Both songs were reportedly recorded during the same session, an all-nighter on 13 October.
[35] Pete explained his early tendency to avoid guitar solos to *Guitarist* in 1990: "...I knew Jimmy Page – Led Zeppelin weren't formed then but I'd seen him in various bands and if anything his playing slowed down as he got older! He was an extraordinary player, arrogant, flash... And Eric, with The Yardbirds, used to play absolutely beautifully and he'd only been playing a year! And Jeff Beck, who always had that quality of making the guitar sound like a voice... That was the kind of market-place I was in, and although I hadn't been belted round the chops by Jimi Hendrix yet, I definitely didn't want to be competing with those players... I was very embarrassed playing on The Who's first album because I tried to play solos and I could hear the jazz creeping in. So I made a conscious effort to keep away from feature solos. And it did feel very much like a competitive area..."

The Who finished the year appearing on *RSG*'s star-studded New Year and Christmas specials, the latter featuring an unlikely Who interpretation of *Jingle Bells*.

Chapter 3

"...this being angry at the adult world bit is not all of us. It's not me and it's not John. It's only half Roger, but it is Pete."
- Keith Moon

By 1966, Pete had moved from his Belgravia apartment and was living in Chelsea. In her 1974 book *The Who...through the eyes of Pete Townshend*, author Caroline Silver described his new abode as, "... a penthouse apartment in the middle of London's smart Chelsea district. Far below, charming gray-roofed houses stretch away, interspersed with neat, green squares, to the river Thames. Tugboats and barges come and go all day on the river; on the far banks are the flashing colored lights of the Battersea Fun Fair. It is the kind of place anyone would envy Townshend for living in, which makes him feel self-conscious and anxious to move somewhere else." Pete lived alone in Chelsea, a recording studio occupying one room, while broken guitars adorned the walls of another.

After penning three consecutive hit singles in the U.K., Pete was emerging as a bright young figure on the British music scene. As he gave an increasing number of interviews to the music media, he became known as an interesting, articulate spokesman for his generation with an often unflinching regard for the truth. On January 5, Pete appeared without The Who on the *A Whole Scene Going* television show, during which he admitted publicly for the first time that he was an active drug user.

More press coverage appeared in the March 26, 1966 issue of *Melody Maker*. The 'Pop Think-In' featured Pete's opinions on various subjects, opinions which, until now, weren't thought of as particularly important by the media. Pete's thoughts on a broad range of subjects, especially popular music and cultural issues, would be printed by a wide range of printed media for years to come. When asked his opinion on the war in Vietnam, Pete commented, "Actually it's turned into a bit of a bore, one of those questions like Korea. That war was never won was it? There will always be teenagers ready to throw themselves under tanks. I wonder what I would do if we were in the same position. I always stand by Young Communist principles. If I was in Russia and in some harsh five year plan - if it was for the good of the country - I wouldn't mind. I would get joy out of seeing something being done, like new libraries being built. But for a youngster to face foreign troops blasting away about something they don't even understand...well really they all ought to get out." The principles of the Young Communist league had been familiar to Pete for a few years now - he had joined the organization in art school.

Inevitably, Pete was questioned on a subject a little closer to home, that of Pop Art. "It's still my favorite form of art," Pete said.

> My favorite artists are Barry Fantoni and Peter Blake. What I like most of all is it's English. Foreign pop art I hate. I don't think you can enjoy it unless it's relevent [sic] to your own country. It has no relevance to the Who except we used it's ideas...I think we did a lot for it in this country. If we hadn't have done it, it might have taken another year to catch on. The number of journalists I had to explain it to, especially on local papers. Pop art encompasses performances, what are called "happenings", and autodestructive performances, including smashing guitars. ...I used to talk to Kit about Pop Art a lot and suddenly he came out with this idea. He told us: "Keith is going to have a bullseye on his T-shirt, Pete is going to wear badges" - all these were his ideas. At the beginning it took a lot of guts to wear them.

Seven months later, Pete appeared in *Melody Maker*'s 'Blind Date' segment, where celebrities gave their opinions on the latest music. Pete's selections (chosen by the magazine and played to Pete as he reviewed them) included Cliff Richard's *Time Drags By* ("What a load of crap," Pete commented), Nancy Sinatra's *In Due Time* ("This must have been written by some C&W writer who doesn't know the modern lyrics scene."), The Temptations' *Beauty Is Only Skin Deep* ("Nice sound. I like this sort of thing."), and the band Oscar performing *Join My Gang*, a song written by Pete ("I like it, I think it's good. I'm still waiting for the money from this.").

Meanwhile, in January 1966, Chris Stamp took a trip to New York to attempt to renegotiate The Who's recording contract. The band's lack of success in the U.S., which stemmed from American Decca's seeming unwillingness to promote them there, had prompted The Who's management to make a move. *I Can't Explain* had reached an unimpressive number 93 in America, while *Anyway, Anyhow, Anywhere* didn't even make the charts. The single *My Generation* reached number 74, while the album (entitled *The Who Sings My Generation* in the States), released in April 1966, also failed to reach the charts. Decca American dealt mainly in country music, and it seemed that the label, staffed mostly with old, conservative types, wasn't ready for The Who. "American Decca was sort of archaic," Stamp told Richard Barnes. "I mean they didn't even know about Elvis Presley, let alone The Who. I realized that we would never break The Who with this company." Thus began the battle between The Who and their record label.

Frustrated with Shel Talmy's dictatorial style of producing, a financially poor record deal for The Who, and American Decca's ineptitude in getting the band noticed in the U.S., Kit Lambert and Chris Stamp consulted an attorney in an effort to find a way out of their contract. While in America, Chris had been offered an advance from Atlantic records, and was eager to begin a relationship with the company. The lawyer informed the management duo that the contract with Talmy could be legally broken.

Kit wrote to Shel Talmy to inform the producer that The Who no longer wanted to be associated with him, and that their contract (which had four years remaining) was no longer valid. "I received a letter in the post saying something to the effect that my services were no longer required," Talmy told *Record World*. "I don't think I ever fell out with the group at any stage but they were very young and they were very influenced, possibly unduly influenced, by their managers. Kit Lambert is not one of my favorite people and I was happy in one way because it meant I would not have to be associated with him. We came very close to blows at one point."

When Talmy balked at the prospect of losing the band, Lambert decided to force the issue by recording their next single himself and releasing it on a different label, in effect removing Talmy from the equation and in the process showing him that they meant business. The Who's follow-up to *My Generation* was supposed to be *Circles*, a song which the band had already recorded with Talmy and was projected for release on the Brunswick label. However, in late January, 1966, Kit Lambert took The Who into Olympic studios in London to record *Substitute*, a new Townshend composition. The band also recorded a new version of *Circles*, renamed it *Instant Party*, and made it the B-side. So, when *Substitute*, The Who's next single, was released in March 1966, it was Reaction (recently signed Who agent Robert Stigwood's label[36]), and not Brunswick, on the record label. (The band used Atco, a subsidiary of Atlantic Records, when the single was released in the U.S. a month later.)

Substitute, about which Townshend later commented he'd made "...after hearing a rough mix of *Nineteenth Nervous Breakdown* by The

---

[36] "Shel Talmy had to be gotten rid of," Pete told John Swenson, "and the only guy who was really powerful enough, who was connected with The Who in any way whatsoever at the time and who wouldn't suffer by it was Robert Stigwood."

Stones", wasn't a difficult song for him to write. "The lyric, so applauded by rock critics, was thrown together very quickly," Pete recalled in 1987. "Smokey Robinson sang the word 'substitute' so perfectly in *Tracks Of My Tears* - my favorite song at the time - that I decided to celebrate the word itself with a song all its own."

Despite its apparent simplicity, *Substitute* was a successful release. "The lyric has come to be the most quoted Who lyric ever," Pete wrote in 1971.

> ...it somehow goes to show that the "trust the art, not the artist" tag that people put on [Bob] Dylan's silence about his work could be a good idea. To me, *Mighty Quinn* is about the five Perfect Masters of the age, the best of all being Meher Baba of course, to Dylan it's probably about gardening...*Substitute* makes me recall writing a song to fit a clever and rhythmic sounding title. A play on words. Again it could mean a lot more to me now than it did when I wrote it. If I told you what it meant to me now, you'd think I take myself too seriously.

"The stock, down-beat riff used in the verses I pinched from a record played to me in "Blind Date," a feature in *Melody Maker*," Pete continued. "It was by a group who later wrote to thank me for saying nice things about their record in the feature...The record I said nice things about [*Where Is My Girl* by Robb Storme] wasn't a hit, despite an electrifying riff. I pinched it, we did it, you bought it."

Substitute also signaled Pete's first lesson in production: "We made this straight after *Generation* and Kit wasn't really in a position to steam in and produce...A blonde chap called Chris at Olympic studios got the sound, set up a kinky echo, did the mix etc. I looked on and have taken the credit whenever the opportunity has presented itself ever since."

After The Who released *Substitute/Instant Party* on the Reaction label, Shel Talmy immediately countered, obtaining a court injunction within six days of the single's release which prevented Reaction from pressing any more recordings of the B-side since he'd already recorded the song with The Who. Further, Brunswick issued their own Who single, *A Legal Matter*, the song sung by Pete which had appeared on the *My Generation* LP. *A Legal Matter's* B-side, entitled *Instant Party*, was in fact the version of *Circles* which Talmy and The Who had recorded prior to the contract squabble. The band now had two singles released in Britain within six days of each other on two different record labels. Both B-sides were different versions of the same song.

"The pop world is evenly split over the promotion of the two Who singles presently on the market," read the March 19, 1966 edition of *Melody*

Maker. "Their single on Polydor's Reaction label, *Substitute*, climbed to number twenty in this week's *MM* chart, but their other release taken from the *My Generation* LP, titled *Legal Matter*, on Brunswick hasn't yet hit the Pop 50. The High Court battle over the Who's recording contract with Shel Talmy, their ex-recording manager, still goes on, but will not now effect the distribution of *Substitute*. The disc now has a completely new B-side, called *Waltz For A Pig*, by the Who Orchestra." 'The Who Orchestra' was actually the Graham Bond Organization, who recorded this song (the 'pig' reportedly meaning Shel Talmy) for Reaction since The Who, under an agreement with Talmy, were not to record until after the court hearing on April 4th.

Pete recalled the court date a few years later:

> …Shel took [the case] to the High Court judge and said things like, 'And then on bar 36 I suggested to the lead guitarist that he play an innuendo, forget the adagio, and play 36 bars modulating to the key of E flat,' which was all total rubbish since he used to fall asleep at his desk while a bloke called Glyn Johns did everything.[37] Eventually we found ourselves in court and we dreamed up even more preposterous replies. 'Shel Talmy certainly did *not* tell us at the 36th bar to play an innuendo,' we said. 'He told us to do such and such, and we suggested blah, blah, blah.' All this in incredible, grand, grandiose musical terms.

Talmy, represented by former Conservative party minister and top-notch attorney Quentin Hogg, gained the upper hand in the courtroom. "…it just looked like the judge was going to go with Quentin Hogg because he was making him laugh and all that," Chris Stamp later recalled. "You suddenly saw British justice."

When the case was introduced to the elderly judge, he reportedly mistook the name The Who for an acronym for the World Health Organization. Clearly fighting a losing battle, Kit and Chris decided on settling with Talmy in order for The Who to move on. The band ended up staying with American Decca on a renegotiated deal which gave them double the royalties they had previously made. Polydor, Reaction's mother label, assumed rights to The Who's European releases. Talmy received a favorable settlement: A five percent royalty on The Who's recordings through 1971, which would include their two best selling albums, *Tommy*, and *Who's Next*. This was the price that The Who paid for artistic freedom in the recording studio. The record deal meant that the band could choose

---

[37] Johns went on to produce *The Who By Numbers*, *Who Are You* and *It's Hard*. He was also named associate producer of *Who's Next*.

their own producer now that Shel Talmy was out of the picture. Of the two records released by The Who during the ordeal, *Substitute* did well, reaching number 5 in Britain while *A Legal Matter* reached only number 32.

During their legal battle with Shel Talmy, The Who had maintained a hectic – and increasingly lucrative – touring schedule. With the recent domestic popularity of *My Generation* and *Substitute*, the band were now commanding live fees of up to £500 per show – a rate which was second to only The Beatles and sometimes The Rolling Stones. The band had embarked on their first headlining theater tour in February, which sent them throughout Britain. After performing with the Yardbirds on a special broadcast of *Ready Steady Go!* (retitled *Ready Steady Allez!* for this show) from La Locomotive club in Paris[38], The Who appeared at the *New Musical Express* poll winners concert at the Empire Pool in Wembley on May 1. Also on the bill were heavyweights such as The Beatles, The Rolling Stones, The Yardbirds, The Small Faces, and Roy Orbison. In their review, the *NME* recognized The Who's act as the most notable of the evening. "The screaming was deafening for The Who," the review read. "..I don't know that it was music; it was more like watching violence put to rhythm."

"The Who by this time were very into their Union Jack period and looking incredible," Chris Stamp told *Moon* author Tony Fletcher in 1999.

> Pete did his feedback thing and we had smoke bombs going off. And we did this destructive ending with Pete's guitar. And Keith, who had knocked over a few drums here and there, really went for it... He did a huge thing with the drums, I think they even fell off the stage, he made a huge mess. He did it to be with Pete, to top Pete, and to also make the Who's presence felt, make sure the Stones and the Beatles had to follow *this*.

The band were now using *My Generation*, their most powerful song, as the final number of their live act. Richard Barnes described a typical rendition of the song in *Maximum R&B*:

> It was the climax of a powerful, loud, uncompromising set and it was at the end of *My Generation* that Pete would start hitting his Rickenbacker on the floor to get strange electronic noises and effects from it. He would set up a feedback pattern and then run the mike stand down the strings to get a screeching loud electronic scraping

---

[38] "The show was going out live in both France and England," Vicki Wyckham told Andrew Motion in 1987, "and the time came for the finale. [As] the cameras... followed, recording the event – into the street go The Who, into the alley and all stop and immediately pee against the wall."

noise...Then, with a mean look he'd start poking the speaker cabinet with the guitar and ripping holes in the fabric covering. The tension and drama of their act was intense. Snarling and scowling, Townshend would unleash his fury on his equipment. He would attack the speaker cabinets with the guitar, swinging it above his head and smashing the cabinet, using the guitar as an axe...The Who were the most outrageous and stunning live act to hit the British scene. They were sheer violence and frustration set to music.

Pete's penchant for flailing his equipment about during live shows caught up with him at a May 20, 1966, performance at the Ricky Tick Club in Newbury. As the band performed *My Generation*, one of Keith's drums fell over, knocking a cymbal onto Pete. "I wasn't hurt, just annoyed and upset," Pete told an interviewer later. "Keith and John had been over two hours late. Then I swung out with my guitar not really meaning to hit Keith. I lost my grip on the instrument and it just caught him on the head." Keith, who sustained a badly bruised face, a black eye and a cut on his leg, refused to play with the band for a week, during which time they used a temporary replacement. Pete reportedly visited Keith's home to offer an apology the weekend after the incident, but Moon wouldn't come to the door. Richard Barnes commented, "...things were not well within the group and several fights and arguments later there was a possible breakaway from the group by Keith and John, who were planning to combine with two members of the Yardbirds to form a new group to be called Led Zeppelin - a name invented by John."[39]

One of the Who's opening acts during a show at Blackpool's South Pier on May 28 (which marked Keith's return to drumming duties after the incident with Pete) was The Rockin' Vicars. This band's guitarist was Ian 'Lemmy' Kilminster, the famous Motorhead frontman. At this time, the Rockin' Vicars had just recorded and released a Pete Townshend composition (otherwise unreleased) entitled *It's Alright*.

Another Townshend song, *So Sad About Us*, was soon recorded by a band that Kit Lambert was producing at the time, The Merseys. The song "did quite well", Pete recalled in 1983. He'd written the song at his old Acton County Grammar School school friend Speedy Keene's house. Keene (nicknamed Speedy for his motorcycling prowess) was "...a talented drummer and emerged as a great writer as soon as I opened my ears to him properly," Pete said. During this period, Keene (who would later emerge as

---

[39] In late 1966, Moon recorded *Beck's Bolero* with Jeff Beck, Nicky Hopkins, and two future members of Led Zeppelin. "I remember Townshend looking daggers at me when he heard it, because it was a bit near the mark," Beck later said. "He didn't want anyone meddling with that territory at all."

the drummer for Thunderclap Newman) drove Pete's anonymity-be-damned Lincoln Continental, chauffering Townshend to Who gigs all over Britain for a reported £15 per week[40]. For a time, Keene and Townshend shared Pete's Wardour Street flat. "We had a lot of things in common," Keene told Dave Marsh in 1983. "We liked really good cars, big cars with big engines. We liked high-energy music... At that time, you couldn't get a long paper between us. We were close."

On June 2, 1966, The Who began the first show of a six-day tour of Sweden and Denmark by breaking through a large paper Union Jack to enter the stage at Stockholm. A show a few days later in Orebro, Sweden had the Who on a bill with eleven other bands. The Who's set began late and the fans rushed the stage. A few songs into the show, the police cut power to the stage, and Pete lost his temper. "With the stage lighting and amplifiers now dead, Pete Townshend furiously stormed over to the power supply room of the building ready to tackle both the police and stagehands," Joe McMichael and 'Irish' Jack Lyons wrote in their book *The Who Concert File*.:

> The power was soon restored, however, and the concert continued with Who roadies defending the mains power switch. But the police once more intervened, cut the electricity for a second time and the concert continued with Keith Moon offering an improvised drum solo. Soon tiring of the solo, Moon joined Townshend and threatened the policemen guarding the power switch but they soon realised that nothing more could be done and The Who withdrew after an aborted set.

Pete's quick temper on stage was becoming increasingly evident, as the above example and the previous guitar-swinging episode with Moon demonstrate. Later in the year, at another show in Sweden, Pete ripped the stage curtain down in a rage as it had been lowered during The Who's performance. Some of the band's equipment-smashing during this period was so violent that it provoked complaints from fans who feared for their own safety. Later examples, such as Pete's assault of Abbie Hoffman during The Who's appearance at Woodstock and his subsequent altercation with a plain-clothes police officer at the Fillmore offer a glimpse of Townshend's tendency to fly off the handle at a moment's notice while on stage. Pete described this frame of mind to an interviewer in 1979: "When I'm on the stage I'm not in control of myself at all," he said.

---

[40] On May 30, 1966, Pete was involved in a car accident. Erroneous reports soon surfaced on the radio that Roger Daltrey had been killed.

> I don't even know who I am...I'm not this rational person that can sit here now and talk to you. If you walked on stage with a microphone in the middle of a concert, I'd probably come close to killing you. I have come close to killing people that walked on stage. Abbie Hoffman walked on the stage at Woodstock and I nearly killed him with my guitar. A policeman came on when the bloody building at the Fillmore in New York was burning down and I kicked him in the balls and sent him off...I'm just not there. It's not like being possessed, it's just, I do my job and I know I have to get into a certain state of mind to do it.

A further example of Pete and the band's violent tendencies while onstage occurred at the newly-renamed Windsor Jazz and Blues Festival, which took place at Windsor Racecourse on July 30. The annual music event had this year been moved from Richmond, its original location, due to complaints about the noise. Pete, dressed in a dinner suit complete with bow tie and girlfriend Karen in tow, led the band through a powerful set which included the Who's high-octane interpretation of the *Batman* theme, *I Can't Explain*, *Anyway, Anyhow, Anywhere*, and *Substitute*. However, Richard Barnes recalled:

> ...they thought that they weren't getting across very well and so finished with *My Generation* where Pete smashed his guitar into his amps and ripped all the fabric off the front and started laying into the speakers inside. The guitar split and then split again, the head was ripped off and then the neck snapped. He continued until the guitar was smashed to small pieces. Keith kicked all his drums over and they were rolling around the stage while Roger smashed the cymbals with his fists, hurled mikes at the back of the stage. Not content with this, Roger then started to kick out all the footlights at the front of the stage. Keith then got a bucket of water and threw it into the audience. The whole stage was covered in yellow smoke from smoke bombs which were being hurled onstage by Kit Lambert and Chris Stamp as they encouraged the onstage demolition. The crowd went absolutely wild...Keith said, "After that show, the roadies came on in little white coats and shoveled the equipment into buckets. The audience had smashed up all their seats and the whole place looked like Attila the Hun had ridden through it."

"In a frenzy of violence the Who beat group caused thousands of pounds worth of damage to their own equipment at the Sixth National Jazz and Blues Festival at Windsor, Surrey on Saturday," reported the August 6 edition of *Melody Maker*. "As well as pushing their own amplifiers and drums over, and smashing guitars, singer Roger Daltrey kicked in the footlights. Microphones went flying, and the stage was left in utter chaos when they finished the evening."

One of the songs featured in The Who's set at the Windsor Jazz and Blues Festival was *I'm A Boy*, which the band recorded a few weeks later at IBC studios. At the time, Pete had been working on an idea named *Quads*. Set in 1999, *Quads* told of a world where prospective parents were able to choose the sex of their children. The couple in Pete's story chose four girls, but were erroneously given three girls and a boy. Undaunted, the couple raised their children as if they had four girls, dressing their frustrated little boy in girls' clothes and denying him involvement in any boyish activities. "The song, of course, is about a boy whose mother dresses him up as a girl," Pete wrote in 1971, "...and won't let him enjoy all the normal boyish pranks like slitting lizards' tummies and throwing rocks at passing cars...*I'm A Boy* was my first attempt at Rock Opera." *I'm A Boy* appears to be the only song which materialized from the *Quads* project, but *Disguises*, recorded a few months earlier, features similarly outlandish lyrics and subject matter. Whether or not any further *Quads*-related songs were written, Pete's ideas for the project went beyond *I'm A Boy*. "[*Quads*] goes on in later life where the three girls become a singing group, and I had amazing visions of Keith, John and I pretending to be the Beverly Sisters," Pete said in 1971. "There was a lot of comedy in it... but I think at the same time it was a heavily serious thing as well because it had these flashbacks to childhood, which I was very into at the time." *I'm A Boy* was released as a single on August 26, 1966, just two weeks after Decca had released *The Kids Are Alright* (the legal settlement allowed Decca to continue to release singles from the *My Generation* album). *I'm A Boy* became the band's first #1 hit[41].

The recording session from which *I'm A Boy* emerged marked the beginning of a period of prolific recording by the band, who hit IBC studios in August to begin recording their next album. With Shel Talmy out of the picture, the band and its management had carte blanche in the studio, and the perceived confinement of recording under Shel Talmy thus gave way to an atmosphere of innovation and enlightenment. "It was a wonderful and unrestrained creative period during which my partner Kit Lambert, The Who and myself were all discovering how to make records for ourselves, and trying out all kinds of ideas, no matter how far out and crazy they seemed to be," Chris Stamp recalled in 1995.

---

[41] The Who traveled to the U.S. for the first time at the end of September to promote *I'm A Boy* through television appearances. Despite their efforts, the record failed to generate interest and didn't make the charts.

The new aura of freedom in the recording studio also proved to benefit the individual members of The Who. "By the time The Who came to record their second album they were skint through smashing up too much expensive gear," Chris Charlesworth later wrote, "...so their music publisher suggested that if each member of the group contributed at least two songs the publishers would advance £500 to each member, a considerable sum in 1966. The offer was accepted and Daltrey, Entwistle, and Moon were sent off with pens in their hands to compose songs." While Entwistle soon proved a capable songwriter with no outside help, Pete assisted Moon and Daltrey in constructing demo recordings of their compositions at his home studio.

These first sessions at IBC studios featured the band recording the Martha and the Vandellas song *Heatwave*, and an interesting take on the *Batman* theme which had cropped up in The Who's live act recently. Two songs featuring Keith on lead vocals were also recorded – a Jan and Dean song entitled *Bucket T.*, and *Barbara Ann*, a song which the Beach Boys had released earlier in the year.

After the *Quads* project had failed to come to fruition, Pete Townshend continued in his quest to write thematically linked music. *A Quick One, While He's Away* proved to be the next incarnation of this desire. Recorded at IBC, Pye, and Regent Sound in autumn 1966, this six-song medley clocked in at over nine minutes and was Pete's most ambitious effort yet, despite its admittedly light subject matter. "Pete Townshend and Kit had been talking for a while about extended themes and ideas in rock'n'roll," Stamp recalled in 1995. "...and they both felt it could be done in an operatic way without renouncing the basic balls of rock. [*A Quick One, While He's Away*] ...was the first shot at that idea, with its themes of love, betrayal and forgiveness." Through its' six phases, *A Quick One* tells the story of a lonely woman whose lover is far away (*Her Man's Gone; Crying Town*) and the arrival of several suitors, one of which is a Welsh train driver (*We Have A Remedy; Ivor The Engine Driver*). The girl becomes involved with Ivor but confesses all upon the return of her lover, who forgives her (*Soon Be Home; You Are Forgiven*). Despite possessing an aura of silliness, *A Quick One, While He's Away* was an effective song[42]. It typified this period for the band, a phase during which they recorded a wide variety of material. The song became a standard feature of The Who's live act in the coming months.

The August studio sessions continued with the band recording an Everly Brothers song, *Man With The Money* at IBC, along with an unlikely

---

[42] "[*A Quick One*] was inspired by an obscene spoof baroque opera my friend Ray Toliday and I had written and recorded at my Wardour Street home studio for Kit Lambert's birthday in early 1967," Pete wrote in a 2001 article in *Q* Magazine. "That was called *Gratis Amatis* and featured – among others – Titania, who had to be "disowned", because she "let her knickers down"."

medley of *My Generation* with Edward Elgar's *Land Of Hope and Glory*, which was intended for release on an upcoming EP. *Run Run Run*, which would become the first song on The Who's new album, was recorded at IBC studios in October, 1966. The song was first recorded by a band known as The Cat and produced by Pete. The effects of Shel Talmy's absence are quite noticeable on The Who's version of this song, John's bass being loud and very much a lead instrument, sharing the spotlight with Pete's guitar.

Boris The Spider, John Entwistle's first composition for The Who, was recorded by the band at Pye Studios in October. "Politics or my own shaky vanity might be the reason," Pete wrote in 1971, "but *Boris the Spider* was never released as a single and could have been a hit."

> It was *the* most requested song we ever played on stage, and if this really means anything to you guitar players, it was Hendrix' favorite Who song. Which rubbed me up well the wrong way, I can tell you. John introduced us to *Boris* in much the same way as I introduced us to our *Generation* - through a tape recorder. We assembled in John's three feet by ten feet bedroom and listened incredulously as the strange and haunting chords emerged. Faced with words about the slightly gruesome death of a spider, the song had enough charm to send me back to my pad writing hits furiously.

The silly *Addams Family*-esque harpsichord of *I Need You* marked the arrival of the first of Keith Moon's two compositions for the new album, both of which were recorded in October at Pye studios. The second, which more than eclipsed the first in silliness and, more importantly, sheer drumming brilliance, was an instrumental entitled *Cobwebs and Strange*. Chris Stamp recalled that the recording of the song, "...involved marching up and down past a mono mike because Kit Lambert, years ahead of his time, thought this might create a 'stereo' effect. Keith played orchestral cymbals, Pete was on penny whistle, Roger blew a trombone, and John played the trumpet."[43] If any instrumental could ever give an accurate portrayal of what was going on inside Keith Moon's head, this must have been it. Pete blew the cobwebs off *Cobwebs and Strange* in 1993, using it as the opener during his *Psychoderelict* solo tour.

During a break from recording in late October, The Who appeared on a *Ready Steady Go!* special which featured the band for an unheard-of 16

---

[43] In addition to telling John Swenson "our manager was completely nuts", John Entwistle said that *Cobwebs and Strange* was ultimately recorded with the band members standing still because as they marched they lost time with the backing track which was being played on a monitor at one end of the studio. "If we'd worn cans we could have gotten tangled up, so we finally had to track it standing still..." Entwistle told Swenson.

minutes (over half the show) during which they dutifully smashed up their equipment. An EP of studio versions of some of the songs played here (*Disguises, Circles, Batman, Bucket T, Barbara Ann*) was released in November, entitled *Ready Steady Who!* The day after the band taped the show, they embarked on an 18 show, 20 day jaunt through the Netherlands, Denmark, Sweden and Germany. Sound man Bobby Pridden, who remains in this capacity with The Who today, was with the band at this point, having joined them beginning in September. Pridden "was forced to take over as head road manager straight away which was a bit scaring at first," he told *Record World*.

> I'd been working with The John Barry Seven before that – a very placid crowd – but I knew what The Who were up to, like smashing their equipment. On that first night it was all fine. The gear went up and it was really nice and then when they went on stage I was so scared. It was the most amazing experience I've ever had. Something clicked, like with Pete, the aggressiveness, the whole thing, the dynamics, the music, everything, and I was quite stunned.
>
> At the end of the act everything got smashed to pieces. Roger just walked off and he said to me: 'Get it fixed for the next gig' and I'm just looking at all those bits and that was when I made my mind up to get into it and do it. I really liked it funnily enough. It was a challenge.

Recording resumed upon the band's return to England in November, with The Who completing *I've Been Away* at Regent Sound, and *Happy Jack* at CBS studios. The latter proved to be the first Who single to break the U.S. singles charts, climbing to number 24 upon its release in the spring (the song reached #3 in the U.K.).

Happy Jack's subject matter, a hermit who lived on the Isle of Man, was culled from Pete's memories during The Squadronaires' residency there during his childhood. "My father used to play saxophone in a band for the season on the Isle of Man when I was a kid," Pete wrote in 1971. "There was no character called Happy Jack, but I played on the beach a lot and it's just my memories of some of the weirdos who lived on the sand." Among other numbers recorded in November was *See My Way*. "…Roger was insistent that Keith play like Jerry Allison, Buddy Holly & The Crickets' drummer, on this track," recalled Chris Stamp, "but after he dampened his drums as far as they would go, Roger still wasn't satisfied with the sound. Eventually Keith and John went outside and found some cardboard boxes to drum on."

December 3, 1966 marked the U.K. release of The Who's second studio album, *A Quick One*. Pete's musicianship had markedly improved since the previous album, thanks to a year packed with live shows. Townshend referred to this release as the Who's first album, casting off the Shel Talmy-produced *My Generation*. He also recalled the album as being fun to record. "Recording *A Quick One* had been mainly enjoyable, especially songs like *Happy Jack* and Keith Moon's *Cobwebs and Strange*," he wrote in a 2001 *Q* article. Renamed *Happy Jack* for American issue (*A Quick One* was deemed too suggestive), the LP reached #4 in the U.K. Apart from the album's title, the only difference between the U.S. and U.K. records was the inclusion of the single *Happy Jack* on the U.S. version due to its success there. *Heatwave* was omitted to make room. The U.S. version of *A Quick One* reached #67.

A Quick One was well received in the music press - *Melody Maker* called the recording, "An incredible new album...at last it fulfills the promise of the Who."

"The release of a new Who album, named after the recent hit, should therefore be reason for celebration," wrote Jon Landau in the July/August 1967 issue of *Crawdaddy*.

> Happily, it is, although the Who of *Happy Jack* are clearly not the Who of *The Who Sings My Generation*. They have metamorphosed with the best of them, and the changes are vast. In fact, the new Who are really a contradiction of the first order. Onstage the group is still famed for its uninhibited exhibitionism and its instrument destruction tactics in which, via various gimmicks, one is led to believe that the world is coming to an end. But listening to *Happy Jack* after being familiar with The Who's live antics, and the first album, one is apt to be surprised. *Happy Jack* is an almost arty, and for The Who, restrained affair. It emphasizes the group's rare talents, in the areas of self-editing (a lost art if ever there was one), humor, lyricism, and other things which one generally expects to find in the wilder groups. The more extroverted side of the group is, in fact, played down.
>
> They're sharp, sarcastic, cynical, but never weighed down with their own self-importance. They are a life-force on a rock scene in which too many people are hiding behind facile, slogan songs about how all the world needs is for everyone to love everyone else. Nor do they have to rely on psychedelic lyrics, or pseudo-poetry, or meaningless attempts at the recreation of the beauty of the Eastern pattern completely out of its natural context, to create music. Rather, they are much more influenced by the

Western classical tradition, both instrumentally and lyrically, than that of any other culture.

The Who don't pretend. Their music is them and they don't have to defend it by coming on too arrogantly, or freaky, within the context of the music itself. They say what they have to say in a manner that is perfectly natural for them, and therein lies their magic and their charm. We would all do well to listen, and to learn.

Pete was quite proud of *A Quick One*. "Just after we'd finished *A Quick One* we became a big clubbing band; we used to go down to the clubs a lot," he said in 1975. "I got to know [Paul] McCartney pretty well, and he was really raving over the album and saying that track *A Quick One* was exactly the sort of thing that The Beatles were working towards. He said they'd been really inspired by it. And when *Sergeant Pepper* came out [June 1967] I remember very smugly thinking, 'It's all because of *A Quick One*.'"[44]

On November 22, 1966, Pete appeared on the American television program *Where the Action Is*, hosted by Dick Clark. The segment, which was filmed in Pete's new Wardour Street flat in London, featured Townshend extolling the virtues of loud music. "One of the reasons for having music fantastically loud," Pete told Clark, "is because you get so many people that'll just turn a deaf ear to what you do, you know, just won't listen to what you do. It doesn't matter how good or bad it is. In fact, the bigger it is normally, the more they'll close their ears to it, so the louder you've got to work. Volume is a fantastic thing. Power and volume!"

Pete's new dwelling on the top floor of 87 Wardour Street lay a little to the south and across the street from the Marquee Club. "Pete was now living in a very big room with a kitchen attached on the top fifth floor of a building on the corner of Wardour Street and Brewer Street, in the heart of London's Soho," wrote Richard Barnes in 1982.

> He'd got a carpenter to build a whole wooden environment into the room. There was a raised platform and a sort of wooden DJ's booth, where he could sit and play records and tapes surrounded by electronic toys and gadgets. [Pete had upgraded his equipment to two Revox 15 tape decks, a "rough patch bay," a limiter and a mixer] His bed was raised up 7ft. from the ground and the

---

[44] In a January, 1967 interview, Pete said, "The only Beatle I've ever suspected of having anything in common with was Paul McCartney...I like all the things he says, and all the songs he writes...They are basically my main source of inspiration – and everyone else's for that matter. I think *Eleanor Rigby* was a very important musical move forward. It certainly inspired me to write and listen to things in that vein."

underneath was used for seating. The whole thing was built as one continuous structure from the same wood, even the floor... Little steps led up to the raised stage area and built-up seats. It looked very strange – something like a modern lecture theatre. Not particularly homely.

...In the center of Pete's pad was a large stone garden pedestal about 3ft. in diameter for holding a small shrub or bush. This served as Pete's rubbish bin and ashtray. One day as we were sitting there he suddenly realized that it was getting quite full. He picked it up - it was quite heavy - and simply tossed the contents out of the window on to busy Wardour Street five floors below. He didn't even look to see where it had all gone.

"Right in the heart of Soho, it was on the top floor of an office block," Pete recalled in 1970. Thoughts of the apartment evoked memories of "...Listening to records on a giant system at 200 watts. Making love in the bed built up near the ceiling, watching *Alice in Wonderland* on the telly, eating baked beans straight out of the tin."

On December 23, 1966, The Who guested on the final episode of the music show which had helped to make the band a household name in Britain, *Ready Steady Go!* With a tip of the hat to one of their most important influences, The Who played *Please Don't Touch* by Johnny Kidd and the Pirates (Kidd had been killed in a car accident back in October) along with a short version of *I'm A Boy*.

The public saw yet another episode of Pete Townshend's explosive temper at the New Year's Eve *Psychedelicamania* (reportedly billed as a 'Giant Freak-Out All Night Rave') show at the Roundhouse, in London. After three consecutive power outages, Pete lost it and commenced to destroy his equipment in a rage. "Pop stars are renowned for their moody temperament, but Pete Townshend went too far at the excessively violent climax to The Who's act," wrote onlooker Bill Montgomery in a letter to *Melody Maker*. "He went into [an] unparalleled frenzy and using the guitar as a sledge hammer sent amplifiers toppling across the stage amidst clouds of smoke, sending hangers-on scurrying for cover. The whole audience reared back from the stage in absolute terror. Excitement on stage, yes, but violence which threatens to involve fans - no thanks!"

"We've got to the stage when we end the night by destroying everything – which is expensive," Pete told an interviewer in early 1967. "I think in pop though, it's good because it has big impact and personally, we find it a great laugh... I smash guitars because I like them. I usually smash a guitar when it's at its best... What I do isn't sadistic. It's aggression. I think aggression has a place in society today – whereas sadism and masochism hasn't."

The Who were now making the jump from clubs to large ballrooms and theaters. The band's status as one of the most popular groups in Britain meant a platoon of screaming teenage girls would be on site at virtually every show, something which did not impress the band. "Sometimes we'd do things to put off the 'screamers' from coming to see us," John Entwistle once recalled. "We'd occasionally sing 'Talking 'bout my Masturbation' and 'Prostitute' instead of 'Substitute'. On one occasion we all walked onstage smoking tampons and throwing tampons at the audience with the string alight, and I actually led Keith on with a sanitary towel over each eye as though he was blind. I led him up on stage and sat him at the drums." While the band members did their part to ensure that the teenybopper crowd would not feel comfortable at Who gigs, Kit Lambert took steps to make sure that The Who were not being generally over-promoted. Upon the release of *Happy Jack*, the band didn't appear on television performing the song as they had with past singles. Lambert opted to make a film to promote the single, more than two decades before the advent of MTV and the general acceptance of the music video as a legitimate promotion device. The final product, a slapstick comedy piece a la Laurel and Hardy, can be seen in the 1979 Who biopic *The Kids Are Alright*.

In January, 1967, Pete was once again featured in *Melody Maker*'s *Pop Think In* column, a segment allowing celebrities to offer their opinions on a variety of subjects. Pete explained that he was enjoying a recently discovered love for colorful clothing. "I used to dress soberly but I've found that color has become more important in my life than it was ever before," he said. This love of color in his clothing could perhaps be attributed to his girlfriend, Karen Astley, a dress design student at Ealing Art School. Pete also had some strong opinions on Christmas Cards, of all things. "I hate them," he explained. "Christmas decorations have still to be exploited. They could be really fantastic – with colors and things. Nobody has done anything very far out yet, have they?"

The Who's first important show of 1967 took place in late January at London's Savile Theatre, with new phenom Jimi Hendrix, who'd only arrived in the U.K. four months earlier. To coincide with the recent release of *A Quick One*, the band decided to dramatically alter their stage show. "...they talked of a completely new act," Richard Barnes recalled in *Maximum R&B*. "The act they had been doing for 18 months would be entirely changed...The Who played better than they had done for months. The group whose trademark was their destruction of their instruments had stopped smashing up their gear. There was no ritualistic guitar and drum obliteration in this show. No smoke bombs. The Who had replaced these ingredients with even better playing and singing. It was the only way to drop part of their act and improve their show." It's possible that another reason for the drastic alteration of the stage act that night was the presence of Hendrix. Pete (along with Jeff Beck and Eric Clapton) reportedly saw

Hendrix at the Bag O'Nails a few weeks prior to the Saville Theater show, and was floored.

Animals bassist Chas Chandler took Hendrix to see Pete as The Who were wrapping up work on *A Quick One* in 1966. "I was completely unaware of what he was about," Pete told *Q*'s David Cavanagh in 2000.

> I met him at a studio. All he had was his guitar and a little road amp, and Chas Chandler brought him to talk to me about amplifiers. He looked scruffy and unassuming. I thought, I must help this poor – I'm going to get politically incorrect now – badly dressed idiot negro, because he's obviously going to die of starvation. I told him I'd been using Marshalls, but that I felt that a new amp called Sound City was better. He turned to Chas and said, 'We'll have one of each.' Then I went to see him play and I fucking wished I'd kept my mouth shut.

Pete often gushed in the press regarding Hendrix. "He could have stolen my wife and I would have been very happy about it," he said later. "I had a very reverent attitude toward him...but I don't think he took us very seriously."[45] In 2004, when Pete was asked why *Tommy* featured very little electric guitar, he said, "The reason for that is Jimi Hendrix – he just made me stop playing, really."

Following four shows in Italy, the band left for the U.S. on March 22, 1967. They arrived in New York, according to Andrew Motion, "...to be greeted by 1,000 screaming teenagers who had been rounded up by Stamp and grouped under a ten-foot banner saying I LOVE THE WHO..." The Who, along with Cream, Wilson Pickett, Smokey Robinson and the Miracles, The Blues Project and several other performers (with Mitch Ryder and the Detroit Wheels headlining), were scheduled to perform five shows a day for nine consecutive days on the *Murray the K Show* at the RKO 58th street theater in New York, from March 25 to April 2. Pete tried to make a big impression at the press reception, wearing "an electric jacket with flashing light bulbs,"[46] he told *Hit Parader*'s Keith Altham the following September. "We worked hard on propaganda for the first three days and I had two stock quotes everyone wrote down," said Pete. "They were 'we

---

[45] In September, 1997, Pete unveiled an English Heritage Blue Plaque on 23 Brook Street, Mayfair, which was Hendrix' residence from 1968-69. "Hendrix becomes the first pop performer to be honored with a blue plaque, which normally celebrate long dead scientists, politicians and poets," reported *The Times*.

[46] The jacket "proved to be something of an anticlimax, because a girl had appeared on TV recently with a dress working on the same principle," Pete told Altham. "Reporters kept asking me where I had got my copy from and I said, 'It's psychedelic and it cost $200 and it's supposed to blow yer mind!"

want to leave a wound' and 'we won't let our music stand in the way of our visual act!'" One of the methods The Who used to ensure that Pete's "stock quotes" held true was to reintroduce their destructive stage habits to the show.

"They were chosen to close the show and wisely so," Al Kooper, who was a member of The Blues Project, wrote in his book *Backstage Passes*.

The first day everyone in the cast stood in the wings to see what all the talk was about.

They launched into *My Generation* and you could feel it coming. Keith Moon flailed away on those clear plastic drums, and it seemed like he had about twenty of them. It was the first time any of us colonists had seen the typical English drumkit. He had huge double bass drums, one of which said THE, and the other of course, WHO. Moon just beat the shit out of them for fifteen minutes non-stop.

Pete Townshend leaped in the air, spinning his arms wildly and just being the most generally uninhibited guitar player ever seen in these parts. Roger Daltrey broke a total of eighteen microphones over the full run of the show. And John Entwistle would just lean up against his amp taking it all in. They reached the modulation part of the instrumental and Townshend spun his guitar in the air, caught it, and smashed it into a placebo amp. No cracks in his Stratocaster so he aimed for the mikestand. Whackkkkk! Crack number one. Then the floor. Whommmmmmppp! The guitar is in three or four pieces and he's still got a signal coming out of it. All of a sudden Moon kicks his entire drum kit over and the curtain rings down in a cloud of artificial smoke.

...I realized my heart was beating three times its normal speed. I figure, as a critic of that show, my electrocardiogram was the best testimonial I could have offered.

"We were smashing our instruments up five times a day," Pete told *Musician* in 1982. "We got two songs – the act was twelve minutes long – and we used to play *Substitute* and *My Generation* with the gear-smashing at the end, and then spend the twenty minutes between shows trying to rebuild everything so we could smash it up again. Or we'd run around pawn shops trying to buy stuff on the cheap..."

With perhaps a nod to Jimi Hendrix, Pete developed an affinity for Fender guitars due to their low cost and solid durability, preferring them to the weaker Rickenbackers he had used until now. "I discovered Fender guitars are very strong and cheap out in the US," Pete said a few months later. "...Telecasters and Stratocasters are just too tough," he added in 1982.

> ...once on the *Murray the K Show*, I chopped a Vox Super Beatle amplifier in two. They're made out of chipboard...and I chopped right through the whole thing. It was a 4x12 cabinet, and it fell into two bits just like that (joins and parts hands symmetrically), I picked up the Stratocaster and carried on playing...*and it was still perfectly in tune!* Now *that's* a guitar for you! I think they're the most beautiful guitars ever designed.

The Who's act must have cost them a fortune[47], but this first exposure in America was critical to their future success, as was their performance at Monterey a few months later. "We really worked the destruction bit to a fine art in our spot," Pete told *Hit Parader*. The band were also terribly irreverent to the show's other performers, including their host, the popular American DJ, Murray the K, and singer Wilson Pickett. Pete recalled the experience in a 1982 interview with *Musician*:

> [Murray the K] used to complain because he had what he called his personal microphone for doing the introductions with, and we were fairly irreverent towards it...[after destroying their own equipment], when we ran out of microphones, his used to come in for a bit of a bashin'. And so we used to actually get daily lectures from him about abusing his personal microphone, which we thought was pretty funny. Then the last thing was when Wilson Pickett called a meeting because we were using smoke bombs as well, and he felt that we were very unprofessional, and that the smoke was affecting everybody else's act. Actually, I think he didn't like following us. But they were all on a different *planet*, basically. We didn't really know what was going on and we didn't take it very seriously. And when it got to the last day we all put funny masks on and went in and sat and listened to [Murray the K] with

---

[47] The trip's expense was significantly enlarged by Moon and Entwistle's profligate champagne-and-caviar room service bills at the Drake Hotel, which reportedly alone exceeded the payment the band received for their Murray the K Show performances.

these masks on...I remember, he asked us to take them off, demanded we remove them.

When asked if the band obliged, Pete replied, "Nope."

Following a potentially huge but aborted booking on the Ed Sullivan show (artists were expected to support an ongoing news readers' strike by refusing to perform), The Who returned to England in early April, 1967, to attend to the business of issuing their next single. *Pictures of Lily*, a song about a young man admiring naked pictures of a turn-of-the-century actress (perhaps Lily Langtry, who indeed died in 1929 as stated in the lyrics), was released in late April, having probably been recorded in early March at Pye studios. "Merely a ditty about masturbation and the importance of it to a young man," Pete wrote in 1971.

"It's all about a boy who can't sleep at night," Pete later recalled, "so his dad gives him some dirty pictures to look at. Then he falls in love with the girl in the pictures which is too bad because she is dead...John and I used to exchange pictures like that when we were at school. We used to go into grubby little shops to buy them," he said, adding, "...looking at dirty pictures is a normal part of adolescence." *Pictures of Lily* reached number 4 in Britain, but only a disappointing number 51 in the States, where it was reportedly banned by many radio stations. "The Who are moving into a class of their own," the *Melody Maker* review announced.

Pictures of Lily also was the first Who record to appear on Track Records, Kit Lambert and Chris Stamp's new money-making venture[48]. "In the coming months," Chris Charlesworth wrote in 1984, "Track would expand considerably and attract such artists as Jimi Hendrix, Arthur Brown, Marsha Hunt and a group called John's Children whose principal writer was guitarist/songwriter Marc Bolan." With two of the most unpredictable and explosive acts leading the way in Hendrix and The Who, and with the similarly quirky Lambert at the helm, Track Records soon established a reputation for frequently veering off the beaten path. But the approach proved fruitful: Within the company's first nine months, they boasted seven top ten records, and a six per cent share of the total British market. After the first year, Lambert's venture showed a £30,000 profit. The advent of Track records meant that Kit and Chris' time away from The Who increased. The result was the appointment of John 'Wiggy' Wolff as the band's "day-to-day" manager.

Pete sensed the dawning of a new phase for The Who upon their return from their first American visit. "...every member of the group is beginning to come into his own," he told *Melody Maker*'s Nick Jones in

---

[48] The tactics used to launch Track Records were vintage Lambert. He observed "the methods of biscuit and washing powder firms that marketed goods roughly the same size as a box of records," he told John Heilpern in 1969, "...and [then] marched into the boardroom at Polydor – one of the biggest companies in the business... and offered them a partnership."

April. "We're having no internal setbacks, and we've started to break into the American scene... The American tour was like it was in London when we first started to get really big. It's like starting again all over..."

Coinciding with this Who renaissance, Pete was also experiencing change in his personal life. Back in early 1966, Pete had become reacquainted with Karen Astley, who had attended Ealing Art School along with Pete a few years earlier. The two quickly became an item. "I... found some other hobbies outside of tape recording: cooking, kissing Karen, restaurants, making love to Karen," Pete would later recall. "...In fact my life with Karen enriched my output as a writer. We made lots of friends and as a couple were more social than I had ever been on my own, my demos had a bigger audience."

One of the stops on the new couple's social circuit was the UFO Club, which opened in December, 1966[49]. According to Dave Marsh, Karen was a waitress at the club. Chris Charlesworth recalled the scene:

> The UFO club was an important underground center in the mid-sixties, a place where ideas were exchanged between counter culture icons of all persuasions... Pete had already experimented with acid and at the UFO he had access to high quality LSD from the Swizz Sandoz laboratories; like the rest of the UFO's hip clientele he could spend an evening gently tripping the night away, his eyes locked into the bubbles on the wall, his mind somewhere else entirely.
>
> Among the other regulars at the UFO club was a stunningly attractive girl called Karen Astley, a clothes designer and illustrator... her family background was steeped in music; her father, Edwin Astley, was a well known composer and classical arranger. Pete became enamored with Karen, she became his first (and only) serious girlfriend.

The UFO club (*Melody Maker*'s Chris Welch said it stood for either 'Unidentified Flying Object,' or 'Underground Freak Out'), which stayed open all night, hosted psychedelic bands (Pink Floyd were regulars) in addition to offering various films. "We showed Marilyn Monroe movies, Kenneth Anger's films, William Burroughs's Cut-Ups – all of which in those days were regarded as very interesting and experimental," 60's chronicler Barry Miles told Pink Floyd biographer Nicholas Shaffner in

---

[49] 'Night Tripper' was the original name of the UFO club (the venue became the UFO a week after its opening). Featured on the club's 'Night Tripper' posters (by psychedelic artist Michael English) was the face of Karen Astley. The UFO club was short-lived – it opened December 31, 1966, and closed on Friday, October 13, 1967.

1981. "You could get fruit juice and sandwiches, but no alcohol – which, looking back, seems extraordinary..." The social scene at the UFO club brought together many like-minded souls, Pete included. While at the UFO, Pete mingled with artists Michael English and Mike McInnerney, singer Arthur Brown, Jimi Hendrix, the Animals, and the Yardbirds.

The UFO was "...believed to be Britain's first psychedelic club," wrote *Melody Maker*'s Chris Welch, who described the club as "the major centre of the social revolution among Britain's youth."

> Happy young people waving sticks of incense danced Greek-like dances, waving frond-like hands with bells jingling, neck scarves fluttering and strange hats abounding.
> There were pretty slides casting beams of light over the jolly throng who stood or squatted in communion, digging the light show or listening to Love being relayed at sensible non-discoteque volume. There were frequent announcements warning patrons to be cool and that the fuzz might pay a call. In fact two young constables did pop in and seemed wholly satisfied that all was well, and in fact all was well.

If Pete's acid-tinged memories of events at the UFO club are to be relied upon, all was *not* well at times. "I remember being in the UFO club with my girlfriend, dancing under the effect of acid," Pete told *Q*'s John Harris in 1996. "My girlfriend used to go out with no knickers and no bra on, in a dress that looked like it had been made out of a cake wrapper, and I remember a bunch of mod boys, still doing leapers, going up to her, and literally touching her up while she was dancing, and she didn't know that they were doing it. I was just totally lost..."

In 1967, Pete moved out of his Wardour Street digs into Karen's flat in Victoria, London. Shortly thereafter the couple moved to an apartment on nearby Ebury Street in lower Belgravia. "I had a studio at Ebury Street on the top floor," Pete recalled in 1977's *The Story Of Tommy*.

> The most fascinating thing about this recording studio in particular, was that it was the room in which *Tommy* - the first few songs from *Tommy* were born. I worked pretty much when I liked, and the sound didn't seem to disturb any neighbors. In the same house, down in the basement, lived an elderly but quiet couple who didn't ever complain. In my studio I had a drum kit, an organ, an electric piano, two old Revox stereo tape recorders, a rather

ancient but well made microphone mixer, and some odd effects that I used to use to enhance my recordings…

The fact that the "elderly couple" who lived in the basement didn't complain is quite amazing when considering that his friend 'Speedy' Keene stated that "[Pete] had two four-by-twelve's up against each wall and a club amp driving it, and to sit and listen to music that loud and powerful, it was a bit too instant. That was the trouble."

Following a short European tour with dates in Germany and Scandinavia, The Who, along with Cream, played at the Pembroke College May Ball in a large marquee at Oxford University on Saturday, May 27. "The undergraduates, mostly upper middle class and upper class students," Richard Barnes wrote in 1982, "were just standing in their dinner suits and summer ball gowns watching in awe as the Who went through their paces." John Entwistle recalled the show with disdain. "We were getting very effed-up with them," he said. "They were real prannies, some of them were trying to dance. I mean, dancing to the Who. They didn't clap or anything. So Moon got up and went and threw his drums into the audience." Moon strained his stomach muscles performing this act, and Entwistle, who had broken a finger on his right hand punching a picture of "a well known pop singer" backstage in Bognor Regis a few weeks earlier, was still unable to perform properly despite limping through a few shows. Keith didn't return until June 9. Recording for the band's next album was put on hold while Keith and John recuperated.

In mid June, the band flew back to the U.S., playing two small club dates, one each in Michigan (Ann Arbor's Fifth Dimension club held only 250 people) and Illinois, prior to heading to San Francisco for two shows at Bill Graham's Fillmore West. Pete thoroughly enjoyed the Fillmore performances, both of which featured the Carlos Santana Blues Band as the support act. "It was a gas," Pete wrote in a *Melody Maker* article upon his return to England. "It was like going back to the Marquee club… And the amplification at the Fillmore is too much. It's a great pity that England doesn't take pop as seriously as those American guys do. The bloke who runs the Fillmore really worried about what we thought of his place and whether the amps were OK… They're really conscientious." Townshend was also impressed with the audiences: "Oh man, they are too much," he wrote. "The vibrations you pick up are incredible. They want to hear what you're playing."

The Fillmore shows meant a major change in The Who's live set, since they were asked to perform for 1½ hours each day. The band's standard performance to date lasted about thirty minutes. "Playing for the Fillmore, which had the first great sound system, forced us to explore all the old and new repertoire we had," Chris Stamp explained in 1995. "We rehearsed any material we could, including *A Quick One*. We only had one afternoon to do this but that night was magnificent. The band had found their enthusiasm for playing again with the longer, less structured sets and *A Quick One* sounded fabulous."

"...now I understand why every group comes away from there saying 'That's the best gig we've ever played,'" Pete told *Melody Maker* a few months later.

> I'd really like to get something going like that in England. The PA system is fantastic. The whole place is very well built for sound and acoustics. It's a rock group's paradise. And the audience! You've just got to play well. You can't help it...They just love music...That's what it's all about. That's why a place like the Fillmore is open seven nights a week with top bands there all the time because the people really understand and dig pop music.

Next on The Who's schedule was The Monterey International Pop Festival. This three-day event, attended by over 200,000 people, proved to define the essence of the summer of love for many. The Who's show took place on June 18, 1967, the third and final evening of the festival, following an afternoon which featured a performance by Indian sitarist Ravi Shankar. Also on the bill for the evening were Jimi Hendrix, The Grateful Dead, Big Brother and The Holding Company, and The Mamas and The Papas. Pete reflected on what he considered a lack of "big names" at the Monterey show in a *Melody Maker* article two weeks later. "The Beatles should have been there," he wrote, "The Stones should have been there."

"I promise this group will destroy you in more ways than one," Animals frontman Eric Burdon announced from the stage before The Who's set. The Who played *Pictures of Lily, A Quick One, Happy Jack,* and *My Generation* followed by Pete smashing his Strat. The band were very displeased with their sound, as they hadn't brought their own equipment with them. They had to settle for inferior Vox amplifiers and were sorry they hadn't gone to the trouble of bringing their own Marshall equipment along[50].

"The Who were in a dangerous mood from the first chords of *Substitute*," recalled Keith Altham[51] in a 2004 *Mojo* article.

---

[50] Hendrix, on the other hand, brought his own Marshall equipment and reportedly sounded far superior to The Who as a result. The lack of Marshall equipment onstage at this event also implied that The Who were behind the times: "The Who were intimately involved in the development of Marshalls but looked like latecomers as a result of what John called Kit's "penny-pinching"," Dave Marsh noted in 1983.
[51] Pete was also wary of the press attention Hendrix was drawing. "Why are you spending so much time with Hendrix," Pete told Altham at the airport after Monterey, according to Altham's 2004 *Mojo* article. "We're paying your fucking fare home. I hope we're going to get something out of this in *NME*."

Apprehension built as the group moved up a gear to tackle Eddie Cochran's *Summertime Blues*. Suddenly, The Who clicked and found that gestalt quality which made them so unique. Against all expectations, the beautiful people began to stir.

As they wound up into an anthemic *My Generation* it finally happened. Townshend went berserk, smashing his guitar on the stage before attempting to fell a stack of amps with it. Splinters and sparks flew as the road crew descended, desperate to save the festival's PA system from being destroyed. This well-meaning attempt at a salvage operation was seen by Moon as a personal affront. The drummer exultantly booted the best part of his kit into the press pit and exited stage left.

There was a momentary stunned silence from the crowd, before they rose in waves to applaud. The Who had experienced their first victory in The Wild West. Only one act could have followed them. Hendrix triumphed, but it was The Who that had drawn first blood.

Pete went to see Hendrix prior to the show about rumors he was going to smash up his guitar. "I had it out with him. I said 'You're not going to go out there and smash your guitar, are you?,'" Pete said in 1982. "He got very nasty about it... He varied between being very nice to me and being a bit arrogant." After The Who's set, Pete watched Hendrix's performance and subsequent guitar destruction. "...I was sitting next to Mama Cass," Pete said, "and she turned to me and said, 'Isn't this guy stealing your act?' and I said, 'Yeah, but, you see, he's so fucking great, who cares.' It was all peace and love at that time and I was very magnanimous and I said to him afterwards 'Is there any chance of gettin' a piece of your guitar?' because he was my hero. He said, 'Yeah, and I'll fuckin' autograph it for you, honky', or something like that."

Backstage at Monterey, Pete reportedly met Owsley Stanley, the inventor of the powerful hallucinogen STP, and on their flight home to England he and Karen sampled a concoction that Stanley had given them. "We took some on the plane coming home, thinking it was acid," Pete said later.

It turned out to be STP, something that I would never ever take. It was bloody terrible. I mean, you wouldn't believe it. You know when they say under Japanese torture, sometimes, if it's horrible enough the person actually gets the feeling that they're leaving their body? In this case, I had to do just that, abandon my body.

…It was actually about a four-hour hump, whereas a normal acid hump is about twenty-five or thirty minutes… you have a hump and then plane off into a nice trip. Well, on this STP trip, the hump was about four to five hours, and it was on an airplane over the Atlantic. I said, 'Fuck this, I can't stand any more.' And I was free of the trip. And I was just like floating in midair looking at myself in a chair, for about an hour and a half. And then I would go back in again and it would be the same. And I was just like, zap, completely unconscious as far as the outside world was concerned. But I was very much alive, crawling alive.

"It was like a hundred years on the airplane across the Atlantic," he said later. "…I never realised what a fragile mind I had. Eventually it tailed off and …then you need a week to repiece your ego, remember who you are and what you are."

This "terrifying trip", as Pete described it in 1977, led him to abandon psychedelic drugs immediately. Meher Baba, a spiritual figure Pete would soon discover and follow, stood firmly against hallucinogenic drugs, but Pete's decision to quit psychedelics had already been made. "It really did make me push the whole thing away," Pete said in 1977. "If I hadn't had that really awful trip on that plane back from Monterey, I probably would still be into drugs. I found it very easy to accept what Baba said about drugs because it just seemed to happen that way. I actually felt physically damaged by it. That's why I never really feel I'm doing anything courageous or selfless by not involving myself in it. It was very easy to do."

"Acid had taken me apart but not put me back together again," Pete later wrote in *Rolling Stone*, "and it is clutching another of Baba's statements about drugs that I justify what I did to my brain: *For a few sincere seekers, the use of hallucinogenic drugs may have instilled in them a state of longing that has brought them into my contact, but further injection would not only be harmful, but have no purpose.*" While he had decided to stop using psychedelic drugs, Pete's pot smoking continued.

In early July, The Who returned to New York to record some tracks for their next album prior to embarking on their first full-scale American tour. Keyboardist Al Kooper was enlisted for this recording session. "We… spent a very fruitful week at New York and covered a lot of ground," Pete wrote in a *Melody Maker* article a few weeks later, "…The tracks were recorded at Talent Masters Studio on 42nd Street which is run by Chris Huston." One of the tracks recorded during this visit was *Rael 1*. Al Kooper recalled the experience in his autobiography:

We recorded most of the song in one day and then adjourned for a noon start the next day. We left rather hurriedly because we were fried from working so intensely...evidently the multitrack tape of *Rael* was left on the counter unboxed. The cleaning woman came in and threw it in the trash but didn't empty it, so it lay there with soda and cigarette ash all over it. When Chris Huston came in next morning...he was horrified. The first 15 seconds of the track had been compromised and would have to be done again. He was the one who was gonna have to tell Townshend. I wanted to see this encounter. So Pete comes boppin' in about 12:15 and Chris takes him in a corner and is talking very hushed to him. All that is audible are Chris' last words, "Pete, I'm sorry but sometimes these things happen..." Townshend is pacing back and forth inside the control room, when all of a sudden he picks up the engineers' chair and throws it through the control room glass partition, damage of roughly $12,000. Then he turned to Chris and said, "Don't worry, Chris...sometimes these things just happen."

The Who returned to Talent Masters Studio during a break in the tour in early August for further recording work. Following the initial Talent Masters sessions, The Who traveled to Oregon to kick off their first full-scale North American tour, an eight week affair including forty-plus shows in 28 states. The band were part of a 'package tour', an unlikely pairing with Herman's Hermits[52], a harmless, but tremendously popular (Pete later said that Herman's Hermits were "bigger than the Beatles" at the time) pop band with teenage heartthrob Peter Noone on lead vocals. The two bands actually did have something in common – their agency, Premier Talent. The first show took place on July 7.

"We have just left New York and are flying to Oregon for our first concert with Herman," Pete wrote in a letter to *Melody Maker*, published the following month.

> I haven't seen Herman's own plane yet but have heard it's amazing - with "Herman's Hermits" and "The Who" painted in dayglo paint along the sides. We're all looking forward to the tour in general excepting a few crisis

---

[52] "...I said [to *Sixteen* magazine in a 1966 interview], 'Listen, you know these Herman's Hermits guys are the biggest band in America... you know, I have a mission, it is to rid the world of this shit!," Pete said in a 1989 radio interview "...And we did it, right out from under Herman's Hermits' noses. We went out with them and undermined them and just made sure they never, ever came back."

points we would rather avoid, like Dallas and Houston, etc. The New York groups have told us such amazing tales of the effect long hair has on shotgun carrying farmers there!

The band played 30-40 minutes most nights, according to *The Who Concert File*, which described The Who's basic set list as *Substitute* (which had recently been released as a single in the U.S.), *Pictures Of Lily, Summertime Blues, Barbara Ann, Boris The Spider, A Quick One, Happy Jack, I'm A Boy* and *My Generation*. The band, not exactly what the crowd would expect as the opener for Herman's Hermits, tore through their set with little or no delay between songs. By the time they reached *My Generation*, with its customary autodestructive finale, the crowd was in a state of shock. "It was spellbinding," Tom Wright (Pete's deported art school crony, who'd been named road manager for this tour and many future outings) told Richard Barnes in 1982. "A lot of times there was no clapping whatsoever, just dead silence. People in the front rows were just sitting there with their mouths opened – stunned."

"America was very good for us," Pete told *Melody Maker* when the band returned home, "because we had to re-think and start again. They were fresh audiences who hadn't heard us live." The American crowds' impression of Pete's guitar smashing was different, too. "In England I used to get people asking me for my guitars and calling me terrible names because I smashed equipment up," he said. "They said I wasn't worthy of having such expensive guitars just to wreck them, so why didn't I give them away. But in the States it was the other way round. They thought it was a gas. They loved it. I became a kind of hero. I was presented with beautiful guitars - just to smash them up. It became ludicrous."

"When we played on the tour with Herman," Pete added, "we were playing to younger audiences. Every night we came off stage sweating and exhausted but really knocked out. When you get those enthusiastic audiences you just don't want to get off stage." The Who also sounded much better on this tour than on previous visits since they finally brought their own Marshall amplification equipment, along with Moon's new custom made Premier 'Pictures of Lily' drum kit.

The Herman's Hermits tour wound on through July and August, with Neil Diamond sharing the bill for two shows in Chattanooga, Tennessee, and Keith Moon's legendary 21st birthday party taking place at the end of August after a show in Flint, Michigan. It was during this tour that Moon found a new toy. "Keith feels he has to be involved in some sort of entertainment," Pete told John Swenson.

And the first really big thing ever was in the Herman's Hermits tour. We went to Georgia, where they sell fireworks, and they sell these things called cherry bombs, and one day I was in his room and his door knocker was all black like he'd been putting these things in and I said 'Could I use your bog?' and he smiled and said 'Sure.' I went in there and there was no toilet, just sort of an S bend, and I thought 'Christ, what happened?' he said 'Well this cherry bomb was about to go off in me hand and I threw it down the toilet to stop it going off.' So I said 'Are they that powerful?' and he said 'Yeah, it's incredible.' So I said 'How many of 'em have you got?' with fear in me eyes. He said 'Five hundred,' and opened up a case full to the top with cherry bombs. And of course from that moment on we got thrown out of every hotel we ever stayed in. The Holiday Inns were phoning round saying 'Don't let this group in – they blow up the hotels.'

Another defining moment in Who history occurred on September 15, 1967, as the band appeared on the *Smothers Brothers* show, which can be seen on the 1979 biopic *The Kids Are Alright*. The Who were in top form during the introductions, with all involved making host Tommy Smothers feel as uncomfortable as possible. Following a ridiculously mimed version of *My Generation*, complete with smoke bombs, Pete proceeded to smash his guitar in front of Keith's drum riser, unaware that Moon had put a mammoth dose of explosive powder – reportedly three times the accepted load for such a stunt – inside one of his bass drums and was preparing to detonate it. The ensuing explosion, which reportedly caused Bette Davis to pass out as she was watching from the side of the stage, caught Pete as he was hunched over, smashing his guitar, with his head only a few feet from Keith's bass drum. The force of the blast knocked him down and as he stood up, engulfed in smoke, his hair badly singed and his hearing damaged, he staggered over to Tommy Smothers, grabbed the host's acoustic guitar from around his neck and smashed it to pieces. "I was looking around and Townshend comes staggering over, as was scripted, but I'm looking at him for injuries," Tommy Smothers told *Mojo* in 2004. "He wandered over and grabbed my guitar and smashed it, too. But I'll bet you his head was ringing. It must have sounded like a siren inside his skull." Townshend "couldn't hear properly for a week afterwards", Chris Charlesworth recalled.

In the next few days after the *Smothers Brothers* show, The Who went to Gold Star studios in L.A., recording *Our Love Was* at Columbia Studios. *I Can See For Miles* was mixed during this visit. Upon their return to England, the band continued recording their next album. In addition to the work they had just completed in California, the band had recorded *Early Morning Cold Taxi* and *I Can't Reach You* in London during the summer. "...I write a lot of songs on airplanes," Pete said in 1968, "but they sound just like songs written in airplanes. Let me see: *I Can't Reach You* - "our love was flowing, our life was soaring" and "I can't reach you; I'm a billion ages past you and a billion years behind you." It's all spacy, cloudy, you know; sun glinting on the wings, big massive jet engines silently soaring through the quiet skies, you know all this stuff is great for lyrics."

Six months later, The Who recorded *Glow Girl*, a song with an airplane crash theme. "I never regarded myself as a person afraid of traveling by air," Pete said in 1968[53].

> When we did the Herman's Hermit tour in an old charter plane, I wrote so many songs about plane crashes, it was incredible. I did a song called *Glow Girl*...I wrote it because we were taking off in a plane which I seriously thought was going to crash... and as I was going up I was writing a list, I thought, that if I was a chick and I was in a plane that was diving for the ground and I had my boyfriend next to me and we were on our honeymoon or we were about to get married, I know what I'd think of. I'd think about him and I'd think about what I am going to be missing. ...I just went through a big list of what was in this chick's purse - cigarettes, Tampax, a whole lyrical list and then holding his hand and what he felt and what he was gonna say to her...The man, he's trying to have some romantic and soaring last thoughts. Eventually what happens is that they crash and they are reincarnated at a very instant musically. What I wanted was the list getting [more and more frantic], she's going through her handbag, ballpoint pen, cigarettes, book matches, lipstick and Excedrin and he's going "We will be this and we will do this and we will be together in heaven and don't worry little one, you're safe with me," and all this kind of bullshit. What happens is The Who do an incredible destruction as the plane hits the ground, explosions...then "It's a girl, Mrs. Walker, it's a girl..." That was supposed to be the end of the thing and you suss out that they've been reincarnated as this girl.

The band had also recorded two Rolling Stones covers, *The Last Time* and *Under My Thumb* during the summer of 1967, and released the songs as a single to protest the recent "savage" sentences imposed on Mick Jagger and Keith Richards for drug possession charges. The Who planned on recording more Stones songs to keep the band in the public eye, but

---

[53] "We all had a narrow escape today," Moon reportedly wrote to his wife during the tour. "One of the engines on the plane caught fire and we nearly plunged ten thousand feet into the heart of Tennessee."

Jagger and Richards were soon released. Pete played bass on both songs since John was overseas on his honeymoon.

While The Who had spent a great deal of time in the recording studio in past months, plans for an album (especially any signature Pete Townshend 'concept') had not been forthcoming. During a visit to the Track Records offices in Old Compton Street, Pete found Chris Stamp poring over a list. "I said to him 'What's that?'," Pete told Chris Charlesworth. ""Oh, just a list of songs that I thought might make up the next album." "Album? What album?" "Well, you've got to have an album out." "But *that* and *that* and *that*." "You're joking. What a boring old album.""

Faced with the prospect of issuing an album of songs most of which Pete considered weak with the exception of *I Can See For Miles*, he pleaded with Stamp to consider delaying the album's release. "Chris was insistent on its release," Pete wrote in a 2001 *Q* magazine article, pointing out that he felt that Stamp's desire for a quality album was secondary to his desire to get another Track release on the market in a timely manner.

> I panicked.
> I can remember pacing around his office, wildly brainstorming, Chris, with a bemused expression on his face, waiting for me to come up with something. I needed an idea that would transform what I regarded as a weak collection of occasionally "cheesy" songs into something with teeth.
> Suddenly I hit on it: we would turn the entire album into a pirate radio segment and actually sell advertising space to manufacturers and fashion houses. My intention was not only to lampoon corporate advertising, but also to get our share of the revenue. Chris immediately got to work and fixed up two art directors for the sleeve and attempted to seell the space between songs on the album to advertisers. With an anticipated sale of less than 50,000 copies companies like Coca-Cola were unwilling to take space and pay for it. They sent a case of 20 cans of their beverage instead.
> No matter, by now I was away…
> I came up with *Odorono*, which turned out to be a fully rounded and rather plaintive song about a singer who, because she has B.O., fails an audition with the impresario Harold Davidson… We spent an additional two weeks on this effort and wrote and recorded a dozen or so jingles. When the brilliant Kit Lambert finally played me the album cut together I was very happy with the result. What made it

fly was of course the proper radio jingles he had managed to get hold of. A dedicated American jingles company made these, but they were not properly licensed and Track released the album under the threat of a lawsuit.

As Dave Marsh wrote, what the entire album seemed to be about was setting up *I Can See For Miles*, one of the best songs I had written by that time. But there are some really good songs on the album, and they are a bit cheesy. The format delivers them in a way that allows the "weaker" songs to work.

…Because we were serious and mischievous at once about the idea it worked very well. It emanated all the art school coolness and irony I longed for at the time (and probably still do).

Pete's decision to use commercials between songs on *The Who Sell Out* was both a satire of and a tip of the hat to the old pirate radio stations to whom he credited much of the band's initial success[54], and which had been rendered illegal as a result of the Marine Broadcasting Act, which was enacted in August, 1967. "You don't realize how good something like the pirates are until they've gone," Pete told Dave Marsh in 1983. "So, to give the album that ethereal flavor of a pirate radio station, we incorporated some 'groovy' jingles." In addition to those previously mentioned, among the commercials The Who recorded for the album were *Heinz Baked Beans*, *Coke*, *Rotosound Strings*, and *Great Shakes*, most of which were recorded at Kingsway studios, London. The majority were thought up by Entwistle and Moon in a neighboring pub.

Most of the material featured on *The Who Sell Out* was recorded in London at Kingsway, IBC, and De Lane Lea studios during October and early November, 1967. Included in the eclectic mix of material was The Who's unlikely version of Grieg's *Hall of The Mountain King,* and a Speedy Keene composition entitled *Armenia City in the Sky* which featured various buzzing noises and backwards guitar.

In early November, Pete recorded *Sunrise* at IBC studios. This jazzy, romantically oriented song which features only Pete playing acoustic guitar and singing, provided a glimpse of his future inclinations in his solo career. "Keith didn't want [*Sunrise*] on the record," Pete told *Sounds* in 1980. "See in a way that's a bit of a giveaway to the fact that at the time I was studying a bit of this jazz thing…I was studying Mickey Baker methods and I had two of his tutors, both of which were magnificent. And it's all

---

[54] Ronan O'Rahilly, who owned the Scene club in Soho, was also the owner of the first pirate radio station, Radio Caroline.

that I've ever needed to get into slightly more complex chord work. And that song I wrote for my mother to show her that I could write real music."

Townshend's next foray into involved storytelling through music came with the advent of *Rael 1 & 2*, which demonstrated a distinct step forward from *A Quick One* in two key areas: first, *Rael*, unlike *A Quick One*, was not at all meant to be funny – the overall feeling was far 'heavier' and, second, the quality of the writing (and consequently the quality of the performance) on *Rael* was far superior to the less polished *A Quick One*. The tangible step forward which took place between these two works can be traced to several factors. Since Kit Lambert had provided him an education in classical music back in 1965, Pete had developed an appreciation for the genre. Add to this the fact that Karen's father was composer Edwin Astley, and one can understand that information and guidance regarding the genre had become readily available to Pete. "I was studying orchestrations and stuff like that, and I'd bought a piano," Pete said in 1975, "and then I did a lot of orchestrations and I bought lots of books about it and I used to speak a lot to Karen's Dad about orchestrations and stuff like that."

Pete wrote in 1977 that he had "dithered tremendously" with *Rael*, which he "intended it to be written for full orchestra and to be a genuine opera. Looking back, I can't quite remember where the Who fitted in, because I had Arthur Brown lined up as the hero." Pete would again entertain thoughts of using the eccentric lead singer of The Crazy World of Arthur Brown when he was writing *Tommy* the following year. Pete described the plot of *Rael* in *The Story of Tommy*:[55]

> ...The story was about 1999 (not as cliched as 2000 you see) and the emergence of the Red Chinese (The Redchins) as world leaders. The only spiritual note was that the Redchins were regarded as being fairly evil because they were crushing the old established religions as they conquered...In 1966, at my studio in Wardour Street I wrote this (one of the first idea-sheets for *Rael*):
>
> Opening is set at sea. In order to create a wide linear feeling in the opening of the opera. The sound of the sea in deep echo is heard. It must be fairly artificial so as not to start too heavily.
>
> NARRATOR SINGING. Someone, a man, is leaving home, (thoughts of home). He is wealthy. He has broken many ties. It is a time of indecision. He is on a boat

---

[55] Rael was "...all about 'overspill' when the world population becomes so great in years ahead that everyone is assigned to their one square foot of earth," Pete told John Swenson. "We played it onstage in Manchester and Scotland and everyone just looked at us with their mouths open – the complication was just too much."

that recently left harbour and is heading out to sea. He wonders if he is doing right.

Basically the story was running into about twenty scenes when Kit Lambert reminded me that while I was pretending to be Wagner, The Who needed a new single. What did I have? I had "Rael." Thus *Rael* was edited down to four minutes (too long for a single in those days ironically) and recorded in New York for that purpose. It later appeared on an album (*Odds & Sods*). No-one will ever know what it means, it has been squeezed up too tightly to make sense. Musically it is interesting because it contains a theme which I later used in *Tommy* for *Sparks* and the *Underture*.

October 14, 1967, marked the release of *I Can See for Miles*, which Pete felt was the best song he had written to date. "I always feel that the best constructed early song that I ever wrote was *I Can See For Miles*," Pete said in a 1978 radio interview. "I put about two solid days into that and when it actually worked…I think the lyrics are great, they create a great sort of impression of images, and the music is harmonically exciting." The single reached a respectable number 10 in the British charts, and number 9 in America, but Pete was thoroughly disappointed at the song's failure to become a smash hit. "That was a real heartbreaker for me," he said. "It was a number we'd been saving, thinking that if The Who ever got into trouble this one would pull us out. On the day I saw it go down (the charts) I spat on the British record buyer. To me this was the ultimate Who record and yet it didn't sell."[56]

"The real production masterpiece in the Who/Lambert coalition was, of course, *I Can See For Miles*," Pete wrote in a *Rolling Stone* article in 1971. "…We cut the track in London at CBS studios and brought the tapes to Gold Star studios in Hollywood to mix and master them. Gold Star owns the nicest sounding echo chamber in the world… I swoon when I hear the sound. The words, which aging senators have called "Drug Oriented," are about a jealous man with exceptionally good eyesight. Honest."

The Who's third studio album, *The Who Sell Out*, was released in December, 1967. It was well received by critics, but didn't fare any better than the band's previous two albums, reaching number 13 in the British charts. The record failed to chart in America, where it was released in January.

---

[56] Kit Lambert's godfather, composer William Walton, heard *I Can See For Miles* and passed word through Kit that the song "indicated real greatness," Pete told the *Washington Times* in 1992. Pete said that Walton's words encouraged him to begin work in earnest on his rock opera *Tommy*.

"...even though it is made up from end to end (give or take some jingle content), *The Who Sell Out* has become a truer account of the Sixties than any other document," Dave Marsh wrote in his essay accompanying the album's reissue in 1995.

Not only because it captures the form in which our passions played out, but because in the very triviality of lyrics like *Tattoo, Mary Anne With The Shaky Hand* and *Odorono* it captures the sad state of our generation's internal affairs that leads inexorably to the smashing revelation of the album's masterpiece, *I Can See For Miles*. *The Who Sell Out* holds a mirror up to reality, and the great part is, it turns out to be a rock'n'roll mirror, something that gives you a totally distorted picture while revealing the truth. If you can't get your mind around that paradox, two things are true: you aren't gonna have nearly as much fun with this album as it has to offer, and you must have missed the Sixties.

Nik Cohn, who reviewed the album in *Queen* wasn't happy that the 'concept' was only applied to one side of the album. "The trouble is that the idea hasn't been carried right the way through; it has only been half-heartedly sketched in," Cohn wrote.

This, of course, is a traditional Who fault – Pete Townshend works something out, the group half completes it and then everyone sits back until another group walks in and steals the whole thing.

In a way, it's an attractive fault, it shows a nice lack of intensity towards success. In this case, however, it's a disaster.

What this album should really have been is a total ad explosion, incredibly fast, loud, brash and vulgar, stuffed full of the wildest jingles, insane commercials, snippets from your man Rosko [pirate deejay], plus anything else that came to hand – a holocaust, and utter wipe-out, a monster rotor whirl of everything that pop and advertising really are.

It is interesting to note the condition of Pete's fingers on *The Who Sell Out* cover photo, holding a giant deodorant applicator - they are clearly scarred from various guitar-inflicted injuries, only a few years into The Who's long history. "This problem is always coming up," Pete said at the time. "At the moment I've lost my fingernail, and that was the most painful thing that ever happened to me. The nail came off when I was playing at Newcastle, as I kept swinging my arm and getting the string caught underneath at full force. I've never known so much pain in all my life. In the end I just blacked out. I couldn't hold a pick or anything, that's how bad it gets...The best thing to do when you hurt your fingers is stick 'em in neat whiskey, which deadens the pain. Obviously it deals with any dirt...and then you drink the whiskey afterwards!"

Reportedly, *The Who Sell Out* was originally intended to include three Eddie Cochran numbers, *Summertime Blues*, *C'mon Everybody* and *My Way*, but these songs (along with a Jaguar commercial[57]) were shelved when Blue Cheer released their own version of *Summertime Blues*. The inclusion of these songs would have made *Sell Out* a much harder-edged album. "Without the hard-rock numbers which were deleted from the record," John Swenson wrote in 1979, "*Sell Out* sounded radically different from the group's stage sound at the time, a fact that may have had something to do with the record's poor commercial showing."

> While *Sell Out* was a clever statement about the basic pop medium, radio, The Who's stage show continued to be all guts and glory, rock on the cutting edge... The live version of *Relax* had almost nothing to do with the album track – onstage it became a fiery hard-rock extravaganza with an extended solo spot for Townshend. During the solo he would experiment with feedback, playing Hendrix-style licks on occasion, and build long, hypnotic statements out of a simple melodic idea, often working out patterns which would eventually emerge as part of the overall structure of *Tommy*.

The Who played two shows at the Saville Theatre on October 22 (supported by Vanilla Fudge), their first live appearances in Britain since June. The band displayed appropriate over-the-top showmanship, with Pete wearing a sparkling 'pearly king' suit made by Karen and covered with hundreds of buttons while he played a double-necked Gibson guitar. Keith wore a full court jester costume. Although the band didn't destroy their equipment, the shows were designed to present the same 45 minute set that had been standard on the Herman's Hermits tour.

The ensuing eighteen-date tour began with a disastrous show in Sheffield on October 28, 1967. The Who were slotted to play on a bill with four other bands for two shows that night, leaving them with enough time for only two songs. "The band's tempers were pushed to the limit," reported

---

[57] "I... wrote a long-winded instrumental called *Jaguar* which was not included on the finished record though The Who made a good job of it," Pete wrote in a 2001 *Q* magazine article.

The Who Concert File, "and Roger Daltrey and Pete Townshend had a disagreement on stage that ended in a scuffle. The concert finished with Pete kicking his speaker cabinets over onto the theatre manager who had ordered the act to be curtailed. Pete then grabbed the manager by the throat and dragged him across the stage."

The following night in Coventry was no better: "The first performance ended in the destruction of the theatre's footlights as well as Pete's guitar when the curtain was lowered during The Who's set," wrote 'Irish' Jack Lyons and Joe McMichael. "Amplification problems had delayed the show by about 20 minutes with only 10 minutes before the second show was due to start. As a result, the tour manager ordered the curtain be brought down. Pete and Roger were left in front of the curtain and *God Save The Queen* was played over the house PA system. Pete shouted for the curtain to be raised, threw his guitar on the stage and began his assault on the footlights."

A short American tour, The Who's fourth of 1967, soon followed[58]. The eleven-date visit featured a November 18 show at the Cow Palace in San Francisco where the band appeared with The Animals, The Association and The Everly Brothers. The tour also included two shows at New York's Village Theater, which would later become known as the Fillmore East. The Vagrants, featuring guitarist Leslie West, opened these shows, showcasing their own autodestruction routine at the end of *If I Were a Carpenter*. "In New York each successive appearance grew wilder and more apocalyptic," John Swenson wrote in 1979. "At the Village Theater... the hostile audience threw shoes and other objects at a hapless Tiny Tim as he bravely tried to entertain the bloodthirsty throng of Who fans with *Tiptoe Through the Tulips*, while the sounds of The Who's road crew nailing Keith Moon's drum kit to the stage came hammering out from behind the curtains. When the band finally played, a near riot broke out in front of the stage."

With 1967 under their belts, The Who enjoyed a burgeoning reputation in the U.S. as a spectacular live act. They had put together a pair of long American tours, which heightened their exposure enormously. They decided to expand their horizons in early 1968, embarking on their first and only tour of Australia and New Zealand, an eight-date nightmare which resulted in Pete vowing never to return. The Who, part of a package tour which included The Small Faces and former Manfred Mann singer Paul Jones, arrived in Australia in mid-January, exhausted from the long flight. "They were greeted off their plane journey," wrote Tony Fletcher in his Keith Moon bio *Moon*, "jet-lagged all to hell, by the obligatory press conference that welcomed every band to a foreign country in the sixties."

---

[58] The Who's PA didn't make it to the November 22 stop in Southfield Michigan. They used the PA of opener the Amboy Dukes. "I really wasn't that worried that they'd trash the speakers," Ted Nugent told *Mojo* in 2004, "but I did have a moment when I saw Townshend kick one of my stacks."

Small Faces keyboardist Ian McLagan, recently busted for possession of pot, was asked the first question. "Mr. McLagan, is it true that you're a drug addict? "I said, 'Oh fuck off,' " he recalls, "and that was it, they started packing their equipment up. And they hounded us after that. Everywhere we went there'd be these arseholes. It was hell." In addition, Ronnie Lane told Dave Marsh in 1983, the media asked, "'How do you feel now that the pound's been devalued?' As if that meant anything to us – and it was supposed to. The whole thing was so bloody and horrible and pathetic. I think Pete Townshend hit this fellow and this is what got the tour off to a good bollocking in the press."

The band's decision to use equipment provided by the local promoters rather than the more expensive option of bringing their own was immediately called into question after they made their first appearance of the tour, on January 20 in Brisbane. Apparently they failed to learn from their bad experience with borrowed equipment at Monterey. *The Who Concert File* reported that the band "were greatly dismayed by the dire quality of the PA system that had been provided." Journalist Andy Neill wrote that "the band had already started to drop the equipment smashing antics in Britain, but felt obliged to resurrect them, to win over new audiences, particularly here in Australia where their reputation for this preceded them. Besides this there was good reason for the band smashing their equipment on this tour, as it was, quite simply, piss poor."

The band's next appearance took place at Sydney Stadium, which boasted a revolving stage. Predictably, by the time The Who took the stage, the revolving stage was no longer revolving – it had become stuck during the Small Faces' set. The band seemed cursed with equipment problems.

As the tour wore on, Pete's impression of Australia worsened. For example, Andy Neill recalled the following:

> Townshend found how backward Australian hotel room service was when, phoning down for breakfast one morning, at what he considered a reasonable hour, he was laughed at by the desk: 'This is Orstraylia mate, we get out of bed in the morning here.' Pissed off he decided to take matters into his own hands! Visiting a local supermarket he purchased a large box of cornflakes and a gallon of milk. Returning to his room he poured the contents into the sink and after sampling a few mouthfuls of his breakfast delicacy, he left the rest to solidify into the sink like concrete before checking out of the hotel.

Yet another unfortunate incident occurred on the airplane that was flying the bands from Adelaide to Sydney towards the end of the tour. Tony Fletcher wrote the following account of the episode in *Moon*:

An altercation between a stewardess who obviously believed the groups' bad press and an entourage that had given up on trying to be polite anymore escalated rapidly until someone called the stewardess by a four-letter word, and the captain landed the plane at the nearest airport to have the entire nineteen-person entourage removed by force. Three hours later, they were finally "escorted" onto another flight to Sydney, airline security riding shotgun. The Australian papers immediately dedicated their front pages to this latest example of the touring party's violence and belligerence and the incident was picked up by a scathing British tabloid press too. The Who vowed never to return to Australia and it was a promise they kept.

Things didn't improve on the New Zealand leg of the tour. "They took nearly 8,000 teenagers for $2.60 to $3.60 each," complained Paul Rodgers in the February 6 edition of the *New Zealand Truth*.

All the kids got for their money was an ear-splitting cacophony of electronic sounds that was neither musical nor funny...the two Wellington performances turned out to be the most hopeless flops ever staged there. Without the aid of recording technicians, this bunch of long-haired boors were worthless. They had no idea of public presentation. From start to finish the shows were a mixture of amateurish bungling, jarring off-pitch guitar chords, inane drum-thumping and thunderous amplification...I'm ashamed to have come from the same country as these unwashed, foul-mouthed, booze-swilling no-hopers. Britain can have them.

"Australia, the nation, was up in arms at what these long-haired monsters were supposedly up to," wrote Andy Neill, "So much so, that the then Prime Minister, Senator John Gorton, sent a telegram to Pete Townshend requesting The Who never set foot in Australia again. Townshend shot back a colorful reply, and to this day has kept his word and never returned!"

Over thirty years later, Pete still hadn't returned to the country. "The Who won't come here, I'm afraid," Roger told Australia's *Undercover News* during a February 2000 visit with the British Rock Symphony. "You Aussies upset Townshend. He's got a very long memory...your bloody Prime Minister said 'get out you pommy bastards and don't come back'...I love Australia, it's a terrific country and we've had heaps of offers but Pete just will not come." It wasn't until 2004 that Townshend finally changed his mind.

In 2000, *Q*'s David Cavanaugh asked Pete what his reply was to Gorton's telegram. "I suppose my reply was to never go back to Australia again," Pete said. "What was actually more insulting was that the telegram said we couldn't go back. We've never seen a copy of it, but I know someone who says he's got it. They also created an extraordinary taxation event for us as well, which meant that they took all our money. It was terribly humiliating and I've never really quite recovered from it, I must say."

Three weeks after their return from Australia, The Who were once again on the road, this time embarking on a nine week tour of North America and Canada, their first as headliner. The tour, which mostly featured shows at ballrooms and colleges, began on the west coast on February 21 with a date at San Jose civic auditorium. Three shows in San Francisco followed, during which recordings were made for a proposed live album (The Who's gigs at the Fillmore East in New York were also taped on this tour).

During a week-long break prior to heading up into Canada, the band stopped by the now familiar Gold Star recording studios in Hollywood to record *Call Me Lightning* and *Little Billy*. The latter, an anti-smoking song recorded for the American Cancer Society, was ultimately rejected, perhaps because at least three of the band members were smokers at the time.

After dates in Vancouver and Edmonton, the band swung back down the Northeast U.S. with dates in Minnesota, Michigan and Illinois before driving all the way to San Antonio five days later. The tour then wound back up the east coast as far north as Canada prior to heading back to New York for two shows a night on April 5 and 6 at the Fillmore East. These dates were The Who's first at the newly renamed Village Theater, which had been taken over by Bill Graham, and Buddy Guy opened both nights (with B.B. King appearing for a few songs on the first night). The nationwide civic unrest which resulted from Dr. Martin Luther King Jr.'s assassination on April 4 dissuaded many from attending these concerts, so the workload was reduced to one show per night. The first night was recorded as part of the plan for the band's upcoming live album. "Only a few hundred people showed up," John Swenson wrote in 1979.

> The band decided to record anyway and waited until the second show crowd had filtered in before playing one marathon set. The show was really a special event. ...The Who were magnificent, opening with an ebullient *Substitute* and *Pictures of Lily*, then a mean *Summertime Blues*, with a long solo spot from Townshend. After a medley of *Fortune Teller/Tattoo* Townshend introduced the

antismoking commercial *Little Billy*... this was the early high point of the show...

I Can't Explain, Happy Jack and *Relax* followed, then came the *Quads* theme, *I'm a Boy*, followed by the miniopera, *A Quick One While He's Away*... At the end of *You Are Forgiven* Townshend kicked the song past its borders and took a long solo comprised of several instrumental passages that would later be used in *Tommy*. As he finished his solo and returned to the *A Quick One* coda the vocal chorus kicked back in again in beautiful, exciting harmony as the three sang counterpoint "Forgiven... forgiven... forgiven," then each one took one of the syllables and shouted it percussively against the chorus, while Townshend smashed the resolution chords brutally. At the song's end the audience realized they had been brought directly into the experience of the songs, an emotional and spiritual moment that virtually defined the magic of rock & roll. Townshend, proudly sensing what he had just elicited, waved a mock blessing at the audience and extended the song's last line to include nto just the song's heroine but the whole audience: "You are *all* forgiven."

The Who came back to earth for three powerful rockers, *My Way, C'mon Everybody*, and *Shakin' All Over*, followed by Entwistle's *Boris the Spider* and closed with what must have been one of their greatest renditions of *My Generation*. "I got to admit," Townshend told the audience "I'm kinda down tonight because of several things. Most of it is being kicked out of three hotels in one day[59]."

...Townshend led the band into *My Generation* with all the blind fury of a general leading his troops to certain death. His gaunt, haggard figure looked especially menacing in front of his stack of buzzing, crackling

---

[59] Moon managed to get the band ejected from the Gorham and Waldorf-Astoria hotels after blowing up his toilet, throwing cherry bombs from a 9th floor window toward policemen on the street below [as if they didn't already have their hands full with the public outcry resulting from the Martin Luther King shooting], and blowing a door off its hinges. The following morning the band was scheduled for a photo shoot for *Life* magazine. "When [publicist Nancy] Lewis finally tracked the band down, they weren't speaking to each other. Or rather, they weren't speaking to Keith," wrote *Moon* author Tony Fletcher in 1999. "Pete, citing his lack of sleep, made it quite clear that he "wasn't going to go for any fucking picture for any fucking *Life* magazine." That Townshend had his fiancée Karen Astley with him, and that she too had suffered because of this extreme example of Moon's behavioral swings, only added to the guitarist's aggravation... Finally, sharing their frustration but with the additional burden of her own responsibilities, Nancy Lewis burst into tears. Only then did Townshend agree to the photo shoot." The resulting photographs included one of the most famous ever taken of The Who – draped in a Union Jack at the foot of Grant's Tomb.

amplifiers with their torn coverings and splintered cabinets. Leaping high to accent certain chords visually, then angling toward Moon for his solos, Townshend played his heart out on this song and Moon responded with a tremendous drum accompaniment. The performance closed on the frenetic note after Townshend had hurled his guitar in the air, smashed it against the amplifiers, the stage, Moon's drum kit, and his own body until it was a barely recognizable mash of wood and wire. Moon's drum kit also went, just for good measure.

The Who's first North American tour of 1968 concluded on April 7 in Toronto, with a show at the CNE Coliseum which featured the Troggs and MC5 as openers.

Chapter 4

"Baba washed the religious preconceptions from my heart with my own tears. I love Jesus far more now than I ever did at infant school as I sang, "Yes, Jesus loves me." Now I know he really was the Christ. Remorse came naturally through Baba, so does love, it can't be forced and it can't be limited. I often wonder though, as I stare at the occasional "evil" character, how my wish to see him fall down a hole is an expression of love. The answer is that it isn't. Only one person on this earth is capable of an absolutely perfect love for all and everything, and that is, when earth is fortunate enough to be his illusory host, the Messiah. The Avatar. He just came and went. Meher Baba."
 - Pete Townshend, 1970

"...I lost touch with The Who's mod audience, and I decided that what I actually had to do was I had to write something for me. And where I was at the time was in a very strange place. I had had a couple of acid trips and hated it – everybody else in the world was wearing funny clothes and blowing their heads off and wearing flares with flowers in their hair, and I felt very out of step with it, but I was interested in the mysticism. I was interested in the spiritual side of it. So I thought maybe what I could try to do was marry the pop single with this idea of this mystical journey, and that's when I started to work on Tommy."
 - Pete Townshend, 1999

Prior to Pete's exposure to Meher Baba back in autumn 1967, his spiritual investigations to date had led him to believe in the existence of extraterrestrial beings and UFOs. "...I was heavily into flying saucers," Pete wrote in *Rolling Stone* in 1970, "...believing them to hold a key somehow to the future of humanity. At the time I sincerely believed I had seen several in the Florida area, today I don't really care." Pete had read the Spaceship sagas of author George Adamski, who had written "that on another planet in our system existed a race of people who were spiritually perfect," Pete recalled in 1977. "He claimed that he was in contact with them. While reading the books I believed this, somehow this man taught me to open my mind. In other words he taught me faith."

A visit to his friend Mike McInnerney's house proved to realign Pete's spiritual inclinations, as the pair sat down for a philosophical conversation. McInnerney, art director for the underground paper *International Times*, was one of the UFO club crowd[60]. According to Dave Marsh, Karen "...had designed the clothes for the McInnerneys' wedding, a real hippie bash, held in Hyde Park."

"I was ranting and raving about," Pete recalled in a 1970 *Rolling Stone* cover story entitled *In Love With Meher Baba*, "...talking too much and finding in Mike someone who talked just as much as I did…Every time I came up with a world-wise theory that had taken me years of thought to get clear he would say, "That's such a coincidence man, this guy Meher Baba said something similar to that in this book, *The God Man*." After I had heard my very last precious revelation hit the dust at the sound of Mike's voice declaring that Baba had already said it I just had to look at the book. What I saw apart from a photo in the front cover of a strange and elderly man, was shattering."

Meher Baba [Persian for 'compassionate father'], a spiritual master born in Poona, India, in 1894, thus entered the life of Pete Townshend. After reading *The God Man* (by C.B. Purdom and still available through Sheriar Press), Pete had discovered a spiritual entity whose teachings grasped his imagination and would affect him and his work profoundly from this point forward. "What was so sneaky about the whole affair was the way Baba crept into my life," Pete wrote in 1970.

> At first his words were encouraging, his state of consciousness and his claims to be the Christ exciting and daring, later they became scary. I began to read his words, read of his astoundingly simple relationship with his disciples…and of his silence for 40 years [Baba took a vow of silence in 1925, which lasted until his death in early 1969. He communicated by pointing to letters on an alphabet board]. It became clear that the party was over. If I read any more lines like "What I want from my Lovers is real unadulterated love, and from my genuine workers I expect real work done," I would have to decide once and for all whether the whole thing was really for me or not.
>
> As is normal with coming to Baba, I didn't have to make any decision. No sooner had the thought entered my head than it left. It's just not that cut and dried. Baba has to be adjusted to over a few months… One thing can be taken

---

[60] "I had an immediate strong feeling for Pete and felt that I would like to give him some books on Meher Baba," McInnerney told Dave Marsh in 1983. "Baba has a way of grabbing you fundamentally and then hanging on. There was a lot of Baba activity in London at the time, and Pete just picked up on it."

for granted; no matter how hard you try, you will never love him as he should be loved.

Baba only asked people for their love, not their possessions or even their lives. Just their love...nothing ostensibly changes when an individual hears about Baba and starts to devote time to thinking about him and his work. No all-pervading joy creeps into life, no formula for solving difficult problems. In some cases it seems to bring problems to a head. At least they are over with that way.

The facts are that any focused attempt to get more out of life, more results from events and emotional chapters, whether it be by following Baba or doing what comes naturally, will start to bring visible results in life. When you are getting things done, you can't help but enjoy life more. When you begin to realize that your own suffering has a purpose, you can bear it with dignity and poise, admit defeat, or that you were wrong, without feeling that your life is worthless.

Pete provided an outline of Meher Baba's life and message with the original pressing of his 1972 solo album, *Who Came First*, from which the following is taken:

Baba's appeal extends to people of every background. His followers include Protestants, Catholics and Jews in the West, Hindus, Muslims, Zoroastrians and Buddhists in the East, and even many who have considered themselves agnostics or atheists. In a word, Baba and what he teaches are universal. He can be understood in terms of the context of every broad religious tradition, yet he is clear in pointing out that he belongs exclusively to none of them... Baba gives no rituals or ceremonies, no particular diets or exercises, no specific form of meditation to his followers. There are no 'churches,' no designated teachers. There is no fee. True religion, in Baba's eyes, is not a card-carrying affair but rather a matter of 'the heart,' the degree to which one lives an honest and loving life. Baba regards the avowed atheist who faithfully carries out his work in the world as far more blest than the man who, claiming to be devoutly religious, shirks his practical, everyday responsibilities. "The greatest sin," he said, "is hypocrisy."

Baba said he was God Almighty on earth, or the God-Man. He claimed, "In the world, there are countless Sadhus, Mahatmas,

Mahapurushas, Saints, Yogis, and Walis, though the number of genuine ones is very, very limited. I am neither a Mahatma nor a Mahapurush, neither a Sadhu nor a Saint, neither a Yogi nor a Wali. I am the Ancient One. The Highest of the High!"

Pete further explained his relationship with Baba in a 1980 interview with *Trouser Press*, commenting, "It's a hard thing to explain, but if you live your life according to the guidelines set down by Meher Baba, you don't need anyone else to tell you how to do things. It's about living a better life and a more loving life in a traditional humanitarian [way], which we are all born with the potential to achieve anyway. But having a focus, someone you really respect but don't necessarily think is a super-being, someone you respect above anyone else demonstrating a real love for you when you think that you're a lump of shit – that's all it needs. It just needs someone to give you back your self-respect, and then it's *your* job from there."

"So I never met Baba," Pete wrote in the 1970 *Rolling Stone* article.

> Never wrote him a letter or received one. How am I hanging on? I'm not hanging on, I'm *stuck* on. People could easily get the idea that I'm an unwilling Baba lover, or "Baba Tryer" as I prefer to call myself. No, it's just that I was unwilling to let go of that incredible piece of happiness, that unqualified stab of love that I didn't even ask for, didn't expect, and it's made my life, which I know to be as colorful as any, gray in comparison. The key is that knowledge of his awesome power, awesome knowledge and bliss he enjoys; that flash, is the basis for the search for my true self.
>
> Baba did not come to teach. He came to awaken. He did not come to form a religion, nor organize any cult, creed, sect or movement in his name. He did not take steps to do so...
>
> I feel that never will I be able to stand back from myself and pretend anymore that God is a myth. That Christ was just another man. That Baba was simply a hypnotic personality. The facts are coming home to me like sledge hammers, not through the words I read in books about Baba, not through even his own words. But through my ordinary daily existence. Meher Baba is the Avatar, God Incarnate on our planet. The Awakener.
>
> As the river flows down outside my home, I look out and remember that eventually it will reach the sea. Each little stream that runs into the Thames feeding it and building it sustains the ocean. Retains the cycle of life that

keeps our planet moist and airy. We too need sustaining, love is the only thing that can do it.

When next you gaze into the deep brown eyes of that girl with a slightly easy smile, try to see the eons that lie behind them. The world weariness that only balance can end. The deep deep desire for peace, eternal peace. The peace that dying *does not achieve*. Try to see it, and then look for it in yourself, you might find, yes, you just might find – you get what you need.

I am the New Christ
You have waited and waited for me for a long time.
I am the real Guide
You will know me
You will see me
My word is power
My thought is action
I am the Truth
Jai Baba!

Pete's attraction to and subsequent immersion in the teachings of Baba took place at a time when it was fashionable to look to the East for spiritual inspiration. "It was trendy for awhile for various celebrities to claim an affinity with assorted Eastern spiritual teachers," John Atkins pointed out in his critical history *The Who on Record*, "but Townshend's interest in Baba was much different from the momentary craze that swept across Western society in the wake of the Beatles' relationship with Maharishi Yogi in 1967. First, Baba was not part of the flamboyant yoga-and-meditation school of gurus who epitomized the incense-clouded era of teach-ins and communal gatherings. Second, Townshend immersed himself fully in the teachings of Baba in what was to become a lifelong devotion. Baba essentially offered, through prayer and faith, a means of self-realization and closeness to God."

On May 21, 1968, just a couple of days after his 23rd birthday, Pete married Karen at the Didcot register office in Berkshire[61]. Shortly thereafter they moved from their £36-a-week flat in Belgravia to a more suitable abode: An 18th century Georgian house on the Thames river embankment in the London suburb of Twickenham. The £16,500 house – restored years earlier after sustaining damage from German bombs in World War II – was

---

[61] "Like most men I thought I'd never get married," Pete told *Disc & Music Echo* in 1969. "I just never felt it was necessary. Karen and I had been living together for about two years and it was okay. But then I realized there were so many problems if you didn't get married. Actually I went to make out my will, because I wanted to leave some things to Karen, and then I thought, "Well, why not get married? Then she would get everything anyway if anything happened to me.""

located less than a mile from Pete's birthplace. It stood on ½ an acre of ground facing Eel Pie Island, which housed the Eel Pie Island Hotel, an established venue which played trad. Jazz in the early sixties prior to becoming one of London's better known R&B strongholds during the Mod years. "Free were on the other night," Pete told an interviewer in 1970. "I opened the double frame windows and listened and they sounded good."

Pete soon added an £8,000 home recording studio upstairs which included a light hooked up to a switch in the kitchen so Karen could call him for dinner. "[I] built my first separate control room/studio in two tiny adjacent rooms," Pete wrote in 1983. The studio included a "gorgeous" grand piano. The only problem with the studio, which Pete and Karen soon noticed, was the fact that it was "slap bang in the middle of the building," Pete recalled in 1977. While the guitar could be played to appropriately obnoxious volume levels through earphones (a major factor in Pete's eventual hearing damage), the drums and piano meant that "when I worked nobody slept," he recalled.

Richard Barnes recalled visiting the couple not long after they'd moved in. "I was very surprised by them. They were both incredibly warm and genuine and down-to-earth," he wrote in 1982. "Pete had lost all his sneering unpleasantness and the 'I'm a Big Shot Pop Star' ego trip had disappeared. He was relaxed, interesting and for the first time in years, very very happy. I didn't know what to put it down to. I thought that it must have been a combination of being married and fairly wealthy and successful. And more importantly their new found relationship with Meher Baba, pictures of whose smiling face with twinkling eyes were hanging around the house."

Another impressed observer was *Disc & Music Echo* reporter Hugh Nolan, who visited Townshend in his new home for an interview. Nolan noted the Baba pictures weren't only in Pete's house, but also in his car. "Baba has made an incredible amount of difference in my life," Townshend told Nolan. "Not so much outwardly – I still shout at cars which get in my way, I still talk too much and I still smash up guitars when I can't afford to. Baba is the Avatar of the Age – the Messiah. He can't do anything but good. He has completely and utterly changed my whole life and, through me, the group as a whole." The changes in Pete's life actually adversely affected some of his professional relationships. "It was very difficult for the people around me to accept that I was living a very different kind of life," he told *Q*'s John Harris in 1996. "Roger and Keith didn't take the piss, John Entwistle would. I think he was embarrassed by it. And I lost Kit Lambert and Chris Stamp. I remember Kit Lambert calling me and Karen Lord and Lady Townshend: "Oh, Lord and Lady Townshend in their house in Twickenham with their babies." "

Meanwhile, The Who were faced with deciding upon their next step. The band's proposed live album (both April Fillmore East shows had been recorded) was scrapped, and recording sessions were held at Advision studios in May in order to record a new single.

In June, 1968, The Who's follow-up single to *I Can See For Miles* was released. *Dogs*, "a comical Townshend single written about the working man's fondness for beer and greyhound racing," according to Chris Charlesworth, "...flopped ignominiously. Their recording career had reached its lowest ebb" (the single reached number 25 in the U.K.; it wasn't released Stateside). The fact that a song of this relative low quality had been released suggested that the band's supply of appropriate material was dwindling. It is interesting to note that, just a few days after they'd recorded *Dogs*, the band went back to Advision and recorded *Melancholia*, a song Pete had written and recorded in demo form the previous year and is regarded by many as superior to *Dogs*. *Melancholia* was rejected by the band, Pete later adding that it "was obviously totally wrong for the band at a time we had just failed to get a hit with the glorious *I Can See For Miles*. I suppose I was really melancholic when I wrote it."

A few months later, the band again tried their luck, this time with *Magic Bus*, a song Pete wrote back in early 1967, and which had already been recorded and released by a group named Pudding that same year. Despite the fact that the song went on to become the "most requested live song for The Who along with *Boris the Spider*," according to Pete (who would later describe the song as "a nothing song," and the lyrics as "garbage"), it fared even worse than *Dogs* in the British charts, reaching number 26, while attaining number 25 in the U.S. The Who's last three singles, *I Can See For Miles*, *Dogs*, and *Magic Bus* had all been disappointments, especially in Britain. The band were fading fast on their home turf, and had reached the point that there was no new material available which they considered appropriate for release. The well had quite rapidly dried up.

Throughout 1968, The Who searched for a new direction. There was talk of a *Monkees*-like TV show featuring The Who, and even an album provisionally entitled *Who's For Tennis*, planned for release during that summer's Wimbledon tennis championship, both of which, thankfully, never came to fruition. "1968 was a strange year for The Who and Pete Townshend," Chris Charlesworth wrote in 1984.

> With a firm foothold in the U.S. at last, their status on either side of the Atlantic differed considerably. In England matters reached a low ebb: hit singles were thin on the ground and box-office takings dropped alarmingly as a result. From commanding fees of three hundred pounds a night upwards, The Who found themselves playing for as little as sixty pounds. They were neither underground nor pop and all but a hard core of fans ignored them as virtual

has-beens, holdovers from a Mod era that was now just a memory.

In America, however, they were at the forefront of the British underground simply because their music was adventurous and their stage shows exhilarating. Much of their income now came from American album sales but it was still necessary to continue touring to maintain a steady financial turnover. They were still in debt – quite how much had never been calculated nor will it ever be, since accounting was not a strong point at New Action Ltd – yet they refused to limit their spending by curbing the destruction on stage (especially in the USA) or even toning down their offstage life-style.

"They were too much in debt [for any type of sabbatical]," George Tremlett wrote in 1975. "In one interview with me, Daltrey had said (I thought at the time, almost despairingly) that their total debts had risen to around £100,000 – more recently, in ...*The Observer*, he said: 'When we got our first hit, *I Can't Explain*, we started earning what was then pretty good money, say £300 a night. But after the first year we were £60,000 in debt. The next year, after working our balls off, we were still £40,000 down. And the biggest choke of all came the year after that when we found we were back up to £60,000 again. Every accountant's meeting was ridiculous. We always owed so much money that we ended up rolling around the office laughing ourselves silly.'" John reportedly had to borrow money just to get home from the Herman's Hermits tour, despite the fact that the band had earned $40,000 on the trip.

In the middle of 1967, Pete began contemplating a new project for The Who. As the band's outlook darkened towards the end of that year, he began to realize that if this latest work failed it could spell the end. "I was petrified that the band was going to finish," Pete recalled in 1977. "When I wrote *Pictures Of Lily* I thought it wouldn't be a hit and although I was getting better at it all the time, I thought I can't write this shit any more. I'd got to come up with something of substance..."

"I felt strongly that I was being tied down too much to single records," Pete said. "I felt that if I had to say everything on a record in three minutes flat then I wasn't ever going to say very much. I wanted to find a way to stretch it a bit more without making it pretentious or pompous and without making it sound like classical music."

"...I was 22 years old," Pete continued, "the Who had begun to fail, we hadn't made it in America, we hadn't had a big hit in the U.K. with *I Can See For Miles*, which was unquestionably the best thing I was ever gonna write in my life. And I thought: It's over. I started when I was 18, and four years later, it's finished. And as a last gasp, I sat down and started to write something wild and pretentious and mad and dangerous."

Pete's inclinations toward composing a new project for The Who coincided with his discovery of the teachings of Meher Baba towards the end of 1967. He thought of writing a series of thematically linked pieces of music focusing on man's spiritual quest. "In my first notes," Pete later recalled, "I talked of an opera that would tell a spiritual story in a parallel way, from the inside and from the outside… but the solid undercurrent riding through all the material was the fact that I was in a 'newfound spiritual mood'." During the band's July-September, 1967, American tour (the Herman's Hermits tour), Pete laid the groundwork. "…I used to rush back to the hotel room to work," Pete wrote in 1977's *The Story of Tommy*, "writing songs or collating lyrics, or scribbling out ideas for the opera that I was working on at the time called *Amazing Journey*."

Amazing Journey started life as a poem of epic proportions if not an epic poem, clocking in at over 230 lines. It formed the nucleus of Pete's new project, outlining a spiritual quest –

> …*The master gravely shook his head and I*
> *Knew that despite his infinite wisdom, infinite power, infinite awareness*
> *That he would not, could not tell me where to look.*
> *Or even what to look for. I had to find the answer myself.*

The poem begins with the narrator describing his 'illness', and the 'amazing journey', a spiritual adventure which he'd experienced in a dream.
> *Sickness will surely take the mind*
> *Where minds can't usually go*
> *Come on the amazing journey*
> *And learn all you should know*

This initial segment brings to mind a phase in Meher Baba's spiritual development, referred to by biographer C.B. Purdom as the opening of Baba's "inner eye". It began when Baba met a Perfect Master named Hazrat Babajan in 1913, an elderly woman (quite an understatement: she was reportedly 122 years old at the time) who kissed him on the forehead. He subsequently fell into a catatonic state, a trance that would leave him almost totally oblivious to his surroundings for nearly nine months, according to Purdom. This was the beginning of Baba's transformation into a Spiritual Master.

"The story is poetry, sometimes good, often terrible," Pete said of the *Amazing Journey* poem in *The Story of Tommy*. "It was all stream of consciousness stuff, but when I read it back then, it staggered me. I realized that I had described a story that I could never have dreamed of myself let alone put to music. But the strangest part of all is that there was no development stage between this Hesse-like tale of mystery and spiritual intrigue, and what we today see to be *Tommy*. I just lived with the story, invented a name for my hero, Tommy, and started to write songs." With *Amazing Journey* forming the new project's foundation, in mid-1968 Pete began to incorporate some songs he'd recently written into the plot. Titles included *She's A Sensation, We're Not Gonna Take It, I'm Free,* and *Welcome*.

Meanwhile, the band needed money. A June 28 show in Los Angeles kicked off The Who's 41-date 1968 North American Summer tour. After heading north to Canada and swinging back down through the midwest, the band experienced an eventful evening on July 14 in Cleveland, Ohio. Pete smashed his only Stratocaster early in the show and had to borrow one from the support act to finish. Meanwhile, Pete and Roger's passports were stolen from the dressing room backstage. Following the resultant customs delays upon their entry into Canada for the next show, the band arrived onstage over two hours late and had to borrow equipment from the promoter because customs wouldn't release theirs. The fact that Pete was playing a borrowed vintage 1958 Stratocaster that night didn't prevent him from destroying it at the end of the show.

As the tour wound on (featuring a stop in Philadelphia, where one of the support acts was UFO club regulars Pink Floyd), The Who played a memorable early August gig at the Singer Bowl in Flushing, New York as the support act for The Doors. The evening led to Pete writing another song, *Sally Simpson*, for his new project. "*Sally Simpson* was about a rock star and it was based on Jim Morrison," Pete told Richard Barnes in a 1975 interview which surfaced in *The Story of Tommy*.

> I met him in New York and he just absolutely amazed me – some bird went up to talk to him or something, one of his bodyguards just punched her in the midriff and she doubled up and he just carried on talking, he didn't see her. Then the same afternoon at this club he actually tried to pull this chick... I wrote that thing and then realized that in a way he was exactly like what Tommy was, and I just re-wrote it.

"Throughout 1968," Chris Charlesworth wrote in 1983, "on tour and at home, in hotel rooms, dressing rooms and even airplane cabins, Pete laboured on the creation of his grand design." Following the writing of *Amazing Journey* and many discussions with the rest of the band in between shows, Pete's ideas for a musical project (which had already been named *Journey into Space* and *The Brain Opera*) gained momentum. Pete sat down and described the venture with *Rolling Stone's* Jann Wenner in mid-

August during the band's three-night run at the Fillmore West (the fact that he went into great detail may be partly due to the fact that he was "very hyped up on coke," as he admitted the following year)[62].

Pete often used interview settings to test his ideas. During the course of his career, Townshend has often broached ideas for a new project in great detail to unsuspecting reporters, in a sense putting himself on the spot and creating expectations among his audience. "What I do," Pete said in 1975, "is force myself to do [projects] by announcing things up front...I said so much [about *Tommy*] that it just *had* to be finished – I had to get it done."

"I'm working on the lyrics now for the next album," Pete told Wenner at around 2 am as the interview began, explaining that the project was provisionally titled *Deaf, Dumb and Blind Boy*.

> ...It's a story about a kid that's born deaf, dumb and blind and what happens to him throughout his life... he's seeing things basically as vibrations which we translate as music...
>
> ...it's a pretty far out thing actually. But it's very, very endearing to me because the thing is...inside, the boy sees things musically and in dreams and nothing has got any weight at all. He is touched from the outside and he feels his mother's touch, he feels his father's touch, but he just interprets them as music. His father gets pretty upset that his kid is deaf, dumb and blind...one night he comes in and he's drunk and he sits over the kid's bed and he looks at him and he starts to talk to him, and the kid just smiles up, and his father is trying to get through to him, telling him about how the other dads have a kid that they can take to football and they can teach them to play football and all this kind of crap and he starts to say, "Can you hear me?" The kid, of course, can't hear him...
>
> The kid won't respond, he just smiles. The father starts to hit him and at this moment the whole thing becomes incredibly realistic. On one side you have the dreamy music of the boy wasting through his nothing life. And on the other you have the reality of the father outside, uptight, but now you've got blows, you've got communication. The father is hitting the kid; musically

---

[62] "We'd been drinking orange juice and in the middle of a long and wandering answer [Pete] asked if I had spiked his drink," Wenner told Dave Marsh. "...when I asked him what he meant by 'spiked,' he said he felt as though he were beginning an LSD trip. I hadn't slipped him anything."

then I want the thing to break out, hand it over to Keith – "this is your scene, man, take it from here."

And the kid doesn't catch the violence. He just knows that some sensation is happening. He doesn't feel the pain, he doesn't associate it with anything. He just accepts it.

A similar situation happens later on in the opera, where the father starts to get the mother to take the kid away from home to an uncle. The uncle is a bit of a perv, you know. He plays with the kid's body...and at this particular time the child has heard his own name, his mother called him. And he managed to hear these words: "Tommy."...and he gets really hung-up on his own name... Tommy is the thing, man.

He's going through this and the uncle comes in and starts to go through a scene with the kid's body... and the boy experiences sexual vibration, you know, sexual experience, and again...it's interpreted as music and it's nothing more than music. It's got no association with sleaziness...or with any of the things normally associated with sex. None of the romance, none of the visual stimulus, none of the sound stimulus. Just basic touch...Slowly but surely the kid starts to get it together, out of ...this incredible simplicity in his mind. He starts to realize that he can see and he can hear, and he can speak; they are there and they are happening all the time. And that all the time he has been able to hear and see. All the time it's been there in front of him, for him to see.

This is the difficult jump... the music has got to explain what happens, that the boy elevates, and finds something which is incredible. To us, it's nothing to be able to see and hear and speak, but to him, it's absolutely incredible and overwhelming; this is what we want to do musically. Lyrically, it's quite easy to do it, in fact I've written it out several times. It makes great poetry, but so much depends on the music, so much. I'm hoping that we can do it.

...There is a doctor involved who tries to do some psychiatric treatment on the kid which is only partly successful...he sees himself in a mirror, suddenly seeing himself for the first time; he takes an immediate back step, bases his whole life around his own image. The whole thing then becomes incredibly introverted. The music and the lyrics become introverted and he starts to talk about himself, starts to talk about his beauty. Not knowing, of course, that what he saw was him..."

It's a very complex thing and I don't know if I'm getting it across...

This synopsis of *Deaf, Dumb and Blind Boy* as it stood at the time was very idealistic, with Pete planning on actually portraying Tommy's emotions through music. "That's really what we want to do," Pete told Wenner. "Create this feeling that when you listen to the music you can actually become aware of the boy, and aware of what he is all about, because we are creating him as we play." The plan was to flash from reality to fantasy using musical interludes, called 'Dream Sequences', between the more conventional songs which described Tommy's experiences. "You've got a double-barrelled plot – one minute you'd see him from one angle objectively, and the other minute you'd see him from the other angle subjectively, so one song followed another song, followed another song, followed another song," Pete said in 1975. "Originally for example the section in *Tommy* where you've got *Cousin Kevin*, *Fiddle About*, *Acid Queen*, and stuff like that, each one was going to be followed by sort of an impressionistic dream-sequence-type piece of music..." The 'dream sequences, some of which were reportedly to feature sound effects (battle sounds following *Overture* and assorted pinball machine sounds where appropriate, for example), never came to fruition, ending up in consolidated form in *Sparks*[63] and the *Underture*, perhaps proving too difficult to execute or simply condensed due to recording constraints. The violent scenes, incidentally, were something that Pete did not feel comfortable writing. "I didn't want to do them," Pete told *Rolling Stone* in 1969. He delegated the responsibility to Entwistle, who came up with *Cousin Kevin* and *Fiddle About*. "I didn't think I could be cruel enough. They're ruthlessly brilliant songs because they are just as cruel as people can be. I wanted to show that the boy was being dealt with very cruelly and it was because he was being dismissed as a freak."

The day after Pete gave the in-depth *Rolling Stone* interview, he ran into fellow Baba follower Rick Chapman in San Francisco. "...he was talking about drugs and things," Pete recalled in 1970, "and what Baba says about it, and he says, "Of course you're not still smoking dope, are you?" So I said, "Yes, sure. What's Baba said about dope?" "Didn't you know that it's been proved now that pot's an hallucinogenic drug, so it falls into Baba's teachings?" he said. So I just stopped. Just because I felt more keen about getting into Meher Baba than I felt about being stoned all my life."

---

[63] In 1962, English Baba devotee Delia DeLeon compiled a booklet of Meher Baba's sayings, entitled *Sparks*.

And then as it started to go down I started to realize how much I credited to drugs. I used to think, "Well, man, I can't play the guitar unless I'm stoned, I can't write a song unless I'm stoned, I can't be happy unless I'm stoned, I can't listen to records unless I'm stoned, I can't do anything unless I'm stoned. Because if I'm not stoned it's not as good." Well, I've... kind of just got out of that, and I get just as much now out of everything perpetually 24 hours a day as I used to out of that high.

"...Baba did emphasize to a young devotee going to see Baba in about 1966," Pete wrote in *Rolling Stone* in 1970, "that the biggest single gesture a man could make for youth, would be to spend his life trying to show the dangers of dope. Remember, Baba was concerned with a set of people that felt the psychedelics held the key to religious experience, to Universal consciousness. God in a pill."

Meanwhile, one of the initial questions elicited from Pete's explanation of his latest project in *Rolling Stone* was regarding his choice of a severely disabled subject. "Tommy became deaf, dumb and blind," Pete wrote in 1977, "when I realized that there was no way to get across, musically or dramatically, the idea of our ignorance of reality, as I had learned it to be, from reading Meher Baba." This statement underlined the theme of *Tommy*, the foundation of the *Amazing Journey* poem.

We have our five senses, and we have our emotions...but there are whole chunks of life, including the whole concept of reality, which escapes us. We don't really know who we are, we don't really know how we got here, and we don't really know what our aim is, we don't understand the concept of infinity, and our minds are unable to accept it. We don't understand suffering or what causes it, we don't understand life itself or what motivates it, we can't accept death and we feel it to be unjust (although it is part of the wheel of life). So I decided that the hero had to be deaf, dumb and blind, so that, seen from our already limited point of view, his limitations would be symbolic of our own.

As the *Deaf, Dumb and Blind Boy* project grew, Pete's ambitions for the project similarly reached new heights. "At one time," Pete recalled in 1979, "I was studying orchestrations and listening to Wagner and all kinds of amazing things trying to get into full scale grand opera and I was going to enlist Arthur Brown whose voice I thought somewhere between a Wagnerian tenor and Screaming Jay Hawkins and have him as the lead singer." Brown, the flamboyant leader of The Crazy World of Arthur Brown, one of Track Records' stable of artists, had a number 1 hit in the U.K. with *Fire* in 1968 (also recall that Pete had considered using Brown for his *Rael* opera back in 1967). The single, produced by Kit Lambert and Pete Townshend, was later recorded by The Who for inclusion on Pete's *Iron Man* album in 1989. Townshend was obviously high on Arthur Brown at the time, planning on using his voice instead of Daltrey's, and perhaps even using other artists for his *Deaf, Dumb and Blind Boy* project while keeping the band happy by "writing a few singles and things."

"...I didn't believe I could do it in the framework of the Who," Pete later explained. "I'd had the idea of rock opera way before, but when I met Arthur Brown, I was convinced that he was the perfect foil for it, he was a great rock singer with an operatic range and all that. I thought about writing an opera for him but it was something outside of the Who – I was hedging my bets. It was Kit that kept pushing me back to the band. He seemed to have greater foresight than we did as to the level that the Who would reach."

It was also Kit who led to the project becoming known as a 'rock opera. "Kit understood before it was seen to be permissible that we could use operatic techniques in rock," Pete told *Uncut* in 2004. "His whole thing was, 'This is opera,' y'know? I used to argue and say, 'No, it isn't, really,' but he'd be, 'No, no, no! This is fucking OPERA!'" Soon, the tag stuck. "As a gag," Pete recalled in 1979, "when we were working on it, we started to call it a rock opera, knowing full well it wasn't a true opera at all."

Within a couple of weeks of the conclusion of the North American tour in mid-September, the first *Deaf, Dumb and Blind Boy* recording session took place at IBC Studios in Portland Place, London. The Who recorded *Deaf, Dumb and Blind Boy* in between performing gigs to provide them with money, a necessary evil due to their poor financial situation. This intermixing of live shows and recording, however, may have helped in the quality of the playing on the album. Songs which were soon to be recorded were often first played at these gigs, resulting in well-rehearsed, high quality takes during the recording sessions.

Among these songs was *The Acid Queen*, a story of Tommy's encounter with a woman who claimed she could cure his affliction, which Pete used to make a statement regarding rites of passage. "The song's not just about acid," Pete said in 1969, "it's the whole drug thing, the drink thing, the sex thing, wrapped into one big ball. It's about how you get it laid on you that you haven't lived if you haven't fucked 40 birds, taken 60 trips, drunk 14 pints of beer – or whatever. Society – people – force you. She represents this force." Another important song was *Sensation*, "...the song Tommy sings after he's regained his senses," Pete told *Rolling Stone*. "He realizes who he is and becomes totally aware...the moment is that of divinity. Tommy is worshipping himself, knowing what he is and speaking the truth... I used all the sensation stuff because after all this time where

Tommy's just been getting vibrations, now he's turned the tables. Now you're going to feel *me*! I'm in everything; I'm the explosion; I'm a sensation." This song, originally entitled *She's a Sensation*, had originally been written about a girl Pete met in Australia.

While Tommy's experiences as a child were aptly outlined in Pete's August *Rolling Stone* interview, many other aspects of the story remained unclear. As the recording sessions continued, the story evolved. Tommy, the central character of Pete's rock opera, became the Messiah. This unlikely jump was explained by Pete in 1974:

> My sort of cameo was that Tommy started off deaf, dumb, and blind, and his coming to know what it was like to be normal was for him what it would be for you and me to become infinitely conscious. It was a big step for him – equivalent to the biggest step anyone can take, which is to stop living in illusion and see reality, infinite reality, for the first time. This is why I originally used it. I had this double story in my mind and then I made him jump. He became a double person, so that not only did he become normal like you and me but he jumped beyond that into what I was paralleling with it – into being a universally conscious person. After that I rewrote the story so that he turned into a Messiah, etc.

"In general terms," Pete explained to *Rolling Stone* in 1969, "man is regarded as living in an unreal world of illusory values that he's imposed on himself."

> He's feeling his way by evolution back to God-realization and the illusion is broken away, bit by bit...When you lose all contact with your illusory state...you don't incarnate again – you just *blend*. Tommy's real self represents the aim – God – and the illusory self is the teacher; life, the way, the path and all this. The coming together of these are what make him aware. They make him see and hear and speak so he becomes a saint who everybody flocks to. The boy's life starts to represent the whole nature of humanity – we all have this self-imposed deaf, dumb and blindness...

Tommy's awareness of the world is completely unjaded, Pete explained.

> He gets everything in a very pure, filtered, unadulterated, unfucked-up manner. Like when his uncle rapes him – he is incredibly elated, not disgusted, at being homosexually raped. He takes it as a move of total affection, not feeling the reasons why. Lust is a lower form of love, like atomic attraction is a lower form of love. He gets an incredible spiritual push from it where most people would get a spiritual retardment, constantly thinking about this terrible thing that's happened to them. In Tommy's mind, everything is incredible, meaningless beauty.

Tommy's newfound universal consciousness resulted in the clarification of the story's ending. Tommy attempts to become the savior of the people, but his followers ultimately reject him. "Rama Krishna, Buddha, Zarathustra, Jesus and Meher Baba are all divine figures on earth," Pete said in 1969. "They all said the same thing; yet *still* we trundle on. This is basically what Tommy is saying [this was also, of course, what *Baba* had said]. But his followers ask how to follow him, and disregard his teaching. They want rules and regulations; going to church on Sundays – but he just says 'live life.'" Pete's song *Welcome* summed up this part of the story. "The institution of the church comes up in *Welcome*," Pete told *Rolling Stone* in 1969.

> The followers want to know how to follow him and he tells them very simply what to do. He's telling them what they want to hear – 'It's going to be all smooth and fun and we're never going to speak, we're going to drink all night and have the time of our life. You can do good things, go out and get new people, and for this you'll win gold stars.' He knows they're completely off the track and is trying by his very presence to make them aware of what they should be doing – coming in to the house and then getting out again. Instead of that they want more action...
> All the time they demand more and so he starts to get hard: 'Well if you *really* want to know what to do, you've got to stop drinking for a start. You've got to stop smoking pot.' And he starts to lay down hard moral facts – like Jesus did – but nobody wants to know.

At this stage, the lyrics and images projected through *Deaf, Dumb and Blind Boy* were simply drenched with Baba references. "The process of writing was controlled by my direct involvement with Baba," Pete recalled later. "His stuff is completely self-contained, and it's a good point to start fucking-up from. On a basic working level, songs like *I'm Free, Pinball*

Wizard and a couple of others are very much Baba, songs of the quiet explosion of divinity. They just rolled off the pen." Pete, however, was quick to point out that his work wasn't coming from above. "...I don't mean divinely inspired," he asserted. "You get a lot of crap from the close devotees of Baba, stories about people rushing up to him and saying, 'My daughter was dying in Poona and I said a prayer to you and you came in a vision and she was well again.' Baba says, 'I'm sorry mate. I don't know anything about that.' It's obviously their faith, their love for him that did the trick. It's like Jesus saying, 'it's your faith that made you whole.'"

While Pete's description of the project to Jann Wenner in mid-1968 included many integral elements of the finished product and subsequent interviews provided some clarification as to the story's ending, the project as a whole was still foundering due to its lack of a clear plot. "...we had been in the studios making it for eight months," John Entwistle told *The Observer*. "We had terrible trouble with the story, in fact, at first it just didn't make sense."

"[*Deaf, Dumb and Blind Boy*] was falling all over the place," Chris Stamp added in 1982. "It was just not coming together and that's when Kit wrote a script." Kit Lambert's input at this point was invaluable – he managed to clarify what was a rather abstract storyline and set the band on course to complete the project. "He was working all through the night on the script," Stamp said, "and when it was finished we went straight round to the printers. We had it printed up as a script to impress the group and had twenty copies made up. It was going to be the first Lambert/Stamp production."

Pete told *Rolling Stone* in 1969 that Lambert's role, although officially only that of producer, was crucial.

> Kit's real contribution will never, ever be known, because, of course, it wasn't production at all, it was far deeper. The word *producer* is, I think, an absurdly misused word anyway. Kit was much more involved in the overall concept of the thing – much more than people imagine. Not all that much, in fact, with the overall sound, although he did produce it and mix it and he did make us work at it. Still, the main thing was that he thought of the idea of rock opera.

"I wasn't aware of the minefield that I was getting into when I playfully called this piece that I was working on a rock opera," Pete said in 1999, "but Kit Lambert was just fantastic, he kind of took me the other way... I'd say, "are you sure it's OK to call this a rock opera", and... he'd say, "well, yeah of course it is," and I'd say, "well the story's a bit dodgy at the moment," and he'd go "yeah, but all opera's got stupid story," and I realized later actually that some of his ambitions of course were to usurp the musical establishment."

Lambert was "...the main sounding board and inspiration for the rock opera," Richard Barnes wrote in *Maximum R&B*. "He and Pete together talked through the project and the structure...They realized that they couldn't get it all on one album, they had about three sides of material, so they decided to make it a double album which greatly helped to clarify the plot." "It was only because Pete had to keep adding bits that it became a double album," John Entwistle told the *Observer*.

Towards the end of 1968, with the completion of *Deaf, Dumb and Blind Boy* (which by this time was now being referred to as *Tommy*) still somewhere on the horizon, Decca and Track records had lost their collective patience with The Who's lack of progress on a new album, and decided to release their own compilations, *Magic Bus – The Who on Tour* (Decca) and *Direct Hits* (Track). Since neither compilation included The Who's Brunswick material (notably *I Can't Explain, Anyway, Anyhow, Anywhere*, and *My Generation*) due to the Shel Talmy case, their worth as definitive Who compilations was highly dubious. "Decca Records really smarmed all over this one," Pete vented in a 1971 *Rolling Stone* article. "Buses painted like Mickey Mouse's last trip. Album covers featuring an unsuspecting Who endorsing it like it was *our* idea...Decca's answer to an overdue *Tommy*: *The Who, Magic Bus, On Tour*. Great title, swinging presentation. Also a swindle as far as insinuating that the record was live. Bastards."

"We were working on *Tommy*, and we kept telling them it would be ready next week, it would be ready next week, it would be ready next week," Pete told the *L.A. Free Press*' Chris Van Ness in December, 1971.

> And it never was. So in the end, in desperation, they got us to do this photo session, which they said was for a publicity handout, of us farting around with this absurd bus. They then got together a few old tapes and threw together [the album], which was a culmination of all the most terrible things American record companies ever get up to. Just exploitation. They didn't care about *Tommy* ever coming out; they just wanted to exploit the Who while the Who were big – though we weren't that big then, really – and make a few bucks, because who knows what may happen tomorrow. Plus the fact that they made it look like a live album. I mean that's the worst thing that's ever gone down.

Another project The Who were involved in towards the end of the year was *The Rolling Stones Rock'n'Roll Circus*, an elaborate TV special planned by the Stones but never released. Along with The Who and the

Rolling Stones, guests included Eric Clapton, John Lennon, Jethro Tull and Marianne Faithfull. It has often been said that The Who's blistering performance of *A Quick One*, a far superior rendition to that which was played in Monterey (attributable to the band's non-stop touring since that date), was the reason that the Stones never released the TV special; they had been upstaged. This performance is included in the 1979 Who biopic *The Kids Are Alright*[64]. The *Rock'n'Roll Circus* "...was, in fact, the most exciting pop show I have ever seen, and one in which I was involved alongside those "maniacs" Keith Moon and Pete Townshend, who organized compulsory audience participation until 5 o'clock Thursday morning," Keith Altham reported in *NME*.

>...Clowns, fire-eater and cowboy on horseback led to The Who. They performed their mini-opera, in which Keith Moon regaled us with his latest impersonation of a human fountain by having beer spilled onto his snare drums while in top gear.
>
>Although he might smile at the thought, Townshend is now almost a piece of pop folklore, with his Catherine wheel arm movements and aggressive leaps. He must make great TV.

Yet another side project in Pete's arsenal was his work producing his art school pal and musical mentor Andy Newman. "...in January, despite his first preoccupation with the opera, Pete branched out with his first production work outside The Who," Chris Charlesworth wrote in 1983.

>Thunderclap Newman was a group assembled by Pete around the wayward talents of Andy Newman... Pete put him in the studio with Jimmy McCulloch, a sixteen-year-old Scottish guitarist, and John "Speedy" Keene, the singing drummer who wrote *Armenia City In The Sky* for The Who's *Sell Out* LP and had lately been working as Pete's chauffeur. With Pete as producer and bass player [he worked under the pseudonym of Bijou Drains] the quartet recorded a Keene song called *Something In The Air*, a memorable single that would top the British charts later in the year. Their album *Hollywood Dream* was equally impressive, indisputable evidence that Pete had mastered

---

[64] "...you know why it was never shown, right?," *The Kids Are Alright* producer Jeff Stein asked *The Hollywood Reporter*'s John Burman in 2003 of the Rolling Stone's *Rock'n'Roll Circus* footage, which was eventually found in a barn after Townshend obtained Mick Jagger's blessing to use it. "...They kicked their fucking ass. So brilliant. The energy at the end of that piece. It feels like the roof is going to come off – Pete and Keith flailing away."

the art of record-making and getting the most out of a studio.

Something In The Air[65], released in mid-1969, was #1 in the UK charts for three weeks[66]. It also cracked the US top 40. The unlikely trio of Keene, McCullough and Newman was Kit Lambert's idea. "Independently all three of them came to me, or I got involved with them with a view to helping them, and then suddenly I realized – or rather, it was Kit Lambert again who said to me, 'You haven't got time for all of them; why not try them together'," Pete told John Swenson in 1979. "I thought, 'Impossible, three more unlikely people you couldn't get,' but they got in a room together, they played together on some film music for a friend of mine, and they were really great, and I played them back the tapes and they said 'Yeah, seems to work,' and they liked it and they were all enthusiastic about it, as a concept."

Riding the momentum of their surprise hit, Thunderclap Newman went on an ill-fated tour. "…I had to go away to America with the Who in the middle of it all and that number one was so unexpected," Pete lamented to *Melody Maker* the following year. "I never even got to see them play a gig, although I hear it was a disaster and the audiences were fantastically disappointed. Andy enjoyed the tour, but people thought they were going to be a rock group, which wasn't the idea… financially it didn't do them any good at all, despite having a number one single. There was nothing to follow it up and I feel very guilty about it."[67]

Returning home from some early February dates in northern England, Pete learned that Meher Baba had died. "Avatar Meher Baba dropped his physical body at twelve noon on 31st January 1969, to live eternally in the hearts of all his lovers," read the cable released by Baba's secretary in India. Pete was especially saddened by the fact that he hadn't become closer to Baba during his lifetime[68]. "…when I got home and the news was broken to me," Pete said, "I felt as if I hadn't had enough time to really make myself ready, to learn to love Baba and hang tightly to his apron

---

[65] The Squadronaires, incidentally, had a popular tune entitled *There's Something in the Air*.
[66] Andrew Motion offers the following in *The Lamberts*: "One of Kit's publicity stunts for Thunderclap Newman and their song *Something In The Air* was, according to Andy Newman himself, to send the DJs at the BBC a pill in a small plastic envelope with a label attached which read 'Take this and it will change your life'. They did take it, 'and it turned out to be a very powerful laxative, which wiped the DJs off the air for about a week'."
[67] Keene, once road manager for John Mayall's Bluesbreakers, wound up producing albums such as L.A.M.F. by the Heartbreakers, and Motorhead's self-titled debut. He died in mid-2002, aged 56. McCullough later saw action with Paul McCartney's Wings.
[68] While the two never met, Baba was reportedly aware of Pete. "I sent Mani the *Observer* color magazine which one week carried the story of The Who and had a photograph of Pete and the others on the cover," London Baba devotee Delia DeLeon wrote in 1991. "While Mani [Baba's sister] was looking at it, Baba came into the room and put His hand on Pete's face. Subsequently Mani gave Pete this photograph when he visited India."

strings as the whirlwind of spiritual events around the closing of his manifestation speeded up." Baba's death prompted Pete to record Cole Porter's *Begin The Beguine* (a Baba favorite) at his home recording studio that month, which would ultimately appear on the Baba tribute album *Happy Birthday*, which was released on Baba's birthday the following year.

Meanwhile, at this point, *Tommy* was ostensibly complete until Pete let his friend, well-known music writer Nik Cohn, listen to an early preview tape. The ensuing incident led to the inclusion of the album's best known track, *Pinball Wizard*. "Nik and I used to go all over Soho playing pinball all the time," Pete told *Uncut*'s Simon Goddard in 2004.

> He was fucking obsessed by it. He'd written a novel called *Arfur: Teenage Pinball Queen* about this girl who he introduced me to one time. She was this podgy little girl who used to hang around Soho, probably a prostitute, about 15, but she was a fantastic pinball player. At that time, the setting for the end of *Tommy* was going to be a church, so we played it to a few people, including Nik Cohn. He kind of liked it but he said, 'It's all a bit *dark*, isn't it!' I just remember saying to him, with maybe an element of sarcasm, 'So if it had pinball in it, would you give it a decent review?' He went, 'Of course I would, anything with pinball in it's fantastic.' And so I wrote *Pinball Wizard*, purely as a scam.

"I knocked it off," Pete said in 1996. "I thought 'Oh, my God this is awful, the most clumsy piece of writing I've ever done: *Ever since I was a young boy, I played the silver ball, from Soho down to Brighton, I must have played them all.* Oh my god. I'm embarrassed. This sounds like a Music Hall song. *Sure plays a mean pinball.* I scribbled it out and all the verses were the same length and there was no kind of middle eight. It was going to be a complete dud, but I carried on. I attempted the same mock baroque guitar beginning that's on *I'm A Boy* and then a bit of vigorous kind of flamenco guitar. I was just grabbing at ideas, I knocked a demo together and took it to the studio and everyone loved it."

Pinball Wizard shifted *Tommy*'s focus back from religion to rock, or, as Richard Barnes put it in 1996, "*Pinball Wizard* made it more Rock Opera than God Opera." At a point when perhaps the whole project had become bogged down in its own deep meaning, *Pinball Wizard* returned the focus to music. The song also provided a means of demonstrating Tommy's first real taste of excitement and success in life. "The whole point of *Pinball Wizard* was to let the boy have some sort of colorful event and excitement," Pete told *Rolling Stone* in 1969.

...*Pinball Wizard* is about life's games...Tommy's games aren't games. They're like the first real thing he's done in his life...this is Tommy's first big triumph. He's got results. A big score. He doesn't know all this; he stumbled on a machine, started to pull levers and so on, got things going, and suddenly started getting incredible affection – like pats on the back. This hasn't happened to him before, and the kids are his first disciples. It's supposed to capsule the later events, a sort of teasing preview. It's meant to be a play off of early discipleship and the later real disciples. In a funny sort of way, the disciples in the pinball days were more sincere, less greedy than later on, when they demand a religion – anything to be like him and escape from their own dreary lives, do things his way and get there quicker.

The 'Holiday Camp' setting at the end of *Tommy* was added to make the pinball theme more palatable. "There may have been some embarrassment because what I felt was that I'd been selling this thing to the band as being really quite deep and then suddenly I felt as though I was losing my nerve," Pete told *Uncut* in 2004.

I remember saying to Keith one day, 'It doesn't feel right any more, this Pinball Wizard thing. Suddenly he's a fucking pinball player!' I didn't think we needed to nail down what Tommy was: he could have been a guitarist or a singer or a preacher or anything – a charismatic individual. But suddenly he was a pinball player and I felt uncomfortable with it being placed in this idea of a pseudo-church. Then Keith said, 'Well, what about a holiday camp?'[69] because I was always going on about holiday camps, I was almost brought up in Butlins. So I ran off, wrote *Tommy's Holiday Camp*, and then wrote a couple of lyrical changes to bring pinball and the holiday camp into the story, so it felt as if this was being lightened up towards the end. But it also seemed more radical, there being more of a sense of commercialism brought in at the end, that he's

---

[69] "...Keith said, "Well I've been thinking that it would be a good idea to set the whole thing in a Holiday Camp."," Pete said 1975. "I said, "What a great idea," and Keith said, "Well O.K. I'll write that tonight." I thought, "God Almighty, if Keith goes off and gets into writing songs about Holiday Camps, I don't know how they're ever going to fit in." So I said to him, "Don't worry Keith, I've already written it." ...when I got home I wrote the short piece called *Ernie's Holiday Camp*. Keith got the credit for it because it was his idea, and also I felt, it turned out just as he himself would have written it."

selling shades and T-shirts and everything in a very absurd, comical, cartoon-y marketplace. Which, of course, pop is! So it all suddenly started to feel natural, that we were on safe ground because we were satirizing our own industry.

Pinball Wizard, the world's first taste of *Tommy*, was released in March, 1969, the same month Pete's first daughter, Emma Kate Townshend, was born. It did well on both sides of the Atlantic, reaching number 4 in the U.K., while attaining number 19 in the U.S. Regarded as by far the best effort since *I Can See For Miles*, the single was met with much praise[70], but some critics were concerned with *Tommy*'s overall moral message even before hearing the finished product. "The band was at pains to point out that the single didn't give a full enough picture of Tommy's character and that the premature judgments would ultimately prove to be inaccurate," John Atkins commented in *The Who on Record*. "Townshend, anxious that his motives in utilizing a disabled character weren't misunderstood, sent a press release to various influential people in London requesting that they reserve judgment until the full album was released."

Following a short series of gigs through Scotland in late April, the band performed *Tommy* in its entirety in public for the first time at Ronnie Scott's Club in Soho, London. The band had dedicated much of the previous two months to rehearsing their overhauled live show, and invited an audience of mostly journalists to witness the result. "…as enormous speaker cabinets were piled high along the walls of the club and hummed ominously at the assembled throng, Pete dryly explained the story line," *Melody Maker* reported. The band soon launched into a non-stop rendition of *Tommy* followed by *Shakin' All Over* and *Summertime Blues*, thrown in for good measure. "The Who gave us a good solid hour's worth of quality listening and excellent showmanship," announced the *Record Mirror* the following week[71]. "In the confined space of Ronnie Scott's club which is more accustomed to the refined rhythms of jazz, the overwhelming intensity of The Who's performance left scores of people literally deaf," *Melody Maker* explained. "Despite the discomfort of those nearest the speakers, nobody wanted to miss a minute of the group's riveting rave-up…"

Tommy, the Who's fourth album, was released in late May. It was a resounding success, eventually reaching number 2 in the U.K. charts and number 4 stateside, where the album stayed on the charts for 47 weeks. "When the double album *Tommy* was released," John Atkins wrote in *The Who on Record*, "…it looked and sounded every bit as epic as Townshend had been promising during the preceding year. It was sufficiently large (in

---

[70] "I didn't think *Pinball Wizard* would be a hit," Pete told *Melody Maker*'s Chris Welch in April, "especially as it's an up-tempo, swinging rockaboogie about a deaf, dumb and blind person."
[71] *Melody Maker*'s Chris Welch clocked the show at an hour and a half.

concept, duration and ideas) to fulfill all expectations, and it was an immediate success with the listening public…"

"*Tommy* is a milestone in rock music, a milestone in the career of The Who and a milestone in Pete's development as a composer," Chris Charlesworth commented. "Despite its faults – muddy production, misleading story line, some flawed songs – the double LP incorporates intriguing ideas and musical devices that Pete had been experimenting with for most of his professional career…Whatever confusion is thrown up by the lyrics, the music – a textbook lesson in rock construction – carries the whole."

"*Tommy* was a magnificent package too," Charlesworth went on. "Wrapped in a triple fold-out sleeve designed by [Mike] McInnerney and containing a lavishly illustrated libretto, it arrived at exactly the right moment to capitalize on the times. Its spiritual references, its suggestion of opaque psychedelia, its aloof pretentiousness (which Pete admitted) appealed directly to the aging rock audience. It was a grand design; everything about it was designed to turn The Who into a legend, which is exactly what it did."

Tommy was met with mostly ecstatic reviews[72], with *Rolling Stone* calling the album "probably the most important milestone in pop since Beatlemania." London's *International Times* proclaimed, "It is impossible to praise this album too much…With *Tommy* The Who have advanced ahead of all other comparable groups," while Nik Cohn wrote, "*Tommy* is just possibly the most important work that anyone has yet done in rock," in the *New York Times*.

Conversely, the *NME*'s Richard Green wasn't impressed. "I really was looking forward to this "pop opera", which has occupied Pete Townshend's mind for so long," he wrote in late May. "But what a disappointment. Running for over an hour, it goes on and on and isn't totally representative of The Who; maybe it's time for a change in style, but if this is it, I long for a return to the old days… Pretentious is too strong a word; maybe over-ambitious is the right term, but sick certainly does apply." Pete responded to this assertion in *Disc and Music Echo*, explaining, "…what I was out to show is that someone who suffers terribly at the hands of society has the ability to turn all these experiences into a tremendous musical awareness. Sickness is in the mind of the listener and I don't give a damn what people think. I'm very pleased with the way the album has turned out… Sure, the boy is raped and suffers, but we show that

---

[72] Pete reviewed the original recording of *Tommy* in 2003 while preparing to remix the album. "When I heard these tracks again last year, for the first time in years," he told *Uncut*'s Simon Goddard in 2004, "I thought, 'Fuck! This was a *band*, a really *good* band.' *Tommy* is probably Keith at the height of his studio powers and John, too, before got into [impersonates frantic bass scales] – all that. It was good, straightforward, powerful, innovative bass playing."

instead of being repulsed and sickened, he has the means to turn all these experiences to his own good." Some good-humored nit-picking came from the *Financial Times*, who noted that *Tommy* was a choral work and not an opera at all, and should be referred to as a cantata.

Despite the mostly positive reviews of his latest work, Pete had several regrets about *Tommy*. One of these concerned the ending. "My whole idea was that Tommy was left behind, poignant," Pete later explained. "You know, *See Me, Feel Me* and you didn't get enough of it. That should be the last thing you hear, whereas the last thing you actually hear is *Listening to You*. I felt that was one mistake. There were lots and lots of others. We could have gone on forever and still not got it right." On another occasion he added, "It's definitely not a total success. I've had a lot of kids come up to me and say, "Well, look man, you've spent two years on it, why didn't you spend three years on it and tighten up some of the bad things about it?"

Pete outlined another regret in a 1987 interview with *Rolling Stone*'s David Fricke. "One of the ironies of *Tommy* was that because of the Woodstock movie the *See Me Feel Me* chorus in the finale became a real anthem for the hippie dream, a theme for the gathering of the tribes."

> Yet the whole point of *Tommy* was that Utopia was not around the corner, that this explosion of positive youth energy was already being co-opted – in this case by a deaf dumb and blind 'guru.' Why is it that rock songwriters are not allowed to be ironic? Why is it that satire can only be comedic? Why can't rock satire be real satire, real irony? I know that a lot of people heard *Tommy*, listened to certain tracks and completely misread them. What people went for in *Tommy* was the celebration, not the denouement. The sad thing is I continue to live with the finale, not the bit in the middle.
>
> What was important at the time, and continues to be important, is that the human individual accepts the fact that he or she is capable of being spiritually swayed. And in order to make the best of that, they really have to listen to what's being said. It's no point being carried away by the uplift.
>
> I suppose the mistake I made in *Tommy* was instead of having the guts to take what Meher Baba said – which was "Don't worry, be happy, leave the results to God" – and repeating that to people, I decided the people weren't capable of hearing that directly. They've got to have it served in this entertainment package. And I gave them *Tommy* instead, in which some of Meher Baba's

wonderfully explicit truths were presented to them half-baked in lyric form and diluted as a result. In fact, if there was any warning in *Tommy*, it was "Don't make any more **records like that.**"

The continually self-deprecating Pete did, however, ultimately concede that the album was something special. "*Tommy* was very arduously put together, and very clumsily put together," he said. "Yet it's got a grace that I just can't account for." He also admitted that he may not have been particularly easy to work with in the studio. "...what other three musicians would have put up with all my bullshit in order to get this album out?," Pete said in 1969. "It's *my* apple, right. It's my whole trip, coming from Baba, and they just sat there, let it come out, and then leapt upon it and gave it an extra boot."

"There's this amazing letter I've got from a kid in Chicago," Pete told *Sounds'* Penny Valentine in August, 1972.

> ...we played there and this kid came up and said "Hey Mr. Townshend, I've got to tell you what happened when I first heard *Tommy*, I was like listening and Baba came to me... I became Tommy and ever since I've been in this amazing spiritual trance." And he wrote this letter about how Baba came out of *Tommy* and how it was all planned and then how upset he's been when he'd found his friends weren't getting the same thing happening.
>
> So I thought fuck it maybe one or two people have got that hit so it's worth doing for that reason. But on the other hand at the same time it's working on a number of other levels – it's entertaining, you know.

While the *Tommy* studio recording received plenty of praise, the rock opera took on a whole new life onstage. The band discovered this fact upon rehearsing their new live set list. "Kit Lambert was furious when he spent months capturing our dynamics on *Tommy* then we went out and played it six times better than we had in the studios," Pete told *Melody Maker* in early 1970.

"We did one day's rehearsal, did the whole thing from start to finish and that was when we realized we had something cohesive and playable," Pete told Chris Charlesworth. "Keith and I went to a pub on the way back and sat there, both incredulous at how quickly it had come together. Roger had become something else and we discussed what would happen and how it would change everything. We knew we had something that was magic and that magic wasn't as clear on the album as it would have been in live performance."

"It made Roger a singer, it made Roger an icon, it made Roger like Jim Morrison or like Robert Plant, or like The Lead Singer. It gave him the right to grow his hair and wear the tassel jacket and swing his mic around instead of just posing and looking angry and, like, 'Don't fuck with me,' which isn't who he is by any means, but it gave him a vehicle, it gave him part that he could play."

"The Who's concerts were already very good, but *Tommy* transformed the act into a legendary event," John Atkins wrote in *The Who on Record*. "Who concerts doubled in duration and brought consistent unanimous acclaim that surpassed every other act in rock...the Who's playing was tighter, more disciplined and charged with excitement. The band members were now fully respected as serious artists, considered the most mature, intelligent and thought-provoking of all the British rock acts of the time."

Three dates at the Grande Ballroom in Dearborn, Michigan kicked off the Who's tremendously successful U.S. *Tommy* tour in early May, 1969. Townshend now took the stage most nights wearing a white boiler suit complete with Meher Baba necklace and button, Doc Martens work boots ("I used to go on wearing a boiler suit and Dr. Martens in defiance of fashion," Pete told the *NME* in 1980), and played his latest weapon of choice, the Gibson SG[73]. Following openers such as *Heaven and Hell*, *Fortune Teller* and *I Can't Explain*, the band performed *Tommy* in its entirety before ending with numbers such as *Summertime Blues*, *Substitute*, *Shakin' All Over*, and *Magic Bus*. Audiences were consistently wowed. "So strong was the new material," wrote Chris Charlesworth in 1984, "that Pete abandoned smashing his guitars on American stages as he had continued to do long after breaking the habit in England. Occasionally, when the mood took him, a Gibson SG bit the dust for old times sake, as if to emphasize that these four really were the same four who toured America with Herman's Hermits two years earlier."

Following the band's first performance of *Tommy* at the Fillmore East on May 16, the day before the album's release in the U.S., Pete met Leonard Bernstein backstage. "...he shook me and said, 'Do you know what you've done!'," Pete recalled in 1994. "Of course, what he was talking about was that I was going the next step in what he had done with *West Side Story*, which was creating a popular song cycle, a musical that was really rooted in street culture." It was also at this show that Pete kicked a plain-clothes police officer off the stage and was charged with third degree assault. The officer had taken to the stage in an attempt to warn the crowd

---

[73] "The first time I started to use the Gibson SG model guitar is when I got fed up with Fenders," Pete told *Guitar Player*'s Michael Brooks in 1972. "...So I went to the manager and said I really need an alternative to this and he said I think you'd like the newest SG and I looked at it. I played it and it rang, it sang to me... and I've used SG's ever since."

of a raging fire adjacent to the hall, which had already consumed a supermarket and a five story apartment building.[74]

The Who's most successful U.S. tour to date reached its conclusion on June 19, at the Fillmore West. "I will never forget that tour, the finale of *Tommy* never failed to mesmerize me along with the audience," Pete wrote in 1977. "It always felt to me like a prayer, I always felt myself full of Meher Baba when we performed it."

The band took it relatively easy upon their return to British soil, performing 10 dates over a six week period, most of which took place the last week of July and the first week of August. They left Europe once again in Mid-August for two American appearances: Bill Graham's Tanglewood Music Shed in Lenox, MA (sharing the bill with B.B. King and Jefferson Airplane), and Max Yasgur's sprawling farm near Bethel, New York.

The Who's appearance at the legendary Woodstock Music and Arts fair took place on Sunday, August 17, 1969. After the band's long summer U.S. tour, Pete had wanted to spend time with his family rather than return for the Woodstock festival. The promoters, however, had other plans. "...we needed one more key act," Woodstock production coordinator John Morris recalled in 1989.

> To get The Who for Woodstock, Frank (Barsalona, The Who's US agent) and I had Peter Townshend to dinner at Frank Barsalona's house. Frank's an insomniac, and I was pretty good at staying awake in those days because I was almost as much of an insomniac. And we wore Peter down to the point where he agreed to do it. Finally. This is after him saying for hours and hours and hours, "No, no, no. I'm not going to do it, I'm not going to do it." Because they didn't want to stay in the U.S. that long. They wanted to get back to their families. Or he wanted to....He was sitting in a corner and finally he said, "O.K., all right. But it will have to be fifteen thousand." And I had to look him straight in the face at six o'clock in the morning and say, "We only have eleven thousand dollars left. That's all that's left in the budget." And I thought he was going to kill me, but he was just too tired. He just said, "Oh, all right, if you let me go to bed. Whatever you say."

The band were sandwiched between Sly and the Family Stone and Jefferson Airplane, and the weather was terrible. And Pete didn't see eye-to-eye with the 'peace and love' Woodstock theme: "All those hippies

---

[74] Townshend was eventually fined $75 for this incident after a June court appearance in New York.

wandering about thinking the world was going to be different from that day," Pete recalled in 1982, "As a cynical English arsehole I walked through it all and felt like spitting on the lot of them, and shaking them and trying to make them realize that nothing had changed and nothing was going to change. Not only that, what they thought was an alternative society was basically a field full of six foot deep mud and laced with LSD. If that was the world they wanted to live in, then fuck the lot of them." Pete clearly wasn't impressed with the aura of the festival. "My impressions of it were quite bad," he told the *San Diego Union*'s George Varga in 1989. "A lot of mud, polluted water, polluted drugs. A moment of pleasure at seeing a picture of my guru, Meher Baba, up on a telephone pole, and then a horrifying scene where a guy high on acid shimmied up the pole, touched the picture, screamed 'It's on fire,' fell and broke his back on an ambulance below. A terrible irony..."

"That was the worst gig we ever played," Roger Daltrey told the *New Yorker*. "We waited in a field of mud for fourteen hours, sitting on some boards, doing nothing, and doing nothing is the most exhausting thing in the world. As a result we gave one of the worst shows we've ever done." The band took the stage at around 3:30 a.m. on Sunday, none too happy about the ridiculously long delay they'd just endured [Pete's wife Karen and baby Emma were waiting in a Manhattan hotel room], and not particularly enamored with the idea of playing, despite the fact that about 500,000 people were in attendance. The famous Townshendian short fuse was burning very quickly. "I immediately got into an incredible state and rejected everyone," Pete recalled later. "And I was telling really nice people like Ritchie Havens to fuck off and things like that."

"We were more arrogant than nervous before we went on," Pete told Dave Marsh. "Pissed off is more like it," Marsh commented.

Backstage, everything from the Coca-Cola to the coffee was spiked with acid, and the band had been flat out tripping against its will for twelve hours...When the Who took the stage, it was jammed with photographers and the camera crew from the movie Michael Wadleigh was making of the weekend's events. Townshend kicked the first cameraman he saw (it happened to be Wadleigh, though Pete didn't know it) into the photographers' pit, a good ten-foot drop.

With the remaining photographers suitably dispersed, The Who began their set in the dark with *Heaven and Hell* and *I Can't Explain* before heading into *Tommy*, which fared well until *Pinball Wizard* got under way and political activist Abbie Hoffman decided to make his grand entrance. "I remember standing on the stage," Woodstock photographer Henry Diltz recalled in 1989, "...and Abbie Hoffman suddenly ran out and grabbed the microphone and said, "Remember John Sinclair and the guys in prison for smoking pot," or something like that... suddenly Peter Townshend was standing there with his guitar and I saw him raise it up, kind of holding it over his shoulder, and walk up behind Abbie Hoffman and just go *boink!* right in the back of the neck. It was almost like a bayonet thrust...one quick little jab right in the back of Abbie Hoffman – who fell down, I remember. It looked like a fatal blow. He was really pissed at this guy taking over the microphone..."

Pete "swatted him with his Gibson SG," Dave Marsh wrote in his 1983 Who bio *Before I Get Old*, "and as the Yippie fell into the photographers' pit, played on. Hoffman screamed unheard curses into the gale of the music, then ran over a hill and out of sight..." Townshend followed *Pinball Wizard* with a brief statement to the audience: "The next fucking person who walks across this stage is going to get fucking killed! You can laugh. I mean it!" This was The Who's contribution to peace and love. Pete reflected on the Abbie Hoffman incident in the booklet that accompanied the 1994 boxed set, *Thirty Years of Maximum R&B*: "What Abbie was saying was politically correct in many ways," Pete wrote. "The people at Woodstock really were a bunch of hypocrites claiming a cosmic revolution simply because they took over a field, broke down some fences, imbibed bad acid and then tried to run out without paying the band. All while [ex-MC5 manager and Hoffman crony] John Sinclair rotted in jail after a trumped-up drug bust. My response was reflexive rather than considered. Later I realized his humiliation on that occasion was fatal to his political credibility."

Pete's mood took a turn for the better when the sun came up.

"*Tommy* wasn't getting to anyone," Pete recalled in 1982. "...By this time I was just about awake, we were just listening to the music when all of a sudden, bang! The fucking sun comes up! It was just incredible. I really felt we didn't deserve it, in a way. We put out such bad vibes...and as we finished it was daytime. We walked off, got in the car, and went back to the hotel. It was fucking fantastic."

"...The Who sliced through the flower power like a chain saw in a daisy garden," wrote *Time* magazine's Jay Cocks in 1979, and "played with an intensity that took the show away from such Mallomar bands as the Jefferson Airplane..." But even years later, Townshend still viewed The Who's Woodstock set as subpar. In 1994, he reportedly blocked MCA's attempt to release a twenty-fifth anniversary CD of the band's entire set at the festival.

Upon their return to England, The Who appeared in front of 200,000 at the Isle of Wight Festival, headlining alongside Bob Dylan on August 30, 1969. "...the Who made a triumphant homecoming at the Isle of Wight Festival," Dave Marsh wrote in 1983. "The band was at the top of the bill with Bob Dylan, who was making his first stage appearance anywhere in several years. The Who were probably the best-received act of the entire weekend. It was their first hour of genuine prestige in their native country."

"The Who made their usual spectacular entrance – this time by helicopter," reported the *NME*'s Richard Green.

> All of us backstage got covered in all sorts of flying muck, and *NME*'s intrepid photographer, Stuart Richman, was almost decapitated by a sheet or hardboard that suddenly took flight!
> The group went straight on stage to be greeted by a roaring welcome. The first number, *I Can't Explain*, began. Roger's long-fringed jacket was open revealing a bare torso; Pete Townshend's outfit consisted of a white boiler suit; John Entwistle maintained a serious expression and Keith Moon had a look on his face as though he was suffering the ultimate torture. *Young Man Blues*, which was written for Mose Allison, began quietly and became a roar-up. Then came the inevitable long selection from *Tommy* – very clever and intricate, but it tended to go on a bit.
> Eddie Cochran's *Summertime Blues* was great, as was *My Generation*. *Shakin' All Over* was obviously dedicated to the bird I was with, as she didn't stop shivering all weekend.
> I was very glad to have seen The Who – they were right on form and must be rated as one of the world's best groups. Their loud sound does not detract from their performance, which is as visually exciting as it is musically together.

"The Who had now assembled the biggest and most perfected sound set-up ever and had developed a top road crew to operate it," Richard Barnes reported in 1982.

> It was pure power that assaulted you from that huge bank of speakers. (It was the first time I'd ever seen warnings about keeping 15' away from the speakers.) At the IOW Festival they launched into practically the whole of *Tommy*. No stopping for rests, just one number straight after the next…Pete was a powerhouse to listen and watch. Jumping, leaping, twisting, swerving, swinging his arm like a rotor, punishing his guitar and forcing everything he could out of it.

One month later, following short visits to Scotland and the Netherlands, The Who were back in North America on a 30-date tour which included a six-night stand at the Fillmore East. Among the tour's opening acts was The Kinks.

By December, The Who could look back on 1969 as the year that had finally propelled them to rock superstardom. "[*Tommy*] not only sold in vast numbers but also put The Who in the position where they could negotiate huge advances on the renewal of their U.S. and other overseas contracts," wrote George Tremlett. "This they did, and by the stroke of a pen they each became dollar millionaires....With *Tommy*, The Who arrived. They never lost money after that."

"...Like a handful of other rock performers, they had achieved legendary status," Chris Charlesworth noted in 1984.

Satisfying as this must have been, Pete was embarrassed by his sudden wealth. As the group's principal songwriter, his income exceeded that of the other three quite considerably but he did not spend money profligately like so many of his fortunate peers.

Instead of securing his financial future he spent money on establishing a Meher Baba Centre in Richmond and financed trips to India by other Baba lovers. He contributed generously to various charities; he continued to live the same Thameside home in Twickenham, stocked his private studio with state-of-the-art equipment, bought a Mercedes Benz car and provided generously for his family without undue ostentation.

He kept around him the same friends from earlier days, cronies from art school, fellow Baba lovers, a few musicians and artists...Above all, he stayed in touch; the remote lives led by other rock millionaires were an abhorrence to Pete Townshend.

Pete had become involved in local Baba centers, the first of which was located at his old flat on Wardour Street, "...a large airy room with oval windows letting in the light from all sides," Delia DeLeon recalled in 1991. "There was a kitchenette and entrance space which became an office." Pete had vacated the flat in 1967, and the Baba center opened there in August, 1968. "...about seventy people attended [the opening], including Baba's youngest brother, Adi, and his wife, Frenee," DeLeon recalled. "...It was an incredible experience to walk into the sun streaming up there through big half circle windows, and hear Don Stevens, our London father figure...give a talk on one of Baba's discourses...," Pete wrote in 1970. "Speedy from Thunderclap Newman lives there now, and the atmosphere has probably returned to its original down-home state, the light warm buzz of Baba's presence less evident and yet still there."

About a year after the opening, Pete's desire to get rid of his studio apartment on Wardour Street necessitated a hunt for a new site for the Baba center. Karen allowed the group the use of her old flat in Eccleston Square, Victoria. The move took place in December, 1969. "This one was, believe it or not, my wife's flat," Pete continued.

> We are a many-flatted couple. Though we do manage to live in one building only today. This one is in Victoria in a basement. It's cool and fairly light for a basement, and it's small. A hundred people have been known to squeeze in there. Only about 20 of them got served with tea. The center is run and financed by a committee which includes myself. The committee sees to it that it is open a couple of days a week, and keeps the bills paid and the library full. It also drinks a lot of tea. One of the dearest women alive is Baba's constant reflection at the London center, Miss Delia DeLeon. She is an actress who is now in her 70's, who met Baba when he looked like the most exciting thing to hit Hollywood...She has the heart of a young girl, and Baba has said that she is very spiritually advanced. Her flippancy and impetuosity are more likenable to a mischievous child than an illusion-wise worker for the Avatar.

A hung-over Pete Townshend spent the morning of January first 1970 at home in Twickenham talking to Chris Welch of *Melody Maker* over breakfast about plans for the future. Certainly, *Tommy* was a huge critical and commercial success, but eventually those successes would become spoiled by overkill if not astutely nipped in the bud beforehand. It seemed that *Tommy* had reached the point where it was being squeezed for all it was worth, and although there appeared to be at least a little life left in the project, the question 'when's enough enough?' was rearing its head.

Pete's comments to Welch on the subject were as follows: "So much has been written, said and done about it, that it is beginning to be a pain in everybody's ass...there are still people who want to hear about it in Europe, but we definitely won't exploit it any further than that and the film we are making which is based on the ideas that went into *Tommy*." Pete went on to explain that a film was being planned (recall that Kit Lambert had written a script during the recording sessions), the contents of which were still up in the air ("The question is – what is the film going to be about, now that the album has been milked to death already?"), and that "there is a single coming. We're going to record it next week and probably have it out in January." The forthcoming record Pete was speaking of was *The Seeker*, which was ultimately released in the U.K. on March 21.

Pete also discussed plans for a new project for the band. "I've got ideas for one. But a lot of my ideas will be channeled into the film. We'd like to do an album of songs next – other people's songs. Then there are plans for a 'live' album. Bob, our roadie, has been recording us on gigs…and he has been getting some incredible results."

"A lull is inevitable," Pete said. "There will be a quiet period for the group as far as the public will be concerned. But the success we have had will make us work harder. We will be taking our stage show to a higher standard of professionalism. We'll use more dynamics and not just put on two hours of noise."

One week later, the band recorded *The Seeker* at IBC studios, with The Who producing. It reached number 19 in Britain, 44 in the U.S. "…*The Seeker* was an almost embarrassing failure after *Tommy*'s critical and commercial success," wrote Chris Charlesworth. "Its lyrics were deeply personal to Pete and seemed to sum up his personal dilemma; not just how to follow *Tommy* but how to exist as a millionaire rock superstar yet stay true to rhetorical ideals already stated and reinforced by the spiritual teaching of Meher Baba."

"I wrote it when I was drunk in Florida," Pete explained to *Rolling Stone* in May. "Quite loosely, *The Seeker* was just a thing about what I call Divine Desperation, or just Desperation. And what it does to people." Conspicuously absent in the role of producer at *The Seeker* recording session was Kit Lambert. As 1970 wore on, it became apparent that Pete and Kit's relationship cooled considerably. A key factor may have been the proposed *Tommy* movie, the content and viability of which Lambert and Townshend soon clashed over. This situation reached boiling point the following spring during the short evolution of *Lifehouse*.

With the dawn of a new decade came a new Who tour which must have thrilled Kit Lambert, as the band took their now world-renowned *Tommy* show to venues which could only seem appropriate given the fact that it was a 'rock opera': The opera houses of Europe[75]. A fourteen day, seven show blitzkrieg of some of the world's oldest and most prestigious opera houses ensued, beginning on Friday, January 16, 1970, at the Champs-Elysees Theatre in Paris and featuring stops at Det Kunglige Teater in

---

[75] "The idea was an adaptation of his original intention to launch *Tommy* by having it performed at the opera houses in Moscow, first, then New York," wrote Andrew Motion in 1987. "This scheme had fallen through because the director of the Metropolitan Opera House in New York, Rudolph Bing, could not easily be convinced of *Tommy*'s merits. Once it had been performed and acclaimed at The Coliseum in London, other cities followed suit, and the band eventually performed in opera houses in Paris, Copenhagen, Cologne, Hamburg, Berlin, Amsterdam and, eventually, New York. It was a triumph of organization, and a graphic illustration of the distance that the band – and rock and roll – had traveled since its beginnings."

Copenhagen, the Stadt Opera Houses in Cologne, Hamburg and Berlin, and wrapped up with a late performance (the show started at midnight) at the Concertgebouw in Amsterdam on January 30.

Pete soon grew tired of the amount of VIPs present at these gigs in small, upper class establishments. "...thousands and thousands of kids were coming to see us and then only about a hundredth of the kids who wanted to see us could," Pete said later. "And we'd go in and play and like the first 20 rows would be Polydor people. Or Prince Rainier and his royal family, and honestly it was such a bad scene. We were going to play the opera houses in Vienna, Moscow and The New York Metropolitan, but I just thought that was the biggest hype bullshit I'd ever heard of. We blew it out." Until June, when The Who *did* play two shows at New York's Met...

"The thing I didn't dig about it is that we didn't play big enough places," Pete continued. "The opera houses over there are very small. There are 1,500 people usually and you could see every face. But you can't win them over. Say there's an old guy in a bow tie out there, he's come up to write a review in some opera paper or some serious music paper and most of the night he sits there with his fingers in his ears. It's just impossible to work when someone's doing that." Keith Moon once told *Rolling Stone*'s Jerry Hopkins that performing in front of such audiences was "...rather like playing to an oil painting."

Pete's relationship with his audience has always been of the utmost importance, something which he'd explore in the coming months through his *Lifehouse* project. "We were most passionate about the audience," Pete said in a 1985 radio interview, "and the audience's role, particularly in concerts, that a good audience has to be one in which everybody loses themselves. You don't go onstage to *find* something, you go onstage to *lose* something. You don't go to a concert in order to be *given* something, you go to a concert in order to become abandoned, to lose yourself."

On February 1, 1970, Meher Baba's birthday, a Baba tribute album entitled *Happy Birthday* was released. "...unaccustomed as I am to making my affection, devotion, love, interest, obsession or whatever you like to call it KNOWN to someone like Baba – who is now after all in the abstract, R.I.P. – the way I know best is music," Pete told *Sounds*' Penny Valentine in 1972. "And also I do feel the need to display my affection and commitment to Baba." The album featured a 28-page book containing "...poems, religious essays, photo and newspaper collages ("All Britain Duped by Sham Messiah," proclaimed a 1932 headline), and a couple of paintings by Mike McInnerney, illustrator of *Tommy*," reported *Rolling Stone* later in the year. "Like the record, the book radiates friendliness and warmth. Even more than the record, it reflects the fact that Meher Baba excluded no one: many different human types are recognizable among the contributors, stupid and smart, complicated and direct."

The album, a limited edition of 2,500 put together by Pete, included his singing and playing on a demo version of *The Seeker* ("which I still dig more than the version done by The Who," he said in May), a song entitled **Poem, and another entitled *Day of Silence*, both of which were written by Pete** and were described by *Rolling Stone* as "peaceful ballads with acoustic guitar and buzzing mandolin." "I wrote *Day Of Silence* on July 10," Pete later commented, "which is the day that followers of Baba choose to spend without speaking, they communicate by using pencil and paper. I wrote the lyrics the day after so I wouldn't break my silence."[76]

Pete was present on most tracks, singing and playing on *Mary Jane*, a catchy farewell to marijuana in response to Baba's anti-drug stance. *The Love Man*, another Townshend composition, and Pete's year-old demo of Cole Porter's *Begin the Beguine* were included along with an excellent Ronnie Lane song entitled *Evolution*[77]. Two strange songs, the Ron Geesin instrumental *With a Smile Up His Nose They Entered*[78], and the very weird spoken-word *Meditation* by Mike da Costa rounded out the album. *Rolling Stone* described the latter as "a poetic freakout...which will surprise anyone who has never tried to meditate...It's a track that can strike you as comic or painful, or both."

Happy Birthday "...emerged from the spirited group of young people who I met when I first came to Richmond," Pete recalled in the essay which accompanied his limited edition boxed set *Avatar* in 1999. "This was a group who seemed to me to gather around Michael McInnerney and his then wife Katie... At the time they lived in part of a beautiful Victorian villa called Willoughby House situated very near Richmond Bridge. There was a large garden and on warm summer days a motley gathering was usual... Not everyone that was attracted to the teachings of Meher Baba was artistic, but enough were to inspire me to suggest that we all get together to make a record."

Although the Who played only two live dates in February, 1970, both were important as they were recorded for a future live album. The Valentines Day show at the University Refectory at Leeds found the Who in top form. The band had decided to record the show, bringing with them Pye's eight track mobile recording unit. They had contemplated issuing a

---

[76] *The Who Concert File* pointed out that the following year The Who played Dunstable Civic Hall on July 10, "a clear case of silence breaking!"

[77] *Evolution* was a different arrangement of the Faces' *The Stone*.

[78] Geesin, a Scottish composer and musician, worked mostly with film music. He and his friend, Pink Floyd leader Roger Waters, scored a film version of Anthony Smith's 1968 book *The Body* in 1970. The flute and organ instrumental included on the Baba LP, *With A Smile Up His Nose They Entered*, was written for Floyd drummer Nick Mason's wife, Lindy. "She was quite a good flautist – but not quite good enough to actually get around it," Geesin told Floyd biographer Nicholas Shaffner. "So then I got a professional to record it on Pete's album."

live album for months now and had recorded every show from their 30-date U.S. tour in October - November, 1969, plus five additional European dates in December. Following the tour, Pete had intended to review the tapes and assemble a live compilation from them, but, "Suddenly someone realizes there are 240 hours of tape to be listened to," Pete told *Rolling Stone*. "...So I said, well, fuck that, I'm not gonna sit through and listen, you'd get brainwashed, let's face it! So we just fucking scrapped the lot, and to reduce the risk of pirating we put the lot on a bonfire and just watched it all go and we said, right, let's get an eight track."

Both the Leeds and Hull shows were a good fit for recording; the venues were small (The refectory at Leeds held 1500, while Hull held 1800) and the band were supposedly fresh, coming off a two week break since their European Opera House tour had ended, although Townshend, in an interview the day of the Leeds show, said the band was "exhausted physically and mentally." The Who's set still featured *Tommy* in its entirety accompanied by the band's most successful singles, four numbers that did well live (*Fortune Teller, Heaven and Hell, Summertime Blues* and *Tattoo*) and a few blues-based numbers, including *Spoonful, Young Man Blues,* and *Shakin' All Over*.

The show was a tremendous success. A few months later, Pete commented that "...it just happened to be a good show and it just happened to be like one of the greatest audiences we've ever played to in our whole career, just by chance. They were incredible and although you can't hear a lot of kind of shouting and screaming in the background, they're civilized but they're crazy...it's a good atmosphere."

The Hull City Hall gig the following night featured a set list which was identical to that of the Leeds show but the general consensus was reportedly that the Hull show simply did not measure up to the previous night's pyrotechnics. Who engineer Jon Astley told the Who fanzine *Generations*, "Pete wanted me to listen to Hull, but it's really not as good a show." It turned out that the decision as to which show would make the cut was made easier when it was discovered that parts of the bass track during the Hull gig did not record due to a faulty microphone. Technically, the recording of both shows was flawed: The *Live at Leeds* album cover even mentioned "Crackling Noises OK - Do Not Correct!" as the high end of Pete's guitar often distorted on the tape and various crackling sounds existed throughout. Pete was not impressed with Pye's unit nor their engineers: "They did a terrible job on the recording," he told *Rolling Stone*. "They fucked it up incredibly...they got crackles all the way through, horrible crackles. But I'm just going to put it out anyway."

Live at Leeds, released in May, reached a very satisfactory number 4 in the U.S., while attaining number 3 at home. The album received a great deal of praise in the press, and was later regarded as one of the finest live representations ever of a rock band. In his *New York Times* review, Nik

Cohn called *Leeds* "...the definitive hard-rock holocaust. It is the best live rock album ever made."[79]

"*Live At Leeds* was specifically designed to prick the pomposity of *Tommy* and display instead The Who's original tough edge," wrote Chris Charlesworth in 1983, "a side of the band that had become submerged amid the grandiloquence of the opera. Many newer fans could be excused for assuming The Who to be art rock dilettantes but *Live At Leeds* put matters back into perspective. It was gut-wrenching hard rock from start to finish, a timely reminder that The Who were first and foremost rockers at heart."

"In those days live albums were always 'live at the Colosseum in Rome' or 'live at the Palladium', 'Hollywood Bowl' etc.," Kit Lambert said.

> I said, 'live' isn't really like that. Touring is much seedier. So why didn't we think of 'live at Grimsby' or 'live at Mud on Sea' – bearing in mind that my father always said Morecambe on a wet Sunday afternoon is not the best place to conduct Scheherazade... I looked at the schedule and said 'You're in Hull on Wednesday and Leeds on Thursday, so it's going to be *Live at Hull* or *Live at Leeds*.' Things didn't go too well at Hull, so it had to be Leeds.

Live at Leeds "was the first Who album to ever come close to approximating the energy and drive of the band's live performances," John Swenson wrote in 1979.

> Daltrey sounded like a different singer altogether, certainly one of the most powerful rock vocalists. You can finally tell just what parts Townshend and Entwistle play in the group's stage sound as well – the only stereo effect on the record is that one channel is all Townshend, the other all

---

[79] Kit Lambert told journalist Alastair Reilly that Cohn wrote the review without hearing the album. "Nik, who had never even heard the album, said 'What would you like me to say? What about: "One of the best live albums ever made"?'," Lambert said. "I said 'Fine Nik, but why don't you come in here and hear it?' 'Oh that's not necessary,' he said, 'I've got a date.' Weeks passed and the album is released. I was over in New York... Eagerly perusing the paper in Nancy Lewis' flat... And having my usual Sunday breakfast, which consisted of an ounce of the very finest cocaine which was sitting on my left knee... When I got to the music pages by Nik Cohn, it said 'and now we get to the question of The Who album.' It said, 'I believe it to be the very finest live album to have ever been made.' I was so surprised that he had said this without ever having actually listened to the album, that I sprang into the air crying 'Eureka!', forgetting of course that I had an ounce of precious cocaine on my knee as I did so. It fell down in a thousand tiny snowflakes into the deep pile of the white carpet and vanished without trace. 'Nancy, quick,' [I said]. She had to grab me by the ankles and mow the lawn with me feverishly up and down, as I tried to snort the remaining £1,000-worth of coke from out of the carpet."

Entwistle. And Moon, as usual, came off with a spectacular flourish, his antic drumming the secret star of the show.

The album's plain brown cover – intended to look like a bootleg – doubled as a folder complete with a 'Tuesday nights at the Marquee' Maximum R&B poster and other assorted pieces of Who memorabilia from the band's early days. "That was just a brilliant idea by some designer who used to work at Track at the time, always coming up with nutty album sleeves," Pete told *Trouser Press* in 1980. "The first super-controversial album sleeve was the one with Lennon and Yoko naked on the front, and Track distributed that; and then they brought out the Hendrix one with all the naked birds on the front, and they were really into album covers and we weren't. We didn't really give a shit, despite the resident art-school member."

The sole detractor from the Who's first live effort was that the album, initially intended to be a two-disc affair, was reduced to only six songs. This situation was rectified in 1995 when MCA issued an expanded version on CD.

Live at Leeds showcased The Who's unique onstage chemistry in several examples of mid-song improvisation. The band's fourteen-minute version of *My Generation*, which included a taste of *Sparks* from *Tommy*, is a prime example. "I still feel that the *Sparks* section that we did on stage in *Live at Leeds* gets close to what's possible for that classical rock thing," Pete said in 1974. "I always imagine a classical conductor with his hair flying. The Who, and Keith especially, are capable of those classical flourishes – the expressive Wagnerian dynamics stuff."

The heavily distorted, full-throttle style of guitar work featured in *Live at Leeds* was viewed by many as the foundation of the heavy metal genre, something which didn't particularly flatter Pete, who later told *Guitar Player* that he'd trade "150 Def Leppards for 1 REM."

"The Who are not Led Zeppelin and we're not Deep Purple and we weren't responsible for heavy metal but a lot of people kind of draw that kind of line from *Live At Leeds* onwards," Pete told *Uncut*'s Simon Goddard in 2004.

I used to see Ritchie Blackmore carrying his guitar up and down my street when I was 14 or 15. ...*He* invented heavy metal. I didn't. He was doing it years before us and probably invented power chords as well. So I dunno why he's such a sullen, dark, evil motherfucker [grins].

We did *Tommy* on the road all over the world, we did *Live At Leeds* and then it was, 'Oh, The Who have invented heavy metal.' And then we were tied into this fucking thing of every show having to be more of a virtuoso explosion of energy than the one before. And after that, I believe The Who were just ruined.

With the live album in the can, the band didn't play another show for nearly two months. One benefit show featuring The Who, planned by John Lennon, was tentatively scheduled to take place on March 17 at the Royal Albert Hall, but it fell through when the venue's management refused to play host. During the break, Pete and the band reworked the live set. "We kicked *Tommy* out of the stage act," Pete told *Rolling Stone* in April. "We're doing rehearsals and recordings for the next two months to get some new numbers into the stage act and record them for a new album at the same time. We'll probably keep some of our numbers from *Tommy* like *Pinball Wizard* and stuff like that. We're doing some shows in England during this period, the next couple of months, to try it all out."

The band re-took the stage on April 18, 1970, at Leicester University in a continuing trend of playing to rather small venues in England. The Leicester show, before about 1600 fans, soon turned ugly. "We were playing in a small hall at Leicester University and there were a load of Hell's Angels idiot-dancing all over everyone," Pete later recalled. "It got to the point where they were causing such uproar we had to stop playing *Tommy*. It wasn't worth it, so to give the rest of the crowd some enjoyment we went into *Shakin' all Over*. The Angels tried to get on stage and one threw a bottle of Newcastle Brown which hit me in the head." Pete left the stage bleeding and received eight stitches at a local hospital. "...I think that if I had not been quite so pissed and quite so bloody," Pete told *Zigzag* in 1972, "I would have got stuck in a lot further and probably got a lot more badly hurt. Because I got hit on the head, and it bled a lot, I thought I'd better get to a hospital, but I was really wild; I broke my guitar across some geezer's collarbone but it didn't seem to do much to him – he had a ring in his nose, I remember."

The band resumed their U.K. university tour seven days later, on April 25 at Nottingham, then traveling to Dunstable, Exeter, Sheffield, Liverpool and Manchester Universities before ending at Lancaster University on Friday, May 15.

Two weeks after the release of *Live At Leeds*, The Who began their only U. S. tour of 1970. A four week affair, the trip began with two performances at New York's Metropolitan Opera House on June 7, 1970[80]. The Met's Opera Company Director, Rudolph Bing, was reportedly persuaded to put aside his initial reservations and accept The Who's booking after he listened to the *Tommy* album and was suitably impressed. "It must

---

[80] "[Kit Lambert's] proudest moment, he liked to boast, was when in 1970 *Tommy* became the first work of contemporary popular music to be performed to a capacity audience in the Metropolitan Opera House, New York," wrote *The Times*' Tony Palmer in Lambert's 1980 obituary. "His father would have savored the occasion."

have been the first time that the Metropolitan Opera House had the smell of pot smoke drifting around its gold chandeliers," Richard Barnes said.

The band received a particularly flattering appraisal of the show from an unlikely source – *Life* magazine:

> Rock music may have reached its all-time peak with the recent performance at the Metropolitan Opera of *Tommy*, the Who's opera about a deaf, dumb and blind pinball wizard who becomes a pop hero and martyr. A great leap across the gaps of generation, class and culture, the performance installed rock as a maturely rounded art in the shrine of the great European classics. It demonstrated the willingness of the Establishment in its most uptight organization to cooperate with the youth culture in its most drastic and uncompromising medium. Best of all, it afforded the Who – a great musical organization long in coming to fame – the opportunity to do brilliantly what no other rock group ever dreamed of doing.
>
> From the moment the boys walked onstage, it was obvious they were determined to give their greatest performance. Flashing their delightfully tawdry show tricks, they worked the Met as if it were a grind house in Yorkshire...Pete Townshend, a gawky, goony airplane mechanic in a white coverall, pogoed across the stage like Bugs Bunny riding an electric broom...Though the boys used every trick in the book to keep the crowd riveted on them, there was no gimmickry in their music. Of all rock groups, the Who has delved the deepest into the rock essence. They have reached now a level of accomplishment in their idiom directly comparable to the attainments of jazz musicians in theirs. Every song is grasped with authority, charged with energy, performed with flawless ensemble and fascinating solo work.
>
> It was just these gifts that forged the 20-odd numbers of *Tommy* into a compelling art work. They have been even more impressively evidenced by the Who's recent concerts, of which *Tommy* is the principal part...
>
> The instant they hit the final chord, the entire audience, thousands of freaks in fringes and tie-dyes, leaped to its feet in a stunning ovation. Townshend stammered a few words of gratitude, Moon and Entwistle engaged in a brief water battle, then the whole group jumped into a cycle of scorching encores. Whipped half-dead from this two-and-a-quarter-hour performance, as well as an equally long

matinee, Pete Townshend gathered his last energies to improvise an elaborate and moving coda, based on melodies from *Tommy*. As the audience sat spellbound, the concert resolved itself as a huge symphonic fantasia. When the gold curtain came looping down and the crystal chandeliers glimmered into light, 4,000 people had become one gargantuan child, stamping and chanting, "More! More! More!"

The audience's demands for more still poured forth even after the day's second show. "We did two shows each two and a half hours long," Pete told *Trouser Press* in 1980.

> That's the longest I've ever played; they were pretty close together and it was five hours of solid rock, not Grateful Dead stuff but heavy, exhausting stuff. We never did encores anyway, and I was told that we didn't have to do an encore if we didn't want to, but I should at least go on and thank the audience for their 15 minutes of spontaneous applause. Of course, their 15 minutes of spontaneous applause was about as spontaneous as an orgasm. It was extremely worked-on... I went to speak and someone threw a can of coke at me.

This prompted Pete to throw the mike stand into the crowd and bark, "After two fucking hours, boo to you too!"

The Who still played *Tommy* at their next stop, two shows at the Mammoth Gardens in Denver, Colorado, despite Pete's recent comments to the contrary to *Rolling Stone* and the Met posters touting the New York gig as the opera's last run-through. Pete had a frightening experience during his stay in Denver. "I had lost my temper with a groupie, who on my arrival at Denver presented me with a bottle of C.C. [Courvoisier Cognac] and maybe even herself (I should be so lucky)," Pete recalled in 1977.

> But I threw her out. I got a little worried that that wasn't the way to do things and wrote the above prayer [*Baba - when my fist clenches...crack it open*] which I later used in the bridge of *Behind Blue Eyes*... later that night in the same hotel, I was awakened by a small group of White Panthers who had come to violently avenge Abbie Hoffman, whom I threw offstage at Woodstock. I came very, very close to getting my head cracked open when I lost my temper with them (they were quite small people), then a giant emerged from the shadows in the hallway. He

was big, black, hated me and he called me chicken shit. Such is life that I ran for it.

When the summer tour arrived in California, Pete met up with some fellow Baba followers. "After I got into San Francisco and had comfortably settled into the hotel," Pete wrote in a 1970 *Rolling Stone* article, "the first person I met to cheer me up was John Sebastian [of Lovin' Spoonful fame]."

With his lady, they sparkled through the coffee shop, Mr. And Mrs. Tie Dye. They came to both shows in Berkeley and tie dyed a boiler suit for me...The show at Berkeley that night [16 June]...was the best we did in the States that tour. The sound was great, if a little loud for such a small place, and the crowd just super-aware and alive...After the show, I met a lot of Baba-friends...They were cool, and it goes without saying that they allowed me my pop star exhilaration that night as Keith and I and the gang destroyed what was left of our minds and bodies and hotel rooms that night.

In the morning I visited the Murshida. Her presence always astonishes me, it's easy to tell just how much high level work Baba is doing through her. Her eyes are calm and tired, but her life frantic and ordered. We talked about her work and my desire to make a film, of the special *Happy Birthday* record/magazine we had made in London to celebrate Baba's birthday. The Murshida had not taken to it with unqualified praise to say the least. I think she forgave me and my pals in the end for allowing our egos to breathe using Baba's name as an umbrella. He is so much like a father, like a friend, that it's easy to forget that he is also God Almighty. Being with Murshida reminded me of the fact, it always does. Next day Rick [Chapman] called me and took me in his '60 Continental into the 30-mile queue into Berkeley from S.F. There was a bus strike I think. First stop was a house called Meherstan which is the "light" center for young Berkeley Baba lovers... I talked a bit about *Tommy*, how it had all come about. I compared their center to our own in London, and we talked pretty formally about life with Baba in general. I talked about dope and my trip, why and how I had stopped using it, and watched knowing smiles from young people flash as I spoke of the new high that I was getting from being with Baba... After Meherstan we went to the home of Robert Dreyfuss, the guy Baba told to tell the West about dope, and I met several Baba lovers of the 20-year-oldish variety who seemed obsessed with chiropractry and small Indian cigarettes rolled out of a single tobacco leaf called *Beedies*, that smell just like dope.

Pete left the following morning to catch up with The Who in Texas. The tour continued on through Dallas and Houston, and included the Who's first performance in Memphis. Upon leaving Memphis on board an Eastern Airlines airplane, Richard Barnes recalled:

> During the tour Pete was talking to Pete Rudge, their U. S. tour manager about the success of *Live At Leeds*. As both were from Britain they easily understood Pete's fairly common term, "I heard it was going a bomb in New York," meaning it's going extremely well. However, they happened to be sitting on an Eastern Airlines plane waiting to take off from the runway at Memphis International Airport at the time of their conversation and a passing stewardess thought they were talking about a bomb on the plane. She told the pilot who radioed the control tower and the plane had to taxi to a secluded part of the airport where the 69 passengers were all taken off and searched along with all the luggage by police. An hour and 20 minutes later the plane left but Pete and co were still being questioned by police and FBI representatives[81].
>
> When they finally arrived at their destination, Atlanta, they found that their rooms booked at the hotel had been let out to some Eastern Star ladies there for a convention. Further, the equipment truck with their 4-ton PA was stuck miles away. The very exhausted Who didn't start the concert at Memorial Auditorium until after

---

[81] *NME* writer George Tremlett's account of the incident is somewhat different: "...The Who were waiting at the airport for a plane at a time when hijackings were becoming frequent," he wrote in his 1975 book, The Who. "An announcement was broadcast over the public address system that the plane would be delayed, and the loudspeaker nearby started to make a humming noise. As a gag, Townshend dropped to his knees in front of the speaker and said with mock tears: 'OK... OK... Turn it off... I confess... I'll tell you where I put the bomb.' A passing stewardess thought this was a real hi-jacker – and at once the airport was sealed off, the plane was cancelled, and Pete was hauled away for two hours' questioning by the F.B.I." "We didn't know it," Entwistle told Tremlett, "but Martin Luther King had been shot in Memphis – and his father was traveling on that plane. Pete would never have cracked a gag like that had he known – but you can see why the F.B.I. were so worried. They really put Pete through it."

midnight. However practically the whole 6,000 audience stayed and waited.

The James Gang opened for The Who on several shows during this tour, and Pete developed a friendship with their guitarist, Joe Walsh, with whom he was duly impressed. "Joe Wash is definitely one of the best guitarists in Rock that I've come across," Pete wrote later that year, adding that "his playing makes my neck tingle like only Jimi Hendrix has affected it before."

The U. S. tour continued, in all 22 shows in four weeks to ecstatic crowds. The resultant reviews were equally liberal with praise. "As they moved methodically across the country, the Who left a wake of mind-blown, disbelieving Who converts," wrote Richard Barnes in 1982.

> ...the press reviews were almost competing with themselves for superlatives to describe the Who live. The *San Francisco Examiner*: "They had just heard the finest two hour concert of contemporary music of their lives. They knew it. The Who knew it...Exaggeration? I cannot exaggerate perfection." The *Maryland Democrat* went even further: "...UNBELIEVABLE! REMARKABLE! OUTSTANDING!...or anything else you want to call better than the best was the Who concert at the Spectrum Philadelphia." The *San Francisco Chronicle* eulogized, "...The Who show at Berkely Community Theatre was absolutely staggering in its emotional and musical power...writing about their music is something of an exercise in futility. It need not be explained to those who were there, it cannot be explained to those that were not. If a single word can sum it up, that word is 'shattering.'"

With the success of *Tommy, Live at Leeds,* and The Who's ensuing live work, Pete's confidence soared. "As well as being a major milestone for The Who, *Tommy* was also very much Pete Townshend's own personal achievement; it was recognition of this which confirmed his reputation as a creative musician and brought him to the very forefront of rock music, not only in Britain but internationally," wrote the *NME*'s George Tremlett. "Like Bob Dylan and John Lennon, he was mentally and intellectually prepared for it – a tough, determined, ambitious, even ruthless person on the surface, but articulate and idealistic, possessing a conscience, intensely political, well-read, classically aware, and content in his private life."

Pete, however, was also aware that he was responsible for continuing The Who's forward momentum on past *Tommy* to their next challenge. "Until we made *Tommy* we had largely been our own bosses,"

Pete said in 1974. "Suddenly all that changed – for the first time in our lives we were really successful, really taken over the by the audience, and we had to do as we were told. America, the great consumer nation, told us, 'There are 50 million kids over here that want to see you perform. What are you going to do about it – stay in Twickenham and work on your next album, or come on over here and perform?' So we went on over and got involved in the standing ovations and the interviews, the 19-page *Rolling Stone* article, the presentations of the Gold Albums, all that. It took two years to work on anything new."

Chapter 5

"CHANGE. Is it really possible to change anything with music, or to even ease society into a position where what they listen to can change what they feel? Rock is capable of doing amazing things...The only time I am spurred to action is when I feel that I can change the world through Rock, via the Who, via music. We want to change people by taking them UP."
- Pete Townshend, 1971

"For me, what's important about Lifehouse is ...the whole business, the whole process, the whole story, is about what makes this whole thing about pop music, rock music and a rock band, different from the music that went before, different from the art that went before, different from popular art of today...what makes it stand out and, in fact, what makes it the vertebrae of modern life..."
- Pete Townshend, 1999

"Was Lifehouse some attempt create Utopia and really get everybody to live at the Young Vic and have Utopia right there on the ground? Or was it just an excuse to stay up late and do crazy things with all this great equipment you've got, or what was it? Beats me."
- Dave Marsh, 1999

In the latter half of 1970, Pete began a monthly *Melody Maker* column entitled *The Pete Townshend Page* which ran for nine months. The column, which often displayed Pete's self-deprecating sense of humor and his refreshing humility, also became a veritable bulletin board of ideas which were whirling around inside Townshend's brain, some of which were soon to become the next project for the Who.

In the first installment, printed in the August 22 *Melody Maker*, a vacationing Pete explained, "I'm beginning my first page of this bulky journal in particularly strange surroundings. On holiday I am, far away from the sounds of London's traffic and Keith Moon on an island in the Blackwater Estuary called Osea..."

> The most exciting thing about Osea Island is probably the causeway that you have to drive over to reach it. It's over a mile long and is just about revealed for a few hours each low tide for the milkman and postman to make a mad dash across, make their rounds and get back again. As you drive over the sea splashes over the front of the car and you feel a bit like a sea captain at the bridge as starfish and crabs come hurtling through the windows. I'm hoping that the messenger who comes all the way from *Melody Maker* to collect this trivia doesn't throttle me when he realizes he'll have to spend twelve hours looking at a ten acre caravan site before he can get back home again...

Despite the levity of the column, Pete was simply limbering up prior to conveying his latest ideas. With the recent success of *Tommy*, Townshend had witnessed firsthand the power of rock music, and his faith in the medium was boundless. "Rock," Pete wrote, "follows with alarming accuracy the moods and whims, the ups and downs of its listening age group. It REFLECTS, like a rather dusty mirror, the changes that are going on, many of which escape the conscious minds of even the men who write the music." However, he wrote, "...whatever Rock causes or excites in men, it is only catalysing emotions and actions around what is already in them."

Pete's confidence in rock's ability to change society was unshakable. "It [rock] can face up to trouble without giving a hint that it really is affected," he commented in early 1971, "and exhibits carefree attitudes on the surface, or maybe even deep down inside, at the same time it is CHANGING things. Usually for the better, unlike most political change." Pete's observations regarding the power of rock music and its' effect on the audience (and vice versa) lay at the root of his next project, which was ultimately known as *Lifehouse*. He spent the next few months gathering his thoughts as he pondered the band's next move. Meanwhile, The Who were back on the road.

Pete had recently bought a motor home, and was traveling in it from show to show. "From the cab of Maxine the Motor Home I begin this month's essay," read the opening sentence of Pete's September installment of *The Pete Townshend Page*. "Maxine is a large and lovely meat wagon with blood red striping, she comes from the US of A and is what we British would call a motor caravan." A photograph of Pete driving 'Maxine' is featured on the cover of his 2000 release, *Lifehouse Elements*. "I bought the thing to ride in at the Isle of Wight," Pete wrote. "You know, ask in the other groups for tea and cakes..."

> When we first arrived backstage at the IOW there was a good, low class mood in the air. It was easy though to detect that it would have little to do with what was going on out in the audience. Before we left our cozy hotel the barmaid had noticed Keith's white clothes and said, "You're not going to wear those nice clean things OUT THERE are you?" As though he was off into battle.
>
> The press had ruined a lot of people's potential happy weekend by exaggerating reports of water shortage and security trouble...I read the papers too and got nervous and we didn't take the baby. When I got there I realised what a fool I was. This wasn't a battle, or an invasion. It wasn't a gathering of anarchists, nor even really a running gamut of tired Rock Artists in the usual festival tradition. It was a weekend on an island for a lot of young HUMAN BEINGS...The fact that the young people of today do things together in large numbers without the organization of a field marshall is regarded suspiciously by all these days.

On Saturday August 29, 1970, a week after the first *Pete Townshend Page* had hit the stands, The Who, billed along with the Doors, played the third Isle of Wight Festival. Pete and the band, who had provided their huge PA system[82] for the whole festival, took the stage at about 2 am on Sunday morning and it was after 5 when their set ended. "At the IOW festival I met Mike Wadleigh the director and innovator of the Woodstock movie," Pete wrote in September. "It was greatly embarrassing for me to hear him announce that the cameraman's bum I had kicked off the stage during our show at Woodstock had belonged to him. Bearing in mind that we have some great work done for us in the Who sequence in the film I figure he cannot be a man that holds a grudge. Lesson for Abbie."

The band left the audience of 600,000 with a memorable performance, although Pete wasn't happy with the show. "...our performance dwindled quietly and ineffectually away at the IOW," he explained.

> We had played far too long, nearly three hours, making it hard for Sly [& the Family Stone] to follow playing to such a weary audience and leaving the stage on an anticlimactic note rather than an excited one...

---

[82] "Their PA alone takes up one gigantic truck – and the guitar amps occupy another," Chris Charlesworth wrote in a November, 1970 *Melody Maker* article entitled 'Whole Lotta Who Gear'. Pete was now using four 4 x 12 cabinets topped with two 100-watt Hiwatt amplifiers. The entire PA system, which Bob Pridden estimated at costing £5,000, had an output of up to 2,000 watts.

We have deliberately cut down our act to leave us more energy to cope with the most important part of the show. The finale. It doesn't matter how well you play, if you don't leave on the right foot you may as well not bother.

The Who followed the Isle of Wight show with several mid-September dates in Germany, the Netherlands and Denmark prior to returning to Britain for a two month, 23-date tour, the highlights of which Pete reported on *The Pete Townshend Page*. "Our show at Purley Orchid Ballroom was quite an experience," Pete wrote of the October 8 show. "I came closer to complete physical exhaustion than I ever have before at a performance and yet we are playing a slightly shorter show on this tour... The last time we played there was so long ago I can't remember, and as we walked through the audience to the stage, surrounded by bouncers, I heard elderly mods asking for *I Can't Explain* and *Substitute* with such zest that I began to believe they were new releases."

The first two days of the tour were an education for me. I took my Motor Caravan and attempted to gypsy the gigs at Cardiff and Manchester... After taking six hours to reach Cardiff I looked in at the Sophia Gardens where we were to perform to find out what time we were due on.
Finding out I had three hours to spare I decided to look for an AA [Automobile Association] approved caravan park that was close to the city centre according to my map. Off I went, driving for nearly an hour with no success. Eventually I dropped into a friendly cop shop where they gave me complicated but explicit directions. I followed them carefully and eventually arrived at the site. Checking in, paying my seven and six and getting a set of keys to the bog I enquired how to get to the Sophia Gardens as I would be getting back late – and would the gates be open? "Oh, there's no need to worry about the gates," the smiling warden said as I contemplated the last ninety minutes driving. "Sophia Gardens is right next door, in fact you can see it from here."
Despite this terrible indignity I hurriedly walked off to the gig with me boiler suit under me arm feeling like a local Welsh lad made good, and checked in. The James Gang were about to play and I went to watch. I got as far as their first few bars. The bass player's amp stopped working after he'd played only three notes and the impact of their incredible opener, *Funk #49*, was dampened. I didn't watch

anymore, feeling like maybe I was a jinx, and waited till they came off stage a little disenchanted with the equipment we had lent them (BLUSH).

The crowd in Cardiff were "incredible," Pete wrote. "It was the first airing of the now shortened *Tommy* in Wales and we enjoyed the show as much as we have ever." The tour drew typically positive reviews. "When Chelsea play at Stamford Bridge, the cheers filter up into the skies like nowhere else," read *Melody Maker*'s review of the October 29 show. "So it was with the Who at Hammersmith Palais on Thursday. Playing on their home ground for the first time in years, the world's most exciting stage act finished their tour with all the stops out."

Full of confidence and new ideas for his beloved rock music (the importance of which he emphasized by writing it with a capital R), Pete Townshend was ready to move forward after two straight years of playing *Tommy* live. "After the James Gang tour," Pete told *Disc and Music Echo* in October, "we'll only be doing occasional gigs, just to keep a hand in. To be very, very honest we're getting a little bit bored with our current material. The first few gigs of the tour were really nice to play. They were such good halls and sympathetic audiences. But the gigs are getting almost like 9 to 5. And *Tommy* is becoming a bit thin...we are always very conscious of what we are doing and we are beginning to wonder whether people are bored with it. So we are getting off the road to concentrate on other things." The Who's last performance of *Tommy* in its entirety (until it was revived in 1989) took place at The Roundhouse in North London on December 20. Elton John opened.

Meanwhile, *Lifehouse* was taking shape. Pete had written a script[83], and had also broached his latest idea to Universal Studios. The concept was, "a rock film which encompassed a fictional story melded together with live concert footage of The Who," according to Matt Kent, who interviewed Pete about *Lifehouse* in August 1999. "The result he felt would move rock away from the commercial excesses it was only really just beginning to find itself exposed to and place it back firmly in the hands of the audience, where he felt it belonged."

The band had been working on a new album at Pete's home studio, recording *I Don't Even Know Myself*, *Now I'm A Farmer*, *Water*, *Naked Eye*, and John Entwistle compositions *Heaven and Hell* and *Postcard* over the previous year. "*Water* is one of the heaviest things The Who have ever done," Pete said in October. "It's relaxed and fantastically solid, not screaming and wailing guitars. The other tracks we did for the LP are *Naked Eye*, which we did for a while on stage, then we dropped, and *Heaven*

---

[83] Daltrey recalled in 1999 that the script "...didn't make any sense, none of us could grasp it, but it had some good ideas in it."

and Hell which we did a good version of. A crappy version of it was on the B side of the last single." The album was scrapped in the autumn as *Lifehouse* gained momentum. "We've pulled it out because of other ideas floating around," Pete recalled. "...We've done six tracks, about 1 ½ sides. But when we started work on it, Kit (Lambert) was ill. Since then Kit's come up with the idea for an album with a film. I've got an LP of music but I don't know if the structure of the story is strong enough to hold a film. We won't get back together until next year, but there's definitely an album there."

An E.P. containing four of the previously recorded songs was planned, then later scrapped, with Pete concentrating on pushing forward with his combined film/album project. "What I want to do," Pete commented at the time, "is to attempt a follow-through and achieve something which will have as big an impact as *Tommy* did."

The *Lifehouse* storyline was based around a central theme which Pete explained in *Melody Maker*. "Here's the idea," he wrote in the September *Pete Townshend Page*:

> ...there's a note, a musical note, that builds the basis of existence somehow...
>
> This note pervades everything, it's an extremely wide note, more of a hiss than a note as we normally know them. The hiss of the air, of activity, of the wind and of the breathing of someone near. You can always hear it.
>
> Andy Newman told me once how people cannot bear to spend too much time in anechoic chambers because of the horror of complete silence. Anechoic chambers are not only completely silent but all sound that is produced within them is sort of swallowed up by absolutely non reflective walls and ceilings. You shout but you hardly hear yourself!
>
> At midnight when you lay in bed, gently falling into sleep, it gets louder not quieter. It doesn't seem to come through the ears and the air, but it is made up of elements that are. Finally, when it reaches deafening proportions you are asleep, drowned in sound... The key to this unexciting adventure that I'm leading you on is that everybody hears it. Moreover I think everybody hears the same note or noise. It's an amazing thing to think of any common ground between all men that isn't directly a reflection of spiritual awareness... It's a note, it's notes, it's music - the most beautiful there is to hear.

Pete's explanation of this theory is relatively clear and understandable. However, the more he explained, the muddier the picture became. "I've got kind of a pivot idea," he told *Disc and Music Echo* in October, "basically based on physics, closely linked with the things mystics have been saying for a long time about vibrations in music." This became the theme of *Lifehouse*.

> It's a cyclic idea, a bit lame at the moment. But I've got some songs which are similar in potential, just like *Amazing Journey, Sensation, Pinball Wizard* and *...I'm Free* were to *Tommy*. From those songs the whole thing devolved [The three songs were *The Note, We're Moving* and *The Two Of Us*, two of which became *Pure and Easy*, and *Going Mobile*]. It's about a set of musicians, a group who look like The Who, and behave remarkably like The Who, and they have a roadie who is desperately interested in ideals for humanity. It's basically a science-fiction fantasy idea. This roadie is wrapped up in electronics and synthesizers. He is fantastically serious about finding 'The Note' and spends all his time converting Egyptian charts and musical mysticism into an electronic circuitry – and discovers all these wonderful and weird oscillations... Anyway, this group find a note which, basically, creates complete devastation. And when everything is destroyed, only the real note, the true note that they have been looking for, is left. Of course, there is no one left to hear it, except the audience, of course, who are in a rather privileged position.

"It's a sort of futuristic fantasy, a bit science fiction," Pete told the *New York Times* in February.

> It takes place in about 20 years, when everybody has been boarded up inside their houses and put in special garments, called experience suits, through which the government feed them programs to keep them entertained[84]. Then Bobby comes along. He's an electronics wizard and takes over a disused rock theater, renames it the Lifehouse and sets it up as an alternative to the government programs.

---

[84] "In *Tommy*, I achieved the hero's spiritual isolation by making him deaf, dumb and blind," Pete wrote during an online chat on www.barnesandnoble.com in May, 2000. "In *Lifehouse*, I achieved the same isolation for the entire human race by placing the majority of them on a worldwide grid [through] which they experienced all their entertainment and important educational life experiences."

Next, he chooses a basic audience of about 300 people and prepares a chart for each of them, based on astrology and their personalities and other data; and from their charts he arrives at a sound for each of them – a single note or a series, a cycle or something electronic – anything that best expresses each individual...I don't want to go into incredible detail, because I'll probably change it all; but the basic idea is that Bobby takes these sounds and builds on them and through them the audience begins to develop. First they attain a state of harmony, then a state of enlightenment and they keep growing all the time.

On the Lifehouse stage there is a rock group, which will be the Who, to comment on the sounds and celebrate them. But they aren't the heroes and neither is Bobby. The real center is the equipment itself, the amps and tapes and synthesizers, all the machines, because they transmit the sounds; The hardware is the hero. Anyhow, the Lifehouse gets more and more intense, until Bobby takes over the government programs and replaces them with the new sounds, so that everyone wearing the experience suits gets plugged into them and shares them, and it goes on – the sounds keep developing, the audience keeps attaining higher states and, in the end, all the sounds merge into one, like a massive square dance. And everyone starts bouncing up and down together, faster and faster, wilder and wilder, closer and closer and closer. And finally it gets too much, the energy, and they actually leave their bodies. They disappear.

Since the history of the *Lifehouse* project is rife with tales of confusion and misunderstanding of the ideas involved, I offer one additional description of the story. In an article entitled 'An Introduction To *Lifehouse*,' Townshend described the story of *Lifehouse* "as it was presented to The Who in 1971," in a 1999 article in *The Richmond Review*:

A self-sufficient, drop-out family group farming in a remote part of Scotland decide to return South to investigate rumors of a subversive concert event that promises to shake and wake up apathetic, fearful British society. Ray is married to Sally, they hope to link up with their daughter Mary who has run away from home to attend the concert. They travel through the scarred wasteland of middle England in a motor caravan, running an air-conditioner they hope will protect them from pollution.

They listen, furtively, to old rock records which they call 'Trad'. Up to this time they have survived as farmers, tolerated by the government who are glad to buy most of their produce. Those who have remained in urban areas suffer repressive curfews and are more-or-less forced to survive in special suits, like space-suits, to avoid the extremes of pollution that the government reports.

These suits are interconnected in a universal grid, a little like the modern Internet, but combined with gas-company pipelines and cable-television-company wiring. The grid is operated by an imperious media conglomerate headed by a dictatorial figure called Jumbo who appears to be more powerful than the government that first appointed him. The grid delivers its clients' food, medicine and sleeping gas. But it also keeps them entertained with lavish programming so highly compressed that the subject can 'live out' thousands of virtual lifetimes in a short space of time. The effect of this dense exposure to the myriad dreamlike experiences provided by the controllers of the grid is that certain subjects begin to fall apart emotionally. Either they believe they have become spiritually advanced, or they feel suffocated by what feels like the shallowness of the programming, or its repetitiveness. A vital side-issue is that the producers responsible for the programming have ended up concentrating almost entirely on the story-driven narrative form, ignoring all the arts unrestrained by 'plot' as too complex and unpredictable, especially music. Effectively, these arts appear to be banned. In fact, they are merely proscribed, ignored, forgotten, no longer of use.

A young composer called Bobby hacks into the grid and offers a festival-like music concert – called the lifehouse – which he hopes will impel the audience to throw off their suits (which are in fact no longer necessary for physical survival) and attend in person. 'Come to the lifehouse, your song is here.'

The family arrive at the concert venue early and take part in an experiment Bobby conducts in which each participant is both blueprint and inspiration for a unique piece of music or song which will feature largely in the first event to be hacked onto the grid.

When the day of the concert arrives a small army force gathers to try to stop the show. They are prevented from entering for a while, the concert begins, and indeed many of those 'watching at home' are inspired to leave their suits. But eventually the army break in. As they do so, Bobby's musical experiment reaches its zenith and everyone in the building, dancing in a huge dervish circle, suddenly disappears. It emerges that many of the audience at home, participating in their suits, have also disappeared.

The abstract ideas Pete presented, especially in the story's ending, were hard for many to grasp. Accepting that the audience simply disappeared was difficult for many to swallow. "There is no dramatic corollary," Pete added in 1999. "I didn't try to explain where they may have gone, or whether they were meant to be dead or alive. I simply wanted to demonstrate my belief that music could set the soul free, both of the restrictions of the body, and the isolating impediments and encumbrances of the modern world."

But Pete's grasp of – and commitment to – the concept was unquestionable. Over the next three months he went in to a creative frenzy, writing and recording demos for about twenty songs – both at his home studio and that of John Entwistle – which tied in with his recently completed film script. Pete's song *The Note* became *Pure and Easy*, which stated the theme of the entire project. "*Pure and Easy* is a very pivotal track for the *Lifehouse* project," Pete said in 1996, "and it begins, "*There once was a note, pure and easy*," and this was inspired by a piece of writing by the Sufi teacher Inyat Kahn, who was also a musician, so a lot of his writing was about vibration and music, about the spiritual search being wrapped up in the idea that we're looking for a note which suits us all. And at some point this got misinterpreted by people that what I was writing about was the lost chord. I don't know what the lost chord is," he laughed. "A minor 7th with the 5th augmented, I expect – and it's probably a good thing that it's lost."

This group of demos were of exceptional quality, with much of the original synthesizer work being retained for use on the finished Who recordings. "The demos I made to accompany the *Lifehouse* film script I wrote in '71 are among the best I have ever produced," Pete commented in 1983[85]. "I had come fully to grips with working multi-track... I had managed to get a good tight drum sound in a room only ten feet by fifteen that was crammed with synthesizers, organs and a seven foot grand piano," although he admitted that he was "still coming to grips with the incredibly rich harmonics" of his new ARP 2500 synthesizer.

Pete, aware that his initial musings on *Lifehouse* were met with confusion, acknowledged to *Record World* that his ideas at present were "abstract," and required "physical testing." He planned to develop

---

[85] Glyn Johns agreed with this assertion. "Pete's demos were always fantastic and were always a challenge," he told an interviewer in 1999. "...very often I'd listen to the song that we were about to cut and I'd go, "How the hell am I going to compete with that?" Really, really brilliant demos..."

Lifehouse by performing some experimental shows in front of a small audience, and set about searching for a suitable venue. After looking at an old cinema, a closed gaming and billiards club, and even considering purchasing and converting a house, Pete settled on the Young Vic Theatre in London, which had just opened in September.[86] The theater held only 450 people and this intimacy attracted Townshend, who also liked the venue's stage, which ran down the center of the auditorium. The Young Vic featured an "…almost Shakespearian-styled stage area and audience tiers," according to *Record Mirror*, who explained that "The room is octagonal, built from roughly scored concrete blocks." In addition, Pete enjoyed the fact that the theater attracted, "a completely mixed up crowd, part theatrical hangers-on, part freaks, part Who fans," as he told the *New York Times* in 1971.

"Pete came along here some months ago to see *Waiting For Godot*," the Young Vic's artistic director Frank Dunlop told *Record Mirror* in January, "and then he brought the rest of The Who, and they were enthusiastic too. It was this that prompted them to give a concert and we threw the doors open and let anyone come who wanted to dance to the music." This show took place on January 4, 1971.

Pete's plans for using the Young Vic were simple. "I knew what I needed and I was just waiting for the money to come," Pete told Matt Kent in 1999, referring to the $2 million reportedly promised him by Universal Pictures to make a *Lifehouse* film produced by Kit Lambert and Chris Stamp. Pete explained that, as one of the Young Vic's board members, he could have bought the Young Vic out with a portion of the funds from Universal, or provided money for the theatre to stage productions. "…I knew exactly what was going on and I knew that they couldn't mount productions without money," he told Kent.

> I said to Frank Dunlop if you give us this theater for a couple of months, so we'd get to the point where we'd have a bit of a daily thing going here… we'd written some songs and we'd play to people who were coming in every day because they want to see how their music was coming on… we could take a portion of money from the budget and put it in the grant for them and you could use it for your first production of *Waiting For Godot* or whatever it is you want to do. That side of it was very, very clear. My problem

---

[86] Kit Lambert introduced Pete to the Young Vic's director, Frank Dunlop. "…through our meeting at AD8, a gay restaurant in Kensington frequented by Rudolf Nureyev, I became a patron [of the Young Vic]," Pete wrote in 1999. "I give this snapshot not to deepen the impression that I enjoyed a bisexual life with ballet dancers, but rather to show that I moved in exalted circles of wildly willful, imaginative and creative people, and when I spoke to anyone about *Lifehouse* socially, they were encouraging and enthused."

with the artistic director then, Frank Dunlop, was that he thought, by holding a press conference when he did the first couple of days, that he could push forward the creative side of the production. What it actually did was to really put me on the spot and it confused the band.

The press conference took place at The Young Vic on January 13. "We are intending to produce a fiction, or a play or an opera and create a completely different kind of performance in rock," Pete said that day.

> We are writing a story and we aim to perform it on the first day we start work in this theater. Tied in with the whole idea is the use of quadrophonic sound and pre-recorded tapes. About 400 people will be involved with us and we aim to play music which represents them... Rock's real power as a liberational force is completely untapped... so a new type of theater, a new type of performance has to be devised to present it... If a film of this is made, it will become the first real rock film... because it will reflect a reality.

"The press conference was the beginning of the end," Pete lamented in his article for the *Richmond Review* in 1999. "I was portrayed by some as confused when I was merely tired, and by some as arrogant when I was merely deeply committed to the idea that the story would work, that The Who could pull it off."

Pete's plans regarding the audience's interaction with the band were involved with his recent discovery of synthesizers, the use of which he'd been studying in earnest of late. He considered the synthesizer the perfect tool for interpreting an individual's personality into music. He'd been experimenting with synthesizers with the aim of being able to "mechanically reflect the basic information about an individual, like height, weight or astrological detail, in music," Pete told *Rolling Stone* in August, 1971.

"While I was working on the *Lifehouse* script I actually did a lot of experiments with sounds that were produced from natural body rhythms," Pete told *Penthouse* in 1983.

> I was working with the musical bursar of Cambridge University at the time. What we did was ask some individuals a lot of questions about themselves and then subject them to the sort of test a G.P. [General Practitioner] might undertake. We measured their heartbeat and the alpha and beta rhythms of the brain; we even took down astrological details and other kinds of shit. Then we

took all the data we'd collected on paper or charts and converted them into music, and the end result was sometimes quite amazing. In fact, one of the pulse-modulated frequencies we generated was eventually used as the background beat to *Won't Get Fooled Again*. Later I used another one of the pulse-modulated frequencies as the foundation for *Baba O'Riley*.

The use of synthesizers in 1971 was a huge step forward for The Who, and one that wasn't without considerable risk for a band who'd been known as a straight ahead, no-frills four-piece. Pete's insistence that rock music needed to change was reflected in his use of the newest technology available. He was truly pushing the envelope. "It really doesn't seem to be worth doing anything to me," Pete wrote in the February 13 installment of *The Pete Townshend Page*, "unless it can either do something for Rock or do something for its audience. The Who's coming performances and film work at the Young Vic will do both. Nothing can't happen. Basically what we do could change our audience, our music, our status, and even the way we walk. If it all doesn't change anything else it will change me."

The Who set about creating new sounds for their audience, not only with synthesizers, but with a quadrophonic PA system, and a complex prerecorded tape rig, all of which were in keeping with the project's futuristic theme[87]. "Great quantities of electronic equipment were moved into the theater," *Zigzag* reported. "We developed an amazing set of hardware," Pete told *Rolling Stone* at the time. "I spent £12,000 on synthesizers alone. You know in FM radio they have cartridges where, as soon as you hit the button, out comes music? We've got this system where I've got this row of foot pedals, and when I hit one something just comes out. It might be a brass band, a full orchestra, a plane going by, an explosion, whatever."

With all of the writing of demos and a movie script, the incorporation of (at the time) mind-boggling technology, and numerous interviews which outlined The Who's plans for *Lifehouse*, exactly what Pete and the band expected to achieve at the Young Vic remained unclear. Pete certainly wanted an unprecedented level of interaction and commitment from his audience. "I don't mean that I seriously expect people to leave their bodies but I think we might go further than rock concerts have gone before," Pete told the *New York Times* in February.

---

[87] Pete's view of the future as presented in *Lifehouse* included some eerily sharp observations regarding the use of computers. His "grid" was an almost dead-on portrayal of the internet. "I saw it all coming," Pete told the *New York Post*'s Dan Aquilante in July, 2000, tongue firmly in cheek. "I mustn't take credit for it. In college in the 1960's, I took a course in cybernetic theory taught by Roy Ascot. It was he who gave me my grip on what the future was."

> I know that when live rock is at its best, which often means the Who, it stops being just a band playing up front and the audience sitting there like dummies. It's an interaction which goes beyond performance. We aren't like superstars, we're only reflective surfaces. We might catch an energy and transmit it, but the audience doesn't take more from us than we take from them, not when the gig really works. That's what we want to take further at the Young Vic: we want to see how far the interaction can be taken. At first we will be playing there every Monday, but if the experiment works, if people keep coming back and going along with it, we might step it up to two or three or four nights a week, whatever is necessary. By the end of six months, anything might happen.

"I had planned to conduct rather simple experiments during these concerts producing pieces of music for some loyal audience members," Pete recalled in 1999.

> I had no hope of producing anything like the expansive music I had envisioned and attempted to describe in my fiction, but certain people around me believed that was my target. Whispers of 'madness' fluttered backstage like moths eating at the very fabric of my project.

While Pete's expectations of what the Young Vic experiments would yield remained open ended, he pushed onward, undaunted. "The aim is change," Pete wrote in the February *Pete Townshend Page*, "A change of life style for the band, a change of focus for our audience and a change in the balance of power that Rock wields. The music we play has to be tomorrow's, the things we say have to be today, and the reason for bothering is yesterday. The idea is to make the first real superstar. The first real star who can really stand and say that he deserves the name. That star would be us all."

> The Young Vic becomes the 'Life House,' the Who become musicians and the audience become part of a fantasy. We have invented the fantasy in our minds, the ideal, and now we want to make it happen for real. We want to hear the music we have dreamed about, see the harmony we have experienced temporarily in Rock become permanent, and feel the things we are doing CHANGE the face of Rock and then maybe even people.

There is a story connected with each person that will walk into the Life House, but for now we have made one up for them, until we know the real one. We have music that will stimulate them to stay with us through lengthy marathon concerts, and perhaps even boring filming. We have sounds ready that will push us a lot further than we have ever gone before, but what the result will be is still unknown.

Our hero is Bobby, the mystic-cum-roadie that puts all the fantasies in our heads into action, and gets results...

The efforts of the super roadie and their astonishing outcome can be watched, and augmented by your own efforts at the Young Vic. I'll tell you when.

As he'd done with *Tommy*, Pete had now talked so much about *Lifehouse*, he had to deliver the goods. He had created quite a buzz in the music industry, fixing countless eyes on The Who in anticipation of their next move. After a preview show at the Young Vic the previous night, The Who began a regular Monday night booking at the theater on February 15, fully intending to increase the frequency of their appearances there to several nights a week as the *Lifehouse* experiment evolved. They dabbled in quadrophonic sound and produced their new music with the assistance of backing tapes, and some live synthesizer work from Pete. However, several factors combined to derail *Lifehouse* in very short order.

While Pete had been talking of his *Lifehouse* ideas for months now, the rest of the band still didn't appear sold on the project. "...I could explain it to Roger and John and Keith, and they'd say, "Oh I get it, you put these suits on and you put a penny in the slot and you get wanked off"," Pete told *Q*'s John Harris in 1996. "I'd go, "No, no, it's much bigger than that." "Oh, I get it, you get wanked off *and* you get a Mars bar shoved up your bum. I get it." "No, no, no, it's bigger than that, man..." When I delivered the first draft of the script, Roger said, "This'll never work, this film." I said, "Why?", and he said, "You could never get that much wire." That kind of thing did send me over the edge."

Daltrey also wasn't particularly enamored with Townshend's newfound infatuation with synthesizers. "Roger...wanted to go back to what was safe," Pete said in 1999, explaining that Daltrey was dubious about the band's use of synthesizers and backing tapes, preferring the traditional guitar/bass/drums approach. "...the fact of the matter was that we had done *Live At Leeds* and we had done guitar, bass and drums," Pete contended. "Cream had done it and Jimi Hendrix had done it... Nobody wanted it, everyone was fed up with four hour guitar solos, so I was really trying to do something new and innovative and also, in a sense, give ourselves something which would honor the fact that we were one of the few bands that could go into a film company and get a budget."

This confusion also applied to the band's management ("It wasn't an idea I can clearly remember everyone thinking *yeah* about," Stamp said in 1999), and even their publicist. "It always worried me that I couldn't grasp fully what the impact of *Lifehouse* was, because of my job as The Who's press agent, and I felt that I should make an effort to understand and comprehend this very complex idea," Keith Altham said in 1999. "And I felt a lot less bad about it when I realized so many other people who were exceptionally brighter than I was… couldn't grasp it either."

The audience wasn't sold on the band's new approach either. Rather than interacting enthusiastically with the band, the audience at the Young Vic seemed content in their traditional roles as mere spectators, happy to enjoy the music of The Who, but not particularly willing to participate in the proceedings. "People were quite happy to sit and listen to what we were doing," Pete recalled in 1999. "In the end it was we who said… 'Ah, fuck it. Let's get this place rocking.'" The audience's indifference "really crushed" Pete, according to *Zigzag*. "That audience should have been directly involved with the shows, responsible for inspiring the music even," the 1974 article read. "It was clearly too much for a random selection of skinheads who, despite being told that the event was experimental, expected The Who to perform as they always had." Or, as John Entwistle put it, "They wanted us to play *My Generation* and smash guitars."

Townshend disagrees. "They were so little they didn't know who The Who were," he said in 1999. "The idea that we played a bunch of Who hits to keep them quiet is bollocks because they wouldn't have known us from Adam, they were schoolchildren."

Another factor contributing to the demise of the *Lifehouse* experiments was the fact that the previously mentioned money Pete was expecting from Universal Pictures never arrived. "I had written a script, which Universal Pictures had read and apparently understood: they had promised me two million dollars," Pete recalled almost thirty years later.

> Then there was silence. I came up against my first real brick wall since I had started writing and acting as spokesman for The Who and many in their audience. Until then I had felt omnipotent, I hope not arrogantly. But that wall that rose up between me and my *Lifehouse* film stood up to every energetic idea I threw at it. I could not work out what to do.

"I was hoping for, at a maximum, to have gone in there [the Young Vic] for a couple of months," Pete said in 1999, "but I thought I would get a couple of weeks out of it, particularly if I could pay for it. What happened was that no money came, I sat and waited and waited and no money came." He pointed out that the theater was available to the band before its opening in September, if only the money would have arrived. "...we had the Young Vic for as long as we wanted before it opened, as long as we wanted," he lamented. "I used to go down there every day, it was empty for week after week after week." By the time The Who decided to begin the Young Vic shows without the money, the band's selection of available evenings was extremely limited. "My intention was to use the place for as long as I could get it and was really bitterly disappointed when Frank Dunlop announced we could only have it for two days a week," Pete told Matt Kent. He felt that the one-show-a-week schedule didn't provide enough continuity for the audience to feel the necessary level of involvement in the experiment.

> What I needed was a daily experience, to be able to say to somebody that came in...'what's your name, where do you live and do you know anything about The Who?'...I did actually say to one of them, 'If I write you a song will you come back tomorrow to listen to it?' and he said 'Yeah, I'll bring my mum and dad.' That was the kind of scenario that I was hoping for, something where we would start to build up what, I felt, would be a real mirror of what was going on already in the best pop music which was, that I write a song about you guys as a generality and then other 'you guys' type people identify with that process. If I did it 'one to one', what would be the difference? I think it would be more special, more acute, more intimate and in a sense, more involving and, maybe...make each one of those people who got a song written about them the center of their own group of a hundred or hundred thousand faces. They would become figureheads in their own right. What I'd end up with is...a single man PR campaign, who consolidates a lot of interest, particularly in younger fans in The Who, who without them there wouldn't be a band.

"It wasn't an act, it was an evolving process – a new kind of music," Pete said. "But they wouldn't buy it." Discouraged and disillusioned, Pete and the band played the last of the experimental *Lifehouse* shows at The Young Vic on March 1. The project had collapsed after only 3 shows. "It bombed, bombed out incredibly because it was too far out," Pete told *Rolling Stone*.

Meanwhile, the press was continuing to report the prospect of a *Lifehouse* movie. "The Who...are about to make their first film," the *New*

York Times reported in early February. "It is called *Bobby*[88] ...Shooting will start this summer, with an American release expected by November... Townshend has gone into retreat, holed up inside his house and private studios in Twickenham, where he's hammering out a story line. Bearded and bleary, he works 15 hours a day...and can still hardly believe that a film is really, truly happening." Pete's plan was to intersperse the normal dramatic storyline of the plot with live footage of The Who at the Young Vic.

From the outset, the film project had been complicated by Kit Lambert's refusal to let go of his ideas for a *Tommy* movie in favor of Pete's new project. Lambert had wanted to do a *Tommy* movie ever since he'd written a script during the album's recording sessions in 1968/69. Pete had supported the notion of a *Tommy* movie for a time, but eventually wished to put it behind him. "We've spent a year trying to get a film together for *Tommy* and it's so long gone now that we've dropped it," Pete told *Disc and Music Echo* back in late 1970. "I think Warner Bros. have the film rights and they can make a film whenever they want, with whoever they want...Kit and Chris are really keen to get some sort of musical film together for the Who. Really, it's the only step we can take to keep us moving forward..."

Unfortunately, and unbeknownst to Pete at the time, Kit Lambert retarded the progress of a *Lifehouse* film by stubbornly pushing his ideas for a *Tommy* film. "The process...was complicated by Kit Lambert who, keen not to let go of his *Tommy* script, talked Universal into producing both films," Matt Kent wrote in 1999. "[Lambert] told me we would all three together [Lambert, Townshend and Frank Dunlop] develop the script I'd written," Pete wrote in 'An Introduction to *Lifehouse*.'

> We never did, and for a while I wondered why. Recently Frank explained that behind my back Kit had confused him, saying my idea was unworkable, that Frank should go through the motions, then let it fade and move on to the more important project, a movie of *Tommy* which Kit hoped to direct as his first feature.

Ironically, Pete's description of the ill-fated *Lifehouse* film is the clearest and most understandable of his explanations of his story's plot at the time. While the movie failed to see the light of day, it obviously already existed within Townshend's head. "The Festival Hall in London is taken over and various experiences take place like orgies and football matches," Pete told John Swenson shortly after the release of *Who's Next*.

---

[88] The *New York Times* reported that Andy Newman had been cast as Bobby.

Everybody gets roughly the same experience at the same time. **This has become kind of a theater – like an art form in itself –** to provide good experiences for people. Art is taken way, way beyond what it is now, something to be appreciated, for it *is* life, it's what you *get*.

And on the other hand is this guy who I called Bobby for a gag, who decides that it's all bullshit and that the only thing to put everything right is rock & roll. He's an old rock & roll musician, and he talks about his memories of the old days, which is basically just me, rapping. He gets this theater together, with all this incredible hardware which we actually *had*, the stuff like cerebragraphs and charts and synthesizers tuned into the heartbeat, video feedback, and everything. He was gonna put on a six-month concert event which people came to and they put up a force field so that no one could get in, and then they just did it – indulged in a good old-fashioned rock & roll concert.

These are regular people, but they're the scum off the surface; there's a few farmers there, that's where the thing from *Baba O'Riley* comes in. It's mainly young people who are either farmer's kids whose parents can't afford to buy them experience suits; then there's just scum, like these two geezers who ride around in a battered-up old Cadillac limousine and they play old Who records on the tape deck... What eventually happens is that the whole thing gets really big, the government decides that the concerts have to be stopped because they see it as a developing thing taking things out of their control, 'cause once people are in experience suits, they're under the government's control.

The guy who happens to be in charge of the government at the time panics totally at the concert and brings his troops to try to break through the force field, but the force field lasts a given amount of time. We go in occasionally and we see the concerts going on and various people's music being played, like today it's Mary's music, and you get Mary's music and then they dance and jump about. They get their food and they get their beds. It ends up, basically, with an amazing day. Bobby gets everybody's pieces of music together; I was gonna use *Baba O'Riley*, which started everything going, started everybody dancing around. *Baba O'Riley* was originally thirty minutes long and the way you hear it now is all the high points just shoved together and there's lots of passages which were just supposed to be shots of the dancing. The pitch gets bigger and bigger, the force field goes down at a given moment, the troops come in and as they walk in, Bobby is on the platform and he gets shot by the government official and falls off the balcony – there's this great balcony at the Young Vic theater where we were doing it – ...all the kids rush in to catch him and as he hits the ground they all disappear, and that was just gonna be the end of it. But the way it's written is that everybody who was taking part in the rock concert disappears but nobody else does and they're just standing there, looking, and they don't know what has happened to the people. They've gone. And that's when *Song Is Over* starts... The synthesizers were supposed to come in over the end while just what is left in the end on the surface is panned over.

Although Kit Lambert had been mostly absent for the Young Vic shows and the relationship between he and Pete had cooled considerably, it was Kit who called Pete with a suggestion in early March. Lambert wanted The Who to fly to New York to record their *Lifehouse* material as it stood, regardless of the failure of the recent experimental shows. "I remember being skeptical," Pete wrote in 1995. "Kit had been doing hard drugs...But he convinced me that he would co-produce with Jack Adams - a solid engineer I had worked with myself in New York." The recording venue slated for the sessions provided further enticement, a "wonderful new studio," according to Pete, The Record Plant.

"The idea itself wasn't going anywhere... we weren't tackling the storyline," Chris Stamp recalled in 1999, "so Kit's idea as their producer was to move to the most sophisticated recording studio, to try and record these songs... He knew about the Record Plant in New York – he'd actually worked there a few times – and so the band flew over to New York to record some tracks... I think probably that what Kit envisioned doing was the same as he had done with *Tommy*, trying to get more and more into Pete's idea and working it out that way."

By mid-March, the band were in New York, recording their new material at The Record Plant. "The New York sessions were great fun," Pete recalled. "We were the first band to use the revolutionary new Studio One... which opened during our sessions. It was a great experience but very stressful. I remember drinking very heavily and Kit was out of control... He was also disappearing to shoot up all the time... I just drank bottle after bottle of brandy as usual - probably imagining I was showing great self-restraint."

"When I got to New York I found that Kit had changed, and not entirely because he had become a heroin user," Pete wrote in the *Richmond Review*.

> I realized later he had been deeply hurt by my failure to see how desperately he wanted to produce and direct a movie of *Tommy* and I had blocked him, fearing I would lose my mentor and friend to Hollywood. I lost him anyway. At the time, in New York, I was still obsessed with my own problems and was unaware of all this. He had completely lost all affection for me and began calling me not 'Pete', but 'Townshend', or 'Pete Townshend'.

Pete's alcohol abuse, the stress of the sessions following the Young Vic debacle, and his frosty relationship with Lambert combined to make The Who's stay at the Record Plant a short lived affair[89]. After recording *Won't Get Fooled Again,* a cover of Marvin Gaye's *Baby Don't You Do It* (which featured Mountain's Leslie West guesting on lead guitar), *Pure and Easy*, and *Behind Blue Eyes* (with Al Kooper on keyboards) over a span of six days, Pete had had enough. He called a group meeting at the Navarro Hotel and upon entering Kit's room, he overheard Lambert venting his frustration over he and Pete's differing views regarding *Lifehouse*. "I heard him raging to his assistant Anja Butler: 'Townshend has blocked me at every front. I will not allow him to do it this time...'", Pete recalled in 1995. "Something inside me snapped. I suppose it was hearing this man that I loved so much calling me by surname, and with such anger. Perhaps I deserved it, but it devastated me."

Pete lost it. "During the subsequent meeting, as Kit stamped around the room pontificating and cajoling, shouting and laughing, I began to have what I now know to be a classic New York Alcoholic Anxiety Attack Grade One," Pete recalled. "Everyone in the room transmogrified into huge frogs, and I slowly moved toward the open tenth floor window with the intention of jumping out. Anja spotted me and gently took my arm. There is no question in my mind that she saved my life. I was by that time a kook."[90]

---

[89] New York City was also not exactly a distraction-free setting for a band who were trying to focus on a single task. "New York is the hedonistic town, so everyone was getting more loaded," Chris Stamp said in 1999. "The more halcyon hallucinogenic days had passed on now to the more sort of neurotic, narcotic days. And there's the night life of New York with after hours bars, the clubs, the sex, the everything. It's just a little bit more un-intimate for sitting down and getting seriously creative as a group of people. So the recordings didn't really work in the Record Plant. So what happened was Pete and the group just felt uncomfortable and went home."

[90] An article in the fall 2000 issue of *Revolver* reported that Pete was on the 24th floor of the building. "I thought, 'I must get some air,'" Townshend told *Revolver*. "And I stumbled

"...I had the first nervous breakdown of my life," Pete told *Rolling Stone* in 1974. "And I'm just not the sort to have nervous breakdowns. What'd happen is I'd spend a week explaining something to somebody and it'd be all very clear to me, then they'd go, 'Right, that's OK – now can you just explain it again.' There were about 50 people involved and I didn't have the stamina to see it through. A creative person has to work in isolation."

"I've worked myself on something you'll never see to the point of nervous breakdown," Pete said later.

> We've worked probably harder in the last year than ever before. I've never come across something like this before – I've always felt an abundance of energy; particularly if it's one of my projects; I've always thought I've got to push it through, put more energy into it than other people. In this particular case it went on and on and after about six months with no product, only problems, and only me involved in it and the rest of the group getting bored, John getting involved in making his own album, Roger ringing me up every day trying to dissuade me from doing the project, saying that what we really needed to do was go out on the road, we eventually gave up and to put it frankly we just went back into the old mold.

"...I just think the mechanics of [*Lifehouse*] could have been realized in a film that would've been bigger than *2001*," Pete told *Q* in 1996.

> It would have been the musical *2001*. That's why on the cover [of *Who's Next*] we're pissing on the obelisk. The band didn't get it, but that was the idea. I thought this was a huge technical magnum opus that could have been absolutely extraordinary. It would have been *Fahrenheit 451*, *Lawnmower Man* and many other films rolled into one. *Woodstock*, even. I couldn't understand how it hadn't happened. This was an extraordinary moment of visionary imagination for me, and it seemed to have been wasted. Now I understand that not everything you imagine is necessarily at the appropriate time. We were incapable of doing it. We could write songs, make albums, tour. That was about it.

---

towards the window. I was about to jump out, when Kit's secretary grabbed me – just like that! I nearly killed myself. *That* is when I gave up on *Lifehouse*."

"Over the next year, Pete was in a maudlin state," Frank Dunlop told *Mojo* in 2004. "I remember him bursting into tears for no apparent reason on more than one occasion. My regret is that with the job I had I couldn't help him as a freelance director would have. I couldn't just go off and get it done. *Lifehouse* was a gigantic effort. I always felt I wasn't useful enough to him."

Pete's frustration regarding the apparent inability of anyone but himself to understand the storyline of *Lifehouse* has remained with him to a certain extent over the thirty years which have passed since its inception. "I was at my most brilliant and I was at my most effective," Pete said in 1999, "and when people say I didn't know what the fuck I was talking about what they're actually doing is revealing their own complete idiocy, because the idea was SO FUCKING SIMPLE! It is not complicated. The only thing that's complicated about it is the fact that it was talked about too early by people who didn't know what they were fucking talking about." A great deal of this frustration must have been lifted upon the release of Pete's 1999 *Lifehouse* radio play, which he has described as "the definitive version."

Following the late March meeting at the Navarro, Pete was inclined to agree with the rest of the band's assertions that they should salvage what they could of *Lifehouse* by recording the new material and issue an album. Since Pete's recent rift with Lambert precluded their working together at this point, it was necessary for the band to seek another producer for the next album. Pete contacted Glyn Johns, a highly regarded professional engineer whose resume included five Rolling Stones albums, four by Steve Miller, Led Zeppelin's first record and the Beatles' *Let It Be*, to name a few. The selection of Johns, Shel Talmy's engineer during The Who's early days, did nothing to ease the tensions between the band and Lambert. Johns clearly disliked Lambert, and since Johns had taken Talmy's side during The Who's early contract dispute, the feeling was mutual. Johns also was no fan of Kit Lambert's abilities as a producer. "I thought they were atrocious," he told Dave Marsh in 1983, referring to The Who's Kit Lambert-produced recordings.

> Absolutely atrocious – amateur night. I think *Tommy* is absolutely atrocious from a sound point of view. Embarrassing. I mean, Kit Lambert didn't have any idea whatsoever about how to make a record – none. The band would dispute that, and more power to 'em. But I mean from an engineering point of view, from a sound point of view. I'm sure he had wonderful ideas and he was a very explosive character. And I know, because Pete's told me on numerous occasions – they all have – that he did come up with great ideas and he was a great influence on the band.

But he didn't know how to make records – not from an engineering point of view, at any rate.

Pete told *Sounds'* Penny Valentine in 1972 that "For the first time the Who were recorded by someone who was more interested in the SOUND than in the image of the group."

> Glyn's not particularly interested in Who image, whereas when Kit was producing us that was all he cared about.
> ...I don't think Glyn produced. I think he engineered. I mean this is why in the end, when it came to the crunch about what to put on the little label, we put co-produced. Because Glyn had done something that was different to what Kit did but Kit definitely PRODUCED the Who. He would produce material out of a band that had nothing to offer. Glyn couldn't do that.

The band decided to record some of the *Lifehouse* material at the Young Vic for possible release, using the Rolling Stones' new mobile recording studio. First, they tested the set-up at Mick Jagger's country home, Stargroves. A trial run of *Won't Get Fooled Again* impressed both parties enough for them to relocate to Johns' regular place of business, Olympic Studios, to record what would become *Who's Next* (indeed, the trial run of *Won't Get Fooled Again* was of sufficient quality that, with a few overdubs, it was retained for use on the finished album). The Olympic Studios sessions began on April 12, 1971, and recording was wrapped up in late June. "...we just went in there for four days," Pete said in 1983. "Just a casual thing, to try out what we wanted to do. We did six numbers in four days – finished. Went in a week later and did another six. Went in a week later, did another six. We were just churning the stuff out. We had enough for two albums when we were finished."

As recording got under way in mid-April, the band planned on releasing a double album of the *Lifehouse* material and proceeding with the film project later in the year after the new material had reached a satisfactory level onstage. However, over the next month, the double concept album of *Lifehouse* gave way to a single non-concept disc. Once more, Pete's storyline had failed to convince a listener, this time Glyn Johns. "Just before Glyn programmed *Who's Next*," Pete told *Revolver* in 2000, "he took me out to a pub. He said, 'Pete, tell me just once more about this *Lifehouse*.' I thought, Oh God! So I told him the story. And he sat there thinking. I thought he was going to say, 'Now I get it!' And instead he said, 'I don't understand a *fucking* word that you said.'"[91]

"We could have put together a really tight concept album I think," Pete told *Zigzag* in 1971.

> Roger thought so too at the time but Glyn Johns was very adamant that from his view as an observer he couldn't see any concept. And I think maybe he could have been wrong. I don't really know. I think that as a producer he perhaps stands a little too much away from the ethereal concepts that a group gets involved in because it's active, it's working and it's exciting and tends to just listen to what comes out of the speakers and take it at its face value without realizing, of course, that a whole lot of people who are interested in The Who are very deeply into everything that we're doing, all of the time.

Certainly *Tommy* had been a tremendous success despite the album's complex and vague story line. "With *Tommy*," Pete told *Revolver*, "I felt I had failed to nail down the story properly in the songs. It needed explaining for people to understand it. With *Lifehouse*, I just fuckin' failed, period. I had written a story before writing the music, and I still failed – *failed* – to make it work."

In late April, during the early phase of recording, the band took the Rolling Stones' mobile set-up to the Young Vic as planned and recorded their April 26 performance. Pete's second daughter, Aminta Alice[92], was born just two nights before the show, prompting him to smoke a cigar during the performance and announce to the crowd that he was a "proud father for the second time." The Who's last Young Vic performance took place the following week, on May 2.

The material Glyn Johns and The Who selected from Pete's *Lifehouse* demo tapes to record from April to early June, 1971, formed the tightest, most consistent Who album to date. Pete's experimentation with synthesizers is instantly apparent with a shower of notes at the beginning of *Baba O'Riley*, which Pete named after Meher Baba and composer Terry Riley, whose innovative use of synthesizer loops inspired Townshend. The song's complex backing track was a result of Pete's exploration into entering an individual's personal data into a synthesizer in the hopes of

---

[91] "...I found it very difficult to understand the script," Johns told Dave Marsh in 1983. "I mean, I could not get a grip on it. In fact, I don't think it's possible for anybody to understand it. I was incredibly impressed with the fact that he had written it. I was incredibly impressed with the professional manner in which it was written. But I didn't understand it. And I told him so."

[92] It may be significant to note that Delia DeLeon's sister was named Minta.

discovering a melody, or pattern. "Among my plans for the concerts at the Young Vic was to take a person out of the audience and feed information — height, weight, astrological details, beliefs and behavior — about that person into the synthesizer," Pete told *NME* in August, 1971. "The synthesizer would then select notes from the pattern of that person. It would be like translating a person into music. On this particular track I programmed details about the life of Meher Baba and that provides the backing for the number."

Pete's 1982 account of how he arrived at the arrangement for *Baba O'Riley* is quite different. "I went out, bought a Larry Berkshire organ, pushed the marimba button, and *played*," Pete told *Musician*. "And people kept saying, "That's incredible synthesizer work on that," and I'd say, "Okay, sure, you're telling me, right?" "

Regarding his previous account of programming peoples' personal statistics into the synthesizer, Pete commented:

> Oh, that was totally misconstrued. What I was actually doing was collating all kinds of detail about six subjects for the *Lifehouse* film. One was Arthur Brown, the other was Meher Baba, and the rest were the four members of the band. I took astrological details and I was going to take heart rates, pulse rates — everything that I could find out about people — to use as controlling parameters for synthesizer music. Now this was back in '72 [actually '71], and the synthesizer, even then, was still pretty much of an unexplored instrument. I realized I was pushing the technology a bit hard, so I backed off. What I did do in the end was create the musical equivalent of a found poem — like taking a few lines out of a newspaper and calling it a poem.

Another notable song, *The Song Is Over*, filled an important role in the *Lifehouse* script. "This would originally have come at the end of the film," Pete told *NME*. "I had a rough script where all the Young Vic audience would dance and dance and all freak out, and then disappear. Then you would have heard this song." Pete added in 1999 that the song signified "the end of a lifetime, the end of an experience." *Getting In Tune*, Pete told *Zigzag* in September, "...is a straight pinch from Imrat Khan's discourse of mysticism of sound where he says music is one way of individuals getting in tune with one another and I just picked up on that." *Going Mobile* was "...originally a song about driving in America," Pete recalled in 2000. "In *Lifehouse* it's a song about escape from duty and responsibility, about being able to run away." Another song, *Bargain*, featured lyrics which mirrored a

1950 Meher Baba quote: "We must lose ourselves in order to find ourselves; thus loss itself is gain."

In 1971, Pete referred to *Behind Blue Eyes* as a "throwaway" song. Thirty years later, it's one of the band's best-known melodies. It is also regarded by many as one of Pete's most personal songs, despite the fact that it wasn't written as such. "Another *Lifehouse* song," Pete recalled in a 1983 description of the song's demo recording. "I remember my wife saying she liked this one from the kitchen below after I had finished the harmony vocals. The band later added a passion and a fire that really made it blossom from the sad song it appears to be into the proud self expose it became on *Who's Next*. Not a personal song at all, or at least not intended to be. It's about the villain in the story feeling he is forced into playing a two-faced role."

As the years passed, the song's autobiographical content became apparent to Pete. "I wrote that for a film script, *The Lifehouse*; it was written about somebody else," he told *Musician* in 1982.

> It was written about a man who actually was a villain, and he seemed to be a villain; he's accused of being a liar and a cheat, when in fact his motives are absolutely pure. So I tried to capture this character that I'd written and then realized it was me afterwards, and about a part of me that I hadn't considered: the inability to be taken literally because of the way people take you to be. You can never define, you can never control how people react to you, however much of a star you think you are. You can never hide what you really are.

Another classic, *Won't Get Fooled Again*, rounded out the album. "I wrote *Won't Get Fooled Again* as a statement against the new politicians, that they weren't gonna fool me with their claim that they had a new way of doing things," Pete said in a 1985 radio interview. "The original song wasn't a very aggressive song, but again as usual when Roger started to sing it, he sounded like he certainly *wasn't* gonna get fooled."

"*Won't Get Fooled Again* was a refutation of the value of revolution," Pete told *Musician* in 1982. "I don't believe in revolution and war. Revolution is the ultimate betrayal…every revolution, even the necessary revolutions, or the Russian or Chinese revolutions; they are betrayals because they equalize, without recognizing other people's aspirations."

The song's classic Townshendian power chord riffing was perhaps executed with extra edge due to the anger which Pete cites as the song's inspiration. "…[*Won't Get Fooled Again*] was a song, really, about telling people who were telling me what to do to fuck off!," Pete told *Hit Parader* in 1975.

> It was a time when I was incredibly exposed...I refused to change my telephone number, and I refused to not open the door. I thought, well, fuck it, if I can't deal with things that come along, then I might as well fucking give up. So I tried to deal with everything logically and intelligently, tried to handle people.
> And about halfway along, I got fed up with being lectured, and I got fed with people telling me what rock and roll was all about, and what rock musicians were supposed to do now, and how rock and roll musicians were supposed to help overthrow the capitalist regime, and how rock and roll was supposed to sort of finance co-ops and communes and do this and that, and how because you were a rock and roll star and everybody looked to you for guidance and inspiration, that your responsibility was a political responsibility and a liberationist responsibility.
> I felt, all of a sudden, 'I quit,' and I thought, well, no, all right, if I do have any kind of responsibility, let's not give it any kind of low level. Let's go to the fucking top of the building, let's call it a spiritual responsibility.
> Let's say that I am responsible for the spiritual well-being of my patients. So fuck off the lot of you. And I take great pleasure in saying it now. It's one of the songs I enjoy most on the stage, because I still feel that way.

Almost a decade later, the song was still being lauded in the press. "*Won't Get Fooled Again*...[is] rock's best and most furious political manifesto," *Time*'s Jay Cocks wrote in 1979. "Its sardonic observations on the bicameral process (*The parting on the left/Is now the parting on the right*) and the bitter truth of its conclusion (*Meet the new boss/Same as the old boss*) make it a fine anthem for any election year, anywhere."

When Pete revisited the song in a 1987 interview with *Rolling Stone*, he called it "...the dumbest song I've ever written."

> It was dumb to deny the political role of the individual, the political responsibility of the individual. Burning your draft card is a political act. Throwing your vote away is an apolitical act. And *Won't Get Fooled Again* was an apolitical song. Luckily, most people didn't listen to the verses. *There's nothing in the street/Looks any different*

to me/And the slogans are all replaced, by the by... They just listened to the catch.

It was an irresponsible song. It was quite clear during that period that rock musicians had the ear of the people. And people were saying to me then, "Pete, you've got to use the Who. You've got to get this message across." It was like Abbie Hoffman said on the stage of Woodstock that John Sinclair was in jail for one lousy joint, and I kicked him off the stage. I deeply regret that. If I was given the opportunity again, I would stop the show. Because I don't think rock & roll is that important. Then I did. The show had to go on... I greatly regret that it's one of the most powerful songs that I've ever written. The Labour party asked me if they could use it in their election campaign. And I said, "Yeah, but please let me rewrite the verses."

Who's Next, the band's 5th studio album, was released on August 14, 1971, in the U.S., where it reached number 4, and hit the jackpot on British soil after an August 25 release: it became the only Who album to hit number 1 at home. Praise for the new album poured forth, with reviewers calling the album "superb" and "brilliant". "Though *Lifehouse* itself was a catastrophe, Pete and The Who had produced the tightest music of their undulating career," wrote Chris Charlesworth.

"...*Who's Next*, regardless of what you may have been led to believe to the contrary, is neither the soundtrack to the realization of Pete Townshend's apparently-aborted Hollywood dream, the greatest live album in the history of the universe, nor a, shudder, rock opera, but rather an old fashioned long-player containing intelligently-conceived, superbly-performed, brilliantly-produced, and sometimes even exciting rock and roll," wrote *Rolling Stone*'s John Ned Mendelsohn, who went on to call the album "...one of the most masterfully-recorded rock records in recent memory."

Who's Next was the first rock album to feature extensive use of synthesizers (the only other performer at the time who used synths to the extent which Townshend did was Stevie Wonder). Pete wrote in 1982, "Someone once said that when you play around with synthesizers you end up suffering from a disease called 'synthesizeritis.' I suffer happily." Roger Daltrey commented in October 1971 that at one point, "it was in the air for Pete not to play guitar anymore, and just play keyboards..." The rather anomalous image that this statement conjures, one of a guitarless Townshend flailing a synthesizer into submission onstage, demonstrates the importance with which he regarded the new technology. "...the crucial element of The Who's music on *Who's Next* was the use of synthesizer loops," Chris Charlesworth added in 1983. "It was the first time that this much abused new electronic toy had been fully integrated into the sound of a rock band, not simply used to add effects and frills."[93]

Who's Next was also praised for its overall sound quality, particularly since *Tommy*, the band's last studio effort, was regarded as subpar in this area. "Glyn Johns gave The Who a clarity of sound they had never achieved before," Charlesworth noted, "a crispness of tone and sharpness in definition that Kit Lambert, for all his creative suggestions, had never been able to supply."

"I still think that *Who's Next* is one of the best sounding Who albums because the demos for that record were so good," Pete wrote in 1983. "There were good songs, and good ideas, but Glyn Johns our producer stuck his neck out to enhance and evolve not just the songs, but also the *sounds* I had produced at home." Another reason for the album's great sound is Pete's use of a guitar sent to him as a gift from Joe Walsh. He commented on it in an interview with *Guitar Player* in 1972:

> [Joe Walsh] said, "I've got something for you…A 1957 Gretsch." …I said, "Great, cheers, man," and it turned out to be a real knockout. I was being polite. I opened the case and it was bright orange and I thought, "Ugh! It's horrible, I hate it." I went home and went into my studio and plugged it in and it totally wrecked me out, it's the best guitar I've got now. It's the Chet Atkins model, with double pickups, f-holes and single cut-away…I used that guitar on every track on *Who's Next*, it's the best guitar I've ever had. It won't stay in tune on stage but if it did, I would use it. It's the finest guitar I've ever owned, it's the loudest guitar I've ever owned. It is so loud, man, it whips any pickup that I've ever come across… If I plugged it in my amp tonight, normally I'd be working on volume 6 or 7, but I would work this guitar on 1.

While *Who's Next* was the most powerful album of the band's career, the list of songs which were set aside following the decision to whittle the record down to a single disc is quite impressive. "We've got two albums, only one of which is being put out," Pete told *Crawdaddy* in August. "The other's being kept till we need it." The most surprising

---

[93] "The whole thing about this album is the two tracks, *Baba O'Riley* and *Won't Get Fooled Again*, use a synthesizer in a completely different way than anyone had ever used one before, where it actually provides a rhythm, it's not just a sound, but it's a rhythm as well," Glyn Johns said in 1999. "It's to the best of my knowledge the first time anybody had used synthesizer like this. First of all nobody I knew anyway knew how to work them. They were really difficult to program and get any kind of sound out of."

omission was *Pure and Easy*, since it was quite central to the *Lifehouse* storyline and obviously a favorite of Pete's. In 1999, Pete said that *Pure and Easy* was "essential to any look at the atmosphere of the story," and that the song was "the *Amazing Journey* of *Lifehouse*."

"It's a song about reflecting creation musically, i.e. there being one infinite consciousness – everything in infinity being one note and lots of other consciousnesses being us and vaguer consciousness being gas and grass and space," Pete told *Zigzag* in September, 1971. "I just wrote a lyric about all this – talking about it as music. That is really one of my favorite songs, it really should have been on *Who's Next*..." Pete further lamented the omission of the song in 1999. "...it is the pivotal song and it was left off *Who's Next*," he said.

> Not through anybody's fault but because the album was put together and it sounded great and we didn't want to fuck with it...[94] I think that if *Pure & Easy* had been in the original mix people would have understood what the other songs were about so much better. They would have known, so much better, what songs like *Won't Get Fooled Again* were about. If you'd heard *Pure & Easy* you would have known why I was so angry about revolution. What was happening was that my sacred heart, which was the music, was being used for political purposes and that made me angry. The worst thing to happen is for your work to be used for political reasons.

Another *Lifehouse* leftover was *Too Much of Anything*, "which if I'd done as a really great rock song would have been a killer – it's about excess and living your vices," Pete said later. "...I deliberately did it in a southerly drawly twang to keep it much lower. I put much more energy into *Love Ain't For Keeping*...I had a few failures, such as *Teenage Wasteland*, which was supposed to have been the overture and didn't quite land and some of the musical experiments which didn't quite land until many years later when I got them to land with *Psychoderelict*."

Pete had a demo of *Mary*, which, he later recalled, "was a song intended to bring some romance into the sci-fi plot [of *Lifehouse*]. Mary was a character in the script. The song wasn't recorded for *Who's Next* by the Who as we decided to make it a single album rather than a double."

With an eye towards polishing up the *Lifehouse* material through live performance, the band began a series of unpublicised shows in May,

---

[94] "Glyn played us the album the way he thought it should be, and we said, 'Great. Put it out.'," Pete told Dave Marsh in 1983.

1971. "What we have to do now is rebuild ourselves because we were so heavily involved in the film idea," Pete told *Melody Maker* in early July.

> We have been doing gigs without any advance publicity here and there, not because we were testing out a new stage act and didn't want any publicity but because we always do gigs like that. They are not very big gigs and they will sell out instantly. If we advertise them in the press there will be lots of people turning up who can't get in. We like playing these small gigs. We did four shows before we started recording to try the new act out on stage [in Sunderland, Birmingham, Liverpool and Dundee]...We are doing another three this weekend [Worthing, Sheffield, Leicester]. We had to go back to gigging and find our feet again after the film business before we could start moving anywhere.

On the way back from the first show (May 7 in Sunderland), the band pulled over and relieved themselves on a slag heap near Sheffield. A photograph of the band at the slag heap eventually became the *Who's Next* album cover. The 'band pissing on the obelisk' photo also was a jab at Stanley Kubrick. "Yeah, it was mean to be a sort of gag when we pissed up against the monument," Pete told *Oui*'s David Rothman in 1980. "It meant that when we asked Stanley Kubrick to direct *Tommy*, he said, "Fuck you.""

The Who presented an array of new material during this run of live shows, including *Love Ain't For Keeping, Pure and Easy, Time Is Passing, Behind Blue Eyes, Bargain, Getting In Tune, Too Much Of Anything, I Don't Even Know Myself, Baby Don't You Do It, Water,* and *Won't Get Fooled Again*. However, the *Lifehouse* material didn't seem to gel onstage as *Tommy* had done so admirably a few years prior. "...the series of concerts through April and May had proved that they could not play *Lifehouse* on stage as a solid central work like *Tommy*," 'Irish Jack Lyons and Joe McMichael wrote in *The Who Concert File*. "Indeed, two of the most important songs, *Song Is Over* and *Baba O'Riley*, seemed technically impossible without a much-expanded line-up. The synthesizer backing tape was mastered on *Won't Get Fooled Again* only and it was some months before The Who actually attempted *Baba O'Riley* on the stage." The fact that the band couldn't get *Lifehouse* across onstage effectively ended any hopes for a film, since live footage of the band was to be a central part of the finished product. Pete still held out hopes for his beloved project. "I still feel that the group should be making the film," he told *NME* in July. "There is so much that the whole Who organization, our whole team could do in a film. This may sound like blowing our own trumpets but I don't think there are very many other groups who have the knowledge of stage rock theater but at the same time the necessary lack of ego to carry it off. At the moment we are leaning heavily on the fact that we are good experienced musicians and can put on a good stage act. But...and I hate to rub it in...what we really need is a film."

After The Who wrapped up the recording of *Who's Next* in early June, they played more sporadic dates across England. Although the band was disappointed with the new material's lack of fire onstage, they could still bring the house down. "In a climax that only The Who can generate," *Melody Maker* reported of the band's July 10 show in Dunstable, "Pete smashed one of his current three Gibsons into fragments to the obvious approval of the capacity crowd. While Keith knocked his drum kit off the platform, Pete hurled the remains of the guitar in the audience bent on rushing the stage for souvenirs...The Who will always be with us. And while they are they continue to wear the crown of the most exciting live band in existence."

Four days later, the band played a rather special date: a garden party at Keith's new house in Chertsey. This odd-looking architectural anomaly was described by *Rolling Stone's* Jerry Hopkins as something that "...looks to be a collection of square pyramids painted a glaring white." *NME*'s Richard Green reportedly remarked that only Keith could have designed such a strange building, and Pete replied, "But he didn't, and that's what worries me. It means that there's another creature with a mind like Moon's walking this earth. Why isn't 'e in the 'oo?"

The next trip to North America meant the beginning of The Who's biggest tour to date, an event for which the band unveiled their new, state-of-the-art, £20,000 PA system. This tour saw the band playing to packed stadiums for the first time, the smaller venues used on previous tours proving simply too small to accommodate ticket demand. The tour kicked off in heavy rain in aptly named Flushing, New York on Thursday, July 29, 1971. The band reportedly attached rubber blocks to their shoes in order to avoid electrocution on the wet stage. John Swenson recalled Pete's guitar bashing that evening in his 1979 book, *The Who*:

> At the end of *Magic Bus*, Townshend broke the neck off his guitar and flung it into the photographers' pit. When a jittery roadie scuttled out to retrieve the body, Townshend threatened him with menacing gestures to stand aside... Townshend then took a second guitar and, grabbing it like a paddle, picked up the body of the broken first guitar, tossed it into the air, and slammed it with the second guitar as it came down. Both guitars broke into pieces at Townshend's feet. He then picked up a microphone stand and beat the mangled guitar bodies into splinters. The audience could hardly believe it, and Townshend walked off

the stage with the certain knowledge that he had successfully revived a legend.

In a rare display of onstage emotion, Entwistle reportedly joined the fray, demolishing a bass. The band's next show in Flushing took place two days later, this time in hot, sunny weather. The rapid change of climate reportedly brought countless cockroaches scurrying across the stage, with many meeting their fate at the hands of Pete's Doc Martens.

Chris Charlesworth recalled the band's set list at this stage in their careers:

> In order to reproduce the music of *Who's Next* on stage, the band performed with pre-recorded synthesizer tapes during *Baba O'Riley* and *Won't Get Fooled Again*. The new set also included *Behind Blue Eyes* and John's *My Wife* from the new LP, a twenty-minute medley of songs from *Tommy* and a backward glance towards *I Can't Explain, Substitute* and, as a show closer, *My Generation*. Occasionally they played *Magic Bus* and a wildly percussive arrangement of Marvin Gaye's *Baby Don't You Do It*, and two unreleased songs, the beautifully cascading *Pure And Easy* and intrinsically spiritual *Naked Eye*, were also fitted in. It was a long show. The Who gave value for money and, unlike others in their status bracket, they rarely played a succession of obligatory encores. A Who encore was a rarity and when it came it often lasted another twenty minutes.

Following shows at 20,000-seat arenas at Saratoga Springs, NY (in front of a record crowd for the Saratoga Performing Arts Center), and Philadelphia, The Who found that their new PA system was painfully loud (even by Who standards) when they played four early August dates at Boston's relatively tiny 4,500-seat Music Hall. "I'm terribly sorry about you with your fingers in your ears," Pete told the beleaguered crowd on the second night. "A very sad sight to see. We have slight problems adjusting from a 4,000 seat hall to a 30,000 seat hall. We're trying to bridge the gap. We're playing four nights. If we're a bit loud in Boston, it's because we're not loud enough in other places. Just don't put your fingers in your ears, otherwise I'll throw me guitar at you!" The excessive volume even wore on Daltrey, who knocked Pete's amplifiers over the following night and walked off the stage after his pleas for Townshend to turn them down were ignored.

Sound problems plagued the entire tour, and the tension onstage was palpable. Pete smashed a Gibson SG at almost every show. He hammered his guitar into the stage lights in a rage in Chicago when the electricity went out after yet another problem with the PA system. Two nights later, the tour was over. "The Who ended their *Who's Next* tour in a hailstorm of furious sound," wrote John Swenson, "leaving yet another American audience dazed in their wake."

As the latest American tour receded into the past, Pete was faced with the fact that any hopes for a *Lifehouse* film were, too, quickly fading. "...To go into it at any length, it gets more and more confused, and that's why we broke down," Pete said in August.

> I could see the finished product, but I couldn't explain how I thought we could get there. We did give the performances... that's the wrong word really...and Universal Pictures promised me a million dollars on the strength of a conversation. But The Who – and this includes me, because I need direction and production as much as anyone else – got more and more confused and tied up in technicalities like quadrophonic PA systems, and we just forgot how to play.
>
> With songs, I outline the idea to them and then make a demo. That's where this experiment fell down. You can't make a demo of a film. I wrote a script, but I'm not a scriptwriter so that wasn't overly well received. We got very very close to what would have been a revolution in rock and roll, but we didn't really have the fodder to carry it off. We had to stop being The Who for so long we realized it was going to take months to rebuild ourselves. So here we are, with no film. And I want to get a film done more than anything else. But we did get a lot of good material for the album.

The upheaval experienced during the struggle to come up with a *Lifehouse* film could have signaled the end of The Who. "...there have been lots of breakups threatened...one fairly recently when we were trying to get the *Lifehouse* film together," Pete told *NME* in 1972. "It sort of ended up me against the world – that sort of thing. In that particular case, I had one idea about what the group should be doing, and the group had another idea."

Ultimately, The Who recognized that their new album was an enormous success, and that their live shows were consistently exceeding all expectations. "I mean we came out of the whole film problem with a fantastic amount of energy and zest just to play and just to have fun," Pete said in early 1972. "We got so brought down by the problem of what we were trying to get into that we ran back and picked up the guitars and banged away – as if to say 'Fuck everybody.'"

The touring resumed in England in September as The Who (along with the re-formed Faces, Lindisfarne and America) participated in a Bangladesh benefit concert at the Oval Cricket Ground in South London[95]. Keith Moon wowed the 30,000-plus audience by somehow managing to play his drums with a cricket bat. The band then returned to their practice of playing small venues with minimal publicity, with appearances at Reading, Surrey and Kent universities in early October, all of which were before capacity crowds of only several hundred each.

This latest stint of shows at small venues served as warm-ups for The Who's first British tour in over a year, which officially began with an October 18 performance at Southampton's Guild Hall. *Melody Maker* supplied a typically praiseworthy review of the show:

> ...huge searchlights beamed down on delirious fans drunk with ecstasy at the group's new finale. A *Magic Bus/Naked Eye* medley runs into 20 minutes of material from *Tommy* finishing with the *See Me Feel Me* reprise. An instant to catch breath and *My Generation* closes – surely the best combination they could pick.
>
> Whining feedback foiled the two openers, *Can't Explain* and *Substitute*, but from then on the group clicked into top gear. *Behind Blue Eyes*, with its strong vocal lines, showed just how good the Who's new PA system can sound, while...*Baba O'Reilly* [sic] and *Won't Get Fooled Again* brought the audience to their feet on each occasion.

A *Southampton Evening Echo* reviewer said of the show, "...Despite the agony of the noise this was one of the best rock concerts I've ever attended."

Early November saw The Who's tour winding through London for the opening of a new 3,500-seat venue, The Rainbow (formerly the Astoria). Pete marked the occasion by wearing a silver lame boiler suit with a Rainbow on the back, after the band were introduced by a troupe of dancing girls. "Thanks for coming," Pete said from the stage. "I suppose you had to come really 'cause there's nowhere else to go is there?"

A few weeks later, The Who returned to America, playing large arenas across the country in an 18-date affair which ended in mid-December. "Traveling vast distances across the American continent was now accomplished in unashamed luxury," Chris Charlesworth wrote in 1983.

---

[95] "Though it received far less attention than the George Harrison benefits staged at Madison Square Garden earlier that summer," Dave Marsh noted in *Before I Get Old*, "the Who and their comrades raised as much or more money for the cause – and theirs got into the hands of the UNICEF officials and to Bangladesh itself much more swiftly."

An army of sound and lighting men accompanied the group; managers, tour managers, press agents, accountants, lawyers, record company executives, press photographers and writers swelled the party. Peter Rudge, a sharp Cambridge graduate lately employed by Lambert and Stamp, was in charge of the operation and the operation ran like clockwork, a tribute to the professionalism so much admired by Roger Daltrey yet privately despised by Pete.

The playing was in the same mold, tight and direct, and much money was invested in PA equipment which delivered a sound as loud and crisp as any group in the world. All The Who's characteristic gestures were still there: Pete's leaps and arm rolls, Roger's microphone twirling, John's vacant stare and Keith's manic energy. As a unit the group played together superbly, perhaps better than at any time in their career. Offstage they mixed only occasionally. Pete withdrew to his hotel suite to write, read or muse on his avatar; Roger found a girl; Keith went crazy; and John stayed sane. Pete expressed the view that The Who was now a "very sophisticated circus act" and when his conscience was pricked at the sight of a huge box office taking he smashed a guitar and sometimes even two.

The band's greatly anticipated December 9 show at L.A.'s 18,000-seat Forum sold out in less than ninety minutes, with fans camping out overnight to secure front row seats, which had been left available for public sale at The Who's behest rather than being reserved for corporate guests. The show, the band's first in L.A. for 18 months, eclipsed previous sellout records set by the Rolling Stones and the Beatles. Pete took the stage wearing a tie-dyed jumpsuit with a crown on his head, which he soon tossed into the crowd. *Melody Maker*'s Jacoba Atlas reviewed the show in the magazine's Christmas edition:

> There are concerts that are magical because of the music, and concerts that are magical because of the presence of the group. When the Rolling Stones played L.A. it was impossible to hear or see because of the jumping and the screaming; but it didn't matter. The same was true for the Who. The sound up front was slightly muddled, towards the middle and the back of the enormous Forum it evened out correctly; kids leapt up blocking viewing and at any moment one sensed that all was going to break loose. But that was what it was all about. It wasn't just the music,

you can get that at home with your stereo and your Who records. In person they gave you more. They gave you what makes them one of the best rock and roll bands in the world. Just about midnight I found myself making that statement without any qualifications whatsoever.

The *L.A. Times* review of the performance printed the following day called it "the greatest show on earth." A December 15 show in Seattle marked the end of the tour, which proved to be the band's last show in the U.S. for two years.

Pete was still unsatisfied with the conclusion of his *Lifehouse* project, and was still pushing to make a film. "During the latter few months of 1971, Nik Cohn had accompanied the band on their U.S. tour to gather material for a film script that would reflect the essential aspects of the band's performance art," John Atkins wrote in *The Who on Record*. "A film featuring the group is the next major project," *Melody Maker*'s Chris Welch wrote in late 1971. "We start in January, and Pete is writing the music," Daltrey told Welch. "The film should have been *Tommy* when the LP came out. That's when there should have been a film. In the film we do what we are good at – and that's playing. We'll get more involved as it progresses. It's going to be called *Guitar Farm* but I don't want to say too much about the story." Meanwhile the band were kept in the public eye with the release of the single *Let's See Action*, one of the *Lifehouse* songs which had been left off *Who's Next*. *Action*, released in October, 1971, reached number 16 in the U.K.

Chapter 6

"We're all very similar as physical bodies, we enjoy the same degree of self-punishment, the same music, and we enjoy playing together, but we have different basic ethics on how to live our lives and they don't cross. Deeply written into Who philosophy is the fact that each member thinks the other guy's way is total bullshit but it's all right by me. I may be putting words in people's mouths but that's probably true. So let's say I'm tolerated in my mystical beliefs although I should imagine there's a bit of fear in the group that I might grow my hair down my back and start putting solo albums out... do a George Harrison basically."
— Pete Townshend, 1972

"I think the idea people have of us now – or at least our present image – is that people are starting to talk of us as a band that are changing. Which is nice. But what they'll realize in time is that we have changed before. I remember that sort of thing was said when we did Magic Bus for some peculiar reason. People said "what the fuck's going on here, lots of acoustic guitars and clicking noises." And I feel Join Together is today's Magic Bus, and I think when we go on and do some more Who then they'll see it in that light."
— Pete Townshend, 1972

The Who decided to take it easy following the hectic touring of the past few years. "We have plans for avoiding what we feel is going to be a very political year," Pete Townshend told *Guitar Player* magazine in 1972.[96] "No schedule, no gigs, there's a rumor that we might play in Moscow one day. We're not planning to come back to America until 1973, and that's about it."

Pete took advantage of his open schedule and traveled to India in February, 1972[97], to witness firsthand the legacy of Meher Baba. "India was

---

[96] The Nixon-McGovern presidential race took place in 1972

[97] Pete relayed a humorous (and perhaps fictional) anecdote from his trip to India during a radio interview with Scott Muni in August, 1978: "...you travel eleven, thirteen hours on the airplane and arrive in India and there's women in sheets and they look at you and they go 'Sahib, Sahib,' and beggars come up and people with no legs and no eyes. I figured at least

an absolutely, totally mind-blowing experience," Pete told *Penthouse* in 1974. He continued:

> ...It all started with a visit...three years ago, to Myrtle Beach, in South Carolina...It's made up of lots of lakes, kind of an inland Hawaii-type situation with lakes and fairly easy jungles leading down to the Atlantic coast. There are three or four thousand acres there that were a gift for an American Baba center[98]. There are lots of little cottages and places where you can go and stay. Baba loved the place. I went there for one day, in the middle of the tour, and spent the night in this cabin, a place where Baba had lived. All of a sudden, for the first time in my life, I felt that I was in his presence...I put my head on the bed and fucking thought the most incredibly...unthinkable, unrepeatable, and unspeakable thoughts I've ever had. It was so awful, it was like being in hell. I completely broke up. I finally went out with fucking tears streaming down my face. Tears of self-pity. And I thought that I'd blown it. There I was, in the presence of the Master for the first time, and all that bullshit, all that filth.

Pete believed that what he had experienced in the cabin was, "...me fighting like mad not to surrender and using the most subtle, most subconscious way that I knew how. It was very, very spooky." Further uneasiness ensued during Pete's visit to India. He related the visit to *Penthouse*:

> I went over there and the first thing that hit me was that India was a fantastically beautiful country. It's the only place where poverty is almost pure. I mean *I* felt like the fucking peasant with my twenty suitcases and my first-class ticket and my charcoal-gray suit. I felt like a pig, I really did. So to cut a long story short, I ended up in the tomb where Baba was buried. There's a ritual that goes on there in which you walk in, put your head down to the ground,

---

I'm alone. I get my bags and I walk over to the hotel in Bombay and I walk in and I check my bags and go off to the room to catch some sleep and some guy comes up to me and says 'Hello dere. Are you... you're not, eh... you're not Peter Townshend? So I said 'Yes.' 'Oh, Peter Townshend of The Who. Oh, please give me your autograph, I'd be most, most grateful. Give me your autograph! Ah, The Who, most wonderful, wonderful music, ah. You know they reflect the feeling on the streets of Bombay.'"

[98] The Meher Spiritual Center remains an active spiritual retreat. Visit www.mehercenter.org for further information.

and walk out again. It's a kind of sacred procedure. Awful in a sense. It's just what Baba would never, ever have wanted...a ritualistic thing. The first time I went in there, I put my head down and tried to really feel like I was in Baba's presence. And I had the same thoughts that I had when I was in the bedroom at Myrtle Beach. And the same thing happened once again, when I went around the second time. By this time I'm really starting to know what I'm going to think as soon as I get in there. So the third time I go inside, I'm standing there thinking, "Well, I'm washed up. I'm never, ever going to be in the presence of God, so I might as well fucking enjoy being with all these people and have a good time during my unhappy years on earth." And suddenly this young guy walks in and he's obviously got dysentery very bad. He's small and fragile, his face is white, and he's shaking like a leaf. Somebody kind of ushers him forward and he looks like...well, he brought out all my maternal instincts, if that's possible for a man. I just felt so much compassion for him...so much sorrow for him...and I see him get down, put his head to the ground, and tears begin to stream down my face. I'm so wrapped up in this kid that by the time I get my head down, I've forgotten about what it was that was in my head. I forgot that whole trip. So I get up after realizing that this guy was just a device to get me out of the way, you know what I mean? It was Baba's compassion that had arranged it. It was nothing else. I felt so insignificant that I might as well have been a speck of dust. It was the most incredible feeling I've ever felt in my entire life. And I went out afterwards and collapsed in thanks. That's what happened in India.

Pete's stay lasted about a month, living with a group of Baba's close followers and visiting Baba's tomb on an almost daily basis. "There is a ritual there, when all his followers stand around the tomb and sing [Cole Porter's] *Begin the Beguine* which was one of his favorite songs," he told *Creem* in 1980. It totally zapped me out when I was there. I stood up after all this and was crying and everything."

Pete later remarked that his spiritual experience in India has made him reluctant to return. "I'm kind of nervous about going back again," he said. "I mean, I've had my little zap. I don't know how much more I could handle. It's like a door was opened for an instant, just so you could quickly glance inside. Then it slammed shut again. And you think, "Christ, is that where we're all going?" Because if it is, we're all right. I'll tell you that right now."

Three years of following Baba had brought a certain amount of composure to Pete's life. This calming influence stood in stark contrast to Pete's 'rock star' lifestyle, and The Who's reputation as major-league partiers. "I don't use dope, for instance, but I'm often with people who do," Pete told *Rolling Stone*.

> ...Baba changed my life in that respect. I don't normally get involved in the usual group road scenes, dirty parties...but it goes on around me.
> I mean, Baba lovers in the States are incredulous. They walk into my room and go 'Jai Baba,' which means 'victory to Baba,' and there's a room full of people...broken guitars on the floor, piles of whiskey bottles, television sets out in the street, lemon curd all over the wall - they just can't equate the two things. I'm not saying I'm sitting there aloof, like the bloody lighthouse in the middle of the stormy sea - I'm affected, I'm involved, and part of the time I'm doing it - it's just that Baba is strong enough to keep hold of you, and it's possible for you to keep hold of him whatever you're doing.

"Previous to being involved with Baba I tended to weigh things up very carefully whereas now I'm much more impulsive," Pete told Chris Charlesworth, "I just sort of chase my Karma around with the feeling that Baba's got his thumb on my head, so everything's all right. At the same time I haven't changed all that much. I've still got a bad temper and I'm fairly aggressive as a musician. Quite simply, I write more honestly now. I'm not afraid to write what I'm thinking despite the fact that in a case like *The Seeker* it made quite an embarrassing record."

Pete shared some of his feelings about Baba upon his return from India, appearing on the television show *How Can You Be So Sure?* in late March. He also set about creating his second Meher Baba tribute album, *I Am*, at his home recording studio in Twickenham, distributing the 1,500 copies of the finished product among its intended audience of Baba followers. The album contained a Meher Baba prayer entitled *Parvardigar* which Pete had set to music, along with an instrumental version of *Baba O'Riley*. Bootlegged copies of *I Am* and its predecessor, *Happy Birthday*, both very limited releases, began to emerge in the U.S. labeled *The Pete Townshend Meher Baba Album*, but had poor sound quality and no accompanying information regarding Meher Baba. To remedy this, Pete broached the idea of letting Decca release *I Am* on a larger scale.

"What Decca said to me, indirectly, was: 'These albums are selling at $11.98 in stores, and there's nothing we can do about it under the Piracy

Act because it's not a legitimate record,'" he told *NME*.

> ...They didn't make any contract pressure or anything. In fact nobody has. Everybody in the business... I don't know for fuck's sake why... but everyone in the business – Track, Decca, Polydor – they've all been so respectful. It's almost as if I was a fucking monk, y'know, and that they regard making these albums as part of my therapy or something. The record companies are giving up incredible amounts of percentages. I think it's because 'Bangladesh' set certain traditions that the industry are very proud of, and rightly so, and they are anxious to perpetuate this. Anyway, they said to me: 'We'll put this out, we'll give you a dollar an album' – which is an incredible amount of money – 'and we'll make sure the thing is done in good taste.' I thought, well why not? How many copies do you want? They said, 'Well we'll take 25,000 to start with.' So I nearly fell through the fucking roof. I said, how many? Christ, that's a lot of albums. So I said listen if we're going to go into it on this scale, why don't I just do a completely fresh album.

Decca and Track agreed to donate 15% of retail to Pete for Baba-related activities, and Pete set about culling some material from *Happy Birthday* and *I Am* for the new album. He also wrote some new material and included work by Ronnie Lane and other Baba followers on the record.

The resultant album, *Who Came First*, released in October, 1972, contained an eclectic mix of performances by Pete. Included was Ronnie Lane's *Evolution*[99], and *Time Is Passing*, "...another track the Who recorded for *Who's Next* that was rejected," Pete told *Rolling Stone*. *There's A Heartache Following Me* proved an interesting inclusion. "...an old Jim Reeves number, the sort of thing I'd never do, though I really enjoyed doing it," Pete said in 1972. "It was one of Baba's favorite songs. He heard someone playing it outside where all the disciples were, and he said that song, that guy's voice, are really amazing...he said that the words of it were very much the words that the Messiah would sing." *Sheraton Gibson* has proved to be one of the more lasting performances from this album, since the song was included on Pete's 1996 greatest hits compilation *Coolwalkingsmoothtalkingstraightsmokingfirestoking*. "*Sheraton Gibson* grew out of a really interesting writing session that I had," Pete recalled in 1996.

---

[99] A version of *Evolution* was also recorded by Lane's band, The Faces. "...this version has got something about it theirs hadn't and I think they're quite happy about us doing it," Pete told *Sounds* in 1972.

I was in a hotel – I don't think it was the Sheraton Gibson[100], but it might have been – and I'd been out and bought Bob Dylan's *Self Portrait*, which was a double album, and it was a bit of a dip in and see record, lots of different styles, and I was inspired by it. And I thought, this guy is a great genius, no question about it, but he's incredibly prolific and humorous and mischievous, and what would happen if I just sat down, put on a tape machine – I had an early, primitive cassette machine with me – and just put myself on the spot and made songs up as I went along? How many could I come up with? And I came up with eight, and I totally made them up, start to finish, every detail, nothing added, nothing taken away, and what you hear is what I wrote. So it uses the kind of chords that fall under the fingers, but what the song actually does evoke is how I felt at the time.

Parvardigar, from *I Am*, was also included[101]. "I don't actually say this prayer, I just happened to put it to music, but a lot of other people do say it," Pete told *Rolling Stone*.

I think it's an important one, which Baba dictated; it's like the replacement for the Lord's Prayer that he had dictated as the New Messiah. Preposterous as it may sound, I thought that by putting it to music a lot of people would just be saying it without thinking about it. It's an amazing piece of music, and the words are pretty amazing – as a prayer, it is the most unbigoted, unbiased prayer, it is praising everything in a very abstract way, so that anybody can get off on it. Even if you're an atheist you could still dig this, because it's in praise of life.

Who Came First was largely viewed as a Meher Baba tribute rather than a Pete Townshend solo album. "[the album is] in a way dedicated to

---

[100] "It was written in the Sheraton Gibson Hotel," Pete commented during a live chat on www.barnesandnoble.com in May, 2000, just to complicate things. He added, "One of the most important early songs [completed during the same session] was an early version of *Bargain*."

[101] A German language version of *Parvardigar* was also recorded. "When I recorded the *Parvardigar* prayer on 31 August 1971 for the album *Who Came First*, someone suggested I should do versions in several languages," Pete wrote in the *Scoop 3* liner notes in 2001. "An Austrian follower Of Meher Baba, Hilde Halpern, did the translation, working literally from my own free adaptation of Meher Baba's *Universal Prayer*. There was no official release of the result."

Baba, but mainly dedicated to the people who want to know the way I feel about him," Pete told *Rolling Stone* in 1972. "I find that when I try to talk about Meher Baba...I can't put it into words. So I thought maybe I should use my talent – with a small 't' – as a musician and try to put the feeling and the mood across that way."

"Meher Baba is an amazing man," Pete told *Crawdaddy* in 1973. "He's dead now, three years since, but one still gets the feeling of a NOW presence. No single thing that has ever happened to me has changed the way I see and do things in this world so much. This album is meant to reflect these changes." He explained that the album is "...not for [Baba] to listen to, his ears aren't around, but so that he will be around whenever it's played."

In addition to providing a glimpse of Pete's spiritual leanings, the inclusion of demo versions of *Pure and Easy*, *Time Is Passing* and *Let's See Action* on *Who Came First* offered the listener several examples of Pete's oft-vaunted home recording prowess. "This record hasn't let me do things musically that I hadn't done before, because it's music that was already in existence," Pete said in 1972. "If I were doing a proper solo album, I would probably show off more – how well I can engineer, or how well I can play the piano. In a way we're using chuck-outs. But then, I do like the idea of people hearing what I do at home."

Pete included *Let's See Action* "because I felt it said more about Baba than it did about the revolution," he told *Sounds* in 1972. "It was written about the revolution but somehow, in retrospect, I felt it was more about the action here (hits his chest) than here (raises his fist in the air). And also I felt the Who's version was a bit joggy, a bit casual."

While *Rolling Stone* called *Who Came First* "...a brilliant and moving album...the music manages to fuse high devotional feeling with commercial mastery resulting in powerful music," Dave Marsh's review, published in *Creem*, was far more critical:

> Baba books and such have always seemed trite to me, without a whole lot to add to the body of cosmic aphorisms, but since he spent most of his life in silence, one doesn't expect much... It's inconsequential stuff...*Who Came First* is there, if you want it, which I don't suppose I do, particularly. It's a curiosity, more than anything, or an idiosyncrasy.

Meanwhile, mid-1972 saw The Who back in the studio. The band booked time at Olympic Studios in May and June 1972, working again with Glyn Johns. Songs completed during these sessions featured *Lifehouse* and post-*Lifehouse* compositions, which likely included *Pure and Easy*, *Relay*, *Join Together*, *Too Much Of Anything*, *Naked Eye*, *Love Reign O'er Me*,

Long Live Rock, Water, Time Is Passing, Mary, Put The Money Down, and *Is It In My Head?* The silly *Waspman* was also recorded at this time.

While much of the work completed at Olympic was of excellent quality, the general consensus was that it sounded too much like an extension of the band's previous album. "We finished an album with Glyn Johns working at Olympic..." Pete said later. "We put a rough assembly together, and it sounded like a shadow, if this is possible, of *Who's Next*."

"...so I said, 'Fuck this,'...well, everybody did unanimously," he told *Rolling Stone* in October.

> We decided to have one side of the album just good tracks, and the other side a mini-opera. So I went off and started working on that, and got really excited about an idea I had, put about 14 or 15 songs together, and went rushing back and said, 'Listen, I'm not going to play this stuff, but I can tell you that what I've got knocks shit out of what we have already done, so let's shelve all that, put a couple out as singles, and I'll incorporate some others and we could do a new opera." So that's basically what I'm working on at the moment.

The change of focus precipitated other changes. "...I thought at the time, and Glyn was courteous enough to agree, although it did mean scrapping all his work, which was pretty amazing, to scrap the album as such and put out odd singles," Pete recalled. However, he didn't stop there. "I also thought it would be better to work in another studio with another engineer and again Glyn was very nice about that," he added. "We'd put in a fantastic amount of work together and it was pretty much an exhausted relationship at that time."

The new "mini opera" which had become the focus of Pete's attention had been fermenting in Townshend's mind for some time. "When [the work done at the Olympic Sessions] fell through in May '72, I said we needed an album, and couldn't put off doing something that was going to last," he recalled later. "You know, we couldn't keep treading water and I had this idea for a project for a long time, and it really came out of the Who been going for ten years and lots of backward looking and I thought it would be nice to have an album that encapsulated everything the Who had ever done, with a big sort of flourish, so we could really start afresh."

The key song which first represented this retrospective project was *Long Live Rock*, which was recorded by The Who during the recent Olympic sessions. The project, named *Rock Is Dead: Long Live Rock*, was later dropped, leaving the title song to eventually resurface on 1974's *Odds & Sods* compilation.

Join Together, a *Lifehouse* remnant recently recorded in Olympic studios, was released as a single on June 17 in the U.K. and July 8 in the U.S., keeping the band on the charts and in the public eye, ultimately reaching numbers 9 and 17, respectively.

In August, Pete took up residence in a suite at Brown's Hotel in Mayfair for the purpose of conducting interviews regarding his latest activities, including a new European Who tour (rehearsals for which were taking place at that time) and the upcoming release of *Who Came First*. "In the suite there are comfortable armchairs, sandwiches, drinks, coffee, a nicely relaxed atmosphere," wrote Penny Valentine of *Sounds*. "Townshend, with a newly grown small beard, looks splendid in his usual day attire of well cut trousers and tight knitted French sweater. He's back from holiday and – as usual – raring to go."

"The really interesting thing about the rehearsals is that we've been stuck in the studios and it's this thing about not playing together for seven months," Pete told Valentine. "So for our own benefit – aside from the numbers from *Who's Next* which Europe hasn't seen us do and will be new numbers to them – we're doing a couple of numbers for the new album we recorded in June. One's *Long Live Rock* and another is *The Relay* – which looks like it might be issued as a single."

The Who ended their road sabbatical in August, 1972, with a 17-date European tour which stretched into mid-September, the opening act being Golden Earring. Pete, still wearing his customary white boiler suit, was now playing a Gibson Les Paul rather than the SG model guitar he'd been playing since the Woodstock era. The band used backing tapes onstage for their *Who's Next* material and for *Relay*, a song which had been recorded during the Olympic sessions and would see release as a single in November[102].

The switch from Gibson's SG model to the much heavier Les Paul was borne of necessity. "They took the old SG off the market like about a year ago, so we used up every old SG in the country," Pete told *Guitar Player*'s Michael Brooks in 1972, adding, "I don't break them deliberately any more, but when I spin them around, when I've had a few drinks, I bang them and they crack and they break."

> They're made out of really light wood, it's a light guitar. ...the factory stopped making those particular SG's. So we said "You're going to have to make 'em for us, you're going to have to customize them for us," and they said okay but it's going to be about $3000 a guitar. So anyway, we had four of them made for the beginning of the

---

[102] *Relay* reached number 39 in the U.K., 21 in the U.S. "I thought we might do a Marc Bolan and get this one out quickly before *Join Together* gets cold. Also because *Join Together* wasn't a huge success," Pete said in August. "Yet another gem from one of the world's greatest rock bands," wrote *Melody Maker*'s Michael Benton.

tour. They brought them up to us but the guitars were totally different. The pickups were in a different position, and on and on, so I said, "Forget it." So I raided every music store in the country practically, looking for old SG's. ...My favorite guitar now for the stage is the Les Paul Deluxe with the small epiphone pickups that you can buy on the shelf for $50.00.

The tour wound through Germany, Brussels (Pete greeted the crowd by saying "Hello Brussels sprouts!"), Scandinavia and other venues in western Europe[103] and Italy. Ollie Lundin recalled the August 24 Gothenburg, Sweden show in *The Who Concert File:*

> The well-behaved Swedish audience was quietly watching as The Who appeared on stage with their gear. Pete Townshend approached the microphone and asked the audience not to panic. The Who was obviously used to a different reaction. Anyway, Pete backed up a few steps and made an enormous standing jump straight up into the air and landed on his knees on the stage floor with a great crash. The music started, extremely loud. After the song, Townshend grinned and pulled up his trouser legs revealing a pair of enormous knee-pads.

The Who played before a daunting 400,000 fans in Paris on September 9 at the French Communist Party's annual festival. "Actually, I didn't know it was for the Communists until we got here," Pete told *Rolling Stone.* "Well, it's our first chance to exploit the Communists, eh?" Eric Clapton attended this show, at Pete's invitation. "Mid-set, The Who reached their peak with *Won't Get Fooled Again* and *Magic Bus,* Townshend vacillating hideously between a resigned poker face and an evil grimace," *Sounds* reported of the Paris show in their September issue.

> "Get on board...Come on," he urged, and then lurched to the front of the stage, dripping with perspiration, and went through the motions of taking the stalk [of one of

---

[103] The Who's hotel in Copenhagen had waterbeds in select rooms, a point of fascination for Moon. He insisted on a room with a waterbed. "We were having coffee in his room and I said how great it would be if we could get the mattress in the lift and send it down to flood the lobby," Pete told Charles Young of *Musician* in 1989. "Of course, it wouldn't move, but Keith tried to lever it out of the frame, and it burst. The water was a foot high, flooding out into the hallway and down several floors." Moon bluffed hotel management into believing it was their fault, resulting in his prompt upgrade to the Presidential Suite. The suite's expensive furniture was reportedly reduced to firewood after the show, with Moon and Townshend playing major roles in the destruction.

the many red flowers which had been thrown on the stage] between his teeth and hurling a grenade into the crowd gesticulating a mighty explosion. It was a positive allusion to the large Vietnam banner that hung over the fete and a clear mnemonic of Pete Townshend, revolutionary.

The band's September 14 show in Rome, their first in the city since 1967 (The Who had a poor following in Italy: *Who's Next* had sold only 7,000 copies there in over a year), was electric despite the fans' cool reception, due at least in part to their fear of retribution at the hands of a rather oppressive government and police force. The situation was described in *Melody Maker*:

> ...despite the long absence the audience sat impassively throughout the kind of set that most groups would swap their PAs for...It seems an almost unbelievable situation: fans are unable to demonstrate their appreciation of an act for fear of arrest and future banning of rock shows...Townshend is the most fluid mover I've seen since those Olympic gymnasts. He twists and turns and spirals around, leaping from one side of the stage to another spinning his arm like a propeller from start to finish. He falls over, somersaults and crashes to his knees like a man on a trampoline. Some day he'll go head first into his stack of speakers, break both legs and an arm, but that's his style and he couldn't change it if he tried...Townshend smashed his guitar into fragments – the first break of the tour – at the end and the Italian fans didn't know what had hit them. He swung it wildly at Moon's kit, and took three heavy blows against the stage floor before the instrument succumbed. The body left the neck and the whole mangled mess arrived in the front row. The police moved in and the ovation was stifled as a result.

So ended the final show of the tour. The band, which hadn't played in Britain since the November 1971 opening of the Rainbow, said that they wanted to finish their next album and come up with a new stage show prior to playing at home. "A lot of the Who has been lost in volume since we left *Tommy* out of the live show," Roger told *Record Mirror* in December. "[The stage show has]...lost some of the light and shade, and I've found it a lot less rewarding without the character of Tommy." Plans for further tours in early 1973 (including one in Japan) failed to reach fruition as progress on the new album was slower than anticipated. Pete told *Disc* at the time that he was working on something "big...we are after something for the main body of the stage act – something like *Tommy* but not an opera – just a theme to run through it."

In October, 1972, a version of *Tommy* featuring the 104-piece London Symphony Orchestra, along with a 60-voice choir was released. The album, produced by American producer Lou Reizner, featured vocal performances by Steve Winwood, Rod Stewart, Ringo Starr, Richie Havens, and all four members of The Who, among others. While the edge of the original album is perhaps lost in this version, it features some fine vocal performances: Roger's singing was arguably at its peak during this period, and Merry Clayton's take on *Acid Queen* is testament to what a great showcase for vocal talent the song can be, something which would be proven again by Tina Turner and Cheryl Freeman. Pete sang *Amazing Journey*, some of *Overture*, and *Sally Simpson*.

While Reizner wished for Pete's inclusion from the project's beginning, Pete was initially hesitant to oblige. Reizner, who had produced Rod Stewart's *The Rod Stewart Album* and *Gasoline Alley*, wanted Stewart for the role of Tommy. "Well, I thought, for Christ's sake it's gonna look super-competitive, with people comparing Rod's interpretations to Roger's," Pete told *NME*. "I spoke to Kit and Chris our managers about it, and they felt that there wasn't too much chance of it actually happening. Nevertheless, I asked Lou if he would use Roger, because he's heard the backing tracks and was extremely keen to get involved[104]." Reizner complied; Stewart's role was reduced to singing *Pinball Wizard* while Daltrey got the opportunity to take another shot at *Tommy* in the recording studio. "When The Who originally did it – as with most recordings – it was a little hurried towards the end," Pete told the *NME*, "so the vocals weren't perfect – plus the undeniable fact that as a singer Roger has improved a fantastic amount..."

Pete slowly got more involved in Reizner's project. "Normally I wouldn't have got drawn into it," Pete commented during recording, "but because Lou Reizner's such a persuasive fellow, I just found myself getting involved. It's simply a matter of me coming along to the sessions, listening to what's happening, and then approving the various tracks. I've got no control over anything anyway." Ultimately Townshend was flattered. "It's great to just sit here and hear the London Symphony Orchestra playing a piece of my music," he said. "And that someone like Lou has enough enthusiasm to spend money [reportedly about £60,000] and gather together all these amazing people, just knocks me out..."

Predictably, *Melody Maker* loved the album. "This is one mighty beautiful package," wrote Chris Welch.

Townshend's masterpiece has finally got the

---

[104] Daltrey's opinion of what he'd heard, as he told the *NME*: "...bloody amazing."

treatment it deserves with an all-star cast, a full symphony orchestra and a presentation that ranks among the best in the history of rock albums...Missing, of course, is the driving beat of the Who and the overall power that comes with having a rhythm section with Moon and Entwistle at the head, but instead we have a character for each part, each bringing his own style to the thoughts of Townshend...

Dave Marsh provided the opposite view: "It was fatuous and bombastic Camp, a betrayal of the spirit of the original – and of the Who."

On Saturday, December 9, 1972, the London Symphony Orchestra and featured guests (as on the recording, although substituting Peter Sellers for Richard Harris) played the new version of *Tommy* at the Rainbow, whose stage had been transformed into a giant pinball machine for the occasion.[105] In addition to performing the parts he played on the album, Pete served as the narrator. The sold-out show caused Pete (who told Dave Marsh he "grew disenchanted" with Reizner's *Tommy* prior to the stage show) a great deal of anxiety, which he duly treated by ingesting copious amounts of alcohol, and his performance suffered because of it. Reportedly, he "missed cues, insulted the audience and Reizner." Richard Barnes wrote that Townshend "...had been rather useless as the narrator and was probably suffering from severe stage fright and forgot his lines during *Sally Simpson*." Dave Marsh recalled the events as follows:

Townshend, who, as narrator, was supposed to help make the story flow, was dead drunk, missed cues, blew lines. Pete was particularly horrible during *Sally Simpson*. In the course of the evening, he insulted the audience, Reizner, orchestra conductor David Measham and, at the end, wiped his ass with the libretto and staggered off the stage.[106]

"...Being on stage at the Rainbow Theatre, having to live the opera through its weak parts as well as its strong left Townshend uneasy,"

---

[105] The event was originally planned to take place at the Royal Albert Hall, but was deemed 'improper' by their management. The event, tickets to which topped out at £200 each (Paul McCartney reportedly bought five), raised "almost ten thousand pounds" for the Stars Organization for Spastics charity, according to *Melody Maker*.

[106] "The story behind that is, unfortunately, a lot more shallow," Pete told *Uncut*'s Simon Goddard in 2004 with a laugh. "I was drinking quite a lot at that time and I forgot to paste the words into this book which I was reading from. I'd only pasted in the first half of it, so what actually happened was I was wiping my arse on the basis that the book was no good. I thought somebody had ripped some pages out. I'd had too much to think about so up to that point I'd been narrating and when I got to that page and there was nothing there I thought, oh, fuck. I just arsed about, basically."

commented *Melody Maker*'s Mark Plummer.

> He found himself nervous about going on stage on his own with no Who. And an excessive amount of brandy beforehand didn't help him at all...It was a mistake for him to get involved with Lou Reizner and the orchestrated *Tommy*. Not from the recording side, but to go on stage with it. He felt he was there to answer for everything wrong with *Tommy*, standing on his own, in the cold on the side of the stage.

"*Tommy* will pay my pension alright, as my Dad keeps telling me," Pete told Plummer, "but on that stage I felt very open. It was me, Pete Townshend, having to answer all the criticisms leveled at *Tommy*. I'm not a nervous person, I don't usually feel nervous; when I'm on stage with the Who I can forget I'm Pete Townshend. I'm able to become part of the Who and go crazy without having to be me."

A repeat performance of Lou Reizner's *Tommy* was held at the same venue the following year, with Daltrey and Moon reprising their roles. Pete decided to stay away. "I was very excited about that event but, having fucked it up the first time around, I didn't do it again," he told *Uncut* in 2004.

> What was interesting about that second time was that I was sat with my wife Karen and it was the first time I'd ever seen Roger from the audience. I remember turning to her and saying, 'He's fucking good, isn't he?' And he was great. I'd always thought Roger was a bit naff, I'd always thought he was a bit of a nuisance – y'know, [smiling] swinging his microphone around and getting in the way of my guitar sound. That was the moment I realized that, through *Tommy*, Roger had made this connection to the audience and become a theatrical performer. I had much greater respect for him after that.

Meanwhile, a new project had grown in the wake of Pete's *Rock Is Dead: Long Live Rock* idea. The new story, while still faithful to the retrospective angle of its predecessor, centered on a young man's youth. "...at the moment I'm pretty excited about it," Pete had told *Sounds*' Penny Valentine in his suite at the Brown Hotel back in August. "...it'll be a decade of the Who in January."

> ...What's happened to the individual members of the group, how they've changed? So I thought a nice way

of doing it was to have a hero who, instead of being schizophrenic, has got a split personality four ways and each side of this is represented by a particular theme and a particular type of song.

I'm the good part of the character needless to say – the choir boy who doesn't make good, the sea scout who gets assaulted by the scout master. Then there's the bad part, which is Roger, breaking the windows in colored people's houses, turning over Ford Populars and things of that nature. Then there's the romantic part which is John Entwistle, falling in love with the girl next door, everything really going well until her mother catches them one day in a compromising situation and flings him out and he goes off frustrated, despairing. Then there's like Keith – totally, irresponsibly, insane. Playing jokes on his girlfriends, telling terrible lies, blowing up the place where he works. And joining all these moods and songs together.

How was Pete to tackle the task of "joining all these moods and songs together"? Further explanation ensued:

I've written a lot of stuff about this period[107] and it's all come out sounding like old Who material – quite unconsciously. And it gave me the idea to consciously do that. To start off with early Who sound and come through – more and more synthesizer, more and more snazzy recording until you get to the point where he finds himself coming together, fitting together like a jigsaw. Going from that period of sort of fucked up amazing spiritual and social desperation, despair with politics and everything – to come together as one piece of music which is the Who[108].

From this point, Pete offered a description of some of the specific events of the protagonist's life:

I was writing one song about being kicked out of home and eventually he has this final row with his dad about cutting his hair, his mother finds dirty books, gradually their son is being eroded before their eyes, turning

---

[107] "When writing *Quadrophenia* I was inspired by the acquisition of a splendid new Bosendorfer 7'4" grand piano which I still have today," Pete wrote in the *Scoop 3* liner notes in 2001. "It was squeezed into the tiny room I used then, but it sounded extraordinary, still does."
[108] The 'one piece of music' reference brings to mind the 'one note' theme from *Lifehouse*.

into something they can't relate to any more, and I used a bit from *Zoot Suit* – remember that very early record we did? – and I sort of glorified it into a big thing *Zoot suit with white jacket and side vents five inches long.*

...at the end I wrote this song where the kid is really fucked up with drugs and chicks and his family, not getting on at school, identifying himself with a militant group, tries to help workers' causes and finds that not only is he powerless but they resent it. And I started to feel that when you write about somebody that has EVERYTHING happening to them you somehow realize how everything does affect everybody.

Quadrophenia, as the work became known, was the story of a young Mod in 1960s London (although the Mod connection – other than the *Zoot Suit* reference – wasn't apparent in Pete's August, 1972 description of the work). The protagonist, Jimmy (whose name did little to end numerous *Tommy* parallels), suffers from a severe identity crisis which is further complicated by the problems he encounters at home, at work, with friends and in his love life. While Pete's decision to make Jimmy a Mod was widely viewed as an affectionate nod to The Who's roots, it also proved a good fit for his screwed-up hero. "There are so many tragic things involved with the Mods," Pete explained in April, 1973.

...the fact that they grew up and became respectable, that's a miserable situation. The fact that they turn into middle aged pop stars, that's miserable. The fact that they're badly educated kids, deprived, and the only things they have are kicking people and dancing, that's miserable. But at the same time it's got this incredible triumph in that this kid's an individual in the midst of a world where the individual doesn't exist.

An essay purportedly written by Jimmy (penned by Townshend), which appeared inside the sleeve of the double album, set the scene for Pete's story by leaving the reader with Jimmy stranded on a rock, out in the sea, contemplating his young life:

...the bleeding boat drifted off and I'm stuck here in the pissing rain with my life flashing before me. Only it isn't flashing, it's crawling. Slowly. Now it's just the bare bones of what I am.

A tough guy, a helpless dancer.

A romantic, is it me for a moment?
A bloody lunatic, I'll even carry your bags.
A beggar, a hypocrite, love reign over me.
Schizophrenic? I'm Bleeding Quadrophenic.

Several of *Quadrophenia*'s songs successfully articulated Jimmy's various internal struggles, from his identity crisis (*The Real Me, Is It In My Head, Dr. Jimmy*) to spiritual desperation (*Helpless Dancer, Love, Reign O'er Me*). *Cut My Hair* demonstrated one facet of Jimmy's struggle: His frustration with his peers.

Why do I have to move with a crowd
Of kids who hardly notice I'm around
I work myself to death just to fit in

While *The Dirty Jobs* and *I've Had Enough* expressed Jimmy's sick-of-it-all state of mind, the songs also demonstrated a yearning for a higher level of satisfaction. "...Mixed up in *Quadrophenia* was a study of the divine desperation that is at the root of every punk's scream for blood and vengeance," Pete wrote later. This spiritual desperation becomes more evident as the album progresses. *Helpless Dancer*, for example, featured the lines *No one can love without the grace of some unseen and distant face*. The album ends with Jimmy pleading for love (*Love, Reign O'er Me*).

The band entered the studio in December, 1972, to begin recording the new, unfinished project (which was now being discussed as a double album due to the amount of material Pete had written) with Kit Lambert in an effort to consolidate and clarify the story line as they had done with *Tommy* (and failed to do with *Lifehouse*), and at the same time perhaps rekindle their collaborative flame, which had all but been extinguished during *Lifehouse* but "things fell apart fairly quickly," according to John Atkins, and the sessions abruptly ended. Lambert, who continued to abuse drugs and alcohol, "didn't make out very well," according to Pete, "and argued with Daltrey. I felt let down and took over despite the fact that I had more than enough on my plate." "[Lambert] ... left me holding the baby for the production, which was bloody difficult," Pete added in 1987.

Lambert had been living in Venice since late 1971 in the Palazzo Dario, an elaborate fifteenth-century house with a marble façade. Townshend stayed away. "A lot of the pop sycophants went, but none of the band," he told Andrew Motion in 1987. "He desperately wanted us to go, but we were not interested, or too busy." Lambert's young boyfriend, Tito, provided another reason for Townshend to stay away. "They really loved each other," he told Motion, "but the boy hated me."

With a stalled studio attempt under its belt with Kit Lambert at the helm, *Quadrophenia* was beginning to mirror *Lifehouse* in ways that Pete obviously didn't desire. Pete expressed his frustration at the album's slow progress to *Melody Maker*'s Mark Plummer in February, 1973. "I've got to get a new act together for the Who," Pete said, "and I don't care if it takes me two years before you see the Who again, we've got to get something fresh." He lamented his inability to "write a strong plot" and reiterated that the band needed new material to rejuvenate The Who's stage show: "We've tried going through all the hits, basing a show on that, but that doesn't work. It's all in the past now; people don't really want to sit and listen to all our past."

As Pete continued to work on *Quadrophenia*, the band simultaneously sought a new recording venue. They had spent a great deal of time recording over the past year and weren't totally happy with any venue in particular. "We tried everywhere," said Pete, "test recorded at every studio but nothing came of it. At Advision we spent hours getting a sound done. At the end we had finished recording and Kit Lambert turned around to the engineer and said 'that'll do for a demo.'"

After the Olympic Sessions the previous year, Pete had commented that the band may need a change of scenery to start afresh. Their inability to find a satisfactory recording venue resulted in the band purchasing an old church in Battersea, South West London, and converting it into their own recording studio. The studio, referred to as 'The Kitchen' in the *Quadrophenia* liner notes, ultimately became known as Ramport Studios. When the band was ready to record *Quadrophenia*, the studio was still under construction. Richard Barnes recalled the situation in 1982:

> They decided to start the new album at Ramport studios even though it wasn't finished. They were determined that Ramport was going to be a top rate studio and had been dissatisfied with the control room so had ripped out all their work and were rebuilding it. The studio itself, however, was finished. So they brought in Ronnie Lane's mobile, parked it outside, and ran cables out from the studios across the pavement and into the mobile, which was used as the control room. A video camera gave the engineer, Ron Nevison, a view of the studio and two way mike link-ups were installed for communication.

While this was not the perfect situation in which to record their latest album, it paled in comparison to the myriad distractions which faced Pete Townshend and The Who during this period. The first of these involved the band's management. "All had not been well on The Who's business front for some time," wrote Chris Charlesworth in 1984.

The style of management provided by Kit Lambert

and Chris Stamp, the stretching of cheques, the snappy ideas, the full tilt promotional thrust that characterized the workings of New Action Ltd., were ideal for the sixties, but in the climate of the seventies, when The Who no longer needed promoting through outrage, when logistical professionalism and sound financial advice was required, the management team was largely redundant.

Peter Rudge now handled all the group's business affairs in America and a new assistant, Bill Curbishley, looked after day to day matters back home.

Roger had never much liked Kit Lambert and when Lambert and Chris Stamp rejected his first solo album, the relationship went into a further spiral. There was an ugly incident with a stopped cheque for monies that were owed to The Who in back royalties[109]. Roger took matters into his own hands and ordered an independent audit of New Action's books. Inevitably there were questions to be answered. Which is not to say that Lambert and Stamp were dishonest. They were simply cavalier in their business dealings and Pete, who with Keith Moon exhibited similar traits, had no wish to sever the connection. The opposing factions lined up and the problem would not go away.

Townshend and Daltrey remained at odds on this topic during the following year. "I know Roger's very conscious all the time of the money set up," Townshend told Charlesworth.

> I think it's quite simply because he can't sleep at night unless he does actually know what were earning. But that's probably because he's never spent the way Keith and I have – which is why we don't care how much we've got. We spend what we want to spend and never ask questions later. I've never got into the red because my writing money has kept me a wee bit ahead of the group but Keith has occasionally gone into the red through overspending. But in the end you just say, 'We're just going to have to do a few more tours or something.'

During the writing and preparations for the recording of *Quadrophenia* Pete was also spending what he described as "a tremendous

---

[109] The band had reportedly requested the money to complete the construction of Ramport studios. Lambert OK'd a substantially smaller sum than they had requested, had a check cut, went to Venice and promptly stopped payment on the check. "The band went absolutely fucking crazy," Bill Curbishley told Dave Marsh.

amount of time" with Eric Clapton in an effort to help him overcome his heroin addiction, which was eventually toppled with the help of Meg Patterson's innovative electro-acupuncture technique. Patterson would soon refine this technique into what became known as Neuro-Electric Therapy and later helped Pete overcome a heroin addiction of his own, in early 1982. "I was having to answer hysterical phone calls from [Clapton's girlfriend] Alice Ormsby-Gore practically every night," Pete said later.

> She always wanted me to go over there. It was an hour and a half's drive, and always at awkward hours of the night...When I got there, usually she just wanted to explain what was happening. Eric would be asleep somewhere and she would be running around hysterically. What was worrying her, what she needed to talk about, was that she was giving Eric all of her heroin supply, most unselfishly. And then she was having to deal with Eric's extremely selfish outbursts accusing her of doing the reverse.
> It was a typical junkie scene. It was despicable. But even through all that, you know, I got to like and love them both very much. It was the first encounter I'd had with heroin addicts. I wasn't prepared for the lies, I wasn't prepared for the duplicity.

Karen was beginning to feel the strain as she watched her husband juggle his various commitments. "...my wife measured it all against time spent with her," Pete wrote, "fairly minimal at the best of times, and very minimal during this period."

Pete's involvement with Clapton culminated in an all-star show at the Rainbow on January 13, Clapton's first performance in over a year.[110] "I just don't know why [Pete] picked on me to do the Rainbow concert," Clapton told *Conversations with Eric Clapton* author Steve Turner in 1976. "It could have been anybody but I'm grateful he chose me. I was just pleased to be doing it because I wouldn't have made up my mind to do it on my own. It had to be someone dragging me around by the scruff of my collar and making me do this and that." Perhaps deflecting credit for saving his friend, or perhaps simply disagreeing with Clapton as to how events transpired, Pete said, "It wasn't my idea to do the show, it was Eric's idea."

> It came about through Bob Pridden, our main road manager, who lives near Eric, and sees him quite a lot. We've exchanged 'hellos' and 'goodbyes,' but never ever

---

[110] Eric Clapton performed live only twice in 1971, both times a guest. His last performance as a headliner had been in 1970.

got together. So I decided to go down and see Eric to revive an old friendship really. I had a look at his home studio, which I really liked, and he started to talk about these tapes. I asked him what had happened to his last album, and he said: "There it is, over there." And there was this pile of tapes on the floor, and I said "what's become of it?" and he said he was waiting for Andy Johns to come back to finish it off. But Andy was working for the Stones and consequently inundated, and I started to get down to helping Eric finish it off.

The real point is I don't think Eric really wanted to finish it off. And a lot of work I did on it was kind of wasted. But he's now talking about getting it finished. There's some good material there...I think it was recorded at a period when Eric was doing sessions for Stevie Wonder and it was at a time when although the band was about to split they were playing particularly well. If it was finished it would make a fine album.

Eventually I got worried about it ever getting done, and Eric seemed so lethargic about the whole idea, and one day he just rang up and said: "I'm going to do this gig at the Rainbow, do you fancy helping out?" He more or less said, "I'll do it if you'll do it." It was a schizophrenic turn-around that is so typical of Eric. One minute he can be completely down on something, and then he'll put in a year's work.

He worked hard on the concert, and although he was surrounded by good, eager, sympathetic musicians, it was still all his songs, and he had to teach us them all. It was two weeks solid rehearsals at Ronnie Wood's place[111]. Immediately after the concert the Who started recording.

There was talk of a tour following this concert with (among others) Ron Wood, Eric Clapton, Pete, and Steve Winwood, but nothing made it past the planning stage.

Clapton's girlfriend, Alice Ormsby-Gore was daughter of Lord Harlech, who in turn was close friends with world-renowned violinist Yehudi Menuhin. Menuhin, a friend of Meg Patterson, referred Clapton and Ormsby-Gore to her to undergo her electroacupuncture technique in an attempt to end their heroin abuse. Clapton soon underwent the procedure, sleeping on a fold-down bed in the Patterson family's crowded Harley Street

---

[111] 'Ronnie Wood's place' was 'The Wick', an historical home on Richmond Hill. Two decades later, Pete purchased the home and lives there today.

apartment. He stayed for five weeks, visited regularly by Pete, among other friends. Pete was especially impressed with Patterson's successful treatment, and soon news of the innovative procedure had spread throughout the music industry. Robert Stigwood and Atlantic Records "contributed generously to my research and sent rock musicians to me for treatment," Patterson wrote in her 1994 autobiography, *Dr. Meg*.

Meanwhile, another task which occupied Townshend's time during spring 1973 was the recording of sound effects for *Quadrophenia*. Water is a central theme throughout the album, and various recordings of rainfall, thunder, and crashing waves were made to facilitate the idea. Pete had wanted stereo recordings, which made finding acceptable existing sound effects practically impossible since they were almost exclusively recorded in mono. The intricacies of sound effects recording were recounted by Richard Barnes in 1982:

> Pete and his driver, Rod, did much of the recording for the effects. Rod bribed a train driver with £5 to blow his whistle as he was leaving Waterloo station – strictly against British Rail regulations – for the beginning of *5:15*. Pete drove down to Cornwall and [*Quadrophenia* engineer] Ron Nevison towed the mobile there to record the sea, wading along the shore, flocks of mallard ducks taking off and so on. Nevison was stopped and questioned by the police when he was trying to secretly record crowd noises at Speaker's Corner in Hyde Park. He sent his girlfriend to ask the brass band on the Kensington Gardens bandstand to play a Souza march which he recorded with his hidden Nagra.

The Who began recording *Quadrophenia* in April, 1973. "In the last couple of years...Townshend, Daltrey, Moon and Entwistle...have become involved in various solo projects and seemed in danger of drifting apart," wrote *Melody Maker*'s Chris Welch. "It's as if they have taken faltering steps away from the parent body, with varying degrees of success now to return to their alma mata, and get down to the hard business of making Who music."

Instead of bringing finished demos to the studio for the band to hear, Pete brought what he described as "rough sketches on tape" of songs. "It was a very ambitious co-operative project," Pete told John Swenson.

> I wanted everybody in the group to write their own songs and stuff. Everybody was supposed to engineer their own image, as it were. I wanted the group to go in and play a piece of music which was completely spontaneous and

then give people their respective segment of the track. Let's take *Can You See The Real Me*, for example. It's a semi-spontaneous backing track with loose words which I structured later on. So you get that real sort of vital Who backing track sound with some words over the top, and then I'd take the guitar part away and build it into something: Keith, the drum part, that kind of thing. What we could do is take all these individual things down and strip them away and get down to the basic backing track as though that was the result of the stuff instead of the starting point. As always the band just looked at me like I was crazy and walked away. I've explained it to a lot of people and everybody seems to be able to understand it but them. Then John wrote a song which he wouldn't play for me because he thought it summed up the whole album in one song.

A result of the band's negative reaction to Pete's "cooperative" approach was for Townshend to adopt the entire project as his own. With Pete not only writing *Quadrophenia* (the only Who album written entirely by Townshend) and playing guitar and keyboards[112], he now assumed the role of producer in Kit Lambert's absence. He was clearly overcommitted.

The band, however, responded positively to the rough demo tapes with one of their best instrumental performances to date. Moon's drumming was "free and fluid", according to Pete, and Entwistle said that he "really let myself go on playing bass. I played very easy on [the album]." Pete was impressed with John's efforts in recording *Quadrophenia*'s various layered horn parts, telling John Swenson "In the past John's always been as much a quiet one in the studio as he is onstage. The experience he's had in arranging stuff on his own albums and zest and energy at the recording sessions was incredible. He worked like fourteen hours at a stretch on each number, multitracking horns. His attitude to Who music has really matured. And that's why there aren't any Entwistle compositions on this album as such because his energies went elsewhere."

Some pieces of music intended for *Quadrophenia* didn't make it onto the finished product. "There were several pieces I wrote for *Quadrophenia* that were left off the completed album," Pete wrote in the 1983 liner notes from his album *Scoop*. "One or two of them were incorporated into the film soundtrack album. This theme [*Unused Piano* from *Scoop*] was never finished, yet somehow it still captures the atmosphere of triumph and futility attempting to co-exist in the heart of the

---

[112] Chris Stainton, of The Grease Band, played piano on *5:15*, *The Dirty Jobs*, and *Drowned*. Who regular Nicky Hopkins was committed to other work. Townshend reportedly wanted Stainton to tour with The Who post-*Quadrophenia*, but Daltrey, keen on maintaining a four-piece Who, talked him out of it.

hero I created. Part of this theme was eventually used as a chorus on *Cut My Hair*." *We Close Tonight*, a Townshend-written piece sung by Entwistle, was also left off the finished product, resurfacing on the expanded edition of *Odds and Sods* in 1998.

Another Townshend composition, *Recorders*, was "...intended as an atmosphere merely to link a couple of tracks on *Quadrophenia*," he wrote in 1983. "It was never used. I borrowed one of my childrens' plastic whirling tubes – it was a popular toy for a few months in England, like the hoola hoop. I also strummed away on some cello strings."

Tommy film director Ken Russell offered David Litchfield of *The Image* the following ridiculous story of an experience he'd had during the recording of *Quadrophenia*:

> We were there the night they recorded a number called *Rain*[113] and there was a cloudburst and they wanted a stereo rain effect. We were in this caravan outside and bit by bit the playing stopped except for the piano and I went in and the floor and the roof had caved in as they were singing and the rain had really deluged them. They were soaking wet and there were firemen with a hose pumping it out except for the actual man in the cubicle playing the piano and he was gamely playing on and he was up to his neck in water and when they opened the door it poured like a waterfall, which was very funny.

Recording wrapped up in early summer, and Pete retreated to the new studio at his Goring-On-Thames cottage to record backing tracks and mix the album, which took nearly four months. "It took much, much longer to mix and blend than it did to record the backing tracks," Pete said. "...Stuff like *The Rock* and *Quadrophenia* were all recorded here at the house, all John Entwistle's horn parts."

A chief reason for the protracted mixing period was Pete's intention to use quadraphonic sound[114]. "...You see, the whole conception of *Quadrophenia* was geared to quadraphonic, but in a creative sort of way," he told *Hit Parader* in May, 1974.

> I mean I wanted themes to sort of emerge from corners. So you start to get the sense of the fourness being literally speaker for speaker. And also in the rock parts the musical thing would sort of jell together up to the thunder clap, then everything would turn slowly from quad into

---

[113] This story has surfaced in other publications, with *Drowned* being referenced as the song in question.
[114] The Beach Boys' 1970 LP *Sunflower* reportedly featured two quadraphonic tracks.

mono and you'd have this solid sort of rock mono...then a thunder clap and back out again...When we came to mix it we spent months mixing it and then found out that MCA was using the CBS quad system and...you might as well forget it...

For a time, even after the release of *Quadrophenia*, Pete planned on eventually releasing a quadraphonic version of the album:

...For a while we'll see our records as two editions...one in a stereo mix, one in a quad mix. That has to be the way it has to be because stereo at the moment is so much more mature and advanced than quad is. Everyday they make an improvement in the quad set-up; you know everyday I get a piece of mail through from CBS telling me that they've got another dB of separation from front to back and that, you know, if we buy the new modified encoder-decoder we'll get better results...

Quadrophenia, The Who's long-awaited follow up to the hugely successful *Who's Next*, was released in November, 1973[115]. From the opening image of waves breaking on the beach to Keith Moon's crashing *Love Reign O'er Me* finale, *Quadrophenia* presented the story of one adolescent's internal anguish in remarkably clear and cohesive fashion. The story line was much clearer than that of *Tommy* (for British audiences, at least), and the album flowed admirably[116]. Pete's guitar was much more subdued in the mix on this relatively piano-heavy album, which, with the addition of John's horns, made it a distinctly different work.

"It's not really a story as such," Pete told *NME* in November, 1973. "There's a big difference between this and something like *Jesus Christ Superstar* or *Tommy*. It's not a story, more a series of impressions of memories. The real action in this is that you see a kid on a rock in the middle of the sea and this whole thing explains how he got there."

Quadrophenia reached number two in North America and the U.K. "Prime cut Who," wrote Charles Shaar Murray in *NME*'s October review. "...you realize that Pete hasn't blown it after all. Face it, he very rarely does...if you're genuinely prepared to work at getting into it and let it work at getting into you, then you just might find it the most rewarding musical experience of the year."

Melody Maker was similarly complimentary. "*Quadrophenia*, the

---

[115] *Quadrophenia* went Gold ($1 million in sales) on its first day of release. The album went Platinum (a million copies sold) within three months.

[116] In 2002, when *Rolling Stone*'s Chris Heath asked which was the last Who album he was unequivocally proud of, Pete answered, "*Quadrophenia*."

Who's new double album is better than *Tommy*," gushed Chris Welch. He continued:

> Pete Townshend's brainchild, a year in the making, sets new standards for British rock music, and will undoubtedly prove as big a world wide success as the famed "rock opera." Released next week, it is a massive project...that tells the story of the life of a Who fan during the Mod era of the mid-sixties. In a series of brilliant performances, the Who capture the aggression, frustration and inherent romanticism of youth, with each member of the band representing a facet of the mythical hero – this time called Jimmy – and his "quadrophrenic" personality.

Lenny Kaye's review in *Rolling Stone* gave the album a slightly cooler reception:

> *Quadrophenia* is the Who at their most symmetrical, their most cinematic, ultimately their most maddening...they have put together a beautifully performed and magnificently recorded essay of a British youth mentality in which they played no little part.
> ...Tea kettles whistle over the ominous voicings of the BBC, hints of the Who in concert cut in and out of Jimmy's fragmented dreamings, slim and checked jackets mingle with seersucker and neatly cut hair. To the American mind, *Quadrophenia* might thus seem as strange as portions *of American Graffiti* could appear to English experience, but it's to be assured that the appeal of semi-nostalgic shared memories must perforce work as well for one as the other.
> ...Pete, for better or worse, is possessed of a logic riveting in its linearity, and if in effect we are being placed in the mind of an emotionally distressed adolescent, neither the texture of the music nor the album's outlook is able to rise to this challenge of portraiture. Despite the varied themes, Jimmy is only seen through Townshend's eyes, geared through Townshend's perceptions, and the aftermath as carried through four sides becomes a crisis of concept, the album straining to break out of its enclosed boundaries and faltering badly.
> This is reflected in the songs themselves, vastly similar in mode and construction, running together with little differential to separate them. Only a few stand on their

> own as among the best the Who have ever done (*The Real Me, Is It In My Head?*, *5:15*, the Townshend theme of *Love, Reign O'er Me*) and of those it's interesting to note that several are holdovers from the lost Who album Glyn Johns and the band worked on before the onset of *Quadrophenia*. Also, given the inordinately complex personalities that make up the group, little is sensed of any Moon, Entwistle or Daltrey contributions to the whole. Their roles are subdued, backing tracks when they should rise to shoulder the lead, pressed on all fronts by the sweep of Townshend's imagination...
>
> Pete has been the Who's guiding force, their hindsight and hellbound inspiration. It is his mastermind that has created the tour-de-force recording breakthroughs of the album, the realistic and panoramic landscape of pre-Carnaby Street England, arranged the setting so that each member of the band could give full vent to his vaunted and highly unique instrumental prowess. Indeed, it might easily be said that the Who as a whole have never sounded better, both ensemble and solo, proving unalterable worth and relevance in an age that has long passed others of their band's generation into fragments of history.
>
> But on its own terms, *Quadrophenia* falls short of the mark...

Whatever unity the recording process had brought within the band, it soon disippated when Pete's abilities as producer were brought into question. Entwistle and Daltrey both voiced their dissatisfaction at the mixing of the finished album. "When the album was completed, it took only a few days for Roger to express his disgust at the result," Pete later wrote in *Rolling Stone*[117].

> I had spent my summer vacation mixing it, and he had popped in once to hear mixes, making a couple of negative comments about the sound but seeming quite keen to let me 'have my head,' as it were, in production. Fundamentally, I had taken on too much, as always, and couldn't handle the strain when things went wrong and people blamed me. I felt I was perfectly entitled to gamble

---

[117] Glyn Johns was not impressed with the final mix of *Quadrophenia*, either, calling the album "...totally unimaginative from the point of view of sound – every track sounded exactly like the last one, and the last one didn't sound very good... not only did these tracks sound similar from a literal sound point of view, but there wasn't nearly enough imagination in the arrangements."

and lose, as no one else seemed prepared to, either with *Quadrophenia* or even the Who's career.

So, I felt angry at Roger for not realizing how much work I had done on the album - apart from writing it - and angry that he dismissed my production as garbage.

This deepening rift between Pete and Roger remained unchecked for two years before the pair showed any signs of burying their differences.

The next challenge facing Pete Townshend and The Who was performing *Quadrophenia* live. Backing tapes were used for the various synthesizer tracks and sound effects on the album, requiring a great deal of rehearsal time for the band to work the new tracks into their live act. Unfortunately, only two days of rehearsal took place at Shepperton Studios prior to the U.K. tour. Add the tension which existed between Townshend and Daltrey into the mix and a volatile situation soon ensued. "On the second day of rehearsals frayed tempers exploded and a nasty exchange of abuse between Pete and Roger led to their first fight in almost a decade," Chris Charlesworth recalled. "...Pete was revived in hospital but suffered temporary loss of memory."[118]

"I've only ever had one fight with Pete and that was during *Quadrophenia*," Roger recalled in 1975.

> It was a bit of a shame because it was a non-argument, and the last thing I wanted to do in the world was to have a fist fight with Pete Townshend. Unfortunately, he hit me first with a guitar. I felt terrible about it afterwards, but what can you say? Pete should never try to be a fighter. But when he was being held back by two roadies and he's spitting and calling me a dirty little cunt and hits me with his guitar I become very angry. And I was forced to lay one on him. But it was only one.

Quadrophenia hit the stage in late October 1973 as the band kicked off a 10-date tour of England prior to a planned 12-date U.S. jaunt scheduled to end in mid-December[119]. The tour began with an October 28 show in

---

[118] The *Quadrophenia* rehearsals were reportedly filmed for use on screens behind the band during the upcoming tour, but footage of the altercation between Pete and Roger has never surfaced. "...that was one of the pieces I was most broken-hearted actually didn't exist, which was an infamous moment, where Pete and Roger were going at it and Roger decked Pete and knocked him out," *The Kids Are Alright* filmmaker Jeff Stein recalled in September, 2003. "And Keith was over Pete's prone body, Pete's unconscious and he's kind of crying, saying, "Pete! Pete! If you're still alive we'll do anything you say from now on." That kind of thing..."

[119] A few weeks prior to the beginning of the tour, The Who played *5:15* on *Top Of The Pops*. In perhaps a demonstration of his frustration during this period, at the end of the show

Stoke on Trent. *Melody Maker* offered a review of the following night's performance in Wolverhampton:

> Musically, [*Quadrophenia*] wasn't as effective as the record, but when it gets worked in it should prove fairly phenomenal. Monday night could have benefited by trimming it down. Prerecorded tapes of seagulls, sea and thunder echoed effectively around the hall and helped create a suitable atmosphere.

As the *Melody Maker* review mentioned, *Quadrophenia* live proved promising. However, the stage show failed to improve, and The Who's latest live act soon imploded. They were using a new quadraphonic P.A. system and a sophisticated array of backing tapes to accommodate the various sound effects and additional instrumentation featured on the album. Keith was now wearing headphones onstage, synchronizing his playing to the tapes[120], and up to twenty guitar changes were necessary for Pete during a full run-through of the new album. This complex, somewhat mechanical environment was foreign to The Who onstage, and Pete's discomfort with his new surroundings soon reached breaking point. "We were exhausted from making the record and all kinds of things by the time we started touring," Townshend recalled in 1996. "I got very wrecked emotionally."

Pete's emotions weren't the only things to be wrecked on the fourth night of the tour, when The Who played in Newcastle. "…Fifty minutes into the Newcastle gig, during *5:15*, Townshend flipped out completely when the tape synch came in fifteen seconds slow," wrote Dave Marsh in 1983[121].

> He stepped to the side of the stage, grabbed Bobby Pridden by the scruff of his neck and pulled the poor road manager bodily over the mixing desk, then tossed him toward center stage. As Pridden sprawled in front of the crowd, Townshend began pulling at the sound board, yanking out wires, demolishing many of the prerecorded tapes it had taken so many weeks work to piece together.

Pete reportedly smashed the Gretsch guitar Joe Walsh had given him in 1970. He later had it repaired.

[120] "FM stations," Pete explained to the crowd in Chicago back in August 1971 as Moon donned his headphones. "It gets boring up there, you see, so he tunes into the local station and grooves to Crosby, Stills and Nash."

[121] In *Before I Get Old*, Marsh suggests that perhaps Townshend was distressed that evening by the arrival backstage of original Who fan 'Irish' Jack Lyons, who hadn't seen the band in "some time." Lyons announced that he was now 30 years old, which stunned Townshend. "Incredible," Pete said later. "I couldn't believe it. I always thought he was younger than me, for a start. You always think the audience is younger."

"The Who rock band lived up to its reputation for violence on stage with an expensive display of guitar and amplifier-smashing at the Odeon Cinema last night," Steve Hughes wrote in the November 6 edition of the *Newcastle Evening Chronicle*.

The concert was stopped in chaos when guitarist Pete Townshend bawled out sound engineers, destroyed pre-recorded backing tapes and smashed... equipment during the group's presentation of its latest rock opera. It was a ridiculous display of unwarranted violence witnessed by thousands of easily-influenced teenage pop fans. Townshend, a temperamental but brilliant guitarist, is quite notorious for sudden fits of violence on stage which have almost become accepted as part of the act by his many followers. But this time stage hands rushed to disconnect electric amplifiers and Townshend's electric guitar after he swiped it into the stage floor.

Tempers flared after drummer Keith Moon had trouble with headphones. He let the drumsticks fly as the sound engineers battled to fix them. Then Townshend intervened, yelling at the engineers behind control panels on the side of the stage. He ripped out backing tapes and heaved over equipment into the side curtains. The three other members of the band... just stared. The safety net was lowered to the stage but the lights stayed out. Fans sat, quietly at first in total darkness and usherettes – obviously quite frightened – frantically flashed torchlights across the audience. After 10 minutes, with absolutely no trouble from the audience, the curtain was raised and Daltrey launched the band into a medley of 'oldies'. Then he yelled four-letter words at the audience, calling them – among many other derogatory terms – bastards and tried to explain everything by singing *My Generation*, a song about the generation gap and how no one understands the younger generation.

Then Townshend hurled his guitar against the upstanding microphone and smashed it into a score of pieces by banging it against the stage floor. He then turned on a row of piled amplifiers at the back of the stage and hurled a top one to the floor. Moon waded through his range of drums, spilling them across the stage and Daltrey took a last kick at his microphone. They all left to thunderous applause.

While Hughes referred to Townshend's antics as an "extremely childish publicity stunt", he added, "Otherwise, they were musically immaculate, as always."

Pridden, who had to be persuaded to remain with the band that night, found himself the next morning repairing the equipment Townshend had damaged. "We had no money and I had to buy a guitar out of my own pocket to keep the flag flying," Pridden told Richard Barnes. "And... [Pete] is on the phone, 'Do you need a hand down there Bob?' I understand it, if I didn't, I wouldn't have been with them all those years." Townshend and Moon appeared on the television show *Look North* the following night to apologize and assure fans that the tour would go on.

While Pete's playing was considered excellent during this tour (*NME*'s Roy Carr wrote "Townshend is 101 per cent pure raw nervous energy; his licks are as fresh and aggressive as in his old auto-destruct days."), *Quadrophenia* onstage simply wasn't working. The Who had played the new work in its entirety at Stoke On Trent ("...it was bloody horrible!", Townshend said from the stage the following night), and as the tour wound on the *Quadrophenia* segment steadily began to shrink as individual songs were dropped. John Entwistle explained his take on *Quadrophenia*'s demise as an onstage work to John Swenson:

> We had to play in time to the prerecorded tapes, and we found that if we couldn't hear them, even though Keith had the backing track on his earphones and could continue drumming in time, the rest of us would be completely lost. It turned out that we weren't able to hear the tapes most of the time, and we started to play sloppily and got bored and we noticed the kids were getting bored too. It's one thing to play to the sort of metronomic backing track of *Won't Get Fooled Again*, but with the complex time changes of *Quadrophenia* we got crossed up too easily. We had to play it perfectly to make it work each time, we had to play it with an incredible amount of energy or it sounded bad, whereas our normal act is set up with songs that even if we play badly will still sound good, so we can afford to have a bad night and still get away with it.

Following three dates in London the previous week[122], The Who's

---

[122] At the Lyceum, where there were more than twice as many fans as available tickets, which obviously resulted in less than ideal conditions. Crowd surges during The Who's set on 11 November reportedly nearly sent the PA tumbling into the crowd. "Luckily, people like me noticed and held [the speakers] in place for five to 10 minutes until the roadies realized what was going on and helped secure them again," photographer Robert Ellis told *Mojo* in 2004.

1973 North American tour[123] began in typically chaotic fashion at San Francisco's Cow Palace on November 20. This time it was Moon, not Townshend, who provided the theatrics, as he abruptly stopped playing and sprawled over his drum kit mid-show. Moon had faltered earlier in the show and was apparently temporarily revived by a cold shower from the road crew while Townshend passed the time by talking to the audience. This time, however, there was no reviving Keith, who was clearly done for the night[124]. The Who managed to continue the show that night after enlisting a drummer from the audience for the last three songs.

"Moon... slept solidly for ten hours afterwards, and stayed in the following evening watching telly on their night off in Los Angeles (a very unusual pastime for Keith Moon, especially in LA), determined to rest his tired frame and be on top form for the opening Forum show," Chris Charlesworth reported in *Melody Maker*. Charlesworth joined the band in the dressing room following the L.A. show, shortly after Keith Moon had taken it upon himself to hurl chocolate cake at his band mates.

> ...Townshend, who was on the receiving end of most of Moon's cake, looked tired but happy...About an hour earlier, 19,500 fans had stomped and cheered for over 15 minutes in the Forum, refusing to leave even though the house lights had been raised and probably well aware that the Who rarely do encores.
>
> But tonight their enthusiasm was rewarded with just that. The group came back and did an encore – actually *Baby Don't You Do It* – only the second time I've seen this happen in watching the Who around 20 times...
>
> Incredible? The Who doing an encore. So on they came again, weary, exhausted, Moon in particular must have been feeling the strain as *Baby Don't You Do It* is a number with much emphasis on the drumming. But they blasted through the song, climaxing with Townshend unstrapping the Gibson and, gripping the fretboard as if it were an axe, bringing it down on to the stage with a resounding crash time and time again until it cracked

---

The Who were oblivious and kept playing – never realizing that a disaster was so narrowly averted."

[123] A venue notably omitted from this U.S. tour was Madison Square Garden. John Swenson wrote in 1979 that the band "didn't want to play" at the venue due to a "lack of confidence" in their live act at the time.

[124] The official explanation was that Moon was suffering from 'jet lag', while Keith was reportedly actually suffering from the effects of PCP, an animal tranquilizer which had been slipped into one of his pre-show drinks. Richard Barnes recalled, "Keith had been drinking with two girls before the show and somebody had spiked their drinks... They were taken to hospital and apparently one of the girls very nearly died from it."

around the 12th fret.

As the tour wound through Texas, Georgia, Missouri, Illinois and Michigan, the animosity between Townshend and Daltrey simmered on. Frustrations peaked once again after an early December show in Montreal. The entire group was jailed for twelve hours as a result of a particularly enthusiastic bout of hotel room demolition[125]. The incident did nothing to ease tension between Townshend and Daltrey. "Pete wound up sharing a cell with Roger, who was furious because he'd retired to bed early and hadn't been involved in the demolition," wrote Charlesworth. "They were released the following morning on three thousand dollars bail and only just made Boston in time for that night's shows."

In response to a rabid demand for tickets for their three shows in London the previous month, The Who played an additional four shows in their home city upon the conclusion of the North American tour just prior to Christmas. Townshend was reportedly especially pleased with these dates, which were performed at the Sundown in Edmonton[126]. Townshend, according to *Melody Maker*, felt that the shows "broke down the barriers between performers and audience." "I felt like a member of the 'oo an' all that," Pete said, "but I also felt like one of the crowd."

When The Who left Britain for seven shows across the English Channel in France they decided to drop their highly-touted quadraphonic PA system due to the amount of complaints that had surfaced from fans whose view was either partially or completely obstructed by the two speaker towers which were positioned among the audience seating. Another change took place at the tour's conclusion – Pete had finally had enough of the problems with the *Quadrophenia* backing tapes: They were either too slow, too fast, or came in at the wrong time and proved to provide more in the way of artist frustration than audience enjoyment. The tapes were scrapped after the last show in France, and *Quadrophenia* itself was not played again until The Who showcased it in their 1996/97 tour.

With the enjoyable, intimate Sundown shows fresh in his mind, Townshend was faced with the polar opposite for The Who's next show: An early February gig at the cavernous Palais des Sports in Paris, which seated 26,000. *Melody Maker*'s Steve Lake gave his account of the show the following week:

---

[125] Pete reportedly got glass in his eyes when he and Moon heaved a marble coffee table through a window.
[126] While he'd been in the front row for the other three shows, photographer Robert Ellis witnessed the final Edmonton show from the balcony. Naturally, this was the night Townshend smashed his guitar. "I'd never captured Pete smashing his guitar on film," he told *Mojo* in 2004. "…Suddenly [Pete] threw his guitar up in the air and proceeded to smash it up. Bastard! I asked him why he'd done it and he said because you weren't there to take the shot."

> Speeding from the Palais des Sports in a chauffer-driven limousine, Pete Townshend expressed bitter reservations... It was too big, he said, far too big. It felt impersonal. He was disgusted, too, with the French lighting crew, who had apparently bungled the explicitly simple instructions Townshend had given them...

After just three songs, a transformer blew, shutting down power to The Who's P.A. system, and emitting a cloud of smoke ("I thought Roger's make-up was burning off," Moon quipped). Fifteen minutes later, power to the P.A. was restored and the concert resumed. Lake continued:

> They determined to compensate the crowd for the electronic misdemeanor... and delivered a set so packed with visual action that it was astounding that they were able to sustain the pace they set for themselves...
>
> *Drowned* from *Quadrophenia* was the absolute killer, reaching crescendo with Townshend demolishing another $350 guitar, bouncing it twice off the stage, and finally snapping it at the base of the neck with a sledgehammer swipe at his speaker stack. Sparks flew from the jack-plug socket.
>
> ...*See Me, Feel Me* wound up the show proper, following hard on the heels of *Pinball Wizard*, and the lighting crew again upped the house lights to reveal twenty-six thousand pairs of upraised arms waving, and flapping back and forth in approximate time. It was a magnificent and moving sight from the stage. Whoever said that rock and roll is essentially about the transference of raw energy was exactly right. The Who were giving it all away and the kids were sending it right back at them...
>
> The Who huddled stage center, arms entwined, sweating profusely. They grinned their appreciation and staggered off, carrying the triumphant Moon aloft. Paris won't forget for a long time.

Mid-April marked Pete's first ever solo concert, at the Roundhouse, Chalk Farm, London, an unnerving but successful experience. The Sunday, April 14 Easter benefit show was organized to raise funds for the Camden Square Community Play Center. Pete was slated to appear along with other acts such as Coast Road Drive, Byzantium, and the headliner, American folk singer Tim Hardin. When Hardin withdrew from the lineup, Townshend was faced with headliner status, and a much longer set than he'd anticipated.

"...I thought it was going to be a very small thing but it turned out to be bloody massive," Pete told Richard Barnes. "And people were ringing me up and saying, 'I hear you're doing a solo gig at the Roundhouse' and I thought, 'Hold on, this is getting out of control,'" he said. In true Townshend fashion, Pete spent the week prior to the show feverishly rehearsing his set. "When I met Pete on the day of his solo concert he was as white as a sheet," Barnes recalled in 1982. "...He told me that he hadn't been able to eat for the last three days."

Townshend practically brought his entire home studio to the Roundhouse show, performing amidst tape recorders, effects boxes, several guitars and microphones and miscellaneous other equipment, including a table with a lamp for his set list and lyric sheets. Included in his performance were Who favorites such as *Substitute, Pinball Wizard* and *Behind Blue Eyes*, and even the original demo tape of *My Generation*. Pete also played *Girl of the North Country* and *Corrina, Corrina* (both recorded by Bob Dylan on his 1963 release *The Freewheelin' Bob Dylan*), and Tim Hardin's *If I Were a Carpenter*. While Pete had played solo at private Meher Baba gatherings, this was his first public appearance without The Who. The show reportedly went well, apart from an obnoxious fan who repeatedly screamed for Townshend to play *Underture*. After repeated warnings, Pete went into the crowd and at least threatened the fan (one account states that Pete actually punched him). Pete reportedly added a few innovative lines to *Magic Bus*: "I'm so nervous I guess it shows - don't say a thing about my great big nose."

On 18 May, The Who headlined a day-long concert at London's Charlton Athletic Football Stadium (reportedly the first time a British football stadium had been used for such an event) in front of a crowd officially set at 50,000, but estimated to be closer to 80,000 due to gatecrashers. Supporting acts included Montrose, Lindisfarne, Bad Company, Lou Reed and Humble Pie. "They had abandoned *Quadrophenia*, retaining just two songs *5:15* and *The Punk Meets The Godfather*, and settled on a set that stretched back through the past," wrote Chris Charlesworth. "Unfortunately, the weather was atrocious and Pete was depressed at the crowd's passive acceptance of what he considered to be a mediocre performance by the group. The group had not played together since the three French *Quadrophenia* concerts in February, yet it was only Pete who complained about their lack of cohesion. Worse was to come."

Chapter 7

"Why we haven't foundered, obviously, is that we have a tradition in the band which nobody dares to transgress. If anybody mentions breaking up they literally have to wash their mouth out with soap and water...it's like swearing in church. It just doesn't come into the picture."
- Pete Townshend, 1974

"If I had ever dug in my heels about Tommy and said no-one has the right to change my conception, it would have killed Tommy dead as a concept. A dead classic. I felt it was still evolving, still unfinished and still alive...
"With Ken Russell I was prepared to make concessions and compromise some points in order to have Ken make his alterations – it just meant another evolution in the concept. I told him I didn't care if he altered all the words if he needed to:
"Listening to you I get the porridge" – whatever he wanted."
- Pete Townshend, 1975

As the recording of *Quadrophenia* was being wrapped up at Ramport studios, the likelihood of *Tommy* becoming a feature film was slowly materializing. Talks concerning the prospect of a movie, which had been on and off since Kit Lambert had written a script in 1969, took a positive turn when Robert Stigwood became involved in the deal. In the distinct absence of Kit Lambert it was Stigwood (who had produced 1973's *Jesus Christ Superstar*) who negotiated a movie deal with Columbia Pictures, stepped in as producer and provided the leadership and financial wherewithal to land stars Jack Nicholson, Tina Turner and Ann-Margret, and director Ken Russell. Russell had been Pete's choice as director for a *Tommy* movie just after the album was released in 1969, but Russell had told Townshend that he was "booked up for the next couple of years," according to Pete.

Over the four years since *Tommy's* release, Pete had been approached by several prospective directors, but none apparently tickled his fancy, nor he theirs. "Everyone wanted to do the film – everyone thought they had the rights," Ken Russell recalled in 1994, "and there were hundreds of scripts as well, and probably dozens of directors for all I know, but none of the scripts or directors had apparently pleased Townshend."

"...what has happened in the past," Pete told *Rolling Stone* in June, 1974, "is that an American director has come over and taken me to lunch, sat me down and said...'You know, Pete, we're talking about a million-dollar movie here, and er, what we wanna know is your thoughts, we wanna know how you wanna make the movie, Pete.' They were saying," Townshend explained, "'OK, you little English poof, you make the film and please make it gross six times as much as the album did.' And I'd sit there and tell them how to make it. They'd go away and decide, 'Well, maybe we were wrong about wanting to make it.' A week later another mogul comes over, takes me out to lunch, and says, 'Pete, we wanna know how you wanna make the movie...'"

"On the day I met Ken Russell I was strolling around London recording street noises in stereo for the *Quadrophenia* album," Pete recalled in *The Story of Tommy*.

> I had my tape machine in a suitcase and the mikes concealed in a holdall.
> At the time I was after 'casual conversation.' I saw an interesting group and sidled sideways up to them pointing my holdall into their midst. The conversation I heard was fascinating. In the group were Ken Russell, Chris Stamp and Mike Carrearas, who were all unhappy that they hadn't been able to locate me that afternoon for a meeting they were about to have. As you can imagine, I just felt all this meant that the film HAD TO BE.

Ken Russell began talking with Pete about making *Tommy* into a movie in mid-1973, with Pete starting work on the soundtrack for the film upon the conclusion of The Who's live dates in France in February, 1974. "The great thing about Russell," Pete said, "was it was his idea to do [the film]. He came up with suggestions, and I realized I was in the presence of the 'Guv'nor.' So all I have to do is run off when he tells me he needs a new song and just do it. It's great working under somebody rather than always having to do the pushing and leading."

Despite this initial burst of enthusiasm, the novelty of working on the *Tommy* soundtrack quickly wore off. The job grew more and more complicated and the responsibilities multiplied as the days passed. Pete had accepted the role of musical director, but only after his fee was increased by a considerable amount, reportedly from $100,000 to £100,000. Townshend said he spent six weeks in "total seclusion" in his studio preparing the *Tommy* soundtrack, a period of "manic involvement" during which he claimed to have put in as many as 23 hours a day. Townshend later referred to composition of the tracks, each precisely timed to fit its accompanying piece of film, as "mind-bending and complex." After all, the *Tommy* film contained no dialogue; it was music from beginning to end. After the tracks were assembled at home in Twickenham, Pete then spent April and May 1974 re-recording the soundtrack at Ramport studios with an all-star cast of musicians. Recording of the *Tommy* soundtrack was completed prior to the movie's filming, which meant that if any changes were made to the original script during the filming process, the soundtrack had to be adjusted. Prior to shooting, the movie was originally budgeted at £1 million, and shooting set to take 12 weeks. Since the movie wound up costing around £2 million, and shooting took over 22 weeks, one can imagine how many adjustments and rewrites must have occurred during filming.

"A lot of what I was dealing with was incredibly complex and time-consuming and a bit of an education," Pete told *Uncut* in 2004.

> I could go and do a film score tomorrow. I won't. I've been offered many. I turned down *Blade Runner* because I thought, 'Fuck, I'm not going to go there again.'
> As a composer you believe you're king, but even when you compose for a movie, even if the movie is your composition, as it was, Ken Russell was the king. So what would actually happen is we'd go into the studio, he'd sit with his eyes shut, we'd play and he'd say, 'No, this bit needs to be longer,' and I'd say, 'Well, what do you want us to do?' and he'd say, 'Just make it longer, I need more time.' So we'd play a longer track and you'd find that would be Ronnie Wood pissing about on slide guitar for 15 or 16 bars and then you'd find that when it's finished, the editor decides that it's not enough music to cut to so he'd loop up stuff, and then I would have to work on these loops.
> I just felt like a dogsbody. I thought, 'Where's the music?' There are bits of the *Tommy* film, in the *Acid Queen* bit, for example, where you see Tina Turner doing all her stuff and you hear this loop going round with some sound effects chucked on top of it in a hurry to try and make it sound a bit different. I didn't feel that I would ever, ever, *ever* be able to work with a director again, and I never have. I loved working with Ken and I loved doing the *Tommy* movie, but once is enough.

The use of other musicians in the recording of the *Tommy* soundtrack was born of necessity, since as The Who were about to go into the studio to cut the soundtrack to Russell's film, Keith Moon reportedly fell ill and couldn't work[127]. "In a way," said Townshend, "it was a blessing in disguise. I mean we were terrified as to how it was going to work out without him, because we only had two months to do the whole thing. So I thought rather than try and replace him with *a* drummer, I'd choose an ideal bunch of musicians for each song." Stars such as Eric Clapton, Tina Turner, Elton John (who brought along his stage band) and Ron Wood were called upon to lend their services, along with other musicians such as pianists Chris Stainton and Nicky Hopkins, and drummers Kenney Jones and Mick Ralphs. "Yes, most people were happy to come and work on the album," Pete later recalled. "...*Tommy* might be a bit of a cliched old hag but he commands respect."

Other stars were considered for major roles in the film, including Stevie Wonder, who was among those considered for the role of the Pinball Wizard. "Well, this is a really awful story because Stevie Wonder was offered the part of Pinball Wizard by Robert Stigwood and I think was interested in doing it," Pete told Richard Barnes in 1975.

> Then Ken said you can't have a blind negro being beaten by a deaf dumb and blind white kid, because, well, it's just racially wrong. When the news got back to Stevie Wonder he was incredibly annoyed. When he came over to England, Eric Clapton and I went to see him and he wouldn't talk to us. He wouldn't talk to Eric at all because I was with Eric, and Eric couldn't work out what was going on. But when Eric saw him again in America he was really nice to him.

Other notables were considered for major roles in the film, including Mick Jagger and David Bowie (both considered for the Pinball Wizard or the Acid Queen), Lou Reed (also considered for the Acid Queen), and David Essex[128]. Pete had originally wanted Tiny Tim as the Pinball Wizard ("I imagined that it would sound really great on a hundred ukeleles," Pete said in 1975), Arthur Brown as the Doctor, and the role of Mother, Pete said, "...by a sort of older jazz singer who could sing rock, like Cleo Laine or Georgia Brown or somebody of that ilk, or maybe even somebody like Joan Baez." In fact, Pete's cast list and Ken Russell's cast

---

[127] Or maybe he wasn't ill at all. Dave Marsh wrote in *Before I Get Old* that "Keith Moon was angry because Uncle Ernie, a major role in the Lambert script, had been whittled down, most of the good bits given to Oliver Reed, and so he made himself unavailable for the rerecording..." Moon had taken on other film work (*Stardust*) and the recording of a Harry Nilsson album (*Pussy Cats*) during this period.

[128] "Ken Russell wanted David Essex in it, which was very weird because everyone else was against it," Pete told Richard Barnes in 1975. "I like him as a bloke, and I really feel bad about the fact that he was ever suggested and did the work that he did and was then turned down, because I don't like the way it reflects on me. Because we are good friends."

list were polar opposites. "...I resisted all the legitimate actors in it," Pete said in 1975. "I resisted them all. I didn't want Ann-Margret in it. I didn't want Jack Nicholson and I didn't want Oliver Reed in it, because none of them were rock people and I wanted people that could sing rock – it was Ken who said that he had to have those people."

One scene in the *Tommy* film required footage of The Who onstage. Naturally, the shooting of this scene didn't take place without incident. "...there was only one real injury" during the filming of *Tommy*, Richard Barnes wrote in *The Story of Tommy*.

> It was when the Who are playing and the crowd had to storm the stage. The signal for this was Townshend smashing his guitar and throwing the neck up in the air, but one take he threw it a bit high, and it came down on a girl's head. "There was blood everywhere," remembers Townshend, "and she was carried off to hospital. But she came back a few hours later and told us she was 'very honored' to have been smashed over the head by Pete Townshend's guitar. I gave her the guitar."

In the same book, Barnes describes a scene in the film with "...Eric Clapton strolling down the aisle doing *Eyesight To The Blind* flanked by a slightly uncomfortable looking Pete Townshend and John Entwistle." Pete told Barnes, "I've piddled about with acting, but I don't feel comfortable doing it." This was despite the fact that "everyone was pissed out of their brains that day," according to Pete.

Once shooting was completed by the end of summer, 1974, the process of dubbing and synchronizing the music to film took place, "a tedious and painstaking job," according to Chris Charlesworth, "which Pete accomplished less than willingly." A number of mixes had to be constructed to suit various film formats, which saw Pete and a team of technicians working all the way to Christmas.

The *Tommy* soundtrack was released in February and March, 1975, in the U.S. and Britain, respectively. The movie soundtrack featured three new Townshend compositions in *Champagne*, *Mother and Son*, and *TV Studio*. While none of the additional Townshend songs can necessarily be considered important, highlights of the soundtrack include Tina Turner's rendition of *Acid Queen*, and Elton John's *Pinball Wizard*. Oliver Reed and Jack Nicholson's distinct shared inability to sing[129] was somewhat relieved

---

[129] "Robert Stigwood rang up and said he'd got Jack Nicholson, and I said 'Who's Jack Nicholson?' and he said he was one of the biggest stars in America at the moment," Pete recalled in 1977's *The Story of Tommy*. "So I said 'Can he sing?' and he said no." Pete quickly responded, "I'm not having another fucker in this film who can't sing. Oliver Reed's

by Pete's extensive use of choir-like backing vocals, which he and close friend/fellow Baba lover Billy Nicholls conjured up in Ramport studios. The album climbed all the way to number 2 in America and 21 in Britain.

Ken Russell's *Tommy* movie, released in March, 1975[130], was, to put it mildly, coolly received by music critics across the board, the film regarded as camp and farcical, or as Dave Marsh pointed out, "a fairy tale for new initiates." Pete, however, took the movie seriously. "Many Who fans feel the *Tommy* film is not what the Who is about," Pete wrote in *Rolling Stone* in 1977, "or even what *Tommy* is about. In truth, it is exactly what it is about. It is the prime example of rock & roll throwing off its three-chord musical structure, discarding its attachment to the three-minute single, openly taking on the unfashionable questions about spirituality and religion and yet hanging grimly on to the old ways at the same time." Townshend was later nominated for a 'Best Score Adaptation' Oscar for his work on the *Tommy* soundtrack.

"The people that didn't understand it or didn't run with it were the people that had preconceptions to the way it was going to look," Pete told *WNEW*'s Scott Muni in April, 1978.

> They'd spent too long living with that album, they had got their own film in their head and they didn't like somebody like Ken Russell coming along and making pictures which didn't fit in. I had to extinguish in my own mind the film which I had for *Tommy*, before I could even begin to talk to Ken about the way it should look. You know, when you're working with a director that's going to be any good at all, you've got to let the man do it. ...And so I decided, right, let Ken do it his way, and I had to let go of my own ideas. And consequently I really enjoyed it and it really came to me afresh. But to a lot of people who hadn't let go their own ideas about it, it was sometimes disappointing and sometimes shocking.

Pete once again espoused the movie's (and Ken Russell's) importance in a 1993 interview with the *New York Post*. "I still love it," he said. "I don't know whether I did the right thing by the piece or Who fans, but Ken Russell is, in my eyes, still one of the great British directors, and a great eccentric. As it recedes further into the distance, you realize that it's a great movie; the cameos in it were great, and whether it's the best thing or not, we probably have him to thank for MTV." Russell, incidentally, called

---

giving me nightmares as it is." In the same book, Oliver Reed is quoted as saying, "I sang a few notes and Townshend fell about laughing in the studio."

[130] Chris Stamp received an Executive Producer credit for the *Tommy* film; Kit Lambert was not recognized.

Tommy "...one of the easiest and most pleasurable films I've ever made."

Pete's exhausting experiences in assembling and producing the *Tommy* soundtrack had pushed him to the brink of a nervous breakdown not unlike the one he'd experienced at the New York *Who's Next* sessions. His "gung-ho" attitude had been replaced by one of sheer resignation. He was truly frazzled. "Had I known how much time is involved in making a feature I think I would have stopped fantasizing about films altogether," Pete said in June. "People talk to me – 'How can you spend two years making an album like *Quadrophenia?*' – but it's nothing like this."

He drank heavily. Brandy was the nectar of choice, and thus began a dependency on alcohol which was to plague Pete for almost eight years. Burned out, suffering from hearing loss and beginning to lose his hair[131], he was on the brink of a breakdown. A hearing specialist had warned him that further live performances could permanently damage his hearing, and in April a confused and concerned Pete told Bill Curbishley that he would never work on the road with The Who again. He was admittedly "mixed up." "...I might even have said that I felt the Who was finished," he said in 1977. Exhausted from his self-imposed workaholic schedule, he decided that his home studio was partly to blame, and "tore it all out," leaving his country studio as his sole demo-recording venue.

Further evidence of burnout followed. At The Who's closed concert for the *Tommy* extras in Portsmouth in May, Pete's mental state was hazy. "...I signed several managerial and recording contracts in a complete fog," Pete recalled in 1977. "The only event I remember is quietly screaming for help deep inside..." Pete didn't realize he'd signed anything until a legal problem arose several months later.

"I got very scared by memory blackouts, as scared as I had ever been on bad LSD trips eight years before," Pete recalled.

> Once in July 1974 – just after the *Tommy* filming – I sort of 'came to' in the back of my own car. Keith and John were with me (we were probably going to a club), but although I knew who they were, I didn't recognize either my car or my driver, who had been working for me for over two months. The shock that hit me as the pieces fell into place was even more frightening than the black holes in my head as the memory lapses began. Eight drug-free years and still this mental demise.

In addition to his poor physical and mental state, Pete discovered that a large amount of his publishing money couldn't be accounted for,

---

[131] Pete's hair loss, according to Dave Marsh, "...terrified him. He still wasn't thirty. He had scalp treatments, which restored most of the loss, but these were painful, time-consuming and, while he underwent them, disfiguring."

roughly half a million pounds. This tipped the scales in favor of Daltrey regarding the band's management dispute which had surfaced the previous year. "He finally sided with Roger," Charlesworth wrote in 1984, "and, along with Entwistle, sued [Lambert and Stamp] for mismanagement[132]. Bill Curbishley took over officially as manager of The Who in the summer of 1974, but the immediate result of these legal proceedings was to tie up The Who's record royalties until a judgement could be reached. Their only source of income, therefore, was from live appearances."

It was in this sorry state that Pete and The Who returned to the stage in mid-1974, for four shows at New York's Madison Square Garden. The June 10-14 shows had all sold out after the band had aired just one sixty-second commercial on a local radio station. "Pete was in a depressive spiral when he checked into the Pierre Hotel on Fifth Avenue at the beginning of the week," Chris Charlesworth wrote in 1984. "He'd been on the wagon for a few days and was sober at the Garden rehearsals but on the opening night things started to go wrong. Equipment malfunctioned, unwanted squeaks belched forth and the PA sound, which in the past had been crisp as anyone's, was muggy and stilted."

The bad start was simply too much for Pete in his current fragile state. Charlesworth, who interviewed Pete during his stay in New York, wrote that "he seemed in a bad way, stressed out with working on the *Tommy* soundtrack, drinking too much and torn between the wishes of the fans, the band and what he wanted to do himself...I think he felt a great responsibility to everyone: the other three, the fans, the film producers and, of course, his family...He needed a break from everything." Pete was even staying at a separate hotel, opting for the luxurious Pierre while the band settled for their regular New York digs, the Navarro.

The Madison Square Garden shows, all reportedly substandard performances, soon demonstrated to Pete that he was in no shape to be on stage with a band regarded as the finest live rock outfit in the world. "In all the years I'd been with The Who I'd never had to force myself," he told Nik Cohn.

> All the leaping about and guitar smashing, even though I'd done it a thousand times, it was always totally natural. And then, on the first night at the Garden, I

---

[132] "We were well out of it," Chris Stamp said later about his and Lambert's condition at the time. "We were fucking out to lunch, no doubt about that. There was no need to be around any more." By 1976, Lambert had returned to London from Italy, and was deeply in debt. "...he was living in unbelievable squalor in his house in Egerton Crescent," a Lambert associate told Andrew Motion in 1987. "There had been a fire, and he was virtually living under a tarpaulin over the fire damage. He had his two dogs and seven puppies with him, and there was dog shit everywhere. You had to hold your nose when you went in. And it was terribly hot – he had to have heaters on all the time because of his druggy state."

suddenly lost it. I didn't know what I was doing there, stuck up on stage in front of all these people. I had no instinct left; I had to do it from memory. So I looked down into the front row and all these kids were squealing 'Jump, jump, jump.' And I panicked...I was lost...The other three shows I was terrified.

Pete began drinking brandy straight from the bottle onstage. "I got smashed or I couldn't have gone on," he told Cohn. "...my drunken legs gave way under me as I tried to do a basic cliche leap and shuffle," he later added. "For the remainder of the week," Charlesworth wrote, "Pete submerged himself in brandy, stayed out most of the night clubbing with Keith and John and joined in heated disputes backstage." At the final show, June 14, Pete smashed three Gibson Les Paul Deluxes, perhaps demonstrating the heights his frustrations had reached. Not content to be left out of the wanton destruction, Keith smashed Pete's only remaining Les Paul, effectively ending the show. Upon his return to London, a miserable Townshend declared that he'd decided to stop touring indefinitely.

Following the disappointing Madison Square Garden performances, Pete's focus once again shifted away from The Who. He and Keith Moon appeared onstage at three of Eric Clapton's shows in the Southeast U.S.[133], before he returned his focus to his Avatar, Meher Baba. In autumn, 1974, Murshida Ivy Duce, leader of a San Francisco-based Baba group named Sufism Reoriented, visited London. Duce was "head of the Sufi movement in the States, as reoriented under Meher Baba's directives," Pete explained. "Murshida Duce is a remarkable woman," he wrote in 1977.

> She heads a group of about 300 initiates, all committed to total honesty and respect for her authority. She has Meher Baba's sanction as the legitimate Murshid along with "in line" decree from her own deceased Murshid, Murshida Martin. Murshida Martin herself took over under the instructions of the famous Inayat Khan, a spiritual teacher and master musician whose books on Sufism present a poetic system for modern life.
>
> 'Sufism Reoriented' today focuses its initiates on developing their devotion to Meher Baba. Meher Baba gave an explicit charter to Murshida Duce and it is under the limitations of this charter that she works today. I am not a Sufi initiate, but her spontaneous help in my life has always touched me.

---

[133] Clapton, following successful rehab and the comeback show at the Rainbow, was back on tour.

"Pete arranged a large reception for them," wrote fellow Baba devotee Delia DeLeon in 1991. DeLeon, a leading British Baba follower, frequently met and corresponded with Meher Baba from 1931 until his death in 1969. She had met Pete back in 1967 through Mike McInnerney, and the two developed a close friendship. Pete shared some thoughts on DeLeon in January, 1990 in the introduction to the book she wrote describing her experiences with Baba, *The Ocean of Love*:

> Delia DeLeon was a follower of long standing when she influenced me and others who looked for spiritual truth during the '60s. It appeared that apart from her love for Him, her spiritual Master, she possessed and wanted nothing. He was her obsession. He was her absolute and singular focus. As I enjoyed a wonderful family and successful career when I first heard about Meher Baba such total devotion was impossible for me, but Delia DeLeon became an example and inspiration for me.

One evening during Murshida Duce's visit, "as he drove me home, Pete broached the idea of my making a film telling stories of my experiences with Baba," DeLeon wrote in *The Ocean Of Love*, published in 1991. She agreed, somewhat hesitantly, to go ahead with the idea, but was shocked at how quickly this idea would become reality. Pete wasted no time in organizing a film crew. "To my horror," DeLeon recounted, "within four days, I was told the film crew would come to my flat to start – no preparations, no scenario, no discussion of questions. They turned up, plus Pete, Billy Nichols, Richard Barnes, and John Annunziato, a photographer who had arrived in London with his wife, Linda. I was recovering from an angina attack but managed to pull myself together, though how I stood up for two days to seven hours of interviewing I will never know." The movie was eventually finished for the opening of Meher Baba Oceanic in July, 1976.

Meanwhile, as Pete and Roger had been tied up working on Ken Russell's *Tommy* film and Keith was basking in a drug- and alcohol-induced haze in his Malibu beach house, John addressed The Who's need for the release of a new album in the near future. Searching through the band's old tape boxes at the Track Records offices, he found eleven songs deemed worthy of release, which would comprise *Odds and Sods*.

The album featured three *Lifehouse* songs which didn't make *Who's Next*: *Put The Money Down*, *Too Much of Anything*, and *Pure and Easy*. *Postcard* and *Now I'm A Farmer*, remnants from the scrapped 1970 EP, were included, along with the band's unused song for the American Cancer Society, *Little Billy*. 1968's *Glow Girl* and the original High Numbers' debut *I'm The Face* are included, as is *Faith In Something Bigger*. Longtime stage staple *Naked Eye* and *Quadrophenia* predecessor *Long Live Rock* round out an interesting collection which leaves one realizing what a great band The Who were to have leftovers such as these.

Odds and Sods was released in September in Britain[134], the following month in the United States. The album did surprisingly well on both sides of the Atlantic, reaching number 10 in the U.K., 15 in the U.S. "Far from exploiting a random set of discards," read the *Rolling Stone* review in December.

> *Odds & Sods* gives the listener a fascinating glimpse of one of our best bands, caught in the process of forging a style...Ironically, the new album accomplishes de facto what *Quadrophenia* strained for – a portrait of rock as a privileged but insular form of life, destined to perish with youth...
>
> *Odds & Sods* has no plot and boasts no premeditated motifs. Instead, its hodgepodge of tracks, thoughtfully paced and annotated, presents pop music raw, the rough edges intact. Rather than fictionalizing the process, *Odds & Sods* simply documents the metamorphosis of Britain's quintessential mid-Sixties rock band.

In April, 1975, the month after *Tommy*'s glitzy premiere (which only added to his current depressed state), and just a few weeks prior to his thirtieth birthday, Pete gave a long interview with Roy Carr of *NME*. Carr found Townshend in a bitter state of mind and questioning his place in music. "I really hate feeling too old to be doing what I'm doing," Pete told Carr. "I recently went to do a BBC-TV interview and when I arrived at the studios there were all these young kids waiting outside for the Bay City Rollers. As I passed them by, one of the kids recognized me and said, 'Ooo look, it's Pete Townshend' and a couple of them chirped 'Ello Pete.' And that was it. Yet the first time the Who appeared at those same studios on *Top Of The Pops*, a gang of little girls smashed in the plate glass front door on the building."

He described the emotions that had begun to take hold of him at the Madison Square Garden shows, that perhaps The Who were becoming has-beens (at one point, he stated "...to some extent The Who have become a golden oldies band..."). This was a point that Daltrey vehemently disagreed with. "It's just that when I'm standing up there on stage playing rock'n'roll," Pete explained, "I often feel that I'm too old for it...When

---

[134] The photo used on the cover of *Odds & Sods* was taken by Graham Hughes backstage in Chicago. "Pete didn't like it and ripped it up," Hughes told *Mojo* in 2004. "Then he realized that shot was the one, so we stuck it back together and that was it – all tears and Sellotape."

Roger speaks out about 'we'll all be rockin'' in our wheelchairs' he might be but you won't catch me rockin' in no wheelchair..."

"I can tell you that when we were gigging in this country at the early part of last year I was thoroughly depressed," Pete lamented. "I honestly felt that the Who were going on stage every night and, for the sake of the die-hard fans, copying what the Who used to be."

> I dunno what's happening sometimes. All I know is that when we last played Madison Square Garden I felt acute shades of nostalgia. All the Who freaks had crowded around the front of the stage and when I gazed out into the audience all I could see were those same sad faces that I'd seen at every New York Who gig. There was about a thousand of 'em and they turned up for every bloody show at the Garden, as if it were some Big Event – the Who triumph over New York...It was dreadful. They were telling us what to play. Every time I tried to make an announcement they all yelled out shhrrruppp Townshend and let Entwistle play *Boris The Spider,* and, if that wasn't bad enough, during the other songs they'd all start chanting 'jump... jump... jump... jump... jump.' I was so brought down by it all! I mean, is this what it had all degenerated into?

Pete's frustrations weren't limited to the band's stage act. He also expressed a great deal of bitterness regarding songwriting. "...I've been working on tracks for my next solo album," Pete continued. "Invariably what will happen is that once we all get into the studio, I'll think 'Oh fuck it,' and I'll play Roger, John and Keith the tracks I've been keeping for my own album and they'll pick the best. So as long as the Who exists, I'll never get the pick of my own material...and that's what I dream of. But if the Who ever broke up because the material was substandard then I'd really kick myself."

"...they are the people who put the pressures on me," Pete said.

> Let me make this clear. I don't put pressures on them. I don't say 'we've got to get into the studio this very minute because I've got these songs that I've just gotta get off my chest.' It's always the other way around. They always rush up to me and insist that we've got to cut a new album and get back on the road.
>
> Believe me, there have been times in the Who's career then I would have gladly relinquished the responsibilities of coming up with our next single or album

to another writer. There've been a lot of people who said they would have a go but somehow it never quite worked out.

The interview was published both in Britain and the U.S. Pete later regretted having been so open with the press, not the only time in his career he would feel this way. "After my total downward spiral during the filming of *Tommy*," Pete recalled in 1977, "and after living with the desperate fear of further humiliation of the Madison Square Garden variety, I did a few interviews with the London-based rock press. My final undoing was to see among them a face I knew and to imagine that it belonged to someone who cared about me more as a person than as a rock performer. I should never have expected that."

> Blaming the group, I blurted out my tears, my depressions and woe to a couple of writers whose syrhpathies were, to put it mildly, a little to the left wing of rock journalism. When they appeared in print, the results were catastrophic. Roger was understandably outraged, and retaliated to my abject misery in his own interviews published a few weeks later...I feel now as though we were both, to an extent, manipulated by a skillful and opportunistic reporting chain, that the derision handed out to me by Roger for my weakness and indulgence did me a lot of good. It hurt me at the time, but when you're so far down, so the saying goes, the gutter looks up. I had, after all, been derisive of Roger in print many times.

Pete's response to his perceived manipulation by the press was to stop granting interviews, a major step for someone who communicated so much through this medium.

In spring, 1975, the same period in which he gave the Roy Carr interview, Pete was busy composing for the next Who album. Not surprisingly, he found himself in a somber mood. However, the long, heartfelt interview with Carr and the songwriting process proved cathartic for Townshend. "I got my head down to try to write a bit for the coming album and came up with some reality tinged with bitterness," he wrote in 1977. "It was hard for me to admit what I knew as I was composing; that what was happening to me was an exorcism. Suicide notes tend to flush out the trouble felt by the potential ledge jumpers. But once the truth is out, there's no need to leap."

Always mindful of the future, Pete and the band held several meetings to discuss The Who's direction at this time. "For two years I was anticipating the punk thing," Pete told *Trouser Press* in 1980, "wondering how it was going to happen, and getting really frustrated when it didn't."

I spent a lot of time personally forcing the band, especially Roger, into conversations about it and around the time of *The Who by Numbers* we used to have really quite heavy conversations about where music was going to go — particularly in this country — and whether we should be involved in it, and the problem with Moon living in America and living that Hollywood lifestyle and whether we should try to force him to come back to England – all those kind of things. Whether our music should change, whether we should let the Who tradition just bash on until it got really boring, whether we should try to force change by starting labels and working with other bands. Before the emergence of punk, the Who was the only band who actually sat 'round a table to decide, "Should we go on or not?" Would we be doing music a favor if we just fucking stopped? We actually considered that.

One idea, which had been announced during The Who's Madison Square Garden shows the previous summer, had the band hoping to record an album of songs written by other songwriters, such as Ray Davies and Frank Zappa. Pete told the *New York Times* that he planned a television show to complement the album, with one scene featuring "The Who and 100 topless lady accordionists," from which remains *Squeeze Box,* which appeared on the band's next album.

Following the meetings, Pete began recording demos of his new material at his Goring-on-Thames studio in April. Along with demos of the ten songs which would ultimately appear on *The Who By Numbers,* Pete recorded *Girl in a Suitcase,* which was later released on 1987's *Another Scoop,* and *To Barney Kessell,* a jazz-oriented composition which Pete dedicated to "a great guitarist." "I play a lot like this," Pete wrote in 1983. "...it isn't really exploratory jazz as I work with fairly well tried chords, but it's a style of guitar I enjoy." *To Barney Kessell* surfaced on 1983's *Scoop.*

Soon after Pete's interview with Roy Carr, The Who began recording their next album, *The Who by Numbers*, at the Shepperton Sound Stage, using Ronnie Lane's mobile set-up for recording. The band opted for this location over their own Ramport studios[135]. This, combined with Pete's decision to record the album without any synthesizers, gives *The Who by Numbers* a guitar-based, back-to-basics feel. With an eye toward producing a quality effort, Pete and Keith both (at least temporarily) curbed their

---

[135] "There's a strong chance we'll never record there again because it's always booked," Pete told *Hit Parader* in 1974. "And we can't get the time. There just aren't any studios in London, there are only about ten. Everybody in the world wants to record there."

substantial alcohol intakes, and Roger managed to keep quiet about Pete's recent derision of the band in the press, although he took much of the criticism very personally (Chris Charlesworth pointed out that Roger was constantly "...fighting back an urge to reply."). In Daltrey's opinion, the friction between himself and Townshend may have improved the quality of the work. "Pete was incredibly down when he first played us those songs, and very cynical about what he had written," Roger commented later. "When I first heard them it made me unbelievably angry. His cynicism and my anger combined made *The Who By Numbers* a good Who album, although I didn't think so at the time. Without the anger it would have been unbearable."

At one point, Pete was surprisingly excited about the record, telling the press, "Track by track, the new album that the Who are making is going to be the best thing we've ever done. But if people expect another grandiose epic then they ain't gonna get it. 'Cause this time we're going for a superb singles album."

The recording sessions continued into May, with the bulk of the material being done in just a few days in the month's final week. Overdubs were added in June, and the final product was mixed in July and August at Basing Street Studios in Notting Hill, London. "Recording the album seemed to take me nowhere," Pete recalled in 1977.

> Roger was angry with the world at the time. Keith seemed as impetuous as ever, on the wagon one minute, off it the next. John was obviously gathering strength throughout the whole period; the great thing about it was that he seemed to know we were going to need him more than ever before in the coming year.
>
> Glyn Johns, who was producing the album, was going through the most fantastic traumas at home with his marriage. I felt partly responsible because The Who recording schedule had, as usual, dragged on and on, sweeping all individuals and their needs aside. Glyn worked harder on *The Who By Numbers* than I've ever seen him. He had to, not because the tracks were weak or the music poor (though I'll admit it's not a definitive Who album), but because the group was so useless. We played cricket between takes or went to the pub. I personally had never done that before. I felt detached from my own songs, from the whole record; although I did discover some terrific sportsmen in our road crew.

The Who by Numbers, released on the Polydor label (and not

Track[136] – a sign of the band's deteriorating relationship with Lambert and Stamp), was released in October, reaching number 7 in Britain and number 8 in the U.S. The album was well received in the press, with Roy Carr concluding in his review that it was no less than "brilliant." A few years after its release, Pete told *WNEW*'s Scott Muni, "I really liked a lot of the stuff on that album."

Many viewed the album more as a Townshend solo venture than a true Who outing[137], and the introspective *However Much I Booze* was a case in point. Roger reportedly refused to sing the intensely personal song, leaving Pete to sing his own words:

> *I see myself on TV, I'm a faker, a paper clown*
> *It's clear to all my friends that I habitually lie, I just bring them down*
> *I claim proneness to exaggeration, but the truth lies in my frustration*
> *The children of the night, they all pass me by*
> *Got to dress myself in brandy, and sleep while high*
> *But however much I booze, there ain't no way out*

The other song featuring Townshend on lead vocals was *Blue, Red and Grey*, a sparse track with Pete strumming a Ukelele accompanied only by John's horn arrangement. This version was chosen over a full band version, which had also been recorded at Shepperton. Reportedly chosen for inclusion on *The Who By Numbers* by Glyn Johns, the song was "about nothing at all," Pete said in 1977.

Although the rest of the songs were recorded by The Who as a complete entity, Pete's bitter angle during the composition of the material was still evident. "All the songs were different, some more aggressive than others, but they were all somehow negative in direction[138]. I felt empty," Pete wrote in 1977. *Slip Kid*, for example, "...came across as a warning to young kids getting into music that it would hurt them," Pete said in 1977. "it was almost parental in its assumed wisdom." *Squeeze Box* was "Obviously recorded for fun and intended as a poorly aimed dirty joke," he

---

[136] Track Records was fading fast and would fold within a few years. As Dave Marsh put it, "Hendrix had died, Arthur Brown had dropped out, Thunderclap Newman had broken up, the rest of the label's talent roster never sold."
[137] In his *Rolling Stone* review of the album, Dave Marsh wrote, "...it is now clear that if Daltrey decided he'd rather make bad movies, the Who could function acceptably as a trio."
[138] Entwistle, who was charged with coming up with a title and cover art for the album, changed his mind when he became aware of its negative tone. "...I figured we'd call the album *Car Tunes* and I'd draw cartoons of the band," he told the *Tampa Tribune* in 2000. However, he continued, "Basically the songs weren't the kind you'd play in the car unless you wanted to drive off a bridge." *The Who By Numbers* title and cover art were inspired by his son's coloring book.

recalled later. "I had bought myself an accordion and learned to play it one afternoon. (That is not meant to be flash, I don't mean I learned to play it properly, just to manage to work it without falling over!). The polka-esque rhythm I managed to produce from it brought forth this song. Amazingly recorded by The Who to my disbelief[139]. Further incredulity was caused when it became a hit for us in the USA." This song became the Who's first top 20 single since *Won't Get Fooled Again*.

How Many Friends, "...was about what was happening to quite a few people around us, about what was happening to Kit Lambert and to Keith Moon, Eric Clapton, who we were seeing a lot of at the time, Viv Stanshall, Legs Larry Smith," Pete told Matt Kent in 1999. "A number of people who I could see, and myself as well, who were having a lot of problems with hangers on." In *A Hand Or A Face*, he said in 1977, "...was cynical and tried to cut down the growing dependence I had on mysticism and psychic phenomena." Even John Entwistle's humorous *Success Story*, a sardonic song about one's rise to stardom, featured some of the "reality tinged with bitterness," of which Pete spoke as Entwistle sang his view of the recording process: *Take two hundred and seventy six, you know this used to be fun*.

"...*The Who by Numbers* isn't what it seems," wrote Dave Marsh in his *Rolling Stone* review.

> Without broadcasting it, in fact while denying it, Townshend has written a series of songs which hang together as well as separately. The time is somewhere in the middle of the night, the setting a disheveled room with a TV set that seems to show only rock programs. The protagonist is an aging, still successful rock star, staring drunkenly at the tube with a bottle of gin perched on his head, contemplating his career, his love for the music and his fear that it's all slipping away. Every song here, even the one non-Townshend composition, John Entwistle's *Success Story*, fits in. Always a sort of musical practical joker, Townshend has now pulled the fastest one of all, disguising his best concept album as a mere ten-track throwaway.
>
> ...From *My Generation* to *The Who by Numbers*, time and aging have been Townshend's obsession, as if he were trying to live down the statement that made him famous: "Hope I die before I get old." If this is his most

---

[139] *Q*'s David Cavanaugh asked Pete in January 2000 which song he wished he'd never recorded. "*Squeeze Box*," Pete replied. "I loved my demo of it, but I find it excruciating listening to Roger singing it." In 1982, Pete told *The Record* that the song "...was as bad as *Ebony and Ivory*."

mature work, that's because he has finally admitted that there is no way out, which is a darker and deeper part of the same thing. Typically, the Who face the fact without flinching. Indeed, they may have made their greatest album in the face of it. But only time will tell.

Meanwhile, Roger's response to Pete's recent negative comments to the press arrived in the August, 1975, issue of *NME*. "I never read such a load of bullshit in all my life," he told Tony Stewart.

> To be perfectly honest, it really took a lot of my Who energy out reading that. Because I don't feel that way about the Who, about our audiences or anything in that way. It was an unbelievably down interview. And I still haven't come out of it properly yet. I've talked to fans, and I think Townshend lost a lot of respect from that article. He's talked himself up his own ass. And there are quite a lot of disillusioned and disenchanted kids about now.
>
> My main criticism was the generalization of saying the Who were bad. The Who *weren't* bad. I think we've had a few gigs where Townshend was bad...and I'll go on record as saying that. I think we had a few gigs where under normal circumstances we could have waltzed it. We could have done Madison Square Garden with our eyes closed, only the group was running on three cylinders. Especially the last night.
>
> I can understand his musical frustration. He must be so far ahead now with just writing songs for the Who. But surely if the Who isn't a vehicle to get those frustrations out he should find another vehicle. But use the Who for what it is. A good rock'n'roll band, that's all. And one that *was* progressing. I say *was* because we haven't done anything for such a long time. Hopefully when we get back on the road we'll still progress. But if we have any more statements like that I don't see how we can. 'Cos I know it's taken a lot of steam out of me and I'm sure it did with the others.

Upon completion of overdubs and mixing of *The Who by Numbers*, Pete used the subsequent time off to try to recharge his batteries. "I decided to try to get some spiritual energy from friends in the U.S.A.," he wrote in 1977. "...My family (particularly of course my wife, who as a matter of personal policy tries to avoid the aspects of the music world that I still find exciting) had suffered a lot from my pathetic behavior of the previous year, but they would naturally be by my side on any trip other than Who tours. So they came with me, or rather I went with them, to Myrtle Beach, South Carolina, where Meher Baba had set up a retreat during the Fifties." Pete then planned on traveling to California to visit Murshida Duce, who had invited him over when she'd visited England the previous year.

Among the reasons for this trip was an idea Pete had recently been nurturing for some type of British Meher Baba center. "For a few years, I had toyed with the idea of opening a London house dedicated to Meher Baba," Pete later recalled.

> In the eight years I had followed him, I had donated only coppers to foundations set up around the world to carry out the Master's wishes and decided it was about time I put myself on the line. The Who had set up a strong charitable trust of its own which appeased, to an extent, the feeling I had that Meher Baba would rather have seen me give to the poor than to the establishment of yet another so-called "spiritual center."
>
> …I was genuinely unprepared for the unfolding that transpired in that six weeks. My mind was clouded with the idea of trying to run a "center" for Avatar Meher Baba; with the difficulties I would have trying to deal with people's whims and complaints; but most of all, with the hypocrisy of trying to do such a contentiously idealistic thing while enjoying the kind of life I had been living.

Pete recalled the vacation in 1977:

> Against this backdrop of good intentions, I set off in August 1975 to Myrtle Beach. As our party (my wife, my two little daughters and a few friends who traveled with us) crossed the threshold onto Meher Baba's home ground, we were all staggered by the impact of the love that literally filled the air.
>
> Despite the strength I felt growing within me, I think I can speak for our whole party when I say I felt exhausted by Myrtle Beach. God's endlessly present love isn't to be taken lightly. It's great to be forgiven, but it hurts to admit you were wrong in the first place. I realized that I would not be reaping such fantastic emotional and mental rewards had I not been in pretty bad shape; a condition for which I had no one to blame but myself.
>
> When you hold out an empty cup to God and demand that He fill it with wine, He fills it faster than you

can ever drink. Then you know that the fault is your own incapacity to receive His infinite love, rather than His capacity to give it. I loosely quote Hafiz here, of course, but this is what I felt was happening. Even my youngest daughter, Aminta, three years old, became starry-eyed with the atmosphere that poured from the trees. I wouldn't say that the warm reception given us by the residents of the Myrtle Beach retreat was not enjoyed and appreciated, but it paled in significance when compared to the welcome we felt in the buzzing dragonflies, the sound of the ocean and the massaging humidity of the warm afternoon.

We spent an unbelievable ten days. I talked to the older devotees of Meher Baba about my plans for a new place in London and they were naturally encouraging. The sun shone, the children enjoyed themselves, we relaxed and relished rejuvenation at the Master's command. The fears I had that I would not be strong enough to see through the imminent testing rehearsals and tour with the Who receded. We traveled then to California.

"...In California," he continued, "we were well looked after, taken into the bosom of the Sufi family there, provided with a furnished house, picnics, swimming pool, outings to state parks, camping trips to the Sierras and all kinds of straight-laced relaxation," Pete recalled later. "You are probably as mystified as I am as to where the spiritually beneficial work was being done in this kind of program, but spirit was what was needed, and spirit was what I got, even if it didn't fit preconceived notions."

He soon sat down for a conversation with the Murshida:

On arrival in California, I went for a talk with her, to gossip, to bring her up-to-date on events at home, to ask her advice about the color of the walls at the newly planned Baba house in London. Instead, to my amazement, I sat and poured out my very soul. I couldn't for a second have anticipated this happening. She sat and listened as I told her every grisly detail: the paranoia, the drunken orgies, the financial chaos, the indulgent self-analysis (continued herein, I'm afraid) and, of course, the dreamy hopes for the future.

Without batting an eyelid she listened to stuff that was making me recoil myself, then went on to talk a little about her own youth, her life with her husband, the trouble some of her students were having at the time. In short, she got me right in perspective.

At the end of this month with her, we packed our bags, said our farewells and headed home, my wife and the kids to school, me to rehearsals with the band. Keith later told me I walked into the rehearsal hall smiling; he related this because he had found it remarkable. Something positive had happened to me.

Upon his return to England, "being strong again and feeling fairly certain that I could now rock & roll right into my grave", Pete returned his focus to The Who.

Earlier, he had set about ending his long-standing feud with Roger. "...In early August, before I left England, I had written Roger a note, telling him that I felt there had been a lot of unnecessary strife between us, and that I hoped I could earn his respect again," he wrote in 1977. A few weeks later, Pete again wrote to Roger, who was busy promoting his new solo album, *Ride a Rock Horse*. "I told him I would support him in whatever he did. I felt it a strange thing to say."

Pete's recent period of reflection had obviously enabled him to rethink his relationship with Daltrey. "...Roger often sang songs I'd written that he didn't care for with complete commitment, and I took him for granted," he said.

I said what I wanted to say, often ignoring or being terribly patronizing about the rest of the group's suggestions, then sulked when they didn't worship me for making life financially viable...In New York, a good friend of mine gave me some advice. I tried to explain that I felt the problems in the Who were mainly about me and Roger, not the myriad business problems that seemed so manifestly cancerous. I was counseled quite simply: "Let Roger win."

The statement isn't as cruel or flippant as it sounds. This person knew the Who and its history and cared about all of us deeply. The advice meant that I should demonstrate to Roger that my letters were sincere by not hanging on to past grievances or differences. Most of all, I should bow to the changing status quo within the group, created by the fans' new identification with Roger as front man, rather than with me as its mouthpiece.

The band soon began rehearsals for their first tour in over a year. Roger had been working on his previously mentioned solo album, John had been touring and recording with his band Ox, and even Keith had completed a solo album earlier in the year. Pete, John and Keith got back together to recreate an ensemble feel. "When we got together to work on our act before touring again Pete was obviously not into it," said Entwistle. "So we went down to Shepperton for two days to rehearse without Roger singing, just Pete, Keith and myself playing instrumentals, all those old things. We had such a good time that we turned around completely and found ourselves playing better than we had in years."

The Who hit the road in October, 1975, for a 20-date tour of Europe with the Steve Gibbons band in tow as the support act[140]. Following some shaky initial shows (*Rolling Stone* called an early October show in Stafford "sloppy"), The Who were in fine form and had hit their stride when they returned home to London for a 3-date stay at Wembley Arena in late October.

By the time the band had tightened up their stage show, they had also settled into a set list which would remain virtually unchanged during the next year of touring. In addition to a sample of early singles and a handful of songs from *Who's Next*, a nine-song *Tommy* medley had surfaced due to the popularity of the new Ken Russell movie. The set list was nowhere near as progressive as Pete had hoped when composing *Quadrophenia*; in fact, most shows during this period featured no songs from the album, and only two from the subsequent *Who By Numbers*. Despite the perceived step back in the set list, The Who's live show was regarded as world-class during this period. "...they played with renewed energy," stated *The Who Concert File*, "easily reclaiming their crown as the world's greatest live rock'n'roll band. Pete rediscovered his mastery of the electric guitar, playing searing solos and slashing rhythm, jumping and windmilling in his inimitable style, all with new found vigor. Overjoyed at his enthusiasm, Roger, John and Keith performed as if their lives depended on it. Many fans still consider that The Who's rebirth in 1975/76 represented some of their finest moments..."

Following a nine show run through the Netherlands, Austria and Germany[141], The Who headed west to kick off their North American tour, a month-long, 20-date affair which took in over $3 million. Reggae band Toots and the Maytals opened all shows. During the tour, The Who became the first band to play at Houston's new 18,000-seat basketball arena, The Summit, and also the first to play at Pontiac's 78,000-seat Silverdome,

---

[140] The Steve Gibbons Band were discovered in Birmingham in 1975 by none other than Peter Meaden, who co-managed them with Who manager Bill Curbishley. Eleven years after being unceremoniously let go by Kit Lambert, Meaden was back on the Who team. He later lent his Mod expertise during the production of the *Quadrophenia* movie just prior to his death in August 1978 from barbiturate poisoning.

[141] Moon resumed his antics on the band's private plane during the European tour. "The toilet was in the back of the plane," Bill Curbishley told Tony Fletcher in 1999. "And on the way back Pete Townshend went in there and Moon locked him in, so Townshend kicked the door off. Moon carried the door down to the cockpit and said, 'I believe this is yours, old chap,' and gave it to the pilot and put it on his shoulders. So the pilot's trying to fly this plane with a fucking door on him!"

which they sold out. The tour was an operation of mammoth proportions, the band traveling with 14 tons of equipment, including a PA system consisting of 72 speakers. "This tour was the first time they used their $36,000 lasers in the act and the first time lasers had been used in a rock show anywhere," wrote Richard Barnes[142]. "They were employed during the *Tommy* section which had been re-introduced and consistently brought the house down."

Pete was in good spirits at the opening of the U.S. tour, telling Nik Cohn, "I've stopped drinking and I haven't lost my nerve onstage, not yet. Keith Moon has started smashing up his hotel rooms again, which is always a good sign." All shows drew rave reviews, with words such as "stunning, phenomenal, awesome, devastating, magnificent, glorious," and "explosive" in almost every newspaper article covering the shows. Mid-December marked the end of the U.S. tour as Pete smashed a Les Paul onstage in Philadelphia.

After a tumultuous year rife with backstabbing and infighting, all glaringly before the media, The Who had ended 1975 with a bang. Over the three months that The Who had been on the road at the end of 1975 both in Europe and North America, they had reclaimed their position as the greatest rock'n'roll band in the world. The live show had received a huge boost from a rejuvenated Townshend whose playing had improved immensely, and the rest of the band seemed to feed off Pete's energy, all, of course, to the delight of thousands of screaming fans.

The band ended the year with three shows at London's Hammersmith Odeon on December 21, 22, and 23. "The Odeon was transformed into a huge Christmas party with a Who Christmas Pack left on every seat, containing Who balloons, streamers, masks and a badge," Matt Kent wrote in a 2004 *Mojo* article. "Monty Python's Graham Chapman (a friend of Moon's) compered the shows and was promptly booed offstage every night. Moon made his grand entrance descending to the stage on a winch." *Melody Maker's* Steve Clark commented, "If you thought rock was dead at that moment in time [during the shows], you must have been born in the wrong age. Easily the year's best display of rock'n'roll."

The Who took a two-month break in January and February, 1976, and Pete took the opportunity to follow up on some of the things he and Murshida Duce had discussed during his visit to the states in August of the previous year. Pete had planned to establish a Meher Baba center in London, and spent January looking for a suitable location. "After viewing

---

[142] The Who's stage lighting became a focal point in 1972 after a contingent of their road crew hit the road in the U.S. with the Rolling Stones while The Who were inactive. "Bobby [Pridden] and our lights man went over there and came back saying we'd got to get our lights together because theirs were amazing," Pete told *Sounds'* Penny Valentine in August, 1972. "To which I said "look what have I been saying", because our lights are expensive but pathetic – which is not the case with the sound because that's expensive and worth it."

several places, he took me to see the *Boathouse* in Twickenham," Delia DeLeon recalled in 1991. "It was in such a very dilapidated condition that we had to climb ladders to view it. His deep instinct was to buy it and rebuild it according to his idea of a Baba center/workshop which would have living accommodations and a theater. Encouragement came from India and America, and I was happy to know this dream could at last come true." Pete's Baba center later became known as *Meher Baba Oceanic*.

Later that month Pete and Delia traveled to India just prior to the seventh anniversary of Baba's entombment, known as the *Amartithi*. Pete had planned to visit India during a break from touring back in October, 1975, but changed his mind not long before leaving. "It was a joyful two weeks," DeLeon wrote in 1991.

> We arrived the day before...[Amartithi] and so were able to take part in this very special day and its prayers and songs...There in that lovely, peaceful place one feels strongly enfolded by Baba's love...All were interested in the progress of Meher Baba Oceanic and gave Pete their whole-hearted support...As Pete and I sat alone in the Tomb that last morning to pay our final respects to Baba, he sang his own arrangement of the Master's Prayer, *Parvardigar*, and it seemed draw the two of us together in a karmic bond, a moment that lingered in my mind many weeks after my return.

Pete also performed for other Baba lovers during his stay. A performance of *Parvardigar* in which Pete misspoke during one verse and prompted a restart was recounted by one Baba follower, and a further performance from this visit, *Drowned* on acoustic guitar in front of a handful of seated onlookers, was captured on film.

A few weeks later, Pete and The Who were back on the road, performing in Zurich, Munich and Paris prior to heading to the U.S. in early March[143]. The tour's American leg (with the Steve Gibbons Band again opening all dates) got off to a bad start when only two songs into the band's set at the Boston Garden, Keith collapsed and was taken from the stage. The remainder of the show was canceled. While a mysterious 'flu' bug was blamed, it wouldn't be a stretch to assume that Moon's lifestyle played at least a small part in his wrecked physical condition. As if to corroborate this

---

[143] Pete had led an effort to get Moon seen by Meg Patterson prior to this next round of touring. Moon was abusing alcohol and cocaine, and "...was not given a choice in the matter, but he didn't seem to want one," according to Tony Fletcher. After receiving counseling from George Patterson (Meg's husband), Moon played his first sober show in ten years on 27 February 1976 in Zurich. By the band's show in Paris three days later, Moon had resumed drinking and destroyed his hotel room after the show.

view, a security guard was posted outside Moon's hotel room as he recuperated from his 'illness', just in case he thought about going out on the town. This didn't sit well with Keith, who was sufficiently healthy to destroy the entire contents of his room. He cut his foot so badly during the frenzy that he reportedly almost bled to death.

The band limped on, injured (but still somehow serviceable) drummer in tow, playing Madison Square Garden on March 11. The tour swung through central U.S. and on to the west coast, finishing with an April 1 show at Boston Garden to make up for the abruptly canceled gig the month before.

Following two mid-May dates in France, The Who launched their 'Who Put The Boot In' tour of three football stadiums, one each in England, Scotland and Wales. The first show, on a May 31 bank holiday in front of 60,000 at Charlton Athletic Football Ground put The Who in the Guinness Book of World Records as 'world's loudest pop group,' after their mammoth P.A. system spewed forth 120 decibels at 50 meters, enough to permanently damage the hearing of those who were close enough to the speakers. The 76,000 watt PA system was reportedly audible in Croydon, ten miles from the stadium[144]. Despite the heavy rain, this is remembered as a great performance. Opening acts for this and the other two shows were The Sensational Alex Harvey Band, Little Feat, The Outlaws and The Streetwalkers.

"It poured with rain all day and everyone was soaked," Richard Barnes wrote in *Maximum R&B*.

> The whole tour was a massive operation involving...30 tons of equipment...Although loud, the sound was clear and sharp. The sound system specially built for the show by Tasco, and costing £7,000 just for that night alone, had never before been used in England. The long throw bass speakers ensured that even people at the back got high quality sound... At the climax of *Listening to You* all the £100,000 lights including the huge arc lights set up behind the group, facing out into the audience, were switched on, and the effect from this simple piece of theatrics produced one of rock's greatest and most climactic moments...

NME called the show's climax "...a masterstroke. They put the proverbial boot in." However, they didn't return for an encore, which

---

[144] The Who's "laser light show could be seen over much of South-east London," Matt Kent reported in a 2004 *Mojo* article.

disappointed the soaked, muddy crowd. The tour continued, stopping at Swansea in front of 25,000, and Glasgow where 35,000 attended.

A month later, Pete's vision of a London Meher Baba Center was finally realized. "Oceanic...was a Meher Baba Centre for 5 years with 16mm film dubbing and editing suites, a cinema and 4 track studio," Pete recalled in 1982. The center also served as a regular meeting venue for Baba devotees and, with Pete reportedly offering upstairs rooms at £1 a night, a very economical source of shelter for a number of American Baba lovers who needed an overnight stay on their pilgrimages to India.[145] "Meher Baba Oceanic was opened on July 3, 1976 with ten days of music, drama, films, and food," Delia DeLeon recalled in 1991. Adi Irani, Baba's secretary and a disciple, attended the opening, and Mehera, Baba's leading female disciple, gave her blessing to the proceedings. "She sent a beautiful pink silk coat once worn by Meher Baba which became the centerpiece of a small collection of precious artifacts that were touched, used or worn by the Master," Pete wrote in a web posting in July 2001.

> Everything began well, and I greatly enjoyed being a part of the constant ebb and flow of international visitors. I also enjoyed hosting musical concerts, plays and film shows as well as the more usual talks and devotional gatherings. I produced a dozen small films related to Meher Baba, and even directed one myself – *Delia*. From 1976 until the middle of 1979 I was (blessed by all but self-appointed) very much in the forefront of all activity in the U.K. surrounding Meher Baba.

All of the films shown at the opening of Oceanic had been sponsored by Pete and produced at Oceanic. They included *The East/West Gathering* and *O, Parvardigar*, both of which are still available through Sheriar Press. "Pete loves Baba deeply and in my view his greatest achievement is probably his beautiful setting of *The Master's Prayer* to music and later the production of the film *O, Parvardigar*, with this as the sound track," Delia DeLeon wrote in 1991. "This film is most important as it shows Baba at different stages of His life, with the lepers, masts, at darshan programs, and with His devotees in different parts of the world." The film about Delia DeLeon which Pete and John Annunziato had been working on was also shown during the opening of Oceanic. "...Pete promised me the 'Delia" film would be shown," DeLeon recalled. "With so much to do, this meant he and John had to work sometimes all night to get it finished." Townshend wrote, directed and narrated the piece.

Baba's *Mandali* sent the following message to the proceedings:

---

[145] Delia DeLeon held regular Tuesday night meetings at Oceanic throughout its existence.

AVATAR MEHER BABA KI JAI!

Beloved Baba's dear children gathered here today, we your Meherazad family are very happy at this joyous occasion which inaugurates MEHER BABA OCEANIC made possible by Beloved Baba's Grace.

Pete Townshend's desire to create Meher Baba Oceanic, with its pure aims and ideals has been inspired by his love for his Beloved Master, Avatar Meher Baba. Working for Baba does not mean that things are smooth and easy, but when you are wholehearted in your endeavor to serve and please Him, Baba always makes it possible. He guides and helps you at every step. We are proud of you dear children, of your selfless dedication in the work that you do in Baba's Love.

Our dear Pete, in his love for Beloved Baba, has played a major role in constructing Meher Baba Oceanic. It is now for you all to help make it Baba's Home, where you can gather and work in His Love, and feel that He is here with you and know that His beautiful presence surrounds you. It is also for you all to make Meher Baba Oceanic a happy and harmonious medium for others to be drawn to Meher Baba's precious Love.

May Avatar Meher Baba's Love and Blessings shower on you all on this special day. Love to you each His dear ones from your Meherazad family.

1976 also marked the release of the third Meher Baba Association album, entitled *With Love*. The album featured two Townshend-penned instrumentals, *His Hands* and *Lantern Cabin*, along with a song called *Sleeping Dog*. Others featured on the limited release of 4,000 included Billy Nicholls, Ronnie Lane, and Peter Hope-Evans of Medicine Head who later appeared regularly with Pete's backing group.

Touring resumed the following month with four shows in the eastern U.S., beginning with two shows in Largo, Maryland, and the remainder taking place in Jacksonville and Miami, Florida. Chris Charlesworth was in tow, and provided the following report:

> They were closing an open air all-dayer in a big stadium in muggy, unpleasant weather after an ill-judged, weak supporting cast had limped on and off stage to little purpose. A greedy promoter had overcharged and Florida was never Who territory, so the crowd numbered 35,000 instead of a potential 60,000. This hurt their pride and they

were angry at what had happened, furious in fact, and having watched The Who at close quarter scores of times by then I knew all too well that anger could bring out the best or the worst in them. Sharp words were exchanged backstage and I kept my distance; only Keith, fueled as ever by Remy Martin brandy, seemed sociable. But come showtime there was an extraordinary transformation and all their fury, all the frustration and pent-up rage that spilled out of Pete and Roger, was channeled into the music, and they played an absolute blinder, as powerful as any show in the classic '69-'71 era. The Who at their almighty best came flooding over everyone in that stadium that night. At then end they smashed their equipment in an orgy of gleeful destruction and the crowd exploded with endless ovations because they'd never seen or heard anything like it before, nor would they ever again. Afterwards, backstage, in the calm of the caravan that served as a dressing room, I clearly remember sitting down next to Pete and remarking to him on how good this show had been. Exhausted, slumped in a corner, his fingers shredded and covered in blood, his skinny, loose limbed body wrapped in a towel, he knocked back a huge plastic beaker of brandy in one gulp. There was a strange, faraway look in those deep blue eyes of his as he looked up at me. He thought for a minute, fingered the Meher Baba badge that hung from his neck, then managed a wry smile. 'We were playing for the people who weren't there,' he said.

The touring continued after a month-long break back in England (recall that the band's royalties were frozen due to the pending litigation with their ex-managers, and that tour revenue was their only source of income). This 9-date leg featured stops along the west coast in early October (The Grateful Dead opened two Oakland, California shows), winding up with a show at Maple Leaf Gardens in Toronto, Canada on 21 October.

"On the Who's tour of the U.S. and Canada in the fall of '76 a lot of things came to a 'glorious' head in Toronto, the last show of the tour," Pete recalled later.

The road crew threw a party for us, and it was the first party I had been to for at least five years which meant anything to me. I don't go to a lot of parties, but I'm glad that I made this one. I suddenly realized that behind every Who show are people who care as much as, or more than, we do. Talking to the individuals who help get the show together enabled me to remember that audiences care, too.

When I sit in an audience, one of the things that makes it enjoyable is the energy I spend *willing* it to be the best thing I have ever seen. I get to see some great concerts that way. Ask any Who fan if they care how well we are playing on any single date. The Who don't count as much as people might imagine, but as performers their response to the audience's energy is vital.

With the band's relative inactivity over the next few years, this show proved to be Keith Moon's last live performance before a paying crowd.

Chapter 8

"You know, I think the Who stopped two albums too late. I think if I'd stopped two albums earlier, when Keith died, I would never have ended up with a drinking problem, and I would have never ended up creating the kind of emotional havoc that I played not only in my family's life but in the life of others."
- Pete Townshend, 1989

"We used to think we were rebels, but what did we do? We went out and we rampaged around like a small commando troop, you know, we went over to America, to Europe, to Australia, we smashed up the hotel rooms, we raped all the women, and we collected all the money and we came back, and we expected to be heroes, not just heroes in rock'n'roll but we expected to be heroes in the world, you know, in society as it stood. Of course, it doesn't happen that way."
- Pete Townshend, 1985

Following The Who's hugely successful 1976 tours of Europe and America (which reportedly grossed in excess of $8 million), Pete Townshend returned home to his family in Twickenham, of whom he had seen very little in the previous year. "…I wanted to return home as a conquering hero because it had been a marvelous tour for us," Pete recalled in 1984. "But when I got to the front door steps I wasn't the hero. I walked back to the kids who didn't even know who I was." Emma and Aminta were now ages 7 and 5, respectively. "They were very cagey and intimidated by me," Pete said. "They were even more perplexed because I wore an American sea captain's uniform which I'd bought in Chicago[146]. I can see their faces still."

---

[146] In October, 1978, Pete told *Melody Maker*'s Michael Watts that he'd worn the uniform "quite happily for two months every day; in fact, I used to walk about playing this Wagner tape *Overture To Tristan Und Isolde*, walking around like a Nazi."

"...the two kids looked at me and screamed," Pete said in 1978. "It was then I started to come to."

The weeks following Pete's return from the 1976 tours provided a timely dose of reality to a man who'd perhaps forgotten his responsibilities as a husband and father while being consumed by his role as a world - renowned musician and songwriter. "Our marriage staggered on for a while but then came a showdown," Pete recalled.

> My old lady just broke down one day and said she'd run out of energy and that was it. It dawned on me that what she was really saying was, 'I don't really love you. I don't care whether you go away or whether you stay. I don't give a damn about you or your life, or the way you don't think about us'. I went away for two days and thought about all she had said. I saw the truth...that if I lost Karen and the family I wouldn't be able to face life at all. What's more, I wouldn't be able to do anything for The Who either.

During the two days of reflection, Pete realized that a profound priority shift was in order if he wanted to save his marriage and keep his family intact.

> I made a conscious decision that my first love, The Who, would in future take second place to my real love – my wife and my daughters. There were things I got from The Who that nobody could ever get from a marriage partnership. But on the other hand what really made me a human being was my relationship with my old lady. I knew that's what I needed to preserve most. From that point of view my family became my first priority...Some people who are heavily into The Who felt this was a great snub on my part because, in effect, I was telling them, 'Listen, you're not as important as my family'. Fortunately others understood my predicament.

One of those who understood was Dave Marsh: "Because they're a Sixties band, the Who feel a special sense of responsibility (shared, perhaps, only by the ex-Beatles, Bob Dylan and the Rolling Stones) not only about musical matters but about questions of lifestyle, image and ethics," Marsh wrote in 1978. "For Townshend, these are especially weighty concerns; rock is not just a livelihood and a fantastic source of energy, it is so much a cornerstone of belief that he sees his spiritual master, Meher Baba, "through two slits, R & R." "

"This sense of responsibility," Marsh went on, "is at the core of Townshend's determination to avoid a lengthy tour...the responsibility he feels for his audience and the rock ideal is outweighed, at least for now, by the responsibility he feels to his family."

"...I just felt burnt-out, clap-ridden and alcoholic," Pete told *Melody Maker*'s Michael Watts in 1978. "...I made up my mind then. 'I've gotta get my priorities right.' And one priority that I sorted out was that I needed stability and I needed my family, and I needed that more than anything else."

"I don't want to do the American tour again," Pete told John Swenson in 1977.

> My kids are getting pretty old now – eight and seven. When I have an extended period at home, they get noticeably happier. It makes me think about those four months away from home every year, to end up with a lot of American tax bills and maybe nothing else. I love being onstage. It's a great kick, but I think I can live without it. Are we really making the fans happy? Every time we go into a town we get complaints we're not playing long enough. If we play at a big stadium we get complaints it's too big and they can't see us. The only answer is to play in small halls for years at a time. I've got other things to do.

When Pete contemplated breaking the news of his newfound dedication to his family to the rest of the band, he expected a great deal of flak. "Instead," wrote *Time* magazine's Jay Cocks in 1979, "sensing that he was in a state of crisis, they supported him."

> The strongest backing, to Townshend's considerable surprise, came from Daltrey. "He said to me, 'I don't care whether we tour or make records or don't make records. I just always want to be able to work with you, always be able to sing your songs and, above everything else, I want you to be happy.' This was Roger Daltrey, right; the person I was seeing as a competitor. It was a revelation. Nobody has ever talked like that to me. Nobody. Not my mother, not my father, not my kids, not my wife. Nobody ever said things like that and meant them."

Another reason for Pete's decision to stop touring following the 1976 tours was the alarming condition of his hearing. According to Pete, the first tangible evidence of his hearing loss came following The Who's

March 21, 1976 concert at Anaheim Stadium. The size of the audience (55,000) demanded the use of a larger-than-normal sound system. "...we had an enormous PA system and a very, very large monitor PA system and we started up, I played a chord, Roger sang one note, and the sound hit my left ear, and I've never really been able to hear properly out of it since," Pete told *WNEW*'s Scott Muni in April, 1978.

> I had really lousy earaches for about three or four months afterwards. ...then I realized that my hearing overall had sort of dropped. I discovered this in the most alarming way: I couldn't stand the sound of my kids' voices... So I went to this ear shrink... and he said, 'You really should be careful. If you're careful, you'll still have your hearing when you're forty.' And I said, 'When I'm *what*? ...Well, I'm 33 now – that's *seven years*.' ...then I went to another guy. He was a little bit less pessimistic. He said, 'Well, if you conserve your hearing, if you wear earplugs on the stage, if you don't listen to music loud at other times, if you keep away from rock concerts, if you don't go to shows, if you don't listen to loud bands, and... this kind of thing, your hearing will tail off at the normal age.' I just started to think very seriously about a life without music. I mean, even without me being a musician, a life without music, and I decided, and I say this before God, that I'd rather go blind than go deaf. It's my life, music. I'm a writer, I'm a composer, my greatest moments are to sit at a piano or pick up a guitar and *fly*, you know. I communicate with people through music, through what I write. ...after the third meeting with a separate doctor, I got three separate opinions, and he said exactly the same thing, he said you've really got to be careful, otherwise you're going to go deaf very soon. I just went back to the band, and I said, Jesus Christ, you know, what do I do?

While the Anaheim concert provided Pete with the necessary motivation to address his hearing problem, he later contended that a substantial amount of damage had already been inficted upon his ears prior to that point, not from the years of playing in front of a literally deafening PA system, or listening to extremely loud music at home and in his car, but from using headphones. "I say the problem is earphones[147]," he told

---

[147] "...even with a relatively small amplifier, you know, if you hook the earphones up to the speaker terminals, you can blow your own head off," Pete told Scott Muni in April, 1978. "On the stage once, I saw Keith Moon, who uses earphones to follow a drum track, I saw his earphones *catch fire*, on God's honor, *catch fire* on his head there was so much level... and

Musician in 1989.

> That's where my problem started. It was not loud guitar onstage rock'n'roll style. It's very important to make this point. It was EARPHONES! EARPHONES! EARPHONES! It was going home after gigs, to my own studio, and playing guitar through the earphones. My sound was an electric sound. You couldn't reproduce it on acoustic guitar. It had to be with earphones. Obviously I couldn't have a Marshall stack in my living room and practice with the babies upstairs. I used earphones for 20 years. That's what caused the damage. It's not helped now with loud music in performances, but I don't see any difficulty doing stadium shows when the sound is kept deliberately quiet onstage. It's also a different situation when your head is clear and you're not drunk. Wearing earphones when you're drunk can increase damage by a factor of 10, I think. Some of the muscles that operate the eardrum are disabled by alcohol.

In 1977, Pete began to address his hearing problems by experimenting with earplugs during rehearsals ("...that's great until you try and sing," he told Muni "...it really is a bit strange."), and staying clear of loud noises, including in the playback booth at recording sessions. "...when the band go back to goof off on the loud playbacks, I have to stay outside," he said. The revelation that his hearing problems were potentially severely debilitating within a short period of time sobered Pete. "...I wish it was a rumor," he told Muni. "I'm going deaf, and I really don't like the sensation. I have to struggle to hear what people are saying a lot of the time."

It also led Pete to consider what damage The Who's enormous P.A. system, already christened the loudest in the world by the Guinness Book of Records, was doing to their fans' ears. "Listen, if I choose to put an amplifier up and blow my own head off, that's *my* business..." Pete told Muni.

> ...But the thing that makes me wake up in a cold sweat is the fact that the sound intensity measured six rows back at an average Who concert has been measured as high as like, 126 db, which somebody has told me is enough, practically, to physically blow your eardrum into the ear cavity. ...I just think about... the kids that have to be out in

---

he's still going, louder, *louder*! I think earphones and concerts, they're the things to watch out for."

the front. I mean, I'm like that. If I go to a concert, I want to be flattened, and I get lost, I lose myself. This is why rock and roll has been so important in my life. It's the only time when I haven't been there. It's the only time that I have been able to forget about the poverty in India, the particular hangup that I might have that week ...you know, the problems of the world. You *fly*, and one of the things that helps you to fly, I think, is that thing that your brain is being shaken like a walnut inside your skull (laughs). But if, while it's making you fly, it's making you deaf, then what the hell? ...And what really makes me, as I say, lay awake at night is the thought that while people are listening to my music, I'm taking away their capacity to listen to it for more than a short period of time. My younger brothers are both about to go and get their ears tested.

"Electric guitar hurts my ears," Pete said in 1978. "It's bad to the extent that if I'm subjected to really loud noise for a long time, I get a lot of pain. And, apparently, pain is the indication of further damage." Townshend had developed Tinnitus, which, according to *Rolling Stone*, is:

> ...an annoying and unceasing ringing, rumbling or staticky sound in the ears that rarely goes away. It can increase in its intensity to a level that has been horrifyingly described as being akin to "holding a vacuum cleaner to your ear."
>
> Tinnitus can cause irritability, sleep disturbance and difficulty in concentration if left untreated. Unfortunately, the treatment usually prescribed involves staying away from the very thing the patient holds most dear and has often devoted his life to – loud rock & roll. The realization that the afflicted musician can no longer cope with the accepted sound level of rock music both in concert and in the studio can cause a terrifying midlife crisis.

Hearing problems continued to plague Pete from this point forward. In 1982, he told *Musician*:

> One reason I don't like playing that kind of heavy metal guitar any more is because it hurts my ears. It's the frequencies at which my ears are irreversibly damaged...they're very, very sensitive. Say you damage your ears at two kilohertz; any loud noise at that frequency produces pain, which is the ear's warning system not to

screw around at that frequency. So I'm in a kind of Catch-22 situation, 'cause what I've done best for twenty years has damaged that part of my hearing.

Pete's hearing difficulties worsened consistently over the next decade, and didn't show any positive signs of improvement until he addressed the situation by ceasing all live performances. "The real reason that I haven't performed live for a long time is that I have very severe hearing damage," he said in 1989, having been off the road for seven years.

> It's manifested itself as tinnitus, ringing in the ears at the frequencies that I play the guitar. It's very, very difficult for me to work at music. There are a lot of kids out there with Marshall stacks and earphones plugged in who drink a bottle of whiskey and play guitar all night, and that's what I used to do, and I've shot my hearing. It hurts, and it's painful, and it's frustrating when little children talk to you and you can't hear them.

Although he has acknowledged some improvement, Pete still complains of his hearing problems today. "My ears were screaming," Pete remarked the day after a June, 2000 Who gig in Chicago. "...I always feel bad about subjecting my body (mainly my ears of course) to such an assault as it gets on stage with The Who."

Meanwhile, with The Who officially grounded for the present, Pete entertained thoughts of a solo project. "Last year after the U.S. tour I was sick of working with The Who," Pete told the *Los Angeles Times* in 1977.

> I suppose it would have been just as easy for me to have rung up Roger Daltrey and arranged to have done an album with him. But I couldn't even conceive of the idea of writing songs. The last Who album, I barely wrote enough songs. *The Who By Numbers* had no leftover songs at all, I'd stopped dead. But I was eager to do something in the studio with Glyn Johns, our producer, without the heavy pressure of a Who gig.

It was in 1976 that former Small Faces bassist Ronnie Lane visited Pete and started the ball rolling. "Basically the album came about because I was in financial trouble, and I went to see Pete, not to ask for anything, just to see him socially," Lane told Dave Marsh in 1983. "Obviously, we talked about each other's state. Mine came up and he said, 'Well, we've talked about working together in the past. Why don't we get an album together?' I said, 'That would solve my problem.' It did." Lane, also a follower of

Meher Baba, had contributed his *Evolution* to Pete's *Who Came First* album in 1972. Also in 1976, Pete had guested on two songs on Ronnie Lane and Ron Wood's *Mahoney's Last Stand* movie soundtrack.

Recording sessions for the project began at Olympic Studios in late 1976, concluding in early summer, 1977. Five new Townshend compositions made their way onto the album, *My Baby Gives It Away*, *Misunderstood*, *Street In The City*, *Keep Me Turning*, and *Heart To Hang Onto*. These solid efforts proved to set the stage for his first real solo album, 1980's *Empty Glass*.

A rather independent thinker, Townshend had a hard time attempting to collaborate with Lane; in fact, although *Rough Mix* was a joint effort, it contained no Lane/Townshend compositions. "...I've never written anything with anybody else," Pete recalled. "I've taken other people's lyrics and set them to music and I've sometimes worked on other people's songs, but I've never written with anybody because I write unconsciously and tend to just let it spill out. And if anybody says, 'Why don't you change so-and-so', I don't know how to approach it..."

Townshend and Lane only sang together on three songs: *Rough Mix*, *Heart To Hang Onto*, and *Till The Rivers All Run Dry*. "We tried to do things together to an extent but I think it was more my failing than Ron's," Pete said in 1984. "Sometimes Ronnie and I would talk about life," he later said.

> That would mean Ronnie insulting me and me hitting him[148]. Sometimes Eric Clapton would come to play. That would mean Ronnie insulting him, Eric hitting him, and then falling over. Glyn and Ronnie often discussed Ronnie's songs. That consisted of Ronnie trying to keep Glyn in the studio till three or four in the morning while he insulted him.

The pair's differences continued after the project. "I couldn't make out why we didn't spend an hour or two or an evening or two to write a song together," Lane told Dave Marsh. "I've got a few ideas. Pete had a few ideas. My ideas weren't finished, and with his help they could have been finished – things like that. And vice versa. So I said, 'Why don't we get together and write some things?' He turned around and said, 'What? And split the publishing?' I was floored. I never brought it up to him again."

However, the two also shared a mutual respect. "As far as Ronnie's stuff was concerned I really enjoyed working on them," Pete later commented.

---

[148] "Me and Pete, we love each other a lot, but we rub each other up the wrong way, as well," Lane told Dave Marsh in 1983. "He's a much bigger fellow than me, as well – he's got a longer reach than I have."

But his contribution to my songs was much, much deeper... I don't think I would have done the album or the kind of material I did if it were not for Ronnie's encouragement... I was able to gently contribute to Ronnie's stuff, getting to play in a way I hadn't done for years, without tension or pressure... Not only would I not have produced the tracks I did with him on the album were it not for him, but his encouragement and enthusiasm made me try more as a musician than as a sensationalist. When I finished a number, it was Ronnie who looked proud. When I did a good vocal, it was Ronnie who got the kick. It's hard to explain, but in a word, friendship says it.

Misunderstood and *Street In The City* were both selected for Pete's 1996 greatest hits compilation *Coolwalkingsmoothtalkingstraightsmokingfirestoking*. *Misunderstood* was "a song which I expect was flown past The Who at some point, and probably Roger said something like, "Well, it's great, Pete, but it's obviously yours, isn't it? I don't know that I can sing that,"" Pete said in 1996. "It's not actually a song about how I felt particularly. I was just writing a song about that kind of James Dean syndrome – you know, I would much prefer to be confused and gorgeous than as I really am, which is, as I think I say in the song, fairly easy to penetrate, but that's another kind of sub-teenage angst all of its own." *Street In The City* was "...a song about walking through a city and picking up paranoia everywhere," Pete said.

> [the song was written by] deliberately going to somewhere like Oxford Street and picking up feelings from people and writing them down quickly...looking up at people on buildings and looking at people in office blocks, and trying to get a sense of, you know, "That man over there painting that wall – I wonder what he's like in bed with his wife," and "That priest – I wonder what his childhood was like," trying to project and create characters.

The strings in *Street In The City* were conducted by Ted Astley, Pete's father in law. "At the time," Pete later commented,

> Kit Lambert and I were talking about doing a project which would eventually embrace his father Constant

Lambert's unrecorded catalog of compositions[149], and we wanted an orchestral collaborator for that, and the way that we thought we would start was with a series of experiments orchestrating compositions of mine, and I suggested my father-in-law Ted Astley, who had done film music, and this was the first thing that we tried.

Ted Astley was "...very much a mentor and a prime influence in my life," Pete told Hugh Foley in 1989.[150]

> He's... an extremely brilliant, gifted man, a wonderful friend, as well, to me. He has what I think all great musicians have, and that is absolutely no snobbery whatsoever about music.
> ...One thing that Kit aways used to say about his father was that the main thing is that he would have loved not only the music of Purcell and Stravinsky and Prokofiev and all the other great ballet composers, but he would have loved the music of The Who, and that musical snobbery was something which he despised. Kit Lambert, in 1976, had this idea that he wanted to rerecord his father's version of *Rio Grande*, which had never been released in stereo. And we did it together, and Ted Astley was going to do the M.D.'ing for us, so for me that was a wonderful moment, in a sense, two major father figures in my life coming together. A couple of the orchestral tracks on *Scoop*, the second *Scoop*, there's one called *The River*, and there's one called *Praying The Game*, those were our early attempts just to try to work out how you could use a modern double string orchestra with acoustic guitar and very interesting stuff there.

Providing additional instrumentation on *Rough Mix* was an all-star cast of guests, featuring Charlie Watts, John Bundrick, Peter Hope-Evans, Eric Clapton, and Billy Nichols. The record was produced by Glyn Johns and Pete's brother in law, Jon Astley. *Rough Mix*, released in November, 1977, received many positive reviews, and, according to Chris Charlesworth, was "a brisk seller...the most successful extracurricular Who project thus far."

---

[149] I'm not sure whether Lambert or Townshend initiated this dialogue, but this appears to be the first instance of the pair working together since the aborted New York *Lifehouse* sessions in 1971.

[150] Dave Marsh wrote in 1983 that Ted Astley "had often been the opening act for the Squadronaires when they played in the Astleys' home town, Manchester."

Dave Marsh, who wasn't impressed with *Who Came First*, was much more receptive to this second sans-Who effort by Townshend. "The Who's Townshend and former Face Lane come by their rock & roll inclinations honestly, and obviously, but spiritual inclination is their long suit here," Marsh wrote in his review of the album.

> Both men are followers of Meher Baba, the Indian spiritual master who died in 1969, and this has given the album a sort of humility – not to say modesty – which is its special virtue...
>
> *Keep Me Turning* is a spiritual parable that is undoubtedly much clearer to its author than to any other listener. The organ, guitar and drum interplay makes the song exciting, but what draws me back time and again is the yearning and vulnerable quality of Townshend's vocal. This is spiritual rock & roll in the very best sense: it doesn't always make sense except in the heart, which won't ignore it. Its wit and charm strike beyond the confusion of its verses to the heart of the chorus, where the devotional imagery is most complete, and the guitar part at the bridge, which is among the most supple and liquid Townshend has ever done.
>
> ...Don Williams' *'Til the Rivers All Run Dry* is a country love song, but in this context – and considering Baba's love for Jim Reeves' *There's a Heartache Following Me*, which Townshend did on his first solo album – it's clearly a tribute to the master.
>
> *Heart to Hang Onto*, written by Townshend but on which Lane sings the verses and Townshend the choruses, wears an even thinner veil. There's a brutal war going on in the song's midsection between Townshend's *Tommy*-like guitar and John Entwistle's brass arrangement. This is the perfect musical expression of the cosmic quest – this is the real *The Seeker*...
>
> The glory of this album and of the work of Pete Townshend and Ronnie Lane throughout their careers is that art and the deepest spiritual aspiration are completely intertwined. Often, of course, that makes for a rough mix, and a rougher life. But it's worth the turbulence, for it touches closer to the heart of the rock & roll experience than almost anything I know.

While Pete was in the midst of recording *Rough Mix,* The Who's legal wranglings with Kit Lambert and Chris Stamp came to a close following a six-month series of negotiations, the last of which was interminably long and reduced Townshend to an emotional wreck. The final meeting involved Townshend, his accountant, Stamp, and businessman Allen Klein, who'd been brought in to resolve the situation. "Klein apparently produced sheets of figures, totally confused everbody, haggled over his cut for collecting the monies, and after 12 hours presented Townshend with a cheque," *NME*'s Tony Stewart reported in 1978[151].

"It was during the height of the Sex Pistols' notoriety, in March of 1977, that a final settlement was reached," Chris Charlesworth wrote in 1984. "Clutching a cheque for seven figures, Pete left the final meeting in a fragile, unhinged state…" Townshend downed a bottle of brandy and, along with Stamp, headed for the Speakeasy Club where John Otway and Wild Willie Barrett were performing. "I burst in, ignored John and Willie who were on their last number, smashed a few glasses, trod on a few toes and hit a few people, all friends of mine," Pete told *NME* in 1978. "I dunno why I went. I should have just gone and banged me 'ead against a wall."

> Then I thought I saw Johnny Rotten.
> Then I said to Chris, *"Oo's that there?"* An' he said, 'It's one of The Sex Pistols. It's…
> And I'd already gone, and I'd got him and cornered him against the bar. I said something like, 'What the fuck are *you* doing here?' And he said, 'Well, what the fuck are *you* doing here?'
> I thought he was Johnny Rotten for about the first five minutes I was talking to him. Then I suddenly realized it was somebody else. It turned out to be Paul, the Pistols' drummer.
> And I sat him down and I was really preaching at the poor little sod. Then Steve Jones, the guitar player, came and sat down and I went, *'Rock and Roll's gone down the fuckin' pan!'* and I tore up the royalty cheque.
> About half way through the tirade Paul looked at me really confused. He didn't really know what I was talking about. And he said, 'The Who aren't going to break up are they?'
> *'Break up!'* I said. *'We're fuckin' finished! It's a disaster!'*
> And he said, *'Ahhh, but we like The Who.'*
> I went, *'YOU LIKE THE 'OO? AHHHHHHHHHHH!'* And I stormed out of the place, and

---

[151] In *Before I Get Old*, Dave Marsh reported that Pete received $1 million "in full settlement of his U.S. copyrights to date," and "several hundred thousand dollars in back royalties."

> the next thing I knew I was being woken up in a doorway in Soho...
> And I got in and me old lady was waiting for me... sitting there with the rolling pin, but too tired to use it. She said, 'Where have you been?'
> I said 'I've been to hell.' And I really did feel that I'd actually been to hell, and that's what the song *Who Are You* is about.

Pete was "disgusted" with Cook and Jones and their lack of interest in picking up the mantle. "I was telling Paul Cook about the shit that I'd been through and the Who were fucking finished and rock & roll was finished, if this was what it was down to," he later told *Rolling Stone*.

> They were the only band that had a chance. And that they had to fuckin' pick up the banner. And they weren't interested in rock ideals. I mean, all Paul Cook and Steve Jones were into was going around the world and making money and fucking birds. Really! To that extent. I've met them since and I've said that publicly and they haven't come up and sort of said, 'Hey no! It's not true. We do care about our music.' They just wanted to be in a band and be successful[152].

Punk, incidentally, was a huge event for Townshend, who later claimed, "I'm sure I invented it." Pete's contention was that the punk movement provided his beloved rock music with a timely catharsis. He explained the process to *Musician* in 1982:

> ...one of the reasons I'm really pleased that the Who kept going this long is because if we hadn't carried on, and had the Stones not carried on, the Sex Pistols would never have existed, and I think the Sex Pistols were incredibly vital.
> ...I think we've suggested some kind of analogy of rock'n'roll being like a river, and what's interesting is that it doesn't matter whether you join that river when it's massive and wide, or when it's a tiny, trickly stream. You're still joining the river, and traveling at the same speed as every

---

[152] Although he was "disgusted" with Cook and Jones, Pete later pointed out that he was impressed with John Lydon. "Since then, I've met Johnny Rotten and *he* is completely different," he said. "He's such a great guy – sort of like meeting a white Jimi Hendrix. I can't explain it. Just the feeling of being in the presence of someone that's really great. And who isn't gonna compromise."

other drop of water in that river. Whether you're nearer the source, or still have a long way to go, none of that matters. In fact, you can even make your presence felt initially by jumping in with a big splash and swimming aggressively the wrong way for some time. Or even building a dam, which will hold that river up for a while. And that's, to some extent, what the Sex Pistols did. They made a big splash, and in a sense, they held it up for a little while. And then when they stood back – it *rushed* forward. The nicest analogy I think of is a tap that is kept stopped for a long time, and when it's opened for the first time for a long time, a whole lot of rust comes out. And then, water starts to run very pure again. And the punk movement, ostensibly, was that rust. But it was also, strangely enough, the first flow of fresh water for a long time...

Although the litigation with Lambert and Stamp drained him, the combined effect of spending time with his family, the completion of *Rough Mix* and the arrival of punk was rejuvenation and inspiration for Pete (who lifted his press interview boycott), but it also enhanced his attraction to working outside the constraints of The Who[153]. *Rough Mix*, Pete explained to Scott Muni in 1978, "gave me confidence to do something on my own..."

> When you know that every album that you do is going to be measured against the band that I believe is the best in the world, it makes you a bit reticent about going and doing it, you know.
> I did the album with Ronnie because I wanted to get my head going again, you know, and it really did, it wasn't meant to be a big deal. It really got me writing. And it was good for him, too, 'cause he was just forgotten.

"[Punk] freed me," Pete told *Rolling Stone*'s David Fricke in December, 1987.

> It allowed me to be myself. It dignified me, in a way, to be cast to one side.
> I felt very uneasy with the way the Who were inevitably on the road to mega-stardom. I believed that the punk movement would free me from that. It did. It freed

---

[153] While punk may have rejuvenated Pete to an extent, it also somewhat overwhelmed him. "The *Who Are You* period should have been a really good period for the band," he later commented. "What kind of upset it was Punk. My response to it was to drink a little too much."

me from it, that it was all crap and that the bottom line was we were all flesh and blood. But the Who as a band didn't believe it.

I ultimately had to stop using the band as a vehicle for my songwriting. In a way, I've got the punk explosion to thank for making that decision. Commercially, leaving the Who was the dumbest thing I've ever done in my life. But artistically, it was undeniably the most logical thing for me to do. It was the most important thing I've ever done for me – to allow me to have a new beginning, to actually grow.

He spent a great deal of 1977 preparing songs for The Who's next album, and by October he told the *L.A. Times* that he had "…40 songs ready for the next Who thing." The "next Who thing" became *Who Are You*, the 1978 release which centered thematically around the direction, and stagnation, of popular music. In typical Who fashion, *Who Are You* provided only a glimpse of Pete Townshend and The Who's original vision. Pete, in what was now standard practice during preparation for Who albums, initially had big plans for *Who Are You*. "I'm keen on trying to steer The Who in the direction of doing grandiose projects of some sort," he said, as if this was something the public didn't already expect from him in the wake of *Tommy*, *Lifehouse* and *Quadrophenia*. "It would be easy pickings to stick out a hard-edged rock album which would sell a couple of million in the States but, frankly, I'd prefer to make a film, despite the fact that my hair fell out when we did *Tommy*." The notion of a *Lifehouse* film project, dormant since the *Tommy* filming, thus returned to center stage. He resurrected and revised the script, and several new Townshend compositions were added to the overhauled story.

Pete was at least somewhat motivated to pursue the *Lifehouse* movie by his desire to stay off the road. "For the band to do a big film instead of an album – and reach fantastic amounts of people – would mean we wouldn't have to play so many concerts," Pete told *NME* in 1978. "The band went along with it, so I've developed the *Lifehouse* script." The second *Lifehouse* script was "pretty interesting," Pete said in 1999. "It was more landed and more grounded than the first one. It was more about music…" This incarnation of *Lifehouse* fleshed out the original storyline, including more details of the characters' futuristic environment. The new script "…was about music, machines and people changing color, the effect of how you could work out what people's karma was without psychic powers, what would happen if psychic power became part of the instrument of government," Pete recalled in 1999.

A lot of those type of things, for example a policeman could come and know whether you are a good man or a bad man without needing evidence. There were also statements about what had gone wrong with Rock and Roll, in other words the people that were in power at the time used big weapons, big machines, loud noise, whereas the people that were really nice, the good people, used acoustic instruments and played in little clubs!

"And I've developed that to a point where now we've already got a budget sorted out and several film companies interested," Pete told Scott Muni in an April 1978 radio interview.

> And I'm really looking round to try and find a director that would be good to work on it. Now is the time to do it from my point of view, you know I really feel hot for the idea and the music is coming out strong. Quite how long it would take, it could take a couple of years, you know, I mean, films, in that respect, in rock terms are very frustrating 'cause they're so slow, but then you know, so are Who albums for God's sake. A couple of songs I think we'll put in just as a taster, there's a song called *The Music Must Change* which will probably be on the album, there's another song called *Guitar and Pen* which is about the way I write basically, how precious the guitar and pen are, and just several songs about music but hopefully we would include some of the stuff which was originally intended for the film like *Song Is Over*, *Won't Get Fooled Again*, *Baba O'Riley*, *Getting In Tune*, *Pure and Easy*, all these songs were written for *Lifehouse* originally. So with that material to jump off from, rework, brought up to date, plus a good body of new stuff I think it could be the great Who film, hopefully. 'Cause although *Tommy* was a great event in The Who's career, the film wasn't really a Who film. I'd like to see the *Lifehouse* film be a Who film from start to finish, a Who production.

In 1979, Pete submitted the reworked *Lifehouse* script to director Nicolas Roeg. "Roeg is loosely interested, I don't know if it's the kind of thing that he would want to do, but I really love the films he's directed, he's English, and his new film *Bad Timing* just smashed me," he told *NME* in 1980.

> I'd done a couple of scripts for [*Lifehouse*], but I can't see the wood for the fucking trees anymore...*Lifehouse* was originally a fiction, almost a

science fiction, concept with a concert at the heart of it. The action was a story about an approaching army heading toward this concert and busting in at the climax. But the two things would be shot separately and inter-related. At one point I was imagining a 10-week concert, not just with the Who but with lots of other musicians as well. The idea was that it was set in the future and this was a sort of illegal concert which they were trying to track down and stamp out. Like an expunged church: the lost art of rock'n'roll. When they finally break in, the concert has reached such a height that the audience is about to disappear [laughs]. It was kind of a nutty idea at the time, but I've since brought it a little bit down to earth, rationalized it a bit. What still excites me about it is that it does contain a concert and a story, and it does contain a lot of my feelings about what rock is and what music is, why music has a spiritual value and why the effect of rock music has a spiritual value.

Included in this incarnation of *Lifehouse* were early tunes such as *Relay* and *Join Together*. Tracks from the *Who Are You* sessions slated for the project included *Who Are You, Guitar and Pen, Sister Disco,* and *Music Must Change*. John Entwistle contributed *905*, a song from his long-planned solo science fiction album, which he'd recently scrapped.

"[*Who Are You* is] ...not a concept [album] as such, but some of the material was written for a film idea which I had way, way back in 1971 which was called *The Lifehouse*," Pete told Scott Muni in 1978.

> ...it's a story about the rediscovery of music at some distant point in the future. It's a mixture of sci-fi and music. I revived the idea, middle of last year and all the band said, hey, great, let's have another bash at it and started to write again, and lo and behold, the same kind of writing pattern came out, you know. I find as a musician, that I really like to write songs about music. So some of the material has come from that area and does have a slight concept feel to it, but other stuff's just come out, just generally songs about the way I feel about punk rock, the way I feel about being middle aged and in love, and... the material is very, very mixed.

Pete was upbeat regarding the prospects of this second attempt at *Lifehouse*. "...Seven years later a lot of what I wrote about has since become accepted," Pete told *NME*, "particularly in America, where they're into metaphysics, the connection between your mood and the way you live your life, and the vibrations in the air. It was all spacey talk when I first started. The rest of the band thought I was insane..."

The Who were in sorry shape as they headed for Ramport studios in late September, 1977, to begin sessions for the new album. Keith, now residing in England again after a long stint in California, was fat and his drumming was not at all up to par. Moon, Townshend and Entwistle were all drinking heavily, as Jon Astley told Who fanzine *Generations*: "At about six o'clock the port would come out and they'd all start sitting around talking about the old days and telling jokes until it was time to go home. Glyn would often get really bored with the lack of progress and leave." The band's physical state, together with several technical problems and a month-long Christmas break meant that the *Who Are You* sessions took far longer than anticipated.

In order to protect his increasingly fragile ears, Pete used special precautions in the recording studio. "I've got things like an earphone kit with a lamp in the line," he told Scott Muni, "so when you're listening to music, if it goes over the peak, this light lights up, and I use that when I'm working in the studio, I use that when I'm doing overdubs, and that's working OK. I'm finding that I'm getting used to the lower levels that I'm working at."

In late October, less than a month into the recording sessions, a major setback occurred when Roger punched Glyn Johns following a heated argument. Jon Astley commented later that Glyn had, up to this point in the recording sessions, "...made it very obvious that he adored and loved Pete and didn't think much of Roger", which certainly didn't help matters, and Glyn was also committed to produce Joan Armatrading's next record very soon, as he hadn't expected *Who Are You* to take so long[154]. Johns also reportedly commented that he was "bored rotten" with *Who Are You*.

In December, 1977, the band performed live for the first time in over fourteen months. The show, which took place at the Gaumont State Theatre in Kilburn, North London, in front of only 1500 fans, was scheduled specifically for the filming of a new biographical feature entitled *The Kids Are Alright*. Jeff Stein, the film's producer, wanted definitive, up-to-date live renditions of *Won't Get Fooled Again* and other songs from *Who's Next* to provide a suitable ending to his film, and no contemporary live footage of the band was available due to their recent inactivity. "...I thought we needed something to bring the film full circle," Stein told *The Hollywood Reporter*'s John Burman in 2003. "...basically, I was lobbying, pleading, begging, cajoling, to get them to do a show and finally they acquiesced and we put on a show at Kilburn... It was a fairly small theater. I thought it

---

[154] Johns' next project was Joan Armatrading's *To The Limit*, one of four Armatrading albums he produced between 1976 and 1979. Some-time Armatrading musicians with links to Pete Townshend and The Who were percussionist Jody Linscott and bassist Pino Palladino.

would be a great, intimate, powerful show and it was just a disaster... it was a train wreck."

"It was among the worst concerts they'd ever performed," wrote Chris Charlesworth, "unrehearsed, mildly intoxicated, nervous and with Keith Moon a serious liability on drums, The Who stumbled along between takes, stopping and starting, a pale shadow of their once staggering selves." Pete commented from the stage that the show was a waste of film, and ultimately he was right – the footage of this gig was deemed unworthy for use in the movie.

"...Pete was in a bad mood, which sometimes, fueled their finer performances," Stein told Burman, "But, the only two things we ended up with after shooting that whole show was a little bit where Pete issues that challenge from the stage, which is basically, "Any of you in the audience want to come up here and take away my badge, come up and try it."[155] ...I used that bit. And there's a moment during *Long Live Rock* in the final bows/end credits where they are all coming up the stairs and they are kind of not very happy and Keith... John throws a punch at the cameraman and Keith is about to throw a chair at us and actually did, but we slammed the door in time."

The recording of *Who Are You* suffered further setbacks in the New Year. Pete visited his parents' home in February when an argument between his mother and father erupted. After several futile attempts to intervene, Pete (who'd been drinking) reportedly smashed a window with his hand in frustration, then, seeing that the two had only momentarily stopped to see what was going on, he rubbed his hand in the glass fragments. The injuries, although not serious, would render him incapable of playing guitar until early March. "We're about three quarters of the way through, and... it's been so slow, you can't imagine," Pete told Scott Muni the following month. "I look with great jealousy at these young bands that are going in and knocking out albums in eight hours, the way we did our first, but it's good. It's really good and we're all happy. We're... relieved to still be together and working and we're enjoying doing it and the music is coming out just great."

The band's first rehearsal following Townshend's hand injury took place at Shepperton Studios on March 6, 1978[156]. The session also served as an audition for keyboardist John "Rabbit" Bundrick[157]. "We played and

---

[155] "There's a guitar up here if any big-mouthed little git wants to fuckin' take it off me," Pete said from the stage.
[156] In March, the *Who Are You* sessions moved to RAK studios after Glyn Johns left due to other obligations. Jon Astley took the helm for the remaining two months
[157] Bundrick, whose buck-teeth inspired the nickname, was a session musician who had previously worked on Johnny Nash's *I Can See Clearly Now* and Bob Marley's *Catch a Fire*. In February 1978, just a month prior to his Who audition, Bundrick underwent Meg Patterson's Neuro Electric Therapy at Patterson's house in Kent, in an attempt to rid himself

jammed for hours on end," Bundrick later commented. "Then at the end of it, I was told by Pete, "You've got the job if you want it."" The following day, Bundrick broke his hand when he fell out of a taxi after leaving Keith Moon's house in the early hours after celebrating his new job with The Who.

Keith Moon caused problems from day one at the sessions, both in his usual mischievous ways and also due to his poor physical condition. Jon Astley remembered an early incident from the *Who Are You* sessions in *Generations*:

> ...Glyn told me to get in early and mike up the kit...and I spent all day doing it...I had a roadie there who was banging drums for me so I could tune everything...It was very, very hard work. And Keith came in and said "Oh, how does the kit sound?" and shook my hand. So I said "Oh, it sounds fine but I'd like you to play it, though, because I've only heard your roadie play it." And he said "Oh, right, fine" and he got behind and played everything, the whole works and it sounded really, really good – I was so pleased. And he stood up and said "Is that alright?" and I said "Yeah, it sounds great." And he just walked through the kit towards me with this horrible gleam in his eye. He set fire to the studio about three days later.

The effects of alcohol and the diet pills Keith had been taking took their toll on his physical ability to play the drums during these sessions. While drumming is an inherently physically demanding occupation, Keith's version of the profession required nothing less than superhuman stamina, and Moon at this time simply didn't have it. Pete recalled the situation to *Musician* in 1989:

> About halfway through the recording of *Who Are You*, he was showing up late and not playing very well and I got into this mood: "I'm not taking any more of his shit." So I rang him up and told him to get the fuck down here. He came running down, babbling excuses. I got him behind the drums and he could not keep the song together. He couldn't play. He'd obviously been out the night before to some club. He'd put his work second. Again. But before I could say anything, he went [imitates chaotic drum solo]. "See?" he said. "I'm still the best Keith Moon-type

---

of alcoholism. While the treatment successfully curbed Rabbit's appetite for liquor, he maintained that he compensated for it by simply drinking more wine and beer.

drummer in the world."

There was nobody to top him doing that. But unless you wanted that, you were fucked. It happened that on that song, we didn't want that. Keith wrestling himself. He was funny, but he was capable of so much more. He was such a wonderful drummer, not just an apeshit drummer. But he had reduced himself to that in the eyes of the world and in his own eyes. A couple of days after that, he started to call me up just to say good night and I love you. He did that about 10 times, and you could tell he was crying a little bit. He'd say, "You do believe me, don't you?" I'd say, "Yes, but you're still an asshole."

Keith wasn't the only band member suffering substance abuse problems during this period. "…A friend from AA came in to talk to Keith once [during the *Who Are You* sessions], worked with him for two or three weeks," Pete recalled.

He said Keith was a heavy drinker with a strange emotional makeup. Then he said *I* was an alcoholic. I wondered how he'd worked that out, because I hadn't had a drink in three or four weeks. I went back in the studio and I said to Glyn Johns, "Do you believe it? Keith's been coming in here every morning for weeks vomiting on the mixing desk, taking pills for this and that, and I'm supporting Keith by not drinking, and I could use a drink, but I haven't had a drink, and this guy thinks I'm alcoholic." Glyn kind of looked at me. Keith's driver was there, and I took him outside, and I asked, "I haven't had anything to drink, have I?" He said, "No, no." I said, "Listen, you don't have to defend my position. Have I had anything to drink?" "Not apart from when you go home." "What do you mean?" "Well, every night after work you go off to the bar and drink a bottle of vodka. Everyone thought you all were just not drinking while you were working. At the end of the session, you drink a bottle of vodka like water." And I suddenly remembered what I'd been doing. I was drinking alcoholically, but I didn't deal with it until several years later.

Meanwhile, the Moon situation had reached boiling point. Roger, Pete, Jon Astley and Keith went to dinner one night and, "They (Roger and Pete) sat Keith down and said 'You've got to get yourself together or you're out of this fucking rock and roll band,'" Jon Astley remembered in 1995.

"They laid it on the line and, lo and behold, within two weeks he was drumming really well...I thought while he's this good I think I'll get him to go back and re-record as much drums as I possibly can. It was over a ten-day or two week period. It was great."

Who Are You was finally finished in late spring, 1978 and was released in August[158]. While the *Lifehouse* link was difficult to detect, *Who Are You*'s most obvious theme was Townshend and the band's dissatisfaction with contemporary popular music and their fear of stagnation. This theme is prevalent throughout the album, but is most obviously represented in *New Song* and *Music Must Change*[159].

Sister Disco, which followed a similar thematic line, also featured some impressive synthesizer work. "It isn't quite Kraftwerk," Pete later wrote, "but in 1976 I don't think they were doing it much better."

Who Are You, the song which was written shortly after Pete's encounter with two Sex Pistols at the Speakeasy in 1977, "...is very misunderstood," Pete said eight years later. "It's actually a prayer, believe it or not, I think, scuppered for once by Roger's overkill. In fact what I was doing was trying to sort of ask who and where, what God was, you know. That's what the song was really about, about the hell of living on the street and going through money trouble and all that stuff, and continually looking up to the sky and saying 'who are you, who are you, who are you?'"

The album garnered a reasonably complimentary review from *Rolling Stone*'s Greil Marcus:

> This is by no means a great record, but despite the doubt, guilt, worry and self-laceration in almost every song, it's a strangely confident one. Again and again, the persona is that of the cripple, the victim of disaster, but *Who Are You* is not the work of cripples, no matter how many breakdowns and bottles the Who have left on their fourteen-year-old trail.
>
> ...*Who Are You* is an LP the Who have been working toward all through the Seventies. The fears of aging, irrelevancy and the dissolution of one's self, one's band or one's audience that peeked out of *Who's Next* and *The Who by Numbers* have finally surfaced whole...
>
> It will be a real disappointment if another three years pass before the next Who album: this one seems to

---

[158] August 1978 marked the death of early Who mentor/publicist Pete Meaden. He was found dead in his parents' North London home of a barbiturate poisoning. Dave Marsh described Pete as "especially saddened."

[159] After discovering that Moon couldn't handle the difficult time signature of *Music Must Change*, Pete left the original percussion track from his demo intact: The sound of his footsteps walking across the tiled floor of his studio.

have left them ready for the new music they claim they can't make – a claim that's obviated by what is new and, more importantly, compelling on *Who Are You*. I said this was, despite its claims to oblivion, a confident record: what makes it so is the Who's refusal to settle for mere "survival," for automatic applause and meaningless *pro forma* hits. Pete Townshend recognizes the fact that, after a decade which seemed happy with its own dead end, bands like the Clash have broken through limits he had half-accepted. In this case, the child really is father to the man, and that means the chance to start all over again is at Townshend's finger tips.

In *Before I Get Old*, Dave Marsh pointed out that "...the music doesn't reinforce the message: There is nothing truly new here, no real departures." Greil Marcus agreed: "*Music Must Change* might be announcing the need for a New Wave, but it's quite consciously two years out of date, and, what's more, the music itself sounds old and stiff-there's not a single musical concession to punk, reggae or even hard-nosed rock."

The album did feature somewhat of a departure from the norm in the form of some jazzy Townshend guitar work. "I've got so used to playing guitars so loud, that when I try and play them soft, I can't," Pete told Scott Muni in 1978. "So a couple of the guitar solos on the latest album, they're almost like jazz solos. I'm a big fan of jazz guitar players. I particularly like people like Pat Martino and people like that, and Kenny Burrell. And I've always liked that kind of playing. So I'm starting to play a little bit more like that. Because that doesn't have to be loud. And so my whole sort of musical perspective is changing."

Who Are You reached number 6 in Britain, number 2 in the U.S. While Dave Marsh wrote, "The playing is grand in the way that *Who's Next* was, which makes it ideal for onstage interpretation", Pete remained adamantly against touring. "The last three years have been the happiest of my life as far as my family goes," Townshend said at the time.

"The problem really with the group at the moment is... we're in middle age as a group, I mean not just as human beings," Pete told Scott Muni during work on *Who Are You*, "and you have to completely review the way you work, you have to review your lifestyle, your energy level is different, and touring in the USA is something which requires more than just a manager to lay the gigs out and an airplane to ride around in."

It requires a whole energetic burst. You can goof off in a studio, but you can't goof off on the road. If you goof off on the road, you miss the date. Without going into it too deeply, last time we were on tour, we missed a couple of dates. And this is the first time it's ever happened to us, and I don't like it... The road is a place where you can only afford to be a hundred percent professional. If you're sick, or if you're tired, or if... emotionally, you just can't handle it, then you shouldn't be there. So The Who will tour if they're in shape to tour. And if they're not in shape to tour, they won't. It's as simple as that. That's why there's a certain conflict in the air at the moment, because what I want to do is I want to get the album done, I feel so confident that the album is going to create a new surge of energy in the band, and hopefully that will give us all the confidence to get out and do it with vigor.

By this time the Who had purchased rehearsal space, sound stages and other buildings at Shepperton Film Studios near Middlesex. When not in use by The Who, the three sound stages and the rehearsal space were often rented out to other bands, while the numerous buildings housed the band's impressive array of state-of-the-art equipment. Space was also provided for lighting engineer John Wolff and sound man Bobby Pridden to experiment and develop new ideas in their respective areas of expertise.

The businesslike aura of this venture by the newly named Who Group, Ltd., was no coincidence. The band were now under the guidance of Bill Curbishley, who remains at the helm of The Who's affairs to this day. Curbishley, "a tough and honest businessman", according to Chris Charlesworth, was a school friend of Chris Stamp and had begun as a Track Records employee in 1971. The band now owned the previously mentioned property at Shepperton studios, a recording studio (Ramport), and their record label, Polydor, boasted that the Who had the most advanced laser and lighting displays in the world.

Not to be outdone, Pete Townshend was becoming quite the businessman himself, starting his own music and literary publishing ventures under the name of The Eel Pie Group. The book-publishing arm of Eel Pie specialized in children's titles, music books and several Meher Baba-related publications. A bookstore named Magic Bus was opened in London and in April 1978 Pete opened office space for Eel Pie Books in New York, in preparation for the mail-order release of one of their titles, *The Story of Tommy*. Written by Pete along with Richard Barnes, the book chronicled the writing of the 1969 album and also the making of the film five years later. "...what I tried to do with this book is to try to cover the areas that haven't been covered before," Pete told Scott Muni in 1978.

> You know when we did the album way, way back, I did something like a hundred and twenty interviews in one tour on the subject of *Tommy*, I talked it right out of myself.

> I explained it, I explored it, I tried to reason it out and tried to justify bits of it that didn't work and celebrate bits of it that did. When we started to do the film with Ken Russell, I decided at that point that I would make a book about the making of a film. I'm fascinated with films and I do make films, and I thought it would be great to have a book, right from the inception to show how a film is made, everything. We did that, we drew all the material together, but the book wasn't really ready to go out, it didn't feel quite right. So I started to add more material to it. I added a large section which I wrote myself on the actual ideas that brought *Tommy* forth as a story, I'd written pages and pages of notes in 1966 and 67 about, really about also the concept of rock opera, whether it would work, whether or not it would survive, whether or not it was reasonable. And I've included all that early stuff in the book, and there's a long interview in the book with this mate of mine, Richard Barnes, who did the artwork, which really I can't take any credit for, but I think it is fantastic. It's a full color book right the way through...

Pete's Eel Pie recording venture focused on offering recording facilities, equipment and guidance to new acts. Townshend leased a studio building in Soho, and "...equipped it with some of the stuff from my country studio which had a leaky roof," he wrote in 1982. The services offered by the company included allowing bands to use the P.A. system, transportation, or even small loans to pay for recording time. "To press 2,000 singles costs nothing," Pete said.

> We'll tell you where to go, give you $500 and that's it. Pay us back off the top. Anyone can make a record now for $20 an hour which – by 1965 standards – would be of exceptionally high quality. But what fucks bands up now is p.a., because the standard of p.a. that people are used to now, even from small bands, is so high. You can go on with a Telecaster copy, but you can't go on with a shitty p.a. and unless the club or the other group have a good one, you've got to spend $350 to hire one. In my company, we try to cut across that by forming a co-op, allowing the bands to use the p.a. and the van free, and if they got a deal they'd put money back in.

Townshend was cautious to point out that Eel Pie should not be mistaken for a charitable organization, despite the fact that it undoubtedly provided many bands with an otherwise unattainable opportunity. Eel Pie recording, he noted in typical self-deprecating form, also served a somewhat selfish purpose. "I'm often called altruistic in the press, but that's not entirely true. There's a side to that that's exploitative, if you like. Whereas The Who deals with superstars and upwards, my company starts from street level. The reason is, I'm keeping my nose to the ground. In the world of million-pound movies you can lose sight of what's springing up in the city suburbs."

Other activities occupying Pete's time during this period included making a "musical film about a violent incident of his youth for a British arts festival," according to Dave Marsh, and assisting John Annunziato's New York-based film-production company, Nunzi Productions (Annunziato and Townshend had previously made the Delia DeLeon movie which had been shown during the opening of Oceanic). Pete also reportedly wrote some of the material on Roger's latest solo recording, *One Of The Boys*, although he didn't receive songwriting credits. He also played guitar on the album, which was produced by John Entwistle.

The Who's recently purchased space at Shepperton Studios became the site of their only live show in 1978 and Keith Moon's last performance with The Who. On May 25, 1978, the band played before an invited-only audience in a gig which was filmed for *The Kids Are Alright*, a second attempt following the subpar Gaumont State Theatre show. Persuading Pete Townshend to play this show proved a monumental task for the film's producer, Jeff Stein. "I think there were two issues," Stein told *The Hollywood Reporter* in 2003.

> One, I know he was afraid he would totally lose his hearing. And two... He said, "Don't make me play live. Because if you make me play live for this film, I'll get that taste of blood in my mouth and I am like Pavlov's Dog. When I get the taste of blood I can't stop. And I'll hit the road again and I can't do it." I think he thought it would kill him. I think (it was) dealing with Keith, dealing with the band, dealing with their place, dealing with, you know, again as I said, were they an endangered species? It was the middle of the punk movement. He didn't want to be perceived as a dinosaur. It must have been devastating.

Despite the long odds of persuading Townshend to play, Stein, who admitted he "was probably a total pain in the ass", pulled it off. The decision was made to perform at Shepperton because of its location outside London's city limits – the Greater London Council wouldn't let the band use its new laser show, and Stein wanted to capture it on film. To compensate for the out-of-the-way location, fans were bused in from London, with an assortment of alcoholic beverages on board to ensure everyone was in the appropriate mood for the show.

Although Stein only needed footage of a few songs (he was specifically looking for definitive versions of *Baba O'Riley* and *Won't Get Fooled Again*), The Who played around eight songs prior to retiring backstage. "They ended with *Won't Get Fooled Again*," Stein told *The Hollywood Reporter*. "And it was weak."

> And I was beside myself." And, I thought, "OK. Here's the moment of truth. You live with this and this is the end of the movie or you go and beg for them to do it again. Besides the fact the Who didn't much like encores, which was why they smashed their shit up at the end of the show. Now, they have to play the same song twice, which wasn't going to go over well. I knew it. I can't even tell you how I felt going backstage, walking through the minefield.

Again, in spite of the odds against him, Stein made his way to the dressing room and managed to get Pete and the band back onstage to perform a second, more acceptable *Won't Get Fooled Again*, the version which was used for end of *The Kids Are Alright*.

Four months later, a *Rolling Stone* article by Dave Marsh pointed to a brighter future once again for the band. "…the Who seem more like a band than they have in years," Marsh wrote. "The conflicts between Daltrey and Townshend have been resolved – they speak of each other as friends rather than as enemies enjoying a temporary truce. Keith Moon seems on the way to recovery from whatever physical and mental demons have plagued him." Pete and Roger's relationship had benefited from a band meeting at a local pub during the Shepperton filming. The band decided, "'Look, this is a band,'" Townshend told Marsh. "'Let's not be afraid of being a band. Let's not be afraid of being the Who. Let's not be afraid to be different. Let's not be afraid to take stances. Let's not be afraid to be affected.' That was a conscious decision that we took after a talk 'round the table…and it was most effective in my relationship with Roger. We decided not so much to stop fighting as to stop deliberately getting in each others' way and giving each other a lot more space."

Any optimism Marsh's upbeat article may have garnered came crashing down within days of its publication, when Keith Moon died on September 8, 1978. Moon had died of an accidental overdose of Heminevrin, a sedative he'd been prescribed by his doctor in an effort to curb his alcoholism. Pete, vacationing with his family, was understandably devastated by the news of Moon's death. "Pete just went into a shell," John Astley told *Generations*. "He was in complete shock." It didn't help matters that it was Pete who, after receiving the news of Moon's death from Bill's wife Jackie Curbishley, had to call Entwistle and Daltrey, and toughest of all, Moon's mother.

"I helped get him a flat in London because he was broke after his stay in California," Pete told *Musician* in 1989[160]. "...I helped him get back on his feet by getting this flat. And a couple of days later he died in it." The sheer abruptness of Moon's death took the band by surprise, although Moon had spent most of his life abusing his body to the absolute limits. "The worst thing is that none of us were there when he died," John Entwistle told *Time* in 1979. "We must have saved his life 30 times in the past, picking him up when he was unconscious and walking him around, getting him to a doctor."

The remaining members of The Who gathered at Shepperton Studios shortly after Moon's death for a long meeting, but the dominant subject was Moon's estate, not the future of The Who. Following the meeting, Pete issued a statement on behalf of the Who:

> Our first thoughts as a band are for those people who were closest to Keith: his mother; his ex-wife, Kim; and daughter, Mandy; and his fiancee, Annette, whom he was due to marry shortly. Next, we think about the fans of The Who. We are poised with an album in the charts, and films in the making, and although there have always been questions, the future looked better prior to Keith's death than ever before.
>
> Next, we think about ourselves and I have to admit that it's now we cry the tears that just can't be held back. We have lost our great comedian, the supreme melodramatist, the man who apart from being the most unpredictable and spontaneous drummer in rock, would have set himself alight if he thought it would make an audience laugh or jump out of its seats. We have lost our drummer but also our alter-ego. He drove us hard many times but his love for every one of us always ultimately came through.
>
> The Who? We are more determined than ever to

---

[160] "...Poor old Keith couldn't get a flat in London," Pete told Scott Muni five months prior to Moon's death. "Nobody would give him a flat anywhere... So I said, 'Listen, Keith. *I'll* get you an apartment. So I go out and I get this apartment for him [which turned out to be owned by Harry Nilsson]... The day after, the *day after* he moves in, I get this letter from the woman downstairs. 'Dear Sir...', and the complaints list, they run fourteen or fifteen pages of complaints. All of a sudden I wake up and I'm like, Jesus Christ, do you know what's happened, I said to my old lady, I said, 'I'm Keith Moon's landlord!' I've put myself in this situation where I'm Keith Moon's landlord! It's a great experience, I can tell you."

carry on and we want the spirit of the group to which Keith contributed so much to go on, although no human being can ever take his place. We loved him and he's gone.

I have always complained that up until now when I have walked into a pub, someone has slid next to me, nudged me, and said, 'Hey, that Keith Moon, what is he really like?' For the first time in my life I will know what to answer. I wish I didn't.

Marsh's article, aptly entitled *The Who Come To A Fork In The Road*, had taken on a much more ominous meaning now that Moon was dead.

In the weeks following Keith Moon's death, Pete Townshend began a flurry of activity, including consulting for the filming of *Quadrophenia*, recording demos, assisting Raphael Rudd and Paul McCartney with their own upcoming releases, writing a TV play, and contributing Who tracks to a charity album. Townshend recorded several demos during September, 1978, which eventually surfaced on 1987's *Another Scoop*: *Brooklyn Kids*, which he recorded in his country house in Berkshire, *Football Fugue* at Olympic Studios, and *The Ferryman* and *Praying the Game* both at Abbey Road Studios in London[161]. The demos all featured orchestrations arranged by Ted Astley.

He also assisted his friend, fellow Baba-follower and musician Raphael Rudd in recording his first solo album a month after Moon's death. "In June 1978 I was a 19-year-old studying for my masters at the Manhattan School of Music in New York City when I received a phone call that changed my life," Rudd wrote in 2001. "It was Pete Townshend of The Who. He'd heard my music and was inviting me to record professionally at his Eel Pie Studios in London. I couldn't believe it... By September I was recording my first solo album, *The Boy*, with Pete keeping an eye on things. It was he who came up with the title, an affirmation of the importance of the artist remaining young at heart."

"Raphael Rudd and I met because of our mutual interest in the Indian spiritual master Avatar Meher Baba," Pete wrote in a brief essay on the sleeve of Rudd's 1996 release *The Awakening – Chronicles*.

> When about five years old Raphael met Meher Baba, who took the child's hands in his own and gazed into his eyes. Later, when Raphael became a musician and dedicated his work to his master, it became clear to everyone that Meher Baba had inspired the child forever. I

---

[161] *I Like It The Way It Is* was also recorded at this time (in Olympic studios). It was ultimately included in the 2001 collection *Scoop 3*, admittedly "suppressed for many years" because of its subject matter: Pete's inability to curb his alcoholism.

didn't meet Meher Baba in the flesh. But I was pleased to be able to work with Raphael on this recording project that was to be dedicated to Meher Baba... I regarded myself as Raphael's musical mentor during that period. Today, we inspire each other on a more equal footing. I am greatly influenced by Raphael's piano style...

Rudd would later return the favor by arranging the horns on *Rough Boys*, the opening track of Townshend's 1980 solo album, *Empty Glass*. He was also responsible for arranging and conducting members of the London Philharmonic and London Symphony for a block of the *Quadrophenia* movie soundtrack and a few other pieces of Pete's solo work. "...Raphael orchestrated the final scene of the film and conducted the orchestra with great authority despite being only twenty-one years old at the time," Pete commented in 1996. Townshend and Rudd also performed together at Oceanic for the Meher Baba followers, once in December, 1979, and again the following December. Both shows were recorded, and an 18-song CD, *The Oceanic Concerts*, was released in October, 2001.

"To this day Raphael and I regard ourselves as fellow voyagers on the path to God – who we see manifested clearly in the perfect life and continuing compassionate spiritual presence of Avatar Meher Baba," Pete wrote in 1996. "This might seem romantic, and it is of course. But whatever we like to believe as spiritual seekers, and however lost or vain we might become in our pursuit of art and fame, we are both utterly certain that we are merely channels for the will of God."[162]

Four weeks after the death of Keith Moon, Pete was committed to participating in a recording session for Paul McCartney's *Back To The Egg* album. Pete was a member of the all-star *Rockestra*, along with John Bonham, Dave Gilmour[163], Kenny Jones, John Paul Jones, Pete's boyhood hero Hank Marvin of the Shadows ("that was a weird one", Pete later commented), and Ronnie Lane. Eric Clapton and Jimmy Page were also scheduled to participate, but failed to show, prompting Pete to comment, "I think they were both scared."

The *Rockestra* session, which was filmed, lasted nine hours. The group recorded two songs, *Rockestra Theme* and *So Glad To See You Here*. In an interview with *Melody Maker*'s Michael Watts a week later, Pete described the session as "...amazing, absolutely amazing."

My dad is a saxophone player and used to be in the Squadronaires, and it reminded me of their old reunions

---

[162] Raphael Rudd was involved in a car accident in Los Angeles in late February, 2002. He was in a coma for five weeks, and died in early April at the age of 45.

[163] Gilmour, incidentally, had "an enormous beer gut", Pete told *Melody Maker*. John Bonham "had a big beer gut as well. He played amazingly, incredible."

where you get a Scotsman and a guy from Newcastle and they talk about, 'oh, that's a great band, and what a player, what a bloody player!' It was really like that, boring old farts forever. Great fun.

Yet another iron Pete had in the fire during the period immediately after Moon's death was his development of the script and music for a play which was slated to be aired on London Weekend Television. Broadcaster and producer Melvyn Bragg, who knew Pete through Ken Russell (and had interviewed Pete when The Who played at Charlton in 1976) had initially asked Pete to write an opera. "…I had this idea about a kid," Pete told *Melody Maker*'s Michael Watts in October, 1978.

> It's purely autobiographical. I thought I'd actually do something that's outfront autobiographical for a change rather than try not to do something autobiographical which ends up that way.
> So it's about a kid who's learning to play the guitar and is in a band, and he gets involved in a relationship with an old guy who has given up a tremendous musical career to do some menial task and is absolutely fascinated by this. And then he also gets tied up in a relationship with his best friend, who becomes a villain, and there's a terrible fight between his best friend and the old man.
> It's set in London, and there's a sequence in Spain in the life of the old boy. I've written four songs for it.

Further activity on Pete's already full plate consisted of readying "previously unreleased Who tracks[164]" for a charity album which was being readied to benefit Meg Patterson's Pharmakon Clinic, a 30-room experimental drug rehab facility which was due to open in Sussex in January. The *FREE Charity Album*, which was originally planned to include new recorded material from Pete and Eric Clapton, but due to scheduling problems (and looking at Pete's schedule during this period, one can see why) was now slated to include pre-existing material from the pair. Others who'd been approached for material were George Harrison, Keith Richards, Jack Bruce and "members of Led Zeppelin", according to *Melody Maker*.

Pete visited the set of Who-funded *Quadrophenia* in Brighton in October. Shooting for the $2.5 million movie began within weeks of Moon's death, and lasted just under sixty days. Pete was joined in Brighton by two thousand extras (a mix of unemployed youths and mods recruited

---

[164] I am yet to discover which tracks were to be on the album.

from a nearby scooter rally) for the recreation of a bank holiday beach fight between mods and rockers. More on the *Quad* movie later.

Meanwhile, of course, questions concerning the future of The Who were mounting. Although the band had already announced that they would continue, observers wondered what form The 'New Who' would take. Would one drummer be chosen to replace Moon, or would the band use session musicians? Would they ever perform live again? "Roger and I have really got to get together and thrash out... not a compromise, but what is really gonna work," Pete told *Melody Maker*'s Michael Watts in an October feature entitled "Townshend: Picking Up The Pieces." "And if we can't do it so that it will work, then we should knock it on the head," Pete said. A chief concern of Pete's in considering a new alignment for The Who was the reduction of the sound level onstage. "The amplifier levels that we use at the moment, John and I, are really deafening and my ears are at a critical stage at the moment," he told Watts. "If I'm careful now I'll only go deaf when I'm 50, but if I'm not careful it'll be when I'm 40. There's no option, unless they dream up something in the next couple of years."

Townshend had already enlisted John Bundrick as keyboard player, and in addition to the requirement of a new drummer, the addition of a brass section and an extra guitarist were being considered. "For a long time I felt inhibited by being a rhythm player, and what I'd really like is to see the band have a keyboard player on piano and organ, and another guitar player so that I'd be free to do synthesizer work on stage and play various styles of guitar," Pete told *Melody Maker*'s Chris Welch in January. "Then we could do some of the more complex material from The Who's history." One name which made the rounds during this period was that of former Jones bandmate and keyboardist Ian McLagan. "I wanted him," Pete told Welch. "He's a good guitar player too. I was very keen to get him." Hiring McLagan would have perhaps created an uncomfortable situation for all involved, since he married Keith's ex-wife, Kim, in October.

Ginger Baker, Kenny Jones, Carl Palmer, Aynsley Dunbar, Tony Newman and Phil Collins all made it known shortly after Moon's death that they would gladly backstop The Who. "When Keith Moon died, I rang Townshend up and said, 'If ever you need a drummer, I would love to do that job'," Collins lamented in 1994.

> He said, 'Yeah, that would be great, man,' but... Kenney Jones was always gonna be the guy that took over. But I just kind of knew that you had to have *fire* to play with The Who and although I don't look it now, I've got *fire*. And I would have loved to have done that job... played with that band – playing that stuff is what I used to do in front of the mirror when I was learning to play the drums.

In November, 1978, Pete offered ex-Small Faces/Faces drummer Kenney Jones the job[165], and the newest incarnation of the Who was born. "John Entwistle was the first to propose Kenney Jones as The Who's new drummer and Pete was in agreement," Chris Charlesworth recalled in 1984. In 1974, after the Faces had gone their separate ways, Jones had played on the *Tommy* movie soundtrack and was well known to Entwistle and Townshend since his days in The Small Faces. Pete had also played with Jones in McCartney's *Rockestra* in October, where one imagines the subject of the position with The Who may have been broached.

"...I felt the band without Keith was a new band," Pete explained to *Musician* in 1989.

> Kenney was a drummer I'd worked with in the past. I liked him for his simplicity and directness and for the similarity of our backgrounds. He came up at the same time and had had a similar success. He was one of the few British drummers who could fill Keith's shoes, and it was courageous of him to do so.

"There was nobody else in my opinion," Pete told Chris Welch in January.

> It's not a question of Keith being replaced. Kenney would be the first to say that Keith was irreplaceable and that nobody could copy him and nobody would want to. Kenney was a much bigger part of The Who, anyway, than most people realize. We've always had this incredible link with the Faces... Kenney worked on the *Tommy* soundtrack and John and I noted that he was the only guy we could play with without thinking 'where is Keith?'
>
> He's a completely different drummer with a much more conventional approach than Keith. ...Keith was very responsive. He'd play off you. Kenney is a much more formal drummer who lays it down. But he's awake, he's alert and the feeling is we are starting a new band. People have got to live with the fact that The Who they knew has gone, and that they'll never see it again.

The lone dissenting voice in the hiring of Kenney Jones appears to have been that of Roger Daltrey. "Roger really resisted Kenney being

---

[165] Jones reportedly changed the spelling of his first name from 'Kenny' to 'Kenney' around the time he joined The Who.

brought as a quarter member," Pete told *Musician*'s Charles Young in 1989. "He wanted Kenney on salary. I said, 'No, I'm not ready for that. It means we're still running the Who. It's like we're on a pilgrimage to find Keith. To be really unpleasant about it, I'm kind of glad Keith is gone. He was a pain in the ass. The band wasn't functioning. This is a chance to do something new.'"

"I had terrible fights with Pete over [Kenney Jones]," Daltrey told *Music Connection*'s John Lappen in 1994.

> Kenney was a good drummer and a nice guy, but nowhere near the drummer for the Who. His wasn't the right style. But no one would listen to me. I used to go home in tears over that. It came to a point where I told Pete that either Kenney goes or I go. Pete looked at me, square in the eyes and said, 'I guess that's no choice at all,' basically telling me I could leave the band. I was devastated. We patched things up but it was me who had to swallow my pride and go back to Pete. He'd never apologize for anything if there was a fight. I've had to eat a lot of shit over the years to help keep it all together.

The new Who began rehearsals at Shepperton Studios in the spring of 1979, beginning the process of learning to play with not only a new drummer, but one whose style was the polar opposite of Moon's. Upon joining The Who, Jones added another bass drum to his kit with no intention of actually using it, telling *Musician* magazine in 1991, "I just used it as a bloody tom-tom stand." Consider the following quote when contemplating the difference in philosophies between Moon and Jones' playing styles:

"There is a definite way to strike drums," Jones told *Musician*, "and there is a very fine line."

> My son is a drummer, and when he plays my kit he dents all the skins. I really lose my temper with him. You don't need to do that. You can strike the drum the right way with a flick rather than making it a strength thing. You can appear to be smashing the fuck out of them, but you're not. You're just putting your emotion into it.
>
> Over the years I've had a lot of people tell me it must be great being a drummer because I can take my frustrations out on the drums. No *way* do I ever do that. The minute I get angry, I stop. I pride myself on playing an acoustic musical instrument. It's not something to get your anger out on.

Jones, however, drew widespread praise for his musicianship with The Who during 1979 and 1980, and Pete was solidly in his corner. "Kenney Jones has been a tremendous blood transfusion," Pete told *Oui* magazine's David Rothman in 1980. "Not just as a player – 'cause he's different from Keith, very much a fundamental backbone drummer – but he's a much more positive individual. Keith was a very positive musician, a very positive performer, but a very negative animal. He needed you for his act, on and off the stage. Kenney fits in very well as a person with the other guys in the band."

Pete publicly expressed a great deal of optimism regarding the new band, although his comments occasionally perhaps bordered on the inappropriate considering that Moon had been dead for just a few months. "We're finding ourselves in a way," he told *Melody Maker* in January 1979. "…Ironically, Keith's passing was a positive thing. It meant that it was impossible to continue to be bound by Who traditions… I feel very excited about the fact that the Who is a well-established band with a tremendous history, but suddenly we're in the middle of nowhere – a new band. I'm really excited about it."

The Who's first show before a paying crowd featuring Kenney Jones on the drummer's stool, and the newly acquired John Bundrick ("our all-new British Texan keyboard player", Pete announced from the stage) on keyboards, took place on May 2, 1979 at the Rainbow Theatre in Finsbury Park nearly a year after their last show at Shepperton studios. The show was originally intended to be a final rehearsal prior to the band leaving for the Cannes film festival in France, but it was agreed that the new Who lineup should be introduced on home turf as a gesture of solidarity with the fans. Despite the show being announced with only 48 hours' notice, the three thousand tickets sold out in well under an hour. A large contingent of Mods was present for the show, which was well-received by the Who-starved audience.

"…Five shadowy figures loped onstage at 8.35 and cut into a willful, almost irreverent execution of *Substitute* that had the entire audience on its feet from the first bar," *Melody Maker* reported. "…Relatively adventurous arrangements of material both obscure and well-worn, irresistibly urgent treatments of their simpler stuff, and a new found enthusiasm for performance suggest that the new Who might prove to be even better than the old Who." The set list was a veritable Who's Greatest Hits, featuring selections from almost every phase of the band's career, from *I Can't Explain* to *Who Are You*, *Pinball Wizard* to *Won't Get Fooled Again*. "Kenney came across as a powerful hard driving stayer," Richard Barnes recalled in 1982.

"The Who are making a new beginning – in one sense a beginning from scratch – and here to help them are armies of young mods, as if summoned from some suspended dimension, awaiting the hour," wrote

NME's Paul Du Noyer.

> In a strange and magical way, The Who are not reliving their history tonight but remaking it afresh.
>
> What *could* have taken place was an act of homage to the past 15 years: a celebration of affection and nostalgia, maybe tinged with a little sadness; an occasion for reverence or ritual, for the outward preservation and the inward destruction of everything Pete Townshend ever meant to rock'n'roll.
>
> What did happen was a fine, great and gorgeous rock'n'roll gig: no more and no less; as superb a show as The Who can ever have produced.

Pete clearly enjoyed himself. Townshend "bounds from one side to another, executes the legendary windmill chord-smash and generally performs like a man tasting freedom for the first time in years," *NME* reported.

The following week, the band was off to Cannes, promoting their two new movies, *The Kids Are Alright* and *Quadrophenia*, which were both premiered at the Cannes Film Festival. They rented a boat on which they entertained prospective film distributors and the press. The Who played before 10,000 fans on May 12 in a Roman amphitheater in Frejus, 25 miles west of Cannes. Impressed with the turnout, they agreed to play an additional performance the following night, despite the fact that the screening of *The Kids Are Alright* took place that same night at Cannes. "We did have discussions about the sanity of that gig," Pete recalled, "but we're up to our necks in investment and emotional commitment, and it's important to get across that we're still very much a live band. The films aren't a tombstone to Keith Moon." Kit Lambert met the band the second night. "Kit Lambert has just spent fifteen minutes telling me what's wrong with The Who," Pete later commented, "– and he was right."

Two shows followed in Paris a few nights later, and two off-the-cuff shows in Scotland in June rounded out the band's live work for the time being. The two Who-backed movies, meanwhile, were well-received.

The Kids Are Alright was a collage of footage of The Who from the early days right up until the May 25 show at Shepperton Studios, assembled chiefly by American Who fan Jeff Stein. Stein, an avid fan who had assembled a book of photographs[166] of The Who back in the early '70s as a

---

[166] "...I still have the guitar Pete's breaking on the last page of the book," Stein told *The Hollywood Reporter*'s John Burman in 2003. "By then I knew him well enough that he spotted me in the front row or two and flung this big chunk of the broken guitar at me and, I'm like, bloodied because it had jagged edges. And my brother was standing there, like punching people out who were trying to grab it from me. It was a beautiful moment."

teenager, had met the band after hanging out backstage after concerts and traveled to England to participate in the aborted Young Vic *Lifehouse* sessions. He approached Pete about the possibility of a Who bio-pic when the band was in New York in March, 1975 for the *Tommy* film premiere. "Pete was staying at the Pierre and I think I went up and knocked on the door to his room and he wasn't there…" Stein told *The Hollywood Reporter*'s John Burman in September, 2003.

> So, I knock on this other door and Yoko Ono opened it, because John and Yoko were staying there. So, I thought, "Whoops. Wrong room," but I think he was visiting him. So, I finally found him and I remember this most distinctly, I was pitching Pete while he was brushing his teeth before he goes to the premiere. So I was like, giving him my impassioned plea and he's brushing his teeth, going, "mmph rrorrog mmmph" and foaming at the mouth, which should have been an omen. (laughs)
> And at that moment, I thought, "OK. That was good enough for me. I think I got Pete's backing. We're getting traction. Let's go."

Stein, who'd been collecting footage since 1973, soon assembled a 17-minute sampler as a preview for the band, consisting of their 1967 catastrophic rendition of *My Generation* on the *Smothers Brothers Comedy Hour*, a 1969 live version of *Young Man Blues* recorded at the London Coliseum and the *Happy Jack* promotional film. Not long after the *Tommy* premiere, the band gathered in New York to see the sample of Stein's work. "We arranged a screening for them at a mixing studio that had a screening room and a pretty amped-up sound system," Stein said in 2003.

> …it was all the members of the band. And Roger had brought his wife. We showed the 17-minute promo and, basically, it was a mini-riot in the screening room. I mean, they were carrying on, laughing and screaming, smacking each other. I remember the coffee table tipped over and everything spilled all over the room. It was chaos…

Sufficiently impressed, The Who provided financial support for Stein's movie, and helped him locate footage. Townshend, "the only person in the Who who actually was tracking stuff and had gotten some stuff together and had stored it," according to Stein, was especially helpful. "Pete was always behind the scenes," Stein told Burman. "He was the man behind the curtain. I could always go to him to help resolve conflicts, whatever."

One capacity in which Pete wasn't willing to provide help, however, was that of interviewee. "...Pete did not want to do any new interviews [for the film]," Stein said. "He thought there was enough material on him – that he was always the one who was their spokesman... He thought, "You know, equal time for the other members of the band." " Pete's position didn't budge 25 years later when the film was released on DVD – he again declined to be interviewed, leaving Daltrey as the only band member to provide updated information.

Although the film was completed prior to Moon's death, it naturally took on a whole new meaning due to the timing of its release. It contained footage of Moon's final Who show, and also featured many humorous snippets and examples of Moon's antics over the years.

"...my favorite review was actually in the *New York Times*," Stein said, "which called the film "willfully uninformative."

> And I thought, if the *New York Times* finds it willfully uninformative I've done my job. I wasn't making it for the people who read the Sunday *New York Times*. I was making it for the people in Queens and Brighton. ...I never wanted to make a linear, straightforward documentary. I didn't want it to be an historical document. I wanted it to be an hysterical document.

"The [*Kids Are Alright*] movie is good," Pete told *Sounds* in 1980. "It's not exactly a documentary of The Who or its history or anything like that; it's just a collection of whatever was available. Some of it's TV trash and some of it is very good live footage and some of it is very bad live footage. Kind of a bit of everything. It's fun though, I think. It's a film about the group, not me." The soundtrack, which included the band's legendary 1967 performance of *My Generation* on the Smothers Brothers TV show, maintained the "collection of whatever was available" theme; it consisted of various and sundry live, studio and television performances from throughout the band's career, although it contained nothing from *Quadrophenia*. The double album reached number 8 in the U.S., 26 in Britain.

The other movie premiered at Cannes was the Franc Roddam – directed *Quadrophenia*, which many observers said was noticeably more violent than Townshend's original story. "*Quadrophenia* is a powerful film," Pete later recalled. "We don't appear in it and there's not a hell of a lot of music, but we're proud of it." The violence of the film stemmed in part from the band's desire for a realistic portrayal of the story, rather than the fantasy route they took when enlisting Ken Russell for the *Tommy* film. Pete had considered Alan Parker or Nic Roeg as producers, but when Franc Roddam's name was thrown into the mix by Who associate (and

Quadrophenia co-producer) Roy Baird, the search was essentially over. Pete had seen Roddam's enormously successful TV play *Dummy*, about a deaf and dumb prostitute, and "liked it a lot," Roddam told *NME*. The admiration was mutual with, Roddam describing Townshend as "...extremely bright, aware and well-informed... a very rich man, but still in touch."

Roddam collaborated with two writers in drafting a script for the film, which, he asserted, "remains true to the spirit of the album, of the Who and the mods, and of revolt itself." "The idea of *Quadrophenia* is that someone is not being allowed to be themselves," Roddam told Watts. "There are pressures from family, school and work, and if you want to move on you have to resist those pressures. ...What I'm doing is a translation of the album, if you like...."

The use of music in the *Quadrophenia* film was similar to its role in Pete's 1999 radio play of *Lifehouse* – it was relegated to an incidental capacity. This was in stark contrast to the *Tommy* film. "In *Tommy* the music dominates the film and is the central driving force behind it, it controls the narrative," Roddam told *NME*. "In *Quadrophenia*, the music contributes to the narrative and supports it but very rarely takes over from it. That's quite a difficult decision because it's putting the music in second place, so it's a very different kind of film."

Some interesting candidates for the role of Jimmy were in the mix as late as a month before filming began. "Johnny Rotten and Sham 69's Jimmy Pursey are being considered for the leading role in the movie *Quadrophenia*," Tony Stewart reported in the 12 August 1978 edition of *NME*. "He asked to talk to me about it," Townshend said of Rotten, "but I don't see how it'll change anything. I don't think he'll do it. In fact I'm 100 per cent certain he won't." Pete saw Jimmy Pursey on television and "thought he looked right for Jimmy" according to Stewart. Pursey also reportedly wanted the role. However, the leading role was soon awarded to Phil Daniels, and a principal supporting role was given to Leslie Ash, neither of whom had much acting experience. The role of the ace face, which was ultimately given to Sting, was reportedly initially offered to Stuart Goddard, better known as Adam Ant.

"It's very difficult when you make a film – when you *produce* a film – because in the last analysis you have to hand it over to the director," Pete told *Rolling Stone* in mid-1980.

> I wrote the script, originally – the first draft screenplay I wrote with Chris Stamp – and there was no riot scene at all. Not at all. For me, *Quadrophenia* was about the fights, and the riots, happening in the kid's *head*. The *threat*: "I'll do anything, I'll go anywhere" – and what you're dealing with is a little wimp. Who's fucking *useless*.

Who couldn't fight anybody. He had his few pills, and his bottle of gin, and he *felt* like he could. It was a study in spiritual desperation: the fact that all that desperation and frustration leads somebody to the point where for the first time in their life they realize that the only important thing is to open their heart. It wasn't about blood and guts and thunder – in the way that the film turned out to be...I suppose the director, Franc Roddam, thought it would make good cinema. And I think to some extent it's possible [the film] has sharpened [the violence] up, but I think it runs a bit deeper.

Roddam reported that Pete was very supportive during the making of *Quadrophenia*. "Townshend, of course, was like a sort of guiding light," he told *NME*. "He was very gracious – gracious enough to say, 'I made the album, the film is yours. I trust you to go away and make it.'"

The *Quadrophenia* film, much like the album, fared better in England than in the U.S. "In America, the film is slow," Pete explained to *Trouser Press* in 1980.

It does good business in the cities, but when it goes out on the road it stays in a cinema for a week and then moves on. Probably because it's a music film it'll make its money back over a period of years, like *Monterey Pop* did. The reason that it's doing incredible business in England is that we were lucky that the mod movement was having its renaissance around the time that the film came out. In fact, it was already well-established, as I understand they certainly didn't have any trouble getting people for the film. A lot of the kids in the film were actually existing mods from Sheffield, Stafford and a few other places, and they had scooters and they had parkas and they had all the kit.

The film was 18 months in the making, and while we were making it we saw the mod thing starting, and some of the kids told us that it had never stopped.

The latest mod revolution was sparked mainly by the popularity of The Jam, whose mod-friendly appearance and starkly British sound owed a great deal to Townshend and The Who. "Outside the Rainbow where we did our first concert," Pete recalled in 1980, "I couldn't resist going up to a row of kids in parkas that all had 'The Who' on and I said, "Have you ever seen the Who play before?" And this kid turned 'round and he didn't know who I was. He was queueing up for tickets and I don't think he cared. He gave me a look like, "Fuck off, cunt" and I suddenly realized that that symbol is just a symbol, just like the bloody swastika was to the Hell's Angels. It meant nothing to them. The people most responsible for the mod fashion thing coming back are the Jam. They started it, and we were just lucky that the film was there..."[167]

"The story of ten days in Jimmy's life will be instantly recognizable to the album owners and, like the vinyl version, the film is rough and energetic, realistic and accessible," wrote *NME*'s Dick Tracy in May, 1979. "It's also a lot of fun, and should produce widespread seat-damaging outbreaks when it reaches British screens next September."

The *Quadrophenia* soundtrack, another double album, featured remixed versions of key songs from the original album, plus songs which fit the period of the story. Selections from artists such as The Kingsmen, Booker T and the MGs, The Ronettes and James Brown filled one of the album's four sides. The album also featured three newly recorded Townshend compositions which all fitted neatly (perhaps too neatly) into the *Quadrophenia* theme, *Four Faces*, *Joker James* and *Get Out and Stay Out*. "The soundtrack, remixed by Entwistle, sounds even better than the recorded original," wrote *Time*'s Jay Cocks in 1979. The album reached number 23 in Britain, number 46 in the U.S.

The production of film versions of *The Kids Are Alright* and *Quadrophenia* (and their associated investments of time and money) "greatly postponed" any planned filming of *Lifehouse*, *NME* reported in May 1979. "I think it's probably killed [*Lifehouse*] stone dead, to be quite frank," Pete said, stating that the film would probably take two years, with an estimated budget of at least £12-15 million.

> ...But I don't know whether it would be possible to make it as a British film, and I wouldn't be interested in making it as an American film, 'cause I live here. Also, I no longer care that much about it, in fact.
>
> When I wrote it I was absolutely passionate about it. It was bound up in that period of the Who when Kit Lambert was still involved in my writing and in a managerial sense. And I felt then was the time the Who should've gone in and made a film. The idea was really to hit *Tommy*, to meet that audience head-on.
>
> Now the only reason I've revived *Lifehouse* was because at one point I figured it was the one way the Who was gonna be able to continue working and communicating

---

[167] Kenney Jones, incidentally, backed a *Quadrophenia* clothing line. "...it's the last thing on earth I would want to do, be involved in clothing lines," Pete remarked. "I never even saw the clothes. I wouldn't mind a Sting suit, mind you, but the suit Sting wore in the film must've cost about 300 quid. But you can get anything you need to be a mod at the shop at the top of the road."

at the level that we had as a performing band and reaching a very wide audience.

While the latest attempt at reviving the *Lifehouse* film had stalled, The Who had produced two successful films, which proved greatly pleasing to Pete[168]. "We're just proud of the fact that we managed to make a film in England. It wasn't entirely English money, but *McVicar* was made with a lot of English money and the *The Kids Are Alright* was made with all our money, and it'll make it back. It's great to be able to cock a snook at all the Americans who say that we're finished as a nation of film-makers. Most film-makers don't have the first fucking idea of what gets kids into the cinema, and it's not just tagging music onto something. It's making films in the British tradition, which is the only kind of film that I think we can make well, which is the kind *of Saturday Night and Sunday Morning* thing. I know it's depressing, but that's our cinema verite, if we ever had one."

"...what these two films do is tie up, once and for all – fully, totally exploit, wring out and wring dry – everything that the Who ever did," Pete told *Oui*'s David Rothman in 1980. "We're almost at the point at which the Who are going to produce their next major creative piece. All this stuff will be gone and done, and the old Who will be – dare I say it? – buried. So, in a way, it's a good thing. We're up against the wall again."

---

[168] Another Who – backed film, *McVicar*, starring Roger Daltrey, was released in 1980.

Chapter 9

"I've long, long gone past the time when I think I've got anything to say. When I was nineteen or twenty, I really felt I had something to say that would...not change the world...but I really felt I had to speak up, I had to act. Now, to be quite frank, I don't give a shit. I just want to be happy and enjoy the people around me and try to enjoy life."
— Pete Townshend, 1980

"It's very, very difficult to live in the present. If you can live in the present, it's a divine quality. It leads to selflessness, it leads to happiness, it leads to a smiling face. It might lead to what a lot of people feel is kind of almost like hippie-esque, dopey consciousness. I don't aspire to that, I aspire to living in the present, accepting what I am and where I am and what's happening to me and trying to make the best of it. That is what I was fighting, I think, for such a long time, was actually what I was. I've always said that happiness is not something which anybody has a right to at all, and if you get 10% of it a day, you should be delighted."
— Pete Townshend, 1985

1979 opened a new chapter for both The Who and Pete Townshend. The newly-aligned Who were enjoying success for the first time since the death of Keith Moon, and Pete was about to record his highly-acclaimed solo album, *Empty Glass*. But while 1979 demonstrated that Pete and The Who's musical pulse had survived the trauma and upheaval of 1978 intact, it also began to shed a glaring light on Pete's personal battle with alcohol, which had been escalating steadily for several years.

The problems, Pete recalled in Dennis Wholey's 1984 book on alcoholism, *The Courage To Change*, began around 1974. "...My wife, Karen, began feeling that there was a potential problem, while I felt it was just the way I was and the way I lived," he told Wholey.

> So we'd have lots of conversations. I would try to justify the way that I ingested alcohol by saying it was part of being a successful person. She didn't buy that at all. What's really peculiar is that I did...I always felt that drinking and work were tied together in a totally appropriate and proper way. This was despite the fact that my great partner, Roger Daltrey, never drank to excess, not from the beginning of our career to the end, and still doesn't...But I felt that I had a bigger responsibility because I was writing songs and was the spokesman for the band. And I wasn't allowed to bring those pressures home. This was the conspiracy that my wife and I carried together. We were accomplices. When I got home, family life was sacrosanct, but it got to the point where that charade could go on no longer.

After Keith's death, Pete's alcohol intake began to affect his ability to perform, a development which although surprisingly uncommon at this point, would seriously affect The Who's live shows in the coming months. An early instance of his deterioration occurred on June 27, 1979, when Pete took part in the opening show of Amnesty International's four-night fund raising event at Her Majesty's Theatre in London, *The Secret Policeman's Ball*. It was Pete's first solo performance in over five years, and he had obviously been drinking. He performed both *Pinball Wizard* and *Drowned* capably, alone with his Gibson acoustic guitar, but his duet performance of *Won't Get Fooled Again* with classical guitarist John Williams was noticeably flawed. Pete lagged seriously at the beginning of the song, mixed up some of the words, and generally looked disoriented. He reportedly blacked out momentarily during the performance, although only a handful of onlookers were said to have noticed. Despite this example, however, Pete played many good shows during this period before his abuse of alcohol and other substances brought all performing to a halt.

A second solo appearance took place on Friday, July 13, 1979, at the Rainbow. This time, the occasion was a Rock Against Racism benefit concert, organized to raise money to pay the legal costs of those arrested in a London area anti-racism demonstration. Pete had become personally involved in the battle against racism through one of his business ventures. "I've got this recording studio called Musician's Co-Op, which people use in a community way," he told *Oui*'s David Rothman in March, 1980.

> Sometimes they pay me money, but usually it's free, because I like their music or what's involved or whatever. There was a band called Mystic, a British reggae band, and they have a community of their own called

People Unite. They were based in Southall, which has a lot of Asians, Africans and West Indians mixed in with the whites. There's a lot of tension there – occasional fights and things like that.

Mystic came to my studio and worked for about two weeks. They're Rastafarians and smoke joints like this long [spreading his arms about three feet wide]. This one guy in the band really impressed me – a guy called Clarence. See, when they'd come into the studio, they wouldn't just have the band record; they'd have apprentices there as well. About five guitar players picking away. I was deeply impressed with the way they lived. My spiritual principles prohibit the dope, but at the same time, they seemed to respect my spiritual stance, and I had to respect theirs. Then I hear that one of the group is in the hospital with brain damage, that somebody had put an iron bar through his skull during a riot against the fascist National Front. I thought, 'Please, God, may it not be Clarence.' Because without him, this whole group of two or three hundred people in the area – young kids and families, who all depended on this band for a living and a raise on debts and everything – would be fucked. It was him. So I've decided that I'm going to stand up and get counted. I think fascism stinks. And I'm going to go onstage and say so. And I'm a bit scared. Not for me. I'm scared for my family, and the people around me.

Pete's public stand against the National Front and other fascist organizations was partly rooted in a sense of duty to his forefathers. "My grandfather, and his father before him, and my father, all fought in a war against fascism," he told Rothman.

We lost uncles, we lost brothers, we lost all kinds of people. Hundreds of thousands of people. In Britain, just as in New York, there's a strong Jewish community. About half of my friends are Jewish. I know how they feel about the last war. And to see that we've allowed a fucking party to reproduce itself. And yet, I don't want to deny anybody their rights. But if the National Front can say, 'Send the niggers back to wherever' and 'Send the Jews back to wherever' and 'Send the Asians back to Uganda', then I can say, 'That attitude STINKS.' And I think the phrase Rock Against Racism is much more universal and powerful than a lot of people realize.

Pete helped organize the show, calling his music industry peers, and was impressed with the fact that "everybody I rang in the music business was right there. Their position was quite clear. With rock, you're on the front line. You represent the sharp edge of a lot of people's ideas. Ten years ago, I had a stand-up row with Abbie Hoffman about politics and rock. I said, 'No way am I ever going to let politics get on the stage of a rock'n'roll concert. It's got fuck-all to do with it'. Now I'm starting to think maybe I was wrong."[169]

Pete topped the bill and supplied the event lighting and equipment through his Eel Pie recording company. Backed by Kenney Jones, 'Rabbit' Bundrick, Tony Butler and Peter Hope-Evans (all of whom saw action on *Empty Glass*), Pete played *Won't Get Fooled Again*, *The Real Me*, *Cat's In The Cupboard*[170], *Bargain*, *Drowned*, *Let's See Action*, *My Generation* and *Tattoo* in a performance which also included a cover of *Blue Suede Shoes*.

The Who returned to the stage on a bank holiday in late August, playing Wembley Stadium in only their second London show with Kenney. AC/DC (whose guitarist, Angus Young, reportedly rated Pete Townshend as the only guitarist he was ever influenced by – a ridiculous but flattering statement), Nils Lofgren and The Stranglers opened the show before a crowd of 77,000. A frustrating situation ensued when local authorities voiced their concerns over The Who's enormous PA system and intricate laser lighting display. "The main problem was that the Greater London Council had put a restriction on the volume level..." wrote Joe McMichael and 'Irish' Jack Lyons in their exhaustive Who live retrospective, *The Who Concert File*. "Consequently, the band sounded muted and dulled, lacking the sharpness and fire for which they were famous. In addition to the restricted sound system, [Who lighting technician] John Wolff's plans to present the Who performing under a breathtaking pyramid of laser light was ruined when the GLC safety inspectors instructed him to switch them off." Two weeks later AC/DC followed The Who to Germany, where, along with Cheap Trick and the Scorpions, they played to 65,000 fans in Nuremburg.

Within ten days, the band was off to reclaim the U.S., as they hadn't played there since October, 1976. After two warm-up shows at a small theater in Passaic, New Jersey, the Who crossed the Hudson River for five straight shows at Madison Square Garden, which would prove a true litmus test for the band. They passed with flying colors. The Who were officially back. "We needed to be reminded," wrote *Time* magazine's Jay Cocks in an article entitled 'A New Triumph for The Who.'

---

[169] When asked by Rothman if he'd like to say anything to Abbie Hoffman regarding the Woodstock incident, Pete said, "No, no. I don't want him coming up onstage again. I'd still kick the fucker off."

[170] Pete announced from the stage that he wrote *Cat's In The Cupboard* the previous week, "and recorded on Monday for my solo album..."

>...Of all the promise and possibility of rock. Of its dangers, and the reasons for facing them down. Of its limits, and the necessity of testing them, trampling them and resetting them still higher. Whether there's a question of age, relevance and survival, or a more general concern about definition and direction, all doubts were settled, and all bets were off, when The Who played five sold-out dates at Madison Square Garden...The Who set new standards, redeemed old promises and put a few ghosts to rest. These concerts may become not only one of the seminal rock events of 1979 but a route dynamited into the new decade.
>
>...The Who endure partly on their own wild momentum, partly on the strength of Townshend's compositions – some of the most brilliant, adventurous and lacerating in all rock – and partly on the indestructibility of the covenant with the fans, who will never let their band off easy...This kind of rock'n'roll communion is strictly hard-core. The limousine crowd does not turn out in force for a Who date...The Who still play for the kids, an audience that has nothing to do with age. These kids are anyone for whom rock'n'roll is far from entertainment and closer to a matter of life and death.

Pete cut the palm of his right hand on his guitar on the fourth night, left the stage to receive stitches, and still returned to finish the show. The final show, on September 18, ended in an onstage pie fight, the band leaving New York triumphant after entertaining over 100,000 fans during their seven-night stay in the area.

Two months later, following four U.K warm-up shows, 2 each in Brighton and Stafford, The Who returned to the States for a full-fledged tour on November 30, the first stop taking place at Detroit's Masonic Auditorium. The band's normal lineup on this tour only featured two songs from their latest album, *Who Are You* and *Sister Disco*, leaning heavily on past material such as *I Can't Explain*, *Baba O'Riley*, *The Punk and The Godfather*, *Behind Blue Eyes*, *Bargain*, *Drowned*, *Pinball Wizard*, *My Generation*, *Won't Get Fooled Again*, *Magic Bus*, *Long Live Rock*, and *Summertime Blues*.

The new tour signaled a change in Pete's thinking. "Before Keith died," Pete told *Rolling Stone*'s Greil Marcus the following year, "I decided that practically all the personal problems I had – whatever they were, whether it was boozing, or difficulty at home with my family – was because of the Who on the road. When we came off the road, I spent two and a half years not touring – under great pressure from the band to tour, but I resisted, and said, "No, I want to try it, and see what happens." I got to the end of that period, and all my problems were still there. Some of them were worse."

Pete had also finally come to terms with the fact that the audience wanted to hear the band's older material, something he had struggled with for years now, and another reason the band hadn't been on tour since 1976. Dating back to his depressing experience at Madison Square Garden in 1974, Pete had despised the thought of just churning out the classic Who numbers in a ritualistic manner which reeked of a complete lack of spontaneity. Initially, he simply didn't know how to deal with it. "...for ages, my reaction to that was just to stop," Pete told *Trouser Press* in 1980. "For two and a half years we didn't do any shows because I just refused to play, but then I started to hang with a few bands and it was probably Steve and Paul from the Pistols who told me, "Why the fuck do you worry about it? Just get up and play. Alright, it's ritualized. Who gives a shit? Just play!"..." Townshend realized that his band's past should never be looked upon as a liability. "...bits of the Who's show are still rooted in tradition, and we go through the motions to a certain extent because people do wanna hear the old stuff," Pete said in 1980. "What you've got to watch is the hypocrisy of pretending that you're not proud of what you've done, and the hypocrisy of pretending that you don't enjoy and are able to lean on the value of those gestures."

From a musical standpoint, the tour went well. 'Irish' Jack Lyons and Joe McMichael offered the following assessment in *The Who Concert File*:

> In general, the concerts were more well-paced and longer than pre-1979 Who gigs, and offered a wider variety of material, including more demanding songs that they wouldn't previously have attempted. Overall, these concerts were a rock spectacle where the music could still produce a very real charge of emotional thrill. The band's dynamics were altered slightly by Keith's absence but the theatrical pull of Townshend, Daltrey and Entwistle out front was still as dramatic and compelling as any other contemporary group. Technical improvements in the band's equipment could be felt as well, not to mention the addition of keyboards and a brass section...People didn't leave these shows disappointed and many younger fans were able to see the band for the first time during the 1979-82 era; not the definitive Who, to be sure, but a reasonable substitute.

During this tour, Pete developed a passion for playing the popular arcade game *Space Invaders*. "Pete was addicted, and we were constantly looking out for machines," Richard Barnes recalled in 1982. "We nearly missed every flight that took off from an airport that had one in the coffee shop. When we arrived in one new town, before he'd even got his cases brought up, Pete was on the phone to the lobby asking about *Space Invaders* machines. He even got Yellow Pages and rung around all the bars to discover if any had one." Townshend was given a *Space Invaders* machine later during the tour. "At each gig it would be set up in the hospitality room," Barnes recalled, "and Pete would challenge the roadies to games. However, if it was therapeutic for Pete, it was the opposite for Roger. He hated the noise and it was agreed that at the end of the tour he would be allowed to smash it up with an axe."

Only two shows into their first full U.S. tour since 1976, The Who were once again faced with a tragedy that threatened to end their careers. In a frenzied rush to enter Cincinnati's Riverfront Coliseum for a Who concert on December 3, 1979, eleven fans died, something of which the band knew nothing until the show was over. The deaths were blamed on several factors: Poor security, a first-come, first-served general admission ticket policy (also known as 'festival seating'), and the fact that only four doors were opened into the venue to allow the crowd of several thousand waiting outside in the frigid weather to enter.

The band was shattered by the news. "If it had happened inside I would never have played again," Pete told *Time* a few weeks later. With Pete already experiencing marital discord, still grieving Keith's death and facing a worsening problem with alcoholism, this latest tragedy seemed to be the last straw[171]. "I just want to work and be happy," a distraught Townshend told a Detroit disc jockey a few days after the Cincinnati concert. "We didn't know anything about the accident. But everything in my life tells me to stop – my two little girls, my brain, body, everything tells me to stop. I'm not going to stop. I just don't care, really. I really don't care what happens anymore."

Unfortunately, Pete managed to magnify the grief caused by the Cincinnati tragedy in early 1980 during an interview with *Rolling Stone*'s Greil Marcus:

> ...the amazing thing, for us, is the fact that – when we were told about what happened at that gig, that eleven kids had died – for a second, our guard dropped. Just for a second. Then it was back up again...It was, fuck it! We're not gonna let a *little thing* like this stop us. That was the way we *had* to think. We had to reduce it, because if we'd

---

[171] "What made me stop thinking the show had to go on was obviously Cincinnati," Pete told *Rolling Stone*'s David Fricke in 1987. "It was a terrible lesson to have to learn. For a long time, I couldn't live with that. It was directly responsible for me literally, emotionally falling apart."

actually *admitted* to ourselves the *true* significance of the event...we could not have gone on and worked. And we had a tour to do. We're a rock & roll band. You know, we *don't fuck around*, worrying about eleven people dying. We *care* about it, but there is a particular attitude I call the "tour armor": when you go on the road you throw up an armor around yourself, you almost go into a trance.

It wasn't that the members of the band weren't deeply affected by the incident, Pete pointed out. "We did go home...and we talked about it with our families and our friends," he said, but then added, "...If I could dare say it, I'd say that Cincinnati was a very, very positive event for the Who. I think it changed the way we feel about people. It's changed the way we feel about our audience."

Pete's attempts to describe the band's survivalist tour rationale and to find a positive aspect of the tragedy failed miserably, no matter how well-intentioned they were. "...I watched Roger Daltrey cry his eyes out after that show," Pete told Marcus. "I didn't, but he did. But now, whenever a fucking journalist – sorry – asks you about Cincinnati, they expect you to come up with a fucking theatrical tear in your eye! You know: "Have you got anything to say about Cincinnati?" "Oh, we were *deeply* moved, terrible tragedy, the horror, loss of life, *arrrghh* – what do you do? We did all the things we thought were right to do at the time: sent flowers to the fucking funerals. All...*wasted*. I think when people are dead they're dead."

Pete later told Dave Marsh that he regretted the "unfortunate" incident, explaining that his comments had been "sensationally framed, without vocal inflections; it actually looks like I actually mean what I'm saying or at least, that I believe what I'm saying is worth saying. When I spoke to Greil Marcus, I was sarcastic and – I thought – self-detrimental about the group's bloodyminded determination to carry on after the tragedy. I was simply trying to illustrate how absurd show-business thinking is. It didn't come off and hurt the feelings of the relatives."

The December 4 show in Buffalo, New York went ahead as scheduled, with a few cautionary changes: The Who did away with their soundcheck (it was reported that the melee in Cincinnati reached boiling point when fans heard the band performing their soundcheck, mistakenly believing that they were missing the beginning of the show), and the show's start time was pushed back ninety minutes to give the audience extra time to enter the facility. "The band had decided to continue with the rest of the tour that morning," Richard Barnes wrote in 1982.

> ...the tour continued almost as planned except for some understandable over-reaction with regard to security. At many of the concerts there were hundreds of police and

security people. In some places, even if a kid stood up to applaud, a uniformed official would threaten him. On arrival at one auditorium the police had dogs trained on the crowd of a few hundred waiting around the stage door as the Who entered. At Buffalo, Roger announced from the stage, "You all heard what happened yesterday, there's nothing we can do, we feel totally shattered, but life goes on. We all lost a lot of family yesterday. This show's for them."

If The Who's first U.S. tour in three years wasn't enough to gain nationwide publicity, the deaths in Cincinnati certainly were. "In a curious way the Cincinnati deaths made The Who more famous than ever," Chris Charlesworth wrote in 1984. "It made headlines all over the world; *Time* magazine put The Who on its front cover."

Meanwhile, the band's shows on this tour were drawing further press attention in the form of rave reviews. The Who's performances during this time were highly regarded, even by such a seasoned Who-watcher as Pete's close friend, Richard Barnes. "...the shows on this tour amazed me," he recalled three years later. "It's difficult to be objective when you see so many shows. Certainly there were bad nights, but when they were good, they were probably the best there is." Pete was typically modest regarding his performances, content to sidestep the accolades with his frank humor. "At the end of a two-hour show the lasers were fucking helpful, because then you could stand still and let them do the stuff," he said in 1980. "Or if I was having a problem playing a decent guitar solo, I could whirl my arm a couple of times and it would have the same effects as a well played guitar solo. And that *da-da-rrraaanggg*! Gesture that I do: every now and then I do it and I think, "Christ, I'm fucking glad that belongs to me." It gets me out of so much trouble!"

Following a sold out concert in Cleveland, Ohio and a performance in front of 41,000 at Pontiac, Michigan's huge Silverdome, The Who descended on Chicago for a December 8 show which was simulcast to nine area movie theaters, all of which sold out. Pete and Roger appeared to thoroughly enjoy the International Amphitheater show, reportedly hamming it up for the expanded audience. This was widely regarded as the best show of the tour.

Following two shows in Philadelphia on December 10 and 11, Pete decided to travel to the Meher Spiritual Center in Myrtle Beach, South Carolina for a few days' rest and relaxation prior to the next show, which was in Maryland on the 13th. Pete and Richard Barnes, along with a friend from San Francisco, chartered a Learjet for the trip to South Carolina. "Pete told them to take off vertically," Richard Barnes recalled in *Maximum R&B*.

Pete had experienced this before and warned us to be ready. As soon as the jet had taken off, the pilot pulled the stick back and we climbed almost vertically up to 40,000 feet. It was so exciting that we asked if they would land and take off again but they couldn't. After spending so much time and $5,000 arranging to get to South Carolina, Pete never set foot in the Baba Center. He spent the whole time trying to catch up on sleep in the Myrtle Beach Hilton a half a mile up the coast from the Baba Center.

This event, while perhaps simply illustrating Pete's exhausted state at this point of the tour, also provides a glimpse that his personal beliefs were suffering as a result of his increasing abuse of alcohol. "...I'm very heavily into Meher Baba, but I also drink like a fish," he told *Trouser Press* in 1980. "I'm still not the most honest person in the world. It's difficult, but I do at least know what's happening to me. I accept that there is a larger reason for me being alive than just being a rock star."

"I was living against a lot of principles of Meher Baba that I initially found enriching," Pete later told *Time Out* magazine. "Meher Baba came down very heavily against drugs, for example. So for a while I pushed him out of my life because I wouldn't live within those principles."

Upon their return to British soil following four more U.S. east coast shows, The Who took part in "...the greatest superstar jam for charity which London has ever seen," according to *Rolling Stone*'s Paul Gambaccini. The concerts for Kampuchea, held over four nights at London's Hammersmith Odeon, were organized by U.N. Secretary General Kurt Waldheim and promoter Harvey Goldsmith to aid starving refugees in Kampuchea (Cambodia). In addition to The Who, headliners included Wings, Queen and Ian Dury. "The Who's evening was both exhausting and exhilarating," Gambaccini wrote of the December 28 program. "Two of Britain's best new groups – the Pretenders and the ska-revivalist Specials – played powerful sets, followed by a marathon Who performance that lasted almost three hours..."

"This stands as probably the best concert they did in this country with Kenney Jones," *The Who Concert File* proclaimed.

The shows which they played in 1981 and 1982 seemed to lack the epic forcefulness that was in evidence here. The atmosphere at the Hammersmith Odeon was clearly electric...From the outset, Pete was clearly out to have a good time. His face looked free from the weary burden of the U.S. tour, replaced by a sardonic buoyancy...Pete seemed intent on proving that...The Who could still bash it out with the best of them.

While the show was highly acclaimed, it further demonstrated Pete's worsening problems with alcohol. He was clearly drunk, contributing erratic – sometimes inspired – but occasionally out of tune guitar work, often forgetting to play his instrument and substituting wild dancing in its place. He also provided less-than-inspiring monologues such as "Aren't you glad you were born in London and not in poxy Kampuchea?"

Pete returned to Hammersmith Odeon for the benefit's final show, asked to perform in an all-star band known as Rockestra, headed by Paul McCartney (recall that Pete had played guitar on Wings' 1979 release *Back To The Egg*, guesting on the *Rockestra Theme* and *So Glad To See You Here*). The sold-out crowd "...reached near-hysterical pitch," according to *Rolling Stone*, when "...reports of a Beatles reunion in the *Daily Mirror* and similar speculation in the *Evening News* brought out fans who were willing to pay scalpers up to $440 for the sold-out show...An hour before Wings were to perform, ABC-TV sent word that it would pay $2000 for two minutes of film of a Beatles reunion, and rumors spread through the audience that John Lennon had arrived..."

However, of course, the rumored reunion did not occur, and Pete took the stage along with notables James Honeyman-Scott of the Pretenders, Kenney Jones, John Bonham, John Paul Jones and McCartney. "With that, Rockestra – resplendent in gold top hats and silver jackets," *Rolling Stone* reported, "except for Townshend in a faded suit – took the stage...Rockestra performed its instrumental theme from the album [Wings' *Back To The Egg*], Little Richard's *Lucille*, and a masterful *Let It Be*. The nineteen-piece band started *Let It Be* quietly, then crescendoed as dramatically as any Phil Spector record."

"Much to McCartney's chagrin," Chris Charlesworth recalled, "Pete was the only member who refused to wear the regulation gold lame jacket but up on stage he appeared disheveled, his unkempt hair a tangled mess, baggy trousers bunched at his ankles, swaying drunkenly as if to taunt the prim and proper ex-Beatle[172]."

The Who's first protracted tour in years had taken its toll on Pete. He was drinking very heavily, and was beginning to appear out of sorts during his public appearances. His already worrisome depressive state seemed to take a sharp downward turn after the Cincinnati incident. "At the center of it all Pete seemed confused, unable to cope with this new burden of responsibility and a delayed shock reaction set in," wrote Chris Charlesworth in 1984. "The eventual outcome was to set off another period of intense depression, one in which he was to sink lower than at any other period of his life."

---

[172] A few years later, a clean-cut, sober Pete wore a gold lame jacket when he sang *Face The Face* on the *White City* film.

"...I had a big, big problem because I had been the big rock idealist and now it was all letting me down," Pete told Dennis Wholey in 1984:

> The industry hadn't fulfilled its promise. Rock'n'roll had changed the length of men's hair and very little else. I felt like a fool because I'd waved the banner so aggressively. And what was really worse, I felt that I was being used by journalists.
>
> I hated the feeling that I was in a band on the downward slide that was killing people in Cincinnati, killing off its own members...We were into making big money and anybody who got in the way or had a problem, we dropped. Nobody seemed to notice. Nobody seemed to think this was a particularly bad thing, or we pretended it wasn't, anyway. I felt it start to kill me. Something was getting its teeth into me...I should have stopped working with the band. I should have stopped and had another look at rock'n'roll, the thing that I loved and cared about so much, which I held above all other things.
>
> I had so many great hopes. I could see that the band wasn't doing what I wanted it to do. I cared about doing it for all the wrong reasons. I carried on doing it for Roger. I carried on doing it for John Entwistle. I carried on doing it for the fans. I carried on doing it because I had a contract. I carried on doing it because I had thirty employees. I carried on doing it, and I shouldn't have. I should have stopped and taken a hard, hard look at the music business and myself and come to the conclusion, which a lot of other people had come to, that the best years of The Who were the early years.

Pete's strained relationship with his wife reached breaking point when Karen decided she could take no more. "...Karen finally said, "Listen, the drinking is starting to affect the family. I won't have that," Pete wrote in *The Courage To Change*.

> I said, "Karen, I can't stop drinking. I can't. Particularly when I'm working." So she said, "Well, then, when you work, you stay away." That sounded reasonable, so I started to do that. If I was recording I'd check into a hotel, do some work, or maybe go to the States for a couple of weeks. I'd come back home and dry out completely, maybe just a glass of wine with a meal on Sunday. Then I'd

go away again for a couple of months and do some work and then come back.

"That was a weird year," Pete recalled. "...some weird things happened to me. My wife and I became estranged...Eventually, I started to find social solace elsewhere. I dropped a lot of our mutual friends. I found a few others. I started to get involved with temporary girlfriends. I could go into a nightclub anywhere in London and everybody in the building would know who I was. I spent very little time at home. That's when it all began. Around that time, Karen and I decided that it would be best if I took my problems elsewhere, permanently."

Pete moved to an apartment located above a shoe shop on London's Kings Road, and also spent time at his country home in Berkshire. "He was boozing heavily and regularly showing up at nightclubs and gigs of the newer groups around London," wrote Richard Barnes in 1982. One of the concerts Pete attended during this time (January, 1980) was a Clash gig in Brighton. "...it was one of the best concerts I've ever seen," Pete told *Trouser Press* in 1980. "It was fucking incredible. They asked me to go on stage and play, which was a bit embarrassing because I'd only had *London Calling* about a week, and I wasn't too sure of many of the chords, so I tuned the guitar to one and just pretended. It was really exciting."[173]

At the beginning of 1980, The Who ended their fifteen-year allegiance with MCA records and signed a new deal with Warner Brothers. *Rolling Stone* reported that the multi-album deal was for around $12 million. The deal gave Warner Bros. the rights to the band's U.S. and Canadian releases, while Polydor retained rights to the band's marketing throughout the rest of the world. "Apparently Mo Ostin, chairman of the board of Warners, was a big reason the group signed with that label," *Rolling Stone* reported in March, 1980. ""Mo's been a Who fanatic for years," said one source. "He's always been keenly aware of them, and he's friends with Pete Townshend and their manager. When the group became available, he went after them."" A few months earlier, Pete had signed a solo deal with Atlantic through which he was committed to recording three solo albums over the next six years.

Pete was once again overcommitted. "...I'd made a whole series of insane decisions: signing a new Who deal for five albums, within two months of signing a solo deal for three albums," Pete told *Q* in 1996.

> In five years, I had to produce eight albums. Write all the songs, tour, do the PR, record... there was no way I could have done it. There was that, and I had started a very

---

[173] Pete witnessed many bands' live shows over the next two years, due to the fact that he spent a great deal of time living away from his family. He guessed that he saw "about a hundred" bands in 1981 alone.

ambitious publishing company, I decided to start a floating studio... started to build a house. That was just fucking mad.

Pete had begun work on a new solo album in early 1979, starting with two songs which were leftovers from the *Who Are You* recording sessions: *Empty Glass* and *Keep On Working*. The rest of the tracks were composed during the past year and recorded in demo form at Pete's 24-track recording studio. Pete's attitude in writing this solo album reflected a change from his prior practice of giving his best material to The Who. "The only distinction I made," Pete told *NME* in April, 1980, "was that if I was really going to do a solo album deal properly...the only way I could do it would be to take the best of any material that I had at any particular time, rather than knock together solo projects of any sort based on material that the Who had rejected. So my album – though I was able to take a lot more risks with the material than the Who would – could have been a Who album if we'd happened to be recording at that time, just as the Who album that we're doing now [*Face Dances*] could have been a solo album...I just decided to write – to write straight from the hip and offer everything to the project that's going on at the time, not earmark stuff. I think that what's quite interesting is the way that *I* do a song as distinct from the way the The Who would do it, and I don't want to deny myself all the Who-type material because y'know, that's what I am."

Recording took place at Wessex studios (with additional work being done at Eel Pie and AIR studios), with Chris Thomas at the helm, a highly-regarded producer who'd recently worked with The Sex Pistols and The Pretenders. "Most of the material is pretty uptempo," Pete told Kurt Loder in 1980. "...I did have a couple of ballads I was thinkin' I might include, but I didn't – mainly at the behest of Chris Thomas. He figured the album should be pretty ballsy, and that's the way it's come out." Thomas has also been credited with enticing "vastly superior vocals out of Pete," as Richard Barnes put it, transforming Townshend's voice into a major asset. "I always had quite a nice voice, but I never owned it until 1980, when I did... *Empty Glass*, with Chris Thomas," Pete told *Rolling Stone*'s Jenny Eliscu in 2000. "He said, "Why don't you just sing?" And I said, "Because I sound like Andy Williams." And he said, "So?" And I sound like Andy Williams – I've got a beautiful voice."

Empty Glass is considered to be the first true Pete Townshend solo effort, since *Who Came First* was a collection of demos and songs by Baba follower-friends of Pete, and half of *Rough Mix* was written and performed by Ronnie Lane. *Empty Glass* was written and sung wholly by Pete, who also played guitar and synthesizer. Other musicians involved with the album included bassist Tony Butler and drummer Mark Brzezicki, who went on to achieve substantial success with Big Country, and others with whom

Pete would work extensively in the years to come, such as drummers Kenney Jones and Simon Phillips, keyboardist John Bundrick and harmonica player Peter Hope-Evans.

"The album was originally going to be called *Animal* or *Sacred Animal*," Richard Barnes recalled. "...but because of the Floyd album called *Animals* and other doubts it was renamed." *Empty Glass*' title was, according to Pete, inspired by eastern literature. "*Empty Glass* is a direct jump from Persian Sufi poetry," he told Greil Marcus of *Rolling Stone* in 1980.

> Hafiz – he was a poet in the fourteenth century – used to talk about God's love being wine, and that we yearn to be intoxicated, and that the heart is like an empty cup. You hold up the heart, and hope that God's grace will fill your cup with his wine. You stand in the tavern, a useless soul waiting for the barman to give you a drink – the barman being God. It's also Meher Baba talking about the fact that the heart is like a glass, and that God can't fill it up with his love – if it's already filled with love for yourself.

"Spirituality to me is about the asking, not the answers," Pete told *Trouser Press* in 1980. "I still find it a very romantic proposition, that you hold up an empty glass and say, "Right. If you're there, fill it." The glass is empty because you have emptied it. You were in it originally. That's why it's only when you're at your lowest ebb, when you believe yourself to be nothing, when you believe yourself to be worthless, when you're in a state of futility, that you produce an empty glass. Normally, you occupy the glass. By emptying or vacating the glass, you give God a chance to enter it. You get yourself out of the way...You ask for help."

So the *Empty Glass* title reflected Pete's faith in the power of prayer. "I can't back this up, but I think that when I've sincerely prayed, I've gotten an answer of some sort," Pete continued.

> Not in the ways I'd ever imagined I'd get an answer, but I've gotten one. If you go on challenging life, saying, "Why won't life do something for me? Why am I the one who's always losing?" then all you're doing is perpetuating life as is, the idea that life revolves around you as the center of the universe, which is not true. It's not realistic and it's not practical. You're just another fucking cog in the wheel and you're nothing. You only mean something and you only become something when you believe yourself to be nothing. That's why I put that little footnote on the cover [*Desire for nothing except*

desirelessness, hope for nothing except to rise above all hopes, want nothing and you will have everything], which was only a repeat of something Meher Baba said: "If you want nothing, then you've got everything."

Pete recalled in 1996 that *Rough Boys*, the album's opening track, was "...made up on the studio floor. Entirely...I just made it up as I went along, and Kenney Jones played along. I had a synthesizer guitar which was running into...two early primitive guitar synthesizers...each of which went to a huge Hiwatt stack in the middle of Wessex studio, so I stood there on my own with Kenney bashing away on the drums, and produced this huge noise, which sounded like about thirty guitars...And what you hear is me going nuts in the middle of the studio."

The Raphael Rudd-arranged horns at the end of the song proved a difficult task. "...the reason it's so complicated at the end harmonically is because I was just playing anything that came under my fingers," Pete recalled. "...it took [Raphael] a long time to analyze some of those chords at the end. Anything that didn't work, we snipped out with a pair of scissors." The song, originally entitled *Tough Boys*, was "...a rant about the British punks (like Sid Vicious) I had come across in recent years who wore outfits I had come to know in New York as the apparel of 'rough' gays," Pete wrote in the *Scoop 3* liner notes in 2001. "Not sure why or when the title changed."

Rough Boys was followed by *I Am An Animal*, "A song about the evolution of the individual in a spiritual way," Pete later commented, "about all the different roles we go through in one lifetime." Next was *And I Moved*, which featured the lines, *And his hands felt like ice exciting, As he laid me back just like an empty dress*. "I don't really know what that's about," Pete told *Trouser Press* in 1980. "Originally I wrote it as a song about a voyeur, but it went through some permutations. A lot of people feel that it's about me and my father or me and Meher Baba or me and a relationship with a woman, but I listened to it last night because I was checking the pressings, and I thought it was a bit like an admission of homosexual tendencies." The fact that the song's central figure is a male who is seemingly seducing the singer is better explained when one considers the following: "*And I Moved* is very peculiar and I think it's probably best not to try to explain it," Pete said, adding, "Originally I wrote it when Bette Midler's manager had written to me and said she was doing an album, she liked what I wrote and asked if I could send her a song. He said, "Make it a bit dirty, because that's the kind of thing she likes. So I sent it to her [along with an "electro-pop" song Pete had written entitled *You're So Clever*] and heard nothing for a couple of months; then I heard from him and he said, "I couldn't really give it to her because it's smutty." I said, "What? You asked for something dirty" and he said, "It isn't dirty, it's smutty." "

The vagueness of *And I Moved*'s lyrics showed a change in Pete's stance on how he appeared to the public. He explained his feelings to *Trouser Press* in July, 1980:

> One thing it does reflect...is that all of a sudden I've initiated this process...of...not caring about looking a bit of an idiot, saying the wrong thing or being told that you're wet...There's nothing more annoying than someone who is so full of their own semi-consciousness that they can't be themselves in front of you...it makes you realize that you're not free. Anything that inhibits freedom is damaging in the end.
>
> It's not just society, but in rock. People in rock imagine that they're so incredibly fucking liberated and anarchistic. But they're not. They're so incredibly closed up and macho. In many ways rock is more reactionary than the rest of society, because the business side of it is so super-corporate, the money flow of it so controlled, and the forefront of it is so commando-trained, so macho, so concerned with uniforms and hardness.

Many listeners thought *Empty Glass* included some admissions of homosexuality or at least bisexuality on Pete's part. "Of course, a literal reading of a songwriter as complex as Townshend can be deceptive," read a retrospective review of the album in a 1989 issue of *Rolling Stone*, "as in *Rough Boys* and *And I Moved*...taken by some as confessions of homosexual lust. "A lot of gays and a lot of bisexuals wrote to me congratulating me on this so-called coming out," Pete commented. "I think in both cases the images are very angry, aren't they? In *Rough Boys*, the line 'Come over here, I want to bite and kiss you' is about 'I can scare you! I can frighten you! I can hurt all you macho individuals simply by coming up and pretending to be gay!' And that's what I really meant in that song, I think." "

One of *Empty Glass*' standouts was *Let My Love Open The Door*, "...one of those songs where you end up shooting to write something really deep and meaningful," Pete explained in 1996, "and what you end up coming up with is something that appears to be froth. This was a song about love, but this is actually about divine love. It's supposed to be about the power of God's love, that when you're in difficulty, whether it's major or minor, God's love is always there for you. But I suppose, because I used the royal "we" – I sang with God's voice – it became a song about, you know, "Hey, girl, I'll give you a good time, if you're feeling blue, come over to my place, and we'll catch a movie," very much a soap opera version of what it was all about..." Eventually released as a single, this song reached a very satisfactory number 9 in the British charts.

The catalyst for *Jools and Jim*, Pete's attack on music journalism, was his reaction to some articles he'd read in the music press. The song was originally entitled *Jools and Tone* after *NME* writers Julie Burchill and Tony Parsons. "I wrote the song after someone from the *Guardian* wrote an article about them to promote their book, and he got very animated about how they didn't give a shit about Sid Vicious going down," Pete told *Trouser Press* in 1980. "Then [*NME* writer Parsons] brought up Keith as well and said, "Fuck Keith Moon, we're better off without him. Decadent cunt driving Rolls Royces into swimming pools; if that's what rock'n'roll's about, who needs it?" To a certain extent I agreed with a bit of it, but I feel that it was a bit of opportunist cock...I just wrote the song as a reaction. "I changed the title from *Jools and Tone* to *Jools and Jim* because it's not directly about them," Pete said, "it's about taking a stance and believing what you read. It's just another "don't believe what you read" song. I think it's one of the best songs on the album. The energy's great and I really like the singing on it."

Keep On Working was Pete's attempt at a Kinks song. "Ray's [Davies] always been a big influence on me," Pete told *Musician* in 1982. "I've never been able to write in the same way, though I've often tried. In fact, I'm terrible at it. I think *Keep On Working* ...tries to be a Kinks song but it just doesn't work. I mean, *Lola* or *Low Budget* is so much better..."

After *Cat's In The Cupboard*, a rocker which could easily be imagined as a Who song, the classic *A Little Is Enough* has remained a staple of Pete's live shows, and "...a really great favorite of mine," he said in 1996.

> ...Around the time when I was making this record, I was having my first difficulties in my marriage and feeling that I'd allowed my career to take far too much priority in my life. My wife had warned me I was taking on too much, and I just wasn't really listening to her, and one day I came back from the studio or a gig or maybe even from a party, weeping, crying – "This is all too hard, I'm depressed, I can't do it, I can't handle show business, nobody loves me, they're not giving me enough money, they're giving me too much money, I'm too big, I'm too small," whatever it was...Anyway, I went to somebody called Adi Irani, who was Meher Baba's secretary for a long time, and he was doing a lecture tour over here, and he said, "You look a bit sad." So I said, "Well, I'm going through my first real hiccup in my marriage," and he said, "Oh, what's it about?" And I said, "My wife doesn't love me anymore." And he

said, "Well, she's there, isn't she?" And I said, "Yeah," and he said, "Then she must love you a little bit," and I said, "Yeah, yeah she probably loves me a little bit." And he said, "Well, when you're talking about love, which is in itself by nature infinite, then a little is enough." And it solved my immediate problem, but also seemed to me to be a very, very wise thought, and a very romantic thought too, you know, if you only have a moment of love in your life, it's enough, because it never evades you and it always returns.

"It was purely personal; instinct, and purely transparent," Pete told *Rolling Stone*'s Greil Marcus in 1980.

> It's very emotional, but it's also very straightforward and clear. Just the fact that you can't fucking have the world. If you're lucky enough to get a tiny piece of it, then – fine. I suppose I wrote the song about a mixture of things. I wrote it a little bit about God's love. But mainly about the feeling that I had for my wife – and the fact that I don't see enough of her, and that when we are together there are lots of times when things aren't good, because of the period of adjustment you require after a long tour; stuff like that. She would always want a deeper, more sustained relationship than I would – but in the end I suppose we're lucky that we do love one another at all. Because love, by its very nature, is an infinite emotion – just to experience it once in a lifetime is enough. Because a lot of people don't – don't ever experience it.

Pete dedicated the *Empty Glass* album to Karen, while *Rough Boys* was dedicated to his daughters Emma and Aminta, and The Sex Pistols.

Empty Glass, a song which Pete wrote for the *Who Are You* sessions and had recorded with the band in April, 1978, was next. "*Empty Glass* provides Pete Townshend's extremely condensed rock & roll version of the Book of Ecclesiastes," Dave Marsh wrote in June, 1980. "The spark-off for the song was when I read Ecclesiastes again, and it was so powerful," Pete told *Trouser Press* in July, 1980. "…You got King Solomon talking about how after he's fucked everybody and had everything and gone through everything, the only piece of advice he's got is that life is useless. But it also contains some great inspirational poetry: "There is a time", and all that. It really reminded me of a lot of Persian Sufi poetry, that it's only in desperation that you become spiritually open…"

Gonna Get Ya rounded out the album. "That song's nonsense," Pete said in 1980. "It's just a word game. I don't think it means anything."

The finished *Empty Glass* was a tight, clean-sounding, upbeat album chock full of catchy songs which were loaded with impressionistic writing. The album was full of energy. Pete credited much of this vitality to the British punk movement. "I had invented punk a thousand times in my head," Pete said in 1980, "and when it finally happened it really inspired me. It came just as rock was getting so rigid and formatted and it was a reaction to boredom...I hold rock above most forms of art because it is one of the few forms of communication where there are people who are idealistic in the medium. And there is a very high percentage of people who listen who are looking for idealism and are disappointed when they get empty crap. I aspire to music that has brains, balls and heart."

Empty Glass, released in April 1980 in the U.K. and a month later in the U.S., was an immediate critical success. "If *Empty Glass*' very title questions Townshend's worthiness to receive grace," wrote Dave Marsh in his review of the album in the June, 1980, issue of *Rolling Stone*, "the shape of his music leaves no question that he's willing to accept whatever fills the cup...*Empty Glass* contains the least stiff-necked music that Pete Townshend has made in ages."

"*Empty Glass* may be an album without much innocence," Marsh went on, "...but that's only because Pete Townshend is past the point where he can fake acceptance. You can hear it in his vocals, which are the most – and probably the only – assured ones he's ever done." Marsh continued with a description of the album's content:

> ...songs of reality and songs of spiritual imagination, songs of doubt and songs of faith, songs of experience and songs of devotion. What's missing (again) is innocence, and it's about time he's lost that. For quite a while now, Townshend has been threatening to dispense with the pose that he never really knew what both hands were up to, what actions they were taking. He's certainly done so here. *Empty Glass* isn't just an album with vaguely religious connotations. It's as consciously spiritual as any rock & roll record ever made. Not that everything is exactly what it seems. Pete Townshend remains rock's master illusionist. The love songs, especially *Let My Love Open The Door* and *A Little Is Enough*, might sound purely romantic on the radio, yet their imagery is shaped by religion. (Whose body is so "edible," after all, as the Lord's?)
>
> Pete Townshend's current songs are mostly quiet declarations, not strident ones – another sharp departure

from his past. And, after all, those of us who still hold much faith and devotion for rock & roll at this point must grasp at any straw. The ones offered here are far stronger than most, because they're bonded with real love.

Empty Glass was a triumph. A *Guitar* magazine retrospective look at the record seven years later described, "...a frightfully revealing and appealing album. While *Glass* may not contain the usual dose of Townshend's manic, mashing guitar, it is surely the guitarist's most personal pop statement, and a rich and diverse musical document."

Empty Glass blew open the door to Pete's solo career. "If I disagree with the fact that [*Empty Glass*] is the best work I've done in a long time, I would be fooling you," Townshend said in 1982. Later, he admitted that The Who seemed much less viable as a result: "I think the only thing that really went wrong was that I realized, as soon as *Empty Glass* was finished, 'Hey, this is it. I'm not able to achieve with the band what I've achieved here.'"

Meanwhile, as 1979 drew to a close, *Lifehouse* was once again showing some signs of life. The project had gained little momentum following The Who's renewed interest in it back during the 1977/78 *Who Are You* recording sessions, but it had resulted in Pete's writing of the previously mentioned second draft of the *Lifehouse* script. Michael Hirst, a scriptwriter Pete had met during the 1978 *The Kids Are Alright* filming at Shepperton Studios, was also working on a script for *Lifehouse*. "Michael helped me to trawl all my short stories into shape," Pete said in late 1999. "...I'd sent him a bunch of short stories and he had been an editor. He sent them back to me with annotations and stuff and encouraged me to write, but we also had a load of meetings on the story of *Lifehouse*."

Hirst's script eventually made it through to director Nicolas Roeg. "I got very, very excited because Nic Roeg was my absolute favorite director," Pete recalled. "Of the two British directors around at the time, Nic Roeg and Ken Russell, for me, it was the toss of a coin but at that time I was more into Nic Roeg than Ken Russell." Roeg, a British director whose resume included *Don't Look Now*, *The Man Who Fell To Earth*, and the recently completed *Bad Timing*, liked Hirst's *Lifehouse* script, but Pete thought "it was a bit weird." Pete submitted his own recently rewritten script to Roeg, who thought "that it was too sci-fi and not well-written enough," Pete recalled, adding, "well, I'm not a screenwriter." Pete wanted to visit Roeg to discuss the script he'd written, and thus began a fiasco of epic proportions. In mid-February, 1980, Roeg, married with children but living in L.A. with a twenty-three year-old actress ("I knew Nic as...a very happy family man who occasionally seemed to have a glamorous actress on the side," Pete said), was in London for a friend's funeral. Pete (who, we must recall, was in the midst of possibly his life's most challenging crisis and therefore not in complete control of his faculties) began courting Roeg's girlfriend, actress Theresa Russell[174], who he'd described as "the most spectacular creature on the face of the planet." He recalled the story in a 1999 interview with Matt Kent:

> Nic's actress girlfriend loved [Pete's script], absolutely loved it and kept pressure on Nic who, unbeknown to me, she was intending to marry...What happened was I completely fucked it up because Nic was in LA and I was going over to LA to do some demo's [for *Face Dances*], so I was going to...talk to him about the script I had written and how Michael Hirst might be able to bridge the gap...I could sense that he wasn't all that mad about it but Jeremy Thomas [Roeg's producer], too, felt that this was a huge project...I rang one day, knowing that Nic had just left LA to come back to London for a funeral of a friend, and I rang his apartment in LA, knowing that he wouldn't be there, saying that I was flying over to do some demo's and his girlfriend came to the phone. I said, 'can I speak to Nic' and she said 'oh, Pete he's just left for London' and I knew that and said 'Oh fuck, I was just coming over and was hoping to see him. Nevermind, maybe I'll give him a ring when I'm there', but my intention was to see her. So, I'd fly over there and get into this whole obsession about realizing that I had to move very, very quickly, that Nic Roeg and she were obviously living together, he was obviously living there and not in London, they weren't working on a project, what was going on, were they in a relationship, were they not?...I rang up a couple of friends and asked advice...I hadn't even met her yet! I decided that in order to find out what was going on it would be OK to take her out, not one to one as I couldn't reveal what was going on, and so I got [some friends] to come with me and her to go and see *The Wall*. We went and got very pissed and it was the first time in my life I'd ever taken cocaine[175] and she took a bit...I completely, totally...without any real encouragement from her at all, apart from the fact that she was herself and she was great to be with...totally fell in love with her...partly I must say fuelled by the fact that it was the first time I'd taken cocaine. What then happens is I jump in a car, it's

---

[174] Theresa Russell, nearly thirty years younger than Roeg, appeared in 1980's *Bad Timing*, the first of several Roeg-directed roles. Several years later, Roeg and Russell were married.
[175] This marked Pete's first foray into drug-taking in twelve years.

Valentine's Day, and I go and buy her some tequila and loads of flowers and she wouldn't let me in, wouldn't let me see her and I completely fell apart. I had the most spectacular emotional crash and came back and immediately became a serial drug addict. I was really in a terrible state…up to that point I had a lot of drink problems and a lot of emotional stuff; Cincinnati, Keith dying…I was drinking, drinking, drinking but this was the thing that really started to push me over the edge.

When Pete returned to England, he had to deal with the wrath of Nic Roeg. "…Nic, of course, was fucking furious with me," Pete recalled. And so closed another chapter in the story of Pete's struggle to complete *Lifehouse*. "…that version of *Lifehouse* was in fucking production," Pete lamented. The movie "was on the way. Jeremy Thomas is a big, powerful producer, he was behind it. Mike Hirst is a great writer, has written some fantastic films since. We would have done it." Dealt this most recent blow, *Lifehouse* once again disappeared from view, not to resurface for another thirteen years.

Pete soon composed a song which reflected his feelings for Roeg's girlfriend. "It is so wonderful to feel in love like that," he said in 1999. "I felt like I was made of dissolving concrete. The song that I wrote about it, which turned into *Athena*, that's all the feelings I was feeling at the time [one line from the song certainly summed up the letdown: *I felt like one of those flattened ants you find on a crazy path*]. I felt like I'd been trodden on. I felt fractured, my emotions were huge. I hadn't felt that kind of feeling for a long time and so I felt bad but I felt alive. It started a whole train for me of looking for that kind of experience, to try to bring myself alive again through pain." Pete recorded a demo of the song, *Theresa*, on February 16, 1980 – just two days after the Valentine's Day incident – at the Warner Brothers recording studio, Amigo studios, in North Hollywood. "When I came to do the vocal on this," Pete recalled in the *Scoop 3* liner notes in 2001, "…I was really out of my mind with frustration and grief because she didn't reciprocate. But as you can hear, I was obviously enjoying myself."

Pete changed the title of the song from *Theresa* to *Athena*, "Because I didn't want to blow the whistle on myself," he said. "I didn't want to do anything which, at that time, would hurt her, would hurt Nic any more than I already had." He also perhaps did it to keep Karen from finding out about his promiscuity. "I'd been through a period of being fairly promiscuous," he continued, "which was unusual for me because I'd always been very loyal to my wife, but when I'd hit an emotional rock bottom after Keith's death I'd started to get quite promiscuous and nobody had ever turned me down. So, when I was finally turned down it hit me hard."

A story obviously based on the Theresa Russell saga, *Champagne on the Terraces*, surfaced in Pete's 1985 book of short stories, *Horse's Neck*:

> ...There had been a girl. She entered his life under the fingernail and prised it upwards until he screamed, while sweetly shrugging off her charisma. Her general demeanor suggested that she was just a girl, just another girl...
>
> He had suggested calling on the girl, to whom he had merely taken a distant fancy; she had been like a challenging whipped-cream and icing-bag job in a confectioner's window. He had known of her involvement with one of his bosses, but he had really seen her as she was. A drunkard had been sobered. He had come to her as a newborn virgin boy; his own mind blank, he had intended to woo blindly...
>
> His clearest memory was their return to the girl's house: they stood at her doorway. He and the girl were left to say their good-byes. Feeling dizzy he'd asked her if he could go in for a minute and sit down. "You can't come in. I'm sorry but I'm in love with someone." The girl said this smilingly, without offense. In dream turning nightmare he had protested. "I feel like hell, it's not for any other reason. I must come in. I can't go anywhere. Please let me come in, I'll just fall on the floor."
>
> "Can't you get it into your thick skull? I love another man."
>
> "Who is talking about love? Please, please. Let me in. I feel awful."
>
> She kissed him and turned away smiling her good night. "Had a wonderful time, I promise, you were great fun. Good-bye."
>
> Away from the doorway he had staggered and then fallen on the fish-slippery pavement. It had started to rain...He'd fallen ungracefully onto his bottom. Humiliation, unmatched in his whole experience, overcame him. A pain grew in the pit of his chest. He had never felt like that before. He'd read about it, heard it sung in love songs, seen people who were suffering, talked to a brother who attempted suicide because of it, but had never felt it. This incredible pain was new to him. It seemed to be a living death that was somehow tied up with the battering of his ego and psyche, and yet he felt a definite physical pain, like being strangled from inside.

> Just a girl. Just a girl. His broken heart was unfeeling, like shattered glass in an acid bath. He had had backed-up words like vomit in his throat. He'd sworn complaints. He'd cursed, kicked, wept, cried, and stubbornly clung on to what he was not. Fuck it! Fuck it! The words were pathetic...
>
> He spent the following day (ironically, Valentine's Day) buying her flowers and trinkets...

Upon Pete's return, he played some demos to his bandmates. "...I was in L.A., and then I came back to London," Pete told *Q*'s John Harris in 1996, "walked into a Who session – didn't even go home to say hello to my little girls – ran through the stuff, and there were all these whispers: "This is okay, but it isn't great."

> And Kenney Jones, who was new in the band, his first response was: "You used all the best material for your solo albums." And my inner reaction was, "Who the fuck are you? You're only in this fucking band 'cos I wanted you in it." Roger had never wanted him in in the first place."
>
> Anyway, I just kind of medicated myself. I turned round to Bobby Pridden and said, "Could you go out and buy me some coke?" and he said, "You don't use coke." I said, "Listen, I do now, go and buy me some." Anyway, he went out and bought me some terrible coke, laced with speed...

After his first experience with cocaine in L.A. in February, 1980, Pete was now finding that the alcohol he was consuming in ever-increasing quantities was no longer getting the job done. "I started drinking about a bottle and a half of cognac a day,"[176] he told *Omni* in late 1982. "And to cut through the drunken stupor I was in I got into this deadly alcohol cocaine oscillation"

"...I adjusted to what was happening in the world," Pete wrote in 1984's *The Courage to Change*, addressing his growing dependency on cocaine:

> ...people weren't drinking quite as much as they used to – certainly not as much as I was. They were using

---

[176] "I went to lunch with the guy who was my driver through that period," Pete told *Q*'s John Harris in 1996, "and I said to him, "I've really got to apologize to you, for all that, drinking two bottles of brandy a day." He said: "No. It was five..." He said," Pete added, ""Pete, I once saw you drop a bottle of brandy, and you got down and licked it up.""

cocaine in the music business – at the dentist, the hairdresser, the lawyer's office, the record company, the recording studio, on the bus, on the taxi. They were using coke everywhere, and I quickly got into this routine, too. Having plenty of money, I was able to supply myself and also about fifty other people who followed me around London…it was a cycle. It was a way of getting out of something, of getting away from the band. It was a way of getting away from rock'n'roll. The only way I could face the work was by destroying myself. I didn't have the guts to stand up and say, "This is a bunch of shit. I've got to go."

Despite Pete's worsening personal problems, The Who were soon back on the road. After a short run through five European cities in late March, the band began the first leg of their North American tour with eighteen dates stretching from mid-April through the first week of May. Despite rumors of the band adding an extra guitarist, Pete had decided to maintain the status quo. "I think we'll keep the horn section for this tour," he told Kurt Loder in April, "It really does add extra color.[177] But apart from that, we're sticking with the same lineup – Rabbit on keyboards, and that's it."

The tour began on the west coast. An interesting snapshot of the band at this stage was provided when *Rolling Stone*'s Greil Marcus took in the first of The Who's three shows at Oakland, California's Alameda County Coliseum on April 18[178]:

> If the show was not quite the Who's Greatest Hits, it was the History of the Who…The band gave the audience what it wanted, but they didn't entice the audience to want more than it had thought of wanting – which is what the Who, like all great rock & roll bands in their great days, have been all about. Technically, the show was superb: shot through with fun and movement…Townshend's crouched leaps were thrilling – spectacular but not gaudy, aggressive but not cruel. No one in the Who ever seemed

---

[177] The Who had been accompanied by a horn section since the beginning of their 1979 North American tour.

[178] It was after one of the shows in Oakland that Pete had the famous 'bloody hand' photograph taken by Annie Leibovitz for *Rolling Stone*. "By the time we got to start taking pictures, the blood was badly congealed," Pete told *Rolling Stone* in 2004. "Annie got me to swing my arm afresh to generate more blood. Then she actually found some fake blood and added a little to create the runny effect. But I have to say, my hand was a fucking mess before she started to embellish it. …I loved how that photo turned out…"

bored by the material. The band changed the show over the next two nights. They cut it down, stretched it out, shuffled the songs, varied the encores – and, according to one fan who saw all three concerts, Townshend never played the same solo twice…As for Townshend, he appeared onstage in an impressive navy blue jacket: he looked like a world-beater. When, after a few numbers, he took it off, revealing a Clash T-shirt with sleeves rolled up, his pants suddenly seemed baggy – and he struck me as just another rock & roll anomaly. Just another Buddy Holly: the kid you laugh at, if you bother to do that, the kid who one day comes out of his shell and changes your life.

Despite the fact that almost all of the venues were sold out as the tour wound on through the central United States and Canada, Pete was losing his enthusiasm. "…I don't think I'd go and watch the Who, even if I lived in America," he said in April. "I mean, I'd sit and wait until the Clash came: I'd go see them. And hope I'd get one of their good nights!" His attitude towards touring had become downright selfish. "We don't give a shit whether the audience has a problem or not," he said.

All we know is that for us, to go on a stage, get instant communication…have an instant connection with the audience, go backstage afterward into a dressing room full of the most beautiful women you can ever hope to lay your eyes on, never have anybody say anything nasty to you, everybody's friendly, everybody's wonderful, people don't throw us out of hotels anymore – I mean life revolves quite nicely – you know what I'm saying? I'm getting paid a lot of money for the privilege. The first ten years in the Who were fucking awful; miserable, violent, unhappy times. It's nice to now sit back and enjoy it.

Following the tour, a newly beardless[179] Pete Townshend spent two weeks at AIR studios in London assembling the demos he'd recorded earlier in the year for the next Who album (recall that he'd laid down several tracks at Warner Bros. Studios in Hollywood in February). Although Pete had told *Rolling Stone*'s Kurt Loder in 1980 that he had found working on *Empty*

---

[179] "I shaved it off about a month ago, mainly for medical reasons," Pete told *NME*'s Charles Shaar Murray in April, 1980. "My face started moulting, so I shaved it off and my kids started screaming and my wife started screaming. I've had a beard since 1970, so my youngest kid has never see me without one except for when I played Widow Twankey in the pantomime. At that time the Kenny Everett false chin was not available, otherwise I would have worn one. The director said I had to shave. Nobody knew who the fuck I was."

Glass "very, very exhausting," he added, "I didn't have any difficulty at all coming up with what I think is some exciting, new-sounding material for the Who quite quickly." The band's new album was eventually entitled *Face Dances*.[180]

Some of Pete's demos for *Face Dances*, such as *You Better You Bet*, demonstrate that Pete was still reveling in the British punk movement – his vocals have a clear John Lydon sneer.[181] "I think I've changed my style slightly through workin' on my solo album," he told Loder. "Because I was singin' every day, my voice improved a hell of a lot, and that affects a lot of the melodies I'm writing and also the kind of diction I can get across." The argument has been made that some of Pete's demos for *Face Dances* are far better than the finished product. Pete's contention was that, despite his having reservations at times, the band would always provide him with a quality effort. "...Sometimes I feel that I get a little too precious about a song," Pete explained in an April 1980 interview with *NME*'s Charles Shaar Murray, "and I feel that I don't really want to hear the band play it because I like the way it is on the demo."

> But I'm always pleasantly surprised. Some of the material that we've been recording with the Who I've sung with a half-English accent – as is the current trend – and I never thought Roger would be able to do it, but he just lunged right in and did it and it sounds much more natural than singing in his normal Bob Seger accent. He was pleasantly surprised and I was pleasantly surprised...The first band that made me feel that it wasn't being deliberately done but that they were just singing was the Sex Pistols. I really got into their albums and played 'em all the time, so when I was ready to do demos it felt quite natural just to do it myself...

Recording sessions for *Face Dances* began in June, 1980, at London's Odyssey studios. The Who had wanted to use their own Ramport recording studios, but their new producer preferred a different location. "As they were using a new drummer and making their first record for a new

---

[180] A last minute replacement for the unimaginative original title *The Who, Face Dances* originated from a phrase Pete coined when he saw a friend in front of a mirror with a match between her teeth, moving the match and her eyes to a beat. The song *Face Dances Part II* on Pete's *Chinese Eyes* album references this incident. "I said to her, 'face dances' and she just laughed," Pete said in 1981. It wasn't until later that Pete remembered the 'face dancers' in Frank Herbert's *Dune* trilogy. "That must have stuck in my head because I really loved the first [book]," Pete recalled.

[181] Townshend enjoyed Lydon's company during this period. In the *Scoop* liner notes, he recalled that the demo of *Cache Cache* was recorded "between drinking bouts with John Lydon and his brother Jimmy one night."

company," Richard Barnes wrote in *Maximum R&B*, "they wanted a new producer. They brought in an American, Bill Szymczyk." Szymczyk's resume included production credits on The Eagles' *Hotel California* and *The Long Run*. Szymczyk, a friend of Pete's, recalled that *Hotel California* was one of Pete's favorite albums: "...really, that's what got me the job with them, that album. Your reputation goes before you, and its like, 'You hear the way that sounds? Do that to me.'"

Face Dances opened with the moderate hit *You Better You Bet*, which reached number 9 in the U.K., 18 in the U.S. The song's sparse guitar and liberal use of keyboards (a consistent theme throughout the album) led some to wonder if Pete was veering away from his signature guitar work. "I always get very worried about the guitar because I tend to come out with the same three or four chords again and again and again," he said on the February, 1981, promotional album *Filling in the Gaps*. "I don't even sometimes know that I'm doing it. So I still look to keyboards, particularly to synthesizers and stuff like that as a way of breaking my own preconceptions, breaking my own habit patterns. *You Better You Bet* was a very spontaneous lyric and a fairly spontaneous, sort of peppy song. I think it's a pop song, really, just a pop song."

Don't Let Go The Coat followed, inspired by a Meher Baba expression ("hold fast to the hem of my robe"). "I wrote this one in London," Pete recalled in 1982. "I was thinking about all the things you cling onto, and that the most important thing for me at that particular time was to cling to some semblance of a spiritual equipoise. The verses of the song talk about 'things might change', and 'things might explode', but just as long as you hang onto that thread, that apron string of a real affection and love for the people around you, and for whatever else you're into, God, whatever it is...Mum and Dad!"

Cache Cache was "a weird kind of song which I wrote to celebrate a wonderful two days I spent living as a tramp in Switzerland," Pete recalled in 1982.

> I decided I was going to give up the music business forever, and I got my wallet and passport, and a bottle of brandy, and went off in a town called Berne. Berne is famous for its big brown bears and these cages up in the hills. I spent about sixteen hours walking around, sleeping under trees and all that, and I was thinking, 'I don't know if I want to be a tramp now,' but I was drunk enough to decide it would be worthwhile just going and visiting the bears. I don't know whether or not I really wanted to get torn to pieces or not, but I think I was in that frame of mind when I really just did not give a damn.

I went up to this bear pit and I went down this bit where all the apple cores are and climbed up the rocks on the other side. I was always thinking 'If I could get in, I wonder why they couldn't get out?' I went into this big sort of cage at the back and walked inside. It really stank but luckily the bears aren't there in the middle of winter. Really, it's just a song about sometimes you can go and say 'Right! I'm going to do something really amazing and stupid and devastating,' and then you end up looking like a complete idiot.

He recalled the writing of the demo in the *Scoop* liner notes:

I had written this about a very screwed up time in Europe, a time that from my point of view still seems strange; The Who too long on the road, me totally schizophrenic and everyone simply reacting by saying that I was schizophrenic. The song is a jibe at them, the band, the managers, the hangers-on, asking them if they know what it's like. It's a bitter piece, but powerful. Roger saw immediately what it was about when I tried to get him to do it on *Face Dances* and made me sing it myself. By the time I came to do The Who version I had forgiven everybody, or realized that they hadn't really been guilty of anything in the first place. When I sang this demo I meant it.

Face Dances may be closest thematically to *The Who By Numbers*: *Did You Steal My Money*[182] is almost the next logical step lyrically from *How Many Friends*, while an examination of a sample of *Daily Records* looks like it was lifted from *However Much I Booze*, exhibiting a similar tone of introspection and self-pity:

I just don't quite know how to wear my hair no more
No sooner cut it than they cut it even more
Got to admit that I created private worlds
Cold sex and booze don't impress my little girls

"I think it was basically about the music drug," Pete recalled in February, 1981. "That's all, just the fact that music does become like a drug and I can't get enough of it. It's not a testament to spending endless hours in smoky recording studios, it's about the business of making records, the

---

[182] "The true story behind this doesn't make anyone look good – especially me," Pete said of *Did You Steal My Money* in 2001. "It is not the time to tell it."

business of using... it's about what I said, music being like a drug to me, to a great extent. When I say music, I suppose I mean songwriting."

It also appears to include some Baba references:

I could be losing you
I could be coming through
I'm unaware of any difference
You still support me now
You love me anyhow
And I am still under your influence

We've had some years of hate
But now we're on the eights
I'm unaware of any difference
I need you even more
My money keeps me poor
I'm still amazed at your omnipotence

Another Tricky Day, which, along with the two Entwistle contributions *You* and *The Quiet One* is perhaps sonically the closest song to the classic, guitar-oriented Who sound on the album, followed the theme of despair:

Another tricky day
Another gently nagging pain
What the papers say
Just seems to bring down heavier rain
The world seems in a spiral
Life seems such a worthless title

How Can You Do It Alone was inspired by Pete's late night encounter with a flasher in London. "I was actually going up Holland Park Road and I wanted a cigarette," Pete recalled in 1982.

> ...it was about two in the morning, and this guy came out of the station and I asked him for a light and he looked very afraid and he stepped back and I said 'listen, all I want is a light from your cigarette' and he said 'Oh, all right'. He opened his coat up and got a lighter out and before he'd known what he'd done, he was completely naked underneath...he was a flasher! He'd obviously just come off the tube doing a bit of flashing. He saw that I saw that he was naked and that I knew what he was up to. I

looked into his eyes and he looked into mine, and the *shame* on his face!

I felt like saying to him, 'listen, don't be ashamed. I don't give a damn.' Then I was walking up the street and I thought I should have asked him, 'how do you do it all on your own? How do you live that solitary...How do you get your kicks?' Because that's more alone than masturbation. So I started to explore that idea and that turned into the song. How can you do anything on your own ultimately?

"I quite liked The Who's rendering of this song," Pete wrote in the liner notes to *Scoop 3*, which included the song's demo. "Roger sang it really well. But it is probably one of those songs that needed my acidic tone to work without awkwardness. Whichever version is your favorite (and you may hate both of them) it's good to be able to compare."

Aside from the songs that appear on the album, the band also recorded *I Like Nightmares*, sung by Townshend, *It's In You*, and *Somebody Saved Me*, a different version of which would appear on Pete's next solo album, *All The Best Cowboys Have Chinese Eyes*. Among the rejected demos was *Dirty Water*, which ended up on 1983's *Scoop*. "...I sang the vocal lying flat on my back on the studio floor," Pete wrote in the liner notes. "The Who didn't record this song as it was too ordinary, but here, as is, it doesn't sound ordinary at all, it sounds nuts." Also rejected was *Zelda*, a song Pete had named after his niece.

During a break in recording[183], Pete recorded a batch of new demos, and was taken aback by the band's reaction to the new material. "I went and wrote four songs while everybody else was resting," he recalled later. "When I played them nobody said anything, not a dicky bird. Eventually Rabbit said, 'I like such and such a song, that has some good bits in it.' He was trying to be positive because he was aware of this big pregnant silence. I just picked up the tape and walked out. I thought, 'I'm not breaking my back for these cunts.'" *Popular*, a "last minute" demo which also didn't make it on to *Face Dances*, evolved into *It's Hard*, which The Who would record in 1982. "The band reaction was lukewarm, we were close to ending the album and were all unsure of what was happening," Pete commented in 1983. "I later removed the 'Popular' chorus, replaced it with 'It's Hard' and managed to sell another song!"

The recording of *Face Dances* was completed in late 1980, with mixing taking place at Bill Szymczyk's Bayshore Recording Studios in Coconut Grove, Florida. Pete visited Bayshore to assist with the mixing process, but wasn't particularly pleased with the result, which was released

---

[183] Recording was interrupted for a few months in autumn, 1980 when Bill Szmczyk was injured in a car accident, shortly after which he was committed to mix The Eagles' *Eagles Live*.

in early March. "None of the band were happy with the album," Richard Barnes recalled. "If we'd been there to mix it, it might have been a bit better," John Entwistle lamented, "but I don't think it was actually on the tape anyway."

Pete explained that his sentiments for *Face Dances* were, "Kind of mixed...I think the chemistry was wrong, and it wasn't just Bill Szymczyk[184]. I don't think we were really quite working together. Roger says that you could feel on *Face Dances* that the band wasn't a band." Daltrey's frustration was squarely aimed at the drummer's stool. "I love *Face Dances*," he later opined. "I love all the songs on *Face Dances*. Imagine if they had been played with a great drummer, as they are when we play live now with a drummer like Simon Phillips or whoever I take on the road with me on my tour, you can hear what the potential of that album could have been. Listen to the drums on that album and you tell me if they're any fucking good." By this point, Jones' successful beginning with The Who during 1979 was being forgotten.

While Szymczyk took more than his share of the blame for the album's marked shortcomings, he consistently defended The Who. "I have to tell you one thing," he later commented, "the songs that Pete Townshend wrote are just amazing, and when I can stand back from it and listen to it as a whole, the album is brilliant, and as a writer, Pete has grown by leaps and bounds. I think that Kenney Jones has been a great addition to the band, and I really love the record, but it was such a big deal to me that I can't be certain that I'm being completely objective about it."

From early on, *Face Dances* fell victim to extremely high expectations. "Bob Seger, who heard the basic tracks of the forthcoming Who album due at the end of '80 termed it 'incredible'," reported *Creem*. In the same article (November 1980), Bill Szymczyk was quoted as saying, "They're tighter personally and musically than they have been for a long time. I think the punk thing really stirred up Pete's juices and his material now just explodes on the tracks. I think he's back to writing the kind of material there was on *Who's Next*." Unfortunately, the album failed to justify the hype.

"It was ineffective; it didn't work," Pete later recalled. "I think the songs weren't right for the band. I can probably get more introspective and examine myself more on [solo] records than anybody else I know and get away with it. I can get all curled up in myself and people don't mind too much. Can't do that with The Who."

---

[184] *Mojo* reported that "Szymcyk demanded that at least three replica recordings be made of each individual track, doing away with any spontaneity." Pete defended Szymczyk in the *Scoop* liner notes. "Much has been said about *Face Dances*, especially by the band, some of it to the irritation of Bill Sz.," Pete commented. "He is a great producer."

"As an album, *Face Dances* neither triumphs nor fails," *Rolling Stone* reported. "Instead, it makes you wonder if the Who, without social – i.e., internal – crises, have any reason for being."

Chris Charlesworth offered his take on *Face Dances* in 1984:

> Though the drumming was unimaginative compared to that of Keith Moon, it would be unfair to blame Kenney Jones for the failure of *Face Dances*. Bill Szymczyk's production was too light and The Who edge, the sharp chord work for which Pete was noted, was nowhere to be heard. Roger Daltrey effected a modern-sounding British accent but seemed unable to identify with the songs and consequently unable to deliver Pete's lyrics with any real conviction. The fault lay fairly and squarely with Townshend's material and the fact that his better songs of the period had already been recorded on *Empty Glass*.

Despite their opinion of the record, The Who's *Face Dances* reached number 2 in the U.K, and number 4 in the U.S.

The band returned to the U.S. in mid-June, kicking off their 1980 summer tour with a show in San Diego, after which Pete punched the wall backstage in what he told an interviewer was a moment of "sheer exuberance." He broke several bones in his right hand, and wore a cast for the rest of the tour. Following the San Diego show, the band performed seven sold out shows in L.A. prior to winding through the southern U.S. for two weeks, playing to packed houses during the unusually hot summer of 1980. The only songs from *Face Dances* which saw (admittedly sparse) action during this tour were *Another Tricky Day* and *How Can You Do It Alone*, and not *You Better You Bet*. They again relied heavily on their past hits, regularly playing staples such as *Won't Get Fooled Again*, *Pinball Wizard*, *My Generation*, *Substitute*, and the like. Other regulars during this tour were *Drowned* and *The Real Me* from *Quadrophenia*, and *Music Must Change*, *Who Are You* and *Sister Disco* from *Who Are You*.

Pete's substance abuse finally began to take its toll as the tour continued. "...his coke and boozing habits had quite an effect on his performance," Richard Barnes recalled in *Maximum R&B*.

> Occasionally he would play brilliantly, and bootlegs of many shows from this tour contain Townshend guitar solos which are among the best he's ever played. More often, however, Pete would be so 'out of it' on stage that he would start to wander off on his own, jamming away at the end of numbers that the other three had thought had finished. Many of these guitar solos...would catch Roger

out and he would be left in the middle of the stage marking time and wondering what was happening. To a certain extent, I suspected that Pete would do this simply to wind Roger up, but many nights he just selfishly played away totally ignoring the other three. An eye-witness report of one of the LA shows appeared in the 'Who Magazine,' a Who fanzine: "Pete appeared a bit more groggy than usual...*Drowned* seemed to go on forever. I thought it was finally over and Pete went into yet another guitar solo. The rest of the band looked at each other as if to say, 'Wah? This isn't the way we played it in rehearsal.' Roger's expression often said 'What the fuck is he doing?' All they could do was try to follow along..."

Pete was also taking a great deal of amphetamines to get him through the tour. However, it would mean that he would talk his head off after a show backstage. He was always the last to leave. One night he spoke for hours to some fans, who couldn't believe their luck at getting backstage and having Pete talk to them. Eventually, even they were exhausted by him and left. After talking about everything to everybody, there wasn't anybody remaining as it was about three in the morning. There was only our bodyguard, a driver and myself left. But Pete ended up talking for another hour to the cleaners as they seemed prepared to listen.

After the last show of the tour, in mid-July at Toronto's CNE stadium, the band attended an all-night party after which, thoroughly exhausted, they flew to New York to board the Concorde for the trip back to England. Richard Barnes recalled the eventful flight home in *Maximum R&B*:

> There was a particularly attractive blonde stewardess on board and every time she passed Pete would make a determined but drunken lunge from his window seat and try to grab her. Every so often, he would stand up and attempt speeches, often attacking his fellow passengers. " 'Ere we all are sitting 'ere traveling faster than a bullet in this supersonic rocket that I paid for with my fucking taxes..." and would quickly collapse. Then he took a liking to my meal and would scoop up a handful of lobster, chew it and start spitting it out at everybody nearby...The pretty blonde stewardess was removed to work behind a curtain up the front of the plane and the passengers nearby were all

moved away. The stewards, however, were all smiles and didn't seem to notice, even when I almost had him in a headlock. The head steward came up and asked if the pilot could have his autograph. Pete started to write it in his wobbly hand and then with a flourish circled the autograph. He went on circling it for about five minutes, so that it looked like a large spiral had been drawn on the page. The steward returned and was delighted, no doubt impressed at what an elaborate autograph Pete had. After leaving the Toronto party a kid in the street had presented him with a packet of cocaine. Pete threw the lot at his nose and it went all over him. Fellow passengers on Concorde probably thought that he had talcum powder all over his face and hair, not realizing that it was really $100 worth of cocaine...Roger and I were concerned about Pete returning to his family covered in spilt wine, brandy, cocaine and bits of food. Roger found a clean T-shirt in his bag, which I took for Pete to change into. Unfortunately, Pete tossed it out of the car window after we left the airport.

Shortly after his return to England, Pete returned to the house in Berkshire which he'd purchased in early 1978. "I lived away from my family for quite a long time," he said in 1982. "...we have a house in the country, and I was living there, mainly...I spent...a lot of time in the country working on a book of short stories and other times just knockin' about with some of the London club scene people. I enjoy a lot of that life, in a way."

It was in the kitchen of this house that Pete recorded *Driftin' Blues*, which surfaced on *Another Scoop*. "I can remember doing it," Pete told *Guitar Player* in 1989.

> I was in my house in the country, I had been living away from my wife for about nine months, had had a string of unsatisfactory relationships with young women, and was feeling like shit because I wasn't able to accept their love, either because I wasn't completely cut off from my wife or just because I wasn't man enough to do it. I was drinking a lot, I'd gone back to using cocaine, which I despised in other people, and I wasn't in very good spirits. I just started to play that song, and suddenly I just felt happy with myself. You know, I felt I had a friend in me. And I suddenly realized what the blues was.

Pete had recorded the song *Dirty Water* at this house back in December, 1979. "I was living alone at the time," he wrote in the *Scoop 3* liner notes in 2001. "I spent a lot of time at my big kitchen table, looking at the River Thames flowing by outside my windows. I used to knock out little songs like this, or short stories that I later published in *Horse's Neck*."

Although Pete maintains that its autobiographical nature has been overstated by some observers, the short story *A Death in the Day of*, from *Horse's Neck*, which appears to have been written in winter, 1980/81, must surely paint a picture of Pete's life at this time, living in solitude, oscillating between drunkenness and sobriety, realizing the mess he was in and his struggle to come to terms with his drug abuse.

> I wake up about four or five in the afternoon; at this time of the year I rise in darkness.
>
> At better times I might awake with a lover, hopefully the one I really care about. The trouble is that the good times are inextricably tangled with the bad. If I am on the wagon I become reclusive and antisocial. I tear out the phone or, if forced to answer, pretend that I'm too ill to move. So if there is a lover, she will have slept with a drunk.
>
> My days in London are not much use to anyone, but fun. I buy clothes, pop in to see friends and endure disturbing business appointments. Everyone is in the same boat: interest rates are running well over 22 percent, I can't really catch up until they fall. In the evening I used to go and see a lot of bands, but at the moment I prefer a quiet dinner with a friend, and then a nightclub.
>
> I have an office which I rarely visit. My secretary is ready to quit. She's seen too much of my self-obliterative nature. My wife, living separately (lucky thing), signs the bills. I have a studio, but most of the time other people use it. I suppose I get pleasure from that. Just now I can't work. Getting up so late, I have a short day. I live in a paradox: I feel comfortable with this unhappiness. I am content with misery.
>
> Living by the river, I can row and I do this frequently. I have a sun bed. I sit under it and listen to Radio 4. In the summer the garden is wonderful. I grow vegetables and prune fruit trees.
>
> I try to write every day. Solitude is vital...I read about six books at once so I can adjust my reading to my mood. If I'm feeling delicate, I might read P.G. Wodehouse or H.E. Bates. If I feel strong, I'll tackle biographies...I read

fairly heavy stuff. To mention all the authors might make me sound pretentious, so I won't, but I never read anything I don't enjoy. Every now and then, for a laugh, I listen to some music.

In spurts I answer fan mail and business letters, play snooker, strum my guitar into a cassette machine, pray for forgiveness and think about what a total mess I've made of a life that had everything, and everyone, going for it.

Pete's desperation is especially evident at the end of the short story:

And so, once more, to bed...The cask of grief that cracks as I lie back always brings tears. Cool tears, spontaneous and free from self-pity, I think. I wonder about the kids of Toxteth and Brixton, and how hard are their lives. I thank God they don't know how absurdly I am wasting my own.

What's the date? Does it matter? Nothing significant about today. What would I write if I were keeping a diary? *Didn't want to live anymore*, or *I've always wanted to try it, just to see what it was like*, or *This showed you, didn't it, you load of bastards?* or *Please water the plants.*

I imagine slashing my stomach and watching my guts emerge; I envisage a mirror image as I draw a rusty razor blade slowly across my throat from ear to ear. Then, simply swallowing a few tablets doesn't seem quite so bad.

If anyone needed further evidence that Townshend's substance abuse problems were gradually tearing The Who apart, the 1981 British tour drove the point home. "Like every arsehole writer I felt that drinking was helping me to work or at least helping with some of the pressure I was going through....," Pete told Chris Salewicz in 1982. "I was drinking myself into oblivion in order not to face up to the fact that there were certain things I couldn't do and certain things I just didn't want to do. I wasn't running away from life but from particular issues." As if Pete's personal struggles weren't a sufficient distraction for The Who at this point, he had also decided to write and record another solo album.

The Who began their most extensive U.K. tour ever, a 26-date affair spanning seven weeks, beginning with a January 25 date at Granby Halls in Leicester. While the U.S. tour had been aimed at large arenas and stadiums, The Who chose to play in smaller theaters for the British tour. The band also elected to play more of their *Face Dances* material on this tour, inserting *The Quiet One, Don't Let Go The Coat, You Better You Bet,* along with an occasional rendition of *Did You Steal My Money* into the lineup. Despite his pathetic condition, Pete managed to turn in an at least capable performance on most nights. "Amazingly enough," reported *The Who Concert File*, "Pete always played well, even on a bad night, but he seemed to try the patience of his fellow band members with tangential diversions and solos inserted in unexpected places! His contempt for The Who and what it had become seemed barely disguised..."

On February 3 and 4, The Who played two shows at the Rainbow, specially organized by Pete and Eric Clapton to raise money for Meg Patterson's financially beleagured Pharmakon Clinic in Sussex[185]. At one of the shows, Pete reportedly drank four bottles of brandy onstage, and embarrassed himself and the band.[186] "...I kept stopping songs and making speeches to the audience," Pete later recalled. "I kept playing long, drawn-out guitar solos of distorted, bad notes. I'd alter the act, making up songs as I went along. And I knew it was London, and I knew that everybody's friends and family were there, and I deliberately picked that day to fuck up the show. I just ceased to care. I threw my dignity away." Pete's antics led Daltrey to throw down his mike and storm off stage, followed by Jones and Entwistle. "Basically I decided to go out and not play," he told Chris Salewicz in 1982. "I was just going to talk until somebody stopped me from talking by knocking me out." The ensuing Townshend-Daltrey confrontation in the dressing room, however, involved no violence. "Far from kicking my head in," Pete recalled the following year, "Roger was worried I was killing myself. Roger's always said over the last year or so when I was going through a lot of shit, "Listen, stop the band if it'll keep you alive. You're the important one to me." I think what I was doing at The Rainbow was testing that." The two shows at the Rainbow raised £20,000.

At this point in the U.K. tour, Pete began to express his distaste for life on the road with The Who. "If touring is just getting up every night to play old favorites that I'd written out of my system years ago," Pete said at the time, "then I don't want to do it."

"Pete was talking as though he had finished with the band," Richard Barnes recalled. "He told Bill Curbishley that he wouldn't do the European tour that was booked. However, Curbishley didn't cancel until the last moment in case Pete changed his mind. Tickets had already been on sale and sold out in some countries, so a massive refunding operation had to be set up. It was obvious that Pete couldn't carry on drinking and never sleeping, and Roger saw no point in doing a European tour with Pete in his

---

[185] Unfortunately, the money didn't reach Patterson's clinic in time to save it – the facility was closed just prior to the concerts taking place. Patterson soon moved to California to continue her research, where she would see Pete within a year to address his heroin addiction.
[186] Accounts vary as to whether this occurred during the first or the second of the two shows.

condition. Pete also needed time to write and record his solo album. He wanted to spend more time with his family."

"The English tour last year was just too much to take," Pete said in 1982. "We weren't playing well enough. And a lot of that was because I was pretty peculiar most of the time. I think we all were, though. And Roger was really having serious doubts about whether or not we should go on." He further recalled the situation in August, 1982 with *NME*'s Paul Du Noyer: "...towards the end of [the U.K. tour], my mind started to turn inside out in a way, and I had almost decided to blow the London gigs. There was so much animosity around the band... anyway, after that, I did cancel a European tour. I just said to everyone I wasn't ready to do it. I didn't really know what was going on in my head, but I could see trouble coming. And I started to work on my own record."

The Who's final date on the English tour took place at the Poole Arts Centre in Sussex on March 16, 1981. Rumors circulated throughout the media that The Who's breakup was imminent and conventional wisdom had it that this was to be the band's last show. "Pete and Roger were both in great moods, laughing on stage," Richard Barnes wrote in 1982. "It was a tremendous show and the audience, which numbered only 2,000 [due to the venue's small size]were wildly enthusiastic...Later at the stage door, a large crowd of fans waited, many in floods of tears, to thank the band and implore them not to break up." One additional date, the only remnant of the canceled European tour, took place in late March, as The Who appeared on Germany's *Rockpalast* TV show, which was, according to Barnes, broadcast to over 50 million people. On the bill with The Who were the Grateful Dead. After The Who's set, Pete joined the Dead onstage for one of their trademark marathon jam sessions, which ended only shortly before sunrise.

Meanwhile, work on Pete's solo album was at a near standstill. Attempts at recording were, according to Richard Barnes, "going very slowly. Progress could usually only be made on Mondays and Tuesdays after a weekend of rest. By Wednesday, he was already exhausted from his destructive nocturnal lifestyle. Producer Chris Thomas remembers one day talking to Pete at the mixing desk only to realize that Pete had been sitting at the controls fast asleep. Pete got stranger and stranger, dropped his friends, had gone in for a succession of unflattering haircuts, taken to wearing makeup...and was 'generally weird.'" Thomas was reportedly growing increasingly concerned at Townshend's cocaine abuse and the effects it was having on his voice.

Further reason for depression struck in late April, as news of Kit Lambert's death reached Pete. "...right in the middle of a period when I was in New York, in early 1981," Pete said in 1984, "Kit Lambert, our ex-manager, died. There had been no contact for a long time, but I still adored him." Lambert, just 45, died from an irreparable brain hemorrhage which he'd sustained from falling down the stairs at his mother's house. The fact that he'd been beaten up in a nightclub earlier was a major contributing factor. "I didn't feel very much at the time," Pete told Andrew Motion.

While he missed Kit's funeral, Pete arranged a memorial service on May 11 (which would have been Lambert's 46th birthday), which took place at St. Paul's, in Covent Garden. "Townshend, who had flown back from New York shortly after hearing of Kit's death, helped …to arrange the service," Motion wrote in *The Lamberts*. "He organized 'about a hundred' members of the London Symphony Orchestra to perform – they played 'some of *Tommy*, music by Constant, and Kit's favorite piece of Purcell, *The Gordian Knot Untied*' – and gave one of the two addresses."

"I attended this very beautiful and extraordinary service," Richard Barnes recalled in 1982. "The two dozen guests were totally outnumbered and overwhelmed by the London Symphony Orchestra…" After the service, a contingent of mourners, including Pete and Chris Stamp, "had a bash in a studio in Covent Garden," Townshend told Andrew Motion.

> We went from this beautiful elevated atmosphere, to this seedy place with cheap wine and beer and all the low lives together snorting coke in some back alley. Chris was saying 'it's what Kit would have wanted', but I wasn't sure. Something around that time happened to me, and I turned away from the light and faced the darkness. I felt I had to experience a shadow of the suffering and isolation that Kit had had. When he died I felt I'd lost the last sense of everything coming into my life; I felt from now on I was never, never going to get topped up again. On one hand it made me want to kill myself, on the other it made everything come together. It was so beautiful.

The effects of Lambert's death on Pete took him further into the depths of drunken depression. "I felt I had even more space then," he recalled in 1984. "I felt I could get away with more. I had even more license."

On May 30, Pete participated in an all day concert arranged by the Trades Union Congress as part of the People's March For Jobs campaign. The set list of the Brockwell Park, Brixton show (billed as 'Rock Against Unemployment') featured *A Little Is Enough* (two versions since Pete apparently wasn't happy with the first), *Cat's In The Cupboard*, *Big Boss Man*, *Substitute*, *Corrina Corrina*, *Body Language*, *Join Together*, and *Let My Love Open The Door*. Pete's band featured drummer Mark Brzezicki, bassist Tony Butler, and harmonica player Peter Hope-Evans.

A much-needed slap in the face arrived for Pete in mid-1981 when he discovered that his Eel Pie business group was in severe financial trouble. Desiring a new mixing desk during work on his new solo album, Pete discovered that he not only had no money for the £130,000 desk, but that he was also over £500,000 in the red. "I was halfway through recording my second solo album when I ran out of money," Pete recalled in 1984. "I went to the bank and said, "Listen, I've got to get this record finished." They said, "No, you can't have any more money." The fact that Pete had kept the same account and used the same branch since the beginning of art school didn't faze the bank. "I said, "Come on...all I have to do is deliver the record and they'll give me two million dollars. So if we can just finish the record…" "No, we're not going to give you any more money."

Pete's Eel Pie companies had virtually run themselves into the ground, and the bank was seeking some security. "...the National Westminster Bank...wanted my bollocks; despite the fact that I'd put every personal penny I had into the company to keep it afloat they wanted more. They wanted my house, they wanted my recording contract, my record label," Pete recalled.

> I was caught in an incredible cleft stick; I'd not wanted to blow the money I had on mansions or Rolls Royces or homes in LA, because I thought it was much better to create jobs or put the money into something which helps other people create, and to accept that this was part of my responsibility. But then I was unable to follow it through, either because I was so fucked up, or distracted, or simply not here because I was on the road with The Who. Also the people I'd appointed to do the work thought there was an endless supply of money...people were spending my money faster than I could earn it.

Pete's royalties simply weren't enough to cover Eel Pie's losses anymore:

> I was selling records. I sold a lot of copies of *Empty Glass*, my first solo album, and The Who's first album for Warner Brothers, *Face Dances*. I had money coming in, of course, because a song writer is buffered. The record was selling in 1979 and I'd be getting money in 1984. I certainly didn't need to steal an old lady's handbag to get my bottle of Remy or my drugs. But then my book publishing company went to the wolves, and it took every penny I had with it – about a million dollars. I had not supervised the company and it had no separate bank of its own. It was badly managed, overstaffed, overinvested, and contracts were too generous to authors; on the other hand,

we did some good stuff and I'm very proud of it. But the company collapsed.

"In the past," Pete recalled, "my answer to financial problems always has been to go out on the road with the Who or to sign a music publishing deal or to get another record advance, which basically accounts for the problem I've had for a long time with overwork and over commitment. It's not altruism. It's fucking stupidity." However, this time the damage was too great. More drastic measures were in order. "I was quite seriously considering the joys of bankruptcy, to live in Paris and have a peaceful life," he told Chris Salewicz. "But in the end I thought, 'No, I'll beat the bastards at their own game. I'll come back from the dead and make some money.'"

"Pete put in a hard-man accountant who cut down the staff of his companies from 37 to 17," Richard Barnes recalled the following year. "He eventually sold off his bookshop in Richmond... and closed down Eel Pie Sound, his PA hire company. His book publishing company had almost more staff than titles and was cut back severely." Eel Pie Books was later sold to Plexus, another London publisher. Eel Pie's role was reduced to that of publishing Pete's music.

Pete later drastically cut back Baba-related operations at Oceanic, which had become increasingly expensive to run. This move must have been a crushing blow to Townshend, who had put so much hard work and money into the center's existence. In a 2001 essay posted on his web site, Pete wrote that Oceanic "...had in any case slowed down to a crawl while I descended into self-obsession. Several of my employees there had gone through problems of their own, and some time in 1982 I impolitely sacked everyone. I then shut down the living quarters and confined the Meher Baba Association to a single room in the building. They moved within a year to new premises they still occupy in Shepherd's Bush in London..."

Pete considered the discovery of his financial mess the turning point of his two-year collapse. "If there was an act of God in this whole thing, which I call a miracle, it was that," he recalled. If nothing else, it rekindled a dialogue between Pete and Karen, who at this point had been living apart for around eighteen months. "I was getting used to living away from my family," Pete told *The Record*'s Alan Du Noyer in 1982. "...It was a mistake, which both my wife and I realize now, but it was something we were trying out. But it didn't protect the kids from my lunacy which I was going through, and it didn't help my old lady, and it didn't help me." He needed Karen's approval on many of the transactions necessary for their financial recovery. "I had to go back to Karen and say, "Can we raise money on the house," Pete recalled in 1984. "Can you sign this piece of paper, which allows the bank to do this and that? Can we sell our country home? Can we at least borrow against our country home?" And she said, "Before I sign this piece of paper, maybe we could talk about us."

"...Throughout that whole period I was seeing my family, spending vacations and weekends with them," Pete recalled in 1984. "At the end of 1981 I started to get into real difficulties and I missed my family a lot. I suddenly realized that I couldn't live without my wife, and she was falling right out of love with me. I couldn't handle that. I also felt that I was really hurting the other women I came across because I was such a pathetic mess...I would wake up in the morning and there would be a beautiful twenty-year-old woman running around. And I would think, What am I doing to this person? She should be out finding a young man."

While the guilt was mounting, Pete's destructive lifestyle continued unabated. "I made a lot of deliberate pleasure trips to New York and L.A.," he recalled in 1982. "Pete would often take Concorde to New York only to spend most of his time sleeping in some hotel suite," Barnes recalled. "He got very friendly with Bowie, and once passed out in the cloakroom of Mick Jagger's Manhattan apartment after a night's drinking with Mick and Charlie (Watts)." One of Pete's supersonic transatlantic flights was a little more exciting than he bargained for. One of the scariest situations he'd ever encountered was "being on Concorde when the engine blew up," Pete said in early 2000. "I understand it wasn't a near-death incident at all, but it certainly felt like it to Elton John. When we got down on the ground, I said to him, 'It must have been horrible for you – some woman up in your cabin was screaming her head off.' He said, 'That was me, darling.'"

In early September 1981, Pete went out drinking in London with friends at the Club For Heroes with near-disastrous results. "...I nearly died there one night," Pete told *Rolling Stone* in 1982. "The first night I went, I was with a couple of friends, and I ended up goin' blue – my heart practically stopped," Pete recalled the following year. "I thought at the time that I'd probably gotten so drunk I didn't know what I was taking, and that I took some terrible drug. But I think I actually drank so much brandy I gave myself alcohol poisoning. I just went black. And that was my hero's entrance to A Club For Heroes. A seven-foot bouncer carried me out like a sack of potatoes."[187] "He'd been drinking with Steve Strange, Phil Lynott

---

[187] Accounts vary as to what happened that evening. In another interview, Pete stated a "so-called friend" had given him "an injection of heroin" in the club's bathroom. "...word had gotten around that I was a heroin addict. So this guy thought I was suffering from withdrawal and that he was doing me a favor, when in fact I'd simply had too much to drink. Anyway, the shot of heroin temporarily killed me – my heart stopped. When they carried me into the hospital, I was dark blue. The nurse actually had to rip off my shirt outside the hospital and beat me back to life." A couple of accounts named Phil Lynott as the guilty party. "I had a very serious overdose one day at the hands of Phil Lynott," Pete said in a 1989 interview. "[Lynott] injected me with something, but fuck knows what it was, he nearly killed me." In 1996, Pete told *Q* magazine, "It was with Phil Lynott. I think it was a speedball. ...It was the first time I'd spent any time with Paul Weller and his girlfriend, and

and Paul Weller," recalled Richard Barnes. The bouncer deposited Pete onto the back seat of his car. "Pete's driver, Paul Bonnick, was used to driving Pete home slumped over the back seat," Richard Barnes remembers. "But this time he noticed that Pete's lips had turned blue." Pete was rushed to the hospital, and by the time he arrived, had "turned completely blue," according to Bonnick.

The comparisons to Keith Moon were now becoming eerily apparent, as Pete continued his plunge. He stopped work on his solo album in October, 1981. "…I gave up," Pete wrote in 1984.

> I went to Chris Thomas, my producer, and said, "Stop the record. I'm going to take three months off." It was crazy, but I was tired. I had worked very hard and done a lot of writing and I wasn't very healthy. There was a doctor looking after me and I was doing a lot of exercise, so I was alive by the skin of my teeth. I was in reasonably good shape, but I was drinking a hell of a lot and not eating very well, staying out late and fucking people around. I felt the best thing to do was stop and regroup. I went to New York and spent a week there. I came back. I got in with a guy who was deeply into free-basing cocaine, and I started to dabble in that, still drinking very heavily all the time.
>
> Then I went to work with Elton John in November 1981. I went to Paris. I took my mother and father and a girl I was seeing at the time and a few friends. I would go to the studio at nine o'clock in the morning, run through a tune with the guys in the band, and Elton would come about midday. We'd work until nine. Then I'd go out to a club, come back to the hotel, and spend some time with this unbelievable woman. God only knows what she was doing there. About five a.m. I would get the energy from somewhere to get out of bed and go and say hello to the minibar. I would drink the soft drinks, the tomato juice, the Perrier, that horrible French lemon juice, then go through the brandy, the wine, and think, Fuck it, the grain; let's have some of the grain. In the end there would be nothing in the

---

they were being so nice to me… Anyway, Phil Lynott said, "I can give you something to perk you up." I held out my arm, had the injection, and the next thing I know was that I was being carted away. The nurse said my heart had stopped beating. They gave me a massive cortisone injection, and it didn't work. They gave me another one under the chest, and they were about to give me an electric shock, and I came round. I think I owe my life to my driver, Paul. He said, "We've got to get Pete to a hospital.'" In a further rehashing of the story, Pete told *Q* magazine in 2000, "I don't know that it was Phil Lynott. I think Phil and I went down to do some coke, but there were five or six other people there."

fridge. It would be about seven or eight a.m., and I had drunk everything. So I would ring up and get some breakfast. The next day I would do the same thing. I don't think I have ever, ever, ever been quite that bad, and yet I didn't feel any remorse about what I was doing. I didn't know that what I was doing was particularly exceptional.

Six months before, I had started to have a glass of brandy in the morning because it was the only thing that would make me feel normal. Wouldn't make me high, wouldn't make me low, just make me feel normal. It would stop my feeling sick.

Richard Barnes wrote in *Maximum R&B* that Pete "...ended a very costly trip to Paris to play on Elton John's album, by throwing up his champagne into the ice bucket in the restaurant of the exclusive Hotel Georges."

Further evidence of his pitiful state occurred upon his arrival in England. "It was Halloween night," Pete recalled in 1984. "We got off the plane and I said, "Take me to a pub. I've got to get some beer." We went in and there were all these people in funny fucking outfits. I drank about five pints of beer, and I still felt sick. I got out to the country...I drank two bottles of brandy, and I was still having D.T.'s. I was in a condition where, like a heroin addict, I needed so much alcohol to balance out the bad reaction I was getting that it would kill me if I drank it all. So, after a couple of days of the shakes, I rang up my doctor and said, "Can you help me?" He said another doctor, who now works in a well-known clinic, was treating people privately. I went to see him and told him I was using hard drugs, too. He said, "Let's deal with the booze first."

Coincidentally, Pete's mother, Betty, had also recently been treated for alcoholism. "She [Betty] was actually the person who made me think about starting to treat myself as an alcoholic...She decided she'd had enough, and she stopped. And I knew, this time, that she'd stopped for life. They said it probably would be a good idea if she didn't go home straight away, so she came to live with me. And two things happened: first, I was really inspired by her, and I wanted to show solidarity by stopping myself, once and for all. But also, a lot of my excuses were taken away. There's absolutely no question of it being genetic, anyway; I couldn't really say, "Oh, it's because everybody in my family is a drunk, that's why I'm a drunk." "

In November, 1981, Pete checked himself into a clinic to address his alcoholism. "...I stopped drinking, and I spent five days in a clinic, initially. A lot of hypnotherapy, individual therapy with various people. But I carried on with the drug thing a little bit. And then I realized that both things were really affecting me, that in order to assist me getting off alcohol, I had used a lot of tranquilizers. One in particular, a drug called Ativan, which is of the Librium-Valium variety. And I became addicted to it."

Still in need of a fix, Pete left the clinic and simply replaced the alcohol with other, more dangerous vices. "I just took anything I could lay my hands on," he told *Time Out* in 1982. "...I hated the sensation of not being drunk."

Pete soon returned to New York and was still actively using cocaine, only now it was often mixed with heroin. "Someone would be free-basing, and you'd see them puff in a bit of burning junk through a straw," he told Chris Salewicz. "And that's it! A lot of people don't realize you are going to get addicted to heroin instantly by smoking it. If you snort it you don't get addicted instantly, but if you smoke it you do. It's not as dramatic as sitting at a party and drawing out a hypodermic and banging it in your arm, but it's the same thing. What was incredible to me was to watch the pushers sweetly come in and say, 'I've got some nice stuff here, but it's not good enough for snorting, it's really for smoking.' And that was it. At least 50 people I know got addicted in the space of six months last year."

He added in 1984:

> ...I went to New York and used a lot of straight heroin and free-based cocaine because I was still in bits. I needed something. I just replaced the booze with drug abuse. I was still very, very fucked up. I came back and went to my doctor and said, "I've got a serious problem with drugs. I'm getting more into drugs. I'm not drinking, but I've got to do something about the other drugs." I mentioned I might go to Meg Patterson, a British therapist living in California. The doctor had prescribed for me a pill called Ativan in quite high doses. I was using the whole prescription at once. Then I would get another supply from a dealer. I wasn't drinking, but I was still using coke, free-basing it. I was smoking heroin, too, quite a lot of it, which I was buying privately and doing completely in secret. Nobody knew except me. I would take two or three Ativan tablets when the heroin wore off, plus sleeping pills. I remember going to see my parents around Christmastime, and my dad said to me, "You say you're not drinking." I said, "No, no, no. I haven't had a drink for a month now." He said, "You're on something and it's a damn sight worse, in my opinion." And he got up and walked out. He was the only person who seemed to know that something was fatally wrong.

Pete's daily intake at this point was alarming: "...I suppose a month before I got NET, I'd been freebasing two or three grams of coke, which required about half an ounce of coke to produce," he recalled in a 1983 *Penthouse* interview. "I was smoking about one gram, sometimes more, of heroin; and on top of that I was usually taking about eight to ten Ativan tablets plus two or three sleeping tablets to get to sleep at night – I was a walking pillbox..."

While it focuses on alcohol rather than heroin and cocaine, Pete's description of an ostensibly fictional character's condition in the short story *Tonight's the Night*, from *Horse's Neck*, is eerily similar to his own state at the time.

> One Christmastime Pete's liver finally gave out. He was trying to give up the booze, taking all kinds of pills and vomiting a lot, seeing little stars and using sleepers to keep himself from being bored. With a bottle he was alone, without it he was catatonically fucked up.

The holidays brought a contrite, dejected Pete back to his family, privately screaming for help but not particularly expecting any. "I went back to Karen and my kids," Pete recalled in a 1985 radio interview, "and I said, 'I don't think I should really stay.'

> I'll go and stay at the country place and I'll come back again tomorrow.' And she said, 'No, stay,' and I said, 'Well listen, the point is that I'm using smack at the moment and I don't think I should be around the house,' and she said, 'No, you stay anyway.' I think that was the thing that really triggered it for me, the fact that I thought I was a worthless piece of crap, not worthy to be in the house that I'd bought, with the family that I'd brought into the world and sustained and fed, and all that stuff, and yet they, particularly my wife, didn't feel that way. I think it was that gesture that meant such a lot to me and I immediately determined that, in fact, in the rest of the sentence I said, 'Okay, I'm addicted now, but I mean to get off as soon as the new year comes.'

Pete was floored by Karen's open heart. "...it's a golden opportunity to demonstrate unconditional love for somebody," he said three years later. "You're faced with somebody who feels such a low sense of their own value that they've turned to drugs, they've destroyed themselves and they stand before you and you say, 'well, still, come home every night, we don't care if you're a junkie, come and stay with us. Steal the silver if you want to. It's you we care about.' Now how many opportunities do you get to demonstrate that kind of unconditional love? …I always urge people that I come across to do what Karen did for me."

Chapter 10

"...it was a waste of time. Heroin is an utter, complete waste of time."
- Pete Townshend, 1985

"From my point of view, I like to be like a reed. You get blown backwards and forwards by the ebbs and flows of what is happening in the world. But you don't break – and I have never broken and I will never break."
- Pete Townshend, 1982

As 1981 drew to a close, the future looked bleak. Over the last two years, Pete Townshend had steadily progressed from alcoholism to full-blown chemical dependency and the daily abuse of cocaine, heroin, and prescription drugs including sleeping pills and Ativan. Still, the pain didn't subside. In early January 1982, Pete overdosed again and was admitted to hospital where his stomach was pumped. Both Bill Curbishley and an assistant of Pete's named Judy, realizing Pete's near-death condition, made separate calls to Meg Patterson for help[188].

By 1982, Margaret "Meg" Patterson, a Scottish surgeon, had been active in the field of drug and alcohol rehabilitation for more than a decade. Patterson had devised a treatment for addiction to various substances which involved the use of a small walkman-size box which sent preset electrical pulses into the patient's brain through electrodes taped behind the ears. The pulses stimulated the brain to produce its own endorphins, as opposed to using the exterior stimulus of the patient's drug of choice. This bizarre treatment, known as Neuro-Electric Therapy (N.E.T.), or the 'Black Box'

---

[188] This account, taken from both Dr. Patterson's autobiography and an email from her husband, George, differs from Pete's account of what happened. "Almost in the first week of using [heroin], I tracked down Meg Patterson in California," Pete told Q's John Harris in 1996. "I said, "I'm using heroin, I want to stop using it, when can I see you?" She said, "Come over tomorrow." I said, "I can't actually manage that." She said, "Come over tomorrow or don't come over at all." So I got a plane and went over there. I was only on it for a couple of months."

treatment, claimed a 98% detoxification success rate and had successfully reformed notorious, high-profile heroin addicts Keith Richards and Eric Clapton.[189]

The treatment, which had originated as 'electro-acupuncture' in Hong Kong's 850-bed Tung Wah hospital in the early 1970s, was initially intended to create analgesia in surgery patients. Dr. Patterson (the hospital's head of surgery) and neurosurgical consultant Dr. H.L. Wen soon discovered an unintended side effect: The treatment proved a reliable means of virtually eliminating the patients' desire for heroin (during this period, Hong Kong was a hotbed of drug abuse. Patterson estimated that approximately 15 percent of the hospital's surgical patients were opiate addicts). Patterson and Wen soon set about locating drug addicts who were willing to be treated for their dependency. After treating over forty drug addicts with the electro-acupuncture technique, Dr. Wen reported in the Asian Journal of Medicine that a 40-minute treatment "consistently stopped all withdrawal symptoms for a period of time," and that "repeated treatments over a 10-day period, according to the addicts, completely removed the desire of the addicts to take their drug of addiction." After witnessing over one hundred patients undergo Dr. Wen's treatment, Dr. Patterson, in a 1976 report to the United Nations Office for Drug Control and Crime Prevention, emphasized that despite the encouraging results, the procedure was performed in a far less than perfect environment:

> It is significant [that those who underwent treatment] received no counseling whatsoever, no social support, no psychotherapy. In fact, their presence in the surgical wards (no other hospital beds being available) was deeply resented by the overworked surgical nurses; also the doctors treating them, all surgeons, were frequently unavailable. In spite of this, there was complete success in taking them off their drugs without any medication. When some patients developed acute withdrawal symptoms while no doctor was available, the symptoms ceased within 15 to 20 minutes of the commencement of a treatment.

Dr. Patterson later returned to England to refine the electro-acupuncture technique into what became known as Neuro-Electric Therapy (N.E.T.). Over the years, the use of acupuncture needles gave way to ear clips containing tiny needles, and eventually to flat electrodes pressed against the skin behind each ear through the use of a headset. In addition to reducing discomfort and the risk of infection, this also enabled Dr.

---

[189] Dr. Patterson died in July 2002 after suffering a stroke. Her NET treatment, still awaiting FDA approval, was, at least until recently, offered at a detox clinic in Tijuana, Mexico, and a pilot program was recently under way in Glasgow, Scotland.

Patterson's patients to move around freely, and even sleep, during their treatment. The electrical current, less than 2 milli-amps, was provided by a portable battery-operated box which enabled the physician to adjust the frequency and wave settings of the stimulus received by the patient depending on withdrawal symptoms and the type of chemical dependency being addressed. The discomfort experienced during treatment was minimal, Dr. Patterson wrote: "...the patient can wear the electrodes quite comfortably on a continual basis for as long as the treatment period lasts, typically five to ten days."

At the time of Pete's overdose, Meg and George Patterson were living in Corona del Mar, just south of Los Angeles. Meg was continuing her N.E.T. research in the hope of obtaining U.S. Food and Drug Administration approval, and was not operating a detox/rehab clinic at the time. She dispatched her clinician son, Lorne, to accompany Pete during his flight to the U.S. "With Bill Curbishley's approval," Patterson wrote in her 1994 autobiography, *Dr. Meg*, "I rented a small flat near us for Pete and Lorne, so Lorne could supervise the treatment day and night – a very demanding task, with no one to relieve him, but I knew that Pete and Lorne got on well together."[190] An American doctor was also enlisted to supervise Pete's treatment, in accordance with government regulations.

George and Meg brought an N.E.T. stimulator with them when they drove to Los Angeles airport to pick up Pete and Lorne, anticipating Pete to be in steep withdrawal. "...I could see from his agitated appearance that he was desperately ill and craving as he came out of the customs area, so I hooked him up to the machine right away," Dr. Patterson wrote in 1994. "I was horrified to discover that he was also hooked on Ativan, a tranquilizer which could well cause convulsions when it was stopped. But it was late at night and not possible to change arrangements. We had two hours' drive to the flat and before we reached there he had demonstrably calmed down."

Pete's memories of detox and rehab were documented in detail in an interview with *Omni*'s Kathleen McAuliffe in late 1982. "The first frequencies they gave me were low ones for heroin," he told McAuliffe. "I think it was kept on that setting for about eight hours." Townshend's recollection of the feelings he experienced during N.E.T. provides some interesting details:

> ...I just got this sense of a natural energy flowing into my body. It was as if all sorts of dormant feelings were being rekindled. The inner joy of recovery, and becoming independent from drugs, it produced this tremendous feeling of rejuvenation. By the second day, in fact, I knew I was on

---

[190] Pete and Lorne met in 1972 when Pete visited Eric Clapton at Meg Patterson's home while Clapton was undergoing his own heroin detox.

> the home stretch. And on the third day I started to look and feel human again. I started to read newspapers and to write about the way I felt. I remember writing things like, "I want to go out for a walk. I don't believe it." I could really feel my passion for life returning.
>
> Another thing was that I'd had traces of returning sexuality...for about a month, maybe two months, before being treated I'd felt no sexual feelings whatsoever, so the treatment definitely had a rekindling effect.
>
> ...But then on the fourth day, I woke up with this aggressive, angry attitude toward life. No, arrogant is perhaps a better word. I believed that I could take on the world. Later on, though – on the fifth day, I believe – I started to get depressed. Meg would then turn the machine up to a high frequency for an hour or so to stimulate the cocaine-type receptors in the brain. And if it was left on too long at this setting, I would start babbling away and everything in the room would start to go *wooooooo*. The intensification of color and sound, often in a very pretty way, was just like acid. But there was no confusion of sense channels – that didn't happen. I really felt up until the next day, when I woke up nauseous and achy. A lot of the withdrawal symptoms had actually returned in their own shape.

Pete was reminded of the severity of 'cold turkey' withdrawal on the second day of his treatment when the 9-volt battery in his electrical stimulator went dead. "We were totally unaware of this [the dead battery] until it became clear that I was going into steep withdrawals," he recalled.

> I got the full belt of the symptoms back – the panic, the nose-running, and fantastic cramps, particularly in my arms and legs. When they got the machine working again, I got only some of the symptoms – and they were less severe. I got a runny nose and I did have muscle cramps. I had a certain amount of difficulty sleeping, but it wasn't too bad, really. I felt fairly warm. But most important of all, I got back the ability to act.
>
> Before, when I tried to stop using heroin unaided, I not only suffered severe withdrawal but was completely unable to get out of bed, even to carry out the most minute task. If the phone rang next to my bed, it might take me ten hours to pick up the receiver. I'd be so far gone I hardly knew what I was doing. The major difference with Meg's

treatment is that you immediately get back the ability to act. I didn't suffer from that horrible kind of paralysis.

Townshend wore Dr. Patterson's 'black box' day and night for the first seven days of treatment, and then wore it only during the day for the last three days, able to obtain restful sleep unaided by this point. This is a striking difference between N.E.T. and other forms of detoxification: Sleep during heroin detox is normally virtually unattainable due to extreme restlessness and cramps. What little sleep is experienced is usually marred with severe nightmares.

After 10 days of N.E.T., detoxification completed and his mood stabilized, Townshend's black box was removed, resulting in "very, very minor withdrawals", and he entered the rehabilitation phase of treatment, undergoing three weeks of psychotherapy with Dr. Patterson, stressing Pete's emotional and spiritual redevelopment. "When you first start to recover you feel superhuman," Pete recalled.

> You get swept away by the euphoria of the natural high and the feeling of being able to handle any crisis... The feeling of *I'm going to get this lot behind me*. But this is where I think Meg is so clever. It seems she understood that, and in the month I stayed with her she helped me to sublimate that and balance it – in other words, not to overreact, and thus swing the pendulum too far in the other direction. She constantly stressed the spiritual rebuilding I had to do, which I'm still dealing with: the importance of getting closer to my children again, and if it was possible – and at the time it didn't look like too hot a situation – to re-establish my relationship with my wife...

By the third week of his treatment, Pete's appearance had improved remarkably. "...people who had seen me taking brisk walks would come up to me on the street and say, "That's California for you. When you first arrived you looked like a corpse. We gave you half an hour to live. And now look at you. All you needed was a few days in California..."

"Pete made a remarkable recovery considering how far gone he had been, both in London and when he arrived in Los Angeles," Dr. Patterson recalled in *Dr. Meg*. "Again, it was not enough simply to detoxify from his drugs of addiction, for his return to drugs had been caused by a variety of problems which had to be sorted out to effect a real cure. Some of these were begun while he was in Los Angeles, such as the agreement of his wife to help him by trying to make their broken marriage work again, and the sorting out of his complex business affairs."

"In retrospect, I realize that the treatment is an education in itself," Pete said.

>NET reeducates the brain to produce its own drugs and in the process you learn something about your human potential. You come to realize that somewhere within you is the power to deal with crises, tensions and frustrations. So the treatment reaffirms one's faith in the self-healing process.

On the last day of his rehab program, Pete and a friend were walking along Laguna Beach, just south of Corona Del Mar where he was staying, when they came upon a medical bottle which had washed ashore. "I said… 'That bottle is full of cocaine,'" Pete recalled in a 1989 radio interview. "…I said, 'I just know that the devil is here now.'" The pair examined the bottle, and Pete's friend tasted it. Sure enough, it was cocaine, probably thrown from an inbound boat whose crew was spooked by an approaching customs craft. "I said, 'Give it back to me,'" Pete continued, "and I just threw it into the sea, and he went, 'NOOOOOOO PETE!'"

The final short story in Pete's 1985 book *Horse's Neck*, retells the emotions Pete felt on this final day of rehab. Pete considered *Laguna, Valentine's Day, 1982* the "most optimistic" story of the collection, and that it served "to kind of explain what I was going through."

>…I sit in a small armchair upholstered in an understated flower pattern and contemplate the view. Before me stretches a vast, shining beach covered with dry sand. There is no wind. In the distance I can see the edge of an ocean that stretches away to a horizon that seems unusually high and straight. I am on a big planet.
>
>There is silence. I don't hear the tinkling celestial sounds I used to hear in the gardens through the door behind me. This is not what I thought Paradise would look like. No one emerges through the other, distant doorways I can see. Strange. All of us believed we were trapped inside that tormenting place of change and strain. Yet the doors are open. I didn't need a key. I just walked through.
>
>What now? In the distance I can see two tiny figures on horses by the water's edge. They are throwing up spray as they ride towards me. I will go and meet them.
>
>…The riders in the distance are much closer now, and I can see that they have a mount for me on a rein. It is a white horse.

The riders have pulled up a good hundred yards off. They wave, but I can't see who they are. A young couple, wearing check shirts and riding boots. They look like a handsome pair. The man releases the white horse and slaps it and it starts to walk towards me. Then the couple turn their steeds and ride back to the surf; they appear to ride straight into the sea, churning up the water. Eventually, they are submerged and, as the white horse reaches me, the last widening ripple they have created shimmers to a stop.

Pete, apparently demonstrating the final step in conquering his demons, penetrates and thus becomes one with what is often a symbol of purity and beauty throughout *Horse's Neck*, the horse[191].

...When my orgasm comes, it is without sensation. I am no longer an animal...At last I can ride. I am in perfect control. I urge the horse into a gallop and the wind cools my face. I am riding towards the water's edge.[192]

After leaving California, Townshend began weekly psychotherapy in Britain in a continuation of his rehab program. "I know that the machine didn't do it. I know I did it," he said in 1983. "What the machine did was train my body to do it. I understand that there were no drugs or anything else from the outside except stimulus. So I did it. I got off heroin, and Ativan and cocaine and everything else. And that's made me complete."

Upon returning from the states Pete moved back in with his family and set about rebuilding the marriage he had slowly been demolishing over the past two years. "Karen said I could stay in the family house in the basement," Pete told Dennis Wholey in 1984. "I stayed there for a couple of weeks and eventually we got close enough together to be able to rebuild the family atmosphere very quickly."

"It was hard for Karen," he continued, "but the kids were able to erase the problems completely. I just hope that, over a period of years, it hasn't left them with any scars. But, certainly, as far as my being there, they made me know it was great "to have you back, Dad." They made a big fuss over me and made it clear that they really enjoyed having me around. The terrible, terrible nightmare turned back into normality."

Pete obviously deeply regretted the toll his drug addiction had taken on his family, especially his children. "...I just wish the consequences

---

[191] Delia DeLeon wrote that "Baba was known as the "White Horse" or "Kali" Avatar by His Hindu followers."

[192] "Somebody said to me when they finished reading this book, 'You know, people are going to think you really fucked the horse!'", Pete recalled in 1989 with a laugh.

hadn't been so fucking hard for the third parties involved," he told *Musician* in 1989.

> ...There are advantages and disadvantages to the life I've led. The kids have financial security but there was a time when they suffered a certain amount of fear and deprivation as a direct result of my behavior. We try to talk about it regularly. Awful, awful thing to contemplate. You don't want to hurt anyone in your life but when you do...At least my old lady knew I was in a rock'n'roll band when we got married. She knew I was an asshole. It's not like that with kids. They're born and they're subjected to all this shit.

Along with regaining the trust of his children, Pete and Karen managed to rekindle their relationship. "...really, apart from a few ups and downs, we never suffered any major problems until the last couple of years," Pete commented in April.

> And we both feel that one of the problems was that I did overcommit when I took on a solo career. It was a great strain. And living in the same house and everything, we literally became estranged – we were like strangers. And it was only when I actually became so ill that I couldn't work that we had the time to sit down and talk. And then we stopped being strangers and we became friends and lovers again, and life is back to the way it was. Our marriage was made in heaven, there's no question about it. But you've got to work at marriage, and it's a different kind of work from what you do normally, and it's got a different end product. I'm sure this stuff is familiar as hell to everybody else, but it's all new to me.
> Anyway, once I stopped taking everything – not just drinking, but doing *anything* at all – and started to be careful about my diet and got into a routine of regular exercise, the transformation was instant. Now I feel superhuman. Also, I had managed, with a lot of assistance from my wife, to reestablish myself in the family, and that's great for me. I mean, it's something I desperately missed.

Another facet of his personal life which sorely needed attention was Pete's relationship with Meher Baba. He duly reaffirmed his faith. "It's very hard to talk about," Pete told *Musician* in September 1982, "because...it's very easy to look like you have some kind of phony humility."

But Meher Baba's teachings on the subject were expressly clear, and my conviction for Meher Baba as the pinnacle and focus of spiritual wisdom in the West is paramount in my life. His statement is that whatever you do, however small or big you feel yourself to be, you're always a channel and a servant of God. Even if you're a *rat*, you've got the hotline to God. Even rats are servants of God whether they know it or not...I'm *embarrassed* to be in God's presence – not afraid. Once I would've been ashamed, but not now.

His personal life thus aligned, Pete resumed work on his solo album shortly after his return from California. Ironically, due to problems obtaining studio time at either of his own recording venues, Pete had resorted to other locations to put his demos on tape. In addition to using the small studio in his "new family home", Pete recorded a small number of demos on a "120 foot long Dutch canal barge on the Thames," he recalled in 1987. Sessions for the album, which became *All The Best Cowboys Have Chinese Eyes*, began in February at Pete's Eel Pie studios with other work being completed at A.I.R. and Wessex studios in London, the same venues used for *Empty Glass*. Also back from the last album were producer Chris Thomas, drummers Mark Brzezicki and Simon Phillips, bassist Tony Butler, and harmonica player Peter Hope-Evans. Chris Stainton, who played piano on several *Quadrophenia* tracks, assumed keyboard duties, along with Pete's sister-in-law, Virginia Astley.

The album ended up taking longer than expected due to Pete's having rewritten a substantial amount of material after the initial demos had been made the previous year. "Originally, I did a series of experiments, basically just rhythm tracks with poetry over the top," Pete told *Rolling Stone*'s Kurt Loder in 1982.

When I took the first tracks to New York and played them for the record company, you would have paid money to have seen their faces! They said, 'Leave it to the avant-garde.' Bowie was with me at the time and he said I should just go ahead and do it, what do the record companies know, anyway. But I came back and rewrote half the album. 'Cos there's little point in sitting and writing material, and getting obsessed with whatever you choose to get obsessed with, and then have nobody to listen.

The new solo album found Pete returning his focus to the principles he considered of the utmost importance in his life. "...when I started *Empty Glass*...I was hoping," he said in 1982.

> I was hoping that I was going to pursue two careers at once, not realizing that they're irrevocably knotted together. I hadn't quite realized how much what I did as an individual would affect the Who, and vice versa. The new album was a big difference, in the approach to it and with the ruthlessness with which I had to deal with the Who, with everything around me, in order to get it made. It's actually a recognition of...a commitment to a set of principles which I've debated over the last ten years: the importance of a family, the importance of my role with my peers and the band, the importance of my freedom of self-expression, and lastly but not at all least, the importance of becoming actively immersed again, for only the second time in my life (and the last time was when I was seventeen) in politics. I really do feel that I can't sit and watch any longer.

Pete's political activism, arguably largely imperceptible thus far into his career, was now aimed at the apathetic views of the public. "I get worried about people, who right now more than ever, believe they are impotent, that they are powerless, that the circumstances of hierarchical control, of apparent control of our planet, are irrevocably destined to fail," he told *Musician*. "I think that is a mistake, because if the individual feels he can't change anything, then what is the point of being alive? ...You can be a RAT – that's what my new album is about – can be a *rat* and still change the world."

Indeed, when *Spin*'s Kristine McKenna asked Pete to define sin, he said:

> Waiting for things to get better. Saying "Look to the future, things will get better." That's as much a sin as saying things will be awful in the future because the future doesn't count. What counts is now, and this moment does shape the future. If you look out at the city you live in and see that it's full of garbage you should whistle a happy tune like a character in a Disney cartoon and start collecting the garbage. To sit at your window and say that someday someone will come and clear up all the garbage is bullshit. And a sin.

Pete's attitude was reflected in his opinion of contemporary music of the early 1980's. "…I suppose what's lacking is the…the depth," he told *Musician* in 1982.

> And the commitment to the depth you put in. You know, if you put in too much, people become almost embarrassed! I don't know how it is over in the States, but over here if you try to get in a conversation about arms buildup or nuclear weapons, people turn away and order another pint of Guinness, and they want to talk about bloody Arsenal! They're gonna be dead tomorrow if they don't start thinking about it…but they're *embarrassed*; "It's annoying – oh, don't talk about *that*! We're impotent, we're neuter." Now *that* is what's happened to rock'n'roll. People have actually started to say, "What's the point of trying to make a really great record, when we know that just a well-constructed, well-produced piece of crap is gonna sell six million copies, and everybody's gonna think we're great." And to be brutal for a second, I think one of the dangers of middle age in rock'n'roll is that it's very easy to take the easy way out. You have to be very angry, in a sense, to stay honest.

Of course, the argument can be made that Townshend has made a career of political activism through his lyrics. Indeed, as he told *Spin* in 1986, Pete feels that this is part of the artist's responsibility:

> …Always to challenge, but first he must gain the public's ear and heart by making an attractive offering. Entertaining first, challenging and inviting debate later…I want to please people, then possibly slip them something that I feel I've been able to make some kind of acute judgment about.

In addition to activism, through *Chinese Eyes*, Pete reflected on his recent battle with substance abuse. The song *Exquisitely Bored*, with its lines (sung by Pete in a distinctly 'Mark Knopfler' voice) *exquisitely bored in California/we take our troubles to the crest* and its reference to *walking in Laguna* seems to be a reference to Pete's recent drug detox and rehab. "…this is the first record I've ever made during which I felt that there was no hope whatsoever to try to repair my lost love for my wife and family or to repair the damage I felt I'd unwittingly laid on my friends and my relationship with the other guys in the band, The Who," he said in 1982. "And the songs, as a result, each a reflection of an aspect of what it's like to feel alone, I think, and yet still be yearning for lost emotions and power." Naturally, due to the solemn nature of many of the songs included on *Chinese Eyes*, it struck many as a particularly sad album. "Unfortunately, a lot of unhappiness comes through," Pete told *Rolling Stone* in 1982. "But there's also a great feeling that I seem determined to win, somehow. You can feel it in a lot of the songs, there's a determination to overcome. And I managed to do it."

While The Who's previous studio effort was entitled *Face Dances*, the song which provided the album's title didn't make the cut and was included on *Chinese Eyes* as *Face Dances Part Two*. The song, Pete said in 1982, "...is the anthem of the soul in solitary confinement...It's like feeling in jail."[193]

> And the face that I sing about is my own, I wrote the words while I was looking in a mirror. The cause of the loneliness is partly obvious, I've become incredibly confused over the years with The Who. I think anybody that's read interviews I've done over the years and seen the work of the band knows the kind of confusion and perhaps it's a kind of self-inflicted torment. I know a lot of people reckon I couldn't live without it. A lot of the values I'd held to be important in the early part of the band's career and in the early seventies – spiritually and morally and creatively – got let down somehow, compromised. I think because I wanted an easier, happier life, I've always found it difficult to say no and I think that applies also to "no" when somebody asks you for a favor and also "no" when somebody is trying to [enter] into your life in someway. And I'd spread myself really thin in this pursuit of the good life and my wife and I lost touch, even living in the same house, and the drinking habits became downright selfish. And the business pursuits I'd got involved in outside of music distracted me from my creative work. And almost two-thirds of the way through this record I came to my senses, thank God, and with a lot of help from friends I got back to my work and my family and my wife and I began again. And lonely breakfasts aren't part of my routine anymore and neither is brandy in the coffee or chain saw hangovers, thank God. It's incredible to think that music began so simply for me when I was a kid in Acton and I had no idea how much it would challenge me when I got older.

---

[193] Pete would explore this theme further in his 1983 *Siege* project, and again in 1985 with *White City*.

And how much the simple thing I call rock and roll could
give and how much it could take – try to take.

The notion of loneliness is reflected in the 'traditional' *North Country Girl*, while the reference to being a kid in Acton was further explored with the song *Stardom in Acton* as Pete contemplated the promise of stardom when he "wriggled to the top" as a youngster.

Another leftover from the *Face Dances* sessions, *Somebody Saved Me*, was also included. It struck many as Pete's eulogy to Kit Lambert, or perhaps even a more veiled reference to Meher Baba:

I lived hippie jokes getting stoned insane
Till the rain looked just like snow
But there was a soul in whom I could depend
He worked himself crazy while I laid in bed
I never leaned on a person like I leaned right then
And when I finally woke up clean
My friend was dead – stone dead

The album's opener, *Stop Hurting People*, was, Pete explained in 1982, a prayer for him to be reunited with Karen. "I wrote it last summer. I suddenly broke down and scribbled it out on a piece of paper, and didn't realize until later quite to what an extent it was a prayer." The song was also a strident declaration of the power of love (*love conquers poses, love smashes stances, love crushes angles into black*), and a statement of Pete's determination to revive his marriage: *A love born once must soon be born again*. The song also featured the lines:

I always wanted to be matched with her, yet her beauty was so different to mine
My beauty needs an understanding and a knowledge of what I am
Hers is enough, earned through eons, for that is what true beauty is – time's gift to perfect humility
May I be matched with you again – I know the match is bad
God help me, may I be matched with you again
Without your match there is no flame

The classic *The Sea Refuses No River*, like the song *Empty Glass* from the previous solo effort, was inspired by eastern literature. "I think somebody described *The Sea Refuses No River* as a suicide note," Pete said in 1996.

In actual fact, what it is is a song of acceptance. This is another one of those songs that grew out of my interest, not just in Meher Baba, but also in the poets that Meher Baba enjoyed when he was a young man in his thirties. His interest in this poetry led me to go and look at it...I was very struck by the use of wine as an analogy for God's love, and therefore by association that the tavern is the heart. The tavern is the place where you receive God's wine, and what you have to do is you have to hold up an empty cup – which is where I got the title of my first album – in order to receive. Anyway, this song is about all of the different qualities of love, and I remember once Meher Baba freely interpreting a poem about the fact that if God's love is wine, then human love is like water, and lust is like the stuff that runs into the sewer, but that in the end it all combines in this huge ocean which is the infinite presence of God, and therefore it's all subsumed and mixed and one. And that's what the song is about.

All The Best Cowboys Have Chinese Eyes, like *Quadrophenia*, was rife with watery metaphors. The Thames river, which flowed directly behind Pete's house in Twickenham and his country home in Berkshire, was especially influential. "It always reminds me of a soul irrevocably plodding on towards God," Pete said of the Thames in 1982.

It's full of food for fish and it provides London with most of its water and yet it's also treated like a rubbish dump...people chuck their cars in and their beer cans, their used contraceptives and everything else. And many rivers still get used as sewers and yet they all get to the sea in the end. And so the analogy with the human soul always appeals to me, the fact that it doesn't matter how clean or dirty you are, you get there in the end. It reminds me constantly, the river, of immortality and of my goal and in a strange way – however I feel – it reminds me of my permanence.

A 1932 Meher Baba quote reflects a similar sentiment:

Baba is like the sun... anyone whose heart is pure can receive the rays. Make the heart pure by thinking of the Master, and then loving Him.
Baba is like the sea, which receives weak or strong, diseased or healty, dotard, sinner or saint.
Baba is like an Infinite Ocean, and in order to realize Him the ego must be annihilated altogether.

The beautiful *Prelude*, which Pete wrote with his old friend Andy Newman, "...is a simple prayer for change in a world that from my viewpoint had gone crazily wrong," Townshend said. In *Communication*, Pete said in 1982, "...I deliberately take the word communication and break it up into bits[194]. I mean I literally hurl the letters of the word at the listener. And then I show a literal example of how not to communicate, which is with flowery, meaningless prose. You know, "briolette tears drip from frozen masks, the back of the whale cracks through the ice floe," blahblahblahblahblah—who needs it?"

Uniforms (Corp d'Esprit) was "...obviously double-edged," Pete told *Musician* in 1982, "because it recognizes that fact [that uniforms can lead to unity in some cases, but herd consciousness in others]. But it also recognizes the fact that there are behavioral uniforms as well."

The final song on *Chinese Eyes*, and another examination of solitude, was *Slit Skirts*. "...*Slit Skirts*...was written at the absolute depths for me," Pete said in 1985. "...I was just barely alive when I wrote that...and I think you can feel when you hear it." He further commented on the song in 1996:

> *Slit Skirts* is about getting to that place in middle age where you really feel that life is never going to be the same – you're never going to fall in love again, it's never going to be quite like it was – and it's a song about getting drunk, about being maudlin and sentimental, and looking back, and, as always, the irony of the intention was lost on most people. I got very, very upset when people said, "This sounds like a song that Pete Townshend wrote when he was getting drunk," (laughs) and I'd very carefully stayed sober in order to write it, so that I could get drunk to listen to it. It evokes that feeling that sometimes I have at my age, which is that one minute I'm sitting there looking at some old crap on the TV thinking, "If I was just ten years younger, I'd probably be in a night club right now," and suddenly you get to the end of the song, and you go from that reflective pseudo-tragic piano motif to the "Slit skirts, slit skirts, we're rocking out now – more champagne!" The futility of it, the bathos of it, and it's not unlike how I was living when I was working on the record.

---

[194] "Just as years ago, when I used to smash guitars because I just couldn't play them the way I wanted to," Pete told *Musician* in 1982, "...now I smash words." During the same interview, he also said that *The Sea Refuses No River* and *Slit Skirts* were demonstrations of Bruce Springsteen's writing form and that the latter song was an attempt "to break that form down, to smash at it."

Body Language, a *Chinese Eyes* reject, eventually surfaced on *Scoop*. "...this song impressed neither record company or producer," Pete wrote in 1983. "...This attempt to fuse streamed poetry with straight lyrics was probably as successful as the other examples on *Chinese Eyes*, and it is still something I enjoy doing. A lot of people think it's 'pretentious.' Yeah, it is isn't it, like lots of people."

Recording of *All The Best Cowboys Have Chinese Eyes* was completed in April. The album's curious title drew questions from the press regarding its meaning. The liner notes did little to explain:

> They were being attacked from all sides, everything seemed hopeless. There seemed to be no language in which they could communicate to their adversaries, to beseech them for mercy. At a crucial moment a natural leader emerged. His horse was dry and cool when all others were frothing and bleeding, his leather clothes dusty and worn. His face was keen and firm, lightly lined and weather beaten. The most remarkable thing about him was his eyes; half shut against the wind blown dust and the noise of guns.

The title *All The Best Cowboys Have Chinese Eyes* was, Pete told Kurt Loder in mid-1982, "...about the fact that you can't hide what you're really like."

> I just had this image of the average American hero- somebody like a Clint Eastwood or a John Wayne. Somebody with eyes like slits, who was basically capable of anything – you know, any kind of murderous act or whatever to get what was required – to get, let's say, his people to safety. And yet, to those people he's saving, he's a great hero, a knight in shining armor – forget the fact that he cut off fifty people's heads to get them home safely. Then I thought about the Russians and the Chinese and the Arab communities and the South Americans; you've got these different ethnic groups, and each has this central image of every other political or national faction as being, in some way, the evil ones. And I've taken this a little bit further – because I spent so much of my time in society, high society, last year – to comment on stardom and power and drug use and decadence, and how there's a strange parallel, in a way, between the misuse of power and responsibility by people who are heroes. If you're really a good person, you can't hide by acting bad; and if you're a

bad person, you can't hide it by acting good. Also – more to the point, really – that there's no outward, identifiable evil, you know? People spend most of their time looking for evil and identifying evil outside themselves. But the potential for evil is inside you.

Pete's focus was on personal responsibility. "This is something that I tried very, very hard to get across on *Chinese Eyes*: not to point a finger and say *they're* the evil ones," he told *Musician* in September, 1982.

It's *us*. We're the ones who are guilty – as a group, and as a race, for allowing things to get out of hand.
I do believe that everybody on the planet, whether they like it or not, is a spiritual aspirant, and that the most valuable demonstration of how he deals with his or her problems can be seen in how he handles the commitments he makes to the most important human beings in his life, whether it's his wife, his offspring, his workmates or whatever. And that includes how the individual deals with his own contradiction and problems…his conscience. That's the place to start.

All The Best Cowboys Have Chinese Eyes was released in May 1982 to mixed reviews. The album was "…a completely listenable and often invigorating set of songs which get his ideas across as clearly as any record he's ever made," Dave Marsh wrote in *The Record*.

What's certain is that Townshend is now making a kind of music that doesn't have much to do with the Who – it still rocks, but it's more devoted to studio intricacy than interplay among band members. It's also certain that this music is a hell of a lot more interesting, even in its use of the same structures and elements, than the tired stuff with which the Who have toyed lately. If you are looking for an explanation of the catastrophe the Who (on record) has become, it's not in any waning of Townshend's abilities.

Referring to lines such as *Love crushes angles into black* and *For that's what true beauty is – time's gift to perfect humility* (from *Stop Hurting People*), and *Just like the stub of that long cigarette full of hash/I'm the first to get booked* (from *Stardom in Acton*), Kurt Loder commented that "This sort of sophomoric spew disfigures most of the album's eleven tracks, which is a shame."

> Because in some ways, *Chinese Eyes* is Townshend's most accomplished and admirable solo LP...Rock'n'roll has less need of gratuitous high-culture flourishes than perhaps any other artistic form – a lesson one might have thought we'd all learned back in the bad old art-rock days. Townshend is a gifted rocker, and that should be enough. That he apparently yearns for some higher form of quasi-literary respectability is sad, not simply because he's so unsuited for it, but because his particular form of pop genius is direct observation.

When Pete returned his eye to Who activities following his return from California, he found that the band had been rehearsing without him, with Roger Daltrey and Andy Fairweather-Low[195] assuming guitar duties in Pete's absence. Pete was armed with "just two songs when I went down to the studio," he told *The Record*'s Jonathan Gross in December, 1982. "The band was working, they were active, they were writing," he recalled, noting that he got the impression that further Who activity would occur with or without his involvement.

> ...If I had said right then and there, 'Listen chaps, I don't feel like making the record', they looked as if they would have gone on and done something without me. And they weren't making any demonstrations to me, either. They were just doing it because they wanted to do it. It was really strange. I thought, 'I'd really like to play with those guys.'

Eager to put the lackluster *Face Dances* behind them, The Who began working in earnest on their next studio album within weeks of the release of Pete's *Chinese Eyes* effort. But, with two solo albums behind him, Pete's outlook for The Who had changed considerably. "...I don't see the Who going on for very much longer," he told *Rolling Stone* at the time.

> I think that with this next album, and with the next protracted period of work we do, we're really gonna throw ourselves into it 100 percent. And then we're gonna stop. I'm pretty sure of that. It's not because we want to, but because we've come to the point where we don't really want to go through all these periods when the public and our fans and the record company and even we don't know

---

[195] Fairweather-Low, who had contributed backing vocals on the *Who Are You* album, received rhythm guitar credit on one track, *It's Your Turn*, on *It's Hard*.

what the fuck's gonna happen next. The tension is just too much. And this period when we work on the band, I'm gonna really think about very little else. I'm worried about it, because I've become accustomed to doing lots of other things. And I like the richness of what I do in other areas. That's become almost as important to me as being in a band. And I think when you get to that point, you have to think very seriously about what it is you're doing it for. Because it's always been too important for us to do just because we enjoy one another's company. And I think basically one of the reasons we're working together at the moment is that we enjoy one another's company. It's as simple as that.

Rather than approaching the band with a collection of demos for the upcoming album, Pete asked for input. "I sat round with everybody and I asked them: What do you want to fucking sing about? Tell me, and I'll write the songs," he told *NME*'s Paul Du Noyer.

It's a piece of piss! I've been writing songs for 20 years. D'you wanna sing about race riots? D'you wanna sing about the nuclear bomb? D'you wanna sing about soya bean diets? Tell me!

...Well, after establishing, quite quickly, that there was very little common ground, we did find that we all cared very deeply about the planet, the people on it, about the threat to our children from nuclear war, of the increasing instability of our own country's politics. There's the fact that we've actually infiltrated the establishment, in a way that younger bands haven't been able to do. It's taken us a long time to do, but now we can see that even the establishment is impotent, it's not just us, and we're really in a danger zone, and not to cry *panic*; panic! But it was something we need to express. Consequently, a lot of material we're doing at the moment is quite anguished.

The result of the band's meeting gave them a sense of purpose, perhaps one that was missing on their previous album. "...it really did unify us a lot," Pete said in 1982, "it made us feel like human beings, part of society, living on a planet, not as isolated superstars who were worried about advancing middle age, money problems, whether they could buy another radiator cap for their Rolls Royces."

Pete's assertion that he was going to focus all of his efforts on the next Who album, combined with the fact that Glyn Johns was back on board as producer, created high expectations in the music world, especially following the lackluster *Face Dances* (which, incidentally, as previously mentioned, also fell victim to similarly high expectations after some enthusiastic comments by Bob Seger and Bill Szymczyk were reported in the press). Pete further fueled the hype in an interview with *Musician* in September, 1982, asserting that *It's Hard* "...is probably the most dangerous one the Who have ever made." He also referred to *I've Known No War*, described by Chris Charlesworth as "melodically uninteresting," and by John Atkins as "marred by a tendency toward the pompous," as "...the key song on the next album. We just started with the word "war" and went from there. It's possibly one of the best Who tracks we've ever done, I believe. It's very archetypal, very 60s issue, but it's also bloody great." Further false hopes were created with the statements, "The new Who songs are violently aggressive, the most aggressive stuff we've ever come up with," and "...from our point of view it's a tremendous record."

Recording sessions for *It's Hard* began in June, 1982, at Turn-Up Down studios, located at Glyn Johns' home in Surrey. Rehearsals had taken place the previous month, with guitarist Andy Fairweather-Low and keyboardist Tim Gorman (from the Glyn Johns produced band Lazy Racer) enlisted in limited roles to augment the band's sound. John Bundrick was out of the band at the time, let go when his alcohol abuse had begun to adversely affect his behavior. Pete and recently sober Kenney Jones were keen to maintain their on-the-wagon status.

During the recording of *It's Your Turn*, *Dangerous*, and *One At A Time*, all John Entwistle compositions, Pete's hearing concerns surfaced again. "The only time I [hurt my ears] recently was on a couple of John's songs, because it was what he wanted," Pete told *Musician* in 1982, "and I came out of those two sessions with my ears ringing for a week. And I thought, "Well, there's another db lost, you know." I'm just very anxious to preserve my hearing."

It's Hard kicked off with *Athena*, the song Pete had written following his embarrassing episode with Nic Roeg's girlfriend in 1981. *Cooks County* was written after Pete had seen a documentary about Cook County hospital in Chicago, a free hospital which was in dire financial straits and had applied for government grants to stay open. "The grants were refused so the hospital was going to close," Pete said.

> It was in a ghetto and it was mainly black people and it was mainly drug abuse and everything else, ghetto-influenced problems, which this hospital dealt with. Of course a lot of these people, you get blasted by a shotgun in a Chicago street and you get picked up by an ambulance, you get taken to hospital and unless you've got a Medicare card or insurance or something you get shoved straight out

again. I just felt so moved by this that I just felt in a sense that I had to scribble out a few lines about it and that's how it came out. I just went in with the poem I'd written 'people are suffering...' and we turned it into this particular track.

Eminence Front, according to John Atkins, was "...undoubtedly the highlight of the whole album...The song is a sharp observation on the cracks that are apparent in the façade of Western affluence, with specific reference to the burgeoning "cocaine-and-caviar" culture of the 1980s."

One Life's Enough, written for Karen, was perhaps the most un-Who like song ever to appear on a Who album. "Where's the guitar?," Chris Charlesworth complained in his 1995 *Complete Guide to the Music of The Who*. He described *Why Did I Fall For That* as "uninspired", and *A Man Is A Man* as "another slight, forgettable ballad..." Pete wrote *Why Did I Fall For That* to address the apathetic attitude of society during the cold war. "...we've just sat back under the nuclear umbrella and lived our lives, taken our drugs, listened to our blues," he said at the time. "I don't want to sound like fucking Pravda or anything, but we have been a pretty impotent, unthinking [generation]."

It's Hard's final song, *Cry If You Want*, described by an obviously disappointed Chris Charlesworth in 1995 as "unmelodious" and "just as forgettable as so many other songs on this weak, insipid album", was a Daltrey favorite. The song featured one of the few examples of *It's Hard*'s promised aggression, this time in the form of a frenzied series of slashing Townshendian power chords as the song faded out.

The cover of *It's Hard* depicted the band members standing in front of a child playing a 'Space Duel' arcade game, perhaps an updated reference to *Tommy*. "I had very little to do with the cover and the title," Pete said, commenting on what was obviously a sore subject. "One of the problems with the band is that we very, very rarely agree on policy. So where we should have had a terrific album cover, we have a rather spineless cover because nobody works hard enough for it. Nobody fights."

It's Hard was released in September 1982, reaching number 11 in the British charts and climbing as high as number 8 in the U.S. The album achieved the dubious distinction of being the first Who album since *The Who Sell Out* not to reach the U.K.'s top 10. "*It's Hard* should never have been released," Roger said later.

> I had huge rows with Pete... when the album was finished and I heard it I said, 'Pete, this is just a complete piece of shit and it should never come out!' It came out because as usual we were being manipulated at that time by other things. The record company wanted a record out and they wanted us to do a tour. What I said to Pete was, 'Pete,

if we'd tried to get any of these songs on to *Face Dances*, or any of the albums that we've done since our first fucking album, we would not allow these songs to be on an album! Why are we releasing them? Why? Let's just say that was an experience to pull the band back together. Now let's go and make an album.' He said, 'Too late. It's good enough...'

"*It's Hard* was a mistake," Pete told *Mojo* in 2004. "I was fresh out of rehab and went straight into the band who were already recording without me. They didn't understand the depth of my problem."

The album received a puzzlingly warm reception from *Rolling Stone*'s Parke Puterbaugh, who called it "...their most vital and coherent album since *Who's Next*," and "...a strong affirmation of this band's ability to reach millions with powerful rock & roll and trenchant, galvanizing politics." Puterbaugh went on to praise *I've Known No War* as "a song that could become an anthem to our generation much the way *Won't Get Fooled Again* did a decade ago," and compared *Cry If You Want* to *I Can See For Miles*. *Sounds*' Gary Bushell was less enthusiastic: "The music on *It's Hard* is worse than the record's cheapo cover. Most of it sounds like the watered-down bits of other Who LPs. It's sort of like a footballer who's got old and fat and out of condition but keeps on kicking a ball about."

Following the *It's Hard* recording sessions, Pete was scheduled to produce The Pretenders' latest effort, but all plans were off upon 25 year-old guitarist James Honeyman-Scott's death from a drug overdose in June. Faced with some unexpected free time, Pete turned his attention to his brother Simon, also a musician.

"All of a sudden, Pete had a big chunk of time free," Simon recalled in 1996.

I was having very little success at the time. I was having a hard time getting noticed. I had a lot of material and a manager who believed in what I was doing. But, I was having a problem getting me, Simon Townshend, accepted. Whether I should have changed my name a long time ago or whatever, is irrelevant. I never have... [Pete] knew I was working intensely on some recordings and demos. He played them and said, "Listen, there are some hits here. Why don't we do some recording? I'll pay for it. If nobody wants to take a bite, I lose 2000 quid. If it works out, perhaps I'll make 2000 quid. Which he did, I might add, in production fees.

Thus, Pete produced The Simon Townshend Band's first album, *Sweet Sounds*.

A rare solo date (his first in fourteen months) took place on July 21 at London's Dominion Theatre[196], marking the first Prince's Trust Gala Benefit. Pete performed *Let My Love Open The Door* and *Amoreuse*, and sat at the piano for a rendition of *Slit Skirts* in addition to playing with the 'house band', which featured Robert Plant, Phil Collins, and Ultravox's Midge Ure. Other guests that evening included Jethro Tull and Madness.

He followed this busy period with a short vacation in Cornwall during which he indulged in a lifelong passion, sailing. Pete also found the time to record three demos, entitled *Cat Snatch*, *Ask Yourself*, and *Baroque Ippanese*, during his stay. By this point, Pete had a well-documented love affair with water, with its use as a metaphor in his lyrics, living close to the River Thames, and his love of the writing of Joseph Conrad as a few examples. His passion for sailing was a natural reflection of this love affair. "I've always loved the sea," Pete told Hugh Foley in a 1989 radio interview, "and I love – *really* love – boats…"

When *Rolling Stone*'s Chris Heath interviewed Pete in 2002, he noted, "…Throughout our conversation, his cell phone is propped up against the window next to us, and at just after five in the afternoon it rings. Each day at this time, he is automatically sent a weather report from Cornwall in southwest England, where his boat *Zephyr* is based. These days, sailing is his other grand passion."

"It is a bit strange, I suppose, but I think it comes straight from the river, and an affinity with the river and an affinity with water," Pete told Heath.

> I love boats. It's the only area of my life where I've actually felt competitive, when I'm racing. And the only sport I win at. I just think, it seems like sort of a nice, gentlemanly way to race, that whole thing that you can be racing intensely and yet only traveling at sort of half a mile an hour. There's something about that that I just love. I'm not a natural sailor. I was around on boats when I was about ten or twelve, and my father and I bought a boat together when I was about twenty, but I don't regard myself as a sort of natural, born-on-boats sort of sailor. But I do sail with people like that. I know if you want to win races what you do is you get a few of those guys around and you put one on the helm. But I understand the wind, I understand hydronautics, I understand a lot about what kind

---

[196] A week earlier, Pete attended the premier of *The Wall* at the Empire Theatre in Leicester Square along with other notables Bob Geldof, Sting, and three members of Pink Floyd.

of boats are likely to win and what aren't, I know about teamwork, I know about putting together a team. I just won my very first race in Antibedes this year with a new boat. We put it in the water, we raced it and we won.

When the question of touring arose following the completion of *It's Hard*, Pete was agreeable but his consent was conditional. "Yeah, I don't see any reason why we shouldn't do a certain amount of work," Pete said prior to recording the album. "But after that, I really think we've had enough. At least for now, we seem to have to know that we're making one last big effort. We have to feel that there is an *end* to it; otherwise, I don't think we could really go in the right mind."

"I think that review would help the Who greatly," Pete had told *Musician* just prior to recording *It's Hard*. "The Who have stopped and regrouped several times in their career, at one point for two whole years. And those times were vitally important for the band. So what we're talking about at the moment is a year of exploitation, but under our own control, of live performances of [*It's Hard*]. And then we're gonna stop. What happens then is an open book."

When asked by *Rolling Stone* if anything would be missing from his life if The Who broke up, Pete replied, "Yeah, I would say about a million dollars a year." Then, seriously:

> I think that, far from there being something missing, the very fact of not being involved in it anymore would allow us to take a different stance on what we've done – to enjoy it, to luxuriate in it, to celebrate it, to cherish it and to draw the best from it. Rather than always see the past as something that threatens our future – which is something that seems to be an irreversible feature of the band today. I don't know: I think the Who will break – not break up, but stop working – before the Stones do.

What became known as The Who's Farewell Tour thus began to take shape. Plans were made for the band to tour the U.S. in the fall, followed by an extensive tour of Britain and other venues in Europe in early 1983. Australia and Japan were penciled in for spring 1983, and, according to *Rolling Stone*'s Kurt Loder in November 1982, "Bill Curbishley, the group's enterprising manager, is already talking about the possibility of playing a quick cluster of dates sometime in 1984 and perhaps fulfilling the Who's longstanding plan to play Eastern Europe – maybe even doing *Tommy* at Moscow's opera house."

A newly sober Pete Townshend looked to the tour as a means of finally showing the world he'd survived the years of drug and alcohol abuse.

A 'dry' tour for The Who was certainly a first. "...I'm never gonna drink again," Pete told Loder.

> In a way, I'm quite looking forward to [the tour] as a test. I'm happy to have sorted out my family problems once and for all. I always felt and hoped that it was possible. I didn't want to be a rock casualty in any sense, because I've always felt that one more rock casualty is just another headline for a couple of weeks, and then everybody gets really...not only bored, but everybody feels *betrayed*. Because although rock casualties make good copy in the *NME Book of the Dead*, they don't make good copy in the lives of rock fans, who have a slightly higher emotional involvement in the musical form than it's just being, you know, like a circus, full of Berlinesque, decadent assholes who don't know how to spend their money, et cetera.

"I didn't want to end up just another rock statistic," he added in *Maximum R&B*. "My kids were still quite young. Up to that point, apart from smashing up a few guitars, there was nothing I'd done which they had to be publicly ashamed of, and suddenly there were lots of things, my alcoholism, people dying at concerts. I'd become a real rock'n'roll seedy figure. I didn't really want to go on in that direction. So I actually agreed to do that last tour really to close the book."

The Who's Farewell Tour began on Friday, September 10, 1982, just one week after the release of *It's Hard*, with two shows at Birmingham's National Exhibition Centre (the second show took place the following night). It had been over seventeen months since The Who's last live performance, and the consensus was that the band were back on top form. "...this elderly group delivered 24 songs in two hours with polish, panache and evident enjoyment," wrote *The Times*' Richard Williams of the Saturday night show.

> Only once or twice was there a suggestion that Pete Townshend, whose devilment is born out of an honest self-dissatisfaction, might wish to send the group hurtling off the rails. In general the performance was as compact and unsurprising as their early shows were erratic and electrifying.
>
> The highlights of any show by The Who, therefore, are likely to be provided by the old songs. This time they included *Substitute*, *I Can't Explain* and the under-regarded *Naked Eye* which has some of his most moving lines. More

recent material such as the inflated *Sister Disco* and the rowdy new *Cry if You Want* sounds tame by comparison.

Townshend probably knows this; Roger Daltrey the singer who has acted as his mouthpiece for almost two decades probably does not.

Nonetheless it was impossible neither to feel a tug when the house lights went up during the inevitable medley from *Tommy*, nor to be warmed by the triptych of encores which included *Shakin All Over*, *Twist and Shout* (with a raging vocal treatment by John Entwistle) and *Summertime Blues*. The latter, an Eddie Cochran song whose words and music played a vital role in shaping Townshend's compositional style, was a particularly appropriate choice; outside there was an autumnal nip in the West Midlands air.

"The Birmingham shows were tight, well balanced and effortlessly professional," Chris Charlesworth recalled two years later. "Two new songs were included in a set that again stretched back into their illustrious history for the most part, and audiences were treated to the rare sight of seeing Roger Daltrey play guitar alongside Pete. Each show climaxed with John Entwistle singing *Twist And Shout* but no guitars were broken and, as far as Pete was concerned, no alcohol consumed." Tim Gorman, who played keyboards and synthesizers on *It's Hard*, performed with the band during the entire tour. "They sounded immaculate and powerful," Who historian John Atkins noted, "and gave great hope for the future, displaying none of the apathy that seemed to set in mid-way through the subsequent US tour."

Following the NEC shows, The Who began the first leg of the U.S. tour, the longest road trip the band had embarked upon in twelve years. The outdoor shows featured an elaborate stage set-up, with 'WHO' spelled out in forty-foot high letters. The stage, situated under the bar of the 'H', featured a 110,000-watt PA system. Eleven tractor-trailers were needed to transport the band's equipment from show to show, while a Boeing 707 was chartered – at around $5,000 per hour – to transport the band and their entourage of about ninety people. Kurt Loder outlined the tour's financial details:

> When ninety people are eating and sleeping off a band's profits, some sort of compensation becomes essential…the Who have signed a lucrative sponsorship deal with Schlitz beer. In return for appearing in two thirty-second Schlitz commercials[197], allowing their music to be used in other Schlitz ads and permitting the Schlitz name to

---

[197] The footage used in the Schlitz commercials was filmed "…at a rehearsal, backstage and at their first concert," according to Stroh VP of Brand Management Hunter Hastings. "You won't see Pete Townshend singing the Schlitz jingle," he added.

be used on concert tickets, the Who will receive a pot of money (described by a Schlitz spokesman as a seven-figure amount and "the biggest corporate-sponsored rock-music entertainment ever undertaken"). Then, there is merchandising – the sale of tour T-shirts and jerseys (ten to eighteen dollars apiece this year), tour programs (five dollars each) and, in an innovative move, an authorized biography called *The Who: Maximum R&B*, a four-color trade paperback that is being sold for fourteen dollars a copy. Every little bit helps.

Dave Marsh, who was writing *Before I Get Old* at the time, wrote an article entitled 'The Who Sell Out' in *The Record* criticizing The Who for accepting sponsorship. Pete fired off a venomous response in the subsequent issue, dated December 1982:

> ...an inference that the Who are now motivated only by greed indicates that this ace rock parasite, now working on a book about the Who, is taking leave of his senses.
> ...I refused to do a tour of such grueling length (ten weeks) without a private plane. The sponsor's fee nearly pays for this plane and makes for better shows without raising ticket prices. We are doing this tour for our fans, for rock and roll and hopefully to make some sense out of twenty years of confusing history in which none of us became millionaires, despite much written to the contrary.
> We are not ashamed to be paid well for what we do, nor for what we have done in the past. I think rock music carries people like Marsh on its back. Until he and others like him realize that until they take a chance, like Cameron Crowe did with *Fast Times At Ridgemont High*, and do something of worth outside of rock and roll criticism, they have to face up to that charge.
> ...A few Schlitz flyers in the arena won't sublimate our passion.

Ticket sales were overwhelming. Two weeks prior to the band's first show in the U.S., they had already sold over half a million tickets for the first fourteen dates. "In almost every city, tickets sold out within a matter of days; in some cities, in a matter of hours," *Rolling Stone* reported.

In Largo, for example, all 18,672 tickets to the Capital Centre show went in ninety minutes. In Pittsburgh, several people were arrested after fans rushed the Civic Arena ticket window for the band's September 28th concert, and the 17,500 tickets were gone within four hours.

But perhaps the biggest success of the first leg of the tour (at press time, the band had not yet announced the second leg) was in New York City, where the Who are scheduled to be the first rock band to play at Shea Stadium since Jethro Tull played there in 1976. All 140,000 reserved-seat tickets for the two shows (October 12th and 13th) sold out in two days...

While strong ticket sales demonstrated the fans' enthusiasm, the quality of The Who's live show was brought into question early in the U.S. tour. When inevitably compared with previous Who live performances, the current tour simply didn't make the grade. "The Who were able to sustain a series of very tight, smooth and musically stable concerts that, again, incorporated a high percentage of songs from their current *It's Hard* LP," reported *The Who Concert File*. "While the concerts suggested no obvious single point of criticism, they sounded sterile and bland for a band whose live reputation was built upon unpredictability and musical spontaneous combustion. The biggest surprise was not what they played, but what they didn't play: the first 23 shows of the year managed well without *My Generation!*"

The standard set list included early singles, such as *Substitute* and *I Can't Explain*, only two songs from *Tommy* (*See Me, Feel Me* and *Pinball Wizard*), three from *Quadrophenia* (*Drowned, 5.15* and *Love Reign O'er Me*), a sampling from *Who Are You* (*Sister Disco* and *Who Are You*), a couple from *Who's Next* (*Behind Blue Eyes* and *Won't Get Fooled Again*), and four from *It's Hard* (*Dangerous, It's Hard, Eminence Front*, and *Cry If You Want*). A cover of The Beatles' *Twist And Shout* was often used as the closer.

Opening acts were of the major league level: The B-52's, Joan Jett, John Cougar Mellencamp, Loverboy, Eddie Money, Jethro Tull, Billy Squier, Santana, The Clash and Midnight Oil[198].

Pete was now favoring Schecter's Telecaster-copy guitars, which he'd begun using back in 1979. "We used to use Gibson Les Pauls," Pete's guitar tech, Alan Rogan told *Guitar World* in 1983. "One day I spotted a Schecter Telecaster-type guitar and I took it down to the shows we were doing in '79 at Madison Square Garden and he used it immediately, then we had backups and spares made of that."

---

[198] The opening acts were also subjected to major-league abuse: Bottles were thrown at The Clash at JFK stadium, David Johansen was booed offstage at Shea Stadium, the B-52's left an Orlando gig early after plastic cups were thrown at them, and a defiant Joan Jett gave the booing crowd the finger in Orlando.

The U.S. leg of the tour began with two consecutive nights at the Capital Center in Largo, Maryland (just outside Washington, D.C.) in late September, 1982. "...there are moments in the show when the desire, drive **and urgency of the Who combine into something truly resonant,"** wrote *The Record*'s **Jonathan Gross regarding the first night.**

> But for the most part, the boys use this indoor date as a warmup, having had only a Birmingham, England date coming in. ...They close with the exultant strains of *Won't Get Fooled Again*, with Townshend offering some of his most graceful leaps of the night. Still, no big deal this one, and the Who pack it up after one encore, which includes the set's most enjoyable tune, *Twist and Shout*, with a vocal by John Entwistle. For a brief moment, it appears Townshend is going to smash his guitar for this next-to-last D.C. area audience (they played two shows here). Alas, he pauses at the top of his backswing and slices instead through a convenient microphone stand. Maybe later for a Fender splinter bomb. Control, Townshend says, is the operative word this year.

The band continued through the east coast and Midwest, playing to over 91,000 at JFK Stadium in Philadelphia and 85,000 at Buffalo's Rich Stadium. Further massive crowds were encountered at the Silverdome in Pontiac, MI (75,000), and CNE Stadium in Toronto (68,000).

Rolling Stone's Kurt Loder caught up with Pete one week into the U.S. tour. "Townshend has already caught a cold, which may explain the two sweaters he's wearing, if not the faded pink handkerchief that's knotted around his wrist," Loder wrote.

> A copy of *Nostromo*, the Joseph Conrad novel, lies on a table near the sofa where he's sitting, and a stack of portable recording equipment – an adjunct to on-the-road songwriting – stands against a far wall. One year after nearly cashing in his chips, Townshend looks a little ragged, but he's obviously sober and straight. His only remaining vice is a penchant for miniature Indian cigarettes, which he smokes steadily.
>
> "I do miss a drink before going onstage," he admits, raking a hand through his disheveled hair. "Even just a small brandy would always stop me from feeling nervous. But once I get on the stage now, I'm okay. I don't miss it," he says, waving the bad old days away. "I don't miss any of it...I think there's a certain amount of relief about the

fact that it's the last tour. There's a tremendous amount of sadness, though, as well, because I know it's not what everybody wants...I think John is probably...*more* than sad. He's not at all vocal, and that makes it very difficult, because he's actually sittin' and tryin' to work out how he feels half the time. But I think I know him well enough to know that he will probably mourn the Who more than anybody in the world. He's losing a vehicle for his talent and *passion* that he knows he'll never be able to find anywhere else."

The aforementioned recording equipment, known as a Portastudio, accompanied Pete throughout the tour. "...today anything is possible, Pete wrote in 1987. "Now if the Portastudio had been invented in 1965 think how much trouble (and money) I'd have saved! But the fun I'd have missed?" He recorded several demos, including *Holly Like Ivy* and *Prelude #556*, both of which appear on *Another Scoop*, during the U.S. tour.

Loder was surprisingly complimentary regarding The Who's live shows. "Buoyed by what they conceive as a spring toward some sort of final curtain," he wrote, "they have been *burning* through their two-hour-plus sets, lashing out the songs from their new album, *It's Hard*, with all the fire of their great, anthemic hits. So far, it seems like a great way to go out – on top, as Roger says."

October saw the Shea Stadium concerts. All 72,000 seats for the first show sold out in under two hours, making it the fastest selling show in the history of ticket agency Ticketron. A second show sold out the following day. An increasingly apathetic Pete wasn't impressed. "...when I was going to Shea Stadium and Robin Denslowe was talking to me saying 'there's a 100,000 people here, you've sold out two dates, you've got the record for selling it out, how do you feel?' and I said 'I'm bored'," he told Matt Kent in 1999. " 'Oh, so you're washed up and arrogant and finished?', 'no, I'm not. This bores me!'"

The tour continued westward, including stops in Boulder, CO, in front of 60,000, and Oakland's Alameda County Stadium (60,300). Stops in San Diego (51,771 fans), L.A.'s Memorial Coliseum (93,000 fans), and a show at Sun Devil Stadium in Arizona (44,312) ended the tour's first leg on Halloween, 1982.

The second leg began a month later with a sold out show in Orlando, Florida, before 65,000 fans. Further shows before giant crowds took place in Houston's Astrodome (60,000) and Dallas (66,000). The Dallas show marked the only time this tour that Pete smashed his guitar, frustrated at the cold wind during the show that caused his guitar to continually go out of tune. Townshend and Daltrey also reportedly argued mid-set during the Dallas show.

Towards the end of The Who's Farewell Tour, "after many hints," according to Richard Barnes, "Pete stunned everyone by announcing he was finally and definitely leaving the group." The remaining plans for tours of Britain, Australia and Japan were scrapped. By mid-December, The Who's Farewell Tour had reached its final stop, a two night stand at Maple Leaf Gardens in Toronto, Canada, the second and final night being featured on North American television as a pay-per-view event. While it wasn't originally planned as the site of The Who's last concert, Maple Leaf Gardens was an appropriate venue for many reasons – a historically important Who-friendly arena (recall that Moon had played his final show before a paying crowd here back in 1976) with sizeable crowd capacity (14,300), plus it was easily accessible for a satellite feed, and, being in Canada, enjoyed a favorable exchange rate. "There were financial and technical advantages to doing it here," Pete told *Rolling Stone*.

While the crowds were appropriately enthusiastic, The Maple Leaf Gardens shows, the first of which was taped in case of technical problems the following night, were described by *Rolling Stone* as near duplicates of each other: "…the band didn't seem concerned about spontaneity: the song blocking and between-tune patter were virtually the same on both nights. Unpredictability, a quality with which the Who established their reputation in the Sixties, was apparently not a priority anymore. But, as the kids who roamed up Young Street after the last concert shouted, "Who cares?""

Variety offered the following assessment of the final show:

> There was little in The Who's pay-per-view concert to distinguish it from performances seen on the stadium tour of North America just concluded. The two-hour-plus performance…capped one of the most commercially successful – and commercially exploited – rock tours in history, and was in fact being billed as the veteran U.K. band's final appearance on this continent.
>
> But aside from a montage of vintage photos of the group, the 20th-Fox Telecommunications-distribbed event stuck to the playbook of the tour. And like the tour concerts, the show lacked the sense of anything special being contributed by the band.
>
> The closeup view of the group afforded by the 11-camera production, however, communicated this more clearly than the stadium shows did. One had only to look at guitarist Pete Townshend's bored expressions to understand that the emotional punch was lacking.
>
> The "very special finale" promised by 20th-Fox, which hinted that Townshend and company would reprise their trademark destruction of instruments from years past,

did not occur. Instead, a very scaled-down version of the fireworks display which ended the stadium shows was reprised.

The purported 2.5 million homes which were projected to order the pay-per-view special were similarly unimpressed. Less than half ordered the event. While The Who's farewell tour had grossed at least $40 million, the band had exited with a string of the worst live performances they'd ever put together.

"The band became *just* a power chord," Pete told the *Washington Post*'s Richard Harrington in 1989.

> And you can't imagine how *boring* an album can be when every song starts off...[windmill and power chords] It sends you to sleep. Somehow in the live context, it's acceptable because of the fact that not everybody receives it at the same time. In a way, it's as if you're rallying a whole group of people, some of whom may not have emotionally arrived yet and you make sure they hear one of the rallying calls and they go out ready to fight.
>
> But *what* are they fighting for? That's the thing that's so extraordinary. We forgot that the Who had already won the battle, that we are a generation that had already taken over society. There's no need to infiltrate the establishment because we've actually inherited the establishment by virtue of growing old. In a sense, we could have just waited quietly in the wings.

Upon the completion of the Farewell Tour, engineer Cy Langston compiled a three-album set of live material spanning the group's career which reportedly drew rave reviews from those who heard it. "Unfortunately," Richard Barnes recalled in *Maximum R&B*, "in their wisdom, MCA Records insisted only tapes from the Farewell Tour be used. The band couldn't believe this but gave in. As a result, *Who's Last*, their farewell album, is thought by the band to be one of their worst[199]." The album reached number 48 in Britain and 81 in the U.S. "To put it bluntly, the Who never sounded worse – more impotent and eviscerated – than on this dismal double album," Kurt Loder opined in his *Rolling Stone* review of *Who's Last*. "...several of the sixteen songs here are available in far superior live versions on such albums as *Live at Leeds* and the soundtracks of *Woodstock* and *The Kids Are Alright*, and even the most casual

---

[199] In late 1984, I wrote a fan letter to Pete. "Glad you liked *Who's Last*," he mentioned in his January, 1985 reply, with an asterisk: "I didn't."

comparison with those previous LPs exposes *Who's Last* as the disgraceful cash-in that it is. ...I can't think of another band as committed and allegedly idealistic as the Who that has ended its career on so sour and sickening a note."

Chapter 11

"I see a society, or a race which I feel lucky to be a part of, and lucky to be a little bit unique, and in my own arena of activity, obviously, especially unique, and I really enjoy that. But at the same time, I don't want to face up to the inevitable fact that if life is as I see it, as I'd like it to be, then I am no better than anybody else (laughs). And that occasionally throws me into a bit of a turmoil, and that's where I'm at odds to a great extent. I don't quite know how to deal with it all the time. Sometimes I've got it in control, and sometimes it gets out of control."
— Pete Townshend, 1982

"I've just made a decision to take on a few things. I won't put my stability or my family at risk, but I have to do something with some risk attached. So far, I've turned away from all big chances and all big risks. I think there is a point where the individual who is involved in the rehabilitation process has to start to run...One has to test the water."
— Pete Townshend, 1984

Despite the conclusion of The Who's Farewell Tour just a month earlier, January 1983 found Pete Townshend working on material for a new Who album at his Eel Pie studios in Twickenham and Soho. Although Pete had made some earnest overtures the previous year to the rest of the band regarding his desire to dismantle The Who, they had decided to record one more studio album before finally calling it quits.

Pete began writing songs based around the notion that "each of us is a soul in siege," he explained in 1987, continuing an idea he'd addressed on *All The Best Cowboys Have Chinese Eyes*. He wrote and recorded several experimental demos for the project, including *Ask Yourself*, *Cat Snatch* and *Prelude, The Right to Write*, in addition to the various pieces he'd recorded on his Portastudio during the Farewell Tour. In searching for an appropriate sound for some of his synthesizer work for *Siege*, Pete came up with what he called a 'Myriad Speaker System'. "I organized a synthesizer whose sixteen unison 'string' voices were reproduced through...sixteen separate small speakers on mike stands at about head height, distributed around the recording studio in formal string section grouping," he wrote in 1987. "As soon as I played a note I knew I'd hit on something. The synthetic string sound was rich and spacious...It's a wonderful system, but is complex and takes many hours to set up."

The *Siege* project was abruptly dropped in March, with Pete deciding that the material was unsuitable for The Who.[200] After several weeks of deliberation, he informed the rest of the band that he was no longer able to write appropriate material for them, and that he was leaving The Who. Since this wasn't the first time a break up had been threatened, Pete's announcement to his bandmates was taken with a grain of salt.

Meanwhile, a 26-song collection of Pete's demo recordings entitled *Scoop* was released in March, 1983. Pete had dreamed of issuing such an album for years. "I'd like to put together an album package of old demo material that I've done which has never been commercially released," Pete said in a radio interview five years earlier. "Every time the Who have made a record I've made a little demo and I thought that'd be quite interesting thing to put together. An anthology of the old material, you know."

Scoop consisted of demo versions of Who songs *So Sad About Us*, *Squeeze Box*, *Circles*, *Melancholia*, *Bargain*, *Magic Bus*, *Cache Cache*, *Behind Blue Eyes*, and *Love Reign O'er Me*. It also contained outtakes and experimentations from various periods in Pete and The Who's history. *Rolling Stone*'s four-star review read, "this album is an open invitation into the root experience of songwriting, a rare glimpse of those secret explosions when words first collide with music." *People Weekly*'s review was published the following month:

> ...a chronicle of Pete's love affair with the recording process... The collection is unpretentious and meant, apparently, to recapture some of the innocence that has been lost in making popular music under constraints of commercialism and band compromise. This is the rock'n'roll equivalent of a writer publishing his notebooks, and because Townshend is as talented as he is, it's a fascinating project.

"...*Scoop* demonstrated how closely The Who have followed their leader's footsteps over the years," Chris Charlesworth remarked, "how Pete's rhythm guitar has suggested percussive lines for Keith Moon and how closely Roger has echoed Pete's guide vocals."

Scoop was followed by two further collections of Pete's demo material, *Another Scoop* in 1987, and *Scoop 3* in 2001. Despite

---

[200] *Siege* was resurrected in 1984 when Pete began writing and recording demos for *White City*.

complimentary reviews and healthy sales, the first two collections did not prove profitable. "...although the first *Scoop* sold more than Mick Jagger's last solo album, I've still got a kind of minus figure on my budget," Pete said in a 1989 radio interview.

> They're expensive to produce because they're quite lavish, the packaging, the double albums, and they're sold at budget prices. Neither I nor the record company are making any money out of it, but you know Atlantic have been great to allow me the space to do it, they really have. I think Doug Morris, who's the president, loves me... most of all because I gave him his first hit in a sense with the *Empty Glass* album. ...So the company has given me that space and it's something that I love greatly. It's one thing that has made me feel that Atlantic is a wee bit more than just a front line record company... understanding that modern rock musicians, although they... tend to be honest enough to put their commercial interests first, in a lot of cases, the music is very much an abstract and that it needs attending to on an abstract level. So I hope that there will be some more stuff, 'cause I produce music all the time, and I write all the time. I write constantly... I've got barrels of stuff.

On July 7, 1983, Pete took a tangible step away from The Who when he held a press conference to announce his new position as an acquisitions editor for London book publishing company Faber and Faber. Matthew Evans, Faber and Faber's chairman, offered Pete the position after noticing the output of Pete's publishing venture, Eel Pie Publishing. Pete explained his new position to Hugh Foley in a 1989 radio interview. "I'm an editor," he said. "...Sometimes I actually physically edit books, you know, I go through text and edit, and talk to the authors about... structural changes, and with some writers I do a good job and with other writers I do a bad job... I do books about music... I try to do high quality photo books if we can do them... It's a natural thing for me to do, I find working with words quite easy." Pete soon settled into his job, visiting his Bloomsbury office twice a week. Future notable projects with Faber and Faber would include editing Animals frontman Eric Burdon's autobiography, Charles Shaar Murray's award-winning *Crosstown Traffic* and working with Prince Charles on a volume of his collected speeches. Pete commissioned Dave Rimmer's *Like Punk Never Happened*, and was commissioning editor for radical playwright Steven Berkoff. He also commissioned a book about one of his favorite musicians, Prince. In a January 2000 interview with *Q* magazine, Pete named Brian Eno and Russell Mills' *More Dark Than Shark* the best book he published at Faber and Faber, commenting, "Russell Mills did illustrations of some of Eno's notebooks, which are hilarious." Also, on a related note, Pete reviewed Joseph Conrad's *Nostromo* for the *Mail on Sunday* in September, 1983.

An aspect of working at Faber and Faber Pete especially enjoyed was the working environment, which allowed him to mingle with people from outside the music business. "When I left The Who I knew I had music, but I was also very keen to have a different life, to work in a different team, to get some different influences," Pete said in 1989.

> I wanted to regularize my life a little bit and meet new people. My work at Faber did that: I got involved with people from the theater, with people involved with medicine, with poets and writers, and with people from the merchandising/production side of publishing. It's a new life really, because people have come to embrace me without having any strong feelings about rock'n'roll at all.

As a result of his position with Faber and Faber, Pete developed a friendship with the Nobel prize-winning author of *Lord of the Flies*, Sir William Golding. In 1989, Pete read a newspaper interview with Golding in which the author expressed his loathing for popular music. "...I was really offended," Pete recalled in a radio interview that year. But when Townshend began to write a letter to Golding expressing his feelings, he realized that Golding identified with Townshend the editor, not Townshend the musician. "So what it's actually allowed me to do is to make friends and creative relationships which don't depend on the fact that I'm famous or skilled as a performer," he said. Another relationship Pete developed as a result of his position at Faber and Faber was with British Poet Laureate Ted Hughes. This friendship would lead to Pete's musical interpretation of Hughes' childrens story, *The Iron Man*, six years later.

In December, 1983, when Warner Brothers terminated The Who's recording contract, Pete released a written public statement on his status with the band, which left very little room for any misinterpretation:

> I will not be making any more records with The Who and I will not perform live again, anywhere in the world, with The Who.
>
> In the first three months of this year, I wrote songs for the next contracted Who album, and I realized after only a short time that they weren't suitable for The Who. In March I informed the other members of the band and our manager that I was in difficulties. Several ideas were thrown around but none helped me.

Therefore in May, I met with the band again and to tell them that I had decided to quit, leaving The Who ball in their court. I did nothing more until September when I felt that, out of courtesy, I should explain my problem to the chairman of Warner Bros USA, Mo Ostin. He was sympathetic and made several suggestions, none of which helped me.

On December 7 we received Warner Brothers' notice of termination of contract. I feel sad that I cannot honor our commitment to Warners – and that many of our fans, both old and new, will be upset after being exposed to rumors that we were recording all this year. The fact is we didn't even book studio time.

My solo deal with Atco will continue, and I hope to record an album next year. I wish Roger, John and Kenney the best of luck with their future work and thank them for their patience.

"When [the announcement] came, it was buried away in the back pages of the bumper Christmas editions that the music press publish once a year," Chris Charlesworth wrote in 1984. "In 1970 the news would have called for banner headlines – "PETE QUITS WHO SHOCK!" – and a sensational front-page story. Now it no longer mattered; if Pete Townshend no longer cared about The Who, neither did the rest of the world."

Pete viewed his decision to leave The Who as a personal choice – he said that the band could continue without him if they wished, while he must surely have realized that since he was the band's principle composer, The Who *sans* Townshend would likely collapse. Upon the band's inevitable break-up, their contract with Warner Brothers had to be addressed. "At the back of my mind there was the possibility that I myself would be able to make enough money to buy *my* way out of the contract and the band could then go on," Pete said later. "What stunned me was that I was going to have to pay back money that had been paid indirectly, for the use of the name to the Keith Moon estate, and directly, to Kenney. We'd just had an installment of something like $1,750,000 and Warner Bros. wanted it back." Pete, John and Roger repaid the the advance, with Pete picking up Keith and Kenney's shares as Kenney reportedly couldn't afford to pay.

Once the pain and turmoil resulting from the breakup of The Who receded, Pete began to relish his newfound freedom. "I feel greatly liberated," he said in 1985. "At the beginning of the Who's career we had the world before us, and a tremendous amount of creative – and every kind – of freedom. When we became an enormously successful group, I think we ended up – *I* ended up – feeling very caged. When I finally did face the future and had the courage to leave the band, I felt like I'd been released and

I still feel very much that way. I feel I can control my own destiny and I still find that a great novelty."

The arrival of 1984 marked the beginning of Pete's third year in a continuing program of weekly psychotherapy, which he'd attended since his return from Meg Patterson's detox treatment in early 1982. "...of course the problems are still there, but therapy helps to draw back the veils that we use to obscure them from ourselves," Pete told *Spin* in 1986.

> Therapy, particularly the old-fashioned kind of analysis, takes a very long time and half the time you don't know what it is you're going to find. I remember missing four weeks of sessions once because I was working on something, so I decided to write down what I might have said to my therapist. I started writing this story about something that happened to me as a child and began to grow very frightened because I knew I was approaching something that was very painful. I finally came to a point which was like a curtain and I knew I shouldn't go any further. By the time I realized how perverse my ideas about beauty had become I was ready to handle it. You must be prepared to accept what you learn about yourself.

The period which had elapsed since the conclusion of Pete's battle with drug addiction had provided him enough perspective to convince him that the wisdom gained from his experiences may help others. It was around this time that Pete recounted the story of his substance abuse to author Dennis Wholey, who was compiling *The Courage To Change*, a book of "Personal Conversations about Alcoholism," which featured the stories of Gary Crosby, Grace Slick and Jerry Falwell, among many others.

Pete also became vocal on the subject of Britain's poor drug rehabilitation facilities during the mid-eighties. Not surprisingly, he was particularly articulate in explaining the plight of drug abusers to the general public. "It's not a problem you can separate from other problems," he told a meeting of Young Conservatives in 1984. "In this society oblivion is one of the only ways you can find balance because everything seems to frantic, so dangerous. With a right-wing government everything also seems so uncaring. People tend to become absorbed in their own emotional physical feelings. Most people go to the pub and get wrecked and that's what I did until my liver more or less gave out. I needed these moments of oblivion and when that stopped working I needed to find something else."

When an individual turns to hard drugs for solace, obtaining help in conquering one's addictions is crucial. Pete, who was able to draw on his own wealth of experience in this area, had very specific ideas as to where one should go for help. "We've got very distorted domestic ideas about how to deal with our problems," he said in 1989. "Ultimately, for the individual who's come to the point where the problem has become a problem that they can see, it's about money. It's about getting treatment, it's about getting skilled counseling, help from people that really understand, always outsiders, never insiders, never friends, never family. Always therapists or people on the street that are working… in community programs, care programs, it's those people who will help you. Those people who just, to them, you're just a number. You're just a human being, and their job is to keep you alive. Those people will keep you alive."

"I don't think there's much you can do to combat the use of heroin," he said in a late 1985 radio interview.

> What I'm most active in doing is raising money to provide beds in clinics to help people that have become victims of drug abuse. When somebody's about to embark on a course of oblivion, it's like somebody's about to throw themselves off the top of a tower block – you say, 'Listen, you shouldn't do that 'cause it's gonna hurt you,' it doesn't work too well, because their whole object is to hurt themselves. So what you have to do is you have to be ready at the bottom of the tower block, so that if they survive, and they want to get well, then you can help them. In Britain, the facilities are very, very, very lean indeed…although we have a national health service, a free medical system, it does nothing particularly for class A drug addicts – cocaine abusers, heroin abusers.
> …we're making a lot of progress. …the British government embarked on an anti-heroin campaign with advertising, and I was co-opted by them as a kind of figurehead, and then the various other people co-opted me into their own campaigns, but my main work is raising money to try and open a large clinic.

The 'large clinic' Pete was referring to was a plan he and Meg Patterson had devised to open a drug treatment facility in London. The plan was later abandoned when Pete and Meg were blackmailed by a devious Rabbi who attempted to use the burgeoning reputation of N.E.T. for his own financial gain. When Meg refused to cooperate with him, he endeavored to mislead her friends and colleagues (he claimed to be her 'worldwide representative'), and threw up legal roadblocks whenever he could; in fact, when Pete refused to cooperate with the Rabbi, he was mailed a letter from the Rabbi's London attorney threatening a lawsuit. It took three years of legal wrangling for Patterson to rid herself of the Rabbi, and he had inflicted a substantial amount of damage to her work by that point.

Further examples of Pete's anti-drug activism during this period took place in the form of a benefit concert in April, 1984 with Siouxsie and The Banshees, and the article he penned a few days later for Britain's *Mail On Sunday* urging better care for the nation's growing number of drug addicts. Pete also formed a charitable organization, 'Double-O Charities', to raise funds for the causes he'd recently championed. Other examples of his involvement with the cause at this time included Pete personally selling fund-raising anti-heroin T-shirts at a series of U.K. Bruce Springsteen concerts, and reportedly financing a trip for troubled former Clash drummer Topper Headon to undergo Neuro-Electric Therapy.

Horse's Neck, Pete's collection of the short stories he had written between 1979 and 1984, was published in May, 1985. "It started when I kept a detailed journal of my dreams for a few months," Pete later recalled, "and I discovered that I don't have the sort of dreams most people have. I turned several of the images into stories and then I went on and did a series of erotic stories as well. My wife was shocked when she discovered them. She said she didn't know I had it in me."

Writing stories as opposed to songs was a completely new experience for Pete. "It was different because I felt unfettered by the need to fit my thoughts into the context of a rock'n'roll song," Pete told *Spin* in 1986. "Except for two stories where I was going for what's known as a shaggy dog ending, *Fish Shop* and *The Plate*, I didn't feel the need to entertain. Most of the book was written with the feeling that I was just laying it out there, and if you didn't like it, tough, because the things I was trying to share were very painfully observed by me and there was no way to sugarcoat them." *Horse's Neck* was "...written from that sort of Charles Bukowski kind of idea that we live in shit, you know," Pete said in 1989, "And that our purpose is to try to, not spiritual ascendance, but just to get out of the shit (laughs)."

Horse's Neck was partly motivated by Pete's sense that, as an editor, he needed to attempt to gain some credibility in the literary world. "...I thought it's wrong of me to be editing peoples' work and telling them what's wrong and everything else and they're sitting there, thinking, 'can this guy write?', he told Hugh Foley in 1989, "And if he does write, do I respect the way he works as a writer?', so I put the book together, and people can see me, warts and all. They can see me really trying, there are great moments in the book, there are also quite kind of sophomoric moments in the book, so you can see that's as good as I can do, and if you can do better, you deserve a deal."

The book contained thirteen short stories, tackling subjects such as childhood, stardom and spirituality. A recollection of a dream entitled *Horses* provides some startling imagery:

I dreamed, once, that I flew over a ruined church set on the edge of a hill. Nothing remained except the foundations of the crypt and the cellar. A horse had slipped on the stony ground from the hillside into the basement ruin and couldn't escape. The terrified animal was running in a mindless circle. Above was the blue sky. One remaining wall with a stained glass window stood high. The floor of the crypt was strewn with rocks and was full of puddles. The horse's fetlocks were bleeding, its body slowly starving. I flew on, helpless to assist. It was a terrible dream and seemed to be portentous.

The circling horse was an oblique warning that I would repeat the same mistake eternally. Would the law of averages allow it? Can anything continue without change? Nothing else in nature behaves so consistently and rigidly as a human being in pursuit of hell.

The house was devoid of furniture, deserted and abandoned, except that the tiny room was occupied by another horse. Its head was not quite touching the low ceiling, but there was still no way the creature could raise its head without bumping the plaster cornice. The animal was pure white like a death mask.

…Confronting the white horse I put out my hand and brushed hard down the flank as if to smooth away the mark of a girth strap. As I did so, the skin fell away, and the dry white bones of the rib cage appeared. Beneath the ribs, living within the body of the horse, moved a massive snake. Its skin shone green and blue. It was bloated and overfed; full of the heart, the liver, and the intestines of my perfect horse, my symbol of purity. It moved within the body of the horse in a circle.

Pete included the same striking image of the horse in the 1982 song *Athena*:

Consumed, there was a beautiful white horse I saw on a dream stage

He had a snake the size of a sewer pipe living in his rib cage

Fish Shop ostensiby provided a vivid glimpse of Townshend's past:

Performing with his band on the stage was my friend Pete, a narrow man with eyes like the eyes a child sees when he stands on his head and looks into a mirror. He was swinging his guitar like a battle-axe, slicing a microphone stand in two and sending the tragic instrument hurtling across the stage, its cable curling.

...He drew people to him, but his true motives were never totally clear. I knew him better than most. I knew the man who hid below the surface. He had learned as an awkward young man how to use people to get what he wanted.

...The band began the song and Pete sang venomously. The words celebrated men being real men; real men didn't need to display their toughness but needed to be able to know compassion and self-sacrifice.

...Pete says that night was important to him. The event seemed to be symbolic: the moment when he finally decided to break away from the little town and the people that he had grown up with.

"That was the most real story that I had in that book," Pete told *Guitar Player*'s Matt Resnicoff in 1989.

Most of the stuff was complete fiction. I was trying to write a Bukowski kind of thing, actually taking people through a really quite nightmarish thing and then out the other side, and little bits of autobiographical things slipped in. You know, you only have one life and only one set of influences. And, if something slips in which anybody can recognize as being real, they immediately think the rest of it must be real.

Pete has repeatedly asserted that the majority of *Horse's Neck* was fictional. "It wasn't as autobiographical as a lot of people took it to be," he said in 1989. "I was upset that the word *autobiographical* appeared even on the jacket of the paperback, 'cause it's not autobiographical at all." He further asserted that most of *Horse's Neck* was fictional in a 1999 article in *The Richmond Review*, stating, "...when I gathered my collection of prose writing, *Horse's Neck*, my editor Robert McCrum urged me to accept that my readers would always come to my writing believing they knew me inside out, and that if I pretended to be able to deceive them with my fictions, I would fail. He was right. Thus it was that fiction mixed with or perfumed by experience became 'autobiographical prose', even though many of the stereotypical rock'n'roll events that I described had never happened."

But the book contains many accounts of events which bear an uncanny similarity to the details of Pete's life, such as *A Death In The Day*

Of, which, if not wholly true, paints a picture which must have been very close to the mark during the time it was written. Another example of a story in *Horse's Neck* which closely mirrors an event in Townshend's life is the previously discussed *Champagne on the Terraces*, which, by all appearances, is an account of the emotional trauma he experienced when Theresa Russell rejected his romantic overtures.

A further example lies in *Thirteen*, which brings to mind Pete's childhood, when his parents entertained at seaside resorts:

> The beach at Filey was a Northumbrian miracle; sandy hollows exposed wind-eroded wombs to a sometimes raging sea. At certain moments you could believe that no one had ever run his fingers through the golden dust, or that no cigarette had ever been discarded. The exploring hand of an inquisitive child would belie that fancy. Even at the water's edge the flotsam of civilization floated gently home. Between the waves the heads of seals would bob, their whiskered noses inspecting the shore. Nearby, a more complete invasion threatened: holiday camps and railways, ice cream parlors and penny arcades at Whitley Bay. Yet in the hollow of a sand dune, a child could well be on a desert island.

Yet another very real story was *Pancho and the Baron*. It appears to reflect Pete's state of mind during his battle with drugs and alcohol, displaying his thoughts in 1981 as he pondered the early demise of Keith Moon ('Pancho') and was informed of the death of Kit Lambert ('the Baron'):

> When I first heard that Pancho had died all I could think of was that I had survived. I had outlasted him. In a sense, I had won.
> …Three years later, in my seedy hotel room in New York, I sat with Able and we talked about the old days. I kept saying over and over again: "I survived." I was about two weeks into a desperate recording session in a small studio there. As a professional drunk I was a great success with the New York musical elite, and I had been entertaining people night after night in my room, at restaurants and nightclubs.
> …"The Baron's dead. He died yesterday. Fell down some stairs. Got beaten up apparently."
> "Shit."
> I got up and looked over Central Park.

"I've survived." That was all I could think of to say before I went to the studio and finished work on another song. "First Pancho, now the Baron."

Later that day Spud, Able and I went out to a nightclub and saw some New York musicians having a good time. When we got back to the hotel I was accompanied by a girl who looked very much like the girl I slept with on the previous night. As she thrashed about all over the bed I started to weep a little.

"What's the matter?" Her face was sincere.

I couldn't think of any reply to the question. I'd survived again and I wasn't even trying. I composed myself, smiled weakly at the girl and nobly finished what I'd started.

Overall, *Horse's Neck* was well-received by critics, referred to by the *Cleveland Plain Dealer* as "...a consistently fascinating and challenging work." *Time* magazine's review was lukewarm, but ultimately complimentary:

> *Horse's Neck* is a sort of album, words without music, consisting of 13 impressionistic pieces drawn from the author's life and times. Each segment sounds a theme: youthful rebellion, sexual obsession, the burden of celebrity, self-realization (once known as growing up).
>
> Townshend, an editor for London publisher Faber & Faber, can be lyric and affecting, but too often he is portentous: "Almost as soon as the window had misted up, a great blast of steam wafted into the street. Pete felt like the witness to some awesome nuclear test of devastating power... We were the frayed rubber band inside the enormous balsa-wood airplane of rock and roll."
>
> Readers looking for the continuity and facts of Townshend's life will be disappointed. Yet there is enough evidence of innovative talent in these pages to indicate that if the author would write acoustical rather than amplified prose, he might have another promising career.

"The audience I had in mind was people who had enjoyed my songwriting, and those are the people who bought the book," Pete told *Spin* in 1986.

> Considering the price of the book in hardback, I'm amazed at how many people did buy it. I'm sure there were

a few new readers, but I wasn't looking for a new audience. If I wanted a new audience, I'd use a nom de plume – and then I'm sure I'd sell zero copies.

In England it was given a mixed reception, and I was pleased with that because I thought the book was mixed. Parts of it were good and parts of it were flat and confused. I reread it once after it was published and some bits of it embarrassed me. The reviews in America did surprise me. It's been quite encouraging, because I imagined that rock critics and literary critics alike might resent the fact that a guy who makes enough dough selling records was trying to infiltrate new territory.

In early 1983 Pete's Eel Pie studios were used by Pink Floyd to record *The Final Cut*. Townshend and Floyd guitarist David Gilmour forged a relationship that would result in several future musical collaborations, the first of which took place in 1984. "He stopped me in the corridor to say how much he had enjoyed my first solo album – I thought that was very nice of him – and also he said that if I ever needed any help with with anything, to give him a ring," Gilmour told *Saucerful of Secrets* author Nicholas Shaffner in 1991.

After the members of Pink Floyd went their separate ways following *The Final Cut*, Gilmour began work on a solo album, which would become *About Face*. "On that second album, I was getting a little stuck for words, as is my wont," Gilmour told Shaffner. "…So I called [Pete] and said, 'Fancy writing a couple of lyrics?' He said, 'Sure, love to, send down the tape.' He sent back the first run of lyrics the next day; he'd been up all night working on it. That was *Love on the Air*." Pete wrote lyrics for two other songs, *All Lovers Are Deranged*, and *White City Fighting*. The latter was left off Gilmour's solo album (Shaffner wrote that Gilmour "couldn't relate to the lyrics personally") and was later used by Pete on his *White City* album.

As with *Rough Mix*, Pete's 1977 effort with Ronnie Lane, this latest joint effort was hardly a true collaboration. "I've always found it very difficult to collaborate and I haven't yet collaborated on a song," Pete said in 1999. "Songs that look like collaborations, like the Dave Gilmour songs that I wrote, were either me writing the music or finding lyrics to music that was already done." In the case of *All Lovers Are Deranged*, Pete "found" the lyrics. A demo song with the same title and lyrics, but different music was recorded by Pete in January 1983 at his Soho studio. "Another lyric based on a true story," Pete explained in the liner notes to *Scoop 3* in 2001. "Two people attempt to conduct a love affair over the telephone, from different sides of an ocean. Not to be recommended."

Pete was still actively involved in the practice of allowing others to use his studio facilities, sometimes at no charge. In addition to giving studio time to his brother Simon, Pink Floyd and Mick Jagger[201] during this period, Pete also allowed much lesser known artists to record at Eel Pie. "...I've been in and out of various levels of this type of work, either running co-ops with people or working directly with one or other new band, or doing special deals for young bands, new bands, sometimes new *old* bands," Pete said in a 1989 radio interview.

> A studio is a studio... when you have a bad week, and there's nobody there who wants to come in and use the studio or if, like me, you don't even really run a commercial studio but you run a studio which is designed expressly to suit a particular artist on a project, if there's no music being made it starts to die... it's an interesting equation, you know, a place like this building right now if there's no music happening for, say, two weeks, and then an artist comes in, it will often take about two weeks to get it trucking again. You know, the people that work in a place like this, the engineers, the maintenance people, the administrative people, they all live for the day when the studio is full of music, full of action. Without the music, they have no purpose, certainly the building itself has no purpose... These are very, very functional places. So, to bring new music in, particularly young players, not only familiarizes them with the process, but it also plants seeds. When I've given free time to people, they've often come back at later dates and bought time just like everybody else. To that extent, it's obviously a commercial thing to do, but... selfishly the reason that I do it has got nothing to do with money. It's to do with the fact that I come in contact with people that are breaking into the music industry. I come in contact with their problems, their difficulties... I see that side of the record companies that only the new artist sees... the last band we had in was Cleveland Watkiss's band... They got a five album deal from Polydor on an album that we did for them for nothing. The first album they're putting out is those tapes, so we're very proud of that. Also, by the by, we get our studio charges. So what would have been a dull period for us has actually turned into cash, it's turned into energy and we had three or four

---

[201] Jagger recorded the solo album *She's The Boss* at Eel Pie Studios. Pete guested on guitar.

weeks of sessions in there where… not just me, but everybody that worked there, got some real feedback.

The subject for Pete's next project, a progression of his 1983 *Siege* project, also evolved from his weekly psychotherapy sessions. The therapy revealed some disturbing shadows from Pete's childhood. "Through therapy… I had come to realize that I had been quite seriously emotionally abused as a child," Pete wrote in a posting on www.eelpie.com in early 2002, recalling that the abuse had occurred during his stay at his grandmother's house when he was a toddler. This newly discovered abuse shed a new light on Pete's past work and his battle with substance abuse. *Tommy* and *Quadrophenia* were both stories of young, desperate men who struggled to express themselves and suffered various degrees of abuse. "Like many other celebrities," Pete wrote in 2002, "…I turned to creative work and finally incomprehensible self-destruction as a means to draw attention to my subconscious difficulty." Pete's 'subconscious difficulty' was also evident in nearly everything he'd written, from early works such as *I Can't Explain* and *I'm A Boy* to his latest work.

Pete's *Siege* project, centered on the notion that "each one of us is a soul in siege", had evolved into a study of the emasculation of the postwar British male. "Throughout history, men have satisfied the drive to create and control by leading, writing, and governing," Pete told *Spin*'s Kristine McKenna in 1986.

> Men gained power through traditionally rewarded acts of heroism, self-sacrifice, and at the most mundane level – and to this day the thing we find hardest to let go of – by doing a hard day's work and bringing home the money. There are so many men who are unable to do that now, and it's backlashing against society in a monumental way. I work with a refuge for battered women in England, and working there has led me to conclude that domestic violence is often the last resort of men who are lost and emasculated. The popular solution is to separate men from wives and children because society refuses to tolerate violence in the home. Yet for millions of years violence has been the way we've run our countries and protected our causes.

The struggle of the British male to maintain relevance (Townshend pointed out that he specifically had the British male in mind, as the problem had not "crystallized" to such an extent in the U.S.) in the 1980s had molded a generation of "desolation and decadence", Pete noted. The footsteps of those heroic soldiers who had assembled the vast British Empire, and those who had bravely and victoriously fought in the two World Wars were impossible to fill, especially in an environment where the notion of conventional warfare had faded during the Cold War and its threat of nuclear annihilation. It had become increasingly more difficult to prove one's manhood through traditional acts of heroism, or even simply through providing for one's family, given the high rate of unemployment at the time. The typical man had no direction, and no avenue to demonstrate his validity. "...in a strongly Feminist climate of the '80s," Pete said, "men were increasingly being made conscious that without wars to fight they must struggle ever harder for some kind of male validity – and had to learn to face that their inbred machismo and violence were unacceptable and abhorrent." Pete's original title for the project was *The Tragedy of the Boy*.

"It's unfortunate that sexuality is a component in the nature of freedom," Pete wrote in early 2002, pointing out that with the advent of feminism and the fact that they retained their primal abilities to give birth and raise children, women were in a stronger and more favorable position than men. "With the advance of feminism in western society... women can shape the future," Pete told McKenna. "I don't object to feminism, but I think men should have a version of it for themselves." Women had gained so much ground that many men deliberately changed their appearance during the '80s, dressing and styling their hair effeminately and wearing makeup. Pete himself had briefly flirted with this aspect of the 'new wave' a few years earlier. "...in some way I experienced triggered identification with those young men who wanted to defy macho conventions of the post-military epoch," he wrote in early 2002.

Pete's drive home from his office at Faber and Faber in Bloomsbury during this period often involved a short cut through an area named White City. Once a collection of spectacular architectural accomplishments aimed at demonstrating the range and breadth of the British Empire, White City was now a dilapidated, depressed area known for its "rough lifestyle", as Pete put it in 2002. It soon occurred to him that this locale provided him with a suitable symbolic setting for his project. The area was essentially born in 1908, when it was the site of the world-famous Franco-British Trade Exhibition, featuring exotic buildings which represented countries from all across the British Empire, and a spectacular arch which served as the area's entrance. The dazzling white plasterwork of the buildings, which were erected especially for the exhibition, inspired the area's name. The White City stadium, the world's largest at the time with a reported capacity of 150,000, was erected for the 1908 Olympiad. In 1936, Hammersmith Council bought the majority of the exhibition grounds, and built apartment buildings. The streets were named after exhibits, such as Commonwealth Avenue, Australia Road, India Way, Canada Way, South Africa Road and White City Road. In 1984, as Pete contemplated his next project, the area was badly deteriorated, depressed, a shadow of its glorious past. The stadium was demolished the following year.

"I used to drive home back through a familiar territory, the White City Estate, which…lies just next to Shepherd's Bush, which is where The Who's career really began," Pete said in a 1985 radio interview with Dan Neer. "…I used to cut back through it, and…I was looking for a place which would act as a symbol setting for a story which I had in mind about life in postwar Britain and suddenly I realized that this place contained all these street names which were connected with the British Empire: Australia Road, Canada Way, and New Zealand Road and South Africa Road and then I thought - 'White City - it's such a wonderful name, and it's a promise of a vision'."

The White City estate provided Pete with a suitable "metaphor for neighborhood" through which he could explore his thoughts on emasculation, and his memories of childhood abuse. By May 1984, Pete's musings on the *White City* project had led him to the conclusion that a film would be necessary in order to fully articulate the ideas involved. "Many of the songs needed images, many of the images needed poetry," he later wrote. His original idea for a story, which "was simply going to be twenty-four hours in the life of somebody who spends a day literally wandering through that area…" he said in 1985, became an examination of the behavior and relationships of the central character, named Jim. Like Tommy and Jimmy before him, *White City*'s protagonist was an embattled, frustrated male who struggled to express himself. "The story is a follow on from *Quadrophenia*," Pete said in 1985. "Jim might be Jimmy from *Quadrophenia* twenty years on."

Like its predecessors, *White City* was naturally strewn with autobiographical elements. In the film, for example, Jim states that he was sent off to live with his grandmother as a child, and that his mother was often involved in affairs with other men. This inclusion of autobiographical information proved cathartic, according to Pete: "Writing *White City* was – for me in therapy – a way of facing some of the anger I felt towards the adults in my childhood, who had done their best, but failed to be perfect parents (if there can be such a thing)," he wrote in 2002.

A script was duly written, the synopsis of which Pete outlined in 2001:

> A violent young man ends up in a wheelchair after a drunken car crash. He descends into anger and self-pity, after driving away his wife with acts of violence. She takes up a job in a women's refuge on the multi-racial White City estate on which they live.
>
> The young man has a friend who takes him to various local pub gigs. At one of these gigs he attempts to

perform, wearing a daft transvestite's outfit and a lot of make-up. He starts well, but booze gets the better of him. He has a terrible row with his mother who runs the pub.

In the middle of the row he suddenly remembers some childhood trauma involving his mother, and rushes to consult his estranged wife who is training some young swimmers at the local swimming baths. She is planning a special event to raise funds for the Refuge.

At the pool the young man comes across a rock star – myself – who had gone out with his wife before they were married. I have offered to perform at the fund-raiser. My obsession at the time is with South Africa and the curse of Apartheid. At every chance I get I engage people (possibly bore them?) with the issues there, attempting to alert people – who really don't need to be reminded – to the fact that racism is everywhere.

During the rehearsals I find myself attracted to my old girl friend and there seems to be a chance we might reunite.

The young man, believing himself to be on the brink of redemption with his wife, is infuriated by me and storms out of the baths.

Later that night, while I am on stage performing, he arrives, dressed absurdly, somehow managing to walk, and to my chagrin convinces his wife to go back to him.

I sulkily leave town, back on the road, hopeful I can find love and help Mandela to rescue Soweto.

Pete soon showed his completed script to Bill Curbishley, who reacted favorably and encouraged him to write songs based around the story. During the summer, Pete busied himself writing songs and refining the story, which he referred to as a 'musical teleplay'[202]. He also began work on the film, contacting Australian producer Richard Lowenstein at the recommendation of a friend at Faber and Faber, producer Walter Donahue. Pete was impressed with Lowenstein's award-winning feature *Strikebound*, and invited him to London to collaborate on the script and shoot the film. Townshend, armed with his script and extensive "location reconnaissance

---

[202] While working on the *White City* demos, Pete also composed a *Siege* canon. A few years later (early 1987), he purchased a "large Synclavier synthesizer," he wrote in the *Scoop 3* liner notes in 2001. "One of the fist things I did on my new Synclavier at this time was conduct a series of exercises round the *Siege* canon I composed on sheet music... I had hoped to complete a symphonic piece based on the canon, but really such a task was – and still is – out of my scope. But I produced a large number of simple variations." A handful of these variations was included on *Scoop 3*.

video movies of the White City estate" which he'd filmed with a pre-production team assembled by Donahue, was, he felt, primed to create a groundbreaking feature-length movie.

However, Lowenstein and Townshend initially didn't see eye-to-eye. "It would be wrong to say Lowenstein and I hit it off," Pete recalled in his early 2002 web entry. "He seemed slightly skeptical of me. He later... referred to my script as 'pretentious'. My script had been intended as a jumping off point for our collaboration on a finished version, but the more we spoke, the more I realized that Lowenstein found my ideas confused. Looking back today, I can see why..." An assessment of a Townshend script using the word 'confused' was nothing new to Pete, who had weathered a storm of confusion and misinterpretation when he attempted to explain *Lifehouse* to his peers. "Indeed, it was – on the surface – a confused tangle of ideas and images," he wrote, "but from my point of view, no more complex than those gathered for my first few songs written for The Who. Songs like *I'm A Boy* or *Join My Gang*, and the background stories for projects like *Tommy*, or *Quadrophenia* all tapped into similar veins."

Lowenstein discussed Pete's take on *White City*'s underlying theme, and reviewed the teleplay. "We talked a few times trying to pin down what was really behind the simple story," Pete wrote in 2001. They began to pare the teleplay down to focus on its central issues. "...we stripped away quite a lot, we stripped away a lot of the music which we felt was superfluous and the whole thing did evolve," Pete said in 1985. "...in small steps, I'd do a bit of recording and then we'd together do a bit of writing for the screenplay. We were inching forward step by step..." But Pete still wanted to maintain the integrity of the teleplay, with its interspersed songs and poetry. "I hoped to demonstrate to him that the song lyrics, and possibly some poetry sequences in the soundtrack, would both deepen and clarify the confused plotting and give it substance and edge," he wrote in 2001. But the pair were already on the clock: Lowenstein had "already been in Britain for two weeks," according to Pete, and the film's budget was in place. Pressure to get the film in the can was mounting. In the interest of getting the film underway, and trusting that Lowenstein was the man for the job, Pete agreed to let go of the teleplay. "At Donahue's suggestion, and with my complete blessing, Lowenstein finally retired to a posh hotel and completed his own shooting script without any further involvement from me," he wrote.

Meanwhile, recording work for the *White City* album had begun at Pete's Eel Pie studios in Twickenham and Soho, and A.I.R. studios in London. Some familiar faces returned, including drummers Mark Brzezicki and Simon Phillips, bassist Tony Butler, harmonica player Peter Hope-Evans and producer Chris Thomas. Another familiar face resumed his position at the keyboards after a two-year absence: John 'Rabbit' Bundrick. Other musicians used on the album were Pink Floyd guitarist Dave Gilmour, bassists Chucho Merchan, Pino Palladino, Phil Chen and Steve Barnacle, the five-man brass section Kick Horns, and ex-Blondie drummer Clem Burke. An interesting addition at backing vocals was Pete's oldest daughter, Emma. Pete's band for the *White City* album was known as Deep End (the stage that the band plays on in the film is located at the deep end of the White City Pool).

The album's opener, *Give Blood*, addressed *White City*'s central issue of emasculation. Pete further described the song's intent in 1985:

> The idea behind the thing was to both honor the old values, the idea that somebody would be prepared to fight for something that they believed in, but to face the fact that that won't work any more, you know, and that we have to find a new way of giving blood, of proving that we are capable of self-sacrifice, and it seems to me that the way that we are confronted with now is just to make some kind of sacrifice for the people that we live alongside, you know, we can't really hope to gain heroism through acts of valor abroad any more, it just doesn't seem to work that way....I think really that the idea was also that 'keep blood between brothers' - you can still shed blood, but do it wrist to wrist.

In contrast with the song's lyrical content, *Give Blood*'s musical structure was arrived at in a relatively simple manner. "*Give Blood* was one of the tracks I didn't even play on," Pete said in 1996. "I brought in Simon Phillips, Pino Palladino and Dave Gilmour simply because I wanted to see my three favorite musicians of the time playing on something and, in fact, I didn't have a song for them to work on[203], and sat down very quickly and rifled through a box of stuff, and said to Dave, "Do one of those kind of ricky - ticky - ricky - ticky things, and I'll shout "Give Blood!" in the microphone every five minutes and let's see what happens. And that's what happened. Then I constructed the song around what they did."

The relationship of *Brilliant Blues* to the theme of *White City* seems to lie in its depiction of the British male's spirit and loyalty in the face of adversity. Pete said in a 1985 radio interview that the song was "dedicated to a Liverpudlian performer called Pete Wiley..."

---

[203] Gilmour told Nicholas Shaffner in 1991 that Pete had double-booked the studio sessions that day. Gilmour was supposed to be performing the guitar track for *White City Fighting*. "Simon Phillips was there for something that I wasn't needed on, so Pete found something else for both of us to do. We did a track together, which was *Give Blood*. That I was on *Give Blood* as well was an accident."

> I particularly like Liverpudlian performers, 'cause when they get big in England, they stay in Liverpool - they **don't leave, and I kind of admire that - sticking to your ground.** ...I just had this idea that in a way the whole statement that the Liverpudlian performers were making by staying in Liverpool, it was a renouncing, this true blue British way... We have two colors in Britain - we have blue for the right and red for the left, and so it was quite simply just to say the brilliant blue doesn't flow in Merseyside, you know, the Mersey is a grey, neglected river with a run-down port and a lot of problems in the area. But when you go to Liverpool they've still got that incredible Merseyside spirit.

While *Face The Face* has drawn comparisons to the T.S. Eliot poem *The Love Song of J. Alfred Prufrock*, which contains the line *We must prepare a face to meet the faces that we meet*, it was only after he'd written the song that Pete discovered the poem. "In that line what he's talking about is... it's a kind of contrast to Dylan Thomas's line, that thing of fighting death: *Rage against the dying of the light*, He's talking about preparing a certain dignity, to meet your destiny, that's really what this song is about. It's both about preparing to meet whatever's gonna hit you, but also seeking it out - seeking out your, certainly not death but seeking your destiny."

"*Face the Face* was done on a new keyboard...and I was very keen to get something very, very fast and upbeat knocked out," Pete said in 1996, "and I knocked out a few sections that I couldn't play all together. I could play bits of it, but try and do it all together and it confounded me, so I did a bunch of building blocks and said to Rabbit, "I want forty of them" – this is a Mozart technique – "five of those, six of these, seven of those," and he wrote it all out and played it to a drum loop... and that became the beginning of the track. This was very much a new age type of recording, and that's why it sounds pretty modern, I think. Simon Phillips overdubbed the drums, we later overdubbed the brass, we overdubbed backing vocals, we overdubbed everything. It was all overdubbed onto Rabbit's synthesizer playing." *Face The Face* was released as a single in late 1985, peaking at number 26 in the U.S. charts.

Hiding Out addresses a more physical aspect of Pete's 'soul in siege' notion. He told Dan Neer in 1985:

> I feel that when people live in these tiny apartments with a TV set, which is their window to the world, their real window to the world, 'cause it's like being in cells, the way people almost choose to live in very confined and personal private places. If you look at a place like Tokyo, where

there's an enormous population, the space in which people live gets smaller, but there's always the fact that you can look out of a window and see the stars. In fact, to somebody who's in jail, just a tiny, tiny, tiny, tiny window so that you can see the sky is all you need to keep you sane. And that's really what the song is about.

Secondhand Love was Jim's statement to Alice that he wanted her to himself, while *Crashing By Design*, with its line *Another man without a woman, too many rages have cost you this time* was an assessment of Jim's life.

I am Secure was Pete's observation of the White City, but also perhaps was a statement about his unique view of life from the elevated platform of rock stardom:

> *My room looks out to the wide open spaces*
> *My heart is touched by awakening faces*
> *I see the panic of people in motion*
> *I can stand here and look out on an ocean*

The song also mentioned apartheid, which provided yet another metaphor for the soul in siege. "The word *apartheid* is a Dutch word, meaning, literally 'living apart,'" Pete said in 1985. "I've always been very interested in the poignancy of the situation in South Africa, where black and white are not even allowed to make love. I wanted to use it in a poetic way, to look at the way that people in modern urban areas are kept apart by the conditions in which they live." Apartheid also provided an ironic example of the decline of the British Empire and its idealistic vision, all of which were represented in the White City estate. "The nationalistic images of Empire sparked by the historical street and building names jarred against the main political issue of the day, which was the dismantling of Apartheid in South Africa," Pete explained in 2002. "Through my friendship with David Astor (once the owner-editor of *The Observer* newspaper in the UK) I had – with Peter Gabriel and others – become involved in fund-raising for the ANC via less radical black South African organizations based in the U.K. I was also supportive of the sanctions imposed against South Africa which I knew Nelson Mandela endorsed."

Next up was *White City Fighting*, the song which was originally slated for Dave Gilmour's *About Face* album. "He didn't feel he could include it on *About Face* because, he said to me 'I don't know what goes on in the White City' - he came from Hampshire or somewhere," Pete said with a laugh in the 1985 radio interview with Dan Neer. "I'm glad he didn't use it because it turned out to be the central track for the album." Gilmour was tickled with Pete's inclusion of his song. "I was extremely pleased about that," he told Nicholas Shaffner, "because I'm probably the only person who's ever written a song on a Pete Townshend album apart from Pete."

The music to the album's final song, *Come To Mama*, began life as *Commonwealth Boys*, an experimental demo recorded in late 1984 which, according to Pete, "didn't fit the story".

Recording and mixing of the *White City* album concluded in early October 1985, although some work remained unfinished due to Pete's commitment to working on the film. "My daily involvement in the film as an actor meant that several pieces of music intended to be in the sound-track weren't even completed in the recording studio prior to filming," Pete recalled later. "Two quite important songs, *After The Fire* and *All Shall Be Well*, emerged from the *White City* song-writing demo sessions but were never completed at the time. The first I gave later to Roger Daltrey to use on one of his solo albums, the second I adapted as a pivotal closing celebration in my next project *The Iron Man*." Other unfinished songs included *Life to Life*, which was later used as the title song on the *Playing for Keeps* soundtrack, and *Night School*, a version of which (complete with goofy video) accompanies the *White City* film.

Shooting for the *White City* film project, now underway with Lowenstein at the helm, involved Pete acting along with the other principals, Andrew Wilde ('Jim') and Frances Barber ('Alice'). "It was the first time I ever had to sit with an actress and pretend to have feelings for her," Pete wrote in early 2002. "I just felt – and looked – shy." In one scene, Pete and Wilde told stories, reminiscing. "I found that much easier to negotiate," Pete recalled. "The rest of my 'acting' was confined to wandering around the White City estate in a Metropolis-label overcoat."

Pete's relationship with Lowenstein improved once filming was under way. "He incorporated into his own script many of the stronger conventional elements of my own, and honed together a solid story," Pete recalled. "I remember working on *White City* with great pleasure... Lowenstein was really wonderful to work with once filming started, and we have remained friends."[204]

Unfortunately, disappointment & frustration ensued. The film, "...with more money and more screen time – would have made an impressive and moving major feature film with substantial music sequences," Pete wrote in a January, 2002 piece on his website.

> With a bigger budget I believe Lowenstein would have made a film for me that provided a British complement to *Purple Rain*. As it was, we shot on 35mm rather than the

---

[204] "I badly needed help from Lowenstein," Pete recalled in January, 2002. "In the U.K. in 1984 no one knew whether I was a distinguished publisher, a reformed junkie, a writer of short stories or a rock star. I was trying to do too many things at once, possibly in a confused battle for some meaning in my post-Who life."

first proposed Super 16 and ran out of money and movie stock with about twenty minutes of film for music video still to shoot. (He had been charged by the record company part of the investors to produce three usable music videos within the story, and I think this too distracted from his ability to produce what would otherwise have been a far more conventional and satisfying full-length movie.)

...there is a very powerful mechanic at work in my teleplay which was never represented in the finished film – perhaps it could never have been so... this teleplay of *White City* could not be made into a movie.

"...I still think the songs from *White City* work better if you imagine the young hero is disabled, and drunk," Pete wrote in the *Scoop 3* liner notes in 2001. But instead, the film became "...an anachronism – too short for cinema release, too long for music video TV, and too insubstantial for my more intelligent and incisive fans."

Pete's solo album, the official title of which was *White City: A Novel*, was released in November, 1985. "Well, I thought, if I could get away with Rock Opera...," Pete told Dan Neer in 1985, explaining the *A Novel* tag. "...there's a bit of a gag, you know, to address the fact that I'd been working as a book publisher lately and that if I was gonna make a record, and a video... that I should call it a novel..."

The album was well-received by critics. "...*White City* is a clear, organic parable of hope triumphing over despair, making this Townshend's best work since *Empty Glass*," wrote *Rolling Stone*'s Rob Tannenbaum. "The values embraced by the album make it Townshend's most relevant work in years..."

The film was also generally well-received. "...this 60-minute tape is haunting," wrote *People Weekly*'s Ned Geeslin.

Jim, convincingly portrayed by actor Andrew Wilde, had a dreadful childhood as the son of an alcoholic father and a promiscuous, bartending mother; he now is estranged from his wife. The images of Jim's life are, in fact, so harsh that Townshend's songs come as a tangible relief from the unrelenting horror of the rest of director Richard Lowenstein's hour-long nightmare. The movie has disarmingly surreal elements, such as a prepubescent girls' synchronized swim team. Like most music videos, this one contains little linear plotting. Unlike most, it is tremendously touching.

Pete's decision to include the synchronized swimming was partially due to the fact that the 'sport' had recently been added to the Olympic games, held in Los Angeles in 1984. "I was very amused with the way America presented the Olympics," he told Dan Neer.

>...To see that synchronized swimming was included and I thought that if Esther Williams has finally made it to the Olympics then maybe in twenty years' time there'd be *cardboard guitar* Olympics or *breakdance* Olympics. I was so struck with it and I found that there were a lot of young kids who'd felt the same way, and in Britain particularly little girls, my daughters were mad keen on it, they used to have all these funny nose clips and I just wanted to bring it into the film because I thought it was so beautiful and so wonderful.

Deep End played live three times, twice at Brixton Academy in a drug rehab benefit (aiding Pete's Double-O Charities) on November 1 and 2 1985, and once at the Midem festival at Cannes in January 1986. All involved with the Brixton shows reportedly had a great time. "...The Deep End, as I called them, played a show or two in Brixton Academy in London, and straight afterwards they all said, 'God, this is the best band that we've ever been in, we must go out on the road!', and I said, 'It can go out on the road – but not with me,'" Pete told Hugh Foley in 1989. He described Deep End on stage as "...me running through solo stuff and jazz stuff and blues stuff and dancing around like a lunatic." The set list included *White City* songs *Secondhand Love*, *Give Blood*, *Hiding Out* and *Face The Face*, in addition to covers of *I Put A Spell On You*, *Nighttrain* and *Barefootin'*, along with Who/Townshend classics *Behind Blue Eyes*, *Won't Get Fooled Again*, *The Sea Refuses No River* and *A Little Is Enough*. In addition, Dave Gilmour sang his own *Blue Light* and *Love On The Air*. A live album, *Deep End Live*, soon surfaced from these shows.

Gilmour was thrilled that Pete asked him to be a part of Deep End. "He asked me if I would do the shows with him because he wanted to move away from being the guitar hero," Gilmour told Nicholas Shaffner in 1991. "He refused point blank to play electric guitar, and people said, 'Oh, come on, at least *Won't Get Fooled Again* – strap on a guitar and do it.' But he refused, he wanted the whole project to be not 'Pete Townshend, guitar hero' but 'Pete Townshend, singer, writer, bandleader.' It was great." Which meant that Gilmour, not Townshend, played lead guitar on Deep End's live performances of *Won't Get Fooled Again*. "It's probably every schoolboy guitar player's dream to play things like *Won't Get Fooled Again* instead of Pete, with Pete singing it," he told Shaffner.

Gilmour again joined Pete in February, 1986 – this time at the Royal Albert Hall in a benefit show organized by bassist Chucho Merchan for the victims of a Columbian Volcano disaster[205]. Pete performed *Eyesight to the Blind*, *Hiding Out*, *I'm One*, and The Beat's *Save It For Later* in his last solo date until July 1993. Also on the bill were The Communards, Annie Lennox, and Chrissie Hynde. Pete's daughter Emma joined him onstage.

While Pete was in the midst of the *White City* sessions, Boomtown Rats lead singer Bob Geldof (with the able assistance of promotion masterminds Harvey Goldsmith in the U.K. and Bill Graham in the U.S.) was busily coordinating *Live Aid*, a live music event staged from London and Philadelphia simultaneously and broadcast on television worldwide to raise funds for victims of a horrific famine in Ethiopia. The majority of the world's top acts participated, over sixty in all, including a reunited Led Zeppelin with Phil Collins sitting in on drums, Queen, U2, Paul McCartney, Black Sabbath, David Bowie, Elton John, Eric Clapton, Mick Jagger, and Bob Dylan.[206] One of the key draws for the London show was a Who reunion, which reportedly was called off several times due to bickering among band members.[207] Geldof recalled that getting The Who back together for this show was "rather like getting one man's four ex-wives together." But together they were on July 13, 1985 at Wembley stadium, in front of a reported 1.5 billion television viewers worldwide. The Who's show consisted of *My Generation*, *Pinball Wizard*, *Won't Get Fooled Again* and *Love Reign O'er Me* and was marred by several technical problems, the most glaring of which was a satellite transmission breakdown which resulted in a large chunk of the band's performance being lost to those watching on television. When the coverage resumed, the audience was treated to seeing Townshend attempting a signature leap and subsequently falling over. Entwistle, without his regular roadie, experienced last-minute problems with his main bass just prior to taking the stage. "I ran for the backup bass but couldn't tune it because there were no transformers backstage," he told *Guitar Player* in 1989. "At that point we were introduced, and I barely managed to get back onstage in time to start *My Generation*. If you listen closely to the video, you can hear me tuning the D string as we go. I just about got it in tune in time for the bass solo."

At the show's conclusion, Townshend and McCartney hoisted Geldof onto their shoulders. "I nearly died of embarrassment," Geldof later recalled. "It was terrible. These people were pop greats... I am still

---

[205] The volcano, Nevada del Ruiz, melted glaciers and triggered a massive flood of water and debris which killed over 25,000 people in November, 1985.

[206] Big-name performers Prince, Michael Jackson and Bruce Springsteen were all conspicuously absent.

[207] It was reported that The Who only finally agreed to play because of the anticipated harsh reaction from the media and the public if they had refused to participate in a fund raiser for such a worthy cause.

embarrassed but intensely proud that I was carried on Paul McCartney's and Pete Townshend's shoulders."

Pete intended *White City* leftover *After The Fire* to be played at the show, but it fell by the wayside due to time constraints. The song ended up being recorded by Roger Daltrey for inclusion on his latest solo work, *Under A Raging Moon*. "I actually wrote it for the *Live Aid* concert," Pete told Dan Neer in 1985.

> I thought it would be really good to have a new song which we could do, but we really didn't have time to do it. I wrote it two or three days before, and then I met Roger in a club, told him I'd written it and that it was ready and he had three days of recording left and managed to squeeze it in. I'm absolutely delighted with the way he's done it...
> I got the idea from thinking about things that people were saying about the aid that was going over to Africa, you know, the fact that this will help put the fire out, but it will still smolder in the future, and it just seemed to me that the line also fitted pretty much the kind of thing that's happened in the past with The Who, you know - the fire might be out, but it's still smouldering.

The Live Aid show brought the obligatory questions regarding the possibility of further Who work. "I think the Who is almost certainly over with as a recording act," Pete told Neer. "I don't want to be a big tease here, but we didn't think that we'd ever get together and do the Live Aid concert so I suppose if an opportunity like that came up again we'd certainly consider it. But what I'm looking forward to is the possibility of working in new ways with the other members of the band, in a way which would bring me the same kind of enjoyment that I get from functioning as somebody that, say, could write songs for Roger, or to work with John or Kenney on musical things in the future. I do want to get away from The Who years. The Who went round in a great big circle and it was a *great* circle, but in the end it stopped working, for me anyway. I certainly wouldn't pursue that."

The second installment of the *Scoop* series was released in March, 1987. *Another Scoop* was a continuation of its predecessor, representing a wide range of Pete's recordings, including one of his earliest demos, *Call Me Lightning*, and his recent *Siege* work, represented by *Cat Snatch*, *Prelude: The Right to Write*, and *Ask Yourself*. Other notable demos such as *Pinball Wizard*, *Substitute* and *You Better You Bet* were included.

Another Scoop was dedicated to Cliff Townshend, who died in June 1986.

"...the greatest strength of *Another Scoop*, like *Scoop* before it," wrote *Rolling Stone*'s David Fricke, "is its revealing portrait of the artist in his private song lab, testing and editing his creative impulses before broadcasting them to the world at large."

> *I want my voice to cut over mountains,* Townshend declares in a 1984 gem called *The Shout. And I want my soul to gush up like fountains to where you reside.*

He needn't worry – these recordings have a resonance that will carry far beyond his studio walls.

On February 8, 1988, The Who regrouped (the term "persuaded to perform" was used by the *Washington Post*) for their first show since *Live Aid*, an appearance at the Royal Albert Hall for the British Phonographic Industry (BPI) Awards, the U.K.'s equivalent of the Grammies. In addition to playing *Substitute*, *Who Are You* and *My Generation*, the band received the BPI's Lifetime Achievement award, for "long-standing services to the music industry."

Pete managed to play the BPI show despite being distracted by family matters. He explained the situation to the *Washington Post*'s Richard Harrington the following year:

> As I was about to leave for Albert Hall, my 17-year-old daughter Aminta was taken to the hospital with pneumonia; she'd been in bed with bronchitis for a while and just as I was about to leave, the ambulance was coming. And it was a real test of the show-must-go-on dictum.
>
> And all these things flashed through my mind: Maybe the reason she's got a weak chest in the first place is psychosomatic...Is she the way she is because I put so many *other* children before her? But I went to the hall and did the gig. And I thought, damn you, Townshend – given the gun, you will *still* kill. I just can't get it out of my blood.

The BPI show, which consisted of renditions of *Who Are You*, *My Generation* and *Subsitute* marked Kenney Jones' last appearance with The Who. Their performance was faded out mid-number due to the show overrunning its allotted time. "Somebody like T'Pau or Rick Astley had been given extra time, and so the whole show over-ran," Richard Evans told *Mojo* in 2004. "The BBC couldn't delay the 9 O'Clock News, so they chopped The Who off in the middle of a song. There was a huge row backstage. It was a farce."

Back in late 1985, with *Horse's Neck* and *White City* completed, Pete considered his next move. Still involved with Faber and Faber, he decided to further strengthen his ties to literature by relating his next project to this area. "The first thing I did to try to give myself some roots in the publishing world was to write a book," Pete said in 1989. "The next thing I thought was I should try to forge some musical links to my publishing life, that I should do something which is actually embedded in the literary world. I was very determined to achieve something that attended to both sides of my career."

Pete wanted to write a musical based on an existing literary work, and he had specific plans regarding the songs. "...I've got this bee in my bonnet about the fact that the term *musical* has moved into the eighties, but the music has been the only thing that hasn't moved into the eighties," he told Hugh Foley in 1989.

> Everything about modern musicals is new, except the music...
> ...I went to see a bunch of musicals over the last four or five years, a lot of which I liked a lot for various reasons, particularly *Les Miserables*... but the music was junk – not just junk, but old-fashioned junk, it just didn't belong... you can understand the mechanic behind it but it doesn't move you. So I wanted music that was a wee bit more up to date. Even my music isn't new – I'd like to see somebody like Thomas Dolby working on a musical too, but maybe if I do it, he'll do it.

The music, Pete noted, was the only facet of the modern musical which hadn't been overhauled to reflect a contemporary feel. "The stage sets were modern, the audience was modern – time had passed for everything except the music," he said.

> The music was from another time, almost as though it hadn't been touched by what has happened in this world...Musicals like *Hair*, *Godspell*, and *Jesus Christ, Superstar* had failed to truly bring rock and roll to the musical stage. So the music had actually gone back to the original rule book written by Rogers and Hammerstein, Irving Berlin, all those wonderful geniuses of the 40's. And it's a great rule book, but it wasn't enough.

Sufficiently motivated, and since he'd already written a 'rock opera', Pete decided to tackle the problem of outdated musical scores. His position was that an individual with a rock background was needed to perform the overhaul. "...I just felt that I had the experience of working with conceptual pieces; I've done it since the beginning of The Who," Pete told *Musician* in 1989. "And I thought, I should really attend to this again. I'm not just a songwriter; I'm a storyteller. And my experience has been acutely a rock and roll one and very, very reflective."

In his search for an appropriate story for his next project, Pete said in 1989, "I looked for a fairy tale. I think that the term fairy tale is something that you can only apply to those universal stories that work at every level – they work for children, adolescents, and older people alike. In *The Iron Man*, I think I've found it."

Pete had read *The Iron Man*, a 1968 children's story written by British Poet Laureate Ted Hughes, back in 1976 when he started Eel Pie Publishing. While many of the company's books were to be focused on music, he said, "we were also hoping to produce better books for children – books in which illustrations were vital and yet in which the prose had a kind of poetic weight, and was not condescending to kids. *The Iron Man* was our model."

The story was that of a great metal giant who emerged from the sea and terrified a rural English farming community because of his intimidating stature and his habit of eating anything made of metal, notably the townsfolk's cars, tractors and fences. The townsfolk trapped the giant in a huge pit and buried him. A year later, the giant managed to dig himself out of the pit and once again terrorized the town. This time an idea brought peace to the area: A small boy named Hogarth suggested that the giant be taken to a local scrap metal yard, where he would have all the food he wanted. All was well until a massive dragon from outer space landed on planet Earth, covering the whole of Australia. It ate all manner of living things – trees, people, animals – and threatened to devour and destroy entire cities and countries if sufficient food wasn't delivered. Not convinced that they could satiate this huge monster, the population of the Earth decided to fight it. A massive war was waged against the Space Dragon, to no avail. It gave the world's population a week to deliver its first meal, threatening to devour entire cities if it wasn't satisfied.

Hogarth pleaded with the Iron Man to do something to stop the Space Dragon, and the Iron Man soon decided to take action. He challenged the much larger Space Dragon to a "test of strength", and if the dragon declined to accept, it would be labeled a "miserable cowardly reptile, not fit to bother with." The Iron Man lay on a massive grid of iron girders and submitted to a fire which turned him red-hot. He told the Space Dragon that if it couldn't withstand the same degree of heat, gesturing toward the sun, then it would have to be his slave. The battle lasted three excruciating rounds until the Space Dragon could withstand no more. "The fires of the sun are too terrible for me," the Space Dragon said. "I submit... I'll do anything you like..."

Upon discovering that the Space Dragon was a "star spirit" whose function was to make "the music that space makes to itself", the Iron Man told the Space Dragon to take up residence inside the moon and sing for Earth. "It's a long time since anybody here on earth heard the music of the spheres. It might do us all good." This the Space Dragon did, and the population of the Earth was deeply affected by the beautiful music that emanated from the moon. "The singing got inside everybody and made them as peaceful as starry space, and blissfully above all their earlier little squabbles," Hughes wrote. "The strange, soft, eerie space music began to alter all the people of the world. They stopped making weapons. The countries began to think how they could live pleasantly alongside each other."

Pete was struck by the fact that Hughes' story was laden with profound meaning and cold war symbolism. "There was so much more to it than there appeared to be on the surface," he said in 1989. "I was deeply struck by the story. It fitted my life at the time, it fitted my childhood, and to some extent I hope that it fits my future. It's a very, very simple story in structure, and yet such a powerful story."

Pete discovered in the depth of *The Iron Man* a great deal he could relate to the contemporary world. "*The Iron Man* is a story that is very pertinent to modern life," he said in 1989. "It is about fear and deprivation of children and the ignorance we display towards both history and nature. You can read many different morals into the tale." But Pete explained perhaps the most important connection he made with *The Iron Man* in a July, 1989 interview with the *Washington Post*:

> What is at the center of *Iron Man* is a little boy who is isolated and afraid. It's the *Tommy* story, it's the *Quadrophenia* story, it's my story, which is why I was attracted to it in the first place. What I found when I got deep into it, it's also about that little boy taking power, taking control of his own life and doing it with such a vengeance that he actually overcomes fear by taking control of the very things that are threatening him. And in a sense, I think that's what I've done in my life and what I intend to continue doing.

"I identify very much with Hogarth myself," Pete told *Musician* in 1989, continuing to explain the personal connection he made with the story. "I have to remind myself sometimes that I'm a big, strong man. We're all big people with nothing to be afraid of. We're the masters of this planet and nothing should frighten us except our own actions and their consequences, our carelessness, the possibility that we are our own undoing."

In 1986, Pete met Ted Hughes since Hughes was published by Townshend's employer, Faber and Faber. The pair discussed *The Iron Man*, and Pete explained his plans to create a musical based on the story. "...I asked him if the rights were available," Pete said in 1989, "and I told him what I was contemplating, turning it into a musical, and obviously as a rock musician, a rock musical – I hate that term." Pete explained some of his plans for his version of the story. "I found that he was very open-minded and certainly not at all concerned about the idea of his story being adapted and perhaps distorted by being swallowed up in the world of rock and roll," Pete recalled in 1989. "He was quite keen to see what would happen."

In discussing the story with Hughes, Pete discovered that Hughes' original intent in writing *The Iron Man* was to calm his son's fears. "His son, Nicholas, was having nightmares when he was a little boy – very, very bad nightmares – and Ted and Sylvia [Plath] were concerned and worried; I suppose worried that maybe it was the strain on their relationship which was causing this," Pete told Hugh Foley in 1989.

> When Ted tried to find out what was going on in this kid's head, he didn't just find that the kid was afraid of all the stuff that kids are usually afraid of like ghosts and the size of the universe, and is there a hairy wolf sitting behind the door, if there is a God, I wish there wasn't, why does the sky go on forever, all that stuff, but also of a new ogre, the possibility of nuclear annihilation. The possibility of being engulfed by chemical waste. He wrote this in '67, and so you suddenly realize that one of the problems of being the child of a particularly intelligent and creative couple must have been that he overheard these conversations. Ted and Sylvia Plath talking about the futility of the world and the way we were fucking it up. And it affected his dreams, and what actually happened... Ted made up the Iron Man story, the Iron Man embodying all the man-made forces that threatened and caused fear, and the Space Dragon, all the abstract, supernatural forces, and has the boy kind of put them together in his own story – kind of smash them together.

Armed with a story and a head full of ideas, Pete traveled to Cornwall and spent an intensive two weeks writing lyrics and music for *The Iron Man*. "...in the two weeks I spent on the actual lyrics," Pete told Dan Neer in 1989, "I surrounded myself with books about robotics and space machinery and dragons and myths and legends and the Beowulf stuff, and all kinds of stuff that I felt was relevant to what I was doing, and just immersed myself..."

In addition to twenty songs, he also ultimately wrote a dramatic scenario, a libretto, an overture and recitatives for the project. "I tried to construct a complete musical work which I could put into the Library of Congress and then anybody who wanted could do it," Pete told *Rolling Stone* in 1989. "It seems mad to spend two and a half years making a record which is in and out of the American shops in three months, so I just thought maybe I could write something which had a chance of having a long life. And I thought maybe I could make it have a longer life by giving it more depth, allowing it to touch a wider audience, allowing it to live in different ways and by not being so central and fundamental to it as an artist myself."

Recording sessions for *The Iron Man* began in early November, 1986 in London. Pete wanted an unprecedented level of control over the album's production, so much so that he decided against using a producer. "Chris Thomas has been a fantastic producer, and I didn't not use him because I had any misgivings about him at all; I actually missed him terribly," Pete told *Guitar Player*'s Matt Resnicoff in 1989. He made the decision because he wanted "complete control over the voicings of all the chords, so that nobody would ever play a note that I didn't want, and the structures would be very, very pure…my first hope was that I would be able to pick up a guitar or sit at a piano with a bunch of vocalists, and the thing would hang together. And it does; you can strip away everything."

Some of the songs Pete used during the *Iron Man* sessions were leftovers from previous projects. *All Shall Be Well* was one such tune, remaining unfinished from the *White City* sessions. "During 1988[208] I was recording a follow up album to *White City*," Pete wrote in 2001. "Chris Thomas was producing for an album that was intended to support a series of story videos that I was planning that would have come out very much like that wonderful movie *Strictly Ballroom* had I the talent of its director Baz Lurhman.[209] However, my father died during the sessions and I had to let the idea go. There were a number of tracks recorded at this time, *All Shall Be Well* and *Lonely Words* are worthy of a mention. There is even another song from these sessions with the same title which has a tango beat. The subtitle of this song was 'Real World', and I used the idea later in a different form as a song for *Iron Man*."[210]

Protecting Pete's fragile hearing was a major consideration during the recording of *The Iron Man*, the results of which can be heard throughout the album. Protecting Pete's ears was a major reason that the songs were

---

[208] While Pete's notes state '1988', he surely meant 1986 as this was the year in which his father died. Also, by 1988 the *Iron Man* project was nearing completion.
[209] Australian director Baz Luhrmann's *Strictly Ballroom* was released in 1992. Luhrmann was also behind the 2001 hit *Moulin Rouge*.
[210] *Real World (Can You Really Dance?)* ultimately surfaced as an instrumental.

created and (chiefly) recorded using acoustic guitar[211]. "I haven't written a song on this record on electric guitar; I just can't do it anymore," Pete wrote in 1989. "I was working mainly with acoustic... I also listened very, very quietly and took my time."

"...on *Iron Man*, it's been a great help to me that I haven't actually done any songs with heavy guitar, and that I've listened to everything very, very quietly," Pete told Hugh Foley in 1989.

> It's actually produced a different kind of dynamics and a different kind of record, which is actually suited to this project, but if I do want to do a very heavy song, I have trouble, because if I sit with a guitar amplifier and thrash away with it, if I want to hear what I'm doing, I have to wear headphones, and even if I don't have the headphones too loud, the very sound of the guitar the way that I play it, which is the sound that's obviously caused the damage in the past, aggravates my current problem, and it sets up dead parts in my hearing spectrum, and also very, very loud ringing to the extent that now I have permanent ringing in my ears – this has developed in the last three years – to such a level that it amounts to something akin to shell shock. You have to constantly tell yourself that it's not happening, whereas what is actually happening is that I can right now hear the most unbelievable row in my head.

The state of Pete's hearing also dictated that he needed to take his time in the recording studio if he wanted to preserve (or even improve) his current level of hearing loss. "If I expose myself to loud electric guitar, particularly my own loud electric guitar, my hearing suffers and I have to take about two or three weeks away from any loud noises," Pete said in April, 1989. "So it's very difficult for me to work at music. I've taken two years to make a record for myself which should have taken about a year. A lot of that has been that I've had to give myself long rests."

---

[211] The electric guitar segments on *The Iron Man* were added at the last minute. "...none of the solos were worked out," Pete told Matt Resnicoff in 1989. "They were all just off the top of my head, and they were all done in two days, because I didn't think the album was going to have any lead guitar on it." Pete had visited George Harrison's house during the time that Harrison was recording with the Traveling Wilburys (Roy Orbison and Mark Knopfler were also there at the time). "They were playing the tracks in George's studio," Pete recalled, "and Mark Knopfler kept coming up to me and saying, "Strumming, man, that's what everything's about: strumming, great strumming!" ...I went back and took the first song, *I Won't Run Anymore*, and I thought, "I'm going to try two guitars on this, strumming." I tried it, and my assistant producer, Jules Bowen, said, "It really picks it up; it sounds lighter." So I went through and put strumming guitars on everything, and then it begged an *electric* guitar. I realized I was going to have to do lead guitars."

Pete considered using other guitarists for *The Iron Man*. When *Guitar Player*'s Matt Resnicoff mentioned that *Over The Top* was similar to Larry Carlton's *Blues Bird* (from the album *Sleepwalk*), Pete replied, "Yeah, I've got that album – probably something else that's gotten into the back of my brain. At one point I actually thought about inviting him onto the record, because I was afraid that I wouldn't be able to play lead guitar. I also thought of Pat Martino, who I desperately want to work with sometime…"

Pete enjoyed coming up with casting ideas for his new project. "It was great fun, not so much actually casting it, but thinking about casting it," Pete told Hugh Foley in 1989. "I suddenly thought, well I've got this list of characters, the Iron Man, some woodland creatures, namely a fox, a badger, an owl, a frog, the boy, Hogarth, the space dragon, the children, and the girl who lived inside the space dragon… This is my interpretation of the story."

Pete ultimately used Roger Daltrey as Hogarth's father, an Australian singer named Deborah Conway as the vixen[212] (who portrayed Hogarth's conscience), and the woodland creatures were portrayed by Chyna, Nicola Emmanuel, Billy Nicholls[213], Simon Townshend, and Cleveland Watkiss. Pete decided to play Hogarth himself, after much experimentation. "I tried all kinds stuff with childrens' voices and girls' voices, and in the end I figured, no, there has to be a centerpiece for the story," he later recalled.

Pete's initial choice for the role of the Iron Man was Lou Reed; in fact, Pete wrote the song *Man & Machines* for Reed's voice. Reed initially agreed; however, he later had to withdraw from the project when it became clear that the songs wouldn't be completed on time, creating a conflict with the recording of Reed's own album, *Songs For Drella*. "I was kind of sorry not to have him," Pete told Dan Neer in 1989, "because at that time I was going to use John Lee Hooker for another role, the father, or a farmer, or something."

> I then just wondered what the hell I was going to do… I had this fixed idea that Lou Reed was the kind of robotic man that I required, and how was I going to replace

---

[212] A former model and singer for the Australian band Do Re Mi, Conway was originally chosen to play Hogarth. "…I went to see her play and she was wearing a slinky red dress and she had her hair flying around, and she's just about one of the sexiest presences I've ever seen on the stage, and I thought, this is not gonna work," Pete told Dan Neer in 1989. "I went up to her afterwards, and I said, 'Listen, would you mind playing something a little more foxy?' And she said she wouldn't, and what would I suggest, and I said, 'Well, how about a fox?' [laughs] I've now bowed to the sexist implications of that and allowed her to be a vixen."

[213] Baba follower Nicholls, who sang on the Small Faces' *Ogden's Nut Gone Flake*, has been a Townshend friend and coworker for decades. Billy's son Morgan, also a musician, has none other than Pete as a Godfather.

him, and I thought, hold on a minute, you're missing the point here. It's not about the person, casting like that is a bit obvious, it's a bit kind of naïve... It's the kind of casting that means that when you do *Tommy* on Broadway you have to have Roger Daltrey and nobody else, like Lou Reed just symbolized something, but wasn't necessarily that person. In fact, when I heard his album, I realized that what Lou was doing in life was actually taking that preconceived image that we have of him and screwing it up and throwing it away, showing us that he's grown as a man, and as a family man in particular. And I suddenly thought well maybe if Lou can't do it maybe John Lee Hooker can do it.

Pete soon became comfortable with his choice. "I wanted a primordial voice," he wrote in a 1997 letter to Charles Shaar Murray, author of the 2000 Hooker biography *Boogie Man*.

The voice from R&B that I remember first being disturbed by was Howlin' Wolf, but JLH's voice is less that of a macho monster, more of a dark, frail masculine soul. He evokes something whale-like in a way, a spirit that is thrashing powerfully beneath the surface, but in grave danger from the world and his own restrained anger and vengefulness. Ted Hughes's Iron Giant in the story has no history; we must project it onto the story for ourselves. Hughes invites us to ponder with him: 'Where had he come from, nobody knows.' The first time I heard the blues by JLH that's how I felt – where does this come from? It was so familiar to me, so resonant, and yet so obviously not of my experience or society.

The Iron Man himself sings in two songs, *Over The Top* and *I Eat Heavy Metal*. Hoping to land the blues master, Pete sent Hooker a demo tape. "When Pete Townshend asked me to do it I laughed at him," Hooker told Murray in 2000. "Iron Man? Gargling gasoline? What do you mean by this? That ain't me. That ain't the blues." But he just said to me, "If anyone can do it, you can."
Since Hooker liked the songs ("[*Over The Top*] is such a pretty song, and that *I Eat Heavy Metal* sounds good"), he agreed to play the part of the Iron Man.[214] To describe Pete as pleased with landing Hooker, whom

---

[214] " 'The Iron Man' had been one of Hooker's nicknames back in Detroit," Charles Shaar Murray wrote in *Boogie Man*. "The honorific bestowed on him by his friends to acknowledge his powers of stamina and endurance during those long years of working in

he'd never met prior to the project, would be an understatement. "...it was a great, great, great thrill for me to work with John Lee Hooker," Pete told *Guitar Player* in 1989. "You know, just to hear him saying my name on the [studio intercom] talkback. I mean, he was the first blues performer I really adored." Hooker's vocals were recorded in New York.

> "It was completely natural," Pete said of the recording session.
> It was tricky to get used to the fact that his young blond girlfriend was younger and prettier than any I had known, but despite his crisp suit, elegant hat and sharp demeanor, there was humility. He couldn't read music or text, and learned each line parrot-fashion. He said it wasn't blues, but he could feel it nonetheless. It was an affirmation for me to sense that he felt at home with what I was doing because I know how deeply everything I do is rooted in his own work.

"This was a very rough day in the studio," recalled Hooker's manager Mike Kappus in *Boogie Man*. "The words and phrases were completely out of John Lee's vocabulary and even with on-the-spot coaching, Pete ended up just having John speak most of the words, later using a synclavier to make them sound sung." Hooker was also slated to sing another song, *Man Machines*, but he "couldn't manage to do this particular song," Pete wrote in 2001.

Pete cast jazz singer Nina Simone as the space dragon. "She was great," he told Hugh Foley in 1989. "What was interesting was I'd done a demo vocal for her, on *Fast Food*, which is the song she sings on this album. I felt like running in to her when she first sang it and saying, 'Listen, you don't have to copy my demo vocal, you do it your way,' until I suddenly realized that, of course, it was the contrary that was true. It was me that had been copying her for twenty five years."

The album begins with *I Won't Run Any More*, where Hogarth faces his fears. "...when he sees the shining lights of the iron man on the top of the hill, the first thing that comes into his mind is, I can't run from this anymore," Pete told Dan Neer in 1989. "I can't run away. The story is about nightmares, in a sense, it's about fear, and what happens in children. And what happens in the story is that you see how we finally get to grips with encountering that."

Over The Top, which describes the Iron Man's reassembly and mindset after he fell over the cliff, along with *I Eat Heavy Metal*, a humorous dissection of his diet, were both sung by John Lee Hooker.

---

steel mills by day and playing in bars by night. Now he was The Iron Man once more: not just to his friends, but to the world."

"...he's got a wonderful sense of humor, and it really conveyed itself through the work," Pete said in 1989. "Certainly it was great fun working with him..." *I Eat Heavy Metal* also provided Pete with some humorous double meaning: "One thing I do know is what music is made of, where *Live at Leeds* came from, and where heavy metal began," he said.

Man Machines, a track which Pete demoed in his home studio back in 1985, was sung by Pete's brother, Simon[215].

An unlikely Who reunion took place in the studio for the songs *Dig* and *Fire*. "I wanted to work with Roger, but I was not keen on working with the Who again and just sounding like the band of '82," Pete told the *Washington Post* in July, 1989. "This was a potential area in my solo work for the Who to come together without that programmed quality, without that need to kill, that need to complete the mission, however you feel about it emotionally..."

>The Who were "...my guests on this record," Pete told Dan Neer.
>
>I really wanted Roger on the record. *Dig* had a synthesizer bass on it. Once Roger was on there, something seemed to be missing and I figured it was really live bass, and I asked John if he minded doing it, and he agreed to do it. We were in the studio together, we worked together on it, we... well, it wasn't quite the old magic, but there was certainly a chemistry there...

The other song recorded by The Who, the old Arthur Brown hit *Fire*, represented the Iron Man's challenge to the Dragon to an ordeal by fire. It also provided "a gift to AOR programmers who won't know what the hell else to do with the record," *Rolling Stone* reported in August, 1989.

"When I first put the collection together, there seemed to be a hole in the fire scene," Pete told *Musician* in July, 1989.

>I said to my manager that the trouble with fire songs is that it's all been said. As recently as Bruce Springsteen, "You can't find a flame without a spark." You go back in history and the fire cliches make you want to vomit. I said the best song is just "Fire, fire, fire, fire/You're going to burn." And Bill [Curbishley] said what a great idea. I said, "No, I didn't mean the actual song." But I sat down and thought that it wouldn't hurt. I used *Eyesight to the Blind* by Sonny Boy Williamson on *Tommy*. Then I got a letter from Arthur in Texas. He's running a small commune there and I thought let's go for it. He wrote asking if I could help

---

[215] Concerns were raised at the time that Simon's voice was too similar to that of his brother.

get him some money through publishing. I wrote back and said I've got a better idea. We'll put *Fire* on the album and pray for a hit.

"*A Friend Is A Friend* is the centerpiece song from *The Iron Man*," Pete said in 1996, in a discussion of the inclusion of the song on his greatest hits compilation, *Coolwalkingsmoothtalkingstraightsmokingfirestoking*.

> There's a point in the story where the Iron Man has been trapped in a pit that's been dug for him by the hero of the story, this little boy called Hogarth, and as they're throwing earth onto his face, his eyes meet the little boy's, and the little boy realizes that there had been a friendship developing between him and this iron giant, and he's worried that he's betrayed it. So it's just a song about the nature of childhood friendship, and what happens when you say to somebody when you're a little kid, "I'm going to be your best friend for ever and ever and ever," whether that is actually true, or can be true. And if it turns out not to be true, how does it make you feel?

The song is "...actually trying to get across the warmth and the mystery of friendship and what it is, the realization of it," Pete told Dan Neer in 1989.

> The words are very clear in the context of the story, but I felt that there's something about friendship that is that it's just a recurring pattern. It's not like love; it doesn't have the pain of love. ...you can actually become friends with somebody who you never know their name, who you meet every day on the train on the way to work. And that that experience, once that has happened, you have a contract. ...it's about how Hogarth has just suddenly realized that the Iron Man and he are in the same place and time, and are both facing the same kind of destiny and that a contract has been written. Hogarth has actually found his first real friend, you know.

The song *All Shall Be Well* represents the love story Pete included in his version of *The Iron Man*. "I think I just felt that you couldn't have a musical without a love story," Pete told Dan Neer.

> ...I also felt that there was a woman somewhere in the story and I just had to find her. ...I found her in two

guises in the space dragon, I found her both as a mother, and also as a lover, and I don't mean that in a Freudian sense... but rather the idea that the first woman that any child, male or female, falls in love with, is their mother. And you fall in love with your mother when she's, in most cases, certainly, in a kind of prime. After a great act of creation, a great act of self sacrifice to bring you into the world... the kind of thing that a mother says, with no guarantees, she's powerless to deliver what she's promising, but she knows she has to say it: 'Hush little baby don't you cry, everything's going to be all right,' and you trust that, and this tearing that Hogarth goes through in this song, he is dealing with burgeoning lust, he's dealing with wanting to tear himself away from his mother, he's dealing with the idea of making new commitments of taking on new challenges, and all under the banner of a world which is in a sense pretending that nothing can go wrong. Or what I wanted the song to do was to make people think well, if this is so, if all shall be well, this is the way we get through life, we say, have a nice day, isn't everything nice, the sun is shining, how are we gonna solve the problems, how are we gonna grow, how are we gonna move forward. And of course what it comes down to is our primal urges, what finally gets Hogarth moving, despite the fact that everybody's telling him now that you've got the Iron Man in the scrap yard, everything's fine, life will be great, is that he wants to fall in love, he wants to find a partner, he wants to create, his animal urges take over, and he's actually quite a dangerous little character at this point.

Was There Life was admittedly "an arch show tune," Pete said in 1989, actually the only one of "about four or five" that were written for the project to make it onto the album. "...the music took me ages to write, and it was tortured and painful, and when I finally got it right, I thought this is the one I'm going to include, and I just know there's a lot of Who fans and in particular Pete Townshend fans are going to hate it, and I thought, I don't give a shit. If you want the rest of the stuff, you listen to this at least once."

Fast Food was the Space Dragon's *I Eat Heavy Metal* – a humorous song which described her desires. "It was fun writing the words for this," Pete later said. "Man actually is the junk food. He is the fast food."

A Fool Says reflected Hogarth's contemplation of the approaching Space Dragon. At first glance, the dragon appeared to be a sparkling star from which emanated beautiful music. As the dragon moved closer, its ugliness became apparent, and the façade of beautiful music became the screams of countless children. Hogarth's love for the approaching object was in vain, and his love could do little to conquer the Dragon, nor to satisfy her demands. "It's not a denial of the value of love, it's just imagining that love can really conquer everything," Pete later said. "It can't – love is an energy, but it's not an act until you turn it into an act. You have to *do* something – you have to be motivated by love to do something. He feels cheated; he feels that he has to do something."

New Life/Reprise rounded out the album. "…I try to musically create the fact that the dragon is subordinated and the horrible screaming that she produces turns back to beautiful music and she flies off back into the sky," Pete told Dan Neer in 1989. "And then the cast gathers for a song called *New Life*, which is really about the fact that now is an opportunity to go ahead and do something new, create a better place. This is a song that I really did write very much with musical theater in mind, kind of a show closing song."

The Iron Man was completed on January 18, 1989. Pete soon went on vacation to Antigua. The album was released in Britain and the U.S. in June, 1989.

"*The Iron Man* resounds with some of his most adventurous playing in almost seven years," *Guitar Player* reported in September. "It's also a perfectly executed pop album."

"This is a Pete Townshend solo album in the most liberal sense of the term," *Rolling Stone* reported in August.

> He appears as part of a sizable cast of vocalists, singing on just about half of the album. There is also a noticeable shortage of ripping guitar… But if *The Iron Man* is short on rock & roll wham, its spiritual tensions are still cut from familiar Townshendian cloth. Hughes populated his original story with the stuff of children's dreams – talking fauna, a dragon from space, a robot with a heart of gold. But the virtues they and the central character – a young boy named Hogarth, played by Townshend – are the same ones that fueled all of the great Who morality plays, like *Tommy*, *Who's Next* and *Quadrophenia*: youth's enormous capacity for courage and love, the power of faith and the drive for a greater common good. The opening number, *I Won't Run Anymore*, is a less combative but no less strident variation on *Won't Get Fooled Again*, executed with rippling guitars. "I'm not gonna run anymore," Townshend sings heartily. "I'm not gonna run like a rat to a piper's tune."
>
> Some guitar hooks and vocal flourishes, like the choruses in *Over The Top* and *Dig*, sound like missed

opportunities, the kind of grabbers that Townshend would have pumped up to anthemic proportions fifteen years ago. It is also jarring to hear a Townshend record so bereft of ironic sting, power-chord rage and torturous self-examination. In remaining true to the innocence and wide-eyed wonder in Hughes's story (yes, dragons can fly and we can all live happily ever after), Townshend has erred on the side of compassion.

The sentiment, however, becomes the middle-aged Townshend. The optimism and hope in songs like *I Won't Run Anymore*, *Dig* and *All Shall Be Well* are refreshingly free of the confessional angst that nearly deep-sixed *White City* and *All the Best Cowboys Have Chinese Eyes*... There are also a few laughs on tap. In *Fast Food*, the iconoclastic, irascible Nina Simone (the dragon, naturally) heats up lines like "I want fast food/Frisky little children/Served up in the nude." *I Eat Heavy Metal* is a neat twist on old blues braggart classics like *Who Do You Love* and *Hoochie Coochie Man*, performed by Hooker, the master of heavy mettle, with a crusty snarl that sounds like he's chewing a cast-iron cud.

The Iron Man is an enjoyable and, in its own way, captivating album about children, for children and for anyone who isn't too cool to share their fantasies. It is not lightweight art pop; nor is it the great Townshend record we've all been waiting for since *Empty Glass*. It is Pete Townshend's *My Generation* for the next generation.

Similar positive reviews surfaced in the press, the *Oakland Tribune* calling the album "Townshend's tightest and most accessible work in years," while the *Atlanta Journal* called it "...a musical and lyrical tour de force."

People Weekly's David Hiltbrand failed to see what all the fuss was about. "...boy, will you be disappointed by this turgid fare," he wrote.

A Friend Is a Friend and *Was There Life* are nearly passable melodies, but only by comparison with the rest of the album. Measured against the body of Townshend's work, these efforts are third-rate. The rest of the songs, whether sung by Townshend or by such guest vocalists as John Lee Hooker or Nina Simone, are stunted and curiously devoid of charm.

An aspect of *the Iron Man* that Pete was eager to explore was its visual potential. At the conclusion of The Who's 1989 tour, he engaged in talks with London's National Theatre about the possibility of staging his work, and he also entertained the idea of an animated film. "I'm keen to do it," Pete told *Musician* in July, 1989. "...I want to see it tested in the theater, get it into workshop as soon as possible. And if it develops, get it funded and out there." Pete told the *Detroit Free Press* the same month that he was "starting to look forward to the idea of getting it finished off. I'm going to try very hard to get it onto the stage, even for a limited season. I think it would actually make a greatly entertaining story."

Pete pointed out to Hugh Foley at the time that he'd "written a whole musical, you know, with an overture, bits of recitative, and a narrative and stuff, and maybe about another 8 or 10 songs which aren't on this first record – I don't think they're the kind of songs which people would miss on an album, they're songs which would only really work on a theater stage." The availability of all the extra music had some observers wondering why Pete didn't expand *The Iron Man* into a double album with more songs and an easier-to-follow plot. "For financial reasons," Pete explained to *Musician* in July, 1989.

> I got a nice deal from Atlantic in the States and Virgin worldwide, but I had to contract all the different singers on the record and I spent two years in the studio. It cost me a lot of money. I couldn't afford a double album because neither company was willing to pay me a double album rate. They would have put it out, but I wasn't willing to risk my own money. It would have taken another six months and another $200,000. John Lee Hooker would have sung five or six songs as opposed to two, and there would have been an enormous amount of detail work. I was working with six singers at once, all of whom were getting 600 pounds a day. The money was just disappearing.

While Pete had originally intended to stage *The Iron Man* by Christmas, 1989, it wasn't until November 26, 1993 that the work was performed in front of an audience – at the Young Vic, the site of the experimental *Lifehouse* shows more than two decades earlier.

Meanwhile, the idea of an animated version of *The Iron Man* was becoming reality. Des McAnuff, who in 1993 staged *Tommy* on Broadway, declared his faith in the work's ability to translate to the big screen early on, and the rights to the story were eventually acquired by Warner Brothers. Animation writer and director Brad Bird, whose work included *the Simpsons*, *King of the Hill*, and *the Critic* was soon on board, and the film was on its way by January, 1997. The $30 million feature was released in

1999 as *The Iron Giant*. Pete was named executive director, McAnuff producer.

"I love animation, but I wanted the film to be a musical," Pete said later[216]. "That didn't happen, but I'm still immensely proud of what has become perhaps the last true cell-animation film to be made on a big budget. We shall see." Ted Hughes, who was sent a copy of Bird's script during the making of the film, was very pleased with the rendition of his work. "I want to tell you how much I like what Brad Bird has done," Hughes wrote in a letter to the filmmakers. "He's made something all of a piece, with terrific sinister gathering momentum and the ending came to me as a glorious piece of amazement. He's made a terrific dramatic situation out of the way he's developed *The Iron Giant*. I can't stop thinking about it…"[217]

---

[216] "[Brad Bird]… was dead set on avoiding a Disney-style musical (which I happen to like) with songs, etc.," Pete commented in an online chat in 2000. "So although we did not argue over this – he is a great filmmaker – I stood down."

[217] Ted Hughes died in October, 1998 at age 68 following an eighteen-month battle with cancer, just thirteen days after being personally awarded the Order of Merit by the Queen.

Chapter 12

"What has bothered me is the echoes of people like Bob Dylan, Tom Petty and Neil Young talking about the evil of nostalgia and sentimentality in rock. Part of me kind of agrees, but I don't really know why. I've been trying to find out in my own mind why nostalgia or sentimentality of any kind is such a bad thing. Certainly there was a lot of it on the Who tour. At least it wasn't the sad variety that we tend to see in the Beach Boys these days."
                                                            - Pete Townshend, 1990

In early December, 1988, Pete Townshend found himself contemplating, of all things, a Who tour. "To be 100 percent honest, the first thing that made me think about touring was the money," Pete told *Musician* in 1989.

> The commercial force behind such a venture is fantastic. I started to think what it would mean to have so much money that I would never have to make records at all. But around Christmas I decided I couldn't face doing it in spite of the fabulous sums of money involved. I said, "No, I want out." I thought what I'd be doing this year was put out my solo album, do a week of interviews, make the videos and go sailing.

Pete had been overcome with doubt. Were The Who too old to tour? Did anyone care anymore? The band had marked their twenty-fifth anniversary in 1988 by posing for photographs on Wardour Street, but, "Townshend says *nobody* ran the photos," *Rolling Stone* reported the following year. Pete shared his doubts in 1989:

I'd spent an immense amount of time thinking about the negative aspects: the trouble that I might have with my hearing, the fact that the Who are a spent force creatively and so couldn't ever go into the studio and produce a decent record. And we're too old, and this group kills people, and music does not belong in stadiums.

In January 1989, Pete traveled to New York for a Rock and Roll Hall of Fame dinner to deliver a speech welcoming new inductees The Rolling Stones[218]. By the end of the evening, Pete was inclined to rethink the touring question. "I saw the Soul Stirrers onstage," Pete said in 1989, "and this 86-year-old guy was onstage talking about music, and I realized that this undeniable American art form of rock'n'roll had given me a reason for being, a focus, a destiny, a past, a present and a future."

Soul Stirrer R.C. Harris' speech had a profound effect on Pete. "...I experienced something there that was very, very important and that was the perspective and the context that I live in and that I'd grown in, and that was a black American heritage," he told Dan Neer in 1989.

> ...I felt a kind of a spiritual buzz from it... [Harris] said 'We've waited a long time for this award, and it's come from you white folk and you rock'n'roll people... but rock'n'roll comes from R & B and R& B comes from gospel music with a swing, and gospel music with a swing comes from the Soul Stirrers.' I looked around me and there's Paul Simon, nodding, 'This is true, this is true', and Bruce Springsteen, 'Yes, yes of course this is very true', and I thought, I'd never even heard of them, you know, and I thought I'm in the presence of the people who created rock'n'roll...
>
> ...And I just thought, faced with all this unbelievable history which was kind of descending on me... that I shouldn't be obdurate about this. If they want to honor The Who, if they want to bring The Who back through the hall of fame, so be it. ...If fans out there are willing to pay us to go and attempt to do something then who are we to argue. And I know I'm going to have trouble with the stadium thing, I know I'm going to have trouble with journalists telling me that I'm a hypocrite, I know I'm going to feel a bit of a hypocrite, I know it's going to be

---

[218] *Rolling Stone* called Townshend's speech "biting." In addition to welcoming the Stones into the Rock and Roll Hall of Fame, Pete "...also slammed them for burying personal differences and planning their own big-money reunion tour."

very difficult for me to work with my hearing problems, I know there are going to be a lot of problems, but I also know that I am still at heart and always will be, a marine. I know that once you give me my gun, I will just go out there and I will kill, and so maybe right now I shouldn't intellectualize this whole thing too much. I should just get down, grab my guitar and go out there and do what I've been trained to do, and hope that it all works out.

"...I just felt that this is the music I was partially responsible for bringing back to America when the Who came over in the Sixties with a catalog of R&B songs," Pete told *Rolling Stone*. "And I suddenly thought, 'This is shit. They want us to come back and tour, and this is their music. It's not my fucking music.' And I suddenly felt that I'd been obstructive, obdurate and obstinate. All the *obs*. And I thought that I should get my shit together."

If this wasn't enough to persuade him, the trip home provided Pete with further inspiration. "...Townshend went to the airport to return to London," *Rolling Stone* reported, "looking forward to flying club class – "no creepy people, none of the bullshit of traveling first" – but switched to tourist class when his flight was delayed by fog."

Trying to find a way to cope with his unfamiliar, claustrophobic surroundings in coach, he decided to pass the time by figuring out how much he'd saved by downgrading his ticket. It turned out to be about $165 an hour... "By the time we landed," he says, "I suddenly realized that the whole nub of the thing, the other thing about coming back to America and touring, was that America was gonna insist on sending me home very, very rich. And that's a good feeling." So Townshend arrived home and told his wife, "Listen, I've procrastinated a lot about two things: one is whether or not to do this tour, and the other is whether or not we should adopt children. And you know, I think I'm gonna do both. Let's get some kids, and let's do this tour." A couple of weeks later, he adds with a laugh, the tour was being booked, and his wife was pregnant.

Thus, in early spring 1989, Pete Townshend and The Who were busy rehearsing in the London suburb of Bray, in an "...airplane hanger of a rehearsal space," according to *Guitar Player*'s Matt Resnicoff. Anyone who may have stumbled upon the band during rehearsals could have easily been forgiven for not recognizing them as The Who. Fifteen musicians now comprised the band, which prompted many observers to question the use of the legendary name. "What you're hearing today is not the Who," Pete explained to Resnicoff during rehearsals. "It's a sophisticated bunch of session musicians who, because of the way they've been picked and the way they've evolved in their relationship to me through my work as a writer, feel very deeply about what they're doing. But nonetheless, they're session musicians, who when this is finished will go back to Mick Jagger or whoever it is they were with. The Who, if you like, is John Entwistle, Roger Daltrey, and Pete Townshend, three kids who met at school when they were 14, and we're still here."

The large collection of musicians was Townshend's idea, chiefly intended to create a "powerful sound without too much volume," thus keeping any discomfort stemming from his hearing troubles to a minimum. "My reasons for wanting a larger band are technical, really," Pete explained. "With a larger number of musicians you can keep the stage sound level a lot lower." Without the ability to reduce the band's onstage volume, Pete would have regarded the proposition of a new Who tour too hazardous to his health. "Contemplating going back on the road with The Who for all the reasons that are involved in it," Pete said in a radio interview in May, "for the celebration, for getting together to celebrate 25 years of our history, our part in rock, to raise money for charities that we believe very strongly in, to honor the audience that want to come and see us play, and to take home their money, if we want to do any of those things, we've got to find a way of doing it, in my case, without actually making my hearing worse..."

In addition to Townshend, Entwistle and Daltrey, the band consisted of a five-piece brass section (The Kick Horns), three backing vocalists, all of whom had performed on *The Iron Man* (Billy Nicholls, Chyna and Cleveland Watkiss), percussionist Jody Linscott, a lead guitarist (Steve Bolton), a keyboardist (John 'Rabbit' Bundrick resumed his role), and drummer Simon Phillips.

"I felt the best thing to do was to make the lineup of the band as anonymous and capable as possible," Pete explained to *Guitar Player*. This statement may explain why Townshend chose Steve Bolton as the tour's lead guitarist.[219] The previously unheard of Bolton, described by *Rolling Stone* as, "...a tall Scotsman with a mountain of hair and a rockabilly wardrobe," played "...merely competent, chorused-out, whammied-up '80s style service to a library of classic crunch," according to *Guitar Player*.

Primarily, it was Pete's hearing problems that led to the additional guitarist, but an underlying desire to function as a rhythm player also influenced his decision. "I can't hear the high notes, or the top octave of the

---

[219] Townshend told *Rolling Stone* that his old friend Joe Walsh offered his services as a backup if Bolton didn't work out. "...Walsh's and the Who's managers decided they might as well draw up a contract just in case," the magazine reported.

piano at all," he told the *Washington Post* in July[220]. "The second guitarist is there because I want somebody to play the solos, but also because I want to play rhythm. That's what I'm looking forward to on this tour because I play *great* rhythm guitar – I'm up there with Don Everly, or whichever one it was."

The acoustic guitar is "...something which I feel is a very, very powerful instrument," Pete told Hugh Foley in a May, 1989, radio interview.

> *Pinball Wizard*, for example, is a front line, famous, loved classic Who track, and it's actually a song that, on the record, is an acoustic track. It's not an electric guitar song at all... the actual rhythm of the song (imitates rhythm), that's what gives it its powerhouse thing, and it's an acoustic played in that slightly kind of Spanishy way that I play. I really feel I'm a definitive rhythm player on acoustic and electric. I've had people that I regard as the top players in the world tell me that – I'm increasingly told that by young guitarists who by the time they're *six* can play faster than Jimi Hendrix ever dreamed of, and I'm proud of that, and I enjoy that and I also think it's a fundamental part of Who music. It's not to say that when the Who go out on the road I won't play some electric, but I don't think I'll ever play the way I used to play.

Conspicuously absent from the new lineup was Kenney Jones, whose drum stool was occupied by widely respected session drummer Simon Phillips. Pete's relationship with Jones had clearly soured over the past few years. "...Kenney...[has] given me an extremely hard time lately," Pete told *Musician* in July.

> Firstly about our not going on the road for so long. And he said I denied him the opportunity to make a good Who album. When I broke the deal with Warner Bros., he felt we were just revving up to make a great album. And he became mesmerized by the Who in a worse way than anyone I've come across. I said to him that I wanted to work with Roger and I think there will be difficulties, but it's not my battle. You've got to sort yourself out with Roger. Got to convince him you can do the job. Nothing seemed to get done. One day Kenney's wife, or girlfriend, or whatever she was, rang me up and she said, "Listen, he's

---

[220] At the press conference announcing the tour, Pete reportedly had problems hearing many of the questions asked by reporters – Daltrey repeated them for him.

not going to wait while you fuck around anymore. He's going to get this band together with Paul Rodgers," and he went ahead and did it...

In explaining his choice of Simon Phillips as Jones' replacement, Pete gave further insight into the formation of the new band. "...what we can do with Simon is probably a lot more ambitious than anything we could do with Kenney," he explained.

> Kenney isn't here. I chose the new drummer. You could go down the rest of the band and I think you'll find that I chose most of them. In fact, I chose the whole fucking lot of them. There's no conflict. This is my band. The only potential conflict is based on how John and Roger feel about working in that environment and calling it the Who. Maybe they would prefer going out as a four-piece and I had a stack and we thrash away like we did in the '60s. I don't know what's on their minds. They're not entirely honest with me all the time. They treat me like a lunatic sometimes.

Townshend, all his doubts about touring now firmly cast aside, was calling the shots. "It's very difficult, when you've changed your mind, to explain why you've changed it," he told *Rolling Stone* in July, 1989. "But this is an anniversary year for the band, and I desperately wanted to do something. I wanna see the Who's catalog out there, I wanna see people buying the early records."

While the rather bloated lineup fielded for this incarnation of The Who had very little in common with the original band, Pete acknowledged that a glimmer of the old magic still remained. "The three of us, when we work together, have part of the magic that the early band had," Townshend told *Rolling Stone*.

> I think, in a sense, Keith's death had a kind of compounding reduction in that magic, and Roger, John and I add up to about fifty percent of the old Who. But it's there...In a sense, the name refers to the audience's feeling about what the band means to them. And that's got very little to do with what the band actually does these days, which is *nothing*. The band has done nothing in years. There *is* no band. It's wrong, really, to call it the Who, because it isn't the Who. It's a bunch of session musicians brought together to play Who material. It's kind of authenticated because of our presence, but that's all, really.

While the presence of a large group of musicians eased the effects of onstage noise levels on Pete's fragile ears, further steps were necessary **during rehearsals in order to minimize his pain.** He had a Plexiglass enclosure constructed in which he could play guitar and see the band, but which shielded him from much of the onstage noise, particularly the high-pitched squeals of feedback which are often experienced during rehearsals when amps and microphones are being repositioned. "...if I'm going to do performances ever again – and I've almost given up hope," Pete said, "I think that a purpose-made booth is the answer, one which would see me through the long, long, long hours of rehearsal and technical rehearsal, where you inevitably get terrible feedback shrieks." As rehearsals continued, Townshend gradually discovered that if he kept the volume on his side of the stage to 98 decibels ("about the level of a loud, fairly squawky hi-fi"), he could leave his plexiglass sound booth without any discomfort.

A result of Pete's extra care and attention toward his hearing over the last few years was that he noticed an improvement in his condition. "...my upper-frequency hearing is actually returning, and that's become a great relief," he said. "I think one of the things about tinnitus and hearing damage is that you psychologically close yourself off. You don't fight for hearing. The reverse happens: You kind of say, "No, no, please, no more loud noises. Stop. Stop! ...yesterday my alarm in my car went off, and I lifted up the bonnet to switch it off, and I couldn't get *near* it. I thought, "If I get close to this fucking alarm, I'm going to blow my brain out." "

While the booth was primarily intended for use during rehearsals, Pete planned to take it on the road as a precaution. "On the stage itself," he told *Rolling Stone*, "I'm really hoping that I'm going to be able to just stand out there and work, and we're trying to build as cosmetic a booth as is possible, so that if I do get noise damage, it will probably be from feedback shrieks. If I get a bad feedback shriek, it disables me for between five and fifteen minutes, so I would then just have to go into the booth. Roger doesn't really want me in this booth at all. He wants me to wear earplugs, but I haven't yet found any that I've felt comfortable with..."

Pete's concern for his well-being while on tour was also evident in other areas. He made it clear in several pre-tour interviews that his trademark windmilling was a thing of the past. "I've got to be careful because I knock my fingernails off and because when you connect [with the strings], you hurt yourself very very badly," he told the *Washington Post*. In previous Who tours, he explained to *Guitar Player* in September, 1989, "...as soon as we'd hit *Baba O'Riley*, I'd go *Djaaang*, swing, swing, all my fingernails would just get broken off across, and from then on I would be in absolute agony for the rest of the tour."

I wouldn't be able to sleep; you know, at night my hand would be throbbing. I'm not allowed to use any kind of opiates at all, so I can't use strong pain-killers, and aspirins don't do anything. And the other thing is, when you swing your arm and you've got a cut finger, blood pours out of it at a great rate, and it goes all over your strings. So one of the other things I decided to do on this tour was be a little bit more careful with my *hands*.

"...There are two ways to windmill," Pete told *Rolling Stone* in July, 1989. "There's the way I windmill, and there's the way that every other asshole windmills. When I windmill," he explained emphatically, "I... break... off... the... ends... of... my... fingers. Flesh flies off. Blood runs under my fingernails. When I windmill, I fucking *windmill*, right? And I can't do that to myself. I really can't. I don't care enough about the audience, and I don't care enough about the music anymore. I care more about the state of my fingernails."

While the windmill was, at least for the time being, not an option, Pete's nearly-as-famous onstage leaps remained in consideration for the upcoming tour. "I haven't really tried to do that lately," he told the *Washington Post*, "but I'm too young and fit to injure myself doing something as easy as that... I'm going to be careful, but I'm still going to kill people."[221]

Pete's decision to put a lid on the windmill came at a time when his guitar playing was experiencing an evolutionary spurt. He had recently bought a Casio MIDI guitar with a locking-nut tremolo system. "I started to play around and thought, 'So that's how they do all this unbelievable string bending; it's this thing that you can wiggle all over the place...'," Pete told *Guitarist* in 1990. "I always used to take the arm off. So I pulled off some solos I was proud of and it kind of brought me back to the electric guitar. I was studying pull-offs and all that stuff and deliberately trying to keep away from the Townshend clichés..." Pete's decision to leave the tremolo arm on his guitars during this tour would have unexpected consequences, resulting in an injury at a show in Tacoma, Washington.

Another concern of Pete's prior to the 1989 tour was his physical conditioning. He hadn't exposed his body to any lengthy touring and

---

[221] The "kill people" mentality reflected Pete's approach to performing live. "At times like this I just see it like a Marine: I'm just going to go out there and kill people," he said. "I don't really know whether I'm going to come back in one piece or not, and I can't really afford to contemplate that. I know that my gun is going to be my best friend and that's it. The fact that *Tommy* is going to be difficult to deal with mentally and artistically is an equal problem to the fact that I'm not sure I'm going to be able to sustain 12 weeks of touring and a 3 ½-hour show without literally getting varicose veins or something. I don't know. There are no guarantees."

performing in seven years, and, at 44 years of age, he wanted to ensure that the band's latest jaunt wasn't hazardous to his heath. "Before this tour, I had to lose 20 pounds," he told the *San Diego Union*'s George Varga in August. "I had to have a heart scan, and I actually had to change my diet. When I come off stage I need a two-hour cool-down period, and I have to sleep 10 hours a night."

Age remained a concern for Pete during the tour. "We have to define our limits," he told Varga nearly two months into the tour.

> I'm surprised at what we've been able to do this time. ...The Stones are never going to stop, and if the Who lives another 25 years, I'm sure we'll be tempted to get up there and party down. And that might be the day somebody has a heart attack on stage. I have to be honest. It's quite possible that I've had a heart attack on this tour! ...So, it's whether or not it repels you, that's what's important. It's about entertainment, and you can't be entertained by people who are repellent because of their age. We can go on stage with 16 layers of makeup[222], and I'm sure on the video (screens that flank the stage) we look two, three, maybe five or 10 years younger than we really are. The people we are really confronted with are the people in the front row who can see the lines, can see the thinning hair and see the makeup. Now if you can make them happy, and if you can mainly convince yourself, I suppose, that you're happy with it, then you can go on. But I think it's still a real problem. There has to be an end to it; rock isn't like blues or jazz.

Further changes were reflected in the set list, which included a wide variety of selections, including many cover versions of other bands' songs, such as Jimi Hendrix' *Hey Joe*, James Brown's *Night Train*, and Bo Diddley's *I'm A Man*. "I'm sounding a bit like a cracked record on the subject," Pete told *Rolling Stone*, "but I just feel that the audience needs a little bit of perspective. I want people who listen to Prince to know *why* he is there. I want the Who to lead irrevocably to Cream and to Jimi Hendrix. I want people to understand the fucking *context*. 'Cause, you know, if you're just presented with Prince out of context, he's not so much a genius as a weirdo."

Pete further explained the issue of context during the radio interview with Hugh Foley in May:

---

[222] The Who reportedly employed a makeup artist on this tour.

Prince is such a kind of quantum genius that the guy doesn't even really know what he's doing half the time. He means something if you know the music of The Who, if you know the music of Jimi Hendrix, if you know the music of Little Richard... It's only then that you can perceive the scale of his genius. If you don't know that music, then he's just another jerk from Minneapolis who wears funny trousers... You have to know the context. It's too easy to belittle some of the fairy tale superstars of this age like Prince, like Madonna, like Michael Jackson, if you take them out of context it's very easy. The reason why they are so enormousy popular is because they understand their context. And so that's something that is happening very much at the moment and which I like to feel that not only have I begun to contribute to a bit in my own work but that The Who will do when they go out on the road, it's something that we're trying to look at in a slightly different way, I'm not saying we're gonna play old blues songs all night... but we're gonna try and evoke the atmosphere we grew up in. So we're going to do four hours of Everly Brothers songs (laughs).

Pete also felt that fans needed to hear some of the more obscure recordings in Who history, and the large band enabled him to do that. In addition to the previously mentioned cover tunes, among the more than seventy songs rehearsed for the 1989 *Kids Are Alright* tour were obscure tracks such as *Mary-Anne With The Shaky Hands* and *Tattoo*, and the band's recent studio work featured on *The Iron Man*: *Dig* and *Fire*. Also included in The Who's repertoire during this period were solo Townshend songs such as *Give Blood* and *Let My Love Open The Door*. "I'm anxious that the traditional Who set doesn't sound or look or feel like a traditional Who set," Pete told *Rolling Stone*.

Wishing to avoid adhering to what he described to the *Detroit Free Press* as the "heavy electric guitar music" of the band's more popular work, Pete wanted to showcase some of The Who's mellower side. "All we're really doing, I think, is letting them hear a little bit more than they hear on the radio or that they heard in the old concerts. We only made eight studio albums, so it shouldn't be that difficult to keep up with us." Another reason for the introduction of more obscure material into the band's setlist was Pete's adverse reaction to contemporary radio, who's Who catalog seemed limited to around four songs. "What I *don't* want to do with the Who, and I think it would be fatal if we did it, is feed radio and reinforce what radio has done to music," Pete said in 1989. "Radio is unbelievably important, but it has become too much of a slave to ratings and demographics, and we tend to become too much of a slave to that response. You go out and play a song like *Behind Blue Eyes, Won't Get Fooled Again, Pinball Wizard*, any of the tracks that get a lot of FM airplay, and the crowd immediately responds."

A result of Pete's wish to provide musical context alongside a large dose of Who material meant that The Who often remained onstage during this tour for over three hours.

Despite all the thought that had gone into the set list, Pete didn't sound particularly excited about it. "The set list is boring," he told *Rolling Stone*, adding that he deferred to Daltrey and Entwistle for song selection. "I don't think any of us are happy with the set," Entwistle remarked. "We have got different ideas about the music, different ideas about how the Who sould sound and what the Who should play, and we'll never, ever agree on that."

The Who's 25th Anniversary *The Kids Are Alright* tour spread most of its 43 dates in 27 cities between two nationally broadcast performances of *Tommy* for charity. In fact, a chief reason for the tour's existence was the two *Tommy* shows: The rest of the tour dates provided the financial wherewithal to pull off the two free fundraisers. "The economics of it started to beg the question: How much is it going to cost us to get a band together to play Radio City Music Hall?," Pete said. "How much does it cost to get the Who Machine in action? When I looked at the budget, I went into shock. A lot of things have changed in seven years, and not just the music."

Together the *Tommy* performances raised $6 million for the Nordoff-Robbins Music Therapy program for autistic and abused children and the nonprofit Rock and Roll Hall of Fame[223]. As a fund raising entity, The Who proved formidable. "I feel that the Who is one of the very few fund-raising outfits of our power and potential with a social conscience, willing to address certain domestic issues," Pete told the *Washington Post*'s Richard Harrington in 1989.

> Since rock-and-roll grows from the streets and sewers – we're not talking in cliches – it also blossoms from the fertilizer of blood and death, deprivation and starvation and, in a lot of cases, domestic melodrama – the angst of youth, the pain, the loneliness and the isolation. It *thrives* on that and therefore it's got a strong linking of hands with Narcotics Anonymous and Alcoholics Anonymous and all these other street causes.
>
> I didn't want to say 'no more' because what if somebody comes to us with a heavy cause and says for every dollar you raise, a life can be saved? What's our

---

[223] Other childrens charities also benefited from this tour.

response? 'No, we won't do it because artistically it's not satisfying anymore?'...

...It seems that charity in the music business has come to consist of the same half a dozen people - me and Peter Gabriel and Sting and Phil Collins and a few others – calling each other on the phone and saying, 'You owe me a favor.' And I've had enough of that bullshit. This way we're taking money from these corporations and making sure it goes somewhere where it can help.

The tour kicked off with a show at Glens Falls, New York on June 21, in front of what the *Detroit Free Press* described as an "astonishingly enthusiastic" crowd of 5,000, prior to two sold-out dates at Toronto's CNE Stadium on June 23 and 24. Most of the shows on the tour began with a 40-minute version of *Tommy*, omitting songs such as *Eyesight to the Blind*, *Sally Simpson* and *Sensation*.

The first full *Tommy* performance followed – The Who's first complete rendition of the rock opera in 17 years – at New York's Radio City Music Hall on June 27. The show began with *Overture*, and the opera was played in its entirety, followed by a selection of Who classics such as *I Can't Explain*, *Baba O'Riley*, *Love Reign O'er Me* and *Won't Get Fooled Again*. Pete appeared on the David Letterman show the same day as the *Tommy* performance, performing *A Friend Is A Friend* with Billy Nichols and Chyna.

The tour rolled through a series of sold out dates at massive East Coast venues[224], including four nights at Giants Stadium in East Rutherford, New Jersey, and two at Washington DC's RFK Stadium. As The Who wound their way through the Northeast and Midwest, Pete's attitude toward touring, shaky at first, began to change. "I'm a late convert, I guess," Pete told the *Detroit Free Press*' Gary Graff on July 18th during The Who's stop at Buffalo's massive Rich Stadium.

> Every now and again I have a slight misgiving about what we're doing, but then I have to remind myself of the size of the misgivings I had before I came out. Without seeing the audiences, I could remain a skeptic. But there's something about how the crowds are responding...that's rebuilding a lot of the faith I had in the music I've loved all my life, that it can keep people together and bring pleasure."

---

[224] "Despite the fact that the news flashes all said Pete Townshend was going to play guitar like John Denver and he couldn't hear a word being said, the show in Boston sold out in two hours," reported *Musician*'s Charles Young.

>...It *is* stimulating. I'm not suffering from the kind of musical boredom that I used to on the road with the Who."
>
>...I think we've succeeded. What happens onstage is that every now and again you think, 'Ah yes, this is the Who,' and at other times you think, 'Oh yes, this is people gathering together to celebrate the Who.' That's good enough, really; it would be cruel for outsiders to say that because we can't do the whole book, we can't do any of it.

"Whatever has happened since the band hit the road is very good, and my view has changed," Pete told the *San Diego Union*'s George Varga a month later, at which point he had markedly increased his use of the electric guitar onstage, eschewing the acoustic despite the presence of Steve Bolton. "I now like to think that I made the right decision," he told Varga.

>Never has a man come under so much fucking pressure to put a band of old war horses back together again, and it's not because I wanted it; it's the *last* thing I wanted. It's what the audience wants. It's not up to me to define when it finishes. It's up to the audience to say, 'No, this is wrong. You now are too old.' But rock has to have the courage to define itself. That's the thing, and it's not up to the performers. I've tried to do it; I tried to do it in *My Generation*, and I've tried to do it since. I tried to say in 1982, 'OK, the Who is finished. It's ended.'

The tour continued south, through North Carolina and Florida before swinging Northwest, stopping in Atlanta, St. Louis and Colorado.

The August 16th show at the Tacoma Dome in Washington provided Pete with further reasons to drop the windmill, which he'd sworn off prior to the tour but had executed consistently anyway since day one. His trademark move was such a powerful and effective gesture, he couldn't resist giving the crowd what they wanted every now and then. "It was like... like Hitler arriving!", Pete said of the crowd's reaction to the windmill, "and all I'm doing is swinging my bloody arm." But swinging one's arm windmill fashion with Townshendian violence and aggression on a Fender Stratocaster with intact tremolo arm was something that even Pete wasn't ready for. As the band performed *Won't Get Fooled Again*, their final song prior to the encore, Pete windmilled and his hand collided with the tremolo arm, which was jutting backwards rather than hanging down in its customary position. "...suddenly I just felt my arm stop," he told *Guitarist* in June, 1990. "I thought I'd just banged my hand but I looked, and it was actually still in there... sort of hanging. I thought, 'Shit! That's gone in quite a way,' then I realized it had gone right through the hand!" The tremolo arm had pierced Pete's right hand between the fourth and fifth fingers[225]. "Well, I picked up the guitar and held it from the tremolo so that everybody could see what had happened," Pete told *Q*'s David Cavanagh in early 2000. "Then I pulled it out and blood started to pump out. And then it fucking hurt. I ran off stage and ended up having oxygen, so I don't remember much after that."

Pete, unable to move his fingers and in "quite severe shock", was rushed to the hospital, leaving the band to perform an encore consisting of *Twist and Shout* and *Hey Joe* without him. "It just so happened that in Tacoma there's this brilliant microsurgeon who irrigated it with a saline solution for an hour and a half," Pete said in 2000. A series of dexterity tests was performed and it was discovered that no nerves or tendons had been damaged. The tremolo arm had pierced the webbing between Pete's fingers and nothing more. "Next day," Pete recalled, "it was healed."

"That night I was sufficiently coward enough to pray," Pete told *Guitarist*.

> I didn't care about rock and roll, or the guitar, or performing, or having money, or being thought of as an important this or an unimportant that or a has-been this or a has-been that. But never to be able to hold a pencil again or, as I said to the doctor, have a good wank... It was just so shocking to realize that for the sake of a catch-phrase I'd put myself in a position where I might have disabled myself for life. I so desperately want what I do *not* to be circus, and it *is* circus. So much of it is tight-rope walking and so little of it has to do with what I write, what I play and the quality of it.

Following two dates in Vancouver and a stop in San Diego's Jack Murphy Stadium, The Who played their second complete rendition of *Tommy*, this time at L.A.'s 5,800-seat Universal Amphitheater on August 24. The televised, pay-per-view performance, which was later released on video, was an all-star affair, featuring Elton John (the pinball wizard), Billy Idol (Cousin Kevin)[226], Phil Collins (Uncle Ernie), Patti LaBelle (the Acid Queen), and Steve Winwood (the Hawker).

---

[225] "...what I was actually doing when I last speared myself on my whammy bar was a kind of humorous impersonation of what a silly fuck I was when I used to do that before," Pete told *Guitar*'s H.P. Newquist in August, 1996. "...My heart wasn't even in it. Maybe that's why I speared myself."

[226] Idol was "a big Who fan," according to Jeff Stein. He was in attendance at The Who's May, 1978 concert at Shepperton studios.

Another date in Los Angeles followed two nights later, this time at the more sizable Memorial Coliseum in front of 65,000 fans. The two Oakland dates which ensued on August 29 and 30 and brought in another 100,000 fans.

Two September dates in Houston and Dallas, Texas, marked the end of the tour's American leg. The shows, which were sponsored by Miller Lite beer and raised $1 million for the Texas Special Olympics, also featured the only opening acts of the entire tour, Texas native brothers Stevie Ray and Jimmie Vaughan and their respective bands, Double Trouble and The Fabulous Thunderbirds.

Nearly a month after the conclusion of the U.S. tour, The Who embarked on their English jaunt faced with the prospect of having to scrap the last few dates due to the imminent arrival of Pete and Karen's baby[227]. The tour consisted of four early October dates in Birmingham followed by a nearly two-week break. Four nights at Wembley Arena ensued[228], the proceedings being brought to a close with two nights around Halloween at the Royal Albert Hall.

Old friend Chris Charlesworth caught up with The Who during their four day stop at Wembley Arena. "I'd lost touch with The Who after Keith died," he recalled after the show.

> I hadn't been to see them with Kenney Jones. All I had to remember of the glory days were the *Leeds* album, a few bootlegs and *The Kids Are Alright* video which I'd virtually worn out. But I decided to buy a ticket for Wembley, to this show, for old time's sake. I was a bit late and they were playing *Substitute* as I found my seat, then they did *Can't Explain*. Of course, it wasn't The Who up there, not The Who that I'd known and loved so much, but it brought all the old memories flooding back and in spite of it all I enjoyed myself...
>
> I liked it when the three of them came back alone after the interval – that was a nice touch – but Roger's voice was shot. It was clear that he was hoarse and having difficulty hitting the right notes. Mid-way through *Behind Blue Eyes* he walked off stage in apparent disgust at himself, not to return. Pete took over on vocals and finished the song, then sang throughout *Won't Get Fooled Again*. In a curious way this set my adrenaline flowing, because I knew it would put them on the back foot and they'd have to

---

[227] Pete's third child, Joseph, was born on 21 November, 1989.
[228] Pete and Eric Clapton appeared on BBC TV the night after the final Wembley show, and treated host Sue Lawley to a rendition of Muddy Waters' *Standin' Around Cryin'*. Pete also performed *I Won't Run Anymore* with a backing band.

improvise. It was the old 'anything can happen at a Who concert' scenario all over again, and it was obvious that Pete was not pleased at this turn of events. Great! An angry Townshend is an exciting Townshend! During *Won't Get Fooled Again* he whacked his Schecter Stratocaster against the monitors at the front but it wouldn't break, so he just tossed it aside and picked up another one.

When the band returned for an encore Pete apologized for Roger, explaining that he had the flu. He made a deeply self-deprecating speech about how they were only doing it for the money which was at least honest. Most big rock bands who reform try to kid fans it's for artistic reasons but The Who had never lied to their fans before and they didn't start now. He paid tribute to Keith, partly because they were in Wembley, where Keith was born. 'We've never been able to replace him,' he admitted. 'I asked Roger if he wanted to come on to do an encore and he told me to fuck off,' said Pete, adding, 'Not for the first time.' Indeed not, I thought. They closed the show with John taking the vocals for *Twist and Shout*.

Charlesworth recalled that his experience at the show led him to get back in touch with Pete, and eventually led to his involvement in compiling *The Who: Thirty Years of Maximum R&B*, a retrospective boxed set.

The *Kids Are Alright* 1989 tour brought in over thirty million dollars, not including the sponsorship the band received from Miller Beer (reported to be in the seven figure range). Some asked if The Who really needed the money, to which Pete replied, "...the sad answer is, 'Yes, we do.' It would be pointless to pretend that we don't... It would also be pointless to pretend that John Entwistle is making the kind of money he used to make in the heyday of the Who. So, money was an important factor. The reality of the money was one of the first things that made us consider whether or not our party was a possibility. But what's been nice is the money *has* led us to the party, and the party has turned out be a good party, (and) an expensive one, in that it's making lots of money, unless that seems like an upside-down statement."

"...what was very important to me about that tour – which in hindsight, I greatly regret doing – what's hard about it was that I fucking *enjoyed* it," Pete told *Q*'s John Harris in 1996.

I think I regret it because finally, as it got closer and closer, I realized that I was doing the job I love to do the most *purely* for the money. And some of the celebration of our 25th anniversary got lost, because I very quickly realized that other people had another agenda. Their motives were not to celebrate the past 25 years but to look forward to the next 25. This was the re-birth of The Who – for Roger, for John, for a lot of the fans, for the record company, the promoters, everybody. It was, "Oh great, we've got one of the few supergroups back that can fill up fucking Pontiac Stadium." The Who got back together and what people were hoping was, through this Townshend will get a taste for it again and we'll be back with the one band who can consistently fill 86,000 seater stadiums. We never ever fucking failed to do it. With a shit record out, with a *dead drummer*, we could still do it. That's the dream that John and Roger have had to let go. But I'm grateful that we did it and I'm grateful that we made the money that we made.

1990 saw a limited amount of Who activity, with the band's induction into the Rock'n'Roll Hall of Fame taking place on 17 January. Pete, Roger and John attended the 5th annual induction ceremony at New York's Waldorf Astoria, with Keith's daughter Mandy also present.

In March, *Join Together*, a boxed set featuring live recordings from The Who's 1989 tour, was released. It reached number 24 in the U.K., and a lowly 180 in the States. "I don't really know what the significance of this album is," Pete told *Rolling Stone* in May. "I don't think it's a groundbreaking live album like *Live at Leeds* was. I don't know whether it will mean anything in Who history."

"*Join Together* is the inevitable live-album curtain call designed squeeze the last dollar out of the Who's twenty-fifth anniversary tour," read the 2 ½ star review in *Rolling Stone*.

>...*Join Together* is not the work of a seminal rock quartet: Instead, it's a meticulously rendered performance of the rock opera *Tommy* plus selections from the Who song book played by a fifteen-piece group that just so happens to include three of the band's original members. Call it the Who Revue, featuring the durable voice of Roger Daltrey, the dour throb of bassist John Entwistle and the deaf-defying antics of Pete Townshend.
>
>...On purely musical grounds, *Join Together* cannot be faulted: The recorded sound is exquisite. It's a highly professional rock & roll record of a kind that was inconceivable when a far angrier Who defined itself by bashing its rebellious way through *My Generation* all those years ago. It's also thoroughly redundant and as predictable as the answer that Pete Townshend himself would no doubt

give if asked to name the Who's best concert album: *Live at Leeds*.

In late 1990, Pete found himself in the news following some comments he'd made in an interview with Timothy White for White's forthcoming book, *Rock Lives*. The two spoke about the homosexual innuendo of *Rough Boys*, of which Pete said, "What, in a sense, *Rough Boys* was about was almost a coming-out, an acknowledgment of the fact that I'd had a gay life, and that I understood what gay sex was about: it was not about faggery at all. It was about violence in a lot of senses. It leans very heavily into the kind of violence that men carry in them. If men have a violence which cannot be shared with women, then it can't be shared with them sexually. And so there's only one place for that violence and that's with other men."

Pete further commented that, "One of the things that stunned me when *Empty Glass* came out was that I realized I'd found a female audience, just by being honest. Not necessarily by saying, "I am gay, I am gay, I am gay." But just by being honest about that fact that I understand how gay people feel, and I identify. And I know how it feels to be a woman. I know how it feels to be a woman because I *am* a woman. And I won't be classified as just a man."

The ensuing reports of Townshend's 'coming out' and his supposed admission of bisexuality naturally drew plenty of media attention, and the fact that he didn't immediately loudly refute the charges provided enough evidence of guilt for many observers. Pete offered a Wildean response to the frenzy: "Scandal is fabulous. No artist ever suffers from it. The people who suffer are the artist's family and friends. When Reuters put out on the wire that I was a transsexual, cross-dressing sheep fucker, I was laughing until I saw my cleaning lady's face. It was a weird day."

Pete further commented on the incident in a 1994 interview with *Playboy*:

> [*Rough Boys*] is ironic because the song is actually taunting both the homosexuals in America - who were, at the time, dressing themselves up as Nazi generals - and the punks in Britain dressing the same way. I thought it was great that these tough punks were dressing as homosexuals without realizing it. I did an interview about it, saying *Rough Boys* was about being gay, and in the interview I also talked about my "gay life," which – I meant – was actually about the friends I've had who are gay. So the interviewer kind of dotted the t's and crossed the I's and assumed that this was a coming out, which it wasn't at all. But I became an object of ridicule when it was picked up in England. It

> was a big scandal, which is silly. If I were bisexual, it would be no big deal in the music industry. If I ran down a list of the men who have tried to get me into bed, I could bring down quite a few big names in the music business. And no, I won't do it.
>
> ...I don't want to deny bisexuality as if I were being accused of child molestation or murder, as if it were some crime or something to be ashamed of, because that would be cruel to people who are gay. But I was bitter and angry at the way the truth had been distorted and decided never to do any interviews again. Not because I had been manipulated but because I didn't trust myself to be precise about what I was saying.

Pete attempted somewhat to address the public's confusion regarding his sexuality in a February 2001 letter to *Mojo* (an earlier issue of the magazine contained some accusations which Pete wished to address). "If it is un-PC to even mention whether someone is gay or not, then I am guilty," he wrote.

> But to give some background to the qualification: I did live with Kit Lambert for six months in 1964 after leaving art college, and he was open about his sexuality with me, and – unlike the wonderfully vulnerable Robert Stigwood – never attempted to seduce me. I sometimes met Kit's rent boys the morning after, and we swapped little purple pills. I genuinely like the gays I knew. They seemed to have a conviction about their entire identity that – at the time – I lacked.
>
> ...The Who had always had a huge male audience who, on the outside, might be entirely populated by lager louts. Keith Moon with his blondes and his press stunts may have seemed to be a lad. Roger was obviously a lad. But what was I? In a couple of early auditions the other guys were urged to "chuck out the gangly one with the big nose". Before I called my beautiful art-school friend Karen Astley I was a Kings Road swan, unsure whether to be gay or not. It was not about fashion, it was about the fact that all the men I admired seemed to be gay, bisexual or just not give a shit. I still don't give a shit. Weren't the '60s great!

Rolling Stone's Chris Heath pointedly asked Pete in mid-2002 if he considered himself fundamentally bisexual. "No, I don't," Pete replied.

I know that I've got – and this has got nothing to do with anything I've actually done, or not done – a very, very feminine side. I think my creative side is very feminine. And I went so far as to say in that interview [with Timothy White in 1989] that I often feel like a woman; I can see what a woman feels – the whole act of submission sexually. But, in a sense, what I was talking about was the act of submission sexually in a male-female relationship, that you can swap roles. But that's very common and corny now, in a sense, to even bring it up. And I suppose what I'm doing is taking all of the feminine attributes and regarding them as being passive, gentle, submissive or whatever. But in the sense that my creative side is archly feminine, it is "I want the baby and I want it now!" It's biological. It's absolute. It's the feminine side that says to you [raises voice], "If I need to take heroin, I'll fucking take heroin – who are you to even raise an eyebrow? If I need to give birth, I shall do it!" But it's got nothing to do with my sexuality.

Further confusion as to Pete's sexual orientation was caused in 2002 when former Doors publicist and manager of the Ramones Danny Fields reportedly referred to Pete in the book *In Their Own Write: Adventures in the Music Press* as a boyfriend of his in the late sixties. Of more concern to Pete was the fact that he knew nothing about the matter until it was broached during an interview with *Rolling Stone*'s Chris Heath in mid-2002. A flabbergasted Pete acknowledged to Heath that he and Fields were friends, but went on to say, "...I just don't know what he is fucking talking about. I have no idea... I haven't spoken to him since this has come out. I'll just look him in the eye and say, "What the fuck are you talking about? Please tell me.""

When Heath asked if he'd had many physical encounters with men over the years, Pete laughed and said, "no, I haven't", adding "...I'm from the Sixties. You know, we tried everything, but..." He later acknowledged to *Rolling Stone* in an email that he distinctly remembered "experimenting, consciously," on only two occasions and that the encounter with Fields, if it happened at all, must have been a case where he "experimented unconsciously". Putting it more bluntly during the interview with Heath, he exclaimed loudly, "...if Danny fucked me, Danny drugged me first. So if you want to fucking print that, then print it. Because that's the truth. It fucking hurts, that he so fucking carelessly said this in the papers. He should have fucking told me what he did to me first."

Pete attributed the few sexual encounters he'd had with men to being in a state of severe inebriation and having impaired judgement. "I think what it had to do with – and to be honest (laughs), I can't remember much about any of it – was to do with the fact that I was actually completely smashed out of my head," he told Heath. "I'm fifty-seven, I've got a young girlfriend, I'm not gay. I'm not interested in men. I don't think I ever really have been."

July 1991 saw a Who reunion of sorts, as the band contributed a track to the Elton John/Bernie Taupin tribute album, *Two Rooms*, which would be released in October. The Who played *Saturday Night's Alright (For Fighting)*, and didn't record the song as a band - in fact, Pete's guitar and vocal work was recorded second only to Jon Astley's programmed drums and keyboards (John and Roger added their parts about a week later). In an interview with *Generations*, Astley later recalled Pete's performance during the session, which took place at Eel Pie: "All in one afternoon we had to do two acoustic guitar passes, a couple of electric guitar passes - one of which was fantastic. It's a funny thing about Pete in the studio; he'll go through the motions and then suddenly he'll get interested and then everyone's just rooted to their seats…it doesn't last long but it's brilliant, he's really going for it and his hand is moving as fast as his brain. He doesn't know what he's going to play next, it's all off the top of his head and then he'll lose interest again. So unless you catch it…I mean, it was a brilliant pass."

Chapter 13

"Tommy is on Broadway. People love it and people hate it, but I am in a new kind of ecstasy."
- Pete Townshend, 1993

"I was very worried that if Broadway failed, it would halt Tommy as a property for probably another 10, 15 years. And that would have been a shame, because my instincts told me this is the right time. One of the things that was very disturbing is that I knew that if it was successful, it would change my life. I was excited that if the show did well, it could feed my future creative life, but I was also frightened that maybe I should be retiring, you know? Maybe I should be just taking the money I already have and slowing down, getting out of show business."
- Pete Townshend, 1993

In September 1991, Pete sailed his 60-foot yacht off the coast of Cornwall to vacation in the Scilly Isles, a tiny cluster of islands about 30 miles west of Land's End. The Townshends stayed in a cottage on Tresco, a small island which contains the ruins of a 10th century abbey and fortifications known as Oliver Cromwell's Tower and King Charles' Tower. Cars are not permitted on the island since it has no proper roads, so Pete's inland transportation consisted of a rented bicycle[229]. It was on Friday, September 13 1991 that Pete fell off his bike and severely broke his right wrist and forearm. "I was on a bike, completely exhilarated, going down this hill, and I hit a pothole and went over the handlebars," Pete told *Playboy* in 1994. Pete's wrist "...shattered into a dozen fragments," he said in 1993. Pete was promptly flown by helicopter to Truro City Hospital for emergency treatment, which involved the insertion of metal pins and plates into the damaged limb, and a cast from fingertips to elbow.

---

[229] On the subject of cycling: Pete later was named to the honorary board of 'Trips for Kids', a non-profit organization based in California which provided disadvantaged children the opportunity to embark on mountain bike outings.

The injury was a devastating blow to Pete – the damage he'd sustained was heavy enough to warrant doubts as to the future of his career as a guitarist. "I really felt my life as a musician was over," Pete said in a 1993 interview. "For a while it looked like I would never be able to play a guitar again with my right hand."

For years, Pete's right hand had taken a great deal of physical abuse, and not all of it as a result of his guitar playing. During the *Who Are You* sessions, he'd smashed a window and rubbed his hand in the glass fragments at his parents' house. Back in 1981, he'd punched a wall backstage during a U.S. tour, breaking several bones. During the 1989 U.S. tour, he'd impaled his right hand on the whammy bar of his guitar performing a windmill. The catastrophic damage now dealt to his right wrist seemed to spell the end of his guitar (and piano) playing. "I fell off and really smashed my wrist up," Pete told Dia Stein on the promotional CD *Interview with a Psychoderelict* in 1993. "I think if they had invented a nylon wrist joint I would be using it, because my wrist is very, very bad. But for a long time I thought I wouldn't play the guitar again, I didn't think I'd be able to type. One doctor I spoke to said that I might have difficulty even writing…"

In November 1991, the PACE Theatrical Group approached Pete about the possibility of taking *Tommy* to the stage. The group, which operated theaters and subscription series in over twenty U.S. cities, had taken shows such as *Evita*, *The Secret Garden* and *Fiddler on the Roof* on the road[230]. Townshend had historically denied the countless requests for stage rights to *Tommy* over the previous two decades; in fact he even stated, "If I did anything smart with *Tommy* it was to register a grand right with the Library of Congress in 1969 and sit on it,"[231] but this time the PACE group found Pete at an interesting juncture in his life: *Psychoderelict*, his latest creative effort, inevitably stalled due to the recent wrist injury, and he was forced to find other creative avenues while he recuperated. "I started [*Psychoderelict*] in 1990," Pete said in 1993. "It was ready to deliver as a bunch of songs in September 1991… rather than put out an album I wouldn't be able to play live, or even feel inclined to talk about much, I held it back." In addition, his recent interest in stage work, which led to *The Iron Man*, perhaps piqued his interest in taking *Tommy* to the stage during this period.

---

[230] The PACE Theatrical Group, which merged with Clear Channel Communications in 2000, produced nearly 100 Broadway shows, and maintained a network in 26 of the 50 largest American cities.

[231] "In the past 15 years," Pete told the *New York Post*'s Lisa Robinson in 1993, "I've blocked every single production [of *Tommy*] - I've been very adamant - until the public were ready, and until Roger Daltrey was ready for a *Tommy* that didn't have him involved in it. Until I could sit down and say to Roger that I wanted to do it my way, but [that] it would be very different. Now Roger and I see very much eye-to-eye; we've had a lot of conversations and we're nicer to each other than we've been in the past."

A combination of these factors persuaded Pete that the time was right to stage *Tommy*. He made an agreement with the PACE group to stage *Tommy*, in partnership with a group of theatrical producers known as Dodger Productions, one of whom was Des McAnuff, director of California's La Jolla Playhouse (and also a guitarist) who ended up producing the work. McAnuff, who won a Tony award in 1985 for the musical *Big River*, already had specific plans for bringing *Tommy* to the stage, and Townshend figured heavily in them. "I wasn't interested in doing another unofficial version of *Tommy*, which is what the other stage versions that I'd heard about seemed to have been," McAnuff commented in the 1993 book *The Who's Tommy* (which is co-authored by Townshend).

> I also knew that we'd have to work hard to adapt *Tommy* to the stage; it wasn't going to be a natural leap, because we were dealing with a song cycle. And in order to maintain the integrity of the piece, I wanted to be able to work with Pete. Of course, I didn't really expect him to say yes, but I immediately began to prepare. I listened to the original album, and the only decision I made firmly at that point was that I wanted to maintain real respect for the original recording. I wouldn't want to update it or make it sound like a nineties version. I wanted to capture the sound and spirit of the original and treat it as a classical piece of rock-and-roll, rather than doing what Ken Russell ended up doing with the film, which was to let people bring their own sound to a song – so that Elton John makes *Pinball Wizard* sound like a Bernie Taupin/Elton John song, and Tina Turner makes *Acid Queen* into a Tina Turner song. That's the only decision I made before meeting Pete.

McAnuff also wanted a more realistic *Tommy* than Russell's rendition. "...we were not interested in exploring *Tommy* as a fantasy," he wrote in *American Theatre* in 1993.

> We believed that the "Amazing Journey" described in the lyric was best achieved by grounding the members of Tommy's family, the Walkers, on some kind of recognizable landscape. ...Ken Russell... had in his 1974 motion picture already given us the fantasy extravaganza (which lives on as a prime example of that particular genre of filmmaking from the '70s) and we were more interested in exploring *Tommy* as a dramatic theatre piece.
>
> ...Pete and I agreed that what we were dealing with was, in essence, a postwar story set against the background

of historical events that led up to the 1960s, so the blitzkrieg of 1940 and the rock-and-roll British invasion of 1963 became the bookends for our timeline.

Des and Pete's first meeting took place in November 1991 at a hotel in London with four other representatives from Dodger Productions and PACE. "He and I managed to have this little private conversation in the middle of the larger meeting, while God knows what was being talked about at the other end of the table," Des recalled in the *Tommy* book, "But we got about fifteen minutes in and agreed to meet again alone."

"From the moment I met Des in London," Pete recalled in 1993, "I felt he was absolutely right. What struck me was that he understood the rock'n'roll ethic that underlays *Tommy*. He never let go of it. He's always held on to the fact that the original songs are all a very important part of the spiritual quality of the piece."

The day after the pair's first meeting, Pete was committed to a recording session (presumably for *Psychoderelict* but Pete's recently-injured right wrist certainly precluded him from playing any instruments) so McAnuff had some time to kill prior to their next meeting. "The breathing space turned out to be great for me," he recalled later.

> I was staying at the Portobello Hotel, and I had thirty-six hours before our next meeting. Pete and I had had just enough of a conversation for me to get a sense of what he was concerned about. He wasn't sure whether the musical danced, and that came up strongly in that first meeting. I thought it did, and I felt that the instrumental sections would be very useful as storytelling... With these ideas in my head, I spent thirty-six hours listening to all of the recordings of *Tommy*. I truly basked in the original and also all the cover versions... I steeped myself in it, took some notes and came up with a kind of outline to start our conversations with about song order and what the bare bones of the story might be.

Indeed, perhaps a strength of McAnuff's during the construction of an onstage *Tommy* was his (and his coworkers') adherence to the original work. "Every designer on *Tommy* listened to the original album over and over," McAnuff wrote in *American Theatre* in 1993. "They paid great attention to the music." He added that the original album "eventually became the bible for everyone on this project."

Pete and Des' meeting the following day proved to be their first creative brainstorming session. "That meeting was about five hours long," McAnuff recalled in 1993. "We just talked and talked and talked and talked about the outline. Pete had a lot of comments, and we switched some things around, and we talked philosophically about the piece. I think quite quickly in that five hours we also made the biggest decisions—the decision about having more than one Tommy[232]; the critical decision to keep Tommy a local hero for as long as possible, to keep that rise to power very brief; and the decision to create a story about a West London family and to ground it in some way—not to make it a fantasy or go in the direction that I think it's gone in other versions."

With that much hammered out and the specter of a Townshend-endorsed *Tommy* stage show looming large on the horizon for the first time, McAnuff flew back to La Jolla to begin work on the project. "By Christmas we'd really made most of our decisions," Des wrote in the *Tommy* book. "We'd pitched the song order back and forth by fax... What we did was tell each other the story, more or less. We would walk through each act, scene by scene, and I would describe some of the visual work that I thought we could do, and Pete would talk about philosophy and then we would discuss themes and characters."

Tommy's transformation from a song cycle with a vaguely discernible storyline into a structured stage musical thus occurred in late 1991/early 1992. Pete made several trips to New York and La Jolla as *Tommy* rolled slowly towards its projected debut in the summer. "...there were substantial gaps in the story line that needed to be addressed in order to realize a full theatrical presentation of the piece," McAnuff wrote in *American Theatre*.

> The delicacy of the original story – about a traumatized youngster who rises to pop stardom as a deaf, dumb and blind pinball virtuoso – was one of the concept album's great strengths. It inspired a willing audience to fill in its own personal detail, and the ambiguities and puzzles that the album served up were consistent with Pete's ambitions to create a spiritual journey. We wanted very badly to preserve the strength of the original recording. At the same time, in order to produce a viable theatre piece, we needed to flesh out and expand the original.

A key piece of *Tommy* which needed attention was the ending. "...I have learned there is a vital difference between the simple rock song and the

---

[232] "Considering his total isolation in most of the story, how were we to find an emotional throughline for the character of Tommy?", McAnuff told the *Washington Post*'s Lisa Leff in 1994. "The basic conflict in the story, we agreed, was between Tommy and Tommy. This gave birth to the idea of the multiple Tommys (i.e., Tommy at 4, Tommy at 10 and the adult Tommy – our narrator). It was the interaction between these characters that created the magical layer which led to many of the most exotic visual elements in the production."

conventional music theatre play – that it's necessary to bring a story to a conclusion, something you never have to do in rock-and-roll," Pete wrote in the 1993 *Tommy* book. "When I originally created *Tommy*, I did it with the understanding that people of the time were exploring the limits of their imaginations," Pete told the *San Jose Mercury News* in July 1994.

> They were in pursuit of spiritual awakening. When they sat down to listen to *Tommy* with a joint in hand or whatever, they were saying to themselves – and probably to me – 'We want to go somewhere.' And I specifically left parts of the story open to allow them to reflect and review.
> But with this version of *Tommy* I approached it from the point of view of the dramatist. Onstage, you have to tie things up in a sense. And I did tie it up at the end. But I didn't add anything that wasn't there to begin with.

Pete was referring to the rewritten ending during which Tommy reunites with his family, embracing each of them, including Cousin Kevin and Uncle Ernie. Together, Tommy and family sing *Listening To You*. Many observers were critical of this ending due to its 'happily ever after' implication. "We've had people come away thinking it's a Nancy Reagan 'family values' message," Pete told the *New York Daily News* in July, 1993. "We'd like to make it clear that it's not."

Indeed, Pete told the *L.A. Daily News* in 1994 that Tommy's return to his family could be for other than benign reasons. He suggested that the reunion may have initially occurred for Tommy "to wreak vengeance. Tommy's embrace of Uncle Ernie is immensely cruel. …You think, 'What's he up to? He's obviously about to embark on retribution." But he snaps out of it. "He ends up accepting who he is, what he is, what he's been through. And (he accepts) the people around him."

Other adjustments drew additional criticism, including the insertion of the line *freedom tastes of normality* (as opposed to *freedom tastes of reality*) to *I'm Free*, and the removal of many religious references. For example, the 'kids' rather than 'disciples' lead Tommy in in *Pinball Wizard*, and the revised *Amazing Journey* disposes of the mysticism of the original. The 'tall stranger' with 'silver sparkled glittering gown whose golden beard flows nearly down to the ground' is removed, replaced with a description of Tommy himself. Another target for those who complained that the Broadway *Tommy* was too soft was the *Acid Queen* sequence: Tommy's father whisks him away before she has a chance to begin her peculiar brand of therapy.

"It was clear I couldn't compete with the acid trip someone had when they first listened to the album," McAnuff told the *Washington Post*'s Lisa Leff in December, 1994. "All I could do was carry out Pete's vision and my own vision of the piece. There was really no other choice. I knew we would take some lumps from people who had a very strong personal relationship with *Tommy*. But as it turns out there has been far less of that than I ever would have expected."

To facilitate the parental decision-making which must have taken place between *Tommy Can You Hear Me* and *Smash The Mirror*, Pete wrote a new song, *I Believe My Own Eyes*. The song was "...a conventional music-theatre number in many respects," Pete wrote in 1993.

> This is because it performs a conventional function. It has a job to do. It has to suggest the passing of time and patience and must strengthen the audience's feeling that the parents are exhausted but still young enough at heart to hope for their relationship. It also must keep the audience's focus on the mirror, about to be smashed by the mother. And it has to attend to the idea that when there are no answers we have to look inside.
>
> There was one other, less specific, part of the brief – and that was that we wanted a ballad, something like *Behind Blue Eyes* from the Who. I trawled all these elements together and came up with the song. By doing so, I surprised myself and everyone else. It is not as popular a song in the show as I had hoped, but it is vital and it works. It is the one piece of new writing I have done for the show that makes me feel I can really write music drama in the future.

It wasn't until this revisiting of *Tommy* that Pete began to realize the story's strong autobiographical nature[233]. "...I didn't realize [the autobiographical nature of *Tommy*] until I did the work on the Broadway show and then I suddenly realized it *was* my story," Pete told *Uncut*'s Simon Goddard in 2004.

> What actually happened was I'd fallen off a bike, smashed my wrist up, thought I couldn't play any more so thought I'd better write a book, an autobiography. But then I thought, I can't write a book until I know what happened to me as a little kid. So I went back to my mum and I said, 'Listen, I can remember being young on the beach, I can remember being in the tour bus with you and dad, I can remember having a lovely childhood and then I can

---

[233] Another autobiographical feature was the Walker family's address: 22 Heathfield Gardens. His parents had lived at 22 Whitehall Gardens in Acton.

remember going to live with my grandmother and I've got two black years. I want to know what happened.' She fussed and kept avoiding it and I said, 'No, Mum, I want to know what happened.' I made her sit down and she kept changing the subject. I kept banging the table going: 'Tell. Me. What. Happened!' And in the end she told me the story. She didn't look good when she told me. I was a very, very clear-cut post-war victim of two people who were married in the war too young, had problems because of the war, so I went to stay with my grandmother, who happened to be off her fucking head. It was a horrible story.

Although Pete wrote in 2002 that he remembered "no specific sexual abuse," he told *Q*'s John Harris in 1996 that "I think it's quite possible that when I was with my grandmother, she had a boyfriend who came into my bedroom. I don't know quite what happened, but I've got that far in my mind. I've tried to bring it out through therapy and I've failed. She used to make me call all her boyfriends – and there were several – "Uncle". I think that's where it [Uncle Ernie] came from." Other autobiographical aspects of the story were revealed to Pete as a result of his questioning his mother about his childhood. "I didn't know that my mother and father had split up," he told Harris.

> I didn't know that my mother had a lover who was prepared to marry her and be my father. I didn't know that my father had said to her, You can fucking go to Aden with this new bloke, but you can't take Peter, I'm keeping him. Where did I get the idea for a woman living with a lover, having a child, the father going off, disappearing, shooting the lover, and on we go to have a dysfunctional family? That's the story of my life, but I certainly wasn't conscious of it.

Regardless of the story's close ties to Pete's life, the audience somehow found a similar connection with *Tommy*. "...We recognized in our excavation of the rock opera that the story was at least to some extent autobiographical – not that Pete was personally traumatized to the point of becoming deaf, dumb and blind, but rather that he was writing an autobiography, perhaps unconsciously, for a generation," McAnuff told the *Washington Post* in December, 1994. "Tommy's physical and metaphysical journey is largely a metaphor, and this, we came to understand, helps explain the *Tommy* phenomenon – the fact that the character became an icon, even a mascot, for a whole generation. It may explain why he lives on with such vitality today."

Interestingly, Pete's involvement with the adaptation of *Tommy's* music to the stage show was seemingly not as extensive as one might imagine of the man who composed the original piece. He reportedly wasn't involved in choosing the seven-member band (two guitarists, bass, French horn, drums, two keyboards), nor did he meet them until two weeks prior to the show's premiere July 9th.

Although *Tommy* had been written over two decades ago, Pete's story of a man's spiritual journey maintained relevance in the 1990's. "This is going to sound incredibly impetuous, but the fact is, I set off on two pathways (in my life)," Pete told the *L.A. Daily News* in July, 1994. "One was the ideological pathway of rock'n'roll. We were going to change the world. We didn't. The second was a spiritual pathway. I thought I was going to grow spiritually by following an Indian master and meditating and being a good boy. And I didn't. If I'm going to grow, do anything of any good, it's all still to be done." Townshend compared himself to Tommy, as seen at the end of the show when he embraces his family and then turns to face the world. Having completed one journey, he's ready to begin the next. "That's the sobering message of *Tommy*," Townshend said. "But it's also very real: Every day is a new day. Every day we have the chance to start over."

"*Tommy* is a spiritual journey," Townshend said, explaining that Tommy's disabilities are metaphors for the deafness, muteness and blindness "that we live in as far as spiritual matters are concerned…We're super-efficient intellectually, super-efficient physically, super-efficient in all kinds of ways, but spiritually we're driving blind. We don't know when we're making progress and when we're not."

Once Pete and Des had hashed out their onstage rendition of *Tommy* with "a fair bit of detail" according to McAnuff, the work began for the La Jolla Playhouse staff to bring the work to life. In addition to its 24 actors, the show would feature nine rear-projection screens to aid in visual presentation (this number increased to eighteen when the show went to Broadway), a nearly full-size airplane out of which actors 'parachuted', a huge pinball machine (one of nine custom-built machines used in the show), dozens of television monitors which showed footage filmed live from the stage, and eight tons of scenery. On average, costume changes took place every three minutes, as cast members donned one of over 1,000 costumes which were made for the show, one of which was a $3,000 white leather jacket.

The La Jolla Playhouse's *Tommy* debut took place July 9, 1992[234] in the playhouse's 492-seat Mandell Weiss Theater. The show was earmarked as a benefit for the London-based Nordoff-Robbins Music Therapy

---

[234] McAnuff and Townshend went sailing near Cornwall just prior to the La Jolla *Tommy* opening.

Foundation, an organization which helps autistic and retarded children. John Entwistle and Roger Daltrey joined Pete in attending the occasion, which was a smash hit. "The show here is one continuous aural and visual orgy," proclaimed the *L.A. Times*, "a movable feast of sound and color, flying props, swirling doors, projections and flashing video for the very senses Tommy was so long denied…a roiling, high-tech piece of theatrical wizardry for the '90s." *Rolling Stone* called the show "…an ingenious and visually smashing telling of the familiar tale of a deaf, dumb and blind boy who is taken for the new messiah… musical director Joseph Church has assembled a fine seven-piece band, with drummer Luther Rix even contributing some powerful Keith Moon-like bashing from the orchestra pit." The *San Jose Mercury News* stated, "…the next big British rock musical to hit Broadway may come from a California theater."

"I wasn't surprised, when I first saw it, as much as I was relieved," Pete told the *San Jose Mercury News* in July 1994 of his reaction to the first show. "I thought, finally someone has done what they said they would do. I had worked with a number of people in the past… but Des made good on his promises."

Nine months after its debut in La Jolla, *Tommy* opened on Broadway at the St James Theater on 22 April 1993[235]. *New York Times* critic Frank Rich's review appeared in the following morning's edition. "The Broadway musical has never been the same since rock-and-roll stole its audience and threw it into an identity crisis," Rich wrote.

> For three decades, from the moment *Meet the Beatles* usurped the supremacy of such Broadway pop as *Hello Dolly!*, the commercial theater has desperately tried to win back the Young (without alienating theier elders) by watering down rock music, simulating rock music and ripping off rock music. The result has been a few scattered hits over the years, typified by *Hair* and *Jesus Christ, Superstar*, most of which have tamed the rock-and-roll revolution rather than spread it through Times Square. Until now.
>
> *Tommy*, the stunning new stage adaptation of the 1969 rock opera… is at long last the authentic rock musical that has eluded Broadway for two generations. …this show is not merely an entertainment juggernaut, riding at full tilt on the visual and musical highs of its legendary pinball iconography and irresistible tunes, but also a surprisingly moving resuscitation of the disturbing passions that made *Tommy* an emblem of its era. In the apocalyptic year of

---

[235] That same month, Pete recorded a cover of *Substitute* with the Ramones.

1969, *Tommy* was the unwitting background music for the revelation of the My Lai massacre, the Chicago Seven trial, the Charles Manson murders. Those cataclysmic associations still reverberate within the piece, there to be tapped for the Who's generation, even as the show at the St. James is so theatrically fresh and emotionally raw that the newcomers to *Tommy* will think it was born yesterday.

In a way, it was. Though the voices and pit band of this *Tommy* faithfully reproduce the 1969 double album, adding merely one song (*I Believe My Own Eyes*), a few snippets of dialogue and some extended passages of underscoring, the production bears no resemblance to the Who's own concert performances of the opera (which culminated in an appearance at the Metropolitan Opera House in 1970) or to Ken Russell's pious, gag-infested 1975 film adaptation. Instead of merely performing the songs, or exploiting them as general riffs of dance and psychedelia, the evening's creators, who also include the choreographer Wayne Cilento and some extraordinary multimedia artists led by the brilliant set designer John Arnone, using the singing actors to flesh out the drama of *Tommy*. Better still, they excavate the fable's meaning until finally the opera's revised conclusion spreads catharsis like wildfire through the cheering house.

...As played by Michael Cerveris with the sleek white outfit, dark shades and narcissistic attitude of a rock star, the grown-up Tommy is nearly every modern child's revenge fantasy come true: the untouchable icon who gets the uncritical adulation from roaring crowds that his despised parents never gave him at home.

...The isolated young Tommy's totemic, recurring cry of yearning – "See me, feel me, touch me, heal me" – flows repeatedly between inner child and grown man, giving piercing voice to the eternal childhood psychic aches of loneliness and lovelessness. It is this primal theme, expressed with devastating simplicity in Mr. Townshend's score and lyrics, that has made *Tommy* timeless... Yet it is the evil of the authority figures the hero must overcome – a distant father, a dismissive mother, a sexually abusive Uncle Ernie and various fascistic thugs – that also makes *Tommy* a poster-simple political statement reflecting the stark rage of the Vietnam era.

As staged by Mr. McAnuff, that anger is present but the story is kept firmly rooted in its own time, from the forties to the early sixties. The slide projections that drive the production design at first recreate in black-and-white the London of the blitz, then spill into the vibrant pop-art imagery of pinball machines, early Carnaby Street and Andy Warhol painting before returning to black-and-white for televised crowd images that recall the early British rock explosion as witnessed on the "Ed Sullivan Show."

...Mr. McAnuff and his designers take the notion of threading a few repeated images abstractly through the action: floating chairs, mirrors, the Union Jack, airplane propellers and disembodied Man Ray eyes, not to mention doors and windows reminiscent of sixties rock-album cover art and the hallucinogenic mythology such art canonized... These dreamy visual touchstones are constantly reshuffled and distorted throughout *Tommy* for subliminal effect, reaching their apothesis in an inevitable (and superbly executed) set piece in which the entire theater becomes a gyrating pinball machine celebrating the rebellious hero's "amazing journey" to newfound freedom.

...Dominating the stage instead of being usurped by the hardware, the performers can shine as well... When the time comes for the entire company to sing the soaring final incantation – "Listening to you I get the music. Gazing at you I get the heat" – *Tommy* has done what rock-and-roll can do but almost never does in the theater: reawaken the audience's adolescent feelings of rebellion and allow them open-throated release. But reflecting the passage of time and Mr. Townshend's own mature age of forty-seven, this version takes a brave step further, concluding with a powerful tableau of reconciliation that lifts an audience of the 1990s out of its seats.

"Hope I die before I get old," sang the Who in *My Generation*, its early hit single. A quarter-century or so later, Mr. Townshend hasn't got old so much as grown up, into a deeper view of humanity unthinkable in the late 1960s. Far from being another of Broadway's excursions into nostalgia, *Tommy* is the first musical in years to feel completely alive in its own moment. No wonder that for two hours it makes the world seem young.

While it was highly regarded by most, *Tommy* had its detractors. "The classic rock anthems are still there – *Amazing Journey, The Acid Queen, Pinball Wizard* – in orchestrations by Steve Margoshes that respect the original voicings and are played by a gutsy pit band," *Newsweek*'s Jack Kroll wrote on May 3, 1993.

> **But the mystery and ambiguity, the poetic richness** of the original has been flattened out. The Gypsy Queen no longer subjects Tommy to her patented drug-and-sex therapy; Tommy's dad whisks him away, keeping the boy free from eros and psychedelia. As before, little Tommy is shocked into catatonia when his father kills his mother's lover. The boy falls prey to his pederastic Uncle Ernie and the bullying Cousin Kevin, until Tommy turns out to be a pinball genius, becoming a savior of youth in a parody of a rock star.
>
> The scenes of little Tommy are the strongest in the show – poignant evocations of an autistic child. But McAnuff has been seduced by Broadway's high-tech rollers into an eclectic style that echoes *Dreamgirls* (tall towers), *Chess* (video screens), *Miss Saigon* (flying airplanes), *Les Miserables* (the people). The audience cheers the special effects, climaxed when Tommy hops onto a flying pinball machine, which explodes in a fireball. But there's almost as much cheering when sodden old Uncle Ernie chug-a-lugs a beer and emits a burp like a sonic boom.
>
> This *Tommy* has energy, and some witty choreography, but no sensuality or soul. Michael Cerveris as the grown-up Tommy epitomizes the cast, attractive but without real charisma. The new *Tommy* spurns charisma. "The point is not for you to be more like me," he tells his followers. "The point is I'm finally more like you." Townshend, the old guitar-buster, has created a new category. Wonk rock.

Time was similarly unimpressed: "...there's not much emotional depth or adolescent rebellion left in the granddaddy of rock operas."

Thanks to word of mouth and gushing reviews such as that by Frank Rich, *Tommy* was a smash hit on Broadway[236]. Attendance was such that Pete told the *New York Daily News* he'd recoup his investment in staging the work by September – only six months after opening. The musical went on to make a reported $150 million, and in 2002, *The Sun* reported that Pete's take was £45,000 per week during this period. In June, 1993, the *Tommy* Broadway show received five Tony Awards, including one for Pete, for Best

---

[236] According to a 1994 edition of the *Chicago Tribune*, one of the few regrets Pete had about the Broadway *Tommy* was that his father didn't live to see it.

Original Score, and one for McAnuff, for Best Musical Director. "You know, the Tony is the first artistic award I've ever had," Pete said later. "I've only ever had performance-related awards before, you know, special services to the music industry, that type of thing. I've never won a Grammy or anything for my creative work. At this time in my life, it's like getting a knighthood." After the awards presentation at the Gershwin Theater, the *Tommy* crew headed to the theater district supper club Laura Belle for a party which lasted well into the following morning. Pete and Michael Cerveris reportedly performed *Pinball Wizard*.

The success of *Tommy* on Broadway obviously had an enormous effect on Pete Townshend, whose biggest triumphs to this point had come through The Who and naturally were conceived as a group effort rather than the workings of an individual. The amount of attention and recognition Pete received as a result of the success of *Tommy* was literally overwhelming. "The thing I had to worry about [prior to the opening of *Tommy* on Broadway] is not that the show was going to flop but that it would be too much of a success. It could destroy me." The praise and attention that showered Pete during this period did cause several problems. He'd started drinking again for the first time in years, his life at home was "failing," and his attraction to New York grew. "When I come to New York now, I have a family," Pete told *Rolling Stone*'s Anthony DeCurtis in late 1993. "I can go to my little yellow theater, and there are people there that love me. I have investors lining up to invest in any crazy idea I come up with. So, I'm pulled to New York - and pulled out of a rather unsatisfactory life at home, where for 25 years I've been married to somebody who doesn't like show business very much. It's quite a good thing that my wife doesn't like show business, but it does make it difficult. I've got a young son, and I don't like to be away from him, but I feel dragged into the excitement and vigor of New York."

Tommy's success also meant that Pete thought about revisiting other areas of his catalog. "I have lots of ideas for plays and musicals that I want to pursue," he told the *San Jose Mercury News* in July, 1994. "And the way this version of *Tommy* has worked out, it makes me think there's hope for some of the pieces I wrote for the Who that nearly worked but didn't – things like *Rael, A Quick One (While He's Away)* and *Quadrophenia*. Maybe I should try them again."

Ironically the stage version of *Tommy* wasn't a hit in London. Despite the fact that it topped two Andrew Lloyd Webber shows to take an Olivier award for 'most outstanding musical production' in early 1997, the West End *Tommy* closed within months of its opening at the Shaftesbury Theatre in March 1996, "...after rave reviews fell on deaf ears," according to *The Times*' Helen Johnstone. "...it became clear that the story of the deaf, dumb and blind boy who becomes a rock messiah was not catching on this side of the Atlantic."

Chapter 14

"I seem to be somewhere else again. I seem to be back in another place and commenting on that job that I did for so long. Now I'm admitting that I can't do it anymore. I have to work another way. I have to be more specific. I don't think it's about getting old, being mature, and being jaded. It's about the fact that perhaps other people are doing it better now and have more energy, vitality, and stamina, and don't fall off their fucking bike."
- Pete Townshend, 1993

"I've been pitching to work in theater for a long time. I started to show an interest in it in 1970. I was hoping to do a theater-film project back then with the Who called Lifehouse. When the Who finished I was keen to move into theater just because of the fact that it was another showbiz area which didn't require me to drag my body around the world like a hunk of meat, which I was rapidly turning into, with holes in various bits and blood pouring out of various parts of my hand most of the time."
- Pete Townshend, 1993

In 1992, as *Tommy* began its run at the La Jolla Playhouse, Pete returned his attention to *Psychoderelict*, the group of songs he'd begun work on two years ealier and had readied for release just prior to the bicycle accident. *Psychoderelict*, in its first incarnation, was "a conventional solo album," Pete wrote in 2001's *Scoop 3* liner notes, "which – I had been warned by my manager and record label – had to be a 'real' rock record." Faced with an uncertain future because of the wrist injury, Pete's reassessment of *Psychoderelict* assumed a new importance. "...I was kind of coming at it as though it was the last thing that I was ever going to do," he told Dia Stein on the 1993 promotional CD *Interview With A Psychoderelict*.

In writing the collection of songs, "I had been obsessed with an idea: that in this highly computerized age the truth is being lost in our easy access to facts," Pete wrote in the *Psychoderelict* press notes. "I saw some moral issues too; is the nature of truth actually changing? Each song I'd written addressed this in a different way. It was a good notion. They were good songs. But the real idea didn't come across."

Shadows of the failure of *Lifehouse* once again loomed large. Interestingly, the path Pete chose for *Psychoderelict* would later help *Lifehouse* reach fruition. Pondering how to articulate the ideas contained in the songs more effectively, Pete recalled the work of one of his favorite authors, Joseph Conrad, whose *Heart of Darkness* was performed as a radio play by Orson Welles in the 1930s. After briefly considering using his favorite Conrad story, *Nostromo*, in radio play format intermingled with the songs he'd written, he decided to use a story of his own which he'd been working on since 1989 called *Ray High and The Glass Household*.[237]

"When I first put the songs together for *Psychoderelict*," Pete told *Guitar Player* in 1993, "I was unhappy with them. I felt that I failed in my original mission. I thought some of this stuff is good and some of it isn't, but it doesn't do what I want it to do. Then I fell off a bike and smashed my wrist... I abandoned the record completely, went off to La Jolla to gun up *Tommy*, sat in at Shakespeare classes, learned what dramaturgy meant, and met dramaturgists... I decided to kick off *Iron Man* again because I thought, "I've got some time now." I was embraced in theater."

Buoyed by *Tommy*'s success on the stage, and the "greater creative scope" granted by his new label, Atlantic subsidiary East West[238], Pete recalled, "I came back to this album and thought, "Fuck it. What I'll actually do is say what this thing is about. I'll use a play or drama to describe what I'm trying to get across. The music can act as highlights." *Tommy*'s successful transformation from a series of songs into a wildly successful stage work had helped persuade Pete that he could successfully articulate his message to the audience through a mix of dialogue and music. "*Psychoderelict* feels like a part of a big continuum, now that *Tommy* is doing so well," Pete said in 1993. "I felt that I could be specific, that I could skip the vague, metaphysical language of music and say what I wanted to communicate, write it out, make it really punchy, and make it work." Previously, Townshend had generally been less direct in delivering his ideas through lyrics, often tending to circumnavigate with the intent that the finished song as a whole would get the meaning across. He often saved his directness for interviewers. "I was obeying the old set of rules," he said, "which is that you don't fuck with people when they're listening to music."

> You don't play them a piece of music and slip them
> a subversive idea that happens to be your idea of the month.
> I do that in interviews. I take an interview as a chance to

---

[237] Pete described *Ray High and the Glass Household* in 2001 as "a novel", and that "part of this book was complete enough to send a first draft to my editor..."

[238] In the midst of working on *Psychoderelict*, Pete was "sacked by EMI who had bought my UK label Virgin to get hold of The Rolling Stones and a few others."

say, "Let's talk about Bosnia or Amnesty International." Interviews are a good place to explore these things because journalists are well-read, they're activists, they're smart, and they know what you're talking about. They can get your crazy rock star ideas in order and ask the right questions if you're going off on the wrong... tangent.

Pete began writing scripts for his project and sent them to his old art school roommate Richard Barnes to review them. "So I wrote scripts and I'd throw them at him and he'd blue pencil them and tell me this was happening, that was happening, and we honed it down to the finely edited form that you have," he told Dia Stein in 1993. "So the story definitely came afterwards, but I think the story was always there, because I'd written the songs around a theme, the theme was, what is the difference between facts and truth? In society, in the press, in music business, in my life, and in rock'n'roll."

Psychoderelict's protagonist is Ray High[239], a washed-up rock star whose best years are supposedly behind him. High, suffering a nervous breakdown, has become a recluse, cutting himself off from most of society. "...what *Psychoderelict* is about," Pete told Matt Kent in 1999, "is a man... I suppose men in particular do this, some women, but mainly men... men who decide to opt out, men who run away, men who go and live on desert islands, men who leave their jobs, men who decide to become Richmond Green drinkers, men who just turn their back on everything around them."

Ray High's self-imposed exile allows him contact with very few people.[240] Only his manager, a reporter, and a fan manage to "penetrate his existence," as Townshend put it. High, at the fan's prodding, reworks an old project he'd abandoned years ago (sound familiar?) entitled *Gridlife*. "We hear Spinner, in a scene from Ray's dream, explain that everything in the universe is composed of music and vibrations, and that soon the whole world will experience their adventure," Pete explained, simultaneously relating the theme of both *Gridlife* and *Lifehouse* in the project's press kit. "Ray's forgotten project from the past is of course based on *Lifehouse*," Pete wrote in 1999.

Ray is cajoled by Rastus [his manager],

---

[239] Pete commented in 1999 that "...the name Ray High was concocted as an amalgam of two rock contemporaries of whom I'm most fond, Ray Davies and Nick Lowe."

[240] True to Pete's traditional form, *Psychoderelict* was originally substantially more complicated. The radio play, according to *The New York Daily News*, "incorporated even more big-issue ideas in its original form, since it started with 12 major characters before being whittled down to the current three. "In terms of presentation, simplifying helped," Townshend admits. "Of course, I'm not known for brevity.'" One of the characters deleted during creative workshops, incidentally, was played by Broadway *Tommy* lead Michael Cerveris.

manipulated by Ruth Streeting [the reporter] and intoxicated by Rosalind [the fan] (for whom he writes a hit song) and manages to get his version of *Lifehouse*... on stage. It is a tremendous success, but he remains a little jaded, and yet nostalgic. I tried to deliver a double irony: Ray prefers to look back to a time when he was still able to look ahead. The play closes as he begins to forget his recent success, pores over new letters and pictures from new fans, and resentfully bemoans his great, lost hippy days of the seventies.

It was deceit and scandal that had delivered High's most recent success, which rendered the experience bittersweet. He preferred to dream about the futuristic visions which had occupied his time while writing *Gridlife* some twenty years earlier. At the end of the play, High yearns for those days, wondering "Whatever happened to all that lovely hippie shit?"
Rolling Stone's Paul Evans described the story as follows:

> Formatted as a sci-fi radio play, substituting an Orwellian air of virtual-reality apocalypse for *Tommy*'s pinball pathway to glory, it's not the coming of age of a deaf, dumb and blind boy messiah but the comeback bid of a shut-down idol. Damned as a "psychedelic flower-child turned alcoholic vegetable" by rock-press vixen Ruth Streeting, Ray High is holed up (a la the aging Elvis), craving a hit and redemption. Alternately an archetypal bitch and mother, Ruth plots with High's manager and flunky father figure, Rastus Knight, to yank Ray back into the spotlight. Predictably, chaos ensues.

Within *Psychoderelict*, Pete examined several areas: The roles of people – especially men – in postwar society (a theme also explored in *Siege* and subsequently *White City*), the effects of the media on the public, and the nature of truth itself. *English Boy*, *Psychoderelict*'s nucleus, was about the effects of a war-free environment on the postwar generations. "It's about the emergence of the modern punk," Pete commented at one point. "Those post-war years in the late 50s and the early 60s in England where they stopped conscripting people into the army," Pete explained in 1993. "They said: "Listen there's gonna be no more war. We've solved that problem. We don't need you anymore." And I think there are a lot of kids running around England trying to find something to do... And the song is really about that... the fact that those boys, those men, those people are kind of made redundant, in a sense, by peace... and now being held up, in some way, responsible for many of the things that are wrong with modern society."

Pete elaborated on this idea in a 1993 interview with *Guitar Player*'s Matt Resnicoff:

> *English Boy* is a story about young men being undervalued and made to blame. What was so awful for me, and it's painful to talk about because I didn't handle it very well, was that my great years in America were so fucking shaky for many men my age because they could have been and they did get drafted. It was *Apocalypse Now*, *Heart Of Darkness*, it was dead people in rivers of mud in the middle of jungles. Mothers, fathers, and families were wondering what the fuck they were doing there. It was Vietnam, and I was trying to pretend that it wasn't happening. I wasn't going to get drafted. I wanted to be a pop star. I felt that politics and pop didn't mix. I had no idea that the music we were playing was so vital to their very survival.
>
> Although it's called *English Boy*, it could just as easily be called *American Boy*. It's about the guys who died in that war…

The song addressed the mixed messages that post war men received, and continue to receive. "*English Boy* is about the idea that you're good enough to go and die in a fucking war for your country, but if there happens to be no war then fucking behave," Townshend told Resnicoff.

> Cut your hair. Wear a grey suit. Do your job. Clean the lavatories. Count the money. Sell the stocks. Fix the car. Keep your fucking mouth shut. That's the establishment picture that young kids grow up with. That's wrong. That's not who we are. If I'm a member of the establishment now, that's not what I want my kids to think of me. I want them to feel free, to be themselves, to be fucking wild, and to make mistakes. It's okay to hurt people. I'll tell you why it's okay, because that's what we do. We fucking drop bombs on the motherfuckers. It's so wrong to drop bombs on the motherfuckers on day one and then the next day turn around with your schoolteacher hat on and say, "Bringing a gun into the classroom? You wicked boy!" What would actually change the nature of that hypocrisy, it seems to me, is just saying, "Let's talk about this. Who are you going to kill?…" You take people into your trust. You don't say, "Listen. This is too big for

you to understand. Keep quiet." That's what *English Boy* is about. "This is my battlefield. It's mine and you can't take it away from me."

As previously mentioned, *Psychoderelict* also examined the effect of the media on society, and the nature of truth. "These new songs are for you if you still believe in truth, or you still believe you can find truth if you try hard enough," Pete wrote in the press kit accompanying the release. "Whether you read newspapers or listen to the radio, you probably think that what you *suspect* is what is really going on is – in fact – close to the real truth. I know I do. We need to be told." This notion was also addressed in *English Boy*.

"*English Boy* was the focus for almost the entirety of the *Psychoderelict* album," Pete said in 1996.

> ...It's about being commentated into existence, and the way that young people become almost parodies of themselves. Something about being a teenager is that there's this temptation to become a parody of your worst self. You think, "Well, everybody's carrying knives and sticking them in people, so I'll do it," whereas in actual fact this is still, or should be, a very isolated situation.
>
> One of the things that happens today is that, because of the incredible effectiveness and the huge appetite of the media for sensational stories, a tiny incident that might happen eighty miles away becomes as significant to me as though it happened in my own neighborhood, and this song is about that, and we allow it to make us afraid when we're walking down the street. We should only be afraid if we've got experience of something. If some old lady's been banged on the head in your street, then be afraid, but if she hasn't then don't be afraid until it happens. Don't go looking for it. So it's about paranoia fed by misinformation and sensation, but primarily about the way that it affects the society of the young, and the way it marginalizes the disenfranchised. Or disenfranchises the marginalized (laughs).

In 1993, Pete explained another media-related theme of *Psychoderelict*, using the media stories of his supposed bisexuality as an example:

> ...On this album, I've tried to make clear that you always try to win over the people who hate you. The more

people hate you, the more you want them. You don't learn from adverse criticism or scandal alone. The press actually hand the story on, then the reaction happens in the bar. In La Jolla, after the opening party for *Tommy*, two girls attached themselves to me. One of them was really game. I'm old and wrinkly and she was young and beautiful. I thought about it briefly, then decided to go to bed. As I said goodnight, one turned to the other and said, "See, I told you he was a fucking faggot." It's not about the story. It's about how the public respond.

Inherent in Pete's decision to convey these hefty ideas through the songs of *Psychoderelict* was his belief in the power of rock music. This belief had wavered during the slide which began with Moon's death in 1978 (or perhaps earlier), but had been buoyed by the success of *Tommy* on Broadway. *Tommy*, *White City* and *Psychoderelict* "...all, in different ways, consider the same things: What we're going through on the planet today, with over-population, global warming and so on; the aging process; the feeling of the loss of a dream," Pete told the *New York Daily News* in July, 1993. "Rock'n'roll can deal with all of that[241]. Unfortunately, it usually doesn't. It's rare when a Bob Dylan grabs an issue and holds our feet to the fire to feel it. What bothers me today is that rock'n'roll has become so *conservative*, so resistant to change. That's something else I'd like to figure out: Why has rock'n'roll straitjacketed itself?"

In addition to the obvious, but superficial, parallels between *Gridlife* and *Lifehouse*, *Psychoderelict*'s roots and thematic elements questioning societal roles and the nature of truth were also entangled with those of *Lifehouse*. This was the result of Pete's recent push to finally get the story told. "After twenty years, I became obsessed with telling the story behind my failure to complete what was a genuinely good idea for the first genuine rock musical film," Pete wrote in the *Richmond Review* in 1999. "The obsession to do this was greater than the desire to complete the original film itself, and led to *Psychoderelict*..."

"Through a series of unfortunate accidents and predicaments, I ended up doing things in a better order than I had planned," he told Matt Resnicoff in 1993.

> I wanted to write songs about the nature of truth, how it's changing in the modern world, how computers – data banks and computer preservation of newsprint in particular – are elevating fact to a level of truth. Facts, as I

---

[241] By 1994, after *Psychoderelict*'s disappointing release, Pete sounded as if he'd given up on the power of rock music. "All rock and roll is toothless," he told *Playboy*. "It's a toothless form."

say on the record, don't always lead to the truth. They should, but they don't always. I think that journalism, particularly criticism, is the foundation of the support system for the musician like me. It doesn't always feel entirely just, because what you work in as a musician is a big picture. It's very difficult to communicate that you desperately need to say something that is very difficult to say, and that is why you've chosen music to start with.

The project also provided Pete an opportunity to include some futuristic-sounding *Lifehouse* instrumental demos he'd recorded more than twenty years earlier. "On the album, the songs associated with *Gridlife* are prefixed *Meher Baba* and originated on eight-track demos first recorded in 1970/71 for *Lifehouse*," he explained in 1993.

The majority of the songs written for *Psychoderelict* were recorded in demo form in late 1990/early 1991 in The Cube, Pete's London home studio from 1985-1997. Recording sessions for the album took place on the Dutch barge *Grand Cru* moored on the River Thames behind Eel Pie studios, which Pete had converted into a recording studio[242]. "I used my usual group of musicians," Pete told Dia Stein in 1993.

> I like to have the same people that I used on *Chinese Eyes*. Jody Linscott on percussion, Peter Hope-Evans on harmonica, John Bundrick, 'Rabbit', on keyboards, and if I can get them, Mark Brzezicki or Simon Phillips on drums, Pino Palladino or somebody like him on bass, and nowadays I like to have a guitar player around. We kicked off with that group of people and they played along with the things that either I was doing in the studio, or that were on tape, and then I started to finish the tracks off. I suppose I play really about 80 percent of the music on it. 'Cause some of the stuff on it I dumped (laughs). But I like them there for spiritual reasons.

Pete had thought of writing a song about pretentiousness for some time prior to penning *Let's Get Pretentious*, "'cause I just like the idea that I had my moment of courageous pretentiousness, jumping in with *Tommy*," he told Stein. "It felt very pretentious at the time to be writing something that was a song cycle, let alone something that later became known as a rock opera. So I've never had a problem with people that call me pretentious… I don't regard it as an insult (laughs). But in the context of the piece, the song

---

[242] "It had once carried live eels (which I thought was amusing because my company is called 'Eel Pie')," Pete wrote in the *Scoop 3* liner notes in 2001.

is actually about what Ray feels is the setting for his manager and the journalist's lifestyle. He feels that it's frippery, it's fluff, it's puff, to use the modern expression."

Outlive the Dinosaur was, Pete wrote in 2001, "...I think one of the smartest songs I've ever written. My hero, a drunken rock-star is living alone in his glass mansion. He takes on all the issues of ecology with a sense of duty and responsibility to our dying planet. And yet he cannot move, cannot reach the outside world, cannot even write a cheque. The word dinosaur was of course first used to describe aging rock stars with vicious irony, and I use it here with vicious irony redoubled."

Now And Then "...is a hard song to talk about," Pete said in a 1993 radio interview.

> It's just a song that I wrote for somebody that I care about and addressed the original idea of the whole album which is really whether or not when you actually feel, or say, that you're in love with somebody that you actually know what you mean. It was the first principle for trying to find out... when we think we're speaking the truth, whether it's possible for us to ever know that we're speaking the truth. And then, if that's true in relationships, then is it possible that when we accuse the totalitarian media of sometimes bending the truth – which obviously, in this particular story I do to some extent – are we actually being hypocrites? Are we actually saying, listen... you have to be exact, you have to be precise, you have to tell us the truth always. Don't censor, don't shield us. We can handle it. When we don't really know how to say what we really feel ourselves because we don't really know how to get in touch with it. That was the first song that set up this idea for the record that, in a way... when you see somebody, when you experience... when you look in their eyes there's something goes between you and you both recognize that and you both might feel very very different things. But if one of you decides that it's – let's say love – what that actually can set up is a very kind of fatal circle.

I Am Afraid, which was inspired by and written and recorded in demo form within a few months of the birth of Joseph Townshend in late 1989, referred to the "future phobia" experienced by Ray in the story.

Predictable, Pete told Dia Stein, was "...about somebody saying, 'What I like about you is that I know what's going to happen,'" Pete told Dia Stein. " 'I *know* what's going to happen. I *know* I'm not going to have an orgasm (laughs). ...I know how it's going to feel. I know how it's going to go today. That is what makes it exciting is I'm certain it's going to go a certain way and that often it doesn't...'"

Fake It, Pete told Matt Kent in 1999, was about fulfilling an audience's expectations, no matter what the cost. The memory of hitting rock bottom in mid-1974 at Madison Square Garden was obviously still fresh in Pete's mind. "It goes back in my career to somebody saying 'jump, jump, jump, jump... '...smash a guitar' and me saying 'but this is crap' and them saying 'but we don't care, do it anyway'.

Fake It and *Don't Try to Make Me Real* were written simultaneously. "What they were supposed to be was a conversation between a man and woman, and the way that men and women traditionally seem to fall into stereotypes of requirement in relationships," Pete told Stein.

The man says often, "Don't try and put me in a pocket. If I say I love you, it doesn't mean I love you. It was something I just said at the time." And in *Fake It*, a woman's saying, "I don't care if you really love me. Bring me flowers, touch me, hold me, because it's now that matters to me. You're passing through my life from one end to the other. Grab me as you're passing – I don't care if it's not true. You tell me anyway." In the play, *Fake It* becomes about information, about law, about justice, about orgasm rather than just about "say you love me, and that'll get me through the day."

Psychoderelict's final song was a reprise of *English Boy* which featured a heavier emphasis on guitar. "I did about 15 solos [for *English Boy (reprise)*]," Pete told *Guitar Player*. "My original idea was that there should be hundreds of guitar solos, but the guy who did the remix, Jeremy Allom, just took one. I'm happy with it... My idea was to have a guitar wall of noise." He described the solo as an "homage" to Carlos Santana. "We were at Woodstock together. We've been together with John McLaughlin, who Carlos works with all the time and who sold me my first Fender amp and a couple of guitars when he worked in a guitar store. I just wanted to evoke that feeling."

Several of the songs Pete had recorded in demo form in The Cube in late 1990 and early 1991 didn't make it onto the finished *Psychoderelict*, mostly as a result of Pete's decision to release a single, rather than double, CD. Among these were a guitar piece entitled *Wistful*[243], which was intended as "an incidental underscore for some dialogue," according to Pete

---

[243] *Wistful* reflected a familiar Townshendian attitude, which Pete described in 2001: "The hero Ray High is playing the guitar while reflecting on the joys of not touring."

in 2001, and *Squirm Squirm*[244]: "At last, a song with a happy inspiration," Pete wrote in the liner notes for *Scoop 3* in 2001.

> One day I was holding my newborn son Joseph and singing him to sleep. It came into my mind that seen from high above we humans must look just like insects, or worms. As he wriggled in my arms I sang to him about the messages we all believe we get sometimes from above. At the time I was gathering material for *Psychoderelict*, which was – among other things – about the loneliness and collapse of a once famous and beloved rock star. The song seemed to contain and reflect both the peace and safety of this child in my arms, and the chaos and danger that surrounded us out there in the crazy world.

Uneasy Street, which was omitted from the final release of *Psychoderelict*, eventually surfaced on the 1996 compilation *Coolwalkingsmoothtalkingstraightsmokingfirestoking*. "There's a very difficult area on *Psychoderelict*, which is unexplored, which is the notion that if *English Boy* is about the exaggeration of evil in society, that there is also real evil in the world, and it's important not to forget this," Pete said in 1996.

> There is real evil at work. It tends to express itself through the individual, who indeed, if charismatic, can inspire masses of people. But *Uneasy Street* was supposed to be about that moment when the hero of the story, Ray High, suddenly realizes that his sexual passion, his desire to be seduced by a glamorous woman that he meets – and the reason the song's not in is that I wrote her out of the play in the end – is a bowing to something in himself which is incredibly self-destructive. In other words, this is not romance, this is not love, this isn't even lust, this is like, "I am going to destroy myself, I am going to go out into the world and find a
> spectacular woman, and give myself to her, and let her do whatever she wants." It's about the fact that this does sit very uneasily in modern life, that if you're talking about a woman doing this it's more common, it's easier to accept somehow, and that in the song this guy meets this beautiful woman, finds her very attractive, and then at the very last

---

[244] *Squirm Squirm* was reinstated into *Psychoderelict* during creative workshops in New York in 1999. The story was being considered for a Broadway run a la *Tommy*.

minute she whips off her mask, and whips off the mask underneath the mask, and turns out to be Satan himself, and that a contract has been written somehow, and the contract is that, you know, "Yes, I am prepared to destroy myself," which is the ultimate evil act. Heavy stuff, but a nice little ditty. (laughs)

Psychoderelict was released in July 1993 U.S. and U.K. It sold poorly; indeed, it soon became Pete's worst selling solo album, selling only about 200,000 copies when expectations were reportedly closer to the 5 million range. "I abandoned my recording contract after *Psychoderelict,*" Pete told David Sinclair of *The Times* in 1998. "I'd always told myself that when I sold less than 200,000 I'd stop. I had imagined myself triumphantly arriving at the Edinburgh Festival with it, so it was a bit of a blow."

"It's a tricky thing to get on the radio, and some of the critics have dismissed it," Pete told the *Orange County Register* in August, explaining that *Psychoderelict* was perhaps somewhat difficult for some music fans, given the format. "Some of it works, some of it doesn't." He also theorized that "...If *Tommy* were released today, it would probably fail. It's not quite fair to say people are lazy. Their listening habits have changed."

Similarly, most reviewers enjoyed the music, but found the dialogue a distraction. "...Townshend is now in the midst of his fourth decade as a bona fide rock star, so it's no wonder that his latest work for Atlantic, *Psychoderelict,* deals with the artistry and business of rock and roll," wrote *Guitar Player*'s Chris Gill in his review of the album.

>...The record breaks rules and challenges listeners, but Townshend hopes his audience will approach it with an open mind. Dialog links the songs together, but because it often interrupts the music, it may annoy listeners who simply want to boogie to the tunes. However, those who tolerate the dialog will discover Townshend's strongest musical work since *Empty Glass.*

People Weekly's Ron Givens agreed:

>This melodrama, overstuffed with who-knew-what-when twists and weighed down by lyrical significance, intrudes upon the songs in the form of dramatized soundbites. Nevertheless, these tunes glow with vitality. The riffs come at you with just the right amount of Who-like snap, Townshend's voice crackles with gusto, and he combines tenderness with sweet pop on *Now and Then* and *I Am Afraid.* Townshend may have thought the play's the

thing with *Psychoderelict*, but he was wrong. Rock and roll is.

Time's Janice Simpson also subscribed to the opinion that *Psychoderelict*'s format got in the way of the songs[245]: "…Tracks like the dynamic opener, *English Boy*, showcase Townshend's talent for mixing metaphysical lyrics with hyperphysical music. The dialogue, presented in the style of a radio drama and performed by actors, wears out its welcome more quickly."

Dave Marsh, reviewing *Psychoderelict* for *Playboy*, was impressed, commenting, "Townshend's songs are excellent, recycling motifs from his great unfinished rock opera, *Lifehouse*. The playing is fine, too, and for once, his story makes sense"

Rolling Stone also gave the effort a thumbs-up, with a 3 ½ star review:

> …Dark and agonized, *Psychoderelict* sputters and bellows, but its clangor gives it power…Yet the story, for all its cliche and bombast, allows Townshend to explore themes that have long obsessed him. …Townshend has flourished a gift for examining life's trials as well as its instances of painful possibility – the pathos of desire, the fight for identity and community, the fanatic urge toward truth. …Townshend's strong voice shines on *English Boy*, a youth cult anthem of the sort he invented with *My Generation*, and the lovely ballad *Now and Then*, while his guitar work fires up big instrumental numbers dedicated to his guru, Meher Baba. Sound effects and dialogue meld with songs to fashion a kind of aural movie; it's a collision that underscores one of *Psychoderelict*'s themes, the tension between truth and technology. Ultimately, the opera's characters place a guarded final faith in music as the avenue toward transcendence.
>
> Driving *Psychoderelict*, that faith continues to make Pete Townshend's career one of rock & roll's finer stories – brave, desperate and open.

"…if you can get past the "high concept," offered *Entertainment Weekly*, "you'll find some meaty songs in a *Who's Next* vein. There's life in the old geezer yet."

---

[245] A 'music only' version of *Psychoderelict* was released in an attempt to make the songs more accessible. "…[*Psychoderelict*'s] complexity meant that it has been largely ignored by radio," Pete said in August. "Even some fans can't cut through the wrappings to get to the music on the disc."

The numerous complements which Pete received for his guitar playing on *Psychoderelict* were welcomed, given the wrist trauma he'd had to overcome recently. "A lot of the guitar playing was post-accident," he said in 1993. The accident and subsequent moments of sobering contemplation during his six-month period of physical therapy had given Pete a new appreciation for the guitar. "...I'm actually becoming a guitar player," he said, as if he wasn't a noteworthy one before. "I love the guitar now, and I never used to. I used to hate it."

Pete realized early in the evolution of *Psychoderelict* that touring may help communicate the piece to the audience. "...I feel it's essential to promote this record," Pete told the *New York Daily News* in July. "The record is very difficult for radio."

"Impetuously and perhaps pompously, I wanted to do something a bit different with the rock format," he told the *Orange County Register* in August. "...I was worried that these great songs would get ignored altogether if I didn't do something drastic to attract attention to the record..." Despite the fact that Pete estimated touring would cost him approximately $500,000, the decision was soon made to take the show on the road. "When I finished *Psychoderelict*, I was *shocked* to find I wanted to perform it live," Pete told the *New York Daily News* in July, 1993. Pete had contemplated settling down once The Who's 1989 tour reached its conclusion, putting an end to his touring days. "My son was born and I took a year off to be with him, and I assumed writing and producing would be enough from then on. But in some way, on some level, it wasn't. I needed what I got from being on stage."

"I'm extremely ambivalent about performing, period," Pete told the *L.A. Times* in June, 1993. "I know when I perform and when I hear music, I love it and I'm energized by it, but I have a great difficulty committing." In order to help make such a commitment, Pete made a decision which unraveled a great deal of the stability he'd built since 1982, the last time he'd battled substance abuse. "I became a drunk for three months," he told the *L.A. Times*, "and in that three months I made about four or five serious commitments which I wouldn't have made sober..." However, he added, "I feel good about [touring]. I think I was a brave guy, and I think I can do the job. I'm certainly confident that I can do the job sober. I'm not trying to make a case for alcoholics going and getting drunk in order to make important life decisions."

The 1993 *Psychoderelict* tour was not a big affair – fourteen dates in mostly smallish venues[246] in eight North American cities – but it was a big deal for Townshend. "As a solo artist, I've only done two, three shows in my life," he told Dia Stein. "Really, I've hardly done anything. As a solo

---

[246] "Playing smaller places, the scope of expression is so much broader," Pete told the *Orange County Register* in August. "You can converse with the audience."

performer I don't exist, really, so I've got no career. So this is a big moment for me. If I actually do this, this will be the first solo tour that I've ever done."

I'm not wildly anxious to get back up on the stage, because I'm not wildly keen to be a performer. I don't feel comfortable as a performer, particularly. I'm much happier as a writer or a band member. It's ironic for me that after years in The Who, being frustrated because I couldn't express what I felt I needed to express because the band was such a big force and had such a big personality, and I had to write for *it*, that I left, got my moment of personal freedom, said my piece, and then missed the fact that whenever I go on a stage now, I'm in the front. ...it's hard work, to have to write it and to have to carry the show as well. This isn't quite like that. This, I would be one of the people in the show, I would have my little rests. I think it would be quite good for me. And I think that I feel comfortable that I could do this where I don't necessarily feel that I could do a tour of just me solo, you know, like a two hour show with me jumping about all over the place.

You know, I don't find performing hard. What Roger does as a performer is so much bigger and harder than what I do. He takes on the whole audience. He makes a pact with them when he walks on – "I am going to hold your attention for two hours and I'm going to give you every ounce of adrenaline and blood and guts in my body." I go out there and say, "Hi guys." What you get is what you see is what you get, you know, and if you like it, fine, and if you don't, then fuck off." I'm a working musician. That's how I see myself. I really do. I see myself as a working musician. I was in a band. And it's the writing that's made me a bit of an icon as a performer.

The first live rendition of *Psychoderelict* took place on July 2, 1993 at the Mayfair Theatre in London, a press-preview show in the same vein as that which The Who had performed at Ronnie Scott's club back in 1969 to unveil *Tommy*. Pete, performing solo for the first time since February, 1986, played his acoustic guitar unaccompanied, but with three actors, John Labanowski (Ray High), Linal Haft (Rastus Knight, High's manager) and Jan Ravens (reporter Ruth Streeting) performing their parts of the story. A Q&A session followed the performance.

Pete Townshend's first ever full-fledged solo tour began with a July 10 date at Toronto's Massey Hall. The musicians (who entered the stage playing *Cobwebs and Strange* on toy instruments[247]) were Townshend regulars Simon Phillips, Pino Palladino, Rabbit Bundrick, Peter Hope-Evans and Billy Nicholls (who was joined by backing singer Katie Kissoon). Guitar augmentation to Pete (who played the majority of the live set on a Fender Telecaster) was provided by Eric Clapton band regulars Andy Fairweather-Low (who'd helped out on *It's Hard*) and Phil Palmer. Two dates at New York's Beacon Theater followed on July 12 and 13, 1993. *Rolling Stone* was impressed, as the magazine's review of the first show revealed:

> Dressed in a natty, humidity-be-damned black suit, Townshend kicked off the American leg of his first full-fledged tour as a solo artist by playing nearly three hours without taking a break; and neither his energy nor his charm wilted a jot during that time...The actors...were on hand to enact the witty spoken portions of the libretto, and behind the stage hung a giant screen on which psychedelic patterns and symbolic images were projected to further embellish the plot and themes.
> Just as the dialogue and song lyrics in *Psychoderelict* benefit from Townshend's uncanny ability to marry tender idealism to brash indignation — "Whatever happened to all that lovely hippie shit?" High asks as the play ends — the music reflects his knack for combining achingly bittersweet melodies with ferocious power chords. Ballads like *I Am Afraid* and the glowing *Now and Then* gave Townshend and his band... the chance to reveal a delicate, graceful virtuosity, while the more sonically and rhythmically charged numbers were tackled with a feverish exuberance.
> In addition to *Psychoderelict's English Boy,* with its effervescent chorus and jazzy bridges, the evening's most invigorating moments included a buoyant rendering *of Let My Love Open The Door* and a radiant *Pinball Wizard,* on which Townshend — who played both acoustic and electric guitar throughout the set — strummed with dazzling dexterity and coaxed sounds from his instrument that were at once clamorous and pretty. Most importantly, Townshend seemed to be having a grand time — poking fun at his serious-songwriter image (the Who's *A Quick One While He's Away* was introduced as a song of "deep, deep social

---

[247] Richard Barnes wrote in 1996 that Pete said this "was to get rid of their egos. With *Tommy* still hot news, however, he soon lost interest in the workshop side and became quite aloof."

significance"), careering across the stage, jumping around and doing windmills against his guitar as if threatening to remind youngsters like Kurt Cobain that trashing one's ax after a night's performance is hardly a new trick. Pete Townshend himself is no more a new trick than Ray High, of course; but with his muse and his sense of humor in good health — to say nothing of his cardiovascular system — High's creator appears in little danger of becoming media fodder any time soon.

The two Beacon Theater shows were recorded, portions of which would later see release as the *Pete Townshend Live* video[248]. A Philadelphia stop followed a few nights later.

Pete's 17 July date at Chicago's Arie Crown Theater became historically important for all the wrong reasons. "I decided to have a bottle of vodka before going on the stage," Pete told *USA Today*'s Edna Gunderson. "I made a terrible mess of it." Richard Barnes recalled that "Pete played a lot of the show flat on his back."

"I hadn't had a drink for 11 years, then I decided I was rich enough, so I deserved one, and I began allowing myself an occasional beer," Pete told David Hinckley of the *New York Daily News* in July, 1999. "Then, for some reason, before a show in Chicago I drank a bottle of vodka. I don't remember a thing, except I'm sure the show was a fucking mess." The resulting guilt Pete experienced from this show was reportedly one of the reasons he returned to Chicago several times to perform fund-raising shows toward the end of the decade.

While thankfully short-lived, Pete's 1993 alcohol relapse was certainly a full-blown affair. "I had *Tommy* on Broadway and it went to my head," Pete told *The Sun*'s Dominic Mohan in early 2002.

> I thought, 'Even if I have got a bit of a problem with alcohol, it doesn't matter,' but of course it did. It doesn't matter how much money I had, I still ended up coming out of a club, seeing a builder's skip and thinking, 'Oh, what a lovely place to spend the night.'
>
> My head went completely. I used to do that all the time. My limo driver would be waiting for me to wake up. There were probably people walking past saying, 'Isn't that the bloke from The Who asleep in that skip?'
>
> There was one day when I just said, 'That's enough.' I didn't go to a clinic, I just stopped. What I'd

---

[248] One segment which didn't make the video was Pete reportedly becoming angry at all the shouted song requests, saying "I play what the fuck I like. You don't think I've worked for 30 years to get to this place to have you fucks tell me what to play."

managed 11 years before I thought I could manage again. It was messing up my life. But I've certainly had help over the years. I've had counselors. I had a therapist for three years, I don't know if that really helped or not. I just know I'm all right now. I don't think about alcohol but I know I wasted a lot of money on it.

Now I suppose to some extent I'm a workaholic, the self-obsession in my work. I think I'm getting better, I'm managing my recovery.

A presciently scheduled twelve day break thankfully followed the disastrous Arie Crown Theatre show. Two days after appearing on *Good Morning America*, Pete's next tour stop took place at L.A.'s Wiltern Theater on 29 July. John Entwistle took the stage for the encore, assuming bass duties on *Magic Bus, Let's See Action,* and *Won't Get Fooled Again*. A second Wiltern Theater date took place the following night, with Pete and co. all standing on one foot prior to the show, "to show that we're all completely sober."

"...The cranky, overly analytical, musical-genius side [of Pete Townshend] was put aside Thursday night," wrote Mark Brown in the *Orange County Register*.

The cheery guy who loves to play smart songs and flail away at his guitar in every way imaginable was there instead. Better than on most Who tours, rawer and more stripped-down than in his 1986 "Deep End" big-band concerts, this rare Townshend solo tour is everything his fans could possibly hope for.

Psychoderelict stands tall among Townshend's work, whether with The Who or without. Grinning like a madman and chasing harmonica player Peter Hope-Evans all over the stage while ripping out guitar leads, Townshend was more than full-on for most songs.

After the show, Pete told Fred Shuster of the *L.A. Daily News* that he was "...far more interested in holding my family together and bringing up decent kids with principles than in being a rock star," he said. "As long as I can hang onto that, I think I'm a worthy member of society. The job that I do as an artist depends on my survival as a person that can tell the difference between decent behavior and otherwise."

Shuster was not impressed with *Psychoderelict* live, calling it "pretentious, dull, stale, silly, amateurish and thoroughly boring".

Psychoderelict reached its nadir during a live-action

sadomasochistic scene shown in silhouette. Townshend's attempts at humor and timeliness only prove just how out of touch and self-indulgent he has become... the bulk of the show was given over to this ninth-rate *Tommy*...

Similarly, the *Oakland Tribune*'s Dave Becker wasn't impressed with *Psychoderelict* after witnessing Pete's 2 August show at the Community Center in Berkley, California. "While the aging-rock-star angle, obviously has more than a few parallels to the life of the 48-year-old Townshend, the self-absorption *of Psychoderelict* isn't nearly as annoying as the fact that it's simply a weak, dumb story," Becker wrote. "Especially coming from the man who set the standard for mixing rock and drama with *Tommy,* the piece is piffle.

The package gained a bit from live performance, mainly because of the spirited playing of Townshend and his band. The album's stronger numbers, especially the rousing single *English Boy,* were given extra spit and fire, although a few electric moments couldn't make up for the tedium of the hour-plus wallow. Townshend himself seemed to recognize the limitations of his new work, murmuring before the performance began that "It's not meant to be the greatest thing since rock'n'roll" and pleading with the audience to "roll with it."

Fortunately, *Psychoderelict* accounted for a minority of Townshend's three-hour performance. The mini-opera wasn't rolled out until the singer-guitarist had riled up the crowd with a skanking version of the English Beat's *Save It For Later* and smoking run through of *Rough Boys*... After tossing off a few Who songs, including a wonderfully moody reading of *Drowned*, it was time for the new material, which received a polite but not-too enthusiastic response from the crowd. Townshend quickly had them on their feet, however, with a wildly freeform version of The Who's *Magic Bus*. Closing with the Who anthem *Won't Get Fooled Again,* Townshend was every bit the rock hero as he led the band to a thundering climax. Watching the middle-aged maestro race around the stage and bash his Telecaster with his patented windmill style, it was easy to believe that rock can grant a certain level of immortality.

Pete returned to the stage for an encore, singing *My Generation* alone with his acoustic guitar. "Townshend's stripped-down treatment turned the powerhouse rocker into a gesture of middle-aged solidarity and showed that great rock'n'roll never gets old," wrote Becker.

Add to the list of those unimpressed with *Psychoderelict* the *San Francisco Examiner*'s Barry Walters: "...The largest chunk of [Townshend's] show was devoted to passionate performances of lousy material," Walters wrote, calling the plot of Townshend's latest work "absolute rubbish... Pointless references to virtual reality are sprinkled throughout the project and the songs sound like 20-year-old outtakes. It's Townshend's worst, a commercial and artistic dud." However, Walters echoed the opinions of most reviewers of the *Psychoderelict* tour in his impression of Pete Townshend's onstage prowess. "The good thing about *Psychoderelict* is that it has enabled Townshend to enjoy himself again," Walters wrote, recalling that Pete appeared "miserable and preoccupied with money" during the 1989 *Kids Are Alright* tour. "Here, he was in excellent voice and pleased to be following his own whims... He spoke to the crowd at length, ran around the stage like in days gone by, shouted out his lyrics and beamed with cranky good will."

The following night saw a repeat performance at Berkley, this time with Broadway *Tommy* star Michael Cerveris guesting on *Pinball Wizard*. "...great, *great*," proclaimed the following morning's edition of the *San Jose Mercury News*.

> ...a stirring reminder that rock at its very best can strike a chord within us and shake us to our shoes... it was one odd and sod after another. There was a smashing rendition of *Rough Boys*, with Townshend slashing out his legendary power chords against the slamming beats of drummer Simon Phillips. That gave way to a shimmering acoustic version of the Who classic *The Kids Are Alright*, with Townshend's vocals displaying a world-weary affection that spanned several rock generations. And when he and the band exuberantly charged into the Who's *Eminence Front*, the crowd was jumping in the aisles.
>
> *Psychoderelict*... was surprisingly effective, musically as well as theatrically... songs such as the energetic rockers *English Boy* and *I Want That Thing* proved Townshend's songwriting is as vital as ever...

Pete again performed *My Generation* alone with his acoustic guitar at the end of the show, and it was again positively received, the *San Jose Mercury News* calling the rendition of the Who classic "stunning... It was one of his *Scoop* albums come to life, a stark onstage "demo" – a one-of-a-kind performance from a one-of-a-kind rock titan."

In the audience during Pete's stop at Berkley was Pearl Jam singer Eddie Vedder, a confessed Who fanatic. "I recognized him in the audience, but he looked bemused, a little lost," Pete told *Spin* in 2001. "[Afterward] I spent an hour with him[249]. It could have been ironic, the play I was performing – about old, worn-out stars trying to pass on their "wisdom" to younger performers." At the time of the Berkley show, "[Vedder] was interested in developing *Quadrophenia* as some kind of stage vehicle," Pete said in 2000. "We became friends because he listens to me when I speak. I just love that! I also admire the way he lives his life. He values friendship and love, and gives those around him space."

The next night marked a benefit show for the La Jolla Playhouse at San Diego's 2,200-seat Copley Symphony Hall[250]. "Townshend was by turns inspired and indulgent, provocative and pretentious," wrote the *San Diego Union*'s George Varga.

> He played guitar with gusto, drawing loud cheers with his patented windmill strumming (which was more simulated than real). And he sang passionately in a wavering voice that grew stronger, weaker and stronger again as the evening progressed.
>
> But the first rocker to ever win a Tony Award on Broadway ultimately emerged triumphant in a generous, 2 ½ hour performance that offered a partial retrospective of his career and allowed him the welcome chance to favor subtlety and nuance over spectacle and bombast.
>
> ...*Psychoderelict*, which — for better *and* worse — he performed Wednesday in its 80-minute, near-entirety. . .its muddled dramatic staging by three London actors underscored the continuing problems in marrying theater and rock live on stage... the standout songs from *Psychoderelict* – *English Boy, Now and Then*, and *I Am Afraid* – rank with his best, and the crowd responded warmly to them.

Michael Cerveris again joined Townshend onstage, providing

---

[249] "Eddie was in great distress," Pete told *USA Today* in October, 1999. "He was worried that he had become a huge celebrity and couldn't sit in audiences unmolested to watch his favorite artists anymore. So he came to an old sage for advice." "I was in a terrible space," Vedder said. "I enjoyed the show incredibly, but I was ready to fall apart mentally. We just kind of stared at each other for the first two minutes. Pete really helped me with a couple things. I had a friend in a bad situation that I didn't understand. In 45 minutes, Pete dispensed information I couldn't have gotten anywhere else. I just appreciate his wisdom and experience."

[250] The *San Diego Union* described the playhouse at the time as "critically acclaimed but financially beleaguered." The show raised approximately $100,000.

vocals that Vargas described as "too slick" on a 12-minute *Tommy* medley which consisted of *Captain Walker/It's a Boy*, *Christmas*, *Sensation*, *Pinball Wizard*, and *See Me, Feel Me*.

Pete returned to the east coast on 7 August for a show at New York's Brooklyn Academy. The date also marked the release of *Pete Townshend Live*, the video recording of his earlier Beacon Theater shows. "…the music from *Psychoderelict* is far superior to the story line," reported the *Boston Globe*, echoing a familiar sentiment by this point.

> …The three actors who play these roles…drift around the stage in a kind of script-induced fog. Townshend's reach exceeds his grasp – he even uses the actors to comment on everything from hippie dreams to technological overkill – but the music redeems the whole enterprise…Townshend rages through new rock songs and ballads that represent some of his best material since his prime with The Who. Although you'll scratch your head at the *Psychoderelict* story line, you'll still be in awe of his music.

The August 9 show at Mansfield, Massachussetts' Great Woods Amphitheater pushed Pete to the limits of his patience as technical problems occurred early into *Psychoderelict*. After dispensing with both the behind-the-stage projections and onstage actors after glitches surfaced during *Early Morning Dreams*, Pete soon ran off into the wings, leaving the band wondering what was next. Perhaps the older Who fans in the crowd knew that they were in for a treat, as Pete has demonstrated many times in the past that his most passionate shows have often occurred when his anger has boiled to the surface, a point Chris Charlesworth noted after a particularly fiery 1976 Who show.

The *Boston Herald*'s Dean Johnson recalled the ensuing fireworks:

> An infuriated Townshend returned for an unscheduled *Magic Bus* that lasted 10 minutes and featured four grinding, sprawling guitar breaks from Townshend. He leaped on amps, scampered Groucho-like around the stage and unleashed his windmill guitar riffs…the rest of the night was so intriguing because no one was sure what was next, including Townshend. After a couple more songs, including a spirited *You Better You Bet*, he did several more new tunes without actors and special effects. Townshend finished with songs that ranged from the English Beat's *Save It For Later* and Dylan's *The Girl From The North Country* to a fiery *Won't Get Fooled Again*, a solo *My*

Generation and *Eminence Front*.

Good rock is all about attitude, and Townshend's spit-and-vinegar show proved he still has it by the truckload. But he was clearly embarrassed. The crowd was cheated out of seeing his new rock opera. A better show resulted, but that provided him little solace.

Two days after a stop in Philadelphia, the final date of Pete Townshend's *Psychoderelict* tour took place on August 12 at one of his favorite venues: Jones Beach Theater, New York. "...the Jones Beach show is the one that I remember as the most successful amalgam of a rock concert and a theatrical piece," Pete told *Cleveland Live.com*'s Ira Robbins in 1996. "It was a little bit circus-ish in a way, a little bit bawdy... By the time we got to the end, the actors were rather parodying themselves and having fun with the thing. But the audience was familiar with it, they were comfortable with it, they knew what was going to happen, they knew that there were going to be people acting, they'd heard from their friends or whatever. By the end of the tour, people knew what was going to happen, and it worked."

Upon the tour's completion, Pete's priorities returned to addressing his recent bout with alcoholism (he began attending AA meetings), and attempting to patch up a yet-again strained marriage. Touring had brought some simmering problems to the forefront. "Going on the road with my album, deciding that it would be my last album — I don't know if it will be or not — and deciding that I would do some shows was partly to see whether I could still do it," Pete told *Rolling Stone* in December, 1993.

> But I also felt I had to prove to myself that having a show on Broadway didn't mean that I wasn't still a rock star. All those things are about turmoil really. The beginning of the year, I was very happy. I was meeting wonderful new people, making regular trips to New York. But toward May, June, I started to get uneasy, and I'm still in that place. I'm still not sure how I'm going to do the things I want to do without traveling an enormous amount — which is again something my wife and I find difficult. So there's a kind of feeling of dread which runs through me, my oldest daughter, my younger daughter and all my friends, including my wife, that we're heading for difficult times, because of the career I want, which is a show-business career, and show business is destructive. It's both disturbing and incredibly exciting.

Ultimately, Pete's marriage didn't recover from this latest rift. The following year, Pete had a girlfriend, and a by 2000 he was publicly lamenting the failure of his marriage.

Chapter 15

> *"...I don't like the Who. Do I have to like them? My feelings about the band are much deeper than that, incredibly ambivalent. I feel like the proud housewife who cooks a lovely dinner, takes it in to this wonderful man she married...who's sitting and watching TV with his shirt hanging out, belching and drinking beer. And she thinks, 'I love him, but I don't like him.'"*
> — Pete Townshend, 1994

Early 1994 brought rumors of a 30th anniversary Who reunion. It was well-circulated that Daltrey and Entwistle periodically prodded Townshend in an attempt to resurrect the band (they "always hold out hope that maybe there's a slim chance I'll come back in to the fold", he said in mid-1994), but they were consistently met with strong resistance. Pete was asked about the prospect of such a reunion the previous year during an interview with the *New York Post*. "[Roger] and I are cooking up something really fucking bizarre, but it's much too soon to talk about it," Pete said, not exactly extinguishing the rumors. "It'll be one of the wildest things we've ever done, something you can do only when you're really old and really rich." Whatever Pete was referring to, it dissipated quickly. By mid-1994, Townshend was bluntly squashing any notion of a Who reunion. "I thought briefly about doing it [30th anniv. Reunion tour]," he told the *Detroit News and Free Press*. "There's never been a tour planned, to my knowledge. There was lots of supposition about it, but nobody ever ran a list of dates or a budget by me. Ultimately it's not something I really want to do. It's an absolute no – forever."

"I think there are days when he doesn't like the Who; he's definitely in his Who denial period now," Daltrey said at the time. "I don't even talk to Pete about the Who anymore. If he changes his mind, he knows my number."

The closest Pete Townshend got to a Who reunion in 1994 was an onstage appearance in late February with Daltrey and Entwistle, his first since the BPI awards show in 1988. On 23 and 24 February 1994, just before his 50th birthday, Roger Daltrey performed a selection of Who songs at New York's Carnegie Hall with a 65-piece orchestra from Juilliard, and guest vocalists including Sinead O'Connor, Eddie Vedder, Linda Perry, The Chieftans, Alice Cooper, Lou Reed and the Spin Doctors. Ringo Starr's son Zak Starkey played drums. *Daltrey Sings Townshend*, a sold-out affair and pay-per-view telecast, was initially to include John Entwistle and Pete Townshend on stage with Roger, but reportedly Pete wasn't comfortable with the idea, citing the fact that he didn't enjoy playing on stage in front of an orchestra (recall the problems with 1972's orchestrated *Tommy* show at the Rainbow), and Pete's unwillingness to go through *a Who's Greatest Hits* show. Richard Barnes recalled in 1996 that "Pete, who had originally supported the idea, decided nearer the date that he wouldn't be involved but after a "robust" phone call from Roger was talked round but he stipulated that the three members of the Who didn't appear together. He performed *Who Are You* and *Won't Get Fooled Again*.[251] Roger sang the rest of the concert and John played bass. The Who did appear together, with everyone else, for the finale, *Join Together*. Michael Kamen wrote and conducted an orchestral piece called *Overture* which included sections of *Quadrophenia* and *Tommy*. The Chieftans backed Roger and Sinead O'Connor on *Baba O'Riley*."

Linda Perry sang what *Rolling Stone* called a "wicked" version of *Acid Queen*, and Eddie Vedder contributed *My Generation* and *The Kids Are Alright*. Vedder, who once told an interviewer that Pete Townshend's influence on him was such that he should be sending him father's day cards, subscribed to appropriately Who-like methods of preparation for the show with a Moon-like wrecking of his dressing room. Circus impresario Jim Rose, a friend of Vedder's, recalled the destruction in *Revolver* six years later:

> I get a call from Eddie; he says, "It's Roger Daltrey's 50th birthday; I got a cake for him, why don't you come with me?" So we went, and everybody was there: Alice Cooper, Lou Reed, Townshend, Sinead O'Connor. So we all met up at Carnegie Hall, we gave Roger the cake, and then Eddie and I went into his dressing room and he hands me a metal chair, and says, "You throw the opening pitch." I look around, and it's just these gorgeous chandeliers and mirrors and gold-plated lights. And I had been drinking.

---

[251] This occurred on the second night.

By the time it was through, there was nothing left. Even the toilet was broken down, just a pipe gurgling water from the floor.

"I think I threw a wine bottle at a mirror and it exploded," Vedder said. "At some point I cut my hand and started writing I HOPE I DIE BEFORE I GET OLD in blood. Which was really good. We got a bill from Carnegie Hall for $25,000... they also said they'd never have rock'n'roll bands in there again."[252]

The *Daltrey Sings Townshend* shows were such a success that Daltrey took the show on the road, bringing Entwistle (for selected dates) and Starkey along, and using Pete's brother Simon on guitar. "He looks so much like Pete it's uncanny," Daltrey told *Music Connection*'s John Lappen in August 1994, obviously realizing that what he'd put together was a surrogate Who. "...I could have used the Who name on this tour; I have Pete's blessing. However I won't do that because it's not the Who."

Daltrey continued to long for a real Who reunion. "I'd love to see the band get back together," he said. "I still feel we have better work to do. But I'm just taking it a day at a time. Pete isn't interested in doing it right now. But tomorrow, who knows? I hear rumors that he might appear at some of the shows on this tour, which pleases me very much."

The appearances didn't happen, though, as Pete stayed away. He was busy reassessing his priorities on the heels of the failure of his staging of *The Iron Man*. "Around the time of his tour, [Roger] was out there doing his thing and I was going through probably one of the worst chapters of my life, having just messed up in London with *Iron Man*," Pete told www.clevelandlive.com in 1996. In the wake of the success of the stage version of *Tommy*, Pete felt the failure of *The Iron Man* especially hard. "Although it was a success in its way, I was emotionally fucked up by it," he said.

> I couldn't work out what had gone on. I knew that *Tommy* was hugely successful and I knew that *Iron Man* had somehow failed and it didn't have to do with the disparity in their budgets, it was something else... I went away to review my life and think about what I was going to do next. Meanwhile, Roger's tour was rolling and I was somehow expected to be a happy-go-lucky part of it all. I couldn't do it. I couldn't do any more than I did, which was to run on the stage and give him a birthday hug, sing a

---

[252] Townshend, who wasn't present for the damage, later commented, "No one thought it was particularly well executed. But after all, he's a fucking surfer!"

couple of songs and then go home. I was not a well boy, I don't think.

The problem for me with Roger's tour was that it was meant as a way of both honoring the work, celebrating the work and using it in the absence of the Who. But I felt comfortable with it. Where I started to feel uncomfortable with it was when Roger's manager started to suggest that I might change horses as well, and move away from what I was doing in my life and turn Roger's tribute to Pete Townshend into the new Who. I'm not suggesting that that was [the manager's] motive, but like a lot of Who fans, his dream was to find some way to get the Who back together. That is still probably Roger's self-confessed dream. That was a real problem for me, because what I felt at the time was that I couldn't see a creative route to that state of affairs. I couldn't see us going into a studio and coming up with songs that were a credit to each of us as human beings.

With Daltrey's longings seemingly lost on an indifferent Townshend, the pair obviously still weren't seeing eye-to-eye after all these years. "No question, it's a strange relationship," Roger commented.

People outside the band just see it as Pete and me fighting. But they don't understand that the fighting between us was the spark for our creativity. What is any artist without opposition? We've never really been chums, but there is a deep love there. If he were ever in trouble, I'd be the first one by his side. We don't need to see or speak to one another. We do fight a lot, we do disagree on a hell of a lot. But what we do have in common outweighs all of that.

The friction between Daltrey and Townshend during 1994 was soon addressed as the pair were persuaded to open a dialogue. "Our counselors kept telling us that we had to sit and talk, and it was frightening," Pete told www.clevelandlive.com in 1996. "In the end, we got the courage, and we sat down and we talked to one another about it. And it was hard, but we resolved it.

In May, 1994 The Who were again back in the news despite the fact that the oft-rumored reunion never took place. An officially blessed boxed set entitled *Thirty Years of Maximum R&B* hit the stores, assembled by long-time Who associates Chris Charlesworth and Jon Astley. Charlesworth had rekindled an interest in The Who and his friendship with Townshend after witnessing one of the the band's shows at Wembley Arena in 1989. "I saw all these CD box sets in the stores by artists who weren't fit to lick The Who's boots, like Journey, so I wrote a stroppy letter about it to Pete," Charlesworth told *Mojo* in 2004. "He rang me up the next day, and said that I should put a Who box together. We kept John and Roger in the loop, sent them lists of tracks, and asked them for suggestions, but what did they contribute? Bugger all. I never heard a thing from them."

"Charlesworth thought the unreleased Polydor boxed set had "too much post Keith Moon stuff,"" Richard Barnes wrote in 1996, "so he, record producer Jon Astley, graphic designer Richard Evans and Polygram's George McManus returned to the archives and repackaged it."

> Unfortunately all the sixties sessions recorded for BBC radio couldn't be included, and the early material, including their first three singles as the Who and first album, could not be properly remixed because of a long-running legal dispute. Press reaction to the boxed set was ecstatic. Britain's *Q* magazine even labeled it 'The best boxed set ever released'.

Pete wrote a sarcastic, occasionally scathing foreword to the set's liner notes entitled *Who Cares*[253] in which he explained his feelings on the project and on the history of the Who in general. He acknowledged that Charlesworth and Astley had done "an OK job", adding that "being dragged through your life like this is strange." He signed off with venomous jab at his critics: "So to my detractors, to detractors of The Who, to critics of Moon and his diabolical certain-death style of rock'n'roll nihilism, I say "Fuck you." And not for the first time. I'm still briefly alive. Be kind, be real, or get out of my face. Pete."

Pete was "delighted" with the 79-song collection, according to a July 1994 report in the *Detroit News and Free Press*. "...and feels it shows the many facets of the band – not just the heavy, arena rock outfit it became during the '70s." The success of the venture led to talk of producing an expanded version of the chronically short *Live at Leeds*. "I've got a huge warehouse full of reels of tapes and movie film," Pete said. "Anybody who's interested enough to come in and wade through it and find stuff to put out can do so. That interests me more than the idea of trying to find new product."

An interesting news story hit the worldwide web the following month. "Back in June 1995," The *Guardian* reported five years later, "many internet users were stunned by a message that went the rounds of newsgroups: "I was very saddened to hear of the death of Pete Townshend,

---

[253] "I said to Pete, Isn't that a bit negative?," Charlesworth told *Mojo* in 2004, "and he said, Well, that's the way I feel."

formerly of The Who. His *Tommy* will be missed by millions." The online rock world might have gone into mourning had not a counter message emerged: "I think you're confusing Peter Townsend, who died but wasn't very famous for almost marrying someone royal, with Pete Townshend, who hasn't died (as far as I know) and was very famous for being in The Who.""

A (thankfully) alive and well Pete attended daughter Aminta's college graduation[254] in October 1994 prior to flying to Los Angeles for the premiere of the touring *Tommy* at the Universal Amphitheater. The *Chicago Tribune*'s Jessica Siegel caught up with Pete backstage, noting that "he was kinda deaf, so I had to talk loud during the interview," and "he still chews at his fingernails, which are bitten to the quick. Occasionally, he smokes[255]." Pete met the cast backstage between acts, and signed autographs. "After writing "You were O.K." on one cast member's playbill," Siegel reported, "Townshend pauses just long enough for dramatic effect before adding "until you joined the show.""

In September 1995, Pete played solo at a benefit show organized by Paul Simon at Madison Square Garden's Paramount Theatre, for The Children's Health Fund. The show also featured Annie Lennox. "Agreeing to appear, I picked up a guitar and I realized that since the middle of 1992 I had probably spent more time at home playing piano than guitar (I was recovering from a serious wrist accident and keyboard practice was more useful physiotherapy)," Pete wrote in the *Scoop 3* liner notes in 2001. "So it seemed to me that I should play piano in public for the first time. On this occasion the Wynton Marsalis orchestra, some of the best jazz musicians on the planet, were in attendance. I was nervous. But I did well." Pete's set included *Save It For Later*, *Slit Skirts*, *Cut My Hair*, *Love Reign O'er Me*, *I Am An Animal*, and *Drowned*. Paul Simon and band joined Pete onstage for *The Kids Are Alright*, while Pete returned the favor by assisting Simon on *You Can Call Me Al*.

In February, 1996, another solo show took place – this time at The Orange, a bar in east London. The occasion was a private party for the cast and crew of the West End staging of *Tommy*. Pete played one song, *Pinball Wizard*, with London *Tommy* star Paul Keating guesting on vocals.

Pete traveled to the U.S. in late April 1996 for a five-date tour. The visit was also to meet with the designers of a *Tommy* CD-ROM, to be released in June 1996[256], to appear on *VH-1 Honors*, and to get the logistics

---

[254] Older sister Emma was pursuing a Ph.D. at Cambridge University during this period.
[255] Siegel also noted that Pete carried a "little red book" in the pocket of his denim jacket: A "…guide to local Alcoholics Anonymous meetings in Los Angeles…"
[256] The *Tommy* CD-ROM featured interviews with the three surviving original band members, Ken Russell, Des McAnuff, and soundtrack producer George Martin. It also featured some original Townshend demos. "I wasn't involved in the authorship of the CD-ROM at all," Pete told *Addicted to Noise*'s Mark Brown in April. "I was a producer and obviously a participant."

of The Who's upcoming *Quadrophenia* show hammered out (the resurrection of *Quadrophenia* is discussed in detail in the next chapter).

The mini-tour was set up to promote *Coolwalkingsmoothtalkingstraightsmokingfirestoking*, Pete's 'best of' compilation which was released in the spring[257]. He visited L.A.'s Universal Amphitheatre for a brief appearance on 28 April followed by a visit the next day to the L.A. House of Blues for two shows, one at 9 pm and another at midnight. Eddie Vedder sat through both L.A. House of Blues shows, and "...mouthed most of the words," according to one reviewer. Also reportedly in attendance were *Cheers* cast members George Wendt and Woody Harrelson, along with actor John Cusack and former Yes bass player Chris Squire. "Townshend appeared to be in good spirits," the reviewer continued, "and had Jon Carin along with him, whose former credits include playing synthesizer for Pink Floyd... [Townshend] peppered the show liberally with lesser known material from his eight solo albums," and performed a "...handful of songs he wrote for the Who."

On 30 April, Pete performed at one of The Who's old haunts, the Fillmore in San Francisco. "...for his screaming crowd, the show was a two-hour high," reported the *Daily Californian*. "When Townshend sang the line "I wish I was home this time" from *Sheraton Gibson* a fan quickly quipped, "You are home, Pete!" The musician's gentle smile cemented the love affair between him and his audience."

While the *Oakland Tribune*'s William Friar reported that the Fillmore show was a mostly acoustic affair, it was clearly the occasions Pete picked up his Telecaster that Friar appreciated most:

> When Townshend wanted to play, he *played*. Lightning-fast riffs. Thundering power chords. Spidery finger-picking. It didn't matter that he never pulled out his trademark windmill strum, and no one really expected him to break a guitar, a rock-concert tradition he started and tired of before many of today's modern rock rebels were even born. However, that didn't stop Tuesday night's audience from begging him to do it. "If I smashed this up, then I'd go to hell," Townshend said, cradling his American-made vintage electric guitar.

Pete was also his quirky, humorous self that night. "Rarely can a rock musician manage to captivate his public without actually playing music," reported the *Daily Californian*'s G.P. Secki, "but Townshend's

---

[257] Pete reportedly let the record company choose the album's title and content, telling them, "You look, you take what you think is cool, because as far as I'm concerned, it's all genius," he told *CNN* in 1996. "Or, if I get up on the other side of the bed, 'Don't do it, it's all rubbish.'"

friendly chit-chat about the most improbable subjects (his masturbation habit, spirituality and paganism, Rod Stewart's sexiness) made the interludes between songs so entertaining that fans kept asking the rock legend to keep on talking. The range of Townshend's well-informed interests was best illustrated by a seamless segue between a discussion about Cybill Shepherd's recent *TV Guide* interview and a song based on a saying of Julian of Norwich, a medieval English saint[258]."

> ...near the end of *Rough Boys*... Townshend's virtuoso playing on the familiar song was one of those priceless moments at a rock concert when you feel you're in the presence of a master. It's like holding a small chunk of history in your hands. And then, as Townshend was about to bring the song to a triumphant climax...he stopped. And calmly retuned one of the strings. He then launched back into the closing chords, but it was a disaster, cracking up both him and his keyboardist. Similarly, during a rollicking encore of the classic Who tune *Magic Bus*, Townshend stopped playing mid-song to take off his shoes, while his keyboardist tried to cover for him. Townshend then proceeded to talk about the incident – again, while he was still ostensibly playing the song.

Pete traveled across the country following the San Francisco show, stopping in New York for two shows at the Supper Club on May 3 and 4. "What a privilege to behold!", wrote Jim Farber of the *New York Daily News*.

> Shorn of The Who's amplification, Townshend's vulnerability came fully to the fore. The gangly singer-songwriter who drove one of rock's most macho bands crept from the shadows, and the result concentrated his message. The force of it came through with particular strength in four numbers from The Who's youth culture epic, *Quadrophenia*. Songs like *Drowned*, *I'm One*, and *Cut My Hair*, which address the gnawing pain of adolescence, seemed all the more moving sung by a lone figure...

---

[258] Pete was referring to the *Iron Man* song *All Shall Be Well*. Julian of Norwich said "...I learned that it is more worship to God to know all-thing in general, than to take pleasure in any special thing. And if I should do wisely according to this teaching, I should not only be glad for nothing in special, but I should not be greatly distressed for no manner of thing: for *ALL shall be well*. For the fullness of joy is to behold God in all..."

Townshend also did quite a bit of talking this night...Townshend's music couldn't have seemed more earnest. No matter how young the perspective in his songs, Townshend made them seem contemporary to a middle-aged man – not only because of their timeless beauty and well-observed lyrics but because of his delivery. By singing in so open and unscarred a style, Townshend demonstrated how the thrills and fears of youth can enlighten a whole life.

The shows, all well-received, were noted for their intimacy and 'back to basics' feel. Pete, accompanied only by ex-Pink Floyd sideman John Carin on keyboards and synthesizers, seemed content and at ease on stage. "[the show] offered a look at the man behind the music, as he bantered with the audience and told stories between songs, more casual and easy - going than I've ever seen him on stage," wrote one reviewer of Townshend's April 30 show at the Fillmore.

Townshend was alternately derided and praised in the press for his set list on this tour, which remained essentially the same for both the California and New York performances. The shows were intended to celebrate Pete's solo career (coinciding with the release of his 'best of' compilation) as songs such as *Let My Love Open The Door, Rough Boys, English Boy, A Friend Is A Friend* and *Slit Skirts* were included. More obscure solo pieces such *as Heart to Hang Onto, Sheraton Gibson* and *Parvardigar* were performed, along with a small selection of Who songs, including *A Legal Matter, I'm A Boy, I'm One, Drowned, Cut My Hair*, and *Love, Reign O'er Me*.[259] While one review ran the headline *Townshend's Greatness: Not Relying Solely on Hits*, another lamented Pete's omission of a few Who staples. "Though Townshend played just over two hours Tuesday [April 30, The Fillmore], he couldn't find room for *Who Are You* or *Won't Get Fooled Again* or *I Can See For Miles* or *Pinball Wizard* or any song from *Tommy*.[260] When you're Pete Townshend and you sell out a show in 20 minutes, you can pretty much do what you want, but that doesn't necessarily mean it's worth paying $30 for."

---

[259] The amount of *Quadrophenia* selections included in Pete's set may have provided a clue at this time that Pete was toying with the possibility of giving the album more exposure, an idea which would reach fruition later in the year.

[260] Not entirely correct. *Eyesight To The Blind* was performed on the night in question.

Chapter 16

"Roger speaks a lot about the magic that happens when the three of us get together to play. I have to say I've yet to experience that (laughs). I'm trying hard not to be cynical. It doesn't feel that magical to me, but I am enjoying performing for the first time in a long time. I must give myself some credit: I've worked very hard learning to do that. The Supper Club dates that I did recently were all part of a program to try and get myself to ease back into being in the public eye and accepting the fact that my audience – my fans, the Who's audience and Who fans – are people that I utterly depend on, and I should accept that with some good grace and enjoy it...."
- Pete Townshend, 1996

"I've never apologized for restoring and reshaping things I've already done. Partly, that's because there's a quality of energy in my early work that's really difficult to emulate. It's not because I can't do it, I think I can do it sometimes, it's because I don't want to do it. I suppose the work that I did when I was young stands on its own two feet, and I don't want to go down the same road again. I've never been afraid of going and looking at that stuff and trying to make it better. I feel like, in a way, what I'm doing is honoring my job as a writer and making up for the fact that, in many respects, a lot of the Who's music was underrated and undervalued."
- Pete Townshend, 1996

On Saturday June 29, 1996 another incarnation of the Who reared its head at Hyde Park in London. Townshend, Daltrey and Entwistle were joined by a five-piece brass section, percussionist Jodi Linscott, drummer Zak Starkey, Rabbit on keyboards, three singers including Billy Nicholls, and Geoff Whitehorn and Pete's brother Simon Townshend on guitar. The event was The Prince's Trust Benefit Concert, featuring alongside The Who, Alanis Morrissette, Eric Clapton and Bob Dylan with Ron Wood.

Pete had agreed to perform at the benefit concert in early 1996, after experiencing a renewed enthusiasm for playing onstage. "I don't perform very much but I'd done this concert with Paul Simon last year for his charity at the Paramount and I enjoyed it," Pete said in April. "I played solo and felt that I could do a concert."

Pete's plans to play solo at Hyde Park were soon dramatically altered when it became apparent that the show was on a much larger scale than any of the concerts Townshend had performed recently. "...when I learned more about [the Hyde Park show] I learned that the expected audience was 150,000 people," Pete said[261]. "And essentially I thought what the hell am I going to do? Stand up there with a guitar? What I did with Paul Simon was play a bit of piano, play a bit of guitar and it was a very intimate occasion. I realized I really couldn't do that and thought about what I could do as an alternative." Pete put it more bluntly in an interview with the *L.A. Times* in May, 2000: "...the promoter, Harvey Goldsmith, told me half a million people were coming and I said, 'I'm scared, I don't think I can do it.'"

At the same time that the Prince's Trust concert lineup was beginning to take shape, a reconstituted *Quadrophenia* was looming on the horizon. Pete had been entertaining the idea of "rescuing" *Quadrophenia* for over two years, even considering a stage show a la *Tommy*, *The Iron Man* and *Psychoderelict*; in fact, during a *Rolling Stone* interview in late 1993 he said, "...if it [*Quadrophenia*] had female voices, I think it would have *West Side Story*-type potential."

"...I really want to see *Quadrophenia* turn into a theatrical property of some sort," Pete said in 1996. "It's a much more cohesive, dramatic work, really, than anything I've ever done."

> The problem with it is it's an inside view. It's an internal story. So it's quite difficult to realize without quite a lot of suspension of disbelief on the audience's part. What I'd really like to see happen is to see it as a touring production that would feature major rock star celebrities like Roger, like a number of other people who may be slightly disenfranchised by their bands breaking up earlier than they would like. Certainly it's a piece that would work well in the Hard Rock Hotel in Las Vegas, in Atlantic City installations, and in sheds on the road, with a band. It would be Who music and Pete Townshend's story. And it might turn out to be a really strong vehicle for Roger. But we'll have to see about that.

The prospect of revisiting *Quadrophenia* onstage arose in the wake of the Broadway *Tommy* success in 1993, when Pete began to evaluate his

---

[261] The Prince's Trust show turned out to be one of the largest single-day events ever staged in Britain.

catalog of work for further stage possibilities. "There were a few projects floating around in my head and *Quadrophenia* was, I suppose, one of them," Pete said in 1996. Pete's interest in reviving *Quadrophenia* was further aroused to a degree by the *Daltrey Sings Townshend* tour in 1994. "I remember when I did Carnegie Hall with Roger in 1994," Pete said in early 1996, "and hearing *Dr. Jimmy* and thinking how wonderful it sounded, but chiefly how wonderfully he sang it and how explosive it was." Another reminder of *Quadrophenia*'s power and beauty came with the arrival in March of Pete's advance copy of the the remastered CD, which was released to the public in July, 1996. "I put it on, and *I Am the Sea* comes up, and it was just spectacular," Pete said. "Something happened in the original mixing process which destroyed the record... Fuck knows what I did. It was some sort of phase problem. *Quadrophenia* now sounds very much like it sounded in the studio, as I remember it."

"...I never really thought about [staging *Quadrophenia*] seriously until about a year ago," Pete said in 1996, "when Bill Curbishley, our manager, came to me with a proposal to do a European tour of a rough treatment that I'd done, which was very, very expensive."

> It was a very ambitious project, a bit like [U2's] Zoo TV, with two bands. I was very excited. Then I told him that I wouldn't appear in it, and he said he didn't think it would sell out, and therefore the funding wasn't available in advance.
>
> And then Des McAnuff came to see me in February or March of this year with a proposal from Robbie Robertson to do a celebration for fifty years of the Vespa motorscooter [a Mod favorite] from the Piaggio company in Rome in August. That's when I started to think about it seriously. I started to think about the fact that a company like Piaggio might be able to put up the money required to do a fairly simple but elegant staging[262]. And then the Prince's Trust thing came up.

Pete eventually settled on performing a "celebrity version" of *Quadrophenia* at the Hyde Park show as an attractive alternative to performing solo. After obtaining sponsorship from Mastercard (which came rapidly, but "not quite enough money", according to Pete), he began to work out the details of the performance. "We're getting *Quadrophenia* done because we went straight to Mastercard, cut out all the people in between, got $400,000 and put the thing up," he said. "It's a strange place to be to

---

[262] The Piaggio anniversary show, which was slated for August in Rome, never took place due to scheduling problems.

realize that all I have to do it stroll into a room with a few old guys and say, "I fancy doing *Quadrophenia* as a dramatic work", and they say, "Hey, we'll give you money." That may sound cynical, but the fact is I can do it, and I trust myself to do it well." The Mastercard-sponsored event was soon dubbed the 'Masters of Music' concert.

Tapping into his recent successful experience with stage work, Pete examined methods to "advance the story" of *Quadrophenia*, since it suffered the same problem as *Lifehouse*, though to a lesser degree. "What happened with *Quadrophenia* is it's a very elegant piece of work that to an extent is confused by its grandiosity," Pete told *Addicted To Noise*'s Mark Brown in April, 1996, in what could have been a statement about *Tommy* or *Lifehouse*. "But it's a very very simple story. A young man has a bad day, basically, and that's really all there is. It's a series of events… He just realized that all he has in his life is himself and some spiritual future. Very much like *Tommy* in a way, the end of it. What's happened to me in my life is I've had kids come up to me like Eddie Vedder and say 'I used to listen to *Quadrophenia* because it was my childhood. I could see my childhood in it.'"

"Knowing that I was going to put the thing up in the UK for the first time, and that the audience in the UK is not as deeply committed to the band and its complete body of work as our fans are in New York, I had to have some kind of visible link to the movie," Pete said in October, 1996. To address this, he decided to use an on-stage narrator for the Hyde Park show, assisted by film projected on a behind-the-stage screen to give the story context and continuity, and to advance some of the less stage-friendly nuances of the plot. The "visible link" to the *Quadrophenia* film was obtained when Phil Daniels, 'Jimmy' from the original movie, agreed to the role of on-stage narrator.

The Hyde Park show band lineup was soon cemented. "Obviously my first choice for a main voice was Roger," Pete said in early 1996. "I asked Roger if he'd appear, and Roger said 'you must get John to play.' Roger had done a tour last year with John on the bass and Zak Starkey on the drums. So they became the nucleus of the band around the time of the announcement, so it kind of amounts, in a sense, to a Who reunion. Though that's not how it's going to look because I'm not going to play guitar, I don't think. I'm going to be in it, performing some songs. It's exciting. But that's where it stands."

Pete said the lineup for the Hyde Park show provided good "karma" for an onstage rendition of *Quadrophenia*. "With Zak Starkey on drums and my brother on guitar," he told www.clevelandlive.com 's Ira Robbins in 1996, "we've managed to spin some karma into the piece which makes it feel very comfortable for me. …When the three of us [Daltrey, Entwistle, Townshend] stand together with a piece like this you can get more of a sense of it having genuine authority... The three of us are 'from the neighborhood'; it just somehow feels right..."

Starkey had strong Who connections, and was, in Pete's hefty opinion, a great drummer. He would also prove to have better Who chemistry with Townshend and Entwistle than previous backstops Kenney Jones and Simon Phillips. "We're really pleased to have him in the band," Pete said in early 1996.

> He's just stunning. He's very easy to play with. Mind you, I'm very spoiled with drummers. I don't fuck around anymore. I only play with people who are really easy to play: Simon Phillips is a different kind of drummer, but he's very easy to play with, he's very much a listening drummer. But what Zak has is a lot of karmic Keith Moon about him, which is wonderful. It's easy to make too much of that – he really is his own drummer. He has his own style. But he's very intelligent. What he did was adapt his own style as an imitator of Keith Moon – he does a garage band imitation of Keith Moon which is probably unbeatable – but he's modified that, moderated it, in a very intelligent and musical way so that he won't be directly compared. He won't evoke uncomfortable memories for the audience. I've known him for a long time. Keith used to be a kind of musical godfather to him. He gave him his first drum kit, which I think is rather strange. Ringo may have actually given him his first drum kit, but I think Keith gave him the first drum kit that he really wanted. It had nude women on it.

Guitar duties were split among Simon Townshend and former Procul Harum/session player Geoff Whitehorn. Pete enjoyed working with his brother again. "I'm glad he's comfortable doing this, because it's a chance to spend time together, which we tend only to do when we're working," Pete said in 1996. "We see each other at Christmas and birthdays and other occasions, but we both shut ourselves out in our respective studios and write, write, write, write. He's been doing it since he was eight, so he's been doing it nearly as long as I have."

The main reason Pete delegated the majority of guitar duties to his brother and Whitehorn was the poor condition of his hearing. "I won't be playing guitar...I can't play guitar the way I used to," he said in early 1996. "I'd fucking kill myself. I'd make myself deafer than I am already...I'm fucking deaf. I'm damaged."

"It's amazing that in the debate about whether or not Pete should tour with The Who that the question of hearing is never thought about, and yet it's the first thing that comes to my mind," Pete told *People online* in 1996. "It makes me angry. When I'm in the back of my car, I can't hear a word my wife and 6-year-old son are saying in the front. On airplanes I can only hear children or people with high squeaky voices if they're looking right at me. I lip-read. I don't have hearing aids in my ears, but it wouldn't hurt for me to wear one, and I eventually will when I can no longer get through the day."

With an eye to strengthening the dramatic aspect of *Quadrophenia*, additional cast members were brought in, including '70s icon Gary Glitter as the Godfather, and former *Young Ones/Comic Strip* star Adrian Edmondson as the Ace Face. "I don't know whether it was inspired, it was just a natural choice," Pete said of the choice of Gary Glitter in 1996. "I wanted somebody who is able to parody the whole idea of a rock star and a rock godfather, and he is that."

So on Saturday, 29 June, 1996, The Who took the stage in Hyde Park as part of the previously mentioned all-star bill. "Eric Clapton, Bob Dylan and other legendary survivors from the 1960s brought rock music back to London's Hyde Park Saturday after a gap of 20 years," read the *Reuters* wire. "Around 150,000 fans braved the unseasonally cold weather to see the aging rockers, and the organizers are confident another 120 million around the world will tune in soon to see the concert on television." The sixteen-piece Who, along with film backdrop, narrator Daniels and actors Glitter and Edmondson, received a "rapturous ovation" for their performance, according to *Reuters*. Prince Charles, not known for a love of rock music, reportedly stopped by the backstage area and was seen "clicking his fingers to The Who." Also spotted among the crowd were Billy Connolly and Mick Jagger, plus a contingent of "young 'mods' on their scooters," according to the *Sunday Times*. The performance raised approximately $1 million for the Prince's Trust. Daltrey had to wear an eye patch for the show after being hit in the eye by a Gary Glitter-wielded microphone stand during a Friday rehearsal.

"[*Quadrophenia* in Hyde Park] …was a reckless move and in a lot of ways it didn't come off," Pete told *The Times*' David Sinclair in 1998. "We played to 200,000 people, half of whom had come to see Alanis Morrissette. I spoke to a lot of young people about it afterwards and they said they didn't really know what was going on. It was all a bit confused."[263]

While the Hyde Park show was not a resounding success in Pete's eyes, it did further demonstrate the potential of *Quadrophenia* as a stage piece. He decided that further onstage testing was in order. "At the moment

---

[263] The following night at midnight, Pete played at a private party at Thunder Drive to celebrate the *Quadrophenia* show. He played a four song, 30-minute set which included *Pinball Wizard* with West End *Tommy* lead Paul Keating, and a rendition of *My Generation* with Joe Walsh on guitar.

I'm considering the idea of bringing it to Giants Stadium or something like that," Pete said at the time. "...But I don't want to tour the world because it's actually a workshop. It might be crap." The band soon settled on testing the work over six nights at New York's Madison Square Garden in mid-July. Predictably, all six nights were sellouts. The only lineup change was Billy Idol in place of Adrian Edmondson.

"It was an expertly synchronized rock extravaganza," wrote the *Boston Globe*'s Jim Sullivan in his opening night review.

> ...What makes *Quadrophenia* resonate today, so long after its inception, is its powerful, universal theme and its killer songs, many of them simultaneously bombastic and introspective. Inner angst meets arena rock; power chords mesh with quasi-operatic singing; sentimentality runs headlong into stridency. It's no wonder that Pearl Jam's Eddie Vedder cites *Quadrophenia* as a seminal album...
>
> There is still no bona-fide Who reunion – these six shows are the extent of it and Townshend doesn't even like to call it The Who. Still, Daltrey must be in heaven. The 14,000-strong Garden audience (a quarter of the house seats weren't sold due to staging) went bonkers over *Quadrophenia* – and got an unexpected encore treat with *Behind Blue Eyes*, *Won't Get Fooled Again* and *Magic Bus*.
>
> *Quadrophenia* hit its stride right away with *The Real Me*, confusion as anthem, with strong leads from Entwistle, Starkey, Daltrey, both Townshends and the five-piece horn section. (Ol' Pete did manage a windmill and a scissor-kick near the end.) A vibrant balancing act – maintained throughout with kudos going to longtime Who sideman keyboardist John (Rabbit) Bundrick. Daniels soon entered, reminiscing about the Mods and their amphetamine obsession. Daltrey sang *Cut My Hair*, about the conformity of the subculture; and Daniels talked about going to see the High Numbers (The Who's early moniker), saying "they weren't exactly Mods" but close enough.
>
> Glitter came on to strut, rant and rave with Daltrey in *The Punk vs. the Godfather*, accompanied by video clips of a young Townshend smashing his guitar – to wild applause. Idol showed up later, arrogant in his first role as the Mod leader, humble in his second as a lackey. Both were cameos. Said narrator Daniels, as Jimmy, chronicling his disillusion: "My folks had let me down, rock had let me down, women had let me down."

In *Doctor Jimmy*, the cockiness and bravado come front and center. The future is pondered during the instrumental *The Rock*. The conclusion follows in *Love, Reign O'er Me*, where Jimmy may find some solace in the rhythm of the sea, even if he contemplates suicide...

Here, in concert as on the album, Townshend wants to dangle the possibility of redemption. By virtue of the fact that he's chosen to have an older Daniels serve as narrator, it's clear Jimmy has survived, however battered.

Variety's Kevin Zimmerman was similarly impressed with the opening night show:

> Townshend stuck with acoustic guitar and was notable mainly while exhibiting his famed wrists of rubber on a solo *Drowned* and trading vocals with Daltrey on a fiery *Helpless Dancer*. Entwistle characteristically stayed well in the back, delivering a thumping bass solo during a roof-raising take on *5:15*. ...Apparently a tuneup for the inevitable Broadway production, *Quadrophenia* nevertheless retains much of its nimble, muscular brilliance. More to the point, perhaps, is the fact that there's clearly life yet in this particular brand of rockers.

Obviously encouraged by the New York shows, The Who soon added a full-fledged U.S. tour to their schedule. "I've enjoyed the concerts so far," Pete told *Cleveland Live.com*'s Ira Robbins in October. I'm not sure how I'm going to feel about being on a long, drawn-out tour again, but I'm sure I'll be okay. I absolutely loved the New York show." Plans also were being discussed for further work upon the completion of the U.S. tour. "We'll probably do a few more shows with it in London and Europe, and after that I really don't know," Pete told Robbins.

> I'm already getting interest from theatrical producers in developing it as a simple sit-down theatrical production with a band on stage, like *Rent*, that kind of thing. I've had a couple of offers already, which I'm thinking about. What I think *Quadrophenia* lends itself to, and what I might be able to pull off where others have failed in the long term is to create a rock'n'roll event of great integrity and authenticity which can sit down somewhere in an installation. Des McAnuff took me to see *Cirque du Soleil Mystere* at Las Vegas in 1994, and I was just blown away by it. I'm a big fan of *Cirque du Soleil*, but what blew

me away was, in the rather bizarre and confused ever-changing scene that Las Vegas now represents in show business, there was this incredibly powerful – I think spiritually uplifting – show doing fantastic business. They do four shows a day, I think, in a twelve- or fourteen-thousand seat arena. I've been looking at a slightly more modest installation, but something that would provide a setting for this kind of musical work. This is what interests me for the future, not so much music theater in the old tradition, but an aspect of music theater that allows technology to play an important part without being subject to the vagaries of Broadway[264].

A few changes were made to the lineup and the visual presentation of the show following the run at Madison Square Garden, including the removal of Geoff Whitehorn from the lineup, with Pete picking up some of the electric guitar duties. "My brother Simon is still playing most of the work, but I decided I would actually get myself a rig like the one I used in '89, which certainly didn't hurt my ears, and play a few solos, basically because I felt that Geoff Whitehorn was getting a bad rap," Pete told Robbins. "I thought he played beautifully and elegantly, and people seemed to think in some way that he shouldn't have been there. So I just thought that I would bow to public opinion and play a bit of electric." It was also decided that the on-stage narration and film presentation were confusing. To correct this, Phil Daniels was dropped, and, as Pete told Robbins, "We're in the process of tidying that up a bit. We're shooting a lot of film, another half-a-million dollars worth of movie."

The tour began in mid-October with four dates in the Northwest, with Pete stopping at Neil Young's Bridge School Benefit on October 19 in Mountainview, CA, the same day The Who played in San Jose. "…it is hard to imagine Young topping last weekend's two concerts," wrote the *San Francisco Chronicle*'s Joel Selvin.

> …with Pete Townshend of the Who dropping by for an unannounced performance Saturday at Shoreline Amphitheatre, David Bowie playfully stealing the show and powerful if somber performances by Pearl Jam, Patti Smith, the Cowboy Junkies and Young himself.
>
> Townshend, appearing at the relatively nearby San Jose Arena with the other members of the Who, dropped by

---

[264] As recently as November 2004, Pete mentioned that he was still entertaining this idea. "I am… talking to Des McAnuff (who must be the busiest man on earth) about a new musical spectacular for Las Vegas," Pete wrote on his web site. "We've been talking about doing this since we mounted *Tommy* on Broadway back in 1993. It's getting closer."

early in the evening for a half-hour of songs he said he "wrote when I was young about being young." Glancing at the songbook, he sang three early Who songs – *The Kids Are Alright*, *I'm A Boy*, and *A Legal Matter* – then added *Drowned*, a song from his other rock opera, *Quadrophenia*, which he is touring across the country, and a rare solo performance of *Behind Blue Eyes*.

Pete also played *Let My Love Open The Door*, and was in good spirits, reportedly telling the crowd, "Muddy Waters said 'My Guitar is my thing!!'...if my guitar was my thing, then I used to bounce my thing all over the stage!"

In the days after the Bridge School Show, Pete rejoined The Who tour for a string of performances in San Jose, Los Angeles and Phoenix. The *San Diego Union-Tribune*'s Dennis Hunt wasn't impressed with the L.A. show. "Remember when The Who was one of the most exciting rock bands around?", he wrote on October 25. "...get ready for a big letdown if you see The Who tonight at the Pond in Anaheim. Hunt disliked many aspects of the concert, citing *Quadrophenia*'s "muddled story line", Gary Glitter ("second-rate"), Billy Idol ("feeble-voiced"), and Daltrey's "totally shot" voice, which "kept cracking in the wrong places and he was having trouble sustaining notes." Hunt also wasn't fond of Zak Starkey's drumming. "Townshend was the best performer of the lot," he offered, "but couldn't carry the show by himself."

The tour wound on through Las Vegas and Denver in late October prior to stopping in Chicago for two shows (October 31 and November 1) at the United Center. "What's this? A flash of inspiration?," wrote *Rolling Stone*'s Steve Knopper in his review of the second show.

> From the Who? The 32-year-old band's short *Quadrophenia* tour, like its 1989 reunion hype extravaganza, is three old rockers and 12 of the best touring musicians money can buy. But unlike 1989 – and certainly unlike the listless 1982 "farewell" tour – singer Roger Daltrey, guitarist Pete Townshend and bassist John Entwistle decided to make *Quadrophenia* count.
>
> As unlikely as it may sound, their best hire was Zak Starkey, Ringo Starr's son, on drums. He mimicked the late Keith Moon perfectly, wearing all white and recreating the chaotic explosions that hold *Quadrophenia* together. His presence alone energized the surviving trio.
>
> The other good choice was *Quadrophenia*, which the band played end-to-end for two hours Friday night at Chicago's sold-out United Center. It holds up after two

decades infinitely better than the impossible-to-kill *Tommy*, the Who's first rock opera, which is still running as a musical around the country. *Quadrophenia*, a tale of mods battling rockers in 1950s England, was about rock nostalgia when it came out in 1973. So it works better than, say, singing, "Hope I die before I get old."

Because of persistent hearing problems, Townshend predominantly played rhythm on an acoustic guitar. Entwistle, as usual, didn't move anything but his fingers. So from the first lines of *The Real Me*, Daltrey was the show's driving force and most energetic personality. Despite the firepower of a 12-piece backing band, with five horns and Townshend's brother, Simon, on electric guitar, Daltrey's voice and microphone-swinging aerobics were the consistent focal point.

His growl enlivened the anthems, such as the punk-like *Helpless Dancer*, *Dr. Jimmy*, the R&B train song *5:15*, and the reflective, romantic finale, *Love, Reign O'er Me*. He even ad-libbed the f-word four or five times, possibly to prove the Who meant what they sang and weren't a bunch of geezers trying to make money. Townshend, wearing a conventional black suit and surrendering all his famous solos to his brother, at first seemed relegated to an irrelevant role.

But on *I'm One*, a great Who song about a loser trying desperately to hang on to his self-esteem, Townshend sang with more soul than he ever managed on the Who's recordings. On his solo version of *Drowned*, like the one on the live *Secret Policeman's Ball* album, he strummed fast chords more for nuance than for power.

The recurring musical themes of *Quadrophenia*, such as the violins that open *Love, Reign O'er Me*, are much more inventive than the irritating repetitive guitar bits in *Tommy*. And its focus on nostalgia works perfectly for a crowd nostalgic for the Who – the show, like the original album, weaves musical bits from *Tommy*, *My Generation* and the band's first single *I'm The Face* into the storyline. The Who's encore – unplugged arrangements of the crowd-pleasing classics *Won't Get Fooled Again*, *Behind Blue Eyes* and *Who Are You* – wasn't nearly as interesting as the preceding rock opera. *Won't Get Fooled Again* suffered without Daltrey's classic scream and the closing line 'meet the new boss, same as the old boss.' The Who haven't cared much about revolution in two decades, but it's a relief to see they still care about more than money.

The first half of November saw the tour move through Michigan and Ohio, and on to the east coast – Pennsylvania, New York, Maryland, Massachusetts. "The surviving members of The Who climbed back aboard the Magic Bus once again on Monday night at the Knickerbocker Arena, and – surprise, surprise – the magic was still there," wrote *The Albany Times Union*'s Greg Haymes, although he noted that the show "was far from a sellout."

The Who's last reunion tour – which kicked off at the Glens Falls Civic Center more than seven years ago – showcased an overblown, lumbering ghost of a band that had helped define rock'n'roll back in the '60s.

With their current *Quadrophenia* tour, the band has reclaimed its rightful status among the Holy Trinity of rock bands, alongside the Beatles and the Rolling Stones.

The Glens Falls show was shaky at best. Was the current tour better? You bet.

...Buttressed by some nifty video narrative, drummer Zak Starkey (yes, Ringo's son) and lead guitarist Simon Townshend (Pete's brother), The Who swaggered through the complex – sometimes convoluted – *Quadrophenia* with confidence and aplomb.

...Daltrey was in incredible voice, soaring on the opening *The Real Me* and rarely touching down during the course of the two-hour show.

Entwistle was his usual stoic self, preferring to remain nearly motionless in the background until he unleashed a devastatingly nimble solo during *5:15*. Not surprisingly, Townshend was the star of the night, although he hammered away on an acoustic guitar for most of the show. His solo, *Drowned*, was a brilliant tour-de-force, and when he finally strapped on his electric guitar and cut loose during the symphonic *The Rock*, it was a galvanizing, cathartic experience.

...After a 90-minute version of *Quadrophenia*, The Who didn't need to pad the show, but they encored with credible renditions of *Behind Blue Eyes*, *Who Are You* and an incendiary duo romp through *Won't Get Fooled Again*, which may have perfectly summed up the hot-and-cold relationship between Daltrey and Townshend.

Ocean Colour Scene opened the show. One additional show, in East Rutherford, New Jersey, rounded out the tour. A full-fledged European tour was soon announced, slated for spring, 1997. Rocker P.J. Proby assumed the role of the Godfather in place of Gary Glitter once the U.S. dates had come to a close.

Two weeks after the conclusion of the U.S. tour, the band played a handful of shows in the U.K. prior to taking some time off. The first two shows, December 6 and 7, took place at Earls Court. "Now, after touring this multi-media presentation across America, Townshend and co are back in Britain for three more shows," wrote the *Daily Telegraph*'s David Cheal in his review of the December 7 show.

> And, if on this, the second of them, there were signs of dryness and tiredness in the voices of lead singer Roger Daltrey and of Townshend himself, the music as a whole was impressively fresh and direct.
>
> The story of *Quadrophenia* concerns a young man's quest for identity and a sense of belonging through the mod-culture of the Sixties. It's an ambitious and at times pretentious saga, but what makes it great is the sheer quality of the music; not just individual songs such as *The Real Me* and *5:15*, but the seamlessness with which they flow into each other, giving the whole enterprise a sense of continuity, building all the while to a soaring climax.
>
> On stage it was rendered, as it had been in Hyde Park, with vitality and fidelity...
>
> The show was marred only by two things. The first was Billy Idol who, during his mercifully brief stints on stage, leapt around and jibbered like an amphetamine-fueled baboon. The night's other guest star, rock and roll veteran PJ Proby was a paragon of decorum by comparison.
>
> The second disappointment of the evening was the uncharacteristic shortage of fire power in the guitar department. Townshend was on an acoustic for most of the show, while his brother Simon played rhythm and lead. Simon is clearly no slouch on the fretboard, but it all sounded a bit thin until Pete finally strapped on his Stratocaster for the climax of the main piece.

An 11 December show at the Nynex in Manchester rounded out all Who activity for 1996. With the completion of the 11 December show in Manchester, Pete and the band took a three-month break. Upon returning home, Pete resumed writing and recording in his home studio, which he referred to as 'The Cube'. "What I'm writing today is very different from anything that I've ever written before," he told Ira Robbins in November.

> I don't know that my audience would feel comfortable with it. I started to demonstrate some of that – I suppose it's the style in which I've been playing for almost the last ten years – in my recent solo concerts. As I grew in confidence I also grew in pragmatic sense of self-preservation, where I would have been quite happy to sit and bang away at the piano all night, or play John Fahey ragtime all night. That's what I do.
>
> I also do a lot of extended compositions – I wouldn't call them jazz, but they're very modal, they're very simplistic. It's a style of composition I've been developing to support dramatic language. I've never been interested at all in film composition, so everything I've been doing is about training myself for another life as somebody who could write for the stage. While I've been trying to learn to play the piano a little bit better, trying to learn to score a bit more elegantly, trying to learn to deal with other players without being quite so dictatorial, show business is changing under me. Las Vegas is a good example. The whole world of theme parks is an area where specially commissioned music from somebody like me is welcomed. So I don't quite know where I'm gonna go.
>
> The piece I'm working on at the moment is quite a modest piece called *Stella*; out of that grew another piece called *Trilby's Piano*, which was a thing about something that happened to me when I was a kid with an aunt of mine – a very positive experience for me. I've started to look at the more positive experiences I've had in my life, and I find it very difficult to compose for that stuff because I've spent most of my time drawing on my negative experiences, or what I would call my growth experiences.

The majority, if not all, of the pieces recorded during this period were written and recorded on piano, specifically a "six-foot Yamaha Conservatory Grand piano that was equipped with a MIDI send", as Pete wrote in the *Scoop 3* liner notes in 2001. An example of the work Pete recorded at this time was *Wired to the Moon* and its successor, *Wired to the Moon (Part 2)*. The former was offered in free mp3 download form on Pete's website, while the latter surfaced on *Scoop 3*. Pete explained the subject matter of the two songs in the liner notes: "I have experienced a number of strange attacks in recent years that I call 'dream attacks'. I fall into a state in which I remember dozens of recent dreams. In fact they start to rerun like several movies, but all at once."

Further recording activity ensued following the band's short European tour, with Pete recording *Prelude 970519* on his birthday, which was the day after the band's final show of the tour, at Wembley Arena. "This piano 'prelude' was intended to evoke serenity, calm, and ultimately – in a very short space of time – readiness to sleep," Pete wrote in the *Scoop 3* liner notes.

So it is intentionally soporific and light. Occasionally, for a month at most, I would try to record at least one piece every day as part of what I called my 'Daily Project'. This idea was inspired by my reading of THE ARTIST'S WAY[265], and the course work I did on the 12-week programme of creative stimulation the authors recommend. If I didn't record any music I might instead try to write a short essay or poem of some kind.

Also during the break, Pete celebrated the eight Olivier award nominations garnered by *Tommy* by throwing an invitation-only party in early February in London's club LA-2. Pete played for an hour and fifteen minutes, treating the 500 guests to a set which hit on nearly all phases of his solo work, with numbers from *The Iron Man*, *Empty Glass* and *White City*, in addition to Who classics such as *Won't Get Fooled Again* and *Pinball Wizard*. John Entwistle attended, along with Roger's family (Roger couldn't attend-he was in L.A.), watching Pete perform with band members Zak Starkey, John Bundrick, Jody Linscott, Billy Nichols, John Carin and Pino Palladino.

It was also during this period that Pete moved to a home in Richmond Hill. Named 'The Wick', the historic home (which has been reported as being bought for prices ranging from £3 million - £8 million, with the higher end being the more oft-reported number) was previously owned by actor Sir John Mills, and later by Rolling Stones guitarist Ron Wood. Richmond Hill is especially noted for its spectacular views of the Thames. "Richmond Hill and its quaint neighbor Petersham village are the Beverly Hills of London, where Mick and Jerry's front window overlooks Pete Townshend's conservatory and they can all chat in the newsagents with David Attenborough, his brother Richard, Jennifer Saunders, the comedian, John Hannah, the actor, or the reclusive pop star Rick Astley," wrote *The Times*' Cally Law in late 2001. "Richmond Hill is a rich man's enclave. Hemmed in on three sides by the Thames and Richmond Park, it retains its period charm and can grow no further... Richmond residents are the

---

[265] *The Artist's Way*, published in 1992, was written by Julia Cameron.

nation's richest earners... the average detached house costs 615,000 pounds." Pete also still owned a home near the Helford River in Cornwall, a popular yacht racing venue.

In April, The Who returned to the road, winding through Denmark, Sweden, Norway, Germany and Austria. May saw the band performing in Belgium, the Netherlands, France and Switzerland prior to a final show on 18 May at Wembley Arena in London.

In mid-June, Pete performed solo at the House of Blues in Chicago in a benefit show for Maryville Academy, a local children's charity. Recall that during the 1993 *Psychoderelict* tour, Pete drank a bottle of vodka prior to going onstage at Chicago's Arie Crown Theatre, and submitted a less-than-stellar performance as a result. "I made a terrible mess of it, and I wanted to go back and put things right," Pete told *USA Today* in 1999. The 1997 show, combined with a repeat performance at the House of Blues the following year, reportedly raised approximately $600,000 for Maryville.

"Early in his three hour-plus set, Townshend paused to present the Rev. John Smyth, executive director of Maryville, a check for more than $200,000," reported the *Arlington Heights Daily Herald*'s Mark Guarino.

Townshend later admitted he particularly wanted to do charitable work in Chicago, "making amends" for his last local solo appearance in 1993 at the Arie Crown when he "got so drunk [he] didn't remember anything about it." He's been sober ever since, he said.

Townshend's relegation to mammoth arenas showed, as he took his time getting comfortable with the more communal environment. He fumbled with his lyric book, flubbed words and chords on the keyboard and admitted his jetlag. Jon Carin helped as a one-man Who, gracing Townshend's guitar with drum rhythms, vocals and keyboards.

But his aloof humor and, in particular, choice of songs he hasn't played live in years or ever, gave the marathon evening more of a campfire feel. Townshend sat to play Gram Parsons' *Christine's Tune*...

A career of blistering guitarmanship led to hearing problems for Townshend in the late '80s when he toured exclusively with an acoustic. On Saturday, however, he frequently sought the electric for blow-up rants of *Acid Queen, Rough Boys* and a twined together *Bargain* and *The Seeker*. He stalked the stage, guided by guitar strumming the speed of bees.

Eddie Vedder invited Pete to a Chicago Bulls game the night before the show, and volunteered to join Pete onstage at the House of Blues, according to *USA Today*. The pair didn't rehearse prior to singing together on *Heart to Hang On To*, *Magic Bus*, and *Tattoo*[266]. "It's a good thing I listened to those records hundreds of times in my youth," Vedder told *USA Today* in 1999. "I've known these songs since I was 17, and they still resonate. When Pete introduced [*Heart To Hang On To*], he mentioned that Ronnie [Lane] had just passed away that week[267]. I hadn't heard about it yet, and I remember thinking, that was the same disease [Multiple Sclerosis] my father was afflicted with."

Further touring ensued in late summer as The Who returned to the U.S., kicking off the latest leg at St. Louis' Riverport Amphitheater on July 19. Ben Waters assumed the role of the Ace Face. The *St. Louis Post-Dispatch*'s Joe Williams described the show as a "...vital and innovative performance..."

"...sound effects, narrative, and video can be sequenced perfectly with live music," wrote *Knight-Ridder*'s John Mark Eberhart.

> The *Quadrophenia* the Who performed at the Riverport Amphitheatre in suburban St. Louis was nearly flawless...
>
> The audience clearly appreciated this long-form work. The video anecdotes could have sapped the energy, but the crowd applauded and laughed. It helped that some material was funny, as when Jimmy observed that his dad loved to eat eels, that eels live on sewage, and therefore his dad must be full of it.
>
> And listeners seemed happy to hear challenging *Quad* songs such as *Helpless Dancer* and *Cut My Hair* instead of a string of obligatory hits.
>
> ...Pete Townshend doesn't have to be electric to electrify; his acoustic work on *Drowned* churned up more rock'n'roll than most players summon with a stack of amps.

The *Chicago Tribune*'s Rick Reger gave a lukewarm review of The Who's overall performance at Tinley Park's World Music Theater on July 20, writing that it "mingled moments of decrepitude with passages of inspired playing," but he opined that it was a better show than the one that The Who had performed the previous fall, despite the fact that Pete forgot to sing half of the bridge in *Cut My Hair*. "There was more emphasis on

---

[266] The performances of *Magic Bus* and *Heart To Hang On To* from this show made it on to 1999's *Pete Townshend Live* CD.

[267] "Ronnie Lane, pop singer, songwriter and bassist, died yesterday in Trinidad, Colorado, from multiple sclerosis aged 51," *The Times* reported on June 6.

improvisation and fiery ensemble playing and less scripted theatricality," Reger wrote. "...when the band dispensed with the excess keyboards, percussion and brass and simplified songs down to bass, drum and guitar, as they did on *I'm One* and *Is It In My Head?*, they mustered that blend of pathos and searing anger that's always defined the Who's sound."

"...I can't write off The Who's performance of *Quadrophenia* Wednesday night at the Marcus Amphitheater as just a dated blast of hot air," wrote the *Milwaukee Journal-Sentinel*'s Dave Tianen in his review of the 23 July show.

> Some of that has to do with the power of Townshend's creation, and more of it has to do with the remarkable intensity Roger Daltrey and Townshend generate on stage, even now.
>
> The calendar says Townshend is 52, but he doesn't look a day past 64. The skin is pale, and any hair that isn't gone is gray. The sense of seniority is heightened by a dark gray suit. Having said all that, Townshend has to be one of the most ferocious, intense coots ever to roar into deep middle age. Although Pete's brother Simon handles some of the guitar chores, Pete is all over the stage, moving non-stop and far more a forceful presence than during the band's '89 tour.

Brian McCollum of the *Detroit Free Press* was not as impressed when The Who played at the Pine Knob Music Theatre on 25 July: "...with a five-piece horn section, two synthesizers and auxiliary percussion, most every song Friday became an awkward anthem," he wrote. "If the Who – and other grown-up rock acts – would recognize the overload, where washes of superfluous sound dilute the essential backbeat, such shows would stand even taller."

The tour wound through Canada with dates in Montreal and Toronto before swinging down the east coast, through Connecticut ("[*Quadrophenia*] came off gloriously...", *The Hartford Courant* reported), New York, New Jersey ("dynamic, riveting," said the *Home News & Tribune*), Virginia, North Carolina and Florida, ending with a 16 August date in West Palm Beach.

Pete was almost immediately back in London working on several projects. The Aug. 18, 1997 Edition of *Publishers Weekly* reported that Pete had signed a "world rights deal" with Little, Brown publishing for his autobiography. The memoir, the contract of which was reportedly "in the seven-figure range" was due out in late 1999. The deal had been in the works for at least a year. "...it's not so much about money as about how much the book would cost to produce if I were to decide to fill it with black and white pictures of my dear old dad or something," Pete said the previous year. "I'll probably start early next year, and it'll take me two years."

>The term autobiography is a bit mischievous; what I'm really doing is writing about my life and my music. About life and music in general. It's going to be an artist's view of the last fifty years and what's been going on with music in that time. I don't pretend to be an arch academic musicologist, but my journey is a unique one, and does give me a very special and acute view of where popular music came from and what it means. I hope this book will elucidate a lot of that stuff simply by me telling my story without any frills. Just talking about my grandparents and my parents and the music that they listened to, and what they did when they were young, and my life and how I grew up and what I did when I was young and the people that I met and then suddenly hey ho here we are. I'm looking forward to it. I've been gathering materials for it, most of which has been a bit of a waste of time, but it's all good memory-jogging stuff.

1999 came and went, with no sign of the promised book. "I've written about 250,000 words and I've taken a break for a while," Pete told *Q*'s David Cavanaugh in 2000. "I've done the difficult part, which was my childhood, and I'm up to the art school years..." He explained the hold-up further in an online chat hosted by www.barnesandnoble.com: "I'm afraid I put it down. My publishers were wonderfully supportive, and I found writing about my childhood very natural. But when I reached the Who years, I started to panic. There is, you see, so much documentary evidence that suggests that the way I remember things is wrong! I need to do more research, speak to friends, find out whether I can really write down what I remember without being dishonest or careless over the truth. I will pick it up again very soon."

Pete also began composing and recording demos in The Wick. One of the first such recordings was *971104 Arpeggio Piano*. "This piece was recorded to DAT tape at my home in London on 4th November 1997," Pete wrote in the *Scoop 3* liner notes. "When I first moved into the house in London in which I now live I chose the tiniest room (an ante-room off the main living room) and set up a... keyboard on which to practice and compose... I used the keyboard every day for about a year, recording to DAT tape or cassette." Another example included on *Scoop 3*, *Variations On Dirty Jobs*, was recorded a few nights later. "I fully orchestrated it earlier this year," Pete wrote in the 2001 liner notes. "Although the chords are similar to *Dirty Jobs* from *Quadrophenia* it is an entirely original composition. It is intended to demonstrate the kind of tonal effect I could achieve should I develop a full orchestral version of *Quadrophenia*."

1998 saw the release of Emma Townshend's *Winterland*, Pete's daughter's debut release. In its three-star review, *Rolling Stone* said the album "carries enough promise to make Townshend an artist worth watching." Pete called the album "pretty great" in a chat on www.barnesandnoble.com in 2000, adding, "I can't tell you how strange it is. Her voice is so beautiful."

On Monday, 8 June, 1998, Pete delivered an address towards the end of a 90-minute memorial service for Linda McCartney, who died in April from breast cancer. The service took place at St. Martins-in-the-Field church. "He paid tribute to the durability and romance of the McCartney marriage[268]," *The Times* reported. "He said, "They achieved it by staying together.""" Other notables present among the 700 who attended were Sting, Elton John, Peter Gabriel, Tracy Ullman, and the other two surviving Beatles, George Harrison and Ringo Starr. Just a few weeks prior to the memorial service, on May 19th, Pete's fifty-third birthday, his father in law, Ted Astley, died at age 76.

A few months later, Pete began a series of solo shows in the U.S., around an appearance at Max Yasgurs' farm in Bethel, New York, the original site of Woodstock. Prior to the Woodstock show, Pete made an August 13 appearance on David Letterman's late night television show, followed with a warm-up performance the next day at Harborlights in Boston. "...the Harborlights show was everything a fan could hope for," reported *The Boston Phoenix*' Brett Milano.

> With a five-piece band in tow, Townshend remained on stage for two hours plus; he pulled favorite Who hits and solo rarities from his catalogue; he was loose and chatty between songs; he did a few tunes (including the folk standard *North Country Girl*) that he's never played live before; and he drastically rearranged nearly everything...
>
> ...As much as you wanted to cheer Townshend for the irreverence with his own oldies, the new arrangements missed as often as they hit. Although the stripped-down band didn't include a drummer, it did have keyboardist Jon Carin, who saddled nearly everything with overloud, monochromatic drum-machine parts; percussionist Jody

---

[268] "...I've lived in a bit of a fantasy, I think," Pete told *Rolling Stone*'s Jenny Eliscu in 2000 when discussing his own failed marriage. "I always wanted there to be a kind of Paul Newman and Joanne Woodward story but they're one of the great exceptions. I did hold Paul McCartney in high esteem because of the way that he conducted his relationship. I have those kind of old-fashioned family values."

Linscott had to make do with slapping cymbals and shaking maracas. More's the pity, because Townshend was in the mood to jam, playing more electric guitar than he had on the last two Who tours...Almost electrifying, but you just can't get funky without a drummer.

The surprise Woodstock homages were a pair of Canned Heat covers, *On The Road Again* and *Going Up The Country* – both beautifully done, with Townshend's falsetto echoing the late Al Wilson's. He and back-up singer Tracy Langran duetted on *The Acid Queen*, the song that occasioned Abbie Hoffman's stage-crashing at Woodstock... But as the night went on there was more dead air on stage, culminating with a glitch-ridden version of *Won't Get Fooled Again* during which Townshend threw down two guitars, stopped the band twice, and finally left the stage.

The following day, Pete appeared in front of 26,000 at *A Day in the Garden*, a 29th anniversary show which took place at the site of the original Woodstock concert[269]. Other guests that day included Ziggy Marley, Ten Years After, Melanie, Stevie Nicks, Don Henley, and Lou Reed. "...there was plenty of the old Woodstock's main ingredient – rock'n'roll – at the three-day music festival held over the weekend here at Max Yasgur's farm, the original Woodstock site," reported *USA Today*'s Jim Bessman.

...The huge stage was the same used by Garth Brooks in Central Park, and there were 30 food vendors and 400 portable toilets, in marked contrast to the absence of both at the first fest. There was a phone bank and a mobile cash machine and a play area for kids, a field hospital and four satellite first-aid stations – and a sturdy chain-link fence to keep '69-style gatecrashers from sharing space with those who'd shelled out up to $69 to get in.

...Pete Townshend's day-ending show was spectacular, with highlights including The Who's *Won't Get Fooled Again*, capped by his trademark windmill guitar licks, and the surprise addition of guitarist Taj Mahal for a blues segment. (Maybe that was to make up for the absence of Ringo Starr's drummer son, Zac Starkey, talked up in

---

[269] The Who were invited to play at a 30th anniversary 'Woodstock 99' festival the following year. "We were earnestly invited to appear," Pete told *USA Today*'s Edna Gunderson in October, 1999. "And I half considered getting The Who together for it, but only half. I feel that I hadn't ever been honest about how important Woodstock had been to me and to The Who."

advance as an addition to Townshend's band.) Also unexpected: Townshend's dedication of *Behind Blue Eyes* to late Yippie leader Abbie Hoffman, whom Townshend yanked off the stage when he interrupted The Who's 1969 set, trying to politicize the Woodstock Nation.

...Townshend also cleverly opened his set with *On The Road Again*, by original Woodstockers Canned Heat, and closed it with the *See Me, Feel Me* grand finale from *Tommy* – which ran till dawn the night The Who did it here in 1969 and this time featured a local 26-piece gospel choir.

The day after the Woodstock show, Pete returned to the House of Blues in Chicago for his second annual Maryville Academy fundraiser. The show, tickets to which were reportedly $175 each, raised over $300,000. "...Townshend did steer clear of most of the cryptic, decidedly uncommercial material that comprised his last two rock operas, *The Iron Man* and *Psychoderelict*," *Rolling Stone*'s Blair Fischer reported.

For most of the night, he strummed an acoustic guitar, which turned any mid-song switch to the electric variety into a nostalgic frenzy. Townshend, of course, fed on the crowd's feedback and unleashed his first trademark windmill during the pulsating conclusion to the otherwise *Kokomo*-flavored *Save It For Later*, the only song anyone seems to know by the English Beat.

An orchestra stand was in place to help Townshend remember the lyrics he penned, a drum machine provided the backbeat for the grungy *Anyway, Anyhow, Anywhere* and *Save It For Later*, and horns and harmonica accompanied pop jigs like *Let My Love Open The Door* and *A Little Is Enough*. Blonde songstress Tracy Langran, a nice surrogate for pictures of Lily, joined Townshend on acoustic guitar for much of the night and lent silky pipes to the ballad *A Friend Is A Friend* and the cheery *Sensation*.

...Long before Townshend lost his hearing, most of his hair and his bandmate, Keith Moon, Townshend was a juggernaut on stage. He ripped into his strings until his fingers bled and he had no compunction about puncturing amplifiers or splintering his guitar on a nightly basis. That, of course, was a long time ago. Preparing to play Canned Heat's *Going Up The Country*, his guitar strap broke and his guitar fell to the ground. Some laughed, but Townshend didn't. Rather, he slowly, calmly picked it off the floor and said, "Just dropping them doesn't do anything." Meet the new boss. Almost the same as the old boss.

Upon his return to the U.K., Pete lent his services to another cause, this time striking (and subsequently fired) Liverpool dock workers. The October 16 *Rock the Dock* concert took place at London's Sound Republic Club, with Pete joined on the lineup by Noel Gallagher and Ocean Colour Scene. Pete played seven songs including *Anyway, Anyhow, Anywhere*, *Pinball Wizard* and *Won't Get Fooled Again*, with Gallagher and Ocean Colour Scene's Steve Craddock joining him for *Magic Bus*.

In November 1998, Pete performed a solo show at the Shepherd's Bush Empire, his first U.K. solo performance in over 12 years. "Pete Townshend does not have any new songs to play," wrote *The Times'* David Sinclair a few days prior to the show.

> He does not even have a recording contract. But on Monday night he will take to an English stage in his own right for the first time in 12 years. "I have to start from the bottom again," he says. "I've got to convince people that it's worth coming to see me play and worth looking at my body of work. I'm still passionate about pop and feel that by doing a show that takes snapshots from throughout my story you get a sense of what it means and what it adds up to.

The night after the Shepherd's Bush show, Pete played a small show (another fundraiser) in Truro, with John Carin, Peter Hope-Evans, Chucho Merchan, and Tracy Langran. Among the set list were *Cobwebs and Strange*, *A Little Is Enough*, *Substitute*, renditions of *Sensation* and *Acid Queen* sung by Townshend and Langran, *Pinball Wizard*, *Drowned*, and *You Better You Bet*. *Baby Don't You Do It*, *Who Are You* and *Magic Bus* were all reportedly performed with the help of rapper Hame. Pete started playing *Sheraton Gibson* but stopped, reportedly because he'd ripped a fingernail off the previous night. Two other shows ensued, the first taking place at London's Vibe Bar on November 16 (for VH1's *Storytellers*), and an early January, 1999 gig at the Oxford Museum of Modern Art in front of 80 people. The occasion was the final night of an exhibition of Gustav Metzger's work.

Chapter 17

> *"What I grew up with was this sense that there was color there somewhere, light, a bright new future. But there was no fucking evidence of it, it was all in one's head. I then got to be 12, 13, 14, and thought - oh, I get this, I have to paint it myself."*
> - Pete Townshend, 1999

> *Ray: When I was a boy I designed the future. It wasn't like the picture in my comic full of rockets and a city on the moon. It wasn't going to be like that. The future was a great big empty place where everyone was watching...*
> *Rayboy: ...and everyone was listening to a man, and he was telling them what to do and what to buy and what to think and even what to dream ...My Dad was always laughing saying 'You playing with your crayons?' and I'd say I was coloring in a picture of tomorrow. 'Come and watch the program', he'd say, pointing at the television flickering in the room. But I'd shake my head, say 'No', because I knew the man was in the telly. He was waiting 'til he had us hooked and then he'd wash our brains...*
> *Ray: ...and so I'd crayon in the future that the man was going to sell us, and the color that I crayoned it was grey...so bloody grey...*
> - Lifehouse, 1999

On Wednesday July 28, 1999, Pete Townshend gave a rare live solo performance at the 1,000-seat Supper Club in New York City's theater district. The 15-song show served to provide publicity for the release of Pete's upcoming live album (it was advertised as a 'listening party') while at the same time raising money for the Maryville Academy[270]. Despite the reportedly indifferent invite-only crowd (many of whom reportedly did more chatting and socializing than listening to Townshend), Pete's performance was fiery and diverse, as he played both electric and acoustic guitar, and even sat at a piano for four numbers. "After taking the stage,

---

[270] *Pete Townshend Live*, recorded during Pete's 1997 and 1998 shows at the Chicago House of Blues was released September 21, 1999. Proceeds from sales of the release went to Maryville Academy.

Townshend immediately launched into *Won't Get Fooled Again*, playing an electric guitar but using the acoustic arrangement he's become known for of late," reported *Launch.com*'s Bruce Simon. "As he approached the end of the song, Townshend turned his guitar up, and he started playing in his trademark windmill style."

Pete set aside his red Fender Stratocaster in favor of a Gibson J-200 for the next two numbers, *Behind Blue Eyes* and *Drowned*. Wearing glasses occasionally during the show, he referred to a songbook on a music stand while playing. Pete's acoustic guitar work on *Behind Blue Eyes*, according to the *New York Post*'s Dan Aquilante, "...was marked with blurred strumming that was so fat you forgot he had no drummer or bassist backing him." The J-200 was soon discarded as Pete picked up his music book and sat at a grand piano for renditions of *Zoot Suit*, *Slit Skirts*, *Let My Love Open the Door*, and an off-the-wall version of the Screamin' Jay Hawkins number *I Put A Spell On You* which, according to Aquilante, "was so eccentric it took a few seconds to decipher that he was playing the usually recognizable song." Bruce Simon opined that the diversity of Pete's set list was perhaps the reason for the songbook. "It seemed as if he was deciding what songs to play on the fly, using the options in the book for reference."

Pete then introduced surprise guest Eddie Vedder[271], with whom he'd taped a performance of *Magic Bus* and *Heart To Hang Onto* at the Ed Sullivan Theater with David Letterman's band earlier that day for broadcast on Letterman's show. The pair shared vocals on the next number, *Heart To Hang Onto*. Vedder and Townshend then both strapped on acoustic guitars and shared vocals on *Let's See Action*, prior to Pete switching to his Stratocaster as the pair performed Pearl Jam's *Better Man*. Pete dug into *Who Came First* for the pair's next two songs, Don Williams' *Till The Rivers All Run Dry* and a rendition of *Sheraton Gibson* featuring Vedder on lead vocals, with Townshend playing acoustic guitar and singing harmony. Following *Magic Bus*, the pair left the stage. "After a short break, Townshend came out alone and picked up his acoustic guitar," Simon reported. "He played about a minute of *I'm One*, this time changing the lyrics to "I'm a loser, just like Eddie." With that, the show ended.

"It was the kind of rock event that fans of either man would have given anything to see," Aquilante wrote, "yet in spite of that, for some bizarre reason, those present – especially in the balcony – loudly squawked at each other throughout the performance. If the show had been a stinker, maybe their lack of respect and courtesy might have been justified. But the

---

[271] Two weeks earlier, Vedder led Washington based band C Average in a set of Who songs at the Yoyo a Go Go Festival in Olympia, Washington. Vedder wore a Daltrey-esque blonde wig and twirled his microphone while his band mates did appropriate early '70s Townshend (white boiler suit, Gibson SG), Entwistle (black hair, black moustache, black outfit, Fender bass) and Moon (large drum kit with THE WHO on the bass drums) impersonations.

concert was terrific. Had the rudesters in the balcony listened more and talked less, Townshend might have stayed longer than an hour."

Spin posted a review on their website the day after the show:

> ...The duo's back-and-forth singing achieved a mesmerizing effect on *Let's See Action*... Though never in short supply of his own classic anthems, Townshend surprisingly deferred to his diminutive collaborator for a sensational rendition of Pearl Jam's *Better Man*, before the pair again traded vocal duties on a hard-edged *Magic Bus*, and an inspired version of *I'm One*, which Townshend acknowledged "...sounds nice when Ed sings it."

The chatty crowd trend continued the following night as Townshend and Vedder performed at the Chicago House of Blues in a benefit for Maryville Academy. "The last couple of days, spending time with Pete has taught me new things about music and new things as a human," Vedder said from the stage. "One of those things is to say what you feel. And I feel like you people talking between songs are driving me nuts." Vedder accompanied Pete for part of a set list similar (but shorter: 12 songs rather than the previous night's 15) to the Supper Club show, and an occasionally bespectacled Pete again referred to his songbook throughout the show. "Townshend tackled *Behind Blue Eyes*, *Drowned* and *Let My Love Open the Door* on acoustic guitar and *Cut My Hair* on grand piano before bringing Vedder out," the *Chicago Sun-Times*' Jim DeRogatis wrote.

> The two shared vocals on *Heart to Hang Onto*... Though it was a perfectly fine rendition, the Pearl Jam tune *Better Man* sounded out of place – especially when Pete was reaching deep into his catalog for songs such as *Sheraton Gibson* from *Who Came First*. The two traded guitar licks and choruses on a rollicking *Magic Bus* before closing with *I'm One*. Townshend was inspired enough to deliver a few gratuitous windmills.

Upon his return from the States, Pete was up to his neck in projects. In addition to the planned writing of his memoirs, reports had surfaced in the preceding months that *Psychoderelict* was being readied for the stage as a successor to *Tommy*. The *New York Daily News* reported that Pete was to begin work on a script with director Ethan Silverman, and that *Psychoderelict* would become a "full-fledged musical," according to the *Wall of Sound* website. "The show is probably a year away," a 'spokesperson' told the *New York Daily News*, adding, "...the plan is to go straight to Broadway." A workshop for the planned *Psychoderelict* musical took place in New York, with actor Peter Gallagher participating. In October 1999, *USA Today* reported "producer John Scher says confidently that *Psychoderelict* will appear next year on Broadway," and "there have been various workshops over the past five years; one is planned for this spring."

However, the project that ultimately consumed the majority of Pete's time and efforts during this period was the resurrection of *Lifehouse*, the first reports of which emerged in early 1999. In the February 7 edition of the *Sunday Times*, Nicholas Hellen reported that Pete had been commissioned by the BBC "to create a musical from unperformed fragments that he first devised at the height of the Who's success. His concept embraces computer technology, science fiction and eastern mysticism in a visionary future cityscape." The project, later referred to as a radio play, and already in rehearsal, was set to debut December 6 on BBC radio 3. Talks were reportedly under way with Daltrey and Entwistle to stage it.

"*Lifehouse* is far from abandoned," Pete had noted back in 1995. "In staging *Tommy*, *Psychoderelict* and *The Iron Man* in 1993 I learned some of the dramatic writing and stagecraft skills I need to go forward. *Lifehouse* - perhaps combined with *Psychoderelict* - will probably emerge as a kind of musical or new-fangled opera rather than as a film. But I assure you it will make sense to you, just as in my mind it always has. Critics will probably call it naïve. I hope so. I wrote it when I was a child."

The BBC's interest in *Lifehouse* lay in the project's relevance to the public's heightened awareness of the often drastic changes wrought in their lives by technology at the dawn of the new millennium. "The story of *Lifehouse* was, in a nutshell, of a family, under considerable stress, who had been affected by the changes in the world, the changes in the way that people communicated and about the tribalization of society, the splitting up of society, which replaces the class system," Pete said in 1999. "Very much an English story." The site of the story's-end concert, according to Pete, takes place "in somewhere like the Millennium Dome, to celebrate the Millennium. This Millennium tag has been added on just because of where we are but it fits very well with the notion that we're at the dawn of a new age and this group of people get together to throw a concert." Pete also pointed out that the play's characters espouse "New Age Millenial notions... These may appear to be rather cosmic ideas, but I implicitly believe in them."

One of the most significant changes in modern life evident during this rebirth of *Lifehouse* was the advent of the internet. This entirely new method of communication, which changed the face of global business and had far-reaching social implications, bore an uncanny resemblance to the 'grid' Pete spoke of back in 1971. "It's extraordinary when you think about what Townshend was writing in 1971," said Kate Rowland, the BBC's head of radio drama, who Pete enlisted to assist him in dramatizing the production. "It was like he was projecting ahead. He didn't use the words 'net' or 'web'. He called it 'grid'. But he was hitting the nail almost right on the head." Rowland's comments were soon widely disseminated through the media, and Pete was the inevitable subject of measured derision for what many observers thought was his taking credit for predicting the internet. "...*Lifehouse* was never meant to be about 'prediction'," Pete wrote in *The Richmond Review* in 1999. "...I've had a certain amount of sarcasm directed at me. That's OK." He made further observations on the subject in August 1999:

> The feeling that you get when you read that early script, which is very naïve and very cobbled together, is that I was trying to describe a world that is maybe in the future without understanding what it would be like. I didn't think I would wake up in the year 1999 and it would be like this... I wasn't pretending to be a seer and I don't like the fact that recently I've been portrayed in that way, that wasn't my notion...

Lifehouse underwent a significant overhaul for the 1999 radio play, with Pete enlisting the help of experienced radio playwright Jeff Young to adapt the story, along with Rowland.[272] Pete's decision to solicit help in readying his story for the radio was partly based on his recent experiences with dramatizing his work. "...I just felt that what I had learnt in projects since I'd done *Lifehouse* – the stage version of *Quadrophenia*, the *Tommy* film, the *Iron Man*, *Psychoderelict* – I'd learnt that I am not a dramatist...yet," he told Matt Kent in 1999. "...I can sit and write a fairly good story, but I don't think that necessarily entitles me to write all the music and whatever. What I wanted to do here was simply to get together a truly great team, who could honor the work I have done in the past, and that other people have done in the past, on this project."

Since the project was now nearly thirty years old, Pete and his consultants – who reportedly hashed out the story during a series of meetings at Pete's Richmond home – decided to change the perspective of *Lifehouse* from a vision of the future to a contemporary story. "...In this playscript – the definitive version of *Lifehouse* – Jeff Young, Kate Rowland and I decided not to try to further predict any problem with the current march of technology, and ignore common phobias about it," Pete wrote in a 1999 article in *The Richmond Review*. "After all, in the current climate, to describe the future is to describe tomorrow, possibly even some daft

---

[272] Pete reportedly began the collaboration by giving Young a batch of old *Lifehouse* scripts in 1998. "Pete felt a sense of loss about never finishing *Lifehouse* and, more generally, about the failures of the '60s generation," Young told *Mojo* in 2004.

science-fiction writer's yesterday. Here we speak not of 'grids', or the virtual reality 'experience suits' of my 1971 story, but of 'tele', 'hackers', 'pirates' and of course 'web-sites'."

However, when updating the story from its fictional post-apocalyptic setting, Pete realized that the play's new backdrop – the reality of today – was much closer to his original idea than perhaps he'd first imagined. "...I've started to realize that I have lived in a post apocalyptic period," he told Matt Kent in 1999. "My life began with a huge atomic bomb, which killed loads of Japanese people and ended a bloody, terrible world war and there's been nothing like it since. It's totally transmogrified the world, transformed it and distorted it. We look out and see green fields and think everything's fine but it is actually an apocalyptic world we live in, the rules have changed."

"There has been no great bomb since that last one dropped on Japan, but there has been a steady erosion of what is natural," Pete wrote in *The Richmond Review*. "As my art school mentor Gustav Metzger says, nature has been replaced by 'environment'. We no longer know the true values of natural life and art. We are slowly destroying ourselves in an 'autodestructive' society."

In revising the *Lifehouse* script and analyzing the play's characters during creative meetings, Young, Rowland and Townshend soon realized that they had to "accept that my phantom presence in the story was more forcefully felt than I had intended," Pete said in 1999. The team arrived at a way to articulate Pete's point of view by incorporating two voices heard by his main character, Ray. The two additional characters reflected Ray's conflicting thoughts – Rayboy, Ray's "childlike voice of around nine or ten years-old, imagining the future, delighting in the certainty that we would all one day blow ourselves to bits," according to Pete, and the Caretaker, "an imaginary friend from that childhood, a kind of Uncle-In-Overalls who replaces the emotionally-distant, war-ravaged father who can only recommend to the kid that he sits and quietly watches the newly acquired miracle of a tiny, grey-screened telly."

Rayboy, whose character was created after Jeff Young studied tape recordings of Pete recalling his childhood, reflected the older Ray's lost aspirations. While the majority, if not all, of Pete's dreams have come true, he pointed out that, "...Ray and Rayboy are still very much of me. Perhaps they are also of my audience and childhood friends: all those... who sometimes turned to me and said that I had a knack of putting into words what they could party-dance away, but found hard to otherwise express. It turned out that what I was best at putting into words for them was the frustration that they could not put anything into words." Thirty-four years after *I Can't Explain*, Pete was still writing for his original Mod fans who couldn't satisfactorily express themselves.

With the script for the radio play which emerged from the creative sessions, Pete finally had a *Lifehouse* story he could hang his hat on. "The play that is going to go on the radio is a final realization, the last stop café of the story," he told Matt Kent in 1999, "...the story that I've always carried in my head and that ran through the original and tied all the songs together... What we have for the radio play is something that is about as close to the telling of that story as I want to get."

The basic story of *Lifehouse* remained essentially unchanged from its original form. "...in the story, what we have now is a family, they live up north – they have run away from the media age – they're supposed to be farmers, which is all very true to the original pattern that I'd placed behind the songwriting," Pete explained in 1999.

> Their daughter grows up in Scotland... she's a good kid, but she runs away and they don't really know why. The father is distraught and takes it very, very badly and the mother doesn't quite know why this is happening and doesn't understand what his reaction is about. It's very suspicious of what the reaction is about; she's worried that he may have driven her away somehow, she's quite down on him because she's not sure he's made a commitment to their new life. He worked in media, television and advertising and run away from it but seems obsessed by it. He's constantly logging on, constantly watching TV, and constantly throwing things at the TV! He gets up one day, gets a bit drunk, jumps in his old van and heads for London to try and find his daughter and he discovers that what's going on in London is a bit of a revolution. That a bunch of young people, renegades, people on the streets have decided to defy the media, who have control of all music, all art, all thinking, all news, all political views, on the basis that the only way 'we' can keep you safe is if we nanny you. Whereas in fact it's all about control.

The young "renegades" Pete mentions decide to voice their defiance of the controlling media by arranging a huge concert. Their defiance is complicated by the fact that the media is supported to a degree by the government. "There's some sense in the story that the authorities, who are, in some ways, in league with the media," Pete said in 1999.

> ...in other words, if I could put faces to the figures, imagine Tony Blair gets a phone call from Rupert Murdoch, who says; 'listen Tony, I hear that these bunch of kids are going to go on air with this *Lifehouse* thing. I have the

rights to that, I own all the media in the UK you mustn't allow this to happen.' 'Well, I'm very sorry Rupert but I don't think there's much I can do'... 'Well fuck that, you stop them, or I will...' kind of thing. What happens is that the bunch of kids get together and it turns out to be a big smash. The philosophy of the *Lifehouse* is very much like the philosophy in the original story; it's a metaphor for what was happening in the earliest, I think healthiest, part of rock and roll, which was when the music reflected the audience. I've taken that metaphor and embellished it a little. What happens at the end of the concert... I don't want to give the ending away but it doesn't end quite as you'd imagine.

The root of *Lifehouse*, then, lies in the power of congregation, as Pete explained in 1999:

In his latest book Ray Kurzweil, who invented the repeatable, triggered digital recordings (called 'samples') so beloved of modern composers, predicts that within twenty years a wise and benign cyborg will be walking down Oxford Street with arms outspread entreating us all to 'follow him'. My future phobia in the 1971 *Lifehouse* was that we might all become like spiritually perfect cyborgs, and perhaps be contented, but our hearts would be empty. We would owe it all to Rupert Murdoch (who was still in Australia in 1971 I think). In a time when rock concerts occasionally did 'catch fire', especially those by The Who, the real heroes of the 1971 *Lifehouse* were the audience, the people who showed up a the Big Show. There was a real sense of danger there. Better to congregate, dance, worship and possibly die than to live in a bubble.

"As everything gets bigger, technology makes the world smaller," Pete told the *New York Daily News* in 1999, reiterating the *Lifehouse* theme. "At some point, there will be an explosion – pollution, political, whatever – and we will relearn that the only way we can survive is congregationally. We can't do it alone." With the current widespread use of the internet, the social implications of people attempting to satisfy their congregational needs through a grid rather than through personal contact could be realistically contemplated. "...people understand virtual reality, the internet and being linked to each other through a grid," Pete told the *New York Post*'s Dan Aquilante in 1999. "We can now start to reflect on the spiritual consequences of living our lives as 100 percent couch potatoes. The conclusion hasn't been decided. Will people stop reaching out? Will they stop congregating?"

Lifehouse, Pete wrote in the *Richmond Review*, "is essentially about the necessity for human beings to congregate regularly in order to share their emotions, and their responses to the spiritual challenges of art, great and small... In this play, as a writer of fiction, and the bearer of post-apocalyptic wounds and generational shame, I suggest that the party might not end quite as they hope. Less seriously, I predict most of us will merely get drunk and laugh a lot, just like any other December 31."

> What's missing today for me is the kind of congregation that went on when I was younger. What *Lifehouse* means, what the metaphor means, is that what works today is what worked in the past, which is that as many people as are able to gather and readdress their personal position and their future will do so. If they do so in a selfless, happy, positive manner, in other words to have a laugh as much as anything else, what comes out of that should be positive.

The music featured in the *Lifehouse* radio play was, perhaps surprisingly, limited to Townshend's original demos and some orchestrations. The decision to exclude existing Who versions of *Lifehouse* songs was made "so I didn't have to wrestle with the record label over the rights to my own songs," Pete told the *New York Daily News* in 1999. The decision also perhaps reflected Pete's confidence in the ability of the revamped script to carry itself without overemphasizing the music. "...the story now has sufficient weight to live with the music – which is some of the most impressive that I've ever come up with in my career," he told *Q*'s David Cavanagh in June, 2000.

"What is probably important to say now is that when you hear this play on the radio, the music will not change your understanding of the story," Pete wrote in the *Richmond Review*. "That was never my intention. Much of the music featured in the play is used by Kate Rowland in an almost incidental way, but I hope in a manner that could not be improved upon. She is especially good at using music in drama... In *Lifehouse*, music itself is a fundamental and rudimentary principle, almost a functional character. To a musician like me, music is what is 'inside us all'. It represents experience, emotion and spiritual potential. I have invested my leading characters with this belief."

Pete's *Lifehouse* radio play was aired in early December. "Dispiritingly, *Lifehouse* sounded almost exactly the way you'd expect a play by a rock star in his 50s to sound," *The Guardian*'s Anne Karpf wrote in her frosty 6 December review.

> Both Mary and Ray are rebelling against a grey future, but so many fine artists have depicted grey futures that this one needed to be a lot greyer to have any impact...
>
> ...Though Townshend's aphorisms strove to be meaningful, they rarely got beyond art-school precious. The dawn chorus isn't the birds greeting each other, but the birds telling each other that they survived the night. Child: "The world is full of smoke." Man: "It's like graffiti in the sky."
>
> Here was a lost boy and a lost girl, and Pete Townshend playing Peter Pan. The only memorable tunes were ones he wrote earlier, specifically for 1971's *Who's Next* album. Neither the echoey, multi-track production nor the first half's slightly fractured narrative managed to give it a modern feel.
>
> Townshend may be a rich and once creative musician, but someone should have had a word in his ear.

Despite reviews such as this, in reading the various interviews Pete gave following the completion of the *Lifehouse* radio play, a sense of satisfaction and almost relief is detected. "For twenty-nine years I have been entangled in this thing called *Lifehouse*," Pete wrote in the *Richmond Review* in 1999.

> I blamed the frustration it caused me on its innate simplicity and my innate verbosity; one cancelled out the other. The story contained ideas that were once regarded as overly ambitious. I felt like a jungle explorer who had stumbled upon an Inca temple of solid gold and become impeded by roots and vines in a knot of undergrowth, only yards from civilization. One day I would emerge crying aloud that I'd discovered something marvelous, but would be patted on the head and indulged in my triumphant ranting. The playscript is the result of this awkward, though not particularly heroic, journey. I have come to the end of a creative adventure in which I struggled as much to overcome my own impatience as obstacles in my path.

The completion of Pete's *Lifehouse* project as a radio play inevitably led to questions about thematically related film or concert work. After losing sight of his dream of a *Lifehouse* film in 1971, Pete was eager to revisit the notion. "I would like to see a film made of *Lifehouse*," he told

the *New York Post* in 1999. "I have dozens of ideas. In fact I'm about to break a long-held rule and going to start making my own films."
Pete also mentioned that there was a "strong possibility" of some live work as a result of the completion of *Lifehouse*. "...I have always hoped that the *Lifehouse* concert referred to in this play can happen in reality," he wrote in *The Richmond Review*.

> I imagine a celebratory gathering at which a large number of individuals hear modest compositions or songs created specifically for them. In a finale, all those pieces could be combined, perhaps with creative and engaging images of each subject. I believe the result would have enormous impact and significance. I recently wrote a proposal to a friend of mine who owns a computer company, that is going to sponsor events of this kind.
> But this is perhaps just my composer's megalomaniacal dream. Such visions must be realized rather than described. That much I have learned on my *Lifehouse* journey, which ends here. Thus I move quickly onto the reality.

The reality was a six-CD boxed set entitled *The Lifehouse Chronicles*, released in February 2000 exclusively on Pete's www.eelpie.com website. A "CD package containing all the music inspired by the *Lifehouse* story over the last twenty-nine years," according to Pete, it contained the entire radio play as broadcast on BBC radio a few months earlier, along with an extensive collection of *Lifehouse*-related demos and orchestral recordings. Assembling the project took "about a year," according to Pete. "For me, one of the things that I want the *Chronicles* to do is to chronicle my own 'experience'," Pete told Matt Kent in 1999. "I was listening to a lot of avant-writing at the time, such as Tim Souster and Stockhausen, and I was trying to find out what these people were trying to do with music."

"...[*Lifehouse* is] a living project and as a result, what I needed to do in order to put it to bed, was to chronicle it up to the present day," Pete told Kent. "It's always been an idea that has stimulated me. When I've gone back to *Tommy*, to *Quadrophenia*, they are stories that are finished; you can only change the shade of them. With *Lifehouse* it was always alive and living, particularly in the area of music creativity and music as a reflection of the human spirit."

A single CD containing a selection of demos from *The Lifehouse Chronicles* entitled *The Lifehouse Elements* was soon released in music stores. "I did it to reach the audience who do not want the bigger more comprehensive package (and thus pay more money), and of course those who do not yet use the Internet," Pete said in 2000.

Pete's plans for a *Lifehouse* concert remained. He planned to release a limited edition of 2001 boxed sets entitled *The Lifehouse Method*, containing the same music as *The Lifehouse Chronicles*, but each also containing an individual code and a ticket to the *Lifehouse* concert. "So, I still have this crazy urge to make the fiction real," Pete wrote in *The Richmond Review*. "Sadly, this particular package will not be cheap. It contains four hours of music – the entire play as broadcast by the BBC – and is lavishly packaged. It also contains that guaranteed concert ticket and my promise that the buyer will be treated there like a V.I.P." Pete had high hopes for the concert, which he considered a "strong possibility" at the time. "Where I'm sitting at the moment with this is that I would very much like, when I do the publicity, to announce that not only will I be doing the *Lifehouse Chronicles* and the radio play but that I was also going to be doing a concert, either with or without The Who, which would embrace some of the hopes of the original concert parts of the story, which was quite simple. In the story there is a concert; in the story that you'll hear on the radio there is a concert."

Interestingly, and probably causing a sigh of frustration (and perhaps resignation) from Pete, this latest version of *Lifehouse* was still met with confusion. "*Lifehouse* was... the most interesting thing [Pete] ever wrote," Dave Marsh wrote in 1999. "However, I don't think that anybody apart from Pete has a clue what it is about." *The Times*' Nigel Williamson was similarly puzzled: "The plot of *Lifehouse* is complicated and at times confused..."

Perhaps too ambitious to be successfully executed, neither the climactic *Lifehouse* concert nor its companion *The Lifehouse Method* ever reached fruition, the only remnants which saw the light of day being two concerts of the music from *Lifehouse* which took place in February, 2000. In a move of which Kit Lambert would have been proud, Pete scheduled the shows at London's Sadler's Wells Theatre, with accompaniment being provided by the 28-piece London Chamber Orchestra. Following two weeks of rehearsals, the sold-out concerts took place on February 25 and 26, both comprising 2 ½ hours of music from *Lifehouse*, and featuring, along with the orchestra, Chucho Merchan, Rabbit Bundrick, Billy Nicholls, Chyna, Cleveland Watkiss, Peter Hope-Evans, Jody Linscott and Phil Palmer. Both shows were opened by Piano Circus playing the Terry Riley composition *In C*. The song order on the first night was *One Note (Prologue), Purcell One Note (Quick movement), Baba O'Riley (orchestral), Teenage Wasteland, Time Is Passing, Love Ain't For Keeping, Going Mobile, Greyhound Girl, Tragedy, Mary, I Don't Know Myself, Bargain, Pure and Easy*, and *Let's See Action* followed by an intermission. The second set consisted of *Hinterland Rag (orchestral), Baba O'Riley, Behind Blue Eyes, Sister Disco,*

Getting In Tune, Relay, Who Are You, Join Together, Won't Get Fooled Again, Tragedy Explained, Song Is Over, and *Can You Help The One You Really Love?*[273] This set list was adjusted slightly the following night.

"...Even when Townshend and his band flubbed their parts – starting a couple songs over from the beginning – the audience's support was unrelenting, and they clapped along and hollered loving approbations," wrote *Rolling Stone*'s Jenny Eliscu, who witnessed the second show.

> From where I was sitting on Saturday, I could see the back of John Entwistle's noggin, and he seemed to be digging it, too.
> ...Townshend offered a brilliant set, full of emotion and resounding proof that the man can still play the fuck out of his guitar. He played only acoustic guitar, having said at a small Q&A session a couple days earlier that if he got his mitts on an electric, he would become too absorbed in his instrument to keep control over the proceedings.
> Aside from a couple of orchestral numbers – each beautiful, but largely a distraction from the rock & roll main event – Townshend's set consisted mostly of familiar favorites... Townshend had his most glorious moments during *Bargain* and a brand new song called *Can You Help the One You Really Love?* He introduced the former by explaining – in the kind of relaxed manner that characterized most of his between-song chatter – that in the course of revisiting his *Lifehouse* demos, he had found that while some songs would benefit from further musical elaboration, others were impossible to better. So, for *Bargain*, he had the tape of his guitar part from a thirty-year-old demo piped through the speakers, and the band played along with it...

The Times' Nigel Williamson wrote, "...Employing a pick-up band, Townshend had given warning that the sound might be "clunky", and at one point he apologetically announced that "some of these numbers could have done with a little more rehearsal." There were rough edges but, as he had claimed, there was also a passion that was undeniable."

> ...he carried the burden of the lead vocals well enough[274]. But many were disappointed that he stuck to

---

[273] *Can You Help the One You Really Love* was a new addition, which Pete described in a chat on www.barnesandnoble.com in 2000: "The story behind the song is this – if you had found *your* Lifehouse (a place you felt your journey might end in joy and fulfillment), would you be able to persuade your parents to join you?"

acoustic guitar, denying us those famous electrified pyrotechnics. He explained that he needed to avoid the rush that still carries him away every time he straps on an electric guitar, for as musical director he needed to stay "on the ground".

...the evening's most powerful moments came when the two ensembles combined. In particular this brought a compelling grandeur to *Pure and Easy*, described by Townshend as the work's "pivotal" song.

Inevitably it was the better known numbers which were best received – *Baba O'Riley*, *Won't Get Fooled Again*, *Going Mobile* and *Song Is Over* were all originally intended for *Lifehouse*. Yet several of the lesser-known songs, particularly *Pure and Easy*, *Sister Disco* and *Mary* were also impressive. It was a flawed but fascinating exercise...

"...there's little, save Townshend's explanatory links, to generate a sense of "concept"", wrote *The Guardian*'s Keith Cameron.

A narrative arc is fleetingly perceptible in the interplay of ballad and rock, orchestra and psychedelia. Elsewhere, one waits for the hits – and it's a bonus to hear them sung by the man who wrote every word.

Lifehouse's guiding ideal is the search for music's transcendence – "the simple secret of the note in us all", according to the deeply hippie *Pure and Easy*, its defining track. Townshend's enduring curiosity about what makes music tick is admirable – even if the frustrating truth may be that its transcendent moments are essentially arbitrary. There were thrilling peaks but as the gig dragged on beyond three hours, nothing he conjured could rival what should have been its grand finale: in the keyboard refrain of *Won't Get Fooled Again*.

As *Lifehouse* neared completion and a sense of finality with the airing of the radio play, Pete continued his historical embrace of technology as he opened his website, www.petetownshend.com in November 1999[275]. The website offered an internet diary updated by Pete and which would

---

[274] Pete had asked Roger Daltrey to provide vocals at the Sadler's Wells shows, but he was in Australia with the British Rock Symphony at the time.

[275] Pete's continued embrace of technology provided a further illustration of his abrasive relationship with Daltrey, who told *USA Today*'s Edward Baig in April 2000 that he didn't own a computer or a cell phone. "I'm determined to get through life without them," he said.

often feature streaming video entries, a chat room, a news section, MP3 downloads of unreleased music[276], details of projects such as *Lifehouse*, a complete concert guide and, later, an updated Who section. The website received over two million hits in its first six months. Matt Kent, who ran the semi-official fan club Naked Eye and had organized Who conventions in the past, was invited by Pete to run the website. "The job offer hit me as a surprise and I can remember it word for word to this day," Kent recalled in 2002.

> October 1998 and the first call on my new mobile phone. 'Hello, can I speak to Matt please.' 'Who is it?' 'It's Pete Townshend.' 'Yes, of course it is, who is it?' 'No, it's Pete Townshend.' After my doubting it a few more times and, I also seem to remember, throwing in a few expletives, it began to dawn on me that maybe it was Pete. 'Oh, hi Pete, what can I do for you?' like it was an everyday occurrence, 'I'm thinking of opening a website and was wondering if you'd like to run it?' After probably wasting a couple of pico seconds thinking about it I accepted and that's what brings me here today. I just happened to be in the right place at the right time.

Pete's website gave his fans an unprecedented amount of information on their favorite musician, and reflected Pete's enjoyment of telling his own story. "I love the internet because it's a place to share," Pete told *New York Post*'s Dan Aquilante in July 2000. "On my web site, I share my process with those who are interested. I am an art school boy, and sharing process is part of how I work. I do love talking about what I do. In concert, some find it irritating as hell. All they want is for me to stop talking and pick up the guitar and play. That's why the internet is so good for me. I can talk."

Pete's newly realized outlet for his artistic ideas proved refreshing, and was a major reason for The Who's return to the road in the near future. "It has sharpened my sense of myself as an artist," he told *The Hollywood Reporter*'s Chris Marlowe in 2001, explaining that he could freely indulge himself before his internet audience, fulfilling his creative needs. "…I am far more willing to attend to my old established and readily recognized methods. This has allowed me to do Who touring in the old manner without feeling I am letting my artistic vision fester."

As rehearsals got under way for Pete's two Sadler's Wells *Lifehouse* shows in February 2000, he began posting regular diary entries on his

---

[276] "I give some stuff away, like I've always done on loss-making tours, the radio and in home taping, and I sell some stuff," Pete told *The Hollywood Reporter* in June, 2001. "The one feeds the other."

website which continued throughout The Who's extensive U.S. summer/fall tour. These usually page-long snippets of thoughts and observations provide a glimpse into Townshend's mind in much the same way that his *Pete Townshend Page* columns did almost thirty years ago. "I spend no time on it at all really," he said in a June, 2001 interview. "I'm an artist. You've seen my guts already, you just don't know it. The diaries are nothing more than what I've always done in interviews. I'm not interested in secrets or facts, just truth."

A few months after the introduction of www.petetownshend.com, Pete opened a commercial website, www.eelpie.com. The site sold Pete's music and various other merchandise, such as copies of the new *Lifehouse* script (autographed versions were available), and books and posters. Since Pete had parted with his record label after *Psychoderelict*, Eel Pie served as his new label. "This site is for everything I do," Pete said at the time. "I will only get back to record labels if I really must." The Eel Pie website soon proved "hugely lucrative for me," Pete told *The Hollywood Reporter*'s Chris Marlowe in 2001, justifying the statement by adding that the site's "dollar gross ran into seven digits in the first year of trading."

In addition to the *Lifehouse*/internet similarities, Pete had been talking about the web for years. In 1986, he gave a lecture about downloading music to an audience at the Royal College of Art[277]. "I think I first told a dark short story about a man who gassed hitch-hikers in the back of his black limousine, then sexually abused them when they were unconscious," he wrote in a January 2001 web diary entry.

> The point of that was that the web brings us sharply up against our own narrow and lonely fantasies. It gives us the illusion of control. But although we can make our target passive in the back of our 'limousine', it is only a perverse few who want sex with unconscious partners.
>
> Listening to music on the web forces us to face our possible lack of social contact with others, and leads us to action. Music on the web should lead people to concerts, congregations, travel, real sex and the ownership of some copyrighted music.

The same month that Pete wrote the above diary entry, he and son Joseph (then 12 years old) logged on to www.napster.com and gave the site a once-over. While he was "amazed how quickly one can gather together good quality tracks," he ultimately judged the site for what it was: Another exploitation of his art: modern-day bootlegging which forced him "into

---

[277] He also "donated an Atari MIDI sequencer to their music department," according to his web diary entry. Regardless of his good intentions, the audience wasn't impressed with his lecture and "walked out", he told *Newsday*'s Letta Tayler in July, 2000.

reliance on what only I can do – that is, to perform live, and to constantly produce new work."

While Pete was ultimately unimpressed with Napster as a money-making venture, he expressed his faith in broadband as the future of entertainment. "…once the cost comes down, there will be no stopping the artists of this world," he told *The Hollywood Reporter* in June, 2001. "Freed from promoters, managers, agents, fixers, middlemen, press, and even accountants, they will perform like buskers whenever they have the need. It's true piracy."

One of the first items sold on www.eelpie.com was a four-CD boxed set entitled *Avatar*, released in February 2000; each of the three Meher Baba albums, *Happy Birthday*, *With Love*, and *I Am*, were reproduced, along with a CD-ROM movie entitled *Parvardigar*. "The three British Meher Baba group albums were never meant to be commercial releases, and neither is *Avatar*," Pete told *In Music We Trust*'s Alex Steininger in 2000. "There are only 2001 copies, so if you have one, you're lucky. There may be a reprint. But it's doubtful."

The release of the *Avatar* boxed set was Pete's first public acknowledgement of his continuing devotion to Meher Baba since his involvement in Raphael Rudd's 1996 album *Awakenings*. "I still read Meher Baba and I still believe he is an authentic spiritual master," he told *Q*'s David Cavanagh in January, 2000[278]. "Currently my connection with him is that I look after and fund archival film work." Pete further addressed his devotion to Meher Baba in *Meher Baba – The Silent Master: My Own Silence*, an essay posted on www.eelpie.com in July 2001 which was interspersed with photos of Baba, and some of Pete's personal photos from the pilgrimages to India he made in 1972 and 1976. Pete's essay indicated that, given his battle with drug abuse, he felt he was an unsuitable public spokesman for Meher Baba, and was uncomfortable in such a role. "Today I avoid making public pronouncements about his status as a spiritual master," Pete wrote.

> He claimed to be the Avatar (another word for 'Christ'), but so do other self-appointed masters in India and elsewhere. I have my own conviction, and I enjoy a very intimate and special relationship with him that – because he passed away in 1969 (two years after I started to follow him, and before I had a chance to meet him) – is entirely spiritual in nature. I enjoy his sense of humor if that doesn't sound too daft. I often feel that I can see mischievous signs

---

[278] "Townshend still prays and meditates every day," *Rolling Stone*'s Chris Heath reported the following year.

of his presence in my daily life, coincidences or delightful moments.

But I feel Meher Baba too in the darker side of life we all face today. My own journey required that I learn some true humility, and also not to take myself so seriously. My drinking and drug crash would have meant little had I been content to be just a rock star, it might even have helped my career. But, as someone who had vaunted so often the spiritual power of music and audience congregation, I fell further when I crashed. I am thus – I hope – more tempered and less melodramatic about spiritual matters. I hope too that I am in a better position now to speak about what it is that really makes me continue to follow Meher Baba.

It is quite simply that I have come to love him unconditionally. That might seem dangerous, but I am asked to give no money; I am asked to make no public statements on behalf of those who carry out the work of carrying his message to the world. I am asked for nothing, except sometimes my presence in India to say goodbye to the remaining older disciples who fondly remember my musical visits in 1972 and 1976. I remember my friends in India fondly too, and I miss them. I hope it is true humility and not lost pride that prevents me from running back like some kind of Prodigal celebrity. I concentrate my efforts on the MEFA film archive project[279], and in finding Meher Baba in the rhythm of my daily life.

I follow him carrying in parallel a powerful residual childhood love for Jesus. But that love does not embrace organized Christianity I'm afraid. All my life Christians I respect have proselytized to me, and I am happy to be their target and know they are secure in their faith. But I will reciprocate with no scriptural sallies of my own. I follow Meher Baba and I do so quietly, if not completely silently.

In addition to outlining the nature of his relationship with Meher Baba, Pete used the essay to communicate his plans to post a "decent biography" of Baba on his web site, plus a selection of film and photographs from his pilgrimages to India.

---

[279] MEFA, or Meher Baba European Film Archive, works to collect and maintain an archive of Meher-Baba related films.

Chapter 18

"Most people out there are just so fucking stupid on this subject. They say to me, 'Why don't you just write songs? You're good at that. You're no good at plays. Some people feel, for example, that some of my song collections are encumbered by literary pretensions. I've been in a fucking rock-and-roll band all my life! People just don't understand what I actually need, and the demands that are implicit on my thinking processes to produce material which has depth... We have to engage life, and for me, stories help me to engage it from a different angle."
"What I've... realized in my journey through life is that what's really important is the human story. It's not what goes on around us but how we respond to it."
- Pete Townshend, 1996

As Pete was readying *Lifehouse* for the radio in October, 1999, reports surfaced that The Who would reunite for a series of concerts. The catalyst which started Townshend, Daltrey and Entwistle talking was the planned *Lifehouse* concert. "...I had originally intended to present *Lifehouse*, in concert form, at the Royal Albert Hall, during the millennium celebrations," Pete told Matt Kent in 1999.

It wasn't just going to be me playing the *Lifehouse* music but a whole day of music that inspired *Lifehouse*, including Terry Riley and some orchestral work. The story is an eclectic mix of music, not just my work. I invited Roger and John to come in at the end and play some of the songs from the original album. What then happened was that it exploded very, very quickly, as everything does when you talk about anything to do with The Who, it just got incredibly out of hand. Robert Rosenberg rang Gateway Computers, who had used one of my songs in a campaign, asked for $20M for sponsorship, or whatever the figure was, and got it arranged in return for a 25 date Who tour and all of a sudden the whole thing was totally out of whack.

"The Who, one of the most influential rock bands of the 1960s and 1970s, is to reform," *The Times* reported on October 6, stating that the band's debut would occur on October 29 in Las Vegas, in addition to announcing, "Daltrey said the band was working on a new album but there was no release date as yet."

Another reason for the resumption of Who activity was a conversation Roger and Pete had at Pete's house back in May, 1998. Daltrey had emphatically expressed his profound disappointment at Pete's neglect of The Who as a living entity, and his feeling that he and Entwistle were pushed aside while Pete enjoyed the unique fruits of being The Who's composer and publisher[280]. So heartfelt and impassioned were Daltrey's words that they brought Pete to tears. "It was pretty scary," Pete told *Rolling Stone*'s Chris Heath in June, 2002. "He felt that I had fucked him over."

> He also went on to say a whole load of other things, which were to do with unspoken contracts from childhood: that we were a band, we were lads from the street, he was going to go into the gutter. We looked at each other in the eyes, we swore to be together for the rest of our lives...
>
> Halfway through the conversation, this stuff that he was saying was making me cry – it was so brutal, it was so nasty and it was so aggressive. And elements of it were true, but lots of it wasn't.
>
> So in the end I stopped him. I said, "Roger, listen, this is hurting too much, you're just going to have to stop. And all I can tell you is to go away, and I swear to you I will think about it." And so he left, and then he called me back about two hours later and he said, "I've been thinking about this, and I went too far – and I'm really sorry." He said, "I just want you to know, I don't care what you do, I don't care if we ever go out again. I'm your friend, I love you, and all I care about is that you're going to be OK." And I said, 'What I feel proud of is that at our age you feel you can come and do it. It's nice that you can be fucking honest." Because years ago I would have had to read this in a newspaper.

"I felt I had been offered unconditional love," Pete wrote in his web diary in August, 2000. "The truth, his truth."

---

[280] Pete was initially skeptical of Daltrey's request to crank up the Who money-making machine. "I wasn't particularly sympathetic," he told the *L.A. Times*' Phil Sutcliffe in May, 2000. Daltrey and Entwistle were, after all, residing in "...mansions about 40 times the size of my house."

> Within a month I had decided that there was unfinished business for Roger, Pete and John. I knew it would cost me very dearly, and it has. But I was not being heroic or patronizing. I was doing what had to be done, out of love, in response to love… I decided that rather than appear to be patronizingly returning to The Who to prop up Roger and John's declining egos or sagging bank-balances, I would turn everything on its head. Roger had asked me to help him and John. I asked them instead to help me.

Pete asked John and Roger to perform with him in the U.S. at the Chicago House of Blues in a benefit for Maryville Academy, "to placate my own uneasy soul," he wrote.

> They both agreed without a moment's hesitation. At the time they agreed there was nothing in it for them but hard work. There were no guaranteed spin-offs, no deals, no tours, no reviews, no assured fan support.
> Not a single journalist feels that this mechanism is worth a serious or uncynical mention. Maybe nobody knows the background yet. It was a selfless and unconditional response from Roger and John to a preestablished plan of mine. I realized these two guys would do almost anything I asked, and ask for little or nothing in return, apart from my company.

Zak Starkey and Rabbit Bundrick were added to the lineup to bring the band back to a five-piece as opposed to the substantially larger versions of The Who fielded in previous years. The Who were subsequently asked to headline *iBash*, a show at the MGM Grand in Las Vegas celebrating the opening of the ill-fated streaming video website Pixelon.com[281], to be broadcast live on the internet. They were reportedly offered $2 million plus an undetermined amount of stock in Pixelon.com to do the show. The band accepted, and soon added two late October shows for Neil Young's Bridge School Benefit in California, since the *iBash* concert revenue would offset their expenses.

The heavily-touted return of The Who took place as scheduled on 29 October 1999 at the MGM Grand Garden on the strip in Las Vegas. Pete, John, Roger, Zak Starkey and Rabbit headlined a bill which also

---

[281] In April 2000, Pixelon.com's founder, Michael Fenne, was discovered to be David Stanley, a bail-skipping felon who was on Virginia's most wanted list for several years for embezzlement and stock fraud. The company, which had amassed $35 million in investment capital but blew $16.2 million on *iBash*, soon dissolved amidst an onslaught of lawsuits.

featured Kiss, the Dixie Chicks, Sugar Ray and Brian Setzer. "The singer's microphone did a lasso twirl and the guitarist's arm windmill-whirled, all before the end of the first song," wrote the *Las Vegas Review Journal*'s Mike Weatherford. "The Who were back, all right."

They've been back now and then, but Friday night they were back the way most people have wanted to see them. No horns, no background singers, no concept albums. Just hunkering down to play the hits, loudly.

...Still vigorous in their 50s, Pete Townshend, Roger Daltrey and John Entwistle recaptured the macho rock side of The Who that's been missing since at least 1989. Past get-togethers have emphasized the concept albums *Tommy* and *Quadrophenia*, and thereby focused on the grand, theatrical side of the band.

But there are many facets of Who history, and it was nice to see the power trio flex its muscles again. Friday's show was more like the *Live at Leeds* album, though longtime keyboardist John "Rabbit" Bundrick played on every song, filling them in without getting in the way. (You wouldn't want to hear *Baba O'Riley* without a synthesizer, would you?)

...Townshend... was plugged in and wailing away, reminding the sold-out crowd he's a phenomenal guitarist as well as a songwriter. He supplied both the power chords and intricate melodies on big-finish tunes such as *Pinball Wizard* and *Listening to You* without the help of a rhythm guitarist.

The 90-minute set kick-started with *I Can't Explain* and finished with *My Generation*, sticking to the standard FM playlist and ignoring everything from its post-Keith Moon catalogue. Ringo's son Zak Starkey stuck faithfully to the Moon drum sound for honest versions of *Who Are You* and *5:15*.

Daltrey sounded great, too, though the only thing that came close to a ballad was the first half of *Behind Blue Eyes*. Along with a little more breathing space, the set could have used some more surprises. But die-hard fans had to settle for only one dusted-off rarity – *Anyway, Anyhow, Anywhere* – and a rhythmic reworking of *Magic Bus* that sounded like it might have been a nod to the funk-metal wave of the mid-'90s.

A few slip-ups, such as a hesitant version of Entwistle's raggedly sung *My Wife*, were easy to forgive from a band that hasn't played together in a few years. They made the show seem, shall we say, more human than a Kiss set earlier in the evening that many observers suspect was lip-synched.

Townshend has resisted doing a hits tour for years now, perhaps fearing The Who would come off like a washed-up oldies revue. But after a playful night onstage Friday, he hopefully will look at recent shows by the Rolling Stones – longtime rivals for the "World's Best Rock Band" title – to see what can happen when veteran rockers get back to work on a regular schedule. With any luck, Friday's show will not be seen as a last hurrah preserved as a digital museum piece, but as a new beginning.

Indeed, *iBash* was a new beginning for The Who. The band's return to the stage in stripped-down form was a resounding success, and led to extensive touring over the next few years. While the MGM Grand show was well-received, the heavily-publicized live web broadcast was a miserable failure – much of the concert was unavailable for internet viewing due to technical problems, perhaps an omen of Pixelon's impending demise. However, the band apparently thoroughly enjoyed the show, playing for well over an hour when they were scheduled for just a 45 minute slot.

The Bridge School Benefit shows took place a couple of nights later at San Francisco's Shoreline Amphitheater. The all-acoustic shows (Entwistle even played an acoustic bass) had The Who closing a lineup which included performances by Brian Wilson, Pearl Jam, Tom Waits and Green Day. The school's students, all of whom suffer from severe speech or physical impairments, sat on a raised platform behind the stage. "Even though the capacity crowd Saturday had already sat through 8 hours of music by eight acts... everybody stayed well past midnight for this eagerly anticipated finale," wrote the *San Francisco Chronicle*'s Joel Selvin.

It was not the Who of yore, 10 years after the storied English rock band's farewell tour, more than 20 years past its prime. This most electric of rock bands played unplugged, as is the custom at the Bridge benefit. Guitarist Pete Townshend even pulled up a chair to play his clattering solo on *Who Are You*. They may look like old bankers, but the Who's members played like juvenile delinquents. It was utterly magnificent – a towering close to an epic concert.

The Who's next stop was for two shows at the Chicago House of Blues to benefit Maryville Academy on November 12 and 13. Despite the fact that they were priced at $300 a seat, the 1300 tickets for the first show sold out within minutes. The second night was added due to the rabid demand, with a similar rapid sellout ensuing.

The House of Blues shows included a silent auction prior to the first evening which included a 12-string guitar Pete had used in the writing of *Tommy*. Eddie Vedder and C Average opened the show with a set of '80s cover tunes prior to The Who taking the stage. Some reviewers pointed out that the set, which included obvious hits such as *Baba O'Riley*, *Won't Get Fooled Again*, *Substitute* and *My Generation*, lacked spontaneity. Adding to the argument was the presence of a TelePrompTer to aid anyone who momentarily forgot the lyrics mid-song.[282] But the set also included rarities such as A *Legal Matter*, *Tattoo* and a Johnny Cash medley which included *I Walk the Line* and *Ring of Fire*. The band turned *Magic Bus* into a jam which ultimately fell apart (Townshend commented onstage that the rendition was "shit"), and the show was wrapped up as Vedder and C Average retook the stage to help The Who with *Let's See Action*. Townshend and Daltrey received lukewarm reviews in the local press – Townshend was accused of appearing to lose interest as the concert progressed, Daltrey of appearing inhibited by the small stage and club atmosphere – while Entwistle was praised for his effort. "On this night, Entwistle was clearly The Who's most dangerous member," *Rolling Stone*'s Kevin McKeough wrote.

> His pummeling, rapid-fire bass lines darted through the songs like a fighter pilot on a bombing run, and he sounded dark and mean as he spit out the words of *My Wife*. His slashing solo on *5:15* earned the wildest cheers of the evening and egged Townshend into his most abandoned solo as well.

At the end of the first evening's show, the band was reportedly offered a sizeable sum of money to do an encore, and obliged with a performance of *Eminence Front*. "We had just finished the show and someone sent a message backstage saying that they would pay $100,000 to the charity if we would play *Eminence Front* again," Daltrey told *The Guardian*'s Bill Borrows, adding with a laugh, "Pete said, 'We're not going on again,' and I said, 'We fuckin' are.'" They then presented a check for $1,000,000 to Maryville's executive director, the Rev. John Smyth.

Buoyed by the success – and their enjoyment – of the recent performances, The Who wrapped up an eventful 1999 with two shows on home turf, December 22 and 23 at the 2,000-seat Shepherds Bush Empire.[283]

---

[282] The TelePrompTer didn't help Pete during *A Legal Matter*, though: He reportedly forgot the words.
[283] "Pete Townshend has revealed why his aging band, The Who, tours at Christmas,"

"The whirlwind opening salvo of *I Can't Explain*, *Substitute*, *Anyway Anyhow Anywhere* and *Pinball Wizard* set the tone for a show that was an uninhibited celebration of the group's glory days," *The Times* reported.

> Executed with a minimum of preparation[284] and, for the most part, without the usual efforts to smuggle in new or unfamiliar material, it was an event which reminded us of exactly why The Who were once the biggest British band after the Beatles and the Rolling Stones, but also why history has tended to mark them down.
> On the debit side there were later, lesser hits such as *You Better You Bet*, Entwistle singing the inevitable *Boris the Spider*, and Daltrey's dreary *After The Fire*. More forgivable were the occasional cocked-up beginnings and an endearingly scrappy version of *Happy Jack*.
> But when they hit their stride with core anthems such as *Baba O'Riley*, *Magic Bus*, *Who Are You* and an epic *Won't Get Fooled Again*, the old magic was still there, even if the fire had dimmed...
> "My ears have gone," Daltrey complained towards the end.
> "You don't need to hear anything these days," Townshend replied, sounding and indeed looking a bit like Spike Milligan. "There's nothing worth listening to these days. It was different when I was a lad."
> Minutes later, the aging rocker smashed his guitar to pieces in one well-practiced but still surprisingly ferocious movement, before leading the group into an encore of *My Generation*, a lyric which has now taken on a somewhat different complexion to when it was written. The dads are all right.

By this point, The Who were reveling in their new back-to-basics lineup. "I enjoyed the shows," Pete told the *L.A. Times* the following May, enjoying his expanded role now that his sound wasn't augmented by other musicians. "We always had an orchestra to hide behind – we never really felt like the Who back then," Entwistle said in April, 2000. "It's much more like the old Who – we're actually playing together." In September, Daltrey added, "the band hasn't been this raw since Keith died."

---

reported *The Times* on Christmas Eve, 1999. ""We always did Christmas because then we didn't have to buy gifts. We'd say, "We're far too busy – we have to learn our lines.""
[284] "We haven't rehearsed anything, we've been too busy in Antigua," Pete said from the stage, according to *The Guardian*.

In addition to disposing of the bloated lineup of past tours, a major reason for The Who's rejuvenation was the addition of Zak Starkey on drums. Starkey, who'd first played with The Who at the '96 Hyde Park *Quadrophenia* show, displayed a style which reminded many observers of Keith Moon. "Kenney Jones, although he's a great drummer, was never the right drummer for the Who," Roger Daltrey said in September, 2000. "With Zak on the drums now, we can get back a lot of fire that has been missing for so long in the band. His style is very similar to Keith's... if you close your eyes, it's so similar musically, it's uncanny. It's eerie. It probably has something to do with Moon teaching him to drum in the first place, I suppose."

While The Who's handful of late 1999 benefit appearances did little to address, in Pete's words, Roger and John's "sagging bank balances", their activities in summer and fall 2000 surely returned all involved parties squarely in the black. Introduced by David Letterman band leader Paul Shaffer as "the most exciting band in rock'n'roll," the band held a press conference from the stage of Manhattan's Supper Club on April 10, 2000 to confirm the widespread speculation and announce a 25-date U.S. summer tour, in addition to the release of a new live album. The tour was organized into three legs, each about two weeks in length, the dates beginning in late June and ending in early October ("Not an arduous one at all," Pete commented). The tour was linked with a similar venture by Jimmy Page and the Black Crowes, so that the bands could share equipment – and thus cut costs as they played on consecutive nights. The alignment with Page and the Crowes led to the inevitable question as to whether there would be any on-stage jamming between the two groups. "Short answer: no, I think," Pete told *Launch.com*'s Gary Graff. "I'm really looking forward to them being days off. You know, I'm definitely going to go and watch. I'm kind of more of a fan of Black Crowes than I am of Jimmy Page, but that's because I grew up with Jimmy Page (laughs). It's an interesting tour... it does create for me what feels like much more of a kind of festival-like atmosphere. I like the feel of it."

The question was soon broached as to how The Who felt about touring without any new material, in effect as a nostalgia act. "That's what it is," Pete said abruptly. Roger, for once, was more eloquent. "What a load of bullshit that is," he said.

> I mean, if you went to see a Beethoven concert tonight, is that nostalgia? If you go to a museum and look at a Renoir exhibition, is that nostalgia? How can it be nostalgia if it's our fucking music? It fucking belongs to us and we can play it when and wherever we like. And if people don't want to come and see it, then that's up to them – we don't force anyone. But it's certainly not nostalgia.

And sometimes you go onstage, and mostly by accident, things happen and a musical direction gets switched in a certain way, and it's just pure fucking magic. And that to me is probably the single most beautiful thing in my life, to have ever achieved something that wondrous. And it happens quite regularly with the Who, so of course I enjoy it and I'm enthusiastic.

"We're picking up where we left off in '81, the last year we were a creative force," Pete told *Newsday*'s Letta Tayler a few months later. "All the stuff that's happened in between has been distraction, really, and procrastination. This is a real 'Well, let's grab it and see what's really there.' And what we know is there is the joy of one another's company... That blood-brother stuff is very important."

Another subject brought up at the press conference was that of The Who's reported plans to try to write some new material. "The plan is to go into my studio, because it's comfortable and it's in the house and there's plenty of room in the house to hide from each other," Entwistle said. "We're just going to go in and try it. I think, hopefully, we can find some common ground on recordings that we've done of these shows. Some of the improvisations may give us inspiration for new songs. A lot of my songs come from what I'm playing onstage, and Pete gets inspired by stuff he sees us work up." Daltrey had also written three songs "which lyrically I think are really good," he said. He added that he'd played demos of the songs to Townshend, and hope that Pete and John would aid in fleshing out the material he'd written. "I don't want us to get back to the situation we used to have with Pete in the latter days," he said, "where he would come up with such a perfect demo that you'd end up just trying to copy it. I want them to be organic from the band." Pete, Roger and John hoped to write together during breaks on the upcoming tour, and perhaps produce an album in 2001. "It's a hope, not a promise," Pete said. "We're in our mid-Fifties, so if we don't do it now..."

Roger insisted that new Townshend compositions could be relevant. "There's a courage and an honesty about [Pete's songs]," he said.

And I know they were written really about problems of adolescence and just a little bit beyond that, most of them, but they equally apply to problems of middle age and onwards too. I think there are other problems of middle age and onwards, but it's frustrated me that Pete has never managed to put pen to paper or pen to guitar and write more about them. It always frustrated me that Pete could do it so well about adolescence and about the young boy growing up, but he can't write about the middle-aged man figuring out his life with all the problems he faces. I mean, what's the fucking difference?

The band's live album, released in April, 2000, entitled *The Blues to the Bush*, featured selections recorded by Bobby Pridden from their 1999 Chicago House of Blues and Shepherds Bush Empire shows. The album, available exclusively at www.musicmaker.com, consisted of 20 tracks including hits such as *Magic Bus*, *Pinball Wizard* and *My Generation*, along with *After the Fire*, which saw live action in 1999. The album's availability solely on the internet also meant that fans could customize their compact disc by dictating song order, or selecting only a few songs for a reduced price.

The album was well received. "...while all three musicians are well into their 50s," wrote *Wall Of Sound*'s Gary Graff in May 2000, "*The Blues to the Bush* sounds more charged and energetic than most of the myriad live albums The Who released after its quintessential *Live at Leeds* in 1970. [the album]...boasts a kind of crisp, off-the-board immediacy that captures a presence many live albums lack. In top form, The Who blows through 20 of its own well-worn favorites with high-octane vigor, reveling in the space of the spartan arrangements rather than trying to fill every possible sonic space." Graff called the majority of the songs "tight and punchy", and wrote that the "extended bluesy version" of *Magic Bus* "may be the best that's ever been preserved on disc."

In May 2000, Pete offered an online auction on his Eel Pie website to raise funds for Oxfam's emergency services to help those affected by floods in Mozambique and a combination of drought and food shortages in Ethiopia. "It will be an opportunity for you collectors of memorabilia, precious guitars and other interesting things to contribute to a very good cause," Pete posted on the site. "I have gathered together a number of items I regard as precious. I will miss them when they're gone, and I sincerely hope they mean as much (or more) to you as they have to me while I've been custodian."

Among the list of items made available for the auction were a selection of gold and platinum awards, the trombone used during the *Psychoderelict* tour, letters to Pete from Paul McCartney, Keith Richards, Arthur Miller and Eric Clapton, the white jacket Pete wore for 1998's *A Day In The Garden*, one of Pete's bicycles, and two sets of authors proofs for *Horse's Neck*. Another interesting item was a Rickenbacker guitar which was "smashed, arranged and mounted by Pete," according to Matt Kent.

Other more important items up for grabs included a "classical Spanish guitar circa 1971" on which Pete composed *Behind Blue Eyes* "and a number of other important songs," according to Pete. "My daughter Minta used it to learn on, and I got it back from her about 3 years ago. It is a very good guitar which I bought in L.A. from West L.A. Music." In addition, a

Rickenbacker Pete Townshend Model 335 was offered. "This is the very first of a numbered line to be built in this limited edition series," Pete wrote. "I have used this guitar around the house. The prototype of this series needed some work, which I did myself, and sent the resulting guitar as a gift to Paul Weller." Another Pete Townshend edition, this time the Gibson SG Special, was offered. "This guitar is the very first of the numbered line to be built in this limited edition series," Pete added. "My son Joseph has the prototype."

The centerpiece of the auction, however, was a 1957 Fender Stratocaster which was given to Pete as a gift by Eric Clapton after Pete had helped arrange Clapton's 1973 comeback show at the Rainbow. However, four days into the auction a message appeared on the auction page: "The Fender Stratocaster has been withdrawn. It has been purchased for an unspecified, but astronomical, price by a syndicate of buyers. David Bowie, Mick Jagger and Pete Townshend have bought the guitar and given it to Tony Blair, the British Prime Minister. Tony Blair is a guitarist himself, and the three rock stars are hoping for Knighthoods and think this gift might help."

On June 6, 2000, The Who played a charity show in New York for the Robin Hood Foundation, an organization dedicated to ending poverty in New York City. Comedian Robin Williams emceed the fundraising event, individual tickets to which cost $2,000, tables upwards of $20,000. Simon Phillips filled in for the previously indisposed Zak Starkey with minimal rehearsals taking place in the days leading up to the show.

Pete arrived in the States in good spirits a few days prior to The Who's 2000 North American tour opener, a June 25 gig at Chicago's New World Music Theater. "I'm feeling pretty good, and I am really looking forward to this first leg of the tour," Pete wrote in his web diary, which was updated regularly during the tour.

> The rehearsals went well, Zak and Rabbit both playing brilliantly as ever. John with a very cool new bass rig, Roger in a really upbeat mood, talking through a new song he's been working on. I'm carrying a full demo studio rig on the road in case Roger or I get to write anything. I am also carrying a large MiniDV editing rig so I can produce some video diaries. I'm hoping to carry a camera onto the stage at some shows, it should be amusing....

The band's first show on the back-to-basics tour was a great success, and was regarded by some even as a return to form, which, by Who standards, is an amazing feat. "Whenever it's tempting to say that the Who have outlived their usefulness and ought to die before any of us get much older, the veteran British rockers offer a glimpse of the fiery spirit that first made them legendary 3 ½ decades ago," wrote *Chicago Sun-Times* critic Jim DeRogatis in his review of the show.

> The band performed before a packed crowd at the New World Music Theatre on Sunday night...The Who didn't entirely redeem itself for the last 10 years' worth of lackluster reunion tours. But it was a lot more inspired and rocked a heck of a lot harder than the first of its shows several months ago at the much more intimate House of Blues.
> What was the difference? ...The key was and always will be Pete Townshend. The Who's mastermind looked like a middle-age church deacon, but he tore into his guitar with a vengeance, bounced about the stage like a speed freak, and seemed to be having genuine rock'n'roll fun.
> The group played many of the same songs as the House of Blues set: *I Can't Explain, Substitute, My Wife, The Real Me*. But Townshend added real six-string heat to all of them, while other tunes like *Magic Bus* and *5:15* were extended into transcendent jams.
> ...Maybe it isn't time to pull the plug on this band just yet, after all. Either that or we've all been fooled again, and we should be glad about it.

"Well we're off," Pete wrote in his web-diary the following day. "It was really noisy last night, the band and the crowd. I came off the stage with my head screaming, and as with the recent indoor shows we've done, it is as much from the noise of the hall as the sound on stage. My amps were set at number '3' ...not like the old days... For a first show it wasn't bad, a little bit out of control maybe, but I had fun."

Despite the improved condition of his hearing he'd reported back in January[285], Pete's ears took a beating as a result of this first show. "My ears were screaming, my head throbbing (with high blood pressure), my limbs aching and the appreciative sound of the audience somehow lost down the short corridor to my dressing room," Pete wrote a few days later. "...I always feel bad about subjecting my body (mainly my ears of course) to such an assault as it gets on stage with The Who."

> ...looking at myself on video after the show, my heart breaks a little for two reasons.

---

[285] "I've had some treatment for it," Pete told *Q*'s David Cavanaugh in January, 2000. "I found a homeopathic practitioner who has really helped reduce it tremendously."

One because I do love what I do so much, and I am grateful to be doing it. But two, because it is so sad that this music I helped to refine seems to demand so much human food – like the Space-Bat-Angel-Dragon in Ted Hughes' Iron Man story, it seems insatiable. While I seem unable to come up with great new songs, I suppose it is enough to feed the Dragon more little pieces of the tips of my fingers, or the edge of my hearing…Sounds melodramatic doesn't it? But that's how it feels you know.

Following a show at Detroit's Palace of Auburn Hills two days later, Pete had already noticed that reviewers were focusing on his renewed energy. "Reviews speak of some new spark in me," he wrote in his web-diary on June 29.

You know there is no new spark. The old spark has always been there, I've chosen not to ignite it. Solo shows of late have helped me refine a good electric guitar sound I can use at medium level and still get off, and the fact that no one is putting me under pressure to be creative for The Who (as a songwriter) helps me a lot. I am still a very active composer, but writing songs for a deeply established rock band (that many musicians I admire don't even like) isn't coming easy to me…If it happens, it happens. If it doesn't, well enjoy the 'new' spark.

Ed Masley's *Post-Gazette* review of the June 30 Pittsburgh show showered Townshend and The Who with praise:

…The Who did more than just get by last night at the Post-Gazette Pavilion with a show that out-rocked any major act that's been through town in years.
Pete Townshend, surprisingly animated, ran on stage looking mod in a sharp black suit and proceeded to bash out the opening power chords of *I Can't Explain* with a youthful abandon he hasn't shown in ages. By the second guitar break, he'd already cranked out a crowd-pleasing flurry of legendary Townshend windmills.
Roger Daltrey was right there beside him, twirling his mike like it was 1968 all over again. And his vocals sounded even stronger than they do on *The Blues to The Bush*…
After three songs, I looked at my notebook and realized I'd already used the words awesome no fewer than

five times, mostly with regard to Townshend. It was that amazing.

Credit Ringo's kid, Zak Starkey, with giving the geezers the kick in the pants they so desperately needed on the drums. His playing stood in raucous tribute to the havoc Moonie used to raise behind the kit, especially his fills coming out of the synthesizer break on *Won't Get Fooled Again*, the part that takes you into what remains the greatest scream in rock.

The music may have been explosive, but the banter had a "storytellers" charm, with Townshend introducing *I Don't Even Know Myself* as a song recorded in his home. "I remember my neighbors next door," he recalled, with a grin, "very appreciative that I had Keith Moon in my bedroom playing drums.

...By the time they hit the encore-closing punk abandon of *My Generation*, you could easily have fooled me into thinking they were still the world's greatest rock'n'roll band after all these years.

The Who made stops in New Jersey (which went "pretty well" according to Pete) on July 1 and Washington DC four days later. "When Pete Townshend confessed his sniffling nose had nothing to do with cocaine use, you believed him," wrote *The Washington Times*' Christian Toto of the band's show at the Nissan Pavilion.

Mr Townshend, who emerged from the shadows in hip shades and a dark trench coat, quickly cocked his arm for his patented windmill moves. Stiff-legged and chrome-domed, the guitarist propped up the evening with his keening background vocals and precise strumming.

...A few numbers wilted under the strain of elongated jams. As much as Mr. Townshend's handiwork should be admired, his guitar solos took precious time that could have been used to squeeze in some lesser-known gems. The guitarist seemed to be enjoying himself too much to care about neglected classics...

Pete, although complaining of ear pain, *was* enjoying himself. "We played in Washington last night, and it was again an enjoyable experience," Pete noted on July 6 in his web-diary.

There is still quite a lot of creative space to be found with this band and material. Rabbit and Zak can be especially inspiring and surprising. But the front line is surprising too sometimes. Roger has been singing powerfully, but also with a lot of new deep feeling. John is visibly cheering up as the prospect recedes of going to jail for tax evasion. He played a blinding couple of bass solos last night – literally beyond belief.

And me? Well I still can't believe myself to be honest. About 8 years ago I had a bad wrist accident that I thought would end my decent playing forever. I thought I was consigned to a computer to write and play music. But I practiced hard, and did 18 months of physio to retrieve still-restricted movement, but that practice opened up a lot of skills to me that I'd never tapped before. I'm enjoying taking off in solos and actually having to land carefully in case I crash-land…

It's going well. We have Camden NJ tomorrow, always a good venue, and Jones Beach on Sunday – just about my favorite place to play anywhere. Then a Summer break with my kids until the West Coast in mid-August.

"This show was hard," Pete commented after the July 7 show at Camden, New Jersey. "Not sure why. Now my ears are blasted, my right ear is ringing badly and the pick up is about 50% down. It will be better by tomorrow afternoon, but despite the fact I am being careful, I am still getting damage on top of that I sustained in the '70s."

The Jones Beach show two days later brought yet another rave review. Both The Who and Jimmy Page and the Black Crowes (who played the same venue the following night) impressed the *New York Times*' Ann Powers. "Both acts performed as if to banish time, with Mr. Townshend and Mr. Page particularly showing their prowess," wrote Powers.

> These are two of rock's most athletic guitarists, and each performed his signature stunts: Mr. Townshend windmilled his strumming arm and ultimately smashed his instrument, while Mr. Page shook and undulated in his usual wizardly fashion. No need for artistic Viagra here! The beasts still howled…Roger Daltrey bellowed on point, played a wicked harmonica, and with his remarkably well-preserved (and eagerly displayed) physique, he made a more convincing Siegfried than some who have graced the stage of the Met…
>
> …Starkey's style is inseparable from Mr. Moon's, and his rapport with the bassist John Entwistle was easy on the band's rapid-fire songs… The reach of classic rock may

sometimes seem to exceed its grasp, but that very striving is its most honorable quality. Age hasn't dimmed it in stars like the Who and Jimmy Page, and changing fashions will not extinguish its power in the lives of those it touches.

Rolling Stone's Anthony DeCurtis was similarly blown away:

> ...The show was simply incredible. ...The fire and force of their performance echoed the great Who shows I had attended in the Sixties and Seventies, shows that are among the best I have ever seen...
>
> But the Who meant something very different to me this time around. When I was young, the Who perfectly caught my anger and my grueling sense of physical discomfort. While the Stones and Beatles always seemed Olympian, remote and somehow perfect, the Who (like the Kinks) seemed very much like me – nervous (that stuttering), vulnerable and really pissed off. When, while discussing his adolescence in 1968, Townshend told *Rolling Stone* that "This seemed to be the biggest thing in my life: my fucking nose, man," I knew that I had found a soul mate. As for "I hope I die before I get old," that just seemed like a weird redundancy to me. I believed to the very core of my soul that getting old and dying were exactly the same thing.
>
> They're not. Watching Townshend stand on stage in the middle of a great rock & roll show and calmly, even gently, explain to a fan who wanted him to smash his guitar that "I'm fifty-five" was inspiring. That about an hour later he smashed the guitar to bits – because he felt like it, not because the audience expected it – made the gesture even more powerful.
>
> In 1967 when I saw the Who for the first time – sporting their frilly shirts and Edwardian jackets – I could not have conceived that thirty-three years later I would see the group again with equal pleasure...

The first leg of the tour ended on 10 July at Jones Beach, Long Island, New York, one of Pete's favorite places to play, "a beautiful and special venue," he wrote in his web-diary the following day.

"Dressed like a distinguished pallbearer at a state funeral, but throwing shapes like a hyperactive punk on speed, he attacks his poor Stratocaster guitar as if it might be forced to yield up the secrets of the universe, thrashing out power chords with his windmilling right arm, bending notes hopelessly out of tune with a whammy bar, squeezing the last drops of feedback from his amplifier before (apparently incensed by the guitar's failure to surrender its mysteries) he lifts the Strat above his head and brings it down on the stage with a force that cracks the neck and sends a shockwave through the stadium," wrote *The Daily Telegraph*'s Neil McCormick of Pete's performance at the Jones Beach show.

> The crowd roar and Daltrey grins with astonishment as Townshend enacts a ritual of autodestruction long absent from his repertoire, smashing that guitar again and again until there is nothing left but some broken bits of wood and a scrawl of electric noise. Then he spits on it and stalks off stage.
> OK... I know Townshend has got through an awful lot of guitars in his time and perhaps this really was nothing more than a moment of high theatre, an act of showmanship certain to delight an audience keen to rekindle the fires of their collective youth... but I'm not sure. If this outburst of musical violence retains the power to astonish, it may be because (now more than ever) it is a genuine expression of Townshend's tormented relationship with his band, his audience, his muse and, ultimately, himself.

In July 2000, as The Who began their summer break from touring, Gibson announced at a trade show that it was issuing a limited edition of 250 Pete Townshend SG guitars. A replica of the instrument that Pete used during The Who's *Live at Leeds* era, part of the proceeds from the sale of the guitars went to Pete's Double-O charities. A special set of ten prototypical models of these guitars was available on Pete's web site, each one complete with a photo of Pete posing with that particular guitar, and a CD containing a snippet of Pete playing it. This level of individual attention came at a premium: The guitars were £10,000 each, which may explain why one still remains, unsold.

In addition to attending Bill Curbishley's wedding, Pete spent some of his break sailing in Cornwall. "Yesterday was my first race aboard 'Deejay' the J24 I part-own with my friend Tim," Pete wrote in his web-diary on August 3. "We were first in a fleet of 12... Sadly, we won't get a cup to add to my collection of about twenty (none of which I can pretend I had anything to do with, I was performing in the USA!), because the committee were 'protested' for restarting the race too early after a false start. Next week is Falmouth Week, a big week for racing in the South West. I am racing on Monday and Tuesday."

"I'm enjoying this break," Pete wrote. "I very much look forward to the next leg of the tour, especially the kick off at The Hollywood Bowl[286]. We haven't played there since the late '60s."

Touring resumed on August 14 as the second leg kicked off at the Hollywood Bowl, The Who's first stop at the venue since 1967. "The Who took to the unadorned shell-like stage with no fanfare, and kicked into early hits *I Can't Explain*, *Substitute* and *Anyway, Anyhow, Anywhere*," wrote *Reuters'* Dean Goodman.

> Bassist John Entwistle took over lead vocal duties from Daltrey to perform *My Wife*, which he dedicated to his ex-wives, one of whom was in the audience, he said.
>
> The generally relaxed show encountered some static during *Magic Bus*, which offered "a bit of a new groove," Townshend said by way of introduction. But it soon crashed to a halt with Townshend complaining that the tempo was too quick, and then taking the song into an extended jam. Touring drummer Zak Starkey apparently took offense at the complaint because Townshend later apologized to him during the encore, and hailed him as coming from the "University of Keith Moon."
>
> Other crowdpleasers included *Baba O'Riley*, which Townshend later referred to indirectly when telling the crowd about his "inestimable wealth" from selling his songs to Japanese car companies, *Pinball Wizard*, *Who Are You*, *Behind Blue Eyes* and *Won't Get Fooled Again*. Three songs were plucked from *Quadrophenia* – a reworked *Drowned*, *The Real Me* and *5:15*.
>
> The show wrapped with their 1965 signature hit *My Generation*, which Townshend introduced simply as "This is it."

The *Los Angeles Times* offered a more enthusiastic take on the show:

> The Who tore into a trio of '60s-era songs to open its set. *I Can't Explain*, *Anyway, Anyhow, Anywhere* and *Substitute* wobbled on slightly shaky legs, with a couple of missed cues and mismanaged harmonies. But the band gathered strength as it settled into material from its early-

---

[286] In 1933, Meher Baba had planned to appear at the venue and speak for the first time in eight years. "He told us we would be with Him forever, and we would get God-Realization, when He broke His silence in the Hollywood Bowl," Delia DeLeon wrote in 1990. However, this plan soon changed – Baba ultimately kept his silence for over forty years.

'70s masterworks *Who's Next* and *Quadrophenia*. The insurrectionary thrust behind such songs as *Won't Get Fooled Again* and *Baba O'Riley* dissipated long ago, but for sheer drama they remain two of rock's most affecting anthems. Townshend, who has recently switched back to electric from acoustic guitar, was a force of middle-aged nature, slashing through power chords with his trademark windmill arm maneuver, plucking out staccato leads, bounding impishly as in the days of yore.

Pete's daughter, Emma, joined him in California in time for the next show, which took place on 16 August at L.A.'s Verizon Ampitheater[287]. During the day, Pete and Emma took a helicopter ride to Irvine. "Flew over the new Getty museum, with a running commentary from my daughter Emma on what is inside, and the beauty of the gardens," Pete wrote the following day in his web-diary.

"I got bored yesterday," Pete wrote in his web-diary the day after the L.A. show. "About halfway through *Magic Bus* I suddenly felt like I'd been doing this for too long. I snapped out of it, I have to laugh at it all. I never expected this to be challenging. It is the ease with which we can knock this stuff out that leaves me aching for musical challenge. All I have to do to raise a cheer is swing my arm. It ain't art. But don't try it at home when you're holding a pick unless you want to lose your fingernails."

The band flew on a private plane from L.A. to San Diego on August 17 for their show that night at the San Diego Sports Arena. "I saw the big islands off the coast for the first time," Pete wrote in his web diary. "...San Diego is one of my favorite places in the world. I vacationed there recently, and I find the climate there most like a perfect English Summer rather than Californian. It's so mild and breezy. Terrific sailing..." That evening's show was well-received by the local press, which included the following review by the *San Diego Union Tribune*'s George Varga:

> Looking not unlike a rumpled deacon in his black suit, Townshend was in fine instrumental form, mixing soaring power chords with searing, blues-tinged leads. He apologized for his raspy vocals, although his singing seemed to improve as the evening went on, and his harmonies with Daltrey on *Behind Blue Eyes* and *The Kids Are Alright* provided two of the concert's most touching moments.
> ...Townshend was only half joking when he advised the crowd that he and his bandmates were

---

[287] Joe Walsh and Nicolas Cage were reportedly among the audience for this show.

"completely, totally, utterly deaf." But the mighty sound he and The Who created should continue to resound for years to come.

Pete was equally happy with the show, describing it as "fantastic" in his web diary entry the following day[288].

> I felt great and played better than I have so far...
> I feel better about life tonight. A couple of people did ask me if I enjoyed myself, and I said 'No!' But I did really, I played so well here and there I delighted myself. And we felt tight and crisp, like a band.

"Long live The Who," proclaimed *San Francisco Chronicle* writer Joel Selvin, after witnessing the band's 21 August show at the Shoreline Amphitheater, which took place two days after a stop in Seattle.

> The sun may long ago have set on the British Empire, but not all its glories have faded. Returning to action with the swashbuckling verve of musicians half their age, the three surviving members of the storied British rock band nearly destroyed a capacity crowd at Shoreline Amphitheatre on Monday with what bandleader Pete Townshend called "Who brutalism." Comeback tours by aging rockers tend to be wobbly affairs, with the musicians propped up by additional players, light shows, set design, anything to distract the audience from the band's lack of vitality.
> Not so the Who, who came out smoking. The inevitable *I Can't Explain* and *Substitute* led to a crunching *Anyway, Anyhow, Anywhere*, punctuated by a cataclysmic Townshend guitar solo complete with trademark windmill arm swings. For all of the nearly three-hour, 19-song concert, the musicians did not just revisit their halcyon years – they re-created the Who in all its splendor and magnificence. ...the band gave a performance as powerful and exciting as anything the Who has done on Bay Area stages since the '70s.
> It was nothing less than a return to form by one of the greatest rock bands of all time... At age 55, bald as a

---

[288] Pete spoke with Eddie Vedder's mother and two of his brothers backstage. "I asked how Eddie is feeling and she said he is doing very well considering the sadness surrounding the band at the moment," Pete wrote in his web diary. Nine fans died at the June 30, 2000 Pearl Jam-headlined Roskilde Festival in Denmark when the crowd surged toward the stage.

banker and still string-bean thin, Townshend was his cranky, peeved, masterful self at Shoreline. "I was so clever when I was young," he told the crowd, strumming the introduction of *Anyway, Anyhow, Anywhere*. "I'm so f--- stupid now." By the end of the exhausting evening, after he had slashed out hundreds of power chords, squeezed off thousands of squealing notes, chirped his harmony vocals behind the ever-youthful Roger Daltrey and presided over a performance that ran the gamut from chaos to precision, Townshend's face was wreathed in smiles. He knew it was good. One of the key reasons was drummer Starkey… Unlike Kenney Jones… Starkey can duplicate Moon's maniacal onslaught, which was an absolutely essential ingredient to the band's incendiary sound.

Although advertised as the Greatest Hits Tour 2000, the program contained some eccentricities. It wasn't just the near-exclusion of anything from the landmark rock opera *Tommy*, outside of an incidental performance of *Pinball Wizard*. The band also turned some lesser numbers into authentic epics – *I Don't Even Know Myself*, *Relay*, *Naked Eye*, *Let's See Action*. Townshend punched out a sublime *Drowned* by himself on acoustic guitar. But the show focused primarily on classic-rock Who – *Won't Get Fooled Again*, *Who Are You*, *Bargain*, *Behind Blue Eyes*, *Baba O'Riley*, even that latter-era turkey *You Better You Bet*.

…Who concerts for the past couple of decades have been largely lackluster, hollow shells of the towering emotional sieges that people who were there 30 or more years ago remember as if they were last month. As with last year's acoustic preview of the full reunion at the annual Bridge concert, the musicians onstage at Shoreline played for keeps. That, of course, was the real trademark of the Who. Townshend's guitar was an instrument he used to wage war. The entire range of human drama – hope, anguish, anger, rapture – was there for all to see. It was never merely a performance. It was life and death. Such urgency is hard to keep up, but Monday's concert was more than a reminder.

Pete explained the reason for the band's incendiary performance at Shoreline in his web-diary entry a few days later. "…when I went on stage I expected a feeling of God's presence," he wrote.

The two shows I'd done there before had been for Neil Young's Bridge School charity and there is no question that on those occasions a very powerful and benign spiritual presence warmed the event. At The Who show this month... there was not a trace of any benign and unconditional spiritual energy. Not that I could feel. It surprised me. I thought it was a defacto element of any Bay Area event. I was not angry, I was suddenly exposed and determined. So what I had to do was work, just to survive.

Following a 22 August date in Sacramento, The Who headed inland for a 24 August stop at the Pepsi Center in Denver. "Granted, Pete Townshend, Roger Daltrey and John Entwistle have taken the stage together and not produced sparks plenty of times in the past," wrote Mark Brown of the *Rocky Mountain News*.

> Thursday night, though, wasn't one of them. Trim, fit and full of fire, the band roared through two-plus hours of rock's classic moments, from *Substitute* to *You Better You Bet*, with Townshend taking flailing electric guitar solos.
> Without the horn sections, backing singers and what-not, Townshend's guitar, Entwistle's bass and Daltrey's voice had to pick up the slack. It wasn't *Live at Leeds*, but it would have been a stunning set from 30-year-olds, much less guys approaching mandatory retirement age. And it's almost eerie the way the youngster of the group, drummer Zak Starkey, has captured the drum sound of his father's late best friend.
> Townshend apologized for giving a greatest-hits set, but the rarities were plentiful, from *I Don't Know Myself*, to a delightful solo acoustic *I'm One*, to the encore of *Naked Eye* and Johnny Cash's *Ring of Fire*. The huge hits were there, of course, with everything from *I Can't Explain* to *Won't Get Fooled Again*, but the band also pulled out hits that are heard on the radio but rarely in concert – a sublime *Getting In Tune*, *Bargain* and a monstrous jam on Entwistle's classic *My Wife*.
> Monstrous jams were the mark of the evening, though, with everything from *5:15* to *The Kids Are Alright* getting extra guitar work as well as extra lyrics. Even the songs that you've heard just too many times in your life – *Behind Blue Eyes*, *Pinball Wizard* – were delivered with punch... it was a roaring rock show from start finish.

The second leg of the tour wrapped up with two shows in Texas, a 27 August date in Dallas, and a performance in Houston two nights later. "This leg is over," Pete wrote in his web diary after the Houston show[289].

> Good show tonight. Very hot and sweaty, just how I like it...I'm home tomorrow to see my son, partner, friends and Flash my dog. I'll be happy to put my feet up somewhere other than a hotel room – but life has not been hard. In Dallas the late meal I had yesterday (Swordfish) was just superb, one of those TRULY GREAT MEALS. Not sure how they do it in hotels with 400 rooms. I've lived well, and the reviews have been generous for a band that hasn't recorded a great new song for twenty years.

Following an almost month-long break, The Who returned to the U.S. in late September for the third and final leg of their North American tour. The first show of the leg took place at the outdoor MARS Music Amphitheatre near West Palm Beach, Florida. "It was hot and humid the way Roger likes it and we all felt excited to be back on stage," Pete wrote in a September 25 web-diary entry. "The audience was especially friendly, and the place was packed." The *Palm Beach Post* review was similarly enthusiastic:

> ...After years of performing with big orchestras, The Who are finally back to being The Who – that snarling, punkish band with plenty of youthful attitude and British cheek. ...despite the well-documented flare-ups between Daltrey and Townshend over the years, they seemed to be having a great time, telling silly one-liners and feeding off the energy of a wildly appreciative audience. The show's club-like set created a surprisingly intimate nature, with the band members close enough that Townshend had to occasionally duck when Daltrey would toss his mike.
> But what made the evening more than a heady nostalgia trip was the band's searing intensity. It's hard to

---

[289] And not soon enough, apparently. "...I am just about as bored as it's possible for a spoiled brat like me to be," Pete wrote in his web-diary a couple of days before the end of the second leg. "I sleep for as many hours as possible so I don't have to pretend I like being awake in the latest hotel room. I bury myself in the absorbing brilliance of a Jeffery Deaver novel and refuse to emerge until the next performance. I do not play golf or go sailing, for if I did I would not have enough energy or desperation left to play a decent show. I do not visit the local sites or go to art galleries. I do not accept invitations to dinner or 'home-cooked' meals. If the most glamorous woman in the world presented herself to me for sex and romance I would be unable to demonstrate even the slightest enthusiasm..."

talk about highlights, because there simply wasn't a low moment in the 20-song set...The Who jammed with unbelievable squall and fury.[290]

A similar rave review was submitted by *St. Petersburg Times*' Philip Booth after the band's performance at Tampa's Ice Palace a few days later:

> About 12,000 fans were treated to sturdy, often exciting performances of familiar favorites during a concert that began and ended with two songs dating back 35 years. *I Can't Explain*, all British Invasion bounce, had Townshend offering four ceremonial bowling-ball strikes on his guitar, and Daltrey executing the first of many microphone-twirling moves. The final *My Generation*, once a counterculture anthem, turned into a sprawling, feel-good jam, bolstered by Townshend's incisive guitar solo, tasty organ work by keyboardist John "Rabbit" Bundrick, and Zak Starkey's typically propulsive, swaggering drumming.
>
> Seldom a disappointing note was sounded in between, thanks in part to the real cohesion of these players, as opposed to the oversized ensembles that have turned previous Who shows into virtual revues.

The positive aura surrounding the band so far during the tour appeared to be in danger of evaporating when Pete ran into trouble during the leg's third show. "I've done something to my wrist at the show in Atlanta," Pete wrote in his web-diary just after the show at Phillips Arena on September 28. "I banged it on my guitar, and not entirely by accident I'm afraid to say...I can hardly type. I have redamaged it where I broke it in 1991... I think there may well be some lumpy shows ahead for me. I am going for an x-ray tomorrow. Ice Ice Ice for now..." He continued his report two days later, prior to a show in Cleveland scheduled for that night:

> Found a good ortho surgeon who with his physiotherapist x-rayed, heated, cooled, steroided, anti-inflammatoried my wrist and told me he really loved *Quadrophenia*. My hand was in good hands... Both the

---

[290] A Fort Lauderdale review of the same show gushed over Pete's playing: "...And there was Townshend to nail the point home, windmilling his arm across the guitar, ripping chords with a tensile power and single-string clarity that no other pair of hands can match. His playing has improved with age. Townshend has added confident soloing to his peerless rhythmic chops."

good surgeon and the physio are coming to see me tomorrow and I'm sure I will be fine for the show in Cleveland. The prognosis is that I can jump around and swing my arm as much as I like, what I have to watch is the flamenco! It's exacerbating the deeper arthritis I built up since the accident. I wish I could show you my x-ray. My wrist looks bionic. One of the old 1991 screws appears to have split the bone. But it's all healed pretty solid.

In any case it works well enough for the relatively unsophisticated jazz fusion pieces and Bach fugues I intend to interpret with the Who tomorrow, so don't panic... Take it from me, I can smash a guitar with one arm.

The band's show in Cleveland's Gund Arena two days later went off without a hitch despite Pete's wrist injury. "This was a good show, my wrist turned out OK," Pete wrote in his web diary. "I played *Sheraton Gibson* (which is about a BBQ I went to with the James gang and their manager Mike Belkin in around 1971). Sadly I didn't play it very well."

The wrist was again not an issue for the final stop of the U.S. tour, three shows in early October at Madison Square Garden. The Wallflowers (featuring Bob Dylan's son, Jacob, whom Pete described as "a very smart and balanced guy") opened for The Who on short notice when Jimmy Page was sidelined with a back injury. Pete's daughter Minta attended the show, as did David Bowie and Lenny Kravitz[291].

"...I'm looking forward to going home," Pete wrote in his web diary on October 7. "This has been just about the most pleasant, easiest and incident free tour I've ever done. I've had fun sometimes on stage, and always off stage... the shows have always been fulfilling for me. I've enjoyed playing my long self-indulgent solos, not just because I'm self-indulgent – it's just rare to be playing with such incredible musicians as Zak, Rabbit and John, I get going and I don't want to stop."

After a three week break, The Who were back at it again, kicking off the U.K. leg of the tour on October 30. Despite both band and fans having to battle through terrible weather[292] to get to the show, at Birmingham's National Exhibition Centre, the band "pumped out a great set," according to Matt Kent[293]. "They were not helped by the uncannily quiet crowd," wrote David Cheal of the *Daily Telegraph* in his review of the show. "...this show was hard to fault, except perhaps for some rather

---

[291] Pete also noted that his girlfriend attended every show of this leg.
[292] "The American tour legs were more like vacations than work, this is work," Pete wrote in his web-diary after a few shows in the U.K. "Tricky travel, lots of problems at home and work. Crap weather and the winter wasteland approaching."
[293] The bumpy plane ride to Birmingham left Pete feeling "slightly queasy", Kent reported on www.petetownshend.com.

aimless extemporization during *The Kids Are Alright*. They were tight, controlled, focused. If only the audience had done their bit and made some noise, this show would have been elevated to another level." The band returned to Birmingham a week and a half later, this time to a more enthusiastic crowd.

The U.K. leg's second show took place in Manchester three nights later. "Definitely THE show of the whole tour so far," Matt Kent commented from the enviable position of one who had seen each show of the tour, and therefore one of the very few individuals qualified to make such a statement. "With the audience on their feet from the very opening chords of *Can't Explain* the band went from strength to strength," Kent wrote in a web update. "The set included the surprise addition of *Mary Anne* as part of the encore and ended with a superlative version of *My Generation*, the best version, in my opinion, since the Leeds days."

"...Before an audience encompassing all generations, the Who delivered a breathtaking show, which not only made sense of their life's work, but also placed it in a new and unexpectedly vital context," reported *The Guardian*'s Dave Simpson.

> They began, appropriately, with three from the early days, when the band was fumbling towards some kind of meaningful future. *I Can't Explain, Anyway, Anyhow, Anywhere,* and *Substitute* were delivered with an energy that would shame bands half their age.
>
> The surviving trio, it must be said, looked pretty good. Townshend is more withered than John Entwistle or Roger Daltrey, but was still magnetic, windmilling with a fury that suggests he's finally over the lingering torpor induced by rehab. With Pete pointing to the ceiling, they delivered a quadruple whammy of *Baba O'Riley, Behind Blue Eyes, Don't Even Know Myself* and *Who Are You* with Ringo's son Zak Starkey handling Keith Moon's parts with aplomb. These songs of early-adulthood alienation and identity crisis take on a newly universal hue when performed by men in their 50s still searching for inner meaning. Similarly, Daltrey's primal howl during *Won't Get Fooled Again* is a pivotal moment, echoed by 10,000 voices in a remarkable collective gesture of post-millenial confusion and catharsis.
>
> Behind the drama, there is much humor. Townshend mock-wearily introduces *You Better You Bet...* as "the Who's last major British hit", before adding, cheekily, "the only one Robbie Williams hasn't pinched!"

Townshend may not relish a role as elder custodian of the nation's youth, but it suits him. As for the band, they are revitalized and again on top of their game. The Who are living, legendary examples of the extraordinary power that music can achieve.

"Of course I knew The Who were old – the three original members having a combined age of 166 and all that – but it still comes as a shock to see a balding, black-suited, stoop-shouldered man with the somber visage of a pallbearer attacking his guitar with such aggression," wrote *The Observer*'s Sam Taylor.

The look on Pete Townshend's face for the first few minutes of Thursday night's triumphant gig in Manchester is really quite disturbing – in a way that it wasn't when he was 25. It's the façade of serene respectability that makes Townshend's clenched jaw and frenzied windmilling arm seem more than an old rock star's stage tricks. You can practically see the demons seeping smokily from his fingertips.

…as a live act, they are up there with the best. You can certainly see why America has embraced them so fervently in their autumnal years. And, professional and energetic as they are, the band's appeal has nothing to do with the supernaturally fresh-faced, full-voiced Roger Daltrey or the white-bearded, supple-fingered John Entwistle, nor the more recent additions – keyboard maestro John 'Rabbit' Bundrick, and Zac Starkey doing a credible impersonation of Keith Moon. It's all about Townshend.

"I feel pretty good," Pete wrote in his internet diary on November 6, two days after completing a two-show stint in Glasgow. "I'm still healthy, though my fingers are completely destroyed again so I can't play as well as I could at the beginning of the tour. I have to work out a trade off compromise: will a great guitar solo make the show or a serious windmill? The windmill often wins."

The poor weather continued the following night for the band's show in Sheffield ("I can't quite make my mind up on this one," Matt Kent wrote in a web update. "It was either great or the worst show on the tour."), prior to arriving home in London for four sold out dates in London – the first at London Arena on November 13, followed by two at Wembley Arena on November 15 and 16 which would round out the band's U.K. tour. An additional date at the Royal Albert Hall on the 27 was a fund raiser for the Teenage Cancer Trust. "The Who are in London," Pete wrote in his internet diary the day of the London Arena show. "We have four major shows ahead of us sold out to the absolute limit with thousands of people still clamoring for tickets. It looks like the Albert Hall will raise twice as much for the Teenage Cancer Society as anticipated, and ending this current phase of Who work with a charity show is appropriate and logical. It is how we began again after all."

The opening act for The Who's London Arena show was Pete's old friend Joe Strummer with his new band, The Mescaleros. Strummer's band set the stage well for Pete and company, providing "one of the most storming warm-ups of the year," according to *The Times*.

The Who didn't fare too badly, either, according to *The Times*' Paul Sexton:

> ...they began with a convincingly brisk and unadorned re-creation of the early days with *I Can't Explain*, *Substitute* and *Anyway Anyhow Anywhere*. Townshend welcomed us to the "bumhole of London" and told us to f*** off – the sort of abuse that was strangely reassuring. What unfolded thereafter was quite unmissable but also troublingly uneven. There were treats, such as *Bargain*, *Behind Blue Eyes* and a genuinely jaw-dropping bass solo by John Entwistle during *5:15*, and in the wake of Townshend's recent revival of the *Lifehouse* project came welcome reassessments of outtakes from its original sessions, *Relay* and *Don't Even Know Myself*. But Roger Daltrey has remained a magnificently lusty frontman for so long, it was hard to face that he was now falling at some vocal hurdles, the strain sometimes showing in his expression, while Townshend seemed bent on distorting some of his undying classics into long and unnecessary jams like some dust-covered FM radio axeman.
>
> During the encore, Daltrey strapped on an acoustic guitar and was considerably more at ease, even mastering a falsetto detail at the end of a winning *The Kids Are Alright*. However, the elongation effect was especially upsetting on the closing of *My Generation*, which started out with fuel injection in the outside lane but ended up puttering along lamely on the hard shoulder.

A couple of nights later, the two-night stint at Wembley Arena began, with Pete feeling "a bit sniffy", according to his November 15 web-diary entry. "An old stamping ground for me and The Who, [Wembley Arena] is just around the corner to where I live, and it's good to be able to invite so many friends and family too." The 2000 tour's final date – which was nearly canceled due to Pete's worsening chest cold – took place at the same venue the following night. Pete's illness dictated that he forego his usual *Drowned/I'm One* solo medley. "It was not the way I wanted to go out, but there we have it," Pete wrote the following day. The band reportedly added the 'you are forgiven' chorus from *A Quick One* to the end of *My Generation*.

Nine days after the tour, Pete was back in action, beginning a two-day rehearsal for the November 27 Teenage Cancer Trust benefit at the Royal Albert Hall, the proceeds of which were slated for facilities and services for cancer-stricken teens[294]. Special guests at the event included Bryan Adams, Noel Gallagher, Eddie Vedder[295], Paul Weller and comedian Phil Jupitus. Weller brought the sheet music for *Sunrise* to the rehearsal as a potential song for he and Townshend to perform during the show. "I had forgotten how pretty it is," Pete remarked, causing him to consider playing the song either with Weller or just solo, but eventually deciding on a Townshend/Weller run through of *So Sad About Us* because "it has more punch."[296]

The sold-out show wound up clocking in at 3 ½ hours, including the Weller/Townshend rendition of *So Sad About Us*, performances of *I'm One* (which *NME* referred to as "stunning"), *Let's See Action* and *Getting In Tune* with Eddie Vedder, *Behind Blue Eyes* with Bryan Adams, and *Won't Get Fooled Again* with Noel Gallagher. The show closed with a medley of *My Generation/See Me Feel Me/Listening To You*, with Vedder, Adams, and teenagers representing the Teenage Cancer Trust.

With the completion of the Royal Albert Hall show at the end of November, all Who activities for the foreseeable future once again ceased. A European tour had been considered, but Pete opted out. "I really do need to catch up on some vitally important solo projects and personal work," he wrote in his web-diary on November 15.

> But I hope we tour in Europe before we pretend to die, perhaps in early 2002? In the meantime perhaps we can play a good live TV show that reaches a large part of Europe – is there still a 'RockPalast'? Or perhaps we can play a charity show somewhere in Central or Eastern

---

[294] The Who, who had already reportedly donated £250,000 from their U.S. tour earnings to the Teenage Cancer Trust, presented the charity with an additional £1,000,000 during the Royal Albert Hall show.

[295] "He's come all the way from Hawaii, come 9,000 miles to see us," Pete said of avid surfer Vedder from the stage. "He's a great friend of mine, my family, this band."

[296] "I suggested to Pete we duet on *Sunrise*, a beautiful song from *The Who Sell Out*," Weller wrote in *Mojo* in 2004. "It was much too complicated for me though, so he saved the day by suggesting we do *So Sad About Us* instead. I managed that one, but just being able to share a stage with The Who was something else," Weller wrote, recalling that "It was amazing to play with my childhood heroes."

Europe that will have the same effect? I don't want Who fans in Europe to think we have deliberately left them out. We left the matter until today to decide, and I have decided I can't go on – not right now. I need rest, but I also need to recharge.

...Roger, John and I intend to go on seeing each other as often as we can to continue to explore what we might do next as a creative band. The Who brand has never been stronger.

So the future's been seen, and it is not the void it once was, neither does it need to be ever again – not while I'm pretending to be alive. So take heart. There will be a pause. Maybe even a long pause. There will probably be no new Who studio album in 2001, it doesn't quite seem possible. But there may well be new Who songs – though today I have no idea quite where they will come from.

What there will not be is an end.

I have profited from this tour in more ways than I can explain. There has been money of course. And there are cynics who will say that's the only reason we got together. It doesn't matter. What matters is that it was – all in all – wonderful... My legs hurt, my teeth hurt, my ears hurt, my fingers hurt, my brain hurts and my whole psyche burns from all the stuff – good and bad and in between – being spouted by Who experts on the internet today. But my heart feels good. It feels like one of those extraordinary days that Keith Moon didn't die. They were always good days.

Chapter 19

> *"My creative energy is located elsewhere. It's a bit like being a painter who suddenly decides to change color or change process. I don't get out my electric guitar and start thrashing away at four in the morning with a bottle of brandy in my hand. I don't allow myself to be that angry any more. These days I'm more likely to get worked up and write a fucking string quartet or something!"*
> - Pete Townshend, 2001

> *"Outside The Who I am working on a number of projects, which may or may not come to fruition. They all require money of course, so I am glad I earned some this summer. I have a music publishing company, a recording studio, a sailboat, a domestic life. I also run a really good charity which usually keeps a low profile, but does a lot of valuable work with addicts, alcoholics and both the victims and 'recovering' perpetrators of sexual abuse. But I myself am always a Grade One addict-accident waiting to reoccur. Certainly what I do on stage always surprises me. It doesn't feel like me sometimes. I have to measure my lust for life very, very carefully and I take impartial advice wherever I can on how to live a relatively normal life (I have a counselor rather than a therapist today). Like most people in the entertainment industry I'm a nut."*
> - Pete Townshend, 2002

In December, 2000, Pete began sifting through the mountain of demos which had accumulated since his last solo album, *Psychoderelict*, hit the stores in 1993. In early January he reported that he had approximately 1400 pieces of music logged, "of which 400 might be potentially good", and only 40 of which were actual songs. During the previous year, Pete had been in contact with Helen 'Spike' Wilkins, the producer of the first two *Scoop* installments, with an eye toward compiling a third effort. "[*Scoop 3*] ... is still a little in the air," Pete told *In Music We Trust* back in 2000. "The producer has had some personal problems and we slowed the whole business down to give her some space. So the next *Scoop* is as yet unfashioned. It will represent the closest thing to a new studio album for me. It will certainly contain brand new music as well as old demos and live material."

"I had a good Christmas and New Year, but I've been finding it rather strange doing creative work again in a home studio," Pete wrote in a January 5 web-diary entry. "I keep wanting to work deep into the night, and feel irritated with anyone who, or any event or commitment that threatens to prevent me working whenever the whim takes me. I am really enjoying it though. My studio is powerful and simple. And I now have a dedicated DV editing suite (which is just a computer on a table!) so I feel very professional."

Despite a couple of power outages at his home in the early New Year, Pete wrote in a web update on January 27 that he was "...having a lot of fun in my studio at the moment... I've been working every day since early January and have managed to complete about seven pieces for *Scoop 3*. Much of that time has been spent listening to the last few batches of old music, so I am being quite productive really."

A little over a month later, Pete added another update which stated that he'd now readied 12 pieces of music for *Scoop 3*, and had spent the "first six weeks of the year going through piano pieces written between 1995 and 1999... They are pseudo-classical-cum-jazz pieces. No words." After taking a short break at the end of February, Pete returned on March 8 with another web entry. "I have now completed about 14 'free' piano pieces and I'm moving on to another period of writing. I have come up with a few lyrics that seem quite cool, but I am going to begin the next batch of recording with a few new acoustic guitar pieces."

The guitar pieces Pete was referring to were recorded on one of his new Collings acoustic guitars which he'd purchased during a recent trip to New York (perhaps while The Who were there the previous October). Pete recorded one piece of music while 'playing-in' one of the guitars a few days prior to Christmas. Named simply *Collings*, it was included on *Scoop 3*. "Helen included it here and I am glad because I am especially proud of it," Pete wrote in the album's liner notes. "The guitar is a special, but quite recent, Collings made in Austin, Texas. It actually played this little piece itself I feel. I used a tuning here that is quite new to me. Reading recently about Bert Jansch one of the guitar heroes of my youth I saw reference to 'DADGAD'; a tuning that allows unskilled folk players to knock out a three chord trick using a single finger... A very useful tuning I find." Another Collings piece recorded during this period was posted on Pete's website for fans to download.

The completed *Scoop 3* album, released in October 2001, continued the series' tradition by presenting further Who/Pete Townshend classics in demo form, along with experimental tracks and some items which were omitted from their respective projects' final release. Fitting the first category are demos of *However Much I Booze* (titled *No Way Out*), *Rough*

Boys (here known as *Tough Boys*), *Can You See The Real Me*, and *Eminence Front*. The album also included *Teresa*, the predecessor to *Athena* which Pete recorded the day after his amorous encounter with – and rejection by – Teresa Russell, along with a heavy dose of recent instrumental tracks.

"...as the songs and song sketches intertwine and twist with the instrumentals," wrote *music.com*'s Stephen Thomas Erlewine in his review.

>...the collection gets a meditative, reflective feel, creating a bit of an aural self-portrait, which ironically enough means that it flows better as an album than any of his projects since *White City*.
>
>However, it may mean that those legions of diehard fans looking for a collection overflowing with unheard songs, starkly revelatory early demos, and covers – like on the first two *Scoop* releases – may be a little disappointed, because there simply aren't as many. But they are here, in the form of previously unheard songs like *Commonwealth Boys* and *I Like It the Way It Is* as well as early versions of *Rough Boys*..., *However Much I Booze*..., and – most remarkably – *Eminence Front* and *Athena*..., in slower renditions that reveal the heart of the songs. Actually, that's true for most of the material here, as the selections from *Who By Numbers*, *Quadrophenia*, *Face Dances*, *All the Best Cowboys Have Chinese Eyes*, and *Iron Man* – even songs that worked brilliantly on the albums – sound more of a piece when delivered in these delicate, passionate, synth-heavy but warm homemade versions, especially when they're bridged by Townshend's evocative instrumentals. It does wind up sounding like a musical diary, and if that isn't enough to satisfy listeners who have eagerly awaited a third *Scoop* for over a decade, they're simply ungrateful, since few musicians would have the guts or the inclination (or the material, for that matter) to release something as raggedly lovely and personal as this.

As a result of Pete's recent work, some pieces of music, such as the aforementioned *Collings*, were offered as free downloads on his website. "For those of you looking forward to conventional songs I'm sure some stuff will surface soon," Pete wrote in a January 2001 web update. "However, I will be less likely to put demos of 'proper' songs up as mp3s, at least until I've shared them with Roger and John, just in case they will work as Who songs. So what goes up will tend to be Who rejects," he wrote, adding that many of his solo gems were 'Who rejects'.

Following up on his promise to get together with Roger Daltrey to work on possible Who songs, Pete offered an early March web entry stating, "Roger and I are not working together yet. He has played me three really good songs, but I don't feel they quite fit the current Who brief." Pete added that he had written some songs of his own, "but I am certain they will not work for The Who without a major change in our musical direction." Two months later, he told the *Daily Telegraph*, "I have my usual clutch of daft ideas. Probably the daftest is to try to write some grand new project that might suit the Who. We shall see."

The Who were invited to perform at the 43rd annual Grammy Awards in Los Angeles in February 2001, but declined since Pete was busy in the studio. The band received a Lifetime Achievement Award. "As one of the key players in the British Invasion and the "mod" movement of the mid-60s, the Who are easily recognized as one of the most powerful and innovative bands in rock history," read the Grammy press release.

In Spring, 2001, Pete's interests returned to the stage, this time focusing on getting *Quadrophenia* up and running. "Trevor Nunn, the director of the National Theatre here in London has at last given his blessing to the development of a script and new score for a theatre musical version of *Quadrophenia*," Pete wrote on www.eelpie.com in March, adding that he was "very, very excited and pleased" at the development. Playwright Joe Penhall was enlisted to rewrite the story for the stage, "with myself interfering a fair bit," Townshend added.

"Joe produced a very striking and original dramatic treatment for the major part of the story," Pete wrote on www.eelpie.com.

With a few clever strokes he solved many of the structural and dramatic problems of staging this work. Then he and I had a couple of creative meetings to establish how to get the most out of the music without overloading any future production with over ambitious production values. As I played some of the songs to Joe on acoustic guitar and keyboard – demonstrating how well some of the pieces work when played in a simple way – he hit on the phrase 'The Cappucino Kid version' of *Quadrophenia*. We decided it was important to try all the songs and music from the piece, however complex they may sound on the Who's album, to test a very simple band line-up. We decided on acoustic guitar, acoustic piano and percussion (not drums). I was certain the music would be wonderful played in this way, but only if we could test it with musicians who would play my music really accurately. This meant using musicians of the caliber of those who toured the piece with the Who for their multi-media stage presentations in the

USA and Europe from 1996 to 1998. I decided to ask John Bundrick (Rabbit) to play keyboards, and my brother Simon to play guitar.

A four day workshop was held in late April at the Bush Theatre (formerly the New Carlton Irish Club where The High Numbers had auditioned for Andrew Loog Oldham in 1964) to work through the new version of the play. In addition to Rabbit and Simon, percussionist John O'Hara, the Bristol Old Vic's music director, was brought in. Music director and old friend Billy Nicholls enlisted two vocalists – Richard Oliver, and Suzi Webb. Webb had toured with The Who on the 1996-97 *Quadrophenia* tour as a backing vocalist. "The workshop went very well," Pete reported on www.eelpie.com. "…Everything sounded terrific played by Rabbit, Simon and John O'Hara (who mainly banged away at bongos and congas). The singers worked hard, aided by Simon on certain character vocals, and we knew with absolute certainly that Joe's 'Capuccino Kid' version was going to work." The proceedings were recorded by Oceanic technical manager Lincoln Fong.

Townshend and Penhall went their separate ways after the *Quadrophenia* workshop, with Pete committed to a benefit performance at the La Jolla Playhouse and working on the completion of *Scoop 3*, and Penhall readying his play *Blue/Orange* for London's West End. When the pair met in July 2001 to review Penhall's newly completed script, Townshend's enthusiasm hadn't waned. "It is excellent," Pete wrote on his website. "I am really excited now that we have a solid theatrical foundation for *Quadrophenia*," he wrote, adding that he would "like to see a production of *Quadrophenia* mounted somewhere in the UK, preferably at The National Theatre." The completed script was duly submitted to Nunn. "Trevor Nunn knows Joe's work, and is a great ally," Pete wrote. "I have invited him to consider this project. But as we stand today, the paper feels right at last, the music has always been great – but now it works in a truly theatrical framework – and all we need now is a starting gun."

"There is exciting news in the wind about *Quadrophenia* and its theatrical life," Pete wrote in a November 2004 web entry, more than three years after the workshop. "The development during 2002 with Trevor Nunn for the National Theatre hiccupped, but various provincial British theatres have shown very serious interest in mounting a production. There is also an investigation of its theatrical potential by a major American producer."

On May 24, 2001, Pete attended the 46th annual Ivor Novello[297] Awards ceremony at Le Meridien Grosvenor House on Park Lane in

---

[297] In 1933 Delia DeLeon took Ivor Novello to see Meher Baba, after which Baba said, "He is my man," according to DeLeon. Baba attended Novello's current play as his guest, and following the show, according to DeLeon, Novello "invited [Baba] to stay at his home whenever He wished."

London. The Ivors are known as the top internationally recognized honors for British songwriters. Others slated for recognition that evening were David Gray, Stevie Wonder, The Clash, Iron Maiden, and Neil Morrissey (better known as the man behind Bob the Builder). It wasn't until around three hours into the ceremony that Pete was called to the stage to receive his Lifetime Achievement award. "Despite enthusiastic applause," wrote the *Daily Telegraph*'s Neil McCormick, "I think it is fair to say the rock legend was not particularly overwhelmed."

Casually attired in short-sleeved shirt and jeans, Townshend announced to the designer-clad assembly: "I did all this crap so I could have my own swimming-pool. And I'm not in it!" He suggested that if they speeded proceedings up a bit, he might still catch a few precious rays of sunshine.

...Townshend was joking, of course, but there was a tangible edge to his remarks. As soon as the last speech was made and the lights in the ballroom went up, Townshend could be spotted pulling on his denim jacket, brushing off the attentions of wellwishers as he made a beeline for the exit, with his beautiful young girlfriend clinging to his arm.

"The problem is they seem to have forgotten they gave me a very similar award at the 'end' of my career 20 years ago," he added, referring to a 1981 award for Outstanding Services to British Music. "As for Lifetime Achievement – I'm far from dead."

June 22 and 23 2001 saw Pete back in San Diego, performing two benefit shows for the financially troubled La Jolla Playhouse. Tickets to the performances at the tiny 550-seat theater cost anywhere from $100 to $1,000, raising over $360,000. Pete played solo for both sold-out audiences, which included fans who'd flown in from as far away as Japan and Australia to witness their hero in such an intimate setting.

"I'm going to be really quiet," Pete told the crowd on the first night, according to George Varga of the *San Diego Union Tribune*. "Then, after a perfectly timed pause, he added: "To start with."

His 102-minute performance found him alternating between acoustic guitars and a grand piano, which at times electronically triggered gently swelling orchestral accents. Exuding a warmth and charm more common to living rooms than rock conerts, he mixed stripped-down versions of such Who gems as *Behind Blue Eyes*, *Cut My Hair*, *Eminence Front*, *I'm One* and the show-opening *Pinball*

Wizard with such choice Townshend solo album cuts as *Slit Skirts*, *Let My Love Open the Door* and the Dylanesque country-blues of *Sheraton Gibson*.

He also included the tender ballad *Heart To Hang On To*, from *Rough Mix*, his 1977 album with now-deceased Small Faces bassist Ronnie Lane. And he paid heartfelt tribute to blues great John Lee Hooker, who died Thursday, by performing a spare, Mose Allison-styled rendition of the vintage Cab Calloway hit, *St. James Infirmary*.

It wasn't until the encore of *Won't Get Fooled Again*, The Who's epic, 1971 anthem of youthful idealism and alienation, that Townshend strapped on an electric guitar, pumped up the volume and executed his patented windmill-like arm motions, to giddy cheers. Replete with stuttering, whammy-bar accents and blistering lead work, the rousing encore contrasted nicely with the acoustic version of *Fooled* performed just three songs earlier.

Following a quiet summer (back in January, Pete had announced plans to "take the entire summer off to go sailing"), October 10, 2001 saw The Who back in action, this time performing a twenty-minute set in front of a mostly uniformed crowd of police, firefighters and other emergency workers – and a TV audience of several million – at the Concert for New York, a star-studded benefit at Madison Square Garden for the victims of the September 11 terrorist attacks on the World Trade Center and the Pentagon. Due to the sensitive nature of the proceedings (well over 3,000 people had died as a result of the attacks a month earlier), there was much deliberation as to the content of the set list. "There was a lot of talk about "Should we play the heavy stuff or not?" and I just said, "We should just do what we do, we shouldn't rationalize this too much"," Pete told *Rolling Stone*'s Chris Heath in June, 2002.

> I went into Eric [Clapton]'s dressing room and into Billy Joel's dressing room, watching the monitors. James Taylor was on, singing *Fire and Rain*, and everybody was crying... I think if we had known what the atmosphere was going to be like in advance, we would have played a different kind of show. When I came off, I thought, "I went out there with a fucking sneer on my face and I machine-gunned the audience! What the fuck?" But it was OK.

They ended up playing *Who Are You*, *Baba O'Riley*, *Behind Blue Eyes*, and *Won't Get Fooled Again*. "Although the majority of performers erred on the side of reverential sentimentality, The Who turned in an emotional yet powerful and electric performance," Matt Kent wrote in a 2004 *Mojo* special edition. For The Who it was an important show that exposed their talents to a new generation of music fans." Pete and Roger joined an all-star gathering at the end of the show, led by Paul McCartney, for renditions of *Let It Be* and McCartney's new song, *Freedom*.

While in New York for this show, Pete was also slated to record a guitar track for the David Bowie song *Slow Burn*, which would see inclusion on Bowie's new album *Heathen*[298]. Pete's playing on the album was "the most eccentric and aggressive guitar I've heard Pete play, quite unlike anything else he's done recently," Bowie told Bruce Simon in 2002. The last time Pete had recorded with Bowie was in 1980, when he played on *Because You're Young*, a track from the album *Scary Monsters (And Super Creeps)*. The following month, Pete was again in the studio, contributing guitar work on three tracks for Mick Jagger's solo album *Goddess in the Doorway*. Other musicians who contributed their services to the new Jagger album were Bono, Wyclef Jean and Lenny Kravitz.

As 2001 came to a close, plans were under way for another U.S. Who tour, much the same in structure as their immensely successful 2000 jaunt. Pete had originally planned to spend much of 2002 writing a novel, entitled *The Boy Who Heard Music*, which he expected to finish by June. He would then have "the rest of the year to go sailing or do whatever I want," he told *Rolling Stone*'s Chris Heath in 2002. It had been nearly six years since Pete had met his girlfriend, singer/songwriter Rachel Fuller[299], and, he told *The Sun*'s Dominic Mohan, "We're going well. There's some stability in my life…"

Pete soon agreed to perform some shows in New York, "to keep [Roger] amused," in Pete's words. "Our manager was on the phone the next day to say, "This is arrogance, to think that you can go back to America now and just play a couple of shows." I said, "OK, just book what you need to book." Soon, a full-fledged North American tour was on the table. Pete found himself in the unusual position of reacting positively to the prospect of a Who tour[300]. "This is something that I'm really quite inclined to do at the moment," he told Heath.

> …It is something I am doing for Roger and John and for other people in the Who's camp. It's not just a

---

[298] *The Guardian*'s Dave Simpson reported in June 2002 that "…Townshend eventually had to mail his contributions by post, after arriving at the studio with "bloodied knuckles" from, implausibly, doing windmills while practicing."

[299] Pete reportedly met Fuller, nearly thirty years his junior, at Sanctuary Studios in 1996 when he was rehearsing with The Who.

[300] Pete later asserted that Rachel Fuller was instrumental in encouraging him to resume touring and playing live.

favor; it's also, in a sense, a thank-you, an acknowledgment of solidarity and friendship.

It sounds patronizing to say that [Roger's] grateful, but I think, in a way, I'm grateful, too, for pushing sixty and being in a band where you can get together with a couple of old mates and rely on some kind of weird cosmic energy to inhabit you and inhabit the audience. And it's pretty bloody reliable. And you can use it for all kinds of things. You can use it for charity events, you can use it to buy yourself a boat if you want to, you can use it to simply go out and enjoy playing music. What you can't use it for is creative work. Unfortunately. So the next bit of the Who's jigsaw puzzle has been the bit where Roger has been fighting hardest, which is to get the Who back into the studio and doing new, fresh creative work. What's been an uphill struggle has been for me to get Roger to accept that it's going to be incredibly fucking hard, and it'll probably be terrible. And he's willing to spend a couple of years producing something which is absolutely terrible. I can't afford to do that.

In early January, Pete announced in a web posting entitled "Oh dear I have to get off my arse" that The Who would be playing three "warm up shows" prior to two previously announced charity concerts in early February at the Royal Albert Hall. "A U.S. tour in three legs is also emerging in sketch-form from the desk of Who manager Bill Curbishley – probably starting in L.A. in June and ending in the Northeast in August. It could all change though…" In its final form, the scheduled North American tour was a 26-date affair, and was expected to draw $1 million per night.

The warm-up shows ultimately took place on January 27 (Pete smashed his guitar at the end of this show) and 28 at the 2,000-seat Portsmouth Guildhall, followed a few days later with a show at the 1,400-seat Watford Coliseum. The Royal Albert Hall shows, organized by Roger Daltrey and Harvey Goldsmith, benefited the Teenage Cancer Trust and took place on 7 and 8 February as part of a five-night run of benefit shows for the charity.

"Those shows saw the band reinstate a number of songs from *Tommy*, as well as reintroducing some old cover versions, including *Summertime Blues*, *Young Man Blues* and *Baby Don't You Do It* into the set[301]," Matt Kent wrote in a 2004 *Mojo* article. "The first night's show at

---

[301] "The actual reality of it is when you start to play something that you haven't played for a long time and in some cases 20 years, it takes you back in a very, very real way to when you were younger, when you were, in my case, sadder and more frightened and more arrogant and when Keith Moon, our drummer, was alive," Pete told *The Sun* the day after one of the

the Royal Albert Hall didn't gel, but the chemistry was right for the following evening, showing that the band still enjoyed the sort of unparalleled rapport with their audience that had marked out their early days in Shepherd's Bush." The second of these shows proved to be John Entwistle's last public appearance with The Who.

The first night found Pete in a raucous mood. "…boy, was Townshend in a strange zone Thursday night," wrote *The Times*' Richard Morrison of the first show.

> When not performing his windmill-action guitar parts with real physical venom during numbers such as *Amazing Journey* and *Pinball Wizard*, he played the role of the bolshie old rocker to the hilt, cheerfully insulting members of the audience, and complaining about his flimsy American guitar as he bashed it sharply against his hip.
>
> …The perennial problem with rock reunion shows, and especially charity rock reunion shows, is that the original edgy spirit and adrenaline-fuelled aggression of a band such as The Who tends to get buried in an all-pervading aura of nice. But that wasn't the case here.
>
> …we…heard the band wallop through a sequence of favorites – *I Can't Explain*, *Substitute* and *Anyway Anyhow Anywhere* – with such genuinely pugnacious glee that it was difficult not to believe that this time they really did mean business.
>
> It was as if they had finally got past the idea of being embarrassed or apologetic about playing these anthems of youthful protest now that they are all – with the exception of the drummer Zak Starkey – in their late fifties, and have reached a point where they once again feel comfortable inhabiting them instead. And while it was too nostalgic, and occasionally too scrappy, to rank as a great performance, it was certainly something special. My Generation, indeed.

The Guardian's John Aizlewood painted a similar picture of Townshend's mood.

> "God, this is boring," sighs Pete Townshend, before embarking upon a version of *5:15* that ends in a 10-minute

---

Teenage Cancer Trust shows. "Yesterday we started to play a song called *Young Man Blues* and I got into it and my hand was completely covered in blood. I was playing the way that I used to play – I used to knock a couple of fingernails off within about five minutes. There's an adrenalin rush – you don't feel anything."

instrumental free-for-all of such dreariness that The Whos leader is not the only one to feel downhearted. Townshend's mean-spirited capriciousness is all part of the Who's volatile marriage, but, like a boorish uncle at a family christening, he can't help but overdo it. The show is singer Roger Daltrey's fundraiser for the Teenage Cancer Trust, whose banners lurk guiltily stage left and right. Daltrey, all oafish charm and hairless chest, does an impassioned charity awareness speech before the encore. Townshend returns to the stage muttering, "I don't know what he said, but it's all lies. Who gives a shit?" The toes of the Royal Albert Hall's crowd collectively curl.

The Who's creative flame may be long extinguished but, as proved by an impressively loud trawl through their former glories, the band can still pack a punch. *Teenage Wasteland* [sic], propelled by John "Rabbit" Bundrick's booming keyboards, retains its operatic grace; *Won't Get Fooled Again* is as articulate as a protest song ever gets; *I'm Free* remains a beguiling anti-authority manifesto.

…They end with a dreadful version of Mose Allison's *Young Man Blues*, Eddie Cochran's *Summertime Blues* and *My Generation*, during which, contrary old cuss that he is, Townshend finally gets a twinkle in his eyes. A nostalgia trip, then, but at least they omitted *Magic Bus* and didn't smash their instruments.

Pete later attributed much of his quirky behavior that evening to a newfound affinity for pretending to be drunk onstage. While this may provide an explanation for his aborting a solo acoustic version of *Drowned* when he forgot the words, it was certainly the reason behind his falling off the stage during *Young Man Blues*. "I need to end the show," Pete explained to Chris Heath of *Rolling Stone* when asked what thought process is involved in the decision of pretending to be drunk. "I enjoy the fact that if I pretend to be drunk for fifteen minutes, the crowd go wild. And, you know, I'm a recovering alcoholic and it's a good laugh to pretend to be drunk. But to be celebrated for it, there's a kind of weird irony of it where, in actual fact, one of the only reasons I can be up there at the moment is because I'm healthy."

As a result of Pete's departure from the stage that night at the Royal Albert Hall, a female fan was injured, which resulted in Pete reconsidering his actions. "Yeah, I've decided to stop doing that," he told Heath.

I actually had to meet with a girl who I hurt. I fell on her with my guitar, and she could have sued me or sued the band or the hall or something, but she didn't – because she's right in the front row, she's obviously a hard-nosed fan. My guitar fell on her neck and damaged her collarbone. And I didn't hear about it until quite recently, and she wrote a letter saying, "I can't believe that you haven't sent a letter saying sorry." And I was – I didn't fucking know about it. And she came and we talked about it. And I was, "What was I doing? Oh, that's right, I was pretending to be drunk" [laughs].

Rehearsals for The Who's 2002 U.S. summer tour took place at Oceanic studios in mid-June, the proceedings filmed for use by tour sponsor JBL. The band introduced some seldom-used live material into the lineup during the rehearsals, including *Eminence Front, Sea & Sand, Another Tricky Day* and *Music Must Change*. Two weeks later, preparing to kick off their second major U.S. tour in as many years, the band was rocked by tragedy. Just before noon on June 27, the day prior to the band's first scheduled show at The Joint in Las Vegas, John Entwistle was found dead in his sixth floor room at the Hard Rock Hotel & Casino, just off the strip. It was later determined that Entwistle, who was already taking medication for a heart condition, had "a significant amount of cocaine" in his system at the time of his death, according to Ron Flud, the Clark County coroner. This combination had brought on not an overdose, but a fatal heart attack. "You've got a lethal drug on board at the time you have a bad heart," Flud told *CNN*. "That's a bad combination."

While grieving was first on everyone's mind, the question of the fate of the tour hung over everyone's heads. Daltrey deferred to Townshend as to the band's direction at this point, and the decision was soon reached to forge ahead with a session player[302]. Pete chose to contact old friend Pino Palladino, a veteran Welsh bassist who'd worked with Townshend on *White City* and had been in the *Psychoderelict* tour lineup.[303] Palladino, about to leave Philadelphia having just wrapped up recording sessions with hip-hop artist Common, was notified of Entwistle's death by his wife. Shocked at the news of the death of his friend, he soon received a call from Bill

---

[302] "I had to push down a lot of emotion," Pete told *Mojo* in 2004. "...It took me all night to decide."

[303] In addition to his work with Townshend, Palladino had played with Daltrey, Jeff Beck, Eric Clapton, Peter Gabriel, David Gilmour, Elton John, Phil Collins, Tina Turner, Melissa Etheridge, Don Henley, Celine Dion, Rod Stewart, Tears for Fears, Gary Numan, Joan Armatrading, Chaka Kahn, B.B. King, Luciano Pavarotti, and Howard Jones, to name a few of the hundreds of artists on his resume. "I'm thrilled the way God planned to have Pino Palladino in an airport waiting in Philadelphia," Pete told the crowd from the stage at Mountain View's Shoreline Amphitheater on July 3.

Curbishley, asking if he could fill in. He agreed to assume the role of Who bassist, despite the obviously awkward and potentially uncomfortable times which may have awaited him. Palladino flew to Los Angeles that evening (June 28). "When I got to the hotel in L.A. that night, Pete met me and said, "We don't expect you to copy John's parts or playing entirely; it wouldn't be right, anyway,"" Palladino told *Bass Player* in 2004. ""We just want you to play as loud as you can bear. This is a loud band and the bass plays a key role, so you'll have to fill that space.""

The decision to continue the tour was immediately alternately praised and questioned among Who fans and the media. "For my part I am not attempting to deliberately establish any sense of memorial or tribute to John," Pete wrote in a web update shortly after the decision was made to continue.

> Unlike others I entirely respect (including many of John's friends and family) I don't feel I know for certain that John would have wanted us to go on. I simply believe we have a duty to go on, to ourselves, ticket buyers, staff, promoters, big and little people. I also have a duty to myself and my dependent family and friends. I also want to help guide Roger and the rest of the band at this time, all of whom have been shaken by John's death.
>
> …My immediate mission is to complete this tour in good heart, and to remember John in my quiet and private times. It is easy for me to smile when I remember John. I loved him unconditionally. I will try hard to not to fall into any of my usual mini-depressions on this tour. Pino is determined to enjoy the music, and so am I.

June 29 and 30 marked Pino Palladino's crash course on playing bass with The Who, as the band ran through a rehearsal each day[304]. "I knew some Who tunes, but not a whole lot, honestly, especially from the bass perspective," Palladino told *Bass Player*'s Chris Jisi in March, 2004. His first night in L.A. was spent listening to Who CDs, making notes and learning songs. "It was pretty scary listening to John's amazing playing," he noted. "We had two short rehearsals to learn about 25 songs. By the second one I realized I had to play a lot more notes than I was used to playing to fill up the spaces between Pete's guitar and Zak Starkey's drums. Pete or Roger would say, "When we get to this section, step out a bit more.""

On July 1, 2002, just four days after Entwistle's sudden death, The Who kicked off their U.S. tour at the Hollywood Bowl, with Counting

---

[304] The dates set for Vegas' The Joint on June 28 and Irvine Verizon Amphitheater on the 29th were rescheduled.

Crows opening. The sold-out crowd of 18,000, which viewed footage of the pre-tour rehearsals with Entwistle on video screens on each side of the stage, gave the band a standing ovation before a single note was played. Pete and Roger, dressed in black, hugged each other prior to launching into *I Can't Explain*, *Substitute*, and *Anyway, Anyhow, Anywhere*, upon the completion of which Daltrey told the crowd, "tonight we play for John Entwistle. He's the true spirit of rock'n'roll, and he lives on in all the music we play."[305]

Rolling Stone's David Wild was on hand and gave an enthusiastic review:

> For two emotional hours, the legendary British rock outfit offered a rousing and frequently moving wake for their longtime band mate often known as "The Quiet One."
>
> Long a group capable of making rock & roll like a matter of life and death, the Who – with British session player Pino Palladino substituting on bass – brilliantly rose to the somber occasion with a show that was by turns, nervy, hilarious and uplifting.
>
> Throughout the evening, Townshend was on fire on guitar[306], finding renewed passion for well-aged classics…
>
> Despite the occasional sound problem and the annoying spectacle of a solitary idiot jumping onstage, the show suggested that anyone writing off the Who in 2002 is premature. Paradoxically, the Who arguably sounded more like a living, breathing band at the Hollywood Bowl than they have anytime since the 1978 death of Moon.
>
> In the end, this long night's amazing journey was less a matter of mourning in teenage wasteland and more a meaningful moment of healing and midlife grace.

Palladino played his first few songs with The Who "off to the side, often in shadow," *Billboard* reported. While Palladino appeared subdued, it was undoubtedly more out of respect to Entwistle than an accurate reflection of his onstage emotions. "…there were times during songs when I'd suddenly realize I'm occupying one of the immortal bass chairs in music," he told *Bass Player*, "or I'd look over and see Pete flailing away and Roger

---

[305] Pete soon added his own comments (after light-heartedly comparing the venue's stage to a "white vagina," and the items hanging from the ceiling to a "testicle factory") – "While noting the absence of Entwistle's "huge harmonic noise," he congratulated Palladino on playing well anyway," *Rolling Stone* reported. ""For fans that have followed us for many years, this is gonna be very difficult," Townshend said [before *Bargain*]. "We understand. We're not pretending that nothing's happened.""

[306] "Townshend, in black sunglasses, furiously attacked his red Fender guitar," according to *Reuters*.

swinging his mike and I'd be like, What in the hell? I'm playing with the Who!"

"At the end of the show," www.billboard.com reported, "[Townshend] and Daltrey embraced and waved farewell to a giant screen beside the stage on which images of Entwistle – ranging from his youth to his older days – were projected."

Two nights later the band played to a sold-out crowd at Mountain View's Shoreline Amphitheater, the site of Neil Young's Bridge School benefit shows. "...Rock'n'roll was never meant to be easy," Daltrey told the crowd during the show, according to the *San Jose Mercury News*. "Nor was life. You just get on with it." The only reported hiccup during the show was Pete stumbling into his amp during *Bargain* [pretending to be drunk again, perhaps?], and knocking it over. The following night saw the band playing to a crowd of around 10,000 at Sacramento's AutoWest Amphitheatre, with the *Sacramento Bee*'s David Barton stating, "...despite the lack of any material newer than 20 years old, The Who seemed young again."

Following a 6 July gig at Washington's The Gorge during which Pete smashed his guitar at the conclusion of *Won't Get Fooled Again*[307], the band headed home for John's funeral. The July 10 service took place at St. Edward's Church in John's home town of Stow-on-the-Wold, Gloucestershire. "The entrance to the church was surrounded by floral tributes including one reading "RIP Ox", referring to the bassist's nickname," the BBC reported on their website. "In the hearse were tributes shaped like a champagne bottle and a guitar." Among the hundreds of mourners were Entwistle's family and girlfriend, as well as Kenney Jones. "The service was broadcast on loudspeakers to the crowd of well-wishers and fans gathered outside," the BBC reported. "Afterwards, singer Daltrey and guitarist Townshend hugged as they left..."

Whispers continued to circulate about whether the decision to continue the tour was appropriate in the wake of Entwistle's death. "...Pete Townshend and Roger Daltrey could be accused of callous indifference and barely disguised greed in canceling a mere two shows before resuming the lucrative trek," the *Chicago Sun-Times*' Jim DeRogatis wrote in late August.

So much for a mate who'd been with them for four decades. But while one can't entirely discount those motives, after seeing the show, it seems they felt they still

---

[307] "...You know, when I used to smash guitars I was an artist," Pete told *Rolling Stone* in April, 2002. "I'd never smash guitars in a rage – it demeaned the whole thing. But now I'll have a quick fit and go, "Oh, fuck everything," smash the guitar and think, "Oh, dear, look at that."" When asked if he'd smash his guitar during the upcoming tour, Pete said, "No. If it happens, I certainly won't be surprised, but it's not something that I plan on doing. I think it would be quite a good thing if I could avoid it."

had something to prove. The argument that continuing the tour is a "tribute" to Entwistle is nonsense – his role was acknowledged only by a brief video montage that preceded the encore; his replacement, Pino Palladino, was barely audible in the mix, and Townshend actually made two rather snarky remarks about the bass giant, noting that he was now floating somewhere above Las Vegas spending even more money (Entwistle was reportedly deep in debt when he died), and the other that his voice was shot, so the band had already recruited Pete's brother Simon to sing backing vocals before they had to replace the Ox on bass as well.

Another example of a 'snarky' comment Pete made about Entwistle: "I think John was in the wrong band," Pete told Simon Goddard of *Uncut* in April 2004. "John wanted to be in, I dunno, Whitesnake. Really. But he loved me and he loved my writing and he loved playing the music but I think he wanted there to be lines of coke in the dressing room and groupies on the end of his knob all the time. And when he was left to his own devices, that's what he did and that's how he died."

Shortly after this latest comment was published, Pete received a letter from Queenie Entwistle, John's mother, who took exception to Pete's remarks. Pete addressed the letter in a web posting. "She was greatly upset by a statement I made in my recent interview with UNCUT magazine," he wrote.

> ...I think I am still very angry about John's death, and some of that came out...
>
> I feel very sad to have upset Queenie and have apologised to her as best I can. She says other fans were also disturbed. Let me just say that I do not think of John in the way it appears I might through that particular comment in the UNCUT interview. (It was very crude indeed I'm afraid...). Morally speaking, he was certainly never worse than I was; I suppose I got beaten in a different way, and - thankfully - my personal crash in rock n roll came early enough that I was able to save my health.
>
> I remember John only as a great genius of the bass guitar... I also genuinely loved him, he was a supporter and proper friend of mine from the age of 13. We first met even earlier than that. He was funny, generous and caring. We shared a great passion for dogs.
>
> John, typically in very few words, thanked me lovingly recently for allowing him his dignity back by

touring with the Who - the one place he really truly shone. I think in 1982 John was as relieved as I was that the Who were going to stop. He very much enjoyed working with his own band, and was always the most sociable and accessible member of the Who, he loved to mix with people and talk. However, recently all of us who worked with him, but who were unfortunately not close to him day by day were worried about his health. He was truly a very quiet and secretive man and none of us were entirely sure what was going on. It has emerged since his death that several people very close to John fought hard to help him - as I felt I did by touring with him. We are all still deeply shocked by our loss, and I think I can speak for many of us when I say that we are angry too. But it is an aimless and probably quite futile anger. For a while I was even angry with the Las Vegas hotel chain in which he died! I had to apologise to them too.

    I am sorry this stuff keeps rearing its ugly head. Jimi Hendrix, Peter Meadon, Kit Lambert, Keith Moon, the Cincinnati Eleven, John Entwistle. I suppose we have to accept that everyone has to die in the end, but in every one of the cases above I have at some point said things in pain that I have later regretted.

    John was a celebrity. He is still celebrated, and in and around the Who, as long as Roger and I continue to work under the Who name, he will be honoured.

    Sorry Queenie.
    Pete

Meanwhile, The Who returned to the stage on July 26 in front of a sold-out crowd of 19,900 at Boston's Tweeter Amphtheatre. "...there were plenty of moments in the concert that can stand with anything that will come off the Tweeter Center stage this season or future ones," the *Boston Herald*'s Dean Johnson wrote in his review of the show. "Peter Townshend remains the most physical guitarist in rock. He assaulted the instrument from the start, violating it in almost every song in an effort to get every last skronk, squeal, and scream out of it. Sometimes he literally just pounded repeatedly on it with the bottom of his fist." Pete and Roger remained onstage after the set and hugged. They returned after the 11pm curfew and played a four-song *Tommy* encore: *Pinball Wizard, Amazing Journey, Sparks,* and *See Me, Feel Me.*

The following night's show in Camden, New Jersey, brought further rave reviews. "I've been going to Who shows for 20 years, and I've never seen Townshend as wholly engaged as he was Saturday," wrote the *Philadelphia Inquirer*'s Dan DeLuca.

> When the band regrouped in 1996 [sic] – after first "retiring" in 1983 – Townshend played acoustic guitar behind a plastic partition, letting his brother Simon handle the heavy stuff. In Camden, Simon was again on board, as was longtime keyboardist John "Rabbit" Bundrick.
> But Pete was on fire. Maybe he was determined to flip off naysayers, sick of hearing *Bargain* on Nissan ads, who figured another greatest-hits tour, begun days after Entwistle's death, was a crass money grab. In any case, he came out windmilling through a trio of '60s singles – *I Can't Explain*, *Substitute*, *Anyway, Anyhow, Anywhere*. And he didn't let up, ripping into each tune like your crazy uncle with a new reason to live.

Following a stop in Hershey, Pennsylvania, Wednesday July 31 marked the first night of a four-night run at Madison Square Garden, the band's return to the site of the Concert for New York the previous October. "It's nice to play for an audience that isn't in uniform," Pete said from the stage. "We're back. We're with you. We remember. And we'll never forget."

"Pete Townshend still cares about the Who's songs," the *New York Times*' Jon Pareles wrote after witnessing The Who's first show at MSG.

> His conviction was in the way he attacked one guitar after another at Madison Square Garden Wednesday night: windmilling through power chords, wrenching out sustained notes and then slicing them off, machine-gunning harsh tremolos and then speeding and squiggling with manic insistence. The Who had something to prove, and he knew it.
> [the band was] ...inevitably cleaner-sounding than the band of the 1960's and 70's, in which Entwistle's steady, growling basslines were the barricade between Moon's eruptive drumming and Mr. Townshend's hair-trigger guitar. But the rhythm section still pushes both Mr. Townshend and Mr. Daltrey. Songs from *Tommy*, which in the late 1960's reflected Mr. Townshend's elevated rock ambitions, were a down-and-dirty blast of hard rock, and all the better for it.

With an audience that was both uncertain about the band's future and willing to give it a chance, Mr. Townshend loudly renewed his covenant.

The third leg of the 2002 North American tour started on August 23, which would have been Keith Moon's 56th birthday, at Detroit's Palace of Auburn Hills. "Every time you come out, you see less of us," Pete told the crowd after *Who Are You*. "Townshend… looks his 58 years but is playing like a man half his age," wrote *The Flint Journal*'s Doug Pullen.

They opened with a triple blast of early '60s British hits, culminating in a bristling Townshend solo on *Anyway, Anyhow, Anywhere* in which he scraped, picked, pounded and windmilled his red-and-white Fender Stratocaster, sending the sellout crowd of 16,000 into a near frenzy with one of his song-ending leaps… The coup de grace was an explosive four-song encore from *Tommy*, the Who's groundbreaking rock opera.

The following night The Who visited Chicago. "…rare is the rock oldies show as vital as the Who's," wrote the *Chicago Sun Times*' Jim DeRogatis.

…This show was about Pete and Roger refusing to go gently into that good night. Both men were in peak form. Townshend's guitar playing has rarely been so inspired or so fiery. While tunes such as *Baba O'Riley*, *You Better You Bet* and *5:15* have been staples of many past reunion shows, their author took them someplace new and exciting Saturday with his incendiary guitar work. Meanwhile, the preternaturally well-preserved Daltrey proudly displayed a washboard stomach and a weightlifter's physique as he reveled in the joys of flexing a voice that, amazingly, has lost none of its range or power. Daltrey also did something I've never seen any '60s icon do. When squealing feedback from the monitors threw him off his game and made him forget the words to the middle section of *Love Reign O'er Me*, after chewing out the monitor mixer, he demanded that the band play the song again in its entirety. On the one hand, this petulant outburst derailed the momentum of the set. On the other, it was refreshing evidence that the Who, unlike peers from Ozzy Osbourne to Paul McCartney, was not simply playing along to a computer-timed program and following lyrics as they scrolled past on a TelePrompTer. This was a band that was living in the moment, with all of the pros and cons that entails.

The Who circa 2002 may still simply be the very best of many Who cover bands. But the best they were. (And one final shout-out is due Zak Starkey, whose playing was the other highlight of the set. Ringo's kid has truly settled into a groove, shaking off the intimidation he showed during earlier treks to evoke the spirit of Moon while making his own mark as a powerful and inventive drummer, more so than Kenney Jones ever did.)

August 25 saw The Who playing in front of 15,000 at Noblesville, Indiana. "When two of the first eight songs are *Who Are You* and *Baba O'Riley*, there's little doubt the show will be a barn-burner," wrote *The Indianapolis Star*'s David Lindquist, who referred to Pete's guitar work during *Baba O'Riley* as "jagged and life-affirming" and Daltrey's vocals "at his blast-furnace best."

Two days later the band stopped in Grand Rapids, Michigan. Robert Plant & Strange Sensation opened. "As painfully candid and ornery as Pete Townshend can be at times," wrote *The Grand Rapids Press*' John Sinkevics, "the Who's guitarist also oozes sincerity with his relentless intensity on stage, forever enshrining him as one of rock'n'roll's most endearing performers."

On Tuesday night at Van Andel Arena, Townshend – amid a stunning 2 ¼-hour display of machine-gun-like guitar riffs and his trademark, arm-swooping windmills – was shrewd enough to recognize that special bond, especially considering fans paid as much as $225 a ticket to see guys whose last bona fide hit single rode the airwaves two decades ago.

"Thank you for dragging your hard-working bodies here to see us play. Thank you for paying your hard-earned cash to see us play," he told an exuberant, very-near-sellout crowd of more than 10,000. "We really appreciate it."

Nobody plays rock guitar quite like Townshend... The godfather of punk himself is still a monster on the instrument, even if he looks like a crazed chemistry instructor on a weekend fling, playing with more energy and sheer rhythmic power than rock musicians (and high school teachers) one-third his age.

He's literally impossible not to watch, whether seesawing back and forth with his guitar pointed like a bayonet at the crowd during *Bargain*, leaping into the air at the end of *Baba O'Riley*, furiously pounding the strings on *The Relay* and *Sea and Sand* or defly tweaking his guitar's whammy bar and twisting the volume knob in one fluid motion to get the perfect unbridled tone on *5:15*. Yes, the kid can still play.

Mid-September brought The Who back to the Hard Rock Hotel in Las Vegas, the site of John Entwistle's death three months earlier, for a makeup of the canceled tour opener. The intimate setting at The Joint dictated ticket prices of $350 and up, but nevertheless the 1600-seat venue was packed. The atmosphere was somber as the band took the stage wearing black with the exception of Pete's blue jeans, but they launched into their usual three-song opener with typical abandon, "thundering from the start," according to the *Las Vegas Sun*'s Spencer Patterson, on their way to what the *Las Vegas Review* called "...a set with a suitable *Live At Leeds* vibe of ragged finesse." Patterson found Townshend in fine form, noting that his voice "sparkled on this night," and that "the virtuoso who spawned a generation of air guitarists windmilled his way through solo after solo, displaying the fast fingers and sense of timing that have earned him a spot in rock'n'roll's pantheon of legends."[308]

The show also featured a pair of montages from The Who's two rock operas, first a four-song run from 1973's *Quadrophenia* and then an encore composed of a medley from 1969's *Tommy*. The *Quadrophenia* segment, in particular, encapsulated the group's tremendous range, beginning with Townshend's solo acoustic rendition of *I'm One*, moving on to a roaring version of *5:15* featuring some of the guitar hero's best work of the night and then concluding with Roger's vocal showcase, the howling *Love Reign O'er Me*.

Notably silent between songs for much of the night, Townshend and Daltrey finally paid tribute to their fallen comrade late in the show during an extended take on *The Kids Are Alright*. "...I met this guy. He had a horn. It became a bass. He gave me his hand. I joined his band. ...We used to share that red wine. It wasn't worth a dime. We'll have to share it some other time. See ya, John."

---

[308] At the following night's show in Irvine, according to the *Orange County Register*, "Townshend launched into a "typically delightful tirade about the Hard Rock in Las Vegas... the hotel at which Entwistle died. He mixed in a few four-letter words as he went off about the joint's huge pictures of "my dead friends," naming Jimi Hendrix and Janis Joplin in particular."

Another rescheduled show took place the following night at Verizon Amphitheater, Irvine, California. "What a surprise it was, to see and hear the effort Daltrey and Townshend put into this show," reported the *Orange County Register*'s Steve Fryer.

> This had all the makings of a we're-only-in-it-for-the-money gig. But from the opening thrash of *I Can't Explain* and throughout the 22-song set, which began 15 minutes early at 8:40 pm when opener Counting Crows canceled because of a member's illness, it was obvious everyone was very much into it.
> ...Townshend, using only Fender electric guitars these days, played with ferocity. He blasted his way through some stinging leads and crunched the chords for some great rhythm work. Townshend, 57, threw in plenty of his trademark windmill-arm routine, did a few mini-leaps, some hopping around and appeared to be having a lot of fun.

Two nights later the band played Los Angeles' Greek Theater, then stopping on September 19 at the Fiddlers Green Amphitheatre in Denver Colorado[309]. "For my money, this was The Who," the *Rocky Mountain News*' Mark Brown wrote.

> While Thursday night's show had its rough moments, it was a stunning rock show overall far better than anyone had the right to expect...
> ...Townshend played more guitar than most fans have ever seen him play, and Daltrey was flat-out nailing high notes that he dodged on the last tour. They blasted through high-octane versions of *Who Are You* and *5:15* and dug out semi-rarities such as *Another Tricky Day* and *Eminence Front*. No one in the packed house looked like they wanted a refund. Even tired songs such as *Love Reign O'er Me* were invigorated.
> Before the show the band ran video of tour rehearsals, featuring touching interview footage with Entwistle. The segment of *5:15* that was filled with his bass improvisations last tour was instead filled with fiery Townshend guitar solos.

---

[309] "As the band took the stage, Townshend cracked wise: 'Tonight is going to be the worst gig we've ever played'," the *Denver Post* reported.

A couple of nights later, The Who performed in Dallas, Texas, at the American Airlines Arena. "...the band performed with energy and conviction," the *Star-Telegram*'s Dave Ferman wrote, "with Pete Townshend often throwing in muscular guitar solos – and several funny between-song comments." The *Dallas Morning News*' Thor Christensen wrote that "Mr. Entwistle's thundering zigzag bass lines were sorely missed," and that Daltrey's vocals were "hoarse", but that the vocals of "Simon Townshend... helped immeasurably."[310]

Two nights later, The Who played the fifth benefit show in less than four years for Maryville Academy at Chicago's House of Blues. Individual tickets went for $400 while balcony boxes cost as much as $25,000. Pearl Jam, minus guitarist Stone Gossard[311], opened the show, including their rendition of *Leaving Here*, which the High Numbers had covered back in 1964. "It takes a lot of guts to come on stage when you know a guy named Pete Townshend is gonna come out later and wipe it with you," Eddie Vedder remarked from the stage.

"Townshend played with remarkable intensity and volume, and took songs such as *Eminence Front*, *Anyway, Anyhow, Anywhere* and *5:15* beyond their expected, time-worn conclusions into the sonic unknown, wind-milling his instrument into stuttering, machine-gunning climaxes," reported the *Chicago Tribune*, who described Daltrey as "hoarse", Townshend "fiery and inspired."

Prior to playing *The Kids Are Alright*, Pete dedicated the song to Maryville director Rev. John Smyth, and spoke of the problems the academy had encountered recently. "Renowned for its work with troubled teens, Maryville has come under fire recently because of incidents of fights, attacks on staff members and suicide attempts at its 270-bed campus in Des Plaines," wrote the *Sun-Times*' Jim DeRogatis. "When I was a teenager, I never, ever realized that one day we would be able to use our music to help kids," DeRogatis quoted Pete as saying from the stage. "There has been some controversy regarding the way Maryville does business, and I can tell you, I never do anything like this without first going through the books and going through the underwear drawer. This one is kosher!"

The following night, the band played at the Xcel Energy Center in St. Paul, Minnesota. "...This is no sad, bloated, Elvis-in-Vegas act, living off the fumes of faded fame," *The Pioneer Press*' Brian Lampert wrote.

The Who remain the real thing, vibrantly in touch
with the passions that have carried them through the years.

---

[310] "[Entwistle's] voice had already tragically died before he tragically died," Pete reportedly said.
[311] Gossard was working a conservation project in Papua, New Guinea; a cardboard cutout stood in his usual position onstage.

From the first crack of Townshend's guitar on *I Can't Explain*, fans at Xcel were treated to rock writ large and loud. Not to mention superb showmanship. Daltrey and Townshend, in particular, remain masters of the rock arena, working with material that sounded as fresh and powerful Tuesday night as it did when they wrote it so many years ago.

...The two-hour-plus show was wall-to-wall greatest hits. Many, like *Anyway, Anyhow*, with a sensational guitar solo from Townshend Sr., were performed with a startling, delightful intensity.

...You still can't keep your eyes off Pete Townshend, who makes up in guitar craftsmanship whatever he may have lost in leaping ability. Both Daltrey and Townshend the elder are inspirations to their generation in their physical conditioning, as well as the passion they still summon for their material.

The *Star Tribune*'s Jon Bream agreed that Townshend was amazing. "The concert could be described as maximum Townshend... He came out with ferocious energy, attacking his guitar on *I Can't Explain* and *Anyway Anyhow Anywhere*, and driving the crowd wild with his windmill wallops and flying leaps. He kept up the intensity on his ax for two more hours."

The September 27 performance at the Tweeter Center in Mansfield, Massachusetts brought further rapturous praise for Townshend and co. "...Put simply the two hour and 15 minute performance was nothing short of rock'n'roll arson," wrote the *Boston Herald*'s Sarah Rodman.

The controlled abandon of Townshend's beyond god-like guitar work and the voluminous energy put forth by frontman Roger Daltrey is the best tribute the pair could offer to late Who bassist John Entwistle...

The majesty of Townshend's wizardry cannot be overstated. Last night the 57-year-old legend was almost overwhelming marrying precision with gut-churning fire on solos as disparate as the skewed caterwauling that closed a raucous *My Generation* to the stone sweetness of the lyrical lines that danced through a supremely funky *Eminence Front*.

In keeping with tradition, the tour ended in Toronto[312]. The *Toronto Sun*'s Jane Stevenson described the sold-out show as "2 hours and 15 minutes of passionate, loud and often exciting music that went a long way towards explaining why the seminal rock band was on the road in the first place. Daltrey spun and danced around the stage, occasionally whipping his microphone, while Townshend delivered his trademark windmill move and some truly breathtaking solos during *Who Are You, Bargain, Baba O'Riley, 5:15, Behind Blue Eyes* and *Won't Get Fooled Again...*"

"...even reduced to half of its original membership, the iconic '60s outfit can still whip an audience of 13,000 Torontonians into a state of sustained adoration and frenzy," reported the *Toronto Star*'s Vit Wagner.

> ...guitarist Pete Townshend, at the not so tender age of 57 hasn't lost any of his capacity for exclamatory punctuation. He might not smash guitars with youthful abandon any more, but his ability to drop one power chord after another remains undiminished.
>
> If anything, thanks to improved amplification, it's a fair bet that Townshend's capacity for windmill-powered electrification has seldom produced greater voltage. After offering an early glimpse of his trademark propeller approach on the night's opening number, *I Can't Explain*, Townshend generated enough power to lend serious weight to *Bargain, Baba O'Riley, Won't Get Fooled Again* and several other of the band's harder-hitting favorites.

Two weeks after the conclusion of the tour, Pete wrote a web diary entry entitled 'Ah Ha! You thought I was sulking' to address future work between himself and Roger Daltrey.

> [Roger] is upbeat and energetic about the future, but as ever – worried that he may be unable for various reasons to sing my songs for very much longer.
>
> ...Because of the power of the shows, and their financial success in a slightly depressed marketplace, there are those who conclude that I will naturally continue to perform with Roger under The Who banner. There are those, who perhaps think they know me better (as a grouch, a spoiler, a self-obsessed creative, an insecure and pretentious self-styled artist etc), who conclude that now it is all over.

---

[312] "It's taken such a long time to come back to this city," Pete said from the stage. "Tonight, in true tradition, this is the last show we're doing on this tour."

The truth is rather less sparked with drama...

Many people think of me as a rock performer first and foremost. A guitar smasher. An arm swinger. An innovator of very loud chord work. But primarily, after art school, I turned my attention entirely to writing rock songs for The Who. Without that creative work I would not have stayed in the band. There have been times I've hated it. When I began to find that song-writing work impossible to do well, I felt there was no point in carrying on with all the other stuff that related to my rock 'image'; it was all real, but very heavy to carry.

...I still don't think I can write new songs for this thing we all call The Who.

Good news? Roger and I met under Bill Curbishley's watchful eye in Boston for a short meeting before we all came home to catch up on our domestic lives. Bill said that The Who are attracting audiences in the U.S. out of all proportion with our visible and measurable status in the record and entertainment industry; if we tour once a year for another four or five years we will make money and make a lot of people very happy. I suggested Roger and I meet as often as possible when we get home, and attempt to write some music together.

...My old friend Tom Wright, who some fans will know as the guy who left his collection of great R&B recordings for me to plunder when he went back to the U.S. in 1963, feels Roger and I need to make a 'last' album. One that is real, passionate, earthy, and innovative – but also accessible...

Anyway, Roger and I haven't managed a meeting yet. But we will do something I'm sure.

That's pretty much where things stand. The Who did well this summer. The money thing just happens around us. It is not what drives us. Not really. Astonishing to think that three years ago Roger and I toured to keep shopaholic John out of debtor's prison.

I'm a nut. But please trust me. I'm going to attempt to get out of my own way, and stay out of my own way. That will be hard for me. It's not exactly a spiritual discipline, but for someone like me who has no regular confining daily schedule of work and responsibility outside the time I spend with my young son, it's hard to remain focused on remaining unfocused.

Chapter 20

"In the past thirty years I have amassed a huge amount of research about the issue of child abuse and the way damage has recently been spreading via the internet. I was concerned for a numbers of years in anticipation of awful problems the 'miracle' of the internet might pose when it finally reached the billions of homes it touches today. I also still have a buzzing head full of opinions, anger, frustration and energy I want to bring to bear on the authorities and treatment charities who I once thought needed my ideas.
But today, without my help, fantastic work is being done by good people who are fighting hard to combat both the spread of sewage on the internet and the terrible psychological effect that it could have on the minds of the children of the future. Every time it occurs to me to say something about what is going on I remind myself what happened to me this year: I was arrested, suspected of wallowing in the very shit that most upset me. It sent me a clear and loud message. I must learn to keep silent and focus my energies elsewhere."
— Pete Townshend, 2003

"To a musician like me, music is what is inside us all. It represents experience, emotion and spiritual potential. In 1971, I didn't think we would just have an internet, I thought I would be able to plug into you and you would be able to plug into me. I did. I still do."
— Pete Townshend, 2004

Reporters descended on Pete's house on Saturday, 11 January 2003, a day after *The Sun* had reported that an unidentified British rock star was one of over seven thousand British citizens under suspicion of viewing child pornography on the internet. The list of suspects, provided by the FBI, was compiled from data that traced a quarter of a million suspected pedophiles worldwide through their credit card information, obtained from targeted web sites. The British segment of this worldwide hunt was known as Operation Ore. That Saturday morning, British media reports named Pete Townshend as the celebrity in question. In the afternoon, Pete, wearing a white dressing robe, appeared on the front porch of his Richmond home and spoke to the media, "...acknowledging that he was the rock legend in question and explaining how he believed this situation had come about," according to *Rolling Stone*. "Later, reporters were handed a written statement." The statement read as follows:

I am not a paedophile. I have never entered chat rooms on the internet to converse with children. I have, to the contrary, been shocked, angry and vocal (especially on my website) about the explosion of advertised paedophilic images on the internet.

I have been writing my childhood autobiography for the past seven years. I believe I was sexually abused between the age of five and six-and-a-half when in the care of my maternal grandmother who was mentally ill at the time. I cannot remember clearly what happened, but my creative work tends to throw up nasty shadows – particularly in *Tommy*.

Some of the things I have seen on the internet have informed my book which I hope will be published later this year, and which will make clear to the public that if I have any compulsions in this area, they are to face what is happening to young children in the world today and to try to deal openly with my anger and vengeance towards the mentally ill people who find paedophilic pornography attractive.

I predicted many years ago that what has become the internet would be used to subvert, pervert and destroy the lives of decent people. I have felt for a long time that it is part of my duty, knowing what I know, to act as a vigilante to help support organizations like the Internet Watch Foundation, the NSPCC [National Society for the Prevention of Cruelty to Children] and Scotland Yard to build up a powerful and well-informed voice to speak loudly about the millions of dollars being made by American banks and credit card companies for the pornography industry. That industry deliberately blurs what is legal and what is illegal, and different countries have different laws and moral values about this. I do not. I do not want child pornography to be available on the internet anywhere at any time.

On one occasion I used a credit card to enter a site advertising child porn. I did this purely to see what was there. I spoke informally to a friend who was a lawyer and reported what I'd seen. I have enclosed my website article about my friend Jenny who committed suicide because of sexual abuse she suffered as a child. I hope you will be able to see that I am sincerely disturbed by the sexual abuse of children, and I am very active trying to help individuals who have suffered, and to prevent further abuse.

Rolling Stone quoted Pete as also telling the press that he'd "…been in touch with Scotland Yard to tell them what I've been doing." Honest, as always, to a fault, Pete didn't help the situation by reportedly stating, "I have always been into pornography and I have used it all my life, but I am not a pedophile. I was worried this might happen and I think this could be the most damaging thing to my career. I think I'm fucked."

While stories circulated worldwide about Townshend the pedophile, many celebrities, while still digesting the very few available facts related to the case, jumped to Pete's defense. British film producer and humorist Martin Lewis went on *CNN* to defend Pete on Monday night. British DJ Paul Gambaccini almost immediately defended Pete, saying "…this is a subject which has concerned him for many, many years, and I therefore do trust him implicitly." Music writer Rick Sky stated, "His argument is that he's been doing research on pedophilia and child pornography on the internet, and I do tend to believe him. It seems very unbelievable that he'd be involved in something like this." "Pete is no pedophile," his neighbor, Chris Hutchins, told the media. "there's no question about that. Pete absolutely lives by his honesty. He's in a program of recovery where to tell a lie could lead him back to a drink or drug problem. If Pete says that it was for his book... then that's true." Among others who defended Pete were Bob Geldof, Bono, David Bowie, Jerry Hall, and Karen Astley. Roger Daltrey said, "My gut instinct is that he is not a pedophile, and I know him better than most. Pete has perhaps been a little naïve the way he's gone about it, but I believe his intentions are good." Old friend Elton John said, "I'm very shocked and I hope it's not as bad as it sounds. I'm a friend of Pete's. I love Pete, and my thoughts are with him."

Pete's assertion in his statement to the press that he had been "shocked, angry and vocal" about child porn was corroborated by the lengthy essay 'A *Different* Bomb', which was posted on his web site back in early 2002 and was presented to the media on January 11 along with Pete's previously mentioned written statement. The essay, a six-page document outlining Pete's thoughts on the scourge of child abuse and its consequences, was written when a friend of Pete's, a victim of abuse at the hands of her father when she was a child, committed suicide. It included Pete's reflections on his own childhood abuse, and characterized the current climate in the media, government and law enforcement towards child abuse as a "witch hunt" – an eerily uncanny observation, given the events of the following year. "In my work fund-raising in the field of drug and alcohol rehabilitation I have come across hundreds of individuals from the UK and Europe whose problems have been triggered by childhood abuse," Pete wrote. "Not always, but often, the abuse is sexual. Sometimes it is quite minor, but even in those cases – for some reason – spectacularly damaging... In some cases, what is so distressing is how little it takes. For me, a few minor incidents seem to have created a dark side to my nature which thankfully emerges only in creative work like *Tommy*."

'A *Different* Bomb' also addressed Pete's disgust with the internet child-porn industry, and detailed the events which led to his involvement in the effort to eradicate it.

> Ethan Silverman, a film director friend, had made an extremely moving documentary about an American couple who adopted a Russian boy. As a charity fundraiser (and, I suppose, philanthropist to boot) I wanted to support the work of such orphanages and decided to see if I could – via the internet – find legitimate contacts to help. (I had tried many other methods and failed). The various words I used included 'Russia' and 'orphanages'. I used no words that could usually be taken to be sexual or lascivious, except – perhaps ill-advisedly – the word 'boys'.
>
> Within about ten minutes of entering my search words I was confronted with a 'free' image of a male infant of about two years old being buggered by an unseen man. The blazer on the page claimed that sex with children is 'not illegal in Russia'. This was not smut. It was a depiction of a real rape. The victim, if the infant boy survived and my experience was anything to go by, would probably one day take his own life. The awful reality hit me of the self-propelling, self-spawning mechanism of the internet. I reached for the phone, I intended to call the police and take them through the process I had stumbled upon – and bring the pornographers involved to book.
>
> Then I thought twice about it. With someone on trial who had once been connected with me[313] – however loosely – I spoke off-the-record to a lawyer instead. He advised me to do nothing. He advised me that I most certainly should not download the image as 'evidence'. So I did as he advised. Nothing.

---

[313] "...in 1997 a man who had briefly worked for me was arrested in the UK for downloading paedophilic pornography," Pete wrote in the same essay.

Shocked at the ease with which he stumbled upon this image back in 1997, Pete wrote that he began "attempting to prepare some kind of document with respect to all this for wider publication." He went on to advocate internet vigilantism as a viable and necessary approach in battling web-based child porn.

> ...The pathway to 'free' pedophilic imagery is – as it were – laid out like a free line of cocaine at a decadent cocktail party: only the strong willed or terminally uncurious can resist. Those vigilantes who research these pathways open themselves up to internet 'snoops'. Many are willing to take the risk. They believe the pathways themselves must be closed. They must be totally and completely eradicated from the internet. If that is not possible they must be openly policed by active and obstructive vigilantes – not just 'snooped' by government agencies and police.

It was acting upon this 'vigilante' attitude that landed Pete in hot water in early 2003.

"...the internet provides a very short route indeed to some of the most evil and shocking images of rape and abuse," Pete concluded in his essay. "The subconscious mind is deeply damaged and indelibly scarred by the sight of such images. I can assure everyone reading this that if they go off in pursuit of images of paedophilic rape they will find them. I urge them not to try. I pray too that they don't happen upon such images as did I, by accident. If they do they may like me become so enraged and disturbed that their dreams are forever haunted."

In October 2002, Pete posted a further web essay entitle A DIFFERENT BOMB – REVISITED, in which he discussed his plans to talk to "someone at a large children's charity here in the UK about creating some safe User Group forum for the rehabilitation of those who, addicted to internet porn, begin to be enticed into unacceptable stuff. I know that 'Just Say No' never worked with heroin, I didn't expect it to. But internet pornography depends on addiction for its massive profits." The essay also included a statement of Pete's determination to continue to push for change.

> ['A *Different* Bomb'] was first posted early this year. At one point recently I decided to take it down at last, but I just heard that another young woman who Double-O had put into treatment for depression and anxiety related to sexual abuse at the age of 8, had started drinking again. Sometimes this all feels so bloody futile. But I am determined to do my bit. I made a lot of money out of that

poor little sap in *Tommy*. Now I understand how easily he could be recreated as a real child in our present society. I feel driven to try to change things.

Meanwhile, further light was shed on Pete's situation in an interview which was published in *The Sun* two days after his implication in Operation Ore was made public. "...I am not making any excuses," Pete told *The Sun*'s Dominic Mohan.

> I am angry about child porn on the internet, and deeply wounded at the inference that I might be a paedophile. I have looked at child porn sites maybe three or four times in all, the front pages and previews. But I have only entered once using a credit card and I have never downloaded. With hindsight it was very foolish but I felt so angered about what was going on it blurred my judgement. I have never purchased any forms of child pornography or wished to own any. I saw the first, awful photo by accident. It repelled me and shocked me to my very core. I was not breaking the law at the time. This was in the winter of 1996/1997. It was then illegal to download, which I did not do, not to search and view. I did not think using a credit card was illegal either at the time. As a public figure I would never have given details had I known I would be breaking UK law. I need to regain the trust of police and authorities involved in protecting children to continue to use my energies and determination to help what they do.
>
> If my therapy revealed anything, it indicated that I might regard myself as the victim of pedophiles. I was stupid to try to deal with my anger about child porn on the internet alone. We must try to stop it but if we can't do that we should invest our energy in helping victims of abuse. I believe I may have suffered some sexual abuse which makes me angry about all this stuff. If my celebrity has a value perhaps it is to get the reality of this problem once and for all back into the public mind... Chasing after people like Gary Glitter and Jonathan King is important, and it is important that the police are able to convince themselves that – if I did anything illegal – I did it purely for research. I am not a paedophile. I agree with what the police are doing. No, I did not expect to be targeted in their swoops. Foolish of me, but not arrogant. I sincerely believed that the police would know my history as someone who works tirelessly to help the abused, and that since 1978 I have run

a charity which has contributed millions to organizations working to prevent violence and abuse.

While most agreed that Pete's actions in taking it upon himself to investigate child porn, especially going as far as to use a credit card on an illicit site, were, in the words of the U.K. Internet Watch Foundation vice chairman Mark Stephens, "incredibly foolhardy, naïve and misguided," most also agreed that Pete's defense of his actions was compelling. It was a fact that Pete had been in touch with Scotland Yard in October, 2002 (former Detective Chief Inspector Jackie Malton called Pete and asserted her willingness to verify that this communication did take place), and wanted to spearhead a website providing information on the dangers of child pornography on the internet, possibly with the involvement of the National Society for the Prevention of Cruelty to Children. Further verification of Townshend's defense that he had previously communicated his desire to prevent pedophilic images from being accessible on the web was provided in March, when the Internet Watch Foundation confirmed that Pete had, in fact, previously reported a list of child-porn web sites to their office. This must have provided a measure of relief to Pete since the IWF initially stated that he had never contacted them.

Pete told *The Sun* that he was committed to campaigning against internet child porn, even at the expense of his music career. "I want to live my life, enjoy my family and continue with my work," he said. "But if all I can do from now on is fight the sexual abuse of children, and to help those who become victims, well that wouldn't be too bad a way of living the rest of my life. ...At heart I think the internet is a wonderful thing. But it is allowing child porn to be circulated freely around the world, crossing borders, allowing laws to be ignored, and there are real children behind the images, children like I was."

On Monday, Pete met with his attorney, John Cohen, and arrived home at 2:30 in the afternoon, using the private drive at the rear of his house, and entering through the back door. Cohen briefed the gathered media a few minutes later, informing them that Pete was scheduled to meet with the police at 3 pm. As scheduled, at the top of the hour, four plainclothes detectives armed with two search warrants arrived, knocked on the door, and entered the house, followed fifteen minutes later by a dozen more officers, one of whom carried a crate containing plastic evidence bags. Pete was interviewed by the four detectives while the remaining officers commenced to scour his home and business addresses in search of potential evidence. "There will be a thorough and detailed search of the premises," a Scotland Yard spokeswoman told the BBC. "It will take as long as necessary."

Four hours later, police were seen leaving Pete's home, loading several personal computers and laptops along with diaries, videos and computer disks into a van. At 7:30 pm, Pete, unshaven and looking weary, was driven away from his house in the back of a car, accompanied by police detectives. "Townshend, 57, was arrested at his London home," *CNN* reported on its website. "He was taken into custody at a southwest London police station, police said." Pete hadn't been charged with any crime. "He has been arrested under the Protection of Children Act of 1978," a Scotland Yard spokesman said, "on suspicion of possessing indecent images of children, suspicion of making indecent images of children and on suspicion of incitement to distribute indecent images of children." After nearly an hour and a half of questioning, Pete was released on bail shortly after midnight. "Mr Townshend has been interviewed this evening by the police," Cohen stated to the press. "He has not been charged with anything and he has been bailed till a future date when he may be required to come back and answer some more questions."

Meanwhile, the support of Pete's friends, family and fans continued to flow in. "We are, and remain, a loving Christian family, and will continue to stand by Pete," his mother, Betty, 79 years old, told the press. "I'm unaware he suffered abuse. If what he says is true, he's carried it privately." Fan support for Pete was demonstrated with the opening of a website, www.petetownshendisinnocent.com, which featured relevant news articles and information, and media contact information to address what many fans considered was unfair coverage of the story. The site even contained a link to purchase "Pete Townshend is Innocent!" t-shirts.

Naturally, regardless of Pete's assertions of innocence, the front-page headlines which proclaimed his arrest on charges of suspicion of possessing indecent images of children damned him in many eyes before he had a chance to speak. The story was perfect media fodder. Daltrey fumed about the media's appetite for the story, telling journalist John Crook, "The list that Pete's name appeared on also had the names of a dozen judges, 30-odd policemen, three MP's – we don't know who the hell they were, because everyone focused on Pete, because his name sold papers."

> …There were people in authority, people other than just the police, who should have known better but who were inflaming the press with sweeping, untrue statements that Pete had actually downloaded this stuff. These people were telling what, well, let's kindly call 'variations on the truth.' What Pete told was the whole truth, from day one, namely that he never downloaded even one image to his computer. That stuff, the pornography, makes him physically sick, he hates it so much.

Queen guitarist Brian May was particularly vocal about Pete's plight and issued a statement addressing the media frenzy over the Townshend story:

> It has deeply saddened me to see a man of such honesty and integrity so appallingly misunderstood and smeared. I believe Pete Townshend will be proved innocent of all bad intentions, but, whether he is or not, he has been carelessly thrust into a hostile glare by elements of the tabloid press in a way which risks permanently damaging both his reputation and his huge contributions to helping the victims of abuse. ...Pete Townshend's integrity is self-evident. He is as appalled by pedophilia as the rest of us. I would like to see some respect for a man who has done so much to improve and inform our view of the world.

Dave Marsh stepped forward in defense of Pete in an interview with *USA Today*'s Elysa Gardner soon after the story broke. "Yes, *Tommy* reflects an interest in this issue, and other things Pete has written have made passing references to it," Marsh said when asked about the presence of references to child abuse in Townshend's lyrics.

> But what they reflect is not great delight but great torment. Pete's been a great friend for more than 30 years, but how we really became friends was I was writing from the point of view of someone who had been abused in a different way, who was a battered child. His records helped save my life. And if people are going to start interpreting his work in light of various things, we ought to make sure that light shines in all the places it ought to, not just in the most scandalous places. This is not a guy who's about hurting people.
> Yes, the cops had a right and an obligation to look into this, but that isn't what happened. They took somebody and dragged him through as much mud as they could dig up. This is basically about criminalizing investigative behavior – saying, 'You're not allowed to investigate certain things.' And any journalist who doesn't feel threatened by that is not paying attention.

Meanwhile, workaholic Pete found himself holed up in his house with no computers, which meant that he couldn't work. He received an offer to create a surround sound 5.1 remix of *Tommy*, and accepted. "I did it because I got arrested last year and I had nothing else to do," Pete told

Uncut's Simon Goddard in April 2004. "That's the only reason. I knew that I'd have to wait two or three months, because the police took 12 computers from my house. I knew that it takes them about a gigabyte a week to look through so I just thought, 'This is gonna take fucking forever. I knew I couldn't work. I thought, fuck, what can I do? So that's why I did it, but I also felt I should go back to the emotional source. *Tommy* was where I started to see evidence of a troubled childhood, one that I wasn't really aware of."

In April 2003, Pete played the original *Tommy* studio master tapes at Oceanic in preparation for the remix. "I put the tapes up in this room and kind of went into shock," he told Goddard. "It's not what I remembered. ...What actually happened with this remix thing is that I rediscovered it[314]. I rediscovered it in its original flawed, incomplete, innocent, naïve, wonderfully gauche form. It's a part of The Who's story and I'm so glad I did it. If I'd done a biography and written about the Who years without having done this remix, I'd have told a very different story. It's not perfect, nothing is, and it was never meant to be perfect. It's probably always going to be the most important thing that I've written."

After what must have been an excruciating period of nearly four months, Pete was summoned to Kingston police station on May 7 for the disposition of his case. He was informed that he would face no charges, but would receive a caution. This meant that Pete would be placed on the Sex Offenders Register for five years, and that any further improprieties would almost certainly result in charges being filed against him. Being on the Register also meant that he was required to check in with the police annually and upon any change of address. After submitting to fingerprinting, DNA sample and a photograph, Pete was free to go.

Scotland Yard had found no downloaded images of child abuse on any of the computers that they confiscated and analyzed. "From the very beginning, I acknowledged that I did access this site and that I had given the police full access to all of my computers," Pete wrote in a web update.

> As I made clear at the outset, I accessed the site because of my concerns at the shocking material readily available on the Internet to children as well as adults, and as part of my research toward the campaign I had been putting together since 1995 to counter damage done by all kinds of pornography on the internet, but especially any involving child abuse.
>
> The police have unconditionally accepted that these were my motives in looking at this site and that there was

---

[314] Once *Tommy* was completed, *Quadrophenia* was the next project slated for a surround sound remix, according to *Mojo* in 2004.

no other nefarious purpose, and as a result they have decided not to charge me. I accept that I was wrong to access this site, and that by doing so, I broke the law, and I have accepted the caution that the police have given me.

Predictably, the fact that Pete was ultimately not charged with any crime didn't make front page headlines. This less-than sensational story, comprising only a few lines in many instances, was generally buried inside the newspapers. "They went through his computers, 14 of them, with military precision without finding one image, which is exactly what he had told them," Daltrey told John Crook in September.

> He explained to them that he works in this field, of trying to get this stuff off the Internet. He was telling the truth, all the way, and the whole thing is appalling to me, the way he has been branded this dreadful thing, which he is not.
> ...I have never known anyone in my life who has helped [victims of pedophilia] more than Pete Townshend. You should see some of the letters he has gotten from [people he has helped], and I am talking about hundreds of people, and he also does just incredible work in prisons. Most people don't even know about that, because Pete doesn't have a publicist following him around calling attention to all he does to help people. He says, 'No, these people have to be protected,' bless him, so imagine how I feel, knowing all this about him, and watching these second-rate journalists feeling they can kick him around all they like...
> I wouldn't lie for him. Child pornography is so completely abhorrent to me, that no way would I defend him if I had even a shred of doubt, but I tell you, no one has done more for these people than Pete Townshend. He did what he said he did exactly for the reasons that he said he did it, and he was found not fucking guilty.
> ...I have to wonder what's going on here... There is a civil liberties issue here, a big one. We can't have the police making judgments on people with no crime. It's not good for democracy, and it's not good for the police, either. This could be done to you tomorrow, or to me, in the same way. Pete did nothing [wrong]. It's disgusting[315].

---

[315] Daltrey called the ordeal "the worst thing I have ever had to deal with in my life" in a February 2003 interview with Virgin Radio.

A few weeks after the resolution of his case, Pete sent an email to *Rolling Stone*'s Jenny Eliscu outlining his plans. "I intend to work my way back to normality," he wrote.

> As a result of all this shit, I've decided to greatly formalize the structure of my charity (Double-O) and the way I work with "survivors" – so that in future my work is more well-known to everyone. I've kept my profile low in this area out of modesty I suppose, and it has worked against me. I am going to complete my autobiography, *Pete Townshend (who he?)*. I put it down and did not plan to finish it until much later. But now I am going to push ahead until it is done. People need to read about my entire life to get a real picture of who I am. I hope to finish it by the end of the year. So it may come out next year sometime. I am also going to get up and play just as soon as I can.
>
> Finally, I'm going out onto the street to meet people, to smile and shake hands with everyone who has been supportive of me in my hometown. But also to give those people who are "undecided" a chance to look me in the eye and make their own decision. Going on TV won't help me. I'm too wounded, too crazy, too happy and grateful, too resentful and too busy. Who fans? I hope that life will go on as usual. Roger has been a rock.

A July 8 report in London's *Daily Mail* stated that Pete was a "changed man" who had by necessity become a recluse due to hate mail and other threats he'd received as a result of the recent investigation. "In today's *Daily Mail* there is an article which states that I walk this neighborhood in fear of my life, that I receive abuse and death threats and go nowhere without a bodyguard," Pete told the *Richmond and Twickenham Times*. "None of this is true. No fear. No abuse. No death threats. No bodyguard. (my driver is a big bloke, but I often walk around Richmond alone)." The newspaper quoted a 'spokesman' of Pete's as saying that while "[Pete] did employ bodyguards soon after his arrest they were shortly dismissed as their services were not required."

Pete reiterated the fact that he hadn't fallen into a reclusive, fearful lifestyle with a web diary entry on July 10, 'Silence Day' for Baba followers. "Silence what I would like for a while – but it seems impossible," Pete wrote.

> I don't want to pick a fight with any British newspaper, but some of them are starting to make things up.

> This year has been a tough one for me, but contrary to what one British tabloid wrote yesterday, I am not depressed, my neighbors are not abusing me – far from it, they go out of their way to show me warmth and understanding – and I have not received death threats. I have a driver who acts as a kind of bodyguard and I have a night security man – but I always have. No change there.
>
> I walk freely in my town, I eat in local restaurants and everyone is very good to me. I take what happened to me very seriously indeed, and I hate the idea that anyone might believe my intentions were criminal, but I do believe great good has come out of it all.
>
> One message I want to send. I know I am not above the law, but the law on the access off indecent images on the internet was changed in this country AFTER I did my research. While doing research I knew the law. I was not breaking it. I'm not stating this to make an excuse. But surely anyone can see if that is a fact, and it is, why would I be ashamed of the subsequent due process of law acting against me?
>
> But I am deeply sorry for the trouble and pain I've caused: even the investigating officer (in Texas) who first found my name on a porn site database was a Who fan, and was saddened.
>
> But I am not sad. I am out of the war against child-porn, but the war continues and that is what matters.
>
> I'm happy, strong, sober, humbled and for the rest of the day I'll try to stay silent.

"Everyone is so kind to me, and they seem to always want to give me the benefit of any doubt," Pete told the *Evening Standard*'s Richard Simpson in early October.

> Not one death threat have I received, though on Day One, before I was actually arrested, I got one really strange letter talking about my big nose. I have never heard any abuse of any kind. A few turned-up noses perhaps – but mostly smiles, congratulations and 'love your music'.
>
> I am not a recluse. I eat out locally without security. I go to parties and I'm going to the threater. I am fine. I don't try to pretend that what happened to me was not serious, nor that it hasn't affected me.
>
> It has not destroyed me, made me frightened, nor has it stopped me doing my work or living my normal life.

What it has done is made me realize I am not above the law, I am not rock'n'roll invincible, and I cannot save the world from internet sewage.

But while the gloom and doom picture of Pete's post-investigation life painted by the *Daily Mail* was markedly different from the truth, his mood when the case broke was indeed dangerously low. "If I had a gun, I would have shot myself," Pete told *The Observer*'s Zoe Smith in a stunning December 2003 revelation[316]. "And if I had shot myself, it would have been fucking awful because it would have confirmed what everybody thought. I know that I caused the most incredible chaos by that one single neglectful careless act – for my ex-wife, for my son who's only 13, for his school friends, for my girlfriend, all of whom had to make a snap decision to wing behind me. And they all did. I'm not sexually attracted to children. I knew there was a developing witch hunt in progress and I thought, "Oh my God, this is going to be hung on me.""

Not long after Pete and his son went sailing in France in September, things began to warm up on the Who front. In mid-November, Pete announced in a web update that he and Roger Daltrey had completed recording Pete's new composition *Real Good Looking Boy*.

> We did it in fairly raw form, but it brought together the band from last year's tour (apart from Pino who is out with Simon and Garfunkel – Greg Lake filled in beautifully. Smashing fellow.) Zak, Rabbit and my brother Simon played brilliantly and Roger and I were bloody useless. But what do you expect of two such creaky old tossers?
>
> I am back in my own studio again preparing songs and visual material for some kind of future project, which I hope will provide a pathway of some kind for Roger and me in the future.
>
> Whatever happens, Roger and I are facing our 'new' Everly Brothers format with excitement and trepidation. I sense great chaotic madness ahead...

Real Good Looking Boy was "a song I wrote quite a few years ago about two young men who worry about their looks," Pete wrote in a February, 2004 web diary entry. "One of them, based on me - hopes and

---

[316] In a 1996 interview with *Q*'s John Harris, when discussing the emotional depths of his early 1980's drug addiction, Pete pointed out that the notion of suicide was pointless for Baba followers. "...what you have to remember intellectually is that it's a completely futile act," he said. "You have to remember that deep down, my rationality was telling me, 'There's no point killing yourself, 'cos you'll be reborn 15 seconds later with exactly the same set of problems.' I believe that."

believes he might look like his best friend who is a conventionally handsome fellow. (He is disavowed of this notion by his mother). The second, based on Roger - hopes and believes he will one day turn out to be like the young Elvis. (He, more happily, sees part of his dream come true). They both find love in later life."

Pete also announced in mid-November that he and Daltrey would play at the Royal Albert Hall in March, 2005. "We will perform something quite surprising I think,"[317] he commented.

Late February 2004 saw Pete in New York City with two purposes. "Firstly, Eel Pie Publishing artist Rachel Fuller has a showcase for Universal Records," Pete wrote in a web entry.

> Secondly, I want to play two new Who tracks to Doug Morris the CEO of Universal. The Who are now handled by Geffen which is based in L.A and - though owned by Universal - has different staff. But Doug signed me to my first real solo deal at Atlantic in 1978 - which led to the making and release of *Empty Glass*, and several more until *Psychoderelict* my last solo album delivery in 1993. He also signed Rachel in 2002. I want him to be the first person in Universal to hear the new Who music...

The "two new Who tracks" were the previously discussed *Real Good Looking Boy* and *Old Red Wine*, a song Pete wrote in New York "about the late John Entwistle," Pete wrote in his web diary. "He loved expensive claret, and often drank it past its prime. There is an irony there somehow: John never seemed to realize how perfectly MATURE he had really become as rock musician. He didn't need the trappings he thought essential, and that - in my opinion - led directly to his premature death." The two new Townshend compositions were heralded as the first new Who music since 1982's *It's Hard*.

With a March 29 appearance at the Royal Albert Hall looming, The Who played three late March warm-up dates at The Kentish Town Forum, the first of which was their first show in the U.K. since John Entwistle's death in 2002. "...as they started with a lean, powerful version of *Who Are You* they sounded like a band that has rediscovered its sense of purpose," reported *The Times*' David Sinclair. In addition to Townshend and Daltrey, the band lineup for these shows consisted of the 2002 touring unit: Pino Palladino, 'Rabbit' Bundrick, Simon Townshend and Zak Starkey.

---

[317] Townshend and Daltrey originally planned to perform an acoustic version of *Tommy* in its entirety, according to *The Guardian*. The idea was later scrapped.

...But it was Townshend Sr whirling his arm in that familiar windmilling motion, and Daltrey twirling his mike like a cowboy lassooing a steer, who dominated as they reeled off a string of hits from their 1960s heyday including *I Can't Explain*, *Substitute* and *Anyway, Anyhow, Anywhere*.

With Entwistle gone, the chemistry between these two old stagers has changed, and while there was little eye contact, it was noticeable how close they stayed together onstage. But the new blood played its part in reinvigorating a set which was comprised mostly of old favourites. Starkey negotiated the twists and mountainous crescendoes that Townshend's songwriting demands with surefooted grace, particularly on *Baba O'Riley*. Daltrey forgot the words to *Love Reign O'er Me*. "It's one of those moments that comes with the bus pass," he joked. But the performances of *Behind Blue Eyes*, *5.15* and *You Better, You Bet* were tidy, economical and all the more dramatic for the avoidance of too many barnstorming heroics.

Paul Weller and Noel Gallagher were reportedly in the crowd for The Who's March 29 show at the Royal Albert Hall for the Teenage Cancer Trust. "...For their main set, the Who play the singles that made them famous: *I Can't Explain, Anyway, Anyhow, Anywhere, Substitute*," reported *The Guardian*'s Alexis Petridis.

They lunge belligerently forth, a series of sudden, sharp impacts that do not appear to be blunted by the cold that turns Roger Daltrey's voice into a bark, nor by the absence of Keith Moon's unique percussive whirlwind, nor indeed by the presence of Pino Palladino, the characterless session musician's characterless session musician, in place of the late bassist John Entwistle.

Neither of the band's surviving members look particularly like rock legends... but their appearance makes their performance all the more surprising. Daltrey attempts to play two tambourines and ends up smashing them both. Townshend runs to the front of the stage, jabs his guitar violently at the audience and windmills his arm in time-honoured style. It should look ridiculous. Instead, it's a thrilling reminder of the unpredictability and menace that underpinned the Who in their prime.

Up in the balcony, a man rips off his shirt and begins miming the drums, while in the stalls, an entire family are frantically pogoing in unison. The Who, it seems, still have the power to move an audience in ways far beyond the standard reverence afforded heritage rock acts.

"...Townshend also spoke out about his traumatic year, which saw him arrested in January 2003 as a part of Operation Ore, the nationwide crackdown on child pornography...," reported *NME*. "Visibly moved onstage, Townshend admitted that he had been "nervous" about stepping out in public again before thanking the packed-out crowd and his bandmates for their support."

On April 8 2004, Pete performed at the Royal Albert Hall for a Ronnie Lane tribute show which served as a fundraiser for both Lane's family and multiple sclerosis research. Lane died of multiple sclerosis back in 1997. Pete performed *Evolution* and *Heart To Hang Onto*. www.billboard.com's Paul Sexton called the show "a thoroughly merited testimonial for an artist who's rarely received his due."

...it was the prospect of seeing Pete Townshend, Ronnie Wood and Paul Weller in an unusual setting that attracted many to take part in the celebration. Clapton and Sir Paul McCartney sent notes of good wishes apologizing for their absence.

The opening "half" of the evening featured well-intentioned but less than inspiring tribute bands Small World and 17 Black in what largely came across as a reprise of a 2001 multi-artist memorial to Lane's colleague, co-writer and Small Faces frontman Steve Marriott. Ocean Colour Scene raised the standard considerably with its short set, which included a well-chosen cover of Lane's later entry, *Done This One Before*.

His band from that era, Slim Chance, reunited after the interval for its first performance in 25 years, featuring a line-up that included former Wings guitarist Henry McCulloch and a version of the 1974 U.K. hit *How Come?* Two punk stalwarts, Glen Matlock (Sex Pistols) and Mick Jones (the Clash, Big Audio Dynamite), joined Slim Chance before a first, rousing appearance by Townshend for *Stone* [*Evolution*]. Then it was the turn of Weller and Wood, fronting a coherent version of Lane's enduring *The Poacher*.

Townshend's one-time Who colleague Kenney Jones, the backbeat of the Small Faces' adventures in mod-pop and onwards into increasingly experimental rock, was then installed on drums, as a succession of vocalists turned the pages of Lane's songbook, including Robert Hart, Sam Brown and 1960s survivors Steve Ellis and Chris Farlowe.

Townshend's *Heart to Hang Onto*, from his 1977 collaboration with Lane, *Rough Mix*, was moving both for his affectionate introduction and its signal that Townshend's artistic mercury is clearly rising again. In a second period that ballooned way out of proportion at some 150 minutes, Wood relived his guitar runs on the Faces' *Ooh La La* and *Stay With Me*.

The spirit was uniformly generous, even if those who arrived wanting to learn more about Lane's life, times and loveable nature will have left largely unilluminated.

On May 19, 2004 – Pete's 59th birthday – The Who played a surprise three-song set at the end of CBS' presentation of highlights of its upcoming season for TV business insiders. The Carnegie Hall gig saw The Who run through the three songs used as themes for the *CSI* series: *Baba O'Riley*, *Who Are You* and *Won't Get Fooled Again*. "Townshend and Daltrey barreled through the songs – Pete windmilling on the guitar, Roger unleashing his trademark screams – as if they were in front of any other audience, say, one composed of people with souls," wrote *Time*'s James Poniewozik. "That, I guess, is what great entertainers do, in popular music or popular TV: they forget, for a while, about the compromises and cynical dealing that keep their business afloat, and occasionally manage to create something wonderful and transcendent." Pete put a positive spin on things, writing in his internet diary on May 23, "...In a very real way the use of Who music in this manner keeps it alive, and brings it to a new audience in an era when our music would otherwise never be heard on the radio or TV..."

The following day The Who played a full set at Boston's Tweeter Center. "It was a little rusty," Pete commented in his web diary on May 23, "But what a welcome we received." The *Boston Globe*'s Tom Kielty was somewhat more impressed:

> The Who's standing as one of rock's most influential and enduring acts is without question. The band has suffered the loss of two founding members... yet it has soldiered on to build on its legend status.
>
> All of which made the more human aspects of the group's performance Thursday at the Tweeter Center that much more compelling. Kicking off its latest US tour, after a surprise Carnegie Hall gig the night before, the band weathered the occasional sound glitch and instrument miscue to deliver a rewarding two-hour set.
>
> Running through one of classic rock's most recognizable catalogs would seem old hat for guitarist Pete

Townshend and singer Roger Daltrey. But what differentiated their performance from the oldies circuit was the focused passion they brought to the material. The fervor has spread to the band's newer members, particularly firebrand drummer Zak Starkey (son of Ringo Starr), who was joined in the rhythm section by bassist Pino Palladino.

Launching into *Who Are You*, Townshend was the epitome of a rock statesman, wearing black wraparound sunglasses and firing the first of countless guitar volleys. Daltrey warmed up his voice, as well as his customary microphone cord tricks, and by the time the band pounded into *I Can't Explain* it was clear that lack of intensity would not be an issue.

While the Who have no shortage of hits to draw from, some of the show's most memorable moments came from relative obscurities. The *Quadrophenia* track *The Punk and the Godfather* received an energetic workout while *Love Ain't for Keeping*, from 1971's *Who's Next*, benefited from Daltrey's acoustic guitar.

The band also introduced two new songs, with mixed results. If the title of *Real Good Looking Boy* was enough to raise the eyebrows of anyone familiar with Townshend's recent legal struggles (the guitarist was investigated following child pornography charges), the song itself was nothing memorable. *Old Red Wine*, however, stood tall against the band's best, starting as a slow ballad before exploding into a brutal guitar burner.

As the set wound down, Townshend attacked the classic *My Generation*, segueing into a wonderfully slowed down version of *The Kids Are Alright* that proved the guitarist is still striving for fresh ways to deliver hooks.

Townshend's windmill arm gestures seemed to approach 90 miles per hour at times, but he still can pick out a single note and deliver it with a frightening ferocity. The enthusiastic treatment he and Daltrey gave the set-ending *Won't Get Fooled Again* was a worthy exclamation point.

May 22, 2004 marked The Who's return to Madison Square Garden. "This was just the best thing that's happened to me in two years," Pete wrote in his web-diary the following day. "So many beautiful, friendly faces, and at a show that sold out in just 20 minutes. Roger connected with the crowd just as he had on the last dates in 2002. I was just happy to be up there, grateful to be alive, and lucky to have such a great team around me." The *Hollywood Reporter*'s Frank Scheck recognized Pete's enjoyment of the show, stating in his review, "The most striking aspect about this performance by the Who, or at least surviving members Roger Daltrey and Pete Townshend, is how much the latter actually seemed to enjoy being there."

"If the young Pete Townshend could have looked into a crystal ball to see himself performing on the Madison Square Garden Stage three days after his 59th birthday, he would've been left slack-jawed with shock," wrote The *Newark Star-Ledger*'s Bradley Bambarger, in a review entitled "Townshend breathes new life into the Who."

Townshend not only avoided dying before he got old (counter to his youthful sentiments and unlike so many of his peers, either in body or soul). As an electric guitarist, he has recovered enough primal virtuosity to rival his prime self -- and far surpass the ambivalent, hearing-impaired performer of the late '80s and '90s. On Saturday, he was as ferocious as any young lion.

Moreover, Townshend the songwriter has shown that his grace, guts and gray matter remain intact, with this tour airing the first new songs he has written for the Who in more than 20 years.

...While providing fine low-end support, Palladino couldn't hope to re-create the full-frequency jet-engine roar of the peerless Entwistle. But perhaps feeling freed, yet again, from a past ideal of "the Who," Townshend filled the sonic hole to overflowing with his live-wire solos. Since taking up the electric guitar again, he has developed a stinging, shimmying new sound, playing a Fender Stratocaster (with whammy bar) rather than the Gibson Les Paul of the '70s. The old dog who invented the power chord has learned some new six-string tricks, incredibly energized and amazingly articulated.

...Particularly effective among the 21-song set list was *Who Are You*, with the metallic salvos devastating and Daltrey in virile form. Among the left-field inclusions, a riveting take on *The Punk and the Godfather* and an acoustic *Drowned* were the highlights of a *Quadrophenia* sequence.

Choosing New York to debut a number in their new "Everly Brothers format," Townshend and Daltrey played the '70s fan favorite *Naked Eye* with each on acoustic guitars. Although the rush of electricity was missed in this of all songs, the duo's performance had a loose, work-in-progress charm.

Appearing on yet another Who hits anthology, Townshend's new song *Real Good Looking Boy* deals with adolescent pains that echo through adulthood, with late resolution. Emotionally acute and sonically rich, the song evokes the past while being texturally fresh. Live, Townshend's harmonies weren't as piquant as they are on the recording, but the band did justice to a subtle, touching, living piece of rock music.

Daltrey can still sing and swing a microphone, and Townshend's windmill strumming still excites. But it's the promise of *Real Good Looking Boy* and *Old Red Wine* -- the latter a moving tough-love tribute to Entwistle, sadly truncated on Saturday as part of a medley -- that provides a viable, valuable route ahead for the Who beyond being an oldies act, however state-of-the-art.

After returning to the U.K. for a month's rest and relaxation ("I'm spending a holiday with my son," Pete wrote in his 23 May web-diary), The Who embarked on a 9-date tour which saw them perform in the U.K. prior to playing their first ever dates in Japan and their first shows in Australia since 1968.

Following early June shows in Birmingham and Cardiff, and before they departed for more exotic climes, the band played at the Isle Of Wight Festival on June 12, 2004, after a 34-year absence. The band followed the Manic Street Preachers on the festival's sunny second day. "As Roger Daltrey and Pete Townshend emerged on stage a huge roar erupted from the 35,000-strong crowd," wrote www.bbc.co.uk reporter Abbie Collins.

Any worries about whether these old rockers still had it in them were immediately quashed when they got stuck straight in with *I Can't Explain*.

From then on it was two hours of back to back hits. They knew exactly what we wanted from them. *Won't Get Fooled Again*, *See Me, Feel Me*, *Pinball Wizard*, *Substitute* and even *My Generation* were all played to perfection. Daltrey's voice was still on form, even if there were a few high notes that he couldn't quite reach.

Looking slick in a black suit and shades, Townshend played his guitar the way he always has, windmilling madly at the end of every song, and he and Daltrey managed those all-important Who harmonies with ease.

…Laughing and joking throughout the set, Daltrey and Townshend found time to poke fun at Paul McCartney and reminisce about the last time they played the festival way back in 1970.

Less than two weeks later, The Who arrived in Japan for the first time for a couple of shows as part of the Rock Odyssey Festival. Other performers on the bill were Aerosmith, the Red Hot Chili Peppers, Paul Weller and Lenny Kravitz. The festival stopped in Tokyo on July 24 (Pete smashed his guitar at this show), and Osaka the following day.

July 28 marked the Australian leg of the tour, the first two dates taking place at the Sydney Entertainment Centre. "Daltrey's foghorn of a voice still packs some heat, though he is no closer to being someone who can do sensitive or subtle," wrote the *Sydney Morning Herald*'s Bernard Zuel.

Townshend windmills his arms, leaps occasionally and, more importantly, can still play with precision and invention. The volume may not be *Live At Leeds* extremes but you may go home with your ears still ringing.

The least likely trouble spot with a band this rich in material is the songs, and not surprisingly the two-hour show (which unusually on this world tour did not have a second encore of *Magic Bus*) hit all bases. There was the killer early days opening trio of *I Can't Explain, Substitute* and *Anyway Anyhow Anywhere*; there was the synth-flecked mid-period songs such as *Who Are You, You Better You Bet* and *Won't Get Fooled Again*; there were *Quadrophenia* and *Tommy* brackets, and new songs both excellent (*Real Good Looking Boy*) and all right (*Old Red Wine*).

OK, we did have to deal with unnecessary and unnecessarily long (but hardly new) noodling in songs such as *Sparks* and *Won't Get Fooled Again*. But as a big rock show it was all professional and hard to find fault with.

The band played a date in Melbourne prior to heading to Hawaii for two early August dates, one each in Honolulu and Maui. The tour wound down with a pair of gigs in California, the first at Shoreline Amphitheater, with the finale taking place at the Hollywood Bowl.

The conclusion of this latest tour brought the usual questions about a new Who album, this time perhaps more marked due to the advent of the two new songs, *Old Red Wine* and *Real Good Looking Boy*. A new Who album had been talked about since the 2000 tour, but nothing had emerged. Pete said that part of the reason for a lack of new product was that the band was so active – a chronic Who problem. "I think we didn't make enough albums because our energy came from playing live," he told *Mojo* in early

2004. "We reflected the energy from our audience. So what we did was often rushed, especially the writing. That is happening again. I should be writing songs today. Instead I'm playing charity gigs and going to Japan and Australia. I'm doing what I want. I'm not complaining, but people – Roger! – should not expect a miracle this year. If we are on the road, even for a month, it breaks my stride as a writer and takes me a very long time to settle."

In November 2004, Pete mentioned *Who2*, a possible collection of new Who songs. "WHO2 will not be a concept album," he wrote in a November 10 web entry. "That is, in itself, a concept for me. Roger and I meet in mid December to play what we have written. If we move ahead from there, we may have a CD ready to release in the spring. My working-title for the project - 'Who2' - is only partly tongue-in-cheek. If the recording works out we will tour with the usual band in the first half of 2005."

Four months later, a further web update announced a setback. "The new Who album has been delayed, not cancelled," Pete wrote on March 21 2005.

> The release date I had hoped for in the late spring or very early summer was whipped from under my nose after three years of writing. Shows we hoped to do in the early summer seemed to fizzle, and we lost our drummer to Oasis until January 2006. All alternatives proposed, and which I have desperately considered, do not fit in with my current commitments. I am committed to record the music for my new story *The Boy Who Heard Music*. I am also completing my autobiography later this year. Sadly, this forces a postponement of the planned Who activity this year for some indeterminate time. I had lots of plans, but no hard schedule. And that is what has created this predicament. It's probably my fault, because I work very slowly in the studio, and either no one believed I was actually recording, or they got tired of waiting. I should say that Roger has done what he calls sketch vocals on several tracks I produced, and the results are very exciting. But I feel I can't tour any more with the Who without a new record. So until that record is actually in my hands, I must hold my breath and live in hope.

In mid-June 2005, a *sans*-Who Pete and Roger played at New York's Gotham Hall[318] for Samsung's *Four Seasons of Hope*, an annual childrens charity fundraiser. "It was a grand and generous gathering of good-hearted, and slightly skeptical business people, some of whom had shelled out $30,000 for a table to be served (but not consume) a beautiful, rare tornado steak and listen to two sixty year old men who call themselves 'The Who'," Pete wrote in a June 22 web-diary entry.

> Roger sang my last published song REAL GOOD LOOKING BOY entirely unaccompanied by me, or Jon Carin who was along for the ride with us on keyboards and memory stick. When Roger plays guitar for his own voice the dynamic is gentler, more intimate, more delicate. It's hard to reconcile that this is the same straining voice that has struggled to be heard over the loudest band in rock for forty years. It was a rare treat, like the Tornado, but better received.

During rehearsals back in London for the Gotham Hall performance, Pete received a request from Bob Geldof for The Who to perform at *Live 8*, worldwide "day of action" designed to draw attention to poverty in Africa, and scheduled to take place at the beginning of the Gleneagles G8 Summit, a policymaking gathering of the leaders of the world's richest nations. Twenty years on from *Live Aid*, this new series of concerts (which took place in early July 2005 in the U.K, France, Germany, Italy, the U.S., Canada, Japan, South Africa and Russia) had similar superstar power. After some discussion with Daltrey, it was agreed that The Who would perform at this 2005 edition of *Live Aid*, twenty years on from the original. A chance to perform at this show, and therefore possibly push the memory of the sub-par *Live Aid* Who performance further back into everyone's memories, must have factored in the decision. "It may have escaped everyone's attention that in photographs of the 1985 *Live Aid* concert I am the only man present with a sensible, classic, short haircut," Pete wrote in a mid-2005 web entry.

> I also look very handsome indeed, especially as photographed by David Bailey and displayed in the Gents at the Caprice. I point this out because, musically on that occasion, we were trounced by *Queen*, who were in the middle of a tour. This time, no doubt, we'll be trounced by U2 who are in the middle of stadium rock's answer to the ANC revolution. What are we in the middle of? We are in

---

[318] In a June 22 web-diary entry, Pete described the venue as "an old bank – an enormous, echoing an enormous, echoing oval room with a gilded ceiling as high as Penn station..."

the middle of 'resting'. Again. I have a feeling my haircut will again prevail. I wonder suddenly, is this truly something I should be bragging about?

It will be the only big show we do this year, or at least the only one we do until someone asks us to do another one. Our career is so *ailing*. We badly need to have our career *revived*. I write this at two-thirty in the morning. Fretting so much about my *ailing* career I can hardly sleep. I have worries. I'm sure I do.

On July 2 2005, The Who took part in *Live 8* in front of 200,000 fans in London's Hyde Park. Other guests for the London show included Paul McCartney, Elton John, REM, Stereophonics, Annie Lennox, Snoop Dogg, Madonna, Coldplay, U2, and a highly-touted Pink Floyd reunion. With Palladino and Starkey unavailable, the Paul Weller band was tapped for drummer Steve White and bassist Damon Minchella to play along with Rabbit on keyboards. The band only played two songs, but the *Daily Telegraph*'s Neil McCormick was impressed. "Still angry after all these years. Tore it up with a snarling *Who Are You* directed at the G8 leaders, and an epic *Won't Get Fooled Again*," he wrote. "Pete Townshend remains the most radical, art-school guitarist in rock, with power chords that really convey power."

As *Live 8* receded into the past[319], Pete busied himself at home and in the studio. His autobiography, *Pete Townshend (who he?)*, was reportedly more than half-finished at this point, with a planned completion date of late 2005/early 2006. Two other key projects were also under way as of Autumn, 2005: Pete was in the midst of creating music for his recently-written play, *The Boy Who Heard Music*, and he continued work on *Who2*.

Pete began writing *The Boy Who Heard Music*, a story rife with the themes explored in *Lifehouse*, in September, 2000. "This is a misleading title because it suggests the story is autobiographical," Pete wrote in a July, 2005 web entry. "It is rather a divergent spur from my life in music: a story about an imaginary concert, not a boy, and so is closer to my script for *Lifehouse*... than my own life story. I was once a boy. So it might be partly about me." Back in November, 2004, Pete wrote that the story was "...a continuation of the LIFEHOUSE chronicles, and features the LIFEHOUSE METHOD (music generated from data gathered from various individuals). I hope to develop this as an animation feature with music in the second half of

---

[319] Sales of The Who's *Then & Now* skyrocketed after *Live 8*, which was watched by nearly 10 million British TV viewers. "Our sales went up 832 per cent over the weekend – that's because we sold one record on Saturday and 832 since," Pete told the press. The Who, among other performers such as Annie Lennox and Paul McCartney, agreed to pledge profits from this surge to charity.

2005. I would also like to see a concert version. With everything LIFEHOUSE-related I know I must dream on."

Work on the *Who2* project continued. Pete readied a demo-DVD for submission to Daltrey in June 2005, which contained "the music tracks of songs I've recorded so far, demos for songs in progress, some videos of me pitching various songs, and printed lyrics and photographs," Pete wrote in the June 22, 2005 installment of his web-diary. "I hope that viewing this DVD will help him to feel that all is not lost by my delaying the work we started last September when we set out to produce a new Who album. It will get finished, as long as we stay healthy." The pair met in August to discuss the Who's future further, and agreed to revisit the situation in February 2006, after Zak Starkey's commitment to Oasis had ended.

References

Books

Atkins, John, The Who on Record, London, McFarland & Company, 2000
Baba, Meher, Discourses, Myrtle Beach, SC., Sheriar Press, 2000.
Baba, Meher, The Everything and the Nothing, Myrtle Beach, SC., Sheriar Press, 2000.
Barnes, Richard, Mods! London, Plexus Publishing, 1991
Barnes, Richard, The Who: Maximum R & B, New York, Plexus, 1996
Black, Johnny, Eyewitness The Who, London, Carlton, 2001
Charlesworth, Chris, The Complete Guide to the Music of The Who, London, Omnibus Press, 1995
Charlesworth, Chris, Pete Townsend: A Career Biography, London, Proteus, 1984
Charlesworth, Chris, The Who: The Illustrated Biography, New York, Omnibus Press, 1982.
Clark, Steve, The Who In Their Own Words, New York, Delilah/Putnam, 1979
DeLeon, Delia, The Ocean of Love, Myrtle Beach, SC, Sheriar Press, 1991
Eliot, Marc, Rockonomics: The Money Behind the Music, New York, Franklin Watts, 1989
Fletcher, Tony, Moon: The Life and Death of a Rock Legend, New York, Avon, 1999
Guiliano, Geoffrey, Behind Blue Eyes, New York, Penguin Putnam, 1997
Helander, Brock, The Rock Who's Who, New York, Schirmer Books, 1996, pp 727-734
Marsh, Dave, Before I Get Old: The Story of The Who, New York, St. Martin's Press, 1983
McMichael, Joe, and Lyons, Jack, The Who Concert File, London, Omnibus Press, 1997
McKnight, Connor and Silver, Caroline, The Who: Through the Eyes of Pete Townshend, New York, Scholastic Books, 1974
Motion, Andrew, The Lamberts: George, Constant and Kit, London, Hogarth Press, 1987.
Murray, Charles Shaar, Boogie Man, New York, St. Martin's Press, 2000
Neill, Andy, and Kent, Matt, Anyway Anyhow Anywhere: The Complete Chronicle of The Who 1958-1978, New York, Barnes and Noble Books, 2002.

Patterson, Meg, Getting Off The Hook: Addictions Can Be Cured By N.E.T., Wheaton IL., Harold Shaw, 1983.
Patterson, Meg, Dr. Meg, Milton Keynes, Nelson Word, 1994.
Purdom, C. B., The God-Man, Crescent Beach, SC, Sheriar Press, 1969
The Rolling Stone Illustrated History of Rock & Roll, New York, Random House, 1980, pp 285-292
Shaffner, Nicholas, Saucerful of Secrets: The Pink Floyd Odyssey, New York, Dell, 1991.
Smith, Larry David, Pete Townshend: The Minstrel's Dilemma, Connecticut, Praeger, 1999
Swenson, John, Headliners – The Who, New York, Ace Books, 1979.
Townshend, Pete, with Young, Jeff, Lifehouse, London, Simon & Schuster, 1999
Townshend, Pete, The Who's Tommy, New York, Pantheon Books, 1993
Townshend, Pete, Horse's Neck, New York, Harper and Row, 1985
Townshend, Pete, and Barnes, Richard, The Story Of Tommy, London, Eel Pie Publishing, 1977
Tremlett, George, The Who, London, Futura, 1975
White, Adam, The Billboard Book of Gold and Platinum Records, New York, Billboard, 1990
Wholey, Dennis, The Courage To Change, New York, Warner, 1984
Wolter, Stephen and Kimber, Karen, The Who In Print, Jefferson, NC., McFarland and Co.

Magazine/Internet articles

(unsigned), "Coming your way – Tamla Motown." Melody Maker, 6 Jun. 1964
(unsigned), "The Who." Melody Maker, 9 Jan. 1965
(unsigned), "Who - And Why." Melody Maker, 20 Mar. 1965
(unsigned), "The Who." Melody Maker, 5 Jun. 1965
(unsigned), "The Who Use Force To Get Sound They Want!", NME, 18 Jun. 1965
(unsigned), "Who Make Drastic Policy Changes." Melody Maker, 17 Jul. 1965
(unsigned), "The Beat Elite." Melody Maker, 25 Sep. 1965
(unsigned), "Who Split Mystery." Melody Maker, 20 Nov. 1965
(unsigned), "Who Hates Who?" Melody Maker, 11 Dec. 1965
(unsigned), "Who In Record Rumpus." Melody Maker, 12 Mar. 1966
(unsigned), "Who's Record Row Still Rages." Melody Maker, 19 Mar. 1966
(unsigned), "Who Record Injunction Is Lifted." Melody Maker, 26 Mar. 1966

(unsigned), "At Last! Entwistle's Silence Is Broken." Melody Maker, 16 Apr. 1966

(unsigned), "Who Cause Thousands Of Pounds Of Damage At Festival." Melody Maker, 6 Aug. 1966
(unsigned), "*I'm A Boy.*" NME, 27 Aug. 1966
(unsigned), "Smash - Up TV Show For Who." Melody Maker, 1 Oct. 1966
(unsigned), "Schhh…You Know Who." Melody Maker, 8 Oct. 1966
(unsigned), "Who - Finally Reaching The Sounds They All Search For." Melody Maker, 19 Nov. 1966
(unsigned), "Who In New Single Delay." Melody Maker, 10 Dec. 1966
(unsigned), "*Pictures of Lily.*" Melody Maker, 22 Apr. 1967
(unsigned), "Who Move Into A Class Of Their Own." Melody Maker, 29 Apr. 1967
(unsigned), "Really Smashing." Guitar Player, Oct. 1967
(unsigned), "The Who Sell Out – And How!" Melody Maker, 16 Dec. 1967
(unsigned), "Tour Extended." Melody Maker, 4 May 1968
(unsigned), "Traffic Warden Takes Magic From Who's Bus!" NME, 19 Oct. 1968
(unsigned), "Scene", The Village Voice, 22 Jan. 1970
(unsigned), "Five Days That Rocked Britain." Melody Maker, 5 Sep. 1970
(unsigned), "Who's Future In The World of Science Fantasy! At Last Pete Tells All! Disc and Music Echo, 24 Oct. 1970
(unsigned), "Quadrophonic Beach Boys." Melody Maker, 7 Nov. 1970
(unsigned) , "Pete's Plan for the "New" Who," Record Mirror, Jan. 1971
(unsigned), "It's About Time For Townshend," Rolling Stone, 5 Aug. 1971
(unsigned), "Pete Townshend at 26. Just an Old Fashioned Guy," NME 21 Aug. 1971
(unsigned), "Pete Townshend Won't Get Fooled Again," Crawdaddy, 28 Aug. 1971
(unsigned), "Time For The Who To Put Their Balls On The Rails," Time Out, 27 Aug - 21 Sep. 1971
(unsigned), "Beaty, Big and Bouncy Who." Melody Maker, 13 Nov. 1971
(unsigned), "Pete Townshend," NME, 1 Apr. 1972
(unsigned), "Townshend Delay." Melody Maker, 23 Sep. 1972
(unsigned), "*Tommy* Repeat For Rainbow." Melody Maker, 27 Oct. 1973
(unsigned), "Who's Quad Christmas!" Melody Maker, 10 Nov. 1973
(unsigned), "Dr. Who Signed." Melody Maker, 8 Dec. 1973
(unsigned), "Random Notes." Rolling Stone, 20 Dec. 1973, pg. 28
(unsigned), "Who La La!" Melody Maker, 16 Feb. 1974
(unsigned), "Chatting With Pete Townshend," Zig Zag, Jul. 1974
(unsigned), "Let's Stay Together." NME, 18 Oct. 1975
(unsigned), "Who Said That!" NME 12 Aug. 1978
(unsigned), "Townshend," Penthouse, Dec. 1974

(unsigned), "Peter Townshend Sees Videodisk As Wave Of Rock Music's Future; Who Plans Video-Angled Albums." Variety, 9 May 1979
(unsigned), "Polygram's 100% Bankrolling Of The Who's Pix Paves Way For Major Move Into Production." Variety, 9 May, 1979
(unsigned), "The Who Set To Show Cannes The What & How Of Ballyhoo." Variety, 9 May 1979
(unsigned), "The Who Survives From 1960s As Disk-Concert-Pix Industry; 'Tommy' Take Tops $60-Mil." Variety, 9 May 1979
(unsigned), "Who Aiming At 'Fever,' 'Grease' Pix-LP Parlay." Variety, 9 May 1979
(unsigned), "Who's Roger Daltrey Scores As Film Thesp, Sparks New Project." Variety, 9 May 1979
(unsigned), "Deaths at Who Date Seen Spurring Tighter Security at Concerts." Variety, 5 Dec. 1979
(unsigned), "Blame For Crush That Killed Who Fans Laid To Four Major Factors; Cincy Mayor Moves On New Rules." Variety, 12 Dec. 1979
(unsigned), "Who Cincy Concert Results In $27-Mil. Negligence Action." Variety, 19 Dec. 1979
(unsigned), "The Who sign with Warner Bros." Rolling Stone, 6 Mar. 1980

(unsigned), "Simon Napier-Bell Producing 'Fictionalized' Kit Lambert Life." Variety, 17 Jun. 1981
(unsigned), "Punitive Damages Nixed In Case Of Concert Tragedy." Variety, 15 Dec. 1982
(unsigned), "The Who - The Final Concert (review)." Variety, 22 Dec. 1982
(unsigned), "*Scoop* (review)." People Weekly, 4 Apr. 1983
(unsigned), "Townshend Splits The Who." Melody Maker, 24 Dec. 1983
(unsigned), "*Horse's Neck* (review)." Time, 30 Sep. 1985
(unsigned), "*Empty Glass* (review)." Rolling Stone, 16 Nov. 1989
(unsigned), "Poet Ted Hughes dies." www.bbc.co.uk, 29 October 1998
(unsigned), "Townshend Eyes Great White Way." www.wallofsound.com, 25 March 1999
(unsigned), "Who-Ray!" www.nme.com, 28 Nov. 2000
(unsigned), "The Who's Entwistle dies on eve of tour." www.cnn.com, 27 Jun 2002
(unsigned), "Fans touched by Who gig." www.bbc.co.uk, 2 July 2002
(unsigned), "Who Launch Tour After Death of Bassist." Associated press release, 2 July 2002
(unsigned), "The Who Play On, Four Days After Bassist's Death." Reuters press release, 2 July 2002
(unsigned), "Final farewell to Entwistle." www.bbc.co.uk, 10 July, 2002
(unsigned), "Cocaine killed The Who star." www.bbc.co.uk, 26 July, 2002

(unsigned), "Townshend 'wrong' over child porn." www.bbc.co.uk, 12 Jan 2003
(unsigned), "Police arrest Who star in child porn inquiry." www.cnn.com, 13 Jan 2003
(unsigned), "Police arrest Townshend." www.bbc.co.uk, 13 Jan 2003
(unsigned), "Who star released on bail." www.cnn.com, 14 Jan 2003
(unsigned), "Who star Townshend bailed." www.bbc.co.uk, 14 Jan 2003
(unsigned), "Who star freed after porn arrest." www.cnn.com, 14 Jan 2003
(unsigned), "Townshend victim of 'witch-hunt'." www.cnn.com, 11 February 2003
(unsigned), "Townshend Affirmed." Rolling Stone, 6 March 2003.
(unsigned), "Who star cautioned over child porn." www.cnn.com, 7 May 2003
(unsigned), "Caution for Who star Townshend." www.bbc.co.uk, 7 May 2003
(multiple authors), "The Who: The Inside Story." Mojo, March, 2004
Addley, Esther, "Bob can't fix it for Dylan at music awards." www.guardian.co.uk, 25 May 2001
Altham, Keith, "Who Admit They're Feuding." NME, 10 Dec. 1965
Altham, Keith, "Who Are Going Around in 'Circles'." NME, 18 Mar. 1966
Altham, Keith, and Smith, Alan, "Mightiest Ever!" NME, 6 May 1966
Altham, Keith, "Lily Isn't Pornographic, Say Who." NME, 20 May 1967
Altham, Keith, "California Screaming." NME, 24 Jun. 1967
Altham, Keith, "Who All Ready To Hit You With New Ideas." NME, 28 Oct 1967
Altham, Keith, "Pete Townshend Keeps The Who Live." NME, 16 Nov. 1968
Altham, Keith, "The Rock'n'Roll Circus." NME, 21 Dec. 1968
Aquilante, Dan, "Townshend Tells All on Lost Who Album." www.nypost.com, 2 July 2000
Arrington, Carl, "Pete Townshend: Who's He?" Creem, Nov. 1980
Atlas, Jacoba, "Caught In The Act: Who In LA." Melody Maker, 25 Dec. 1971
Bailey, Andrew, "Roger Daltrey: A Who Sings His Heart Out in the Country." Rolling Stone, 26 Apr. 1973, pg. 12
Benton, Michael, "Who's Next Monster." Melody Maker, 23 Dec. 1972
Bierbaum, Tom, "Hope The Who Date Will Hype Pay-View Status." Variety, 15 Dec. 1982
Bohn, Chris, "You Better You Bet." NME, 28 Feb. 1981
Borrows, Bill, "Dinosaurs rule the earth." www.guardian.co.uk, 23 Nov. 1999
Brooks, Michael, "Peter Townshend." Guitar Player, May/Jun. 1972
Brown, Mick, "Who's Still Angry? Roger Daltrey is." Rolling Stone, 2 Jun. 1977

Browne, David, "*Tommy* (review)." Entertainment Weekly, 7 May 1993
Burman, John, "*The Kids Are Alright*." www.hollywoodreporter.com, 24 Sep. 2003
Burr, Ty, "Rock Opera Wizard." Entertainment Weekly, 25 Jun. 1993
Bushell, Gary, "*It's Hard*." Sounds, Sept. 1982
Carr, Roy, "*Join Together*." NME, 17 Jun. 1972
Carr, Roy, "Pete Townshend: *Who Came First*." NME, 7 Oct. 1972
Carr, Roy, "Pete Townshend." NME, 24 May 1975
Carr, Roy, "That Was Then." NME, 4 Oct. 1975
Cavanagh, David, "Pete Townshend." Q, Jan 2000
Charlesworth, Chris, "I See A Mad Moon Rising!" Melody Maker, 7 Nov. 1970
Charlesworth, Chris, "Whole Lotta Who Gear." Melody Maker, 7 Nov. 1970
Charlesworth, Chris, "Where To Now, Who?" Melody Maker, 17 Jul. 1971
Charlesworth, Chris, "Caught In The Act: The Who." Melody Maker, 23 Oct. 1971
Charlesworth, Chris, "Rock Comes In From The Cold - At The Rainbow." Melody Maker, 13 Nov. 1971
Charlesworth, Chris, "*Meaty, Beaty, Big and Bouncy*." Melody Maker, 4 Dec. 1971
Charlesworth, Chris, "Thumbs Down In Rome…" Melody Maker, 23 Sep. 1972
Charlesworth, Chris, "Personal Opinion." Melody Maker, 23 Dec. 1972
Charlesworth, Chris, "Giving It All Away." Melody Maker, 7 Apr. 1973
Charlesworth, Chris, "A Piece Of Cake." Melody Maker, 8 Dec. 1973

Cheal, David, "A whiff of the old magic." www.telegraph.co.uk, 1 Nov. 2000
Clarke, Steve, "Silver Screen: *The Kids Are Alright*." NME, 30 Jun. 1979
Clayson, Alan, "Speedy Keen." www.guardian.co.uk, 6 June 2002
Cocks, Jay, "A New Triumph For The Who." Time, 1 Oct. 1979
Cocks, Jay, "Rock's Outer Limits." Time, 17 Dec. 1979
Coleman, Ray, "Who's Next." Melody Maker, 21 Aug. 1971
Collins, Abbie, "Isle of Wight Festival 2004 Review Day 2." www.bbc.co.uk, 21 June 2004
Collins, Michael, "Pete Townshend: Busy Days." Rolling Stone, 20 Jun. 1974
Connelly, Christopher, "1982: Who Won, Who Lost; Winner: The Who." Rolling Stone, 17 Feb. 1983
Coon, Caroline, "Squeeze Box." Melody Maker, 17 Jan. 1976
Cott, Jonathan, "A Talk With Pete Townshend." Rolling Stone, 14 May 1970
Cox, Tom, "Peter rabbits." www.guardian.co.uk, 3 December 1999

Crook, John, "Daltrey Blasts Press, Politicos for Townshend's Ordeal." www.zap2it.com, 30 Sep 2003.
Dawbarn, Bob, "Dogs." Melody Maker, 15 Jun. 1968
DeCurtis, Anthony, "Opera Man: The Rolling Stone Interview with Pete Townshend." Rolling Stone, 23 Dec. 1993
DeCurtis, Anthony, "Opinion." Rolling Stone, 24 Jun. 1993
DeCurtis, Anthony, "Getting Old With the Who." www.rollingstone.com, 20 July 2000
Denselow, Robin, "Townshend Prays, Writes New Opera." Rolling Stone, 26 Oct. 1972
Di Perna, Alan, "*Tommy.*" Guitar World, June 1999
Di Perna, Alan, "Machine Gun." Guitar World Acoustic, no. 38, Summer 2000
Di Perna, Alan, "Smoke Stack Lightning." Guitar World, September 2002
Dodd, Vikram, "John Entwistle, The Who's bass guitarist, found dead in hotel." www.guardian.co.uk, 28 June, 2002
Du Noyer, Paul, "Interview: Pete Townshend." The Record, August 1982.
Du Noyer, Paul, "*It's Hard.*" NME, 4 Sep. 1982
Eason, John, "Web life: Urban myths." www.guardian.co.uk, July 20, 2000
Elder, Bruce, "The Danger Behind the Daltrey Mask." Melody Maker, 16 Aug. 1980
Eliscu, Jenny, "Pete Townshend Opens the *Lifehouse* Door." www.rollingstone.com, February 20, 2000
Eliscu, Jenny, "People of the Year: Pete Townshend." Rolling Stone, December 14-21, 2000
Eliscu, Jenny, "Pete Townshend Says Who Reunion a Cure for Loneliness." Rolling Stone, June 16, 2000
Eliscu, Jenny, "Pete Townshend Speaks Out." www.rollingstone.com, May 20, 2003
Epstein, Dan, "Feel Me: Pete Townshend and Raphael Rudd – *The Oceanic Concerts* (review)." Guitar World Acoustic, no. 48, 2001.
Evans, Allen, "My Generation." NME, 17 Dec. 1965
Evans, Paul, "*Psychoderelict* (review)." Rolling Stone, 19 Aug. 1993
Fantoni, Barry, "Various Artists: *Tommy.*" Melody Maker, 9 Dec. 1972
Fletcher, Tony, "Red, White and Who." Revolver, Fall 2000
Flippo, Chet, "Entwistle: Not So Silent After All." Rolling Stone, 5 Dec. 1974
Flippo, Chet, "Rock & Roll Tragedy." Rolling Stone, 24 Jan. 1980
Fricke, David, "*Scoop* (review)." Rolling Stone #393, 1983
Fricke, David, "*Another Scoop* (review)." Rolling Stone #498, 1987
Fricke, David, "Pete Townshend." Rolling Stone, Nov 5 – Dec 10 1987
Fricke, David, "*The Iron Man* (review)." Rolling Stone, 10 Aug. 1989
Fricke, David, "Then & Wow." Rolling Stone, 29 April 2004

Fu, Lily, "Recording Academy Names Lifetime Achievement and Trustees Award Recipients." www.grammy.com, 9 Jan. 2001

Gambaccini, Paul, "Quadromania: The Who Fuss, Fight and Hit the Road." Rolling Stone, 4 Dec. 1975

Gambaccini, Paul, "British rockers unite in Concerts for Kampuchea." Rolling Stone, 21 Feb. 1980

Garbarini, Vic, "Pete Townshend: Behind Chinese Eyes." Musician, Aug/Sep. 1982

Gardner, Elysa, "Pete Townshend (performance review)." Rolling Stone, 2 Sep. 1993

Geelsin, Ned, "*White City* (review)." People Weekly, 16 Dec. 1985

Gilbert, Pat, "Bigger Than Mod." Mojo, Sep. 2000.

Gill, Chris, "Psychodrama: Pete Townshend stages his return." Guitar Player, Sep. 1993

Givens, Ron, "*Psychoderelict* (review)." People Weekly, 5 Jul. 1993

Glasner, Joanna, "Perilous Fall of Pixelon." www.wired.com, 16 May 2000

Goddard, Simon, "See Me, Feel Me." Uncut, April 2004

Goldman, Albert, "Gap-bridging triumph of rock: The Who at the Met." Life, June 1970

Goldman, Vivien, "*Don't Let Go The Coat*." NME, 9 May 1981.

Graff, Gary, "Not F-F-Fade Away." Guitar One, September 2000

Graff, Gary, "Older, Wiser Townshend Focuses on 'Unfinished Business'." www.yahoo.com, 16 June 2000

Graff, Gary, "Pete Townshend Says No Jamming With Page & Crowes." www.launch.com, 13 June 2000

Graff, Gary, and Simon, Bruce, "The Who Rehearse? Only A Little, Says Pete Townshend. www.launch.com, 1 June 2000

Graff, Gary, "The Who – The Blues to the Bush." www.wallofsound.com, 10 May 2000

Graff, Gary, "Townshend's *Lifehouse* Triumph." www.launch.com, 28 February 2000

Green, Richard, "Who Try To Ward Off Trouble." NME, 22 Mar. 1969

Green, Richard, "Who's Sick Opera." NME, 24 May 1969

Green, Richard, "200,000 Roar Approval." NME, 6 September 1969

Green, Richard, "Who 'Leeds' The Pack." NME, 16 May 1970

Green, Richard, "Woodstock: Best film ever made about pop." NME, 23 May 1970

Gross, Jonathan, "The Who: A Last Stand." The Record, December 1982.

Halfin, Ross, "Mods & Sods." Guitar World, September 2002

Harris, John, "Did loads of drugs, made loads of money, smashed loads of guitars." Q, June 1996.

Heath, Chris, "The Rolling Stone Interview." Rolling Stone, August 8, 2002

Heath, Chris, "Townshend Fights Back." Rolling Stone, February 20, 2003

Henke, James, "Who to rake in millions on tour." Rolling Stone, 14 Oct. 1982
Henry III, William A., "*Tommy* (review)." Time, 3 May 1993
Hewitt, Paulo, "The Punk and the Godfather." Melody Maker, 11 Oct. 1980
Hewitt, Paulo, "The Kids Are Alright." Melody Maker, 17 Jan. 1981
Hiltbrand, David, "*The Iron Man*: The Musical (review)." People Weekly, 18 Sep. 1989
Holder, Noddy, "Blind Date." Melody Maker, 28 Aug. 1971
Hopkins, Jerry, "Keith Moon Bites Back." Rolling Stone, 21 Dec. 1972
Hopkins, Jerry, "One-man Wrecking Crew." Rolling Stone, 19 Oct. 1978
Hughes, Rob, "The Wild Bunch." Uncut, October 2001.
Jisi, Chris, "Mister Fantastic!" Bass Player, March 2004.
Johnson, Derek, "*I Can't Explain.*" NME, 15 Jan. 1965
Johnson, Derek, "*Anyway, Anyhow, Anywhere.*" NME, 21 May 1965
Johnson, Derek, "*My Generation.*" NME, 29 Oct. 1965
Johnson, Derek, "*Substitute.*" NME, 11 Mar. 1966
Johnson, Derek, "*A Legal Matter.*" NME, 18 Mar. 1966
Johnson, Derek, "*The Kids Are Alright.*" NME, 19 Aug. 1966
Johnson, Derek, "*Ready Steady Who / La-La-La-Lies.*" NME, 11 Nov. 1966
Johnson, Derek, "*The Seeker.*" NME, 21 Mar. 1970
Johnson, Derek, "*See Me, Feel Me.*" NME, 17 Oct. 1970
Johnson, Derek, "*Let's See Action.*" NME, 16 Oct. 1971
Jones, Jonathan, "Schools of thought." www.guardian.co.uk, 19 March 2000
Jones, Nick, "Well, What is Pop Art?" Melody Maker, 3 Jul. 1965
Jones, Nick, "The Price Of Pop Art." Melody Maker, 28 Aug. 1965
Jones, Nick, "Who: Where To?" Melody Maker, 10 Sep. 1966
Jones, Nick, "*Psychedelicamania* at Roundhouse." Melody Maker, 7 Jan. 1967
Jones, Nick, "Pictures Of The Who." Melody Maker, 29 Apr. 1967
Jones, Nick, "Second Thoughts On Monterey." Melody Maker, Jul. 1967
Jones, Nick, "The Last Time / Under My Thumb." Melody Maker, 8 Jul. 1967
Jones, Nick, "I Became A Hero - Smashing Guitars!" Melody Maker, 14 Oct. 1967
Jones, Nick, "Who Killed Flower Power?" Melody Maker, 28 Oct. 1967
Karpf, Anne, "Lifehouse." www.guardian.co.uk, 6 December, 1999
Kaufman, Mike, "I Am Completely Unstoppable." Mojo, July 1996
Kaye, Lenny, "*Quadrophenia*: Who's Essay On Mod Era." Rolling Stone, 26 Dec. 1973
Kent, Matt, "Mozambique update." www.petetownshend.com, 31 March 2000
Kent, Matt, "Mozambique Auction." www.petetownshend.com, 2 April 2000

Kent, Matt, "*Lifehouse* Interview." www.petetownshend.com, August 1999

Kroll, Jack, "From the Who to the Whom." Newsweek, 3 May 1993

Lappen, John, "Roger Daltrey." Music Connection, 15 Aug. 1994

Lewis, Alan, "A Happy Resting Place at Plumpton." Melody Maker, 16 Aug. 1969

Loder, Kurt, "Townshend cuts solo disc; Who set North American dates." Rolling Stone, 17 Apr. 1980

Loder, Kurt, "The Rolling Stone Interview: Pete Townshend." Rolling Stone, 24 Jun. 1982

Loder, Kurt, "*All The Best Cowboys Have Chinese Eyes* (Review)." Musician, Aug. 1982

Loder, Kurt, "Last Time Around." Rolling Stone, 11 Nov. 1982

Loder, Kurt, "Who's Last (review)." www.rollingstone.com, undated.

Logan, Nick, "Won't Get Fooled Again." *Melody Maker*, 26 Jun. 1971

Logan, Nick, "Who Enter Period of Self Examination," NME 17 Jul. 1971

MacFarlane, David, "Pay-TV concert flops as Who wrap up tour." Rolling Stone, 3 Feb. 1983

Marcus, Greil, "The Who On Tour/Magic Bus." Rolling Stone, 9 Nov. 1968, pg. 21

Marcus, Greil, "The Who: Who Are You (review)." www.rollingstone.com, undated.

Marcus, Greil, "The Different Drummer." Rolling Stone, 19 Oct. 1978

Marcus, Greil, "The Rolling Stone Interview: Pete Townshend." Rolling Stone, 26 Jun. 1980

Marlowe, Chris, "Online revenue g-g-generation: A Q&A with Pete Townshend." www.hollywoodreporter.com, 15 June 2001.

Marsh, Dave, "The Who: The Who By Numbers (review)." www.rollingstone.com, undated.

Marsh, Dave, "The Who Come to a Fork in the Road." Rolling Stone, 5 Oct. 1978

Marsh, Dave, "Keith Moon 1947-1978." Rolling Stone, 19 Oct. 1978

Marsh, Dave, "Rock & Roll Religion the Hard Way." Rolling Stone, 26 Jun. 1980

Marsh, Dave, "All The Best Cowboys Have Chinese Eyes (review)." The Record, Aug 1982.

Marsh, Dave, "*Psychoderelict* (review)." Playboy, Oct. 1993

Marsh, Dave, "Betrayed by Rock'n'Roll." Mojo, July 1996

Marten, Neville, "Behind Blue Eyes." Guitarist, June 1990

Martin, Gavin, "*Face Dances*." NME, 21 Mar. 1981

Masley, Ed, "Who's return is awesome." www.post-gazette.com, 30 Jun 2000

Mattingly, Rick, "Kenney Jones Faces the Law." Musician, June 1991

McAnuff, Des, "See me, feel me, touch me." American Theatre, Nov 1993.

McAuliffe, Kathleen, "Brain Tuner." Omni, Jan. 1983

McAuliffe, Kathleen, "The *Penthouse* Interview: Pete Townshend." Penthouse, August 1983

McCormick, Neil, "Smash, bang, crash – the Who are back." www.telegraph.co.uk, 3 August, 2000

McCormick, Neil, " 'I look my age – but I certainly don't feel it' " www.telegraph.co.uk, 2 June 2001

McKenna, Christine, "Free Drinking and Heavy Thinking." Spin, March 1986

McKeough, Kevin, "The Who Are Just Alright in Chicago." Rolling Stone, Nov. 1999

McKnight, Connor, and Tobler, John, "Chatting With Pete Townshend, Zigzag, no. 43, 1974

McNeill, Phil, "Pete Townshend & Ronnie Lane: *Rough Mix*." NME, 17 Sept. 1977

Mendelsohn, John Ned, "*Who's Next*." Rolling Stone #90.

Miller, Debby, "The Who to begin 'final' U.S. tour." Rolling Stone, 30 Sep. 1982

Miller, Jim, "The Who: Talkin' about a Generation." Rolling Stone, 5 Dec. 1974

Milward, John, "*Join Together* (review)." Rolling Stone, 17 May, 1990

Mohan, Dominic, "Cops can come and get me." www.thesun.co.uk, 13 Jan 2003

Mohan, Dominic, "My chauffeur used to wait while I slept off the booze in a skip." www.thesun.co.uk, 11 Feb 2002

Molenda, Michael, "British Accents." Guitar Player, Mar. 1998

Molenda, Michael, "Union Jacks." Guitar Player, Mar. 1998

Moore, John, " '60s Tommy still speaks to young." www.denverpost.com, 6 Jan. 2002

Morley, Paul, "Laser Laser on the Wall Who are Complacent After All." NME, 25 Aug. 1979

Morris, Chris, "No Takers For Classic Who Tapes On eBay." www.billboard.com, 27 July 2000

Murray, Charles Shaar, "Townshend: The true saga of Clapton's Rainbow gig." NME, 24 Feb./3 Mar. 1973

Murray, Charles Shaar, "Four-Way Pete." NME, 27 Oct. 1973

Murray, Charles Shaar, "Listening To You, I Forget The Story." NME, 29 Mar. 1975

Murray, Charles Shaar, "Just Who is the world's greatest rock band?" NME, 1 Nov. 1975

Murray, Charles Shaar, "*Who Are You*." NME, 19 Aug. 1978

Murray, Charles Shaar, "In Search of Ancient Mods." NME, 9 Jun. 1979

Murray, Charles Shaar, "Wanna be a hero?" NME, 5 Jan. 1980

Murray, Charles Shaar, "Conversations with Pete." New Musical Express, 19 Apr 1980.

Murray, Charles Shaar, "Pete Townshend: *Empty Glass*." NME, 26 Apr. 1980

Murray, Charles Shaar, "Townshend Talks!" Trouser Press, Jul/Aug. 1980 (reprint of 'Conversations with Pete' above)

Murray, Charles Shaar, "Pete Townshend: *All The Best Cowboys Have Chinese Eyes*." NME, 3 Jul. 1982

Newquist, H.P., "Pete Townshend: The Chronicles Of An Angry Guitarist." Guitar, August 1996.

Patterson, Margaret A., "Casa Filadelfia Detox Center." www.rlministries.com, 2001

Patterson, Margaret A., "Effects Of Neuro-electric Therapy (N.E.T.) In Drug Addiction: Interim Report." www.undcp.org, 1976

Pond, Steve, "Schlitz sponsors the Who's U.S. tour." Rolling Stone, 11 Nov. 1982

Pond, Steve, "The Who Reboards the Magic Bus, but will it still be Magic?" Rolling Stone, 13 Jul. 1989

Poniewozik, James, "CBS: The World Looks Just the Same, and History Ain't Changed." Time, 20 May 2004

Puterbaugh, Parke, "The Who: It's Hard (review)." www.rollingstone.com, undated.

Resnicoff, Matt, "Godhead Revisited: The Second Coming of Pete Townshend." Guitar Player, September 1989.

Resnicoff, Matt, "Flailing Your Way to God." Guitar Player, October 1989.

Roberts, Chris, "Mecca for Mods?" Melody Maker, 25 Jan. 1964

Robinson, Lisa, "It's probably the sack!" NME, 30 Aug. 1975

Rogers, Sheila, "Random Notes." Rolling Stone, 17 May, 1990

Rothman, David, "A Conversation with Pete Townshend." Oui, March, 1980

Rudis, Al, "When We Fight It Can Get Vicious." Melody Maker, 9 Feb. 1974

Salewicz, Chris, "Pete Townshend Stops Hurting People; Stops Hurting Himself: Action For The 80's." Creem, Nov. 1982

Scapelliti, Christopher, "To Die For." Revolver, Fall 2000

Selwood, Clive, "Muddy Hell." Melody Maker, 30 Aug. 1969

Sexton, Paul, "Ronnie Lane Benefit." www.billboard.com, April 8, 2004

Sharken, Lisa, "Long Live Rock!" Guitar Player, September 2000

Sheff, David, "Pete Townshend: *Playboy* Interview." Playboy, February, 1994

Shelden, Michael, "We'll go on until we drop dead." www.telegraph.co.uk, 15 July 2003

Simon, Bruce, "Townshend and Vedder Rock NYC." www.launch.yahoo.com, 29 July 1999

Simon, Bruce, "The Who Set For New York City Charity Gig." www.launch.com, 28 April, 2000

Simon, Bruce, "David Bowie's Heathen To Feature Pete Townshend & Dave Grohl." www.launch.yahoo.com, 5 April, 2002

Simon, Bruce, "Pete Townshend's Mother Stands By Her Son, Says She's Ignorant Of His Abuse Claim." www.launch.yahoo.com, 15 January 2003

Simon, Bruce, "Queen Guitarist Standing With Pete Townshend, Unhappy With Media Coverage." www.launch.yahoo.com, 17 January 2003

Simpson, Dave, "The Who: Manchester Arena." www.guardian.co.uk, 3 November 2000

Simpson, Dave, "Ground control." www.guardian.co.uk, 5 June 2002

Simpson, Janice C., "Pete, we can hear you." Time, 12 Jul. 1993

Sinclair, Tom, "*Psychoderelict* (review)." Entertainment Weekly, 18 Jun. 1993

Skanse, Richard, "Roger Daltrey Says Who Reunion Not Nostalgia, But Magic." www.rollingstone.com, 16 Jun. 2000

Smith, Alan, "The Who use force to get sound they want!" NME, 18 Jun. 1965

Spencer, Neil, "World Class Axe in Pistols Niterie Fracas." NME, 29 Jan. 1977

Spencer, Neil, "Roddam's mod(ern) vision." NME, 18 Aug. 1979

Stewart, Tony, "*Relay*." NME, 23 Dec. 1972

Stewart, Tony, "Roger and Out." NME, 14 Apr. 1973

Stewart, Tony, "Who's last?" NME, 9 Aug. 1975

Stewart, Tony, "Rainy Day Rock Fans." NME, 5 Jun. 1976

Stewart, Tony, "Pursey, Rotten In Line For Who Film Role." New Musical Express, 12 Aug 1978.

Stewart, Tony, "The Who & Various Artists: *Quadrophenia* Soundtrack." NME, 22 Sep. 1979

Strauss, Neil, "Toasting Townshend." Rolling Stone, #679, 7 Apr. 1994, pg 20

Sullivan, Mike, and Lea, Michael, "Cops swoop on Townshend." www.thesun.co.uk, 14 Jan 2003

Sutcliffe, Phil, "Indeed, He Can Explain." www.latimes.com, 28 May 2000

Sweeting, Adam, "Pete Townshend: *Scoop*." Melody Maker, 19 Mar. 1983

Swenson, John, "The One-Time Guitar-Smasher Looks Back." Guitar World, November, 1983

Tannenbaum, Rob, "*White City: A Novel* (review)." www.rollingstone.com (undated)

Tayler, Letta, "Who's this sad-eyed dreamer?" Newsday, July 9, 2000

Taylor, Sam, "Careful with that axe, Pete." www.guardian.co.uk, 5 November 2000

Thigpen, David, "*Tommy* Sells Out." Rolling Stone, 10 Jun. 1993

Tickell, Paul, "Why Do They Bother?" NME, 21 Mar. 1981

Townshend, Pete, "Pop Think-In." Melody Maker, 26 Mar. 1966

Townshend, Pete, "Blind Date." Melody Maker, 8 Oct. 1966
Townshend, Pete, "Pop Think - In." Melody Maker, 14 Jan. 1967
Townshend, Pete, "Dear Melody Maker." Melody Maker, 12 Aug. 1967
Townshend, Pete, "Don't Hold Me Responsible For What I Do Or Say!" Melody Maker, 22 Aug. 1970
Townshend, Pete, "Another Fight In The Playground." Melody Maker, 19 Sep. 1970
Townshend, Pete, "On The Road Again." Melody Maker, 17 Oct. 1970
Townshend, Pete, "TV Miming: Who Is Being Fooled?" Melody Maker, 14 Nov. 1970
Townshend, Pete, "In Love With Meher Baba." Rolling Stone, 26 Nov. 1970
Townshend, Pete, "Is Rock Dead?" Melody Maker, 12 Dec. 1970
Townshend, Pete, "Do You Suffer From Media Frustration?" Melody Maker, 16 Jan. 1971
Townshend, Pete, "Change - By Taking People UP." Melody Maker, 13 Feb. 1971
Townshend, Pete, "Learning To Walk - The Second Time Around." Melody Maker, 13 Mar. 1971
Townshend, Pete, "Things Are Different Across The Sea." Melody Maker, 17 Apr. 1971
Townshend, Pete, "We're Sorry!" Melody Maker, 24 Nov. 1971
Townshend, Pete, "*Meaty, Beaty, Big and Bouncy.*" Rolling Stone, 9 Dec. 1971
Townshend, Pete, "Rock Recording." Hit Parader, May 1974
Townshend, Pete, "Pro's Reply." Guitar Player, Sep. 1974
Townshend, Pete, "Pete Townshend's Back Pages." NME, 5 Nov. 1977
Townshend, Pete, "The Punk Meets the Godmother." Rolling Stone, 17 Nov. 1977
Townshend, Pete, "Townshend's Rebuttal." The Record, December 1982.
Townshend, Pete, "Songwriting." Making Music, June, 1989.
Townshend, Pete, "An Introduction to *Lifehouse*." The Richmond Review, 1999
Townshend, Pete, "Chat Transcript." www.barnesandnoble.com, 21 May 2000
Townshend, Pete, "The Who Sell Out." www.q4music.com, 31 Jan 2001
Townshend, Pete, "*Quadrophenia* heads for theaterland." www.eelpie.com, March 2001
Townshend, Pete, "Meher Baba – The Silent Master: My Own Silence." www.eelpie.com, July 2001
Townshend, Pete, "Peter Blake." Mojo, March 2002
Townshend, Pete, "A *Different* Bomb." www.petetownshend.com, January 2002
Townshend, Pete, "*White City* Teleplay." www.eelpie.com, 13 March 2002

Townshend, Pete, "Pete Townshend's Statement In Full." www.bbc.co.uk, 11 Jan 2003
Tracy, Dick, "*Quadrophenia*." New Musical Express, 12 May 1979.
Turner, Steve, "Peter Meaden [obituary]." New Musical Express, 12 Aug 1978.
Turner, Steve, "Who Said That!" New Musical Express, 12 Aug. 1978
Valentine, Penny, "*Happy Jack*." Disc & Music Echo, 10 Dec. 1966
Valentine, Penny, "The Townshend Talk-In." Sounds, 12 Aug 1972.
Van Ness, Chris, "The Who Have a Smashing Time." NME, 8 Jan. 1972
Vercammen, Paul, "Meet the new boss." www.cnn.com, 15 May 1996
Weales, Gerald, "The Who's *Tommy* (review)." Commonweal, 4 Jun 1993
Watts, Michael, "It's [still] a mod, mod, mod world." Melody Maker, 14 Oct 1978.
Watts, Michael, "Townshend: Picking Up The Pieces." Melody Maker, 14 Oct 1978.
Weisbard, Eric, "Ten Past 'Ten.'" Spin, August 2001
Welch, Chris, "The Who Fulfilled - And A Mini-Opera, Yet!" Melody Maker, 10 Dec. 1966
Welch, Chris, "It's A Knockout!" Melody Maker, 31 Dec. 1966
Welch, Chris, "Jimi Hendrix versus The Who." Melody Maker, 4 Feb. 1967
Welch, Chris, "Love, Beauty, The Fuzz and The UFO." Melody Maker, 17 Jun. 1967
Welch, Chris, "I Can See For Miles." Melody Maker, 14 Oct. 1967
Welch, Chris, "Who Needs To Take Pop Seriously?" Melody Maker, 30 Dec. 1967
Welch, Chris, "Would You Let Your Daughter Marry A Venusian?" Melody Maker, 4 May 1968
Welch, Chris, "Tackling The Most Serious Project Of Their Lives." Melody Maker, 9 Sep. 1968
Welch, Chris, "Bus Ride Back To Pop 30 For Who." Melody Maker, 21 Sep. 1968
Welch, Chris, "*Pinball Wizard*." Melody Maker, 8 Mar. 1969
Welch, Chris, "Rock At Its Most Electrifying." Melody Maker, 6 Sep. 1969
Welch, Chris, "Where Now For *Tommy*?" Melody Maker, 10 Jan. 1970
Welch, Chris, "*Summertime Blues*." Melody Maker, 18 Jul. 1970
Welch, Chris, "The Life And hard Times Of Arthur Brown." Melody Maker, 23 Oct. 1971
Welch, Chris, "Squire Daltrey." Melody Maker, 23 Oct. 1971
Welch, Chris, "5.15." Melody Maker, 6 Oct. 1973
Welch, Chris, "Townshend Tops *Tommy*!" Melody Maker, 20 Oct. 1973
Welch, Chris, "Talking 'bout My Generation." Melody Maker, 27 Oct. 1973
Welch, Chris, "The Who: Another Victory." Melody Maker, 3 Nov. 1973

Welch, Chris, and Ward, Jeff, "Who Eat Humble Pie!" Melody Maker, 25 May 1974

Welch, Chris, "Odds & Sods." Melody Maker, 28 Sep. 1974

Welch, Chris, "Daltrey: Grandfather of Punk Rock." Melody Maker, 30 Apr. 1977

Welch, Chris, "A Face in the Who." Melody Maker, 21 Apr. 1979

Wells, John, "Third Time Lucky Name." NME, 26 Feb. 1965

Wells, John, "*Magic Bus*." NME, 12 Oct. 1968

Wenner, Jann, "Rock and Roll Music." Rolling Stone, 20 Jan. 1968

Wenner, Jann, "The Rolling Stone Interview: Pete Townshend." Rolling Stone, 14-18 Sep. 1968

Wickham, Vicki, "Ten-Dollar Seats for The Who!" Melody Maker, 20 Jun. 1970

Wild, David, "The Who Rock On." Rolling Stone, 2 July, 2002

Wild, David, "Who's On Broadway?" Rolling Stone, 18 Mar. 1993

Wild, David, "*Tommy* Scores Again." Rolling Stone, 3 Sep. 1992

Williams, Mark, "Why Pete didn't need a wheelchair…" New Musical Express, 12 May 1979

Wilson, Tony, "Scuffles at the Proms." Melody Maker, 12 Jul. 1969

Wilson, Tony, "Now Pete's Brainchild Is Set For The Big Screen." Melody Maker, 19 Jul. 1969

Wood, Christina, "Rockin' Good Software: The PC Takes On MTV." PC World, July 1994, pp. 66-68

Newspapers

6 July 2005, The Daily Mirror, Give 8. Cameron Robertson.

5 July 2005, The Daily Mirror, Live 8 Heroes. Cameron Robertson.

4 July 2005, The Daily Telegraph, Guess who stole the show? Neil McCormick.

30 July 2004, Sydney Morning Herald, The Who, Entertainment Centre. Bernard Zuel.

24 May 2004, The Star Ledger, Townshend breathes new life into the Who. Bradley Bambarger.

24 May 2004, Reuters, Concert Review. Frank Scheck.

22 May 2004, The Boston Globe, Still no substitute for the Who. Tom Kielty

31 March 2004, The Guardian, Review. Alexis Petridis.

30 March 2004, New Musical Express, The Grown Ups Are Alright.

24 March 2004, The Times Online, Review. David Sinclair.

28 December 2003, The Observer, My suicide thoughts over porn – Townshend. Zoe Smith

7 October 2003, Evening Standard, <u>Townshend: My life has changed</u>. Richard Simpson.

22 September 2003, Knight Ridder/Tribune News Service, <u>Can explain: Roger Daltrey demonstrates 'Extreme History' on TV</u>. Luaine Lee.

11 July 2003, Richmond and Twickenham Times, <u>Rock star hits back</u>. Hannah Thorpe.

16 January 2003, USA Today, <u>Arrest has Townshend fans searching for clues, too</u>. Elysa Gardner.

3 November 2002, The Observer, <u>Kurt Cobain's Journals</u>. Pete Townshend.

30 September 2002, The Globe and Mail, <u>The Who's back, and why not</u>? Robert Everett-Green.

29 September 2002, Toronto Sun, <u>Two for The Who</u>. Jane Stevenson

29 September 2002, Toronto Star, <u>The Who is alright</u>. Vit Wagner.

28 September 2002, Boston Herald, <u>Fiery Performance shows Who still matters</u>. Sarah Rodman.

26 September 2002, The Chicago Tribune, <u>Who's next</u>? (unsigned)

25 September 2002, Chicago Sun-Times, <u>Moon, Entwistle gone, but long live the Who</u>. Richard Roeper.

25 September 2002, Chicago Sun-Times, <u>The Who try to make it all right for the kids</u>. Jim DeRogatis.

25 September 2002, St. Paul Star Tribune, <u>The Who's main two show their intensity</u>. Jon Bream.

24 September 2002, St. Paul Pioneer Press, <u>Despite lineup changes, The Who still the real thing</u>. Brian Lampert.

22 September 2002, The Dallas Morning News, <u>Half a Who</u>. Thor Christensen.

22 September 2002, Star Telegram, <u>Who's Coup</u>. Dave Ferman.

20 September 2002, The Denver Post, <u>Who are they? An enduring pop force</u>. G. Brown.

20 September 2002, Rocky Mountain News, <u>Townshend, Daltrey reign o'er Green</u>. Mark Brown.

16 September 2002, The Orange County Register, <u>No one needs to ask who's Who</u>. Steve Fryer.

16 September 2002, Las Vegas Review, <u>Band takes 'then there were two' approach</u>. Mike Weatherford.

16 September 2002, The Las Vegas Sun, <u>The Who heats up The Joint with classic hits</u>. Spencer Patterson.

28 August 2002, The Flint Journal, <u>A seemingly grateful Who gets its groove back</u>. Doug Pullen.

28 August 2002, The Grand Rapids Press, <u>This is… What The Who Do</u>. John Sinkevics.

26 August 2002, Indianapolis Star, <u>Rock legends let loose again</u>. David Lindquist.

26 August 2002, Chicago Sun Times, Who at the Tweeter Center. Jim DeRogatis.
2 August 2002, New York Times, The Song Isn't Over for the Who, Aging but Defiant. Jon Pareles.
29 July 2002, Philadelphia Inquirer, Who shows who's standing tall. Dan DeLuca.
27 July 2002, Boston Globe, The Who knows why its rock lives long. Steve Morse.
27 July 2002, Boston Herald, Who knows how to rock'n'roll. Dean Johnson.
6 July 2002, Sacramento Bee, The Who keeps making rock'n'roll history. David Barton.
3 July 2002, San Jose Mercury News, After loss, the Who wows Mtn. View crowd. Brad Kava.
2 July 2002, The Times, The Who rediscover their old edgy spirit. Richard Morrison.
9 February 2002, The Guardian, The Who, Royal Albert Hall London. John Aizlewood.
5 Nov 2001, The Times, The midlife rambler. Nigel Williamson.
21 Oct 2001, The Times, Driven to distraction in Richmond. Cally Law.
25 Jun 2001, San Diego Union-Tribune, Pete smashes barriers instead of instruments. George Varga.
15 Nov 2000, The Times, Who you kidding? Paul Sexton.
29 Oct 2000, The Times, Cornwall's most expensive view. Christian Dymond.
29 Sep 2000, The Cleveland Plain Dealer, Never say never. John Soeder.
27 Sep 2000, St. Petersburg Times, The Who in vintage form. Philip Booth.
26 Sep 2000, Palm Beach Post, The Who older, wiser, but its music still snarls, thrills. Larry Aydlette.
24 Sep 2000, The Tampa Tribune, Connect the dots to bassist's art show. Curtis Ross.
30 July 2000, The Sunday Times, On Record. Dan Cairns.
8 July 2000, The Washington Times, You know Who still rock wizards. Christian Toto.
26 June, 2000, Chicago Sun-Times, The Who at the New World Music Theatre. Jim DeRogatis.
11 Apr 2000, USA Today, To Online Fans, from you-know-Who. Edward C. Baig.
29 Feb 2000, The Times, Son of Tommy Comes of Age. Nigel Williamson.
28 Feb 2000, The Guardian, I really want to know. Keith Cameron.
28 Dec 1999, The Guardian, A band that won't fade away. Caroline Sullivan.
24 Dec 1999, The Times, The Who, Shepherds Bush Empire. Unsigned.

15 Nov 1999, Chicago Tribune, Look Who's back playing all the hits. Greg Kot.
15 Nov 1999, The Times, Who's Who on Pete. Unsigned.
14 Nov 1999, The Chicago Sun Times, Who almost too good for reunion gig. Jim DeRogatis.
31 Oct 1999, Las Vegas Review Journal, The Who show muscle in marvelous return. Mike Weatherford.
8 Oct 1999, USA Today, Pete Townshend gives back to the Pearl Jam generation. Edna Gunderson.
6 Oct 1999, The Times, Who Make Comeback. Unsigned.
1 Oct 1999, USA Today, Pete Townshend's *Psychoderelict* Broadway-bound. David Patrick Stearns.
30 July 1999, Chicago Sun-Times, Pete and repeat. Jim DeRogatis.
30 July 1999, New York Post, Townshend Live & Kickin'. Dan Aquilante.
30 July 1999, New York Daily News, Look Who's Playing. David Hinckley.
11 July 1999, The Times, Ted Hughes's Iron Man wins film friends. Christopher Goodwin and Richard Brooks.
7 Feb 1999, The Sunday Times, Townshend writes a new rock opera. Nicholas Hellen.
6 Nov 1998, The Times, As Mod for it as ever. David Sinclair.
    9 Jun 1998, The Times, Sir Paul pays a last tribute to Linda, his diamond lady. Unsigned.
15 September 1997, The Times, Hendrix joins Handel with pop's first blue plaque. Unsigned.
16 August 1997, Tampa Tribune, The Who fulfill quest with *Quadrophenia*. Curtis Ross.
5 August 1997, The Home News & Tribune, Who's on first with rock show: Townshend, Daltrey wow Jersey crowd. Chris Jordan.
4 August 1997, The Hartford Courant-Connecticut News, The Who's *Quadrophenia* a glorious production. Roger Catlin.
1 August, 1997, Knight-Ridder/Tribune News Service, The Who Revives *Quadrophenia* Album in hopes of a Broadway successor to *Tommy*. John Mark Eberhart
26 July 1997, Detroit Free Press, Fans didn't see Who they expected. Brian McCollum
25 July 1997, Milwaukee Journal Sentinel, Never mind their age – The Who can still rock. Dave Tianen
23 July 1997, Minneapolis Star Tribune, The Who shows it's still passionate in Target Center show. Jon Bream
22 July 1997, Chicago Tribune, The Who's Mixed Bag. Rick Reger
21 July 1997, St. Louis Post-Dispatch, The Who still plays on? Yes...and with pizzazz. Joe Williams
3 July 1997, Baltimore Sun, Feeling *Tommy*'s Pain. Mike Guiliano

16 June 1997, Arlington Heights Daily Herald, Townshend Makes Strong, Sober Chicago comeback. Mark Guarino

17 February 1997, The Times, Ghost of The Who's Tommy returns to win Olivier award. Helen Johnstone.

21 January 1997, Oakland Tribune, Magic of *Tommy* still shines through. Paul Sterman

24 November 1996, Baltimore Sun, Guiliano's 'Townshend': from the Who's mouth. J. D. Considine

25 October 1996, San Diego Union-Tribune, Don't get fooled: New Who a shell of old Who. Dennis Hunt

21 October 1996, San Francisco Chronicle, A Who's Who of music. Joel Selvin.

19 October 1996, L.A. Times, Blasts from Britain's Past. Richard Cromelin

21 October 1996, San Jose Mercury News, 'The Who's *Tommy* goes to Vegas. Mark De La Vina

18 July 1996, Boston Globe, Resurrected *Quadrophenia* Resounds. Sullivan, Jim

17 July 1996, Reuters, *Quadrophenia* (performance review). Zimmerman, Kevin

30 June 1996, The Sunday Times, Rock legends roll back the years. Unsigned.

27 June 1996, Reno Gazette-Journal, Reno Audiences finally get a chance to see, feel and touch *Tommy*. Wayne Melton

16 May 1996, Baltimore Sun, *Tommy* needs shot of wizardry. J. Wynn Rousuck

6 May 1996, New York Daily News, Townshend Triumphant. Jim Farber

2 May 1996, Oakland Tribune, Townshend Rocks-When he wants to. William Friar

2 May 1996, San Jose Mercury News, Townshend's greatness: Not relying solely on hits. Brad Kava

26 March 1996, Providence Journal-Bulletin, Two Broadway hits aim for fresh successes here. Bill Gale

18 December 1995, Philadelphia Inquirer, A Bit of Broadway will be lighting up the stage in Camden. Author Unknown

1 September 1995, Owensboro Messenger-Inquirer, *Tommy* Opens Thursday. Keith Lawrence

2 October 1994, Chicago Sun-Times, See Me, Hear Me, Touch Me: *Tommy* Reborn for the 90's. Hedy Weiss

27 December 1994, Washington Post, *Tommy*'s Musical Mentor. Lisa Leff

23 December 1994, Baltimore Sun, 'The Who's Tommy' goes high-tech, for better or worse. J. Wynn Rousuck

24 December 1994, Richmond Times-Dispatch, 'The Who's Tommy' in D. C. proves a spectacular show. Roy Proctor

23 December 1994, Washington Times, Who could hate this *Tommy*? Author unknown
18 December 1994, Washington Times, Townshend's journey. Jeffrey Staggs
29 November 1994, Philadelphia Inquirer, Want theatrical effect? Then Try out *Tommy*. Douglas J. Keating
30 October 1994, L. A. Times, Nothing But Blue Skies. Barbara Isenberg
2 October, 1994, Chicago Tribune, Pete Townshend: So Why Did a Guy Who Hates Pinball Write a Rock Opera About it? Jessica Seigel
15 August 1994, Newark Star-Ledger, TV is taking a look back. George Kanzler
11 August 1994, Houston Chronicle, 'Lost' but not forgotten. Mike McDaniel
18 July 1994, L. A. Daily News, Images, sound make *Tommy* soar. Daryl H. Miller
10 July 1994, L. A. Daily News, Changing Direction. Daryl H. Miller
5 July 1994, San Jose Mercury News, The Pete Principles. Harry Sumrall
17 July 1994, Detroit News and Free Press, Daltrey, Townshend split on value of nostalgia. Gary Graff
9 June 1994, San Francisco Examiner, Sure plays a mean pinball. Robert Hurwitt
2 June 1994, Oakland Tribune, Broadway's version falls short on vocals. David Barton
20 May 1994, Seattle Times, *Tommy* terrific. Misha Berson
12 May 1994, L. A. Times, 'The Who's Tommy': Is Wizardry Enough? Chris Willman
12 May 1994, L. A. Daily News, In keeping its energy intact, *Tommy* stays true to the Who. Daryl H. Miller
21 January 1994, Detroit News, Too-tame *Tommy* is flashy, but drowns in '90s need for normalcy. Reed Johnson
7 December 1993, Boston Herald, Rock opera *Tommy* a theatrical wonder. Iris Fanger
1 December 1993, Boston Globe, Townshend's other musical comes to Ch. 2. Steve Morse
28 November 1993, Boston Globe, *Tommy* grows up. Matthew Gilbert
10 October 1993, Dallas Morning News, Free at Last. William Snyder
11 August 1993, Boston Herald, Townshend unleashes fury, bad-boy attitude. Dean Johnson
6 August 1993, Boston Herald, 'Wizard of the windmill' reaches out to a new generation on his first tour. Tristram Lozaw
6 August 1993, San Diego Union-Tribune, Rocker's benefit concert mines musical riches. George Varga
4 August 1993, San Jose Mercury News, Things they do look awful cool. Harry Sumrall

4 August 1993, Orange County Register, Townshend enjoys acting his age. Mark Brown

4 August 1993, Oakland Tribune, Townshend's *PsychoDerelict* upstaged by his older material. Dave Becker

3 August 1993, San Francisco Examiner, Townshend's Dud. Barry Walters

2 August 1993, L. A. Daily News, Pete's generation. Fred Shuster

1 August 1993, Orange County Register, Townshend fans get who they want, and more. Mark Brown

31 July 1993, L. A. Daily News, Townshend offers stale rock opera. Fred Shuster

11 July 1993, New York Daily News, Full-Tilt Townshend. David Hinckley

4 July 1993, Washington Post, Talkin' 'Bout His Regeneration. Richard Harrington

20 June 1993, New York Daily News, For Pete's Sake... Jim Farber

18 June 1993, L. A. Times, 'What Did We Do With the Future?' Richard Cromelin

16 May 1993, Boston Globe, See me, feel me, touch me, stage me. Michael Walker

2 May 1993, Hartford Courant, *Tommy* splendid yet preposterous, 'Brothers' drags. Malcolm Johnson

25 April 1993, Philadelphia Inquirer, Rock opera *Tommy* explodes on Broadway. Clifford A. Ridley

24 April 1993, San Jose Mercury News, A Who-less *Tommy* falters. Michael Kuchwara

23 April 1993, New York Daily News, We've got a *Tommy* ache. Howard Kissel

23 April 1993, New York Daily News, *Tommy* Scores. Jim Farber

23 April 1993, New York Post, Score's a score for pinball wizard. Dan Aquilante

23 April 1993, New York Post, *Tommy* Terrific. Clive Barnes

23 April 1993, New York Times, Capturing Rock-and-Roll and the Passions of 1969. Frank Rich

22 April 1993, Philadelphia Inquirer, See it, feel it, hear it. Ann Holson

18 April 1993, L. A. Times, Will New York Embrace the Pinball Wizard of La Jolla? Patrick Pacheco

15 February 1993, New York Post, *Tommy* Tunes up for B'Way. Lisa Robinson

24 July 1992, Washington Times, *Tommy* plays his pinball again. Michael Phillips

24 July 1992, Washington Times, No one asks Who is most popular boy of rock opera. George Vargas

14 July 1992, San Jose Mercury News, See it, hear it, feel it. Judith Green

12 July 1992, Orange County Register, Kinder, gentler 'Tommy' lacks fire. Jeff Niesel
11 July 1992, L. A. Times, The Wizardry of High-Tech Makes It Work. Sylvie Drake
11 July 1992, L. A. Times, They've Taken a Generation's Magic Away. Robert Hilburn
5 July 1992, L. A. Times, The Resurrection of *Tommy*. Michael Walker
5 July 1992, San Diego Union, *Tommy* for a new generation. Michael Phillips
5 July 1992, San Diego Union, For pop fans, *Tommy* remains the one and only. George Varga
20 August 1989, San Diego Union, Who Knows its limits. George Varga
11 August 1989, Salt Lake City Deseret News, Pete serves up treat for lovers of music and stories. Ray Boren
23 July 1989, Atlanta Journal, Townshend Proves Mettle With Spirited *Iron Man*. Keith L. Thomas
23 July 1989, Detroit Free Press, Pete Townshend takes a stab at a rock musical. Gary Graff
23 July 1989, Detroit Free Press, Who Cares. Gary Graff
2 July 1989, Washington Post, Who's Laughing Now. Richard Harrington
28 June 1989, Oakland Tribune, Who's Townshend keeps tight focus on *Iron Man*. Larry Kelp
13 September 1982, The Times, The Who – National Exhibition Center, Birmingham. Richard Williams
6 November 1973, Newcastle Evening Chronicle, The Who – A Ridiculous Display Of Unwarranted Violence. Steve Hughes.
7 February 1971, New York Times, The Who, From *Tommy* to *Bobby*

Printed in the United States
59404LVS00003B/2